Why You Need This New Edition?

6 Good Reasons Why You Should Buy this New Edition of *Broadcast/Broadband Copywriting!*

Electronic media have evolved significantly since the publication of the seventh edition of *Broadcast/Cable Copywriting*. Therefore, this Eighth Edition continues to offer readers an accessible overview of the fundamentals of writing for the electronic media while incorporating new content and a new title---*Broadcast/Broadband Copywriting*---to signal the field's widening scope.

The book presents updated and expanded discussions of copy lengths, psychographic methodologies, retail advertising, brand character's role in campaign construction and the relationship between emotional and rational appeals. These and a multitude of other topic conversations reflect contemporary trends and research. In addition to this fresh material, readers will also discover:

1. a new examination of **virtual agencies, digital portfolios, and online and mobile scripting procedures**

2. an exploration of opportunities and challenges presented by specialized assignments in **place-based, donor spot, classified ad and game show writing**

3. discussions of **broadband writing** interspersed throughout the text

4. updated insights from **top international industry practitioners**

5. a **new Outro Chapter** that succinctly summarizes copywriting's agonies and ecstasies

6. over **60 fresh examples** of effective copy creation

PEARSON

Eighth Edition

BROADCAST/BROADBAND COPYWRITING

Peter B. Orlik

Director and Professor, School of Broadcast & Cinematic Arts
Central Michigan University

Allyn & Bacon

Boston   Columbus   Indianapolis   New York   San Francisco   Upper Saddle River
Amsterdam   Cape Town   Dubai   London   Madrid   Milan   Munich
Paris   Montreal   Toronto   Delhi   Mexico City   Sao Paolo   Sydney
Hong Kong   Seoul   Singapore   Taipei   Tokyo

Acquisitions Editor: Jeanne Zalesky
Editor-in-Chief: Karon Bowers
Assistant Editor: Megan Lentz
Marketing Manager: Wendy Gordon
Production Assistant: Maggie Brobeck
Project Manager: Holly Shufeldt

Art Director: Jayne Conte
Cover Designer: Axell Designs
Cover Photo: Getty Images, Inc.
Full Service Project Management/Composition:
Yasmeen Neelofar/GGS Higher Education Resources

Library of Congress Cataloging-in-Publication Data

Orlik, Peter B.
   Broadcast/broadband copywriting/Peter B. Orlik. -- 8th ed.
     p. cm.
   Includes bibliographical references and index.
   ISBN 978-0-205-67452-7 (alk. paper)
   1. Broadcasting--Authorship.   2. Broadcast advertising.   I. Title.

PN1990.9.A88O7 2009
808'.066791--dc22

                                        2009021789

**Allyn & Bacon
is an imprint of**

PEARSON

www.pearsonhighered.com

ISBN-10:   0-205-67452-6
ISBN-13: 978-0-205-67452-7

Dedication

To Chris, Darcy, and Blaine for three decades of support on this project and your many sacrifices that made it possible.

NEW TO THIS EDITION

Electronic media copywriting is constantly expanding, as evidenced by evolutionary changes that have occurred in the title and contents of the book you hold in your hand. First published in 1978 as *Broadcast Copywriting*, the name and focus were enlarged in the 1990 Fourth Edition to *Broadcast/Cable Copywriting* in order to more fully address new opportunities provided by the wired medium. In this Eighth Edition, we once again broaden our scope to now encompass *Broadcast/Broadband Copywriting* and more explicitly explore the multiplying creative tasks presented by the digital world.

Make no mistake, broadcast radio and television wordsmithing is as challenging and important as it was when the First Edition was released. But there are now *additional* challenges for the electronic media copywriter posed by the cable and broadband worlds. Therefore, the aim of this new edition is to present once more the long established principles and practices of effective copywriting—and then apply them to both legacy and emerging electronic delivery systems. To help accomplish this objective, we have included **over 60 new copy examples** as contemporary illustrations of effective marketing communication.

Among the subjects entirely new to this edition are discussions of:

- virtual advertising agencies
- digital portfolios
- the quest for engagement
- preparation of radio "cheat sheets" and classified ads
- quip and quiz show copy
- online banners and spots
- mobile phone ad construction
- noncommercial copy for pledge drives and underwriting
- a concluding Outro chapter to summarize copywriting's agonies and ecstasies.

Topics included in previous editions which have been expanded and updated include:

- copy lengths as modified by the broadband world
- the relationship of emotional to rational appeals in light of new research
- updated VALS segmentations and other psychographic methodologies
- an enhanced look at retail advertising and place-based applications
- a widened perspective on special venue writing
- heightened examination of brand character and its role in campaign planning.

Finally, broadband considerations are not restricted just to sections specifically devoted to the online world, but are integrated and referenced throughout the text.

CONTENTS

INTRO

Some writers are motivated by their profession's artistic tests. Others are energized by its financial incentives. Broadcast/broadband copywriting offers the stimulating opportunity to have it both ways: to experience constantly evolving challenges to your verbal artistry and personal eccentricities while enjoying significant monetary rewards for successfully meeting those challenges. "Copywriting," confesses creative director Steve Hayden, "is perhaps the only non-criminal activity that allows you to make a comfortable living off your character defects."[1]

Whether you are an experienced media professional seeking to hone your writing focus or a novice wordsmith striving to secure initial employment in the electronic media, this book is designed for you.

Broadcast/Broadband Copywriting, Eighth Edition, introduces you to the special requirements and pitfalls of creating the continuity, commercials, online and off-air presentations that are the life's blood of the electronic communication profession. Unlike the limited-access world of full-length entertainment and documentary script creation, **electronic media copywriting** is a widespread enterprise that requires many thousands of practitioners. It is a function that every local outlet must perform; an activity in which every advertising, public relations, marketing, and other corporate entity that communicates via electronic pathways must engage. And it is the same fundamental skill now being exploited on the superhighways of the Internet.

Despite their comparative brevity, our creations exemplify all the requisites of media form and content that electronic journalism and feature-length entertainment programming demand. Thus, guided exposure to the elements of the copywriter's repertoire will simultaneously acquaint you with the stylistic techniques you'll need if you are aspiring to a career in news writing or program-length construction.

On the other hand, like many wordsmiths before you, you may discover that the opportunity, the compensation, and the challenging diversity of *copywriting* are difficult to abandon in favor of the more sober environment of the newsroom or the much less secure world of long-form program writing. Do not be surprised if you decide to spend your *entire career* as a copywriter and/or continuity supervisor, creative services manager, Web producer, or agency creative director.

Over the years, electronic media copywriting has become much more than the audio/visual hawking of goods. Audiences now view the best commercials as entertainment in their own right, with entire television specials and Websites built to showcase the copywriter's art. For a writer, "Where else can you touch the worlds of music, art, literature, entertainment, psychology, anthropology, technology and commerce?" asks Keith Reinhard, the long-time head of the DDB agency. "All in a single business, sometimes in a single day?"[2]

"We're creative people who must quickly adapt to ever-changing markets," adds Euro RSCG's chairman Ron Berger. "We're risk takers who keep business going by energizing profits and building stockholder value. And all the while, we're producing work that has more influence on our culture than any other business."[3]

Like any art, copywriting requires continuous practice. "Writing," Professor Dennis Brown reminds us, "is not like riding a bicycle, a skill which if learned once is not forgotten. It is more like music—we must practice constantly not just to improve but to maintain our competence."[4] *Broadcast/Broadband Copywriting,* Eighth Edition, strives to assist in such productive and continuous training.

As in the previous editions, this volume is divided into four main parts. After an appraisal of the copywriting marketplace (Chapter 1) and how our jobs reflect communication process considerations (Chapter 2), Part I continues with an inventory of the tools (Chapter 3), human motivations (Chapter 4), and audience characteristics (Chapter 5) that the writer must learn to manage. Part I concludes by examining copy creativity, definition, and validation, as well as prominent regulatory and stylistic constraints (Chapter 6). This first section thereby sets the stage for Part II, which probes audio's key elements (Chapter 7), commercials (Chapter 8), and additional endeavors (Chapter 9). The parallel Part III then uses a similar chapter trio (Chapters 10, 11, and 12) in the exploration of all types of video environments. Finally, Part IV delves into the interlocking process of campaign construction—first, for the more specialized world of public service appeals (Chapter 13) and then for electronic media marketing as a whole (Chapter 14). This section concludes with an Outro (Chapter 15) that gives you things to think about when considering whether to enter—or remain in—the electronic copywriting arena.

Throughout the book, a great many rules and precepts are advanced. Even though each has been tested time and time again in the intensely competitive electronic media, each (except for those ordained by government or industry regulations) can also be broken, given a specific and unique set of circumstances. Knowing the general rules, however, ensures that when you do decide to ignore one, your decision is not inadvertent but is based on a careful, conscious, and calculated appraisal of why this proven principle does not apply to the assignment at hand.

You are cautioned not to view the separate chapters of this book as independent and self-standing wholes. Do not, for example, think that you will acquire all of the information pertinent to writing *audio commercials* simply by reading the chapter bearing that title. Instead, the fifteen chapters in this Eighth Edition are mutually supportive. Each contributes additional perspectives to what is covered in others. Thus guidelines introduced in conjunction with *television commercials* are at least partially applicable to *public service announcement* writing, and vice versa. In the constantly mutating world of electronic copy, nothing remains totally distinct for very long.

Like the seven previous editions, this latest version of *Broadcast/Broadband Copywriting* deepens your comprehension of the subject through numerous examples and illustrations. Many of these models are quite current. Others are more historic and are featured because they have made enduring contributions to the practice of effective electronic communication.

It is especially gratifying to be able to include samples contributed by many of my former students (in order of appearance): Christopher Conn, Craig Allen Munn, Dan Nelson, Tim Swies, Nick Cain, Anthony Clark, Don London, Lisa Drummond, Nisa Phelps, Phil Tower, Paul Boscarino, Kevin Oswald, Brad Maki, Kris Kelly, Jerry Downey, Mike Feltz, Ryan Hopak, John Schroeder, Tricia Hoover, Jamie Jendrejewski, and Catherine (Jenkins) Abate. These true professionals have firmly established themselves in the communications business and continue to excel there as they did in the classroom we once shared. Early on, they all comprehended that, in the words of creative director Sally Hogshead, "The process of creating brilliant ads isn't glamorous. It's sitting down and working. Hard. For a long time. Long after the night crew has stopped vacuuming the hallways."[5]

Before we begin our journey down copywriting's corridors, one housekeeping announcement is necessary. In an effort to increase the number of examples while still keeping the length of the book manageable, we have condensed the format of the sample scripts. **In actual practice, all copy segments that are single-spaced in this book normally would be double-spaced, and all copy herein double-spaced would be triple-spaced.**

Now, let's proceed, in the words of creative director Curvin O'Reilly, to "*Have some fun.* Despite all signs to the contrary, advertising is still the toy department of the business world. Enjoy."[6]

A NOTE TO MY ACADEMIC COLLEAGUES

Thank you for considering this text. It was originally conceived over three decades ago at my students' urging. I subsequently discovered, as did *Tuesdays with Morrie* author Mitch Albom, that "Sometimes you write a book to teach others and wind up teaching yourself."[7] I hope some of the things my students taught me have been adequately expressed in the chapters that follow.

A separate *Instructor's Manual*, available online at **www.pearsonhighered.com/irc**, provides a model syllabus and a series of suggested exercises designed to apply the techniques presented in the Eighth Edition.

ACKNOWLEDGMENTS

First and foremost, I thank my wife, Chris, for her eternal belief in this project and its author, as well as for her patience, understanding, and continuous encouragement during the evolution of all eight editions.

Appreciation is also expressed to the many professionals in the electronic media industries who collectively provided the wealth of script and other illustrative material for the Eighth Edition of *Broadcast/Broadband Copywriting*. Many of their names appear in the text following the copy or other creative achievements they made available.

Gratitude is also extended to Pearson's Mass Communication Acquisitions Editor, Jeanne Zalesky, and Editor-in-Chief, Karon Bowers, for their administrative support, as well as to Lori Rathje and Joan McDonald at Central Michigan University's School of Broadcast & Cinematic Arts for their format and data processing assistance. Kudos are further delivered to Project Manager Holly Shufeldt and Production Editor Swapnil Vaidya for the care they took with a necessarily complex format. In addition, I want to thank the following reviewers for their supportive comments and suggestions: L. Markene Bennett, San Antonio College; Kathy Brady, the University of Wisconsin, Whitewater; and A. J. Miceli, Gannon University.

Finally, deep appreciation goes to our two children, Darcy and Blaine, who have grown up with this thirty-year project and put up with all of its distractions. In spite of their father, both are now building their own successful careers as marketing and media professionals.

Thank *you*, the reader, for your company, as we now explore the specific components and techniques of electronic media copywriting. Our ultimate goal is to help you to capture those elusive "best ideas" in a client-benefiting way. This is anything but easy. "A good ad is a greased pig when it comes time to put your hands on one," observes veteran wordsmith Mark Fenske. "Masters of disguise, good ads sneak out of you in bars, the shower, dreams, even in advertising meetings, and run away to lost pages in your workbook or torn up sheets in office wastebaskets."[8] In the chapters that follow, let's see if we can't learn to construct nets that snag the little buggers before they escape forever.

P. B. O.

The Copywriting Marketplace

Writing, of whatever type, can be a draining and dreaded task. But it can also be a passion, an adventure, and even a compulsion that occasionally brings great satisfaction as a payoff to the pain. One group of people write simply because it is demanded of them by employers (or teachers). A second group sets down words because they like to write. And a special third group may internally be compelled to pen things due to changes in the brain that Alice Flaherty and colleague neurologists label *hypergraphia,* "an overpowering desire to write."[1]

Wonderful and woeful documents can come from all three groups—because linguistically talented as well as linguistically challenged people are found in all three categories. But in addition to talent, a key factor in writing success is the *underlying nature* of the motivation that propels the activity. Flaherty has found that "people driven by intrinsic motivations such as curiosity and enjoyment have a different relationship to the product of their work from those moved by extrinsic motivation including praise, money, and the constantly varying world of punishments. Someone who is fascinated by language attends to overall details and to the overall texture of a writing project."[2] In short, if you focus more on the pleasurable process of sculpting relevant ideas and less on the praise, pecuniary reward, or possible punishment your writing will bring, you are much more likely to derive satisfaction from the project and its result.

This is certainly true of *copywriting,* where the money can be good but the punishment can be great—up to and including the loss of employment. But fixating on the dollars or the dangers can only cause you to lose focus on the assignment at hand and miss the immense satisfaction of deriving an idea and an execution of it that connects with clients and consumers. The more you probe and practice copywriting, the greater can be your sense of accomplishment. You don't need to be afflicted with hypergraphia to succeed.

Therefore, in order to anticipate the prerequisites and pressures of electronic media copywriting, we should, at the outset, learn something about the employment situations into which the copywriter is thrust. When we refer to copy jobs, we are not talking about the singular and comparatively inaccessible world of the entertainment

1

scriptwriter, a world that regularly employs only a few hundred people. Nor are we referring to the separate reportorial sphere of the media journalist. Instead, our focus encompasses that multitude of situations in which nonnews *copy*, the life's blood of all electronic media activities, is created.

Copy is the short piece of written craftsmanship that propels, promotes, defines, and ultimately helps to pay the bills for every carrier of electronic media programming. Unlike full-length (long-form) program scripts, which tend to be the exclusive province of a handful of East or West Coast specialists, pieces of copy must be created by writers at virtually every station, cable system, and other local electronic medium. Copy must also be generated by the many agencies, networks, broadband programmers, corporations, and institutions that seek to make an impact on and through those telecommunications delivery vehicles.

The typical piece of copy is ten, fifteen, thirty, or sixty seconds long. Nevertheless, like the full-length script, it must tell a tale or reveal a truth within the time allotted. This is why some writers view copy creation experience as invaluable preparation for a career in news or long-form program writing. As Guy McCann points out, "A copywriter practices a disciplined form of creativity which requires study of a subject, identification of benefits and the generation of useful ideas that achieve precisely defined objectives. A copywriter, it might be said, must have a pragmatic inspiration when required and on schedule."[3]

Some wordsmiths aspire to media management and realize that success both in media *and* in management depends on the deft supervision of written words. They quite rightly view copywriting experience as a valuable preparation for later administrative and production-directing roles. For example, Paris Barclay, Emmy Award–winning director of such shows as *West Wing* and *ER*, testifies, "My twelve years in copywriting taught me to analyze the industry more systematically than some of my peers."[4] Other writers, meanwhile, see copywriting as a total career in itself. Along the way, these folks learn that, although job contexts differ, traditional writers and *copy* writers share several key traits. As author and ad agency owner Lois Wyse put it, both novels and pieces of copy "require the ability to express ideas in succinct, powerful and caring terms."[5] But merely "having the urge to write [or even being a hypergraphiac] doesn't necessarily make you a writer," adds Professor Howard Good. "Writing requires attention, discipline, and a strong backside."[6]

Assuming *your* backside is hardy, study and practice in the contexts and techniques of copywriting can pay significant professional dividends, whatever your own long-term expressive goals may be. This is because the copywriting craft "involves a knowledge of language, visual imagery and, most important, the human psyche," points out agency executive Bob Cox. "Much of this is instinctive, but the rest must be learned."[7] Pursuing such learning is anything but tedious. For advertising professionals in general, and copywriters in particular, "it's quite a laboratory we work in," marvels agency CEO Charlotte Beers. "We're required to go to plays, concerts, see movies, sit in bars, read, listen and enjoy great diversity of human beings. Not a bad job description."[8]

Most of this book strives to further assist this comprehensive learning process through a focus on proven copy procedures and techniques. In the next few pages, however, we examine the major employment contexts from which copy is generated. In preparing to enter any business, it helps to know how you fit in to the various ways in which that business can be organized.

FREELANCE

This term has a decidedly mercenary origin. It was first applied to warriors too poor or unaccomplished to have their own land or liege lord. They hired themselves and their lances out to anyone who would employ them in order to establish a reputation and accumulate a little wealth. Set designer Dane Krogman recounts that the Duke of Argyll organized freelancers when he unified the Scots against the English. "But it didn't do any good. They got beaten and went back to being lances for hire. It's the same thing for anybody who's a freelancer today—you're true and loyal to whoever's paying you the most money for that particular day."[9]

Freelancing is one way for young copywriters to test, even on a part-time basis, their ability to create marketplace material that successfully serves a commissioned need. Initially, this might be constructing anything from public service spots for the local Food Bank to commercials promoting a home-town merchant. Ultimately, if such small assignments are successfully dispatched, the freelancer may move beyond writing to become a one-person advertising agency: "pitching" area business folk on the need for broadcast or broadband exposure, creating the commercials, supervising their production, and even handling the actual time buys on media outlets. Part-time freelancing is a prudent way for the fledgling writer, like the obscure warrior, to fashion a reputation and make a little money before attempting to slay the fiercer dragons lurking in full-time employment and comprehensive media campaigns.

For seasoned writers, too, freelancing on a full- or part-time basis can be professionally, psychologically, and economically satisfying. As veteran writer Susie Burtch long ago observed, "You don't have to hold the client's hand or be on the phone all day. I earn a full-time salary, there's no overhead, I'm my own boss and set my own hours. And as far as I'm concerned, you just can't get a better deal."[10] "Many freelancers do not want a full-time job," points out McCann-Erickson Worldgroup chief creative officer Marcio Moreira. "They prefer being able to choose assignments, work from home, manage their own time. Some do not thrive when confronted with the inner workings of agency life."[11]

Over time, freelancing by senior creatives has been given a further boost by the twin business trends of outsourcing and downsizing. "A few years ago you called in freelancers to do the stuff you didn't want to do," says creative executive Court Crandall. "Now you call them in when you want something good."[12] "Agencies have figured it out," chimes in Kit Mill, president of Paladin Freelancers. "Hire for valleys and use freelancers for the peaks."[13] Now, for a price ranging from $500 to $2,500 a day, agencies and their clients can hire top writers who have left agency careers to strike out on their own. Thus, "freelancing has become not only respectable, but a preferred, even fashionable way of life," states industry reporter Ann Cooper. "Agencies are offering freelancers more and more choice assignments."[14]

On the other hand, when a freelancer hits a dry spell, there is no continuing paycheck to fall back on. As industry commentator Alison Rogers discovered, it has long been the case that "the personality traits common among the most successful freelancers are quick-wittedness for the busy times and optimism for the slow times."[15] "If not knowing when and how much the next paycheck is going to be bothers you, then stay out of it," freelancer Mike Sellers warns.[16] Even under the best of conditions, cash flow and work flow are uneven, and this problem can be compounded by clients who are quick to issue deadlines, but slow to pay your invoice. In addition, freelancers often "are not kept around to finish the work they begin," asserts freelancer Steve Smith. "As a result, the work often suffers, the client suffers and the freelancer suffers. The client doesn't get the execution from the people who understand it best. The freelancer doesn't get the work to put in his or her book."[17]

To circumvent these difficulties, some freelancers choose to specialize in a particular product or media category. They become experts in agricultural or high-tech or health-care accounts. They learn how to use radio to promote financial services. Or they develop specialized skill in fashioning online content, trade-show scripts, or video training tapes.

Still, despite such precautions, freelancing may end up as full-time anxiety for part-time pay and zero recognition. Mark Fenske, one of the best-known freelancers in the business, comments that "freelance creative is just like having a regular agency job, except the money's not as good, you don't get the good projects, your work is not your own, you've got nowhere to sit and there's no vacation time. Since my life's ambition is to be a scorned, ignored and self-tormented artist, it's been perfect for me."[18]

An emerging alternative to choosing between freelance and full-time work is the *virtual agency*, in which two or three regular agency employees choose from a pool of freelance talent to service a particular client or project. Virtual agencies thereby assemble more stable working groups who collaborate long term rather than for a single assignment. The broadband world also has given birth to "crowdsourcing" firms like OpenAd.net that build communities of copywriters who they then make available to clients. In addition to contracting for the services of the copywriters registered with these firms, clients can also browse online through concepts these writers have previously created but which were never produced. Such broadband crowd-sourcers thus not only assist their client writers to get more assignments, they also help them monetize past 'spec' creations.

Nevertheless, these virtual agencies and talent pools, like conventional free-lancing, lack the synergy that comes from face-to-face sharing with creative partners or the client on a continuous basis. "The bad thing is there is no way to exchange thoughts or interact with the client," admits cyber-creative Denis Crosley. "It's all or nothing. . . Great work comes from the agency and client collaboration."[19]

Whether done independently or in affiliation with a virtual agency or crowd-sourcer, freelancing clearly has its pitfalls as well as its prizes. Therefore, given the option, many copywriters do not freelance. They conclude that they acquire fewer bruises when they fight today's creative battles as a full-fledged and salaried member of a company team. Nevertheless, a number of agencies and client in-house advertising departments continue to rely on freelancers who must be paid only when needed and who don't consume expensive fringe benefits.

ADVERTISING AGENCY

At the opposite end of the spectrum from solitary freelancing is a copywriting slot in a full-fledged advertising agency. Here, you need not worry about soliciting assignments, procuring artwork, paying the phone bill, or finding a photocopy machine. Account executives attend to clients, art directors help with layouts and storyboards, creative directors provide a steady stream of assignments, and a variety of support staff assist with financial and information technology systems.

Agency life is what most people visualize when they think of copywriting. Much popular sociology, and not a few theatrical movies, are fixated on the foibles of the slickly or hiply dressed agency scribe who spouts catchy clichés and snappy slogans that would sour in the mouth of a backwoods con artist. Contrary to this conniving stereotype, asserts Ketchum Advertising's Jim Colasurdo, "In reality, copywriters are the ones in threadbare clothing or stylishly self-conscious 'I'm OK, you're OK' garb that can only be classified as 'Early Earth Shoe.' Nothing fits right, and sometimes even socks don't match. Many have the confidence of baby seals just before the hunters close in."[20]

Whatever their true demeanor, agency copywriters tend to be among the top professionals in their field from the twin standpoints of talent and take-home pay. In most cases, they have had to prove themselves in one or more other media jobs before an advertising agency would even consider hiring them as wordsmiths. During 2008, for instance, the average starting salary for agency copywriters ranged from approximately $37,000 at very small agencies to $97,000 at the largest shops.[21] Even the low end of this range was significantly more than the starting compensation offered to many copywriters working at radio stations. As these numbers suggest, clients—and advertising agencies themselves—expect that agency writers are highly skilled and compensated accordingly.

Assuming that you do make it into an agency creative department either directly or, more probably, via the freelance, in-station or other apprenticeship route (such as the agency's own traffic department), you will encounter one of two main types of structures. You may be working in a unit in which all copywriters serve the total media needs of the clients to whom they are assigned. In this case, you might be helping to create newspaper and magazine layouts, direct-mail pieces, and point-of-purchase (POP) displays and billboards—all in addition to copy for radio, television, and broadband dissemination. This diversity forces the copywriter to be much more of a generalist and to be equally familiar with the distinct requirements of print and electronic communication.

Alternatively, you may find yourself in one of the fewer number of agencies that segregate writers according to the media for which they fashion messages. This pattern goes back at least to the 1950s, when the new vehicle of television caused many clients to demand advertising that reflected the talents of video specialists (or, at least, of writers who were striving mightily to become such specialists). Later, when integrated, cross-media campaigns came to the fore, many agencies abandoned this dual-pool organization. Then, with the start of Internet advertising, writers specializing in "Web" work were assigned to "new media" units. But now, many of these have also been merged into cross-media creative departments, as many clients and agencies feel that a consistent convergence-era message can only be achieved when the same message makers are working cross-platform. Nonetheless, some full-service shops continue to believe that specialists are the only way to maximize the impact of their electronic communications. These agencies share this attitude with the small *boutique* shops that devote most of their attention to the creative aspect of advertising—especially messages designed for broadcast, broadband, and other interactive media.

The differences in working climates between such small firms and the giant agencies can be substantial. As small-agency executive Tony Benjamin argues, "Because small agencies generally (though not always) work with small budgets, they can't afford to allow execution to overshadow content. As a result, _ideas_ have to work uncamouflaged by excessive production values. This means goodbye to the useless helicopter shots, the unnecessary high-tech visuals, the mandatory Jamaican locations, the mega-dollar celebrity endorsers and the overpriced models. Instead, small shops unglamorously create advertising that stands or falls on ideas alone."[22]

In the small organization, fewer people stand between the copywriter and the client, and the client companies themselves tend to be smaller. Because there are fewer decision makers to appease, and because the budgetary stakes are lower, the urge to pioneer new creative techniques can be fed more easily. "You're 'on' all the time, but it's a positive on," says small agency CEO John Leonardi. "It's because you want to be 'on,' not because you're afraid being 'off' will result in pissing off the creative director or account management team."[23] Further, argues award-winning copywriter Luke Sullivan, "Because small agencies are not owned by a holding company, they can make their own decisions about the clients to work with and clients from whom they ought to 'part amiably.' (Whenever you read this phrase in the trades, replace it with 'We ran screaming from them with our hair on fire and our guts trailing in the grass behind us.')"[24]

When a small agency achieves a series of breakthrough campaigns, it acquires notoriety and starts to grow. However, warns small shop owner Jerry Fields, "As soon as a small or mid-size agency starts developing a highly visible image based on its creative work and/or successful new-business track record, it's not long before some mega-agency with deep pockets makes them an offer they can't refuse. Swallowed up in the many-splendored layers of the conglomerate agency management and politics, all the creative and entrepreneurial elements that destined the small agency for greatness disappear."[25]

For the copywriter, this change might not be all bad, because larger agencies offer more back-up support, which helps compensate for the interference from added layers of managerial overseers. Still, says creative vice-president Barry Rosenthal, "There are people above you, beside you, and below you who all chime in with their opinions and directives. Your job is to somehow satisfy all the people who count and still create an effective spot or campaign."[26] In addition, large agencies frequently pit their creative teams against each other for the privilege of producing a major broadcast or broadband message.

In the small agency, conversely, you do not encounter several other copywriters working on competing versions of the same project. "The decisions you make are yours and yours alone," says Linda Kaplan Thaler, who left one of the country's largest agencies to found The Kaplan Thaler Group. "You may screw up, but it's _your_ mistake. Still, I sometimes miss the days of finding someone important to blame when you have the meeting from hell."[27]

No matter what particular structure and bulk a given advertising agency exhibits, and no matter how few or how many functions it serves besides actual message creation, the prime function of copywriters is still to _write_. As creative director Steven Penchina describes the agency scene, "You hole up in your office with your art director . . . and sweat it out. Trying out an idea, honing it, refining it, loving it, throwing up on it, starting over again and again, killing yourself and praying that by 2 o'clock in the morning of the presentation, you'll get that last 10 percent of inspiration that gets you over the hump. It's torture. It always was and always will be. But when you succeed, you'll cherish it. And your client will cherish it."[28]

CORPORATE IN-HOUSE

Certain types of firms prefer to fashion their own advertising rather than to contract it out to a separate agency. They therefore set up units within their organization—often in conjunction with their public relations or marketing divisions—to plan and execute the advertising effort. This pattern is especially popular with utility companies, financial institutions, retail chains, film studios, and some packaged goods manufacturers— particularly in the beauty products field. Their managements feel that corporate policy, image, and attitude can best be communicated by writers who thoroughly understand and "live" the business. "It's no surprise," comments trade reporter Joan Voight, "that top in-house creative directors are clustered in the fashion, media and beauty industries where image is as prized as substance."[29] And what better way to stimulate respect for that style than by making the writer a full-time employee of the organization and dependent on it for that weekly paycheck?

This rationale exposes the greatest weakness of the in-house system: *lack of objectivity*. Executive creative director Andrew Cracknell argues that "the point of having a separate agency is to provide an objective view of the client's problem. Get too close and you begin to lose your edge. . . . This kind of close contact can result in campaigns that talk about products to people instead of talking to people about products. Creatives start to see through the eyes of manufacturers—instead of the consumer who has no interest in the minutiae behind the product."[30]

Writers who are *part of* the enterprise they are publicizing are leery of criticizing its marketing plans and reluctant to question a defective campaign or outmoded corporate slogan. In-house writers come to know their company's sacred cows so well that a whole system of preferred or untouchable subjects can, by accretion, clog the entire creative process and strangle the universal need for constant creative evolution. "The in-house agency," reveals advertising executive Lynne Seid, "generally forgets what drives the brand in the market and gets more involved in what will sell the campaign inside the company."[31] What's more, the in-house pattern can be stifling to the writer who is forced to deal exclusively with the same product or service year after year without the opportunity to grow through exposure to new and different assignments and clients.

Giving it its due, the in-house system generally does offer writers a greater chance of job stability and a heightened opportunity to analyze fully the products and services their copy will promote. Such in-depth knowledge can result in clearer and more accurate messages because of the writer's continuous familiarity with the subject. Inadvertent deception arising from writer misunderstanding of client data is minimized, and corporate decision makers can be kept more closely in touch with consumer opinions about both the advertising and the product or service being marketed.

In-house (also known as *client-side*) copywriting can offer excellent preparation for a career at an outside agency as well. In addition, the competition for entry-level in-house jobs generally is less intense. Writers who wish to make the jump from client-side to agency work, however, must not wait too long. For whatever reason, some agencies conclude that people who have spent more than two or three years on the client-side must be second-rate talent. There is little rational justification for this prejudice, but it persists nonetheless. Many copywriters—skilled ones—have spent entire careers happily and lucratively at corporate in-house billets. You may do likewise. Just be sure that such a setting is where you want to be before you lose your mobility.

GOVERNMENT/INSTITUTIONAL IN-HOUSE

Much of what has been said about the corporate in-house situation carries over to the government/institutional environment. Working for a nonprofit organization does not make the writer's problems significantly different from those an in-house counterpart faces at a profit-making enterprise. The lack of objectivity is still a real danger and is perhaps heightened by the fact that an allegedly praiseworthy public or charitable institution is doing the communicating. In their haste to promote a worthy cause, writers may distort or exaggerate that cause's actual mission.

Still, the in-house setting is the only practical organizational pattern for many small charities, institutions, and foundations that cannot afford outside talent but must rely on the work of regular employees who often perform other functions as well. The municipality, the college, the religious organization, and several like establishments need people who thoroughly understand their institution's role and philosophy and can explain them in a consistent manner whatever the specific issue involved.

This is another generalist environment to which the copywriter trained only in print, broadcast, or broadband message-making may have difficulty adapting. But if you have a strong commitment to that church, charity, or civic organization, such a setting can be personally gratifying and, given the breadth of jobs you may have to perform, professionally stimulating as well. Just remember to reserve a place in your pencil box for well-sharpened objectivity. Mayors and bishops can be just as short-sighted as marketing vice-presidents.

OUTLET-BASED

Copywriters within a station, cable system, network, or Web publisher experience a more varied brand of in-house work. Despite the prevalence of canned (preproduced) video and audio material from outside suppliers, most electronic media outlets must generate copy of their own for broadcast and/or broadband dissemination. These self-created writing efforts include such items as station/system identifications (known as "IDs"), program promotions, public service copy, and, most lucratively, commercial messages to serve the needs of client advertisers. Outlet employees who turn out such writing may or may not be called copywriters, but they draw the scripting assignments nonetheless.

The paradox has been that those major-market stations/systems with the largest staffs have needed in-station writers least. Virtually all their "spot load" (schedule of commercials) accrues from substantial national or regional advertisers whose agencies deliver the commercials prepackaged and ready for airing. Large outlets, in short, have had the greatest capability to hire advertising copywriters, but the least need for them.

Nonetheless, with cable systems continuing to bolster their local advertising efforts and with the competition for fragmenting audiences accelerating in all branches of the electronic media industry, even major-market facilities are reinvesting in copywriter positions to handle promotions and commercial assignments. The consolidation of radio stations brought about by ownership deregulation has also aggregated part-time or piecemeal duties into full-time and higher-paying slots that serve the needs of multiple outlets. Station companion Websites, as well as self-standing ones, also call for writers to both create and repurpose promotional and client advertising copy.

Burgeoning media options available to consumers and advertisers require not only greater efforts by conventional outlets to hold an audience but also aggressive marketing by new broadband delivery systems to become a part of people's listening/viewing habits. At many broadcast stations, the old promotions unit (which used to consist of a secretary sending out bumper stickers) has been upgraded into a creative services or marketing department that handles everything from on-air promotion, to client and press information packets, to the overall design of the outlet's programming and online extensions. Some facilities have even abolished the program director's position and placed that responsibility in the hands of the marketing director. Such fundamental changes in emphasis have meant new prestige and job opportunities for copywriting professionals.

For both advertising and promotion tasks, small operators are also becoming increasingly aware that copywriting slots can pay for themselves. These stations and cable systems have either scraped together enough money to hire one person for full-time writing chores or have retained only those full-time salespeople and air personalities who can be counted on to generate effective copy in conjunction with their other duties. This trend demonstrates that good writing skills are important to electronic media employability, regardless of whether or not you see yourself as primarily a copywriter. "Retaining skilled creative personnel and arming them with knowledge and technology is a vital supplement to a competent sales force," states television station general manager Gary Cozen. "When creative becomes a top priority, clients will pay for quality."[32]

Full-time in-station/system copywriters may discover that writing duties also encompass at least some responsibility for producing, announcing, and actually pitching spots to clients or their representatives. In the case of outlet promotion materials, this selling job is directed to one's own bosses, but it makes the workload no less demanding. If you are the only real writer around, be prepared to persuasively shepherd your concept from the keyboard right through its placement onto the airwaves or the Web.

Outlet-based writers also face two conditions not present in the agency setting: (1) extremely short deadlines and (2) the need to serve competing clients. At an advertising agency, assignments are usually time-lined over a number of days. At a local station/cable office, they may be required within the hour! A retail client wants to change his or her 11 o'clock commercial to reflect a spur-of-the-moment sale, or a station salesperson demands a sample (spec) spot to impress a potential client over lunch. Both of these demands must be attended to immediately while still keeping up with the normal flow of writing assignments.

There is also the problem of competing clients. Most electronic media outlets number several different banks, eateries, gas stations, grocery stores, auto dealers, and other local businesses among their continuing clientele. Because these enterprises are often too small to hire ad agencies, the station/system copywriter must create commercials for each of them. No advertising agency ever handles more than one account in a given product category. But outlet-based writers must service competing clients all the time—which means keeping each one satisfied and differentiated from its rivals.

OTHER EMPLOYMENT OPTIONS

The previous five categories encompass the majority of electronic media copywriting positions, but a number of other options also may be available. Both broadcast and cable *networks* employ their own promotions writers to craft promos and the other brief material used between program segments. This type of writing can be an especially high-stakes adventure. If it actually had to pay for the airtime it uses, the promotions department of any of the networks would be that network's own biggest client. With such multimillion-dollar time investments at stake, network promotion writers must be especially clever.

Similarly, specialty service firms such as Film House, The Chuck Blore Company, and Peters Communications use high-talent writers to create promotion and image packages that enhance programming flow and appeal on behalf of local outlets around the country. Station slogans, comedy bits, musical sell lines, and "concept" channel identifications may all be a part of the specialty service's highly attractive output.

Mention must also be made of commercial, industrial, and educational production houses. Although much of their activity revolves around the creation of full-length projects, many of these projects are of ten- to twenty-minutes duration. Because such audio, video, and PowerPoint presentations mirror the same syntax and format as commercials and promos, copywriters are uniquely qualified to prepare these as well. The same can be said for the dynamic sound and visual content that broadband Internet technology now makes possible and the Websites it enables require. The Web has progressed from a medium whose content was produced by "techie" specialists to one being served by the very agencies and people who have long created messages for conventional broadcasting. "The dot.com world has become as creatively alluring as traditional advertising," BBDO chairman Phil Dusenberry first observed a decade ago. And, as he accurately went on to predict, "Some people defect from traditional advertising to that world. But in time, they'll end up in the same place because it's going to come together."[33]

CONTINUITY—THE COPYWRITER'S MAIN PRODUCT

In most of the employment contexts we have just explored, the electronic media copywriter is engaged in the task of creating *continuity*. This term, which is so central to the writer's role, has both a broad and a narrow definition. To understand our writing responsibilities, we must be aware of each definition's parameters.

In the broad sense, *continuity* encompasses all short, nonprogrammatic aired material. Thus, within this use of the term, everything that is not an integral part of a self-contained information or entertainment show can be called continuity. This definition therefore excludes news copy, but it does include commercials and public service announcements, as well as promos, station/channel IDs, time/weather blurbs, broadband "bumpers," and similar between-program matter.

Commercials and PSAs (public service announcements) are *excluded* under continuity's narrow designation. This much more restrictive use of the term defines continuity as *brief, nonprogrammatic, and nonspot aired material designed to promote, interlock, and increase attention to the aired features and commercials.* This definition, therefore, primarily embraces the role of promotion writers. Commercial copywriters, conversely, exercise the wider responsibilities that are reflected in continuity's broad definition.

Many outlets maintain a *traffic and continuity* department or at least one person designated to prepare program logs and the associated scheduling of all material segments to be aired. Under such an arrangement, a natural relationship exists between the scheduling (traffic) function, which sets down all the programs and announcements in sequence, and the writing function, which seeks to make the flow between all those disparate parts as smooth as possible. The traffic and continuity staffer thus is often both organizer and writer. In each of these contexts, the emphasis is on the *segue.* Originally borrowed from music, the term *segue* is now used in our profession as verb and noun—both to describe the process of one event merging without a break into another and to denote the result of this process.

The electronic media place a high premium on these segues in order to give the consumer as little excuse as possible to tune out mentally, as little time as possible to punch the scan button or to click the mouse. The writer who constructs stimulating and informative copy is just as important to segue achievement as is the technical director or on-air talent. Conversely, dead air and deadly copy can be equally lethal to the maintenance of program and audience flow. The aim, of course, is to give the audience the feeling that pleasing and interesting stimuli are proceeding in an unbroken stream that deserves the continuing investment of their time as well as the more or less constant devotion of their attention.

The fashioning of meaningful, audience-holding transitions is a vital part of the copywriter's craft and a core duty, whether you deal with continuity in the broad or narrow sense. What is more, transitions are as essential within a full-length entertainment or information program as they are to the interlocking of a newscast with the game show that follows it. Skill-honing in constructing between-program transitions improves your ability to sculpt the unified full-length scripts that you might later be called on to write. Even in its most limited sense, continuity writing is therefore both a valuable training ground for more expansive writing efforts and a means of gainful employment in its own right.

It is not necessary to justify continuity writing (in either the broad or narrow sense) as a mere preliminary to "bigger" things. Indeed, it might be argued that the writer who can surmount the immense time problems inherent in a thirty-second spot and still create an attention-holding and memorable vignette possesses and exhibits a cogent talent that few novelists or playwrights ever attain.

PORTFOLIO CREATION

Just as the novelist or playwright collects scenario ideas and character sketches for possible exploitation in some future project, continuity writers should be gathering, preserving, and upgrading the copy assignments on which they have worked in order to advance to better accounts or jobs in the months and years ahead. This means developing a professional portfolio. Unlike plays, novels, and movie scripts, a piece of copy does not prominently display the name of its author. In fact, the writer of commercials and other continuity remains anonymous to all but the supervisor and perhaps the client. This absence of attribution is the price we pay for the relative security of a salaried position and a regular paycheck. To secure that first and subsequent media job, therefore, copywriters must compile their own tangible record of what they have done to serve as a promise of what they will do.

"The book is everything," reveals agency head David Suissa. "The book tells you what kind of attitude they have. It's all there in the work."[34] Therefore, your portfolio should reveal as much or more about you as it does about your work. "I would like the books to have personality," advises BBDO/Chicago creative manager Linda Waste. "I see too many books that don't tell me anything about the person. A really creative, idea-driven candidate will have poured a part of themselves into their work and you can see it in their book. I'm not talking about fancy packaging and a bunch of shock value creative that shows a person is 'edgy.' I'm talking about telling me who you are and what your style of thinking is through what you choose to put in your book."[35]

While there is a natural tendency to concentrate on copy samples for unusual or even bizarre clients, too many of these easier-to-pen pieces will turn off most employers. "Easy equals unimpressive," creative director Mark Gale warns. "Be assured I have already seen spec campaigns for (1) the local bondage store; (2) the barbecue restaurant with insanely spicy food; (3) Porsche. If you need a little spec [copy written for a hypothetical client that was never produced] for your book, choose something potentially mundane—the kind of product most of us work on far more often than we would like to admit."[36] Industry recruiter Monica Buchanan agrees: "I prefer to see hard subjects, like insurance, rather than a piercing or tattoo place."[37] This tracks with earlier research into employer portfolio content preferences by advertising professor Brett Robbs, who found that "while a portfolio can include some work for clients like dog trainers and coffee shops, respondents indicated it should have a number of campaigns for categories like financial services, technology, packaged goods, hard goods, and business to business—categories that also give candidates an opportunity to demonstrate a range of stylistic approaches.... It's those sorts of assignments, respondents say, that provide a real measure of a student's ability."[38]

You will find that portfolio development is easier if you do not have to think up both the market problem and the copy solution. Whenever possible, use and improve exercises encountered in class or stimulated by this textbook. Such exercises will help you determine the limitations within which you must work. Dreaming up your own assignments for portfolio exhibits, on the other hand, can be not only tedious but also misleading. It is much too easy to create a problem for a solution you have already conceived or to avoid instructive pitfalls by bending the task around them. As opposed to the playwright or novelist, the continuity writer can seldom choose the subject. So get your assignments from somewhere or someone else as your new portfolio begins to take shape. Learn to work within the unyielding subject constraints that are an intrinsic part of the continuity writer's world—and let your portfolio reflect this reality.

The upgrade of a bad piece of produced advertising is sometimes advocated as an effective portfolio exhibit. The next time you encounter an ad that you think is a failure, transcribe its copy and then show how you would improve it. When your portfolio sets the original and your enhanced version side-by-side, your conceptual and marketing abilities are graphically revealed. If the portfolio leads to a job interview, these kinds of exhibits are also very potent discussion inciters.

Just make certain that such comparative displays are the only bad advertising in your book! Successful freelancer Yvonne Smith reveals that "it says something about the judgment of the person who ruined an entire portfolio by including that one bad thing. Judge the person on the worst thing in the book. You [the prospective employer] may get something equally bad."[39] Similarly, counsels creative director David Butler, "If a book is really up and down, it's almost like the person can't tell a good ad from a bad ad, and you form an opinion, justly or unjustly, that they can't edit themselves."[40] The creative director for a mid-sized New York agency adds, "We look at the best piece in each portfolio for potential and the worst piece for risk of hire. If the risk seems too great, we pass."[41] In fact, "if a piece isn't good, it shouldn't be in your book," concludes top creative headhunter Dave Willmer. "By including it and acknowledging shortcomings, you'll come across as apologetic and unsure—not the image you want to convey."[42]

Once you have accumulated a group of copy samples that are of as uniformly a high quality as possible, you are ready to compile them. The traditional format to hold this compilation is the portfolio case. These cases come in a variety of sizes and are available at many art and office supply stores. Copywriters usually can and should make do with smaller sizes than are used by art directors. Cases are similar to a zippered vinyl or leather briefcase with paired handles, but they open flat to expose a binder arrangement of multiple rings to which mounting pages are fastened. Individual exhibits are set on these pages, which are then held in place and protected by attached plastic covers (see Figure 1.1). The case's design makes it easy to remove old exhibits and replace them with newer, improved examples.

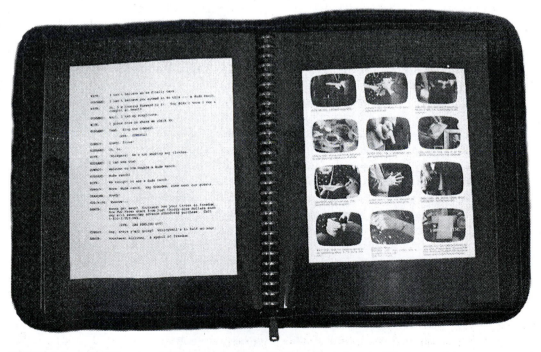

FIGURE 1.1   A traditional portfolio case. A radio script is on the left and a TV commercial photoboard on the right.

Although there are now several other formats for portfolio presentation, the standard case still has its advantages. When cases are "sitting on a conference table, they're reminding me to be familiar with them or ask someone's opinion," admits Mullen Advertising's chief creative officer Edward Boches. "They have more presence in my office." Further, Deutsch executive creative director Kathy Delaney reveals, "If you have something concrete, you usually do spend a little more time with it."[43] However, the hard copy book is expensive for you to put together, and you may have to create one or more equally expensive spares to prevent your job-seeking from being brought to a halt if one executive asks to keep your book for a while. Unfortunately, if the case is lost, so is a significant financial investment.

Therefore, a variety of digital portfolio formats are now becoming much more common. A DVD can constitute a self-standing portfolio, or it can be slipped into a conventional case to convey as-produced audio and video work. Just be sure it has an easy and glitch-free menu, and check it on several machines for stability. Crashing a prospective employer's computer with an electronically infirm disk is unlikely to lead to an interview. A PDF book is another alternative and can be easily emailed with a digital resume. The PDF is obviously easy to store and cheap to copy and send. However, be certain that the file is not so large as to clog the recipient's email box. In addition, some employers may be leery of opening an unsolicited attachment for fear of infecting their computer with a virus. Therefore, PDF books should be sent only after you have made initial contact with the hirer who has agreed to receive it.

Setting up your own portfolio Website is an alternative way to get your work in front of employers. The URL makes it easy to access and easy for the initial recipient to call to the attention of others at the company for evaluation. But keep in mind that the hiring executive is still seeking to get a clear idea of your talent and style in as brief a time as possible. A Website with mounds of material to wade through is just as off-putting as a thick portfolio case. Be selective. The more examples you set before the employer, the more chance there is of including a lame piece of copy that can pollute the whole book. Keep the Website lean and extremely easy to navigate. "Our research shows many employers spend five minutes or less reviewing online work," says recruiting director Dave Willmer, "so make sure your pieces load quickly and contact information is easy to find."[44]

Finally, you may wish to follow the advice of freelance copywriter Ty Lifeset, who reveals, "I opted to go digital. I put my whole portfolio on an interactive CD the size of a business card. Now when I'm in a bar or a coffee shop or any occasion where I could network but wouldn't normally bring my portfolio for fear of paper cuts, spills and whatever else, and someone asks me about my portfolio, I simply reach in my pocket and give it to them. . . . So far, it's been received very well and has brought me numerous gigs along the way."[45]

Different employers may prefer different portfolio formats, so as your career progresses, you may find yourself developing several alternate vehicles to convey your work. But whatever its format, the ultimate test of a portfolio, maintains David Butler, is "the quality of the work. Can we look through a book and find a significant number of ads that make us say, 'Gee, I wish I'd done that.'"[46] "It really comes down to the work inside," agrees GSD&M's creative recruiting manager Jamie Flynn . . . "because it's about the work."[47] As Dave Willmer, whose firm has placed hundreds of copywriters, concludes, "Most creatives have a good story to tell; it's simply a matter of developing a book that does it justice—both at face value and when reading between the lines."[48]

Above all, do not wait until you are actually in the job market to get your portfolio started. Under the pressure of finding immediate employment, the range of your work will be too limited and the scope of your talent too blurred. Granted, the stress of fulfilling assignments is a constant part of the copywriter's lot. But pressure to come up with what those assignments *should be* is not. Further, no writer—novice or veteran—can create, in a short period of time, a copy catalog sufficient to demonstrate either versatility or breadth of experience.

Thus, to give yourself every advantage, it is strongly recommended that you begin your portfolio NOW. A promo or a thirty-second spot need not have been actually aired in order to demonstrate your wordsmith's skill any more than a novelist's character sketch or a poet's sonnet must be actually published before it has merit. The important thing is that the spot, sketch or sonnet exposes a true writer's insight and execution.

Writing style and character are in a continuous process of evolution. They exist, as composer Aaron Copland said about music, "in a continual state of becoming."[49] Not even a hint of this growth can be captured in a portfolio created within a single month. So begin your portfolio now. Improve it gradually throughout your career. Keep thinning it out so that only the hardiest hybrids from each copy species remain. Then, let that portfolio help propel you toward whatever sector of the copywriting marketplace best suits your own aims, goals, and documented abilities.

"Creating advertising is a never-ending thing," cautioned BBDO chairman Phil Dusenberry. "The difficulty is trying to top yourself. What do you do for an encore to all those commercials? Advertising is very much a what-have-you-done-for-me-lately business. You always have to be sharpening your sword, trying to be better tomorrow than you were yesterday."[50] Being "better" requires surmounting both your own past limitations and the constraints imposed by the characteristics of the electronic media. These constraints are explored in the following chapter.

2   Copywriting and the Communication Process

L ike anyone professionally engaged in reaching large and diverse populations, the broadcast/broadband copywriter must be acutely aware of the dynamics of the communication process. We must understand that, though our message may be intended to reach thousands or even millions of consumers, these consumers will usually be alone or in very small groups when they receive it. We may be targeting a "mass," but each person must feel that she or he is being addressed individually. In addition, the fact that the copywriter's messages employ exotic electronic media does not lessen that writer's need to appreciate the most basic components of human communication. Wordsmiths who concentrate mainly on the electronic implements of their delivery system tend to construct messages attuned to media and marketing organizations rather than to the audiences those organizations are attempting to impact.

In the final analysis, copywriters are paid not to fill "media," but to touch *individual people through* those media. Therefore, there must be no misconception as to the primacy of each consumer in determining what we write and how we write it. The unemployment lines continue to be fed by practitioners who write "for" radio, television, and the Internet rather than for other human beings.

COMMUNICATION FUNDAMENTALS

No matter how simple or sophisticated its delivery system, all communication aimed at people includes and activates the four components pictured in Figure 2.1. Any or all of these components can exist in multiple forms and still not change the fundamental functioning of the process.

1. Originator

Limiting our discussion to *human* communication (this is not, after all, a text on computer programming or animal husbandry), we assume the *originator* to be a human

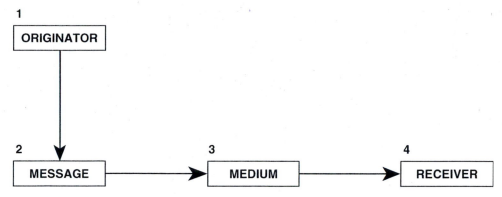

FIGURE 2.1 The Basic Communication Process.

being with some desire to communicate with another human being or beings. In our business, this desire is most often stimulated by money. Whatever the nature of the desire, the originator's task is to establish a temporary linkage with another person in order that they both will focus on the same object, event, or idea.

The duration of this linkage and the clarity of this focus are influenced by every component of the process but initially depend on the originator's overt and covert behavior. We have all experienced situations in which an originator's overt action clashes so strikingly with his or her covert (underlying) behavior that real doubt is cast on that originator's motives. The man who shakes your hand warmly but studiously avoids eye contact becomes as suspect as the woman whose warm vocal "hello" is accompanied by physically backing away. Links have been established, of course, but with much different impacts than the originators intended—or thought they intended.

In certain instances, originators might fool *themselves* as to the fundamental factors influencing their communications. (More than one inadvertently bad peanut butter advertisement can be traced back to some poor copywriter who never could stand the stuff.) Every originator has some financial, social, or professional stake in the results of every communication he or she initiates. The most successful people are those who have learned to probe their own motivations before seeking to influence others.

This influencing may consist of nothing more than attaining attention (which, in the often raucous environment of electronic media, is no small task). Once such attention/linkage has been established, the originator has satisfied the basic mechanical requirements of the communication process. Whether the outcome of this linkage is favorable or unfavorable to the originator is a more long-range and often subjective judgment. As we discover in later chapters, it is not too difficult to secure momentary attention. Holding and parlaying such attention toward ends acceptable or advantageous to the originator, however, are much more extensive and intensive tasks.

2. Message

A *message* is the commodity one must possess in order to be justifiably labeled an originator. It is a commodity one must also *transmit* in order actually to *function* as an originator. This does not mean that originators are always aware of the content they are transmitting—or even that they are transmitting at all. Human beings, in sensory proximity to each other, can receive messages that are products of that proximity rather than of any conscious desire on the part of the alleged originator to communicate. What is interpreted as a "come hither" look on the part of that handsome male across the dance floor may result only from a slippage of his contact lens. Similarly, though she is not aware of the fact, the dozing student in the back of the classroom is originating a distinctly unpleasant message as far as her instructor is concerned—and one that will not have its impact diminished merely because it was inadvertent.

Except in total isolation from others, it is very difficult if not impossible for us to avoid assuming the more or less continuous role of originators transmitting a steady stream of intended and unintended messages to people with whom we come into contact. When the situation instills in us an *active* desire to transmit, we tend to make special efforts to avoid the simultaneous sending of seemingly conflicting communications.

3. Medium

The vehicle through which originators project their messages can be simple or complex. It can emanate exclusively from the originator's own body or use external mechanisms. In fact, some authorities divide media into two broad categories: *communication* and *communications* vehicles. The first category consists of intrabody devices. Thus oral behavior using the human vocal apparatus, as well as physical gestures and other visible body movements (nonverbals), constitutes *communication*. Writing on a blackboard, typing a letter, or marking a forest trail with piled rocks, on the other hand, are all considered *communications* because they rely on message-carrying instruments external to the human anatomy.

A key advantage of communications media is that they extend our ability to communicate in time and/or space. A note left on the refrigerator or on the dining room table will convey the originator's message, even though it may have been written hours or days ago and the originator might be miles away when that memo is discovered.

Mass communications vehicles constitute a special subgroup of communications media because their extreme efficiency not only extends our ability to communicate in time and space, but also makes it possible to reach large and diversified audiences quickly, if not instantaneously. As the copywriter soon learns, however, the optimum use of mass communications requires that each person within the "mass" audience is led to feel that he or she is being addressed directly and singly. In fact, the electronic media in particular are at their most effective when they simulate a *communication* rather than *communications* experience. The script that assists an announcer in seeming to talk "across the table" to you (a communication setting) has a much greater chance of success than one that bellows at "all you folks out there in video-land" and thereby calls more attention to the medium than to the message it carries.

Such a sense of personalized intimacy is at least as important in Internet messages, where folks don't just like—but *expect*—the feeling of a one-on-one experience. While some glossiness can be sacrificed in the online environment, a sense of personal communication is obligatory. As Agency.com vice-president of creative services Chris Needham muses about Web writing, "I'm not sure it's about the absolute most gorgeous image and the absolute perfect tagline. It's dirtier than that. It's all about building connections between people rather than the thing itself beautifully broadcasting out what it is."[1]

4. Receiver

The receiver is the *detector* of the message the originator has transmitted via some medium. We say detector, rather than *target,* because receivers spend much of their time picking up messages that are not really aimed at them. In the most alarming sense, this occurs in bugging and other forms of electronic eavesdropping, where a conscious and technologically sophisticated effort is made to intercept messages intended for others. Usually, however, detection of messages by unintended receivers is simply a case of sensory proximity. We have all overheard conversations of people at adjoining restaurant tables, in nearby bus seats, or barking into cell-phones virtually anywhere. We have all glanced over others' bulletin board notes and postings. In doing so, we became receivers even though the originator of the message sent via the communication or communications vehicle was not seeking to establish a link with us.

Straightforward originators usually do not worry about whether people other than those at whom they aim have, in fact, become receivers of the message. Their only concern is whether they have made authentic receivers of the people they have actively tried to reach. (We must, however, take special care with the media placement of advertising for "adult" products in an effort to minimize the chance that these messages will be apprehended by children.) Well-fashioned and well-delivered communication is more than accidental or mechanical meshing of originator, message, medium, and receiver. Instead, this success requires

> AN ORIGINATOR (with a conscious desire to communicate)
> A MESSAGE (of significance)
> through A MEDIUM (that is appropriate)
> to A RECEIVER (attaching like significance)
> *who RESPONDS in an originator-advantageous manner.*

THE ELECTRONIC MEDIA COMMUNICATION PROCESS

Keep in mind that the originator, message, medium, and receiver are components basic to any and every application of the communication process. When we move beyond simple one-to-one interchanges, additional sub-elements come into play. Thus in the copywriter's electronic media world, we encounter the system represented in Figure 2.2.

1. Originator

Unless the same person owns, operates, and prepares all the advertising for an enterprise, the origination function in the electronic media is shared by a SOURCE working in cooperation with a message CONSTRUCTOR. This source is usually referred to as the *client*. It may be a bank, cereal manufacturer, car dealer, or fast-food palace. In noncommercial assignments (resulting in *public service announcements,* or PSAs), the source may be the United Way, the Red Cross, or even the local Society for the

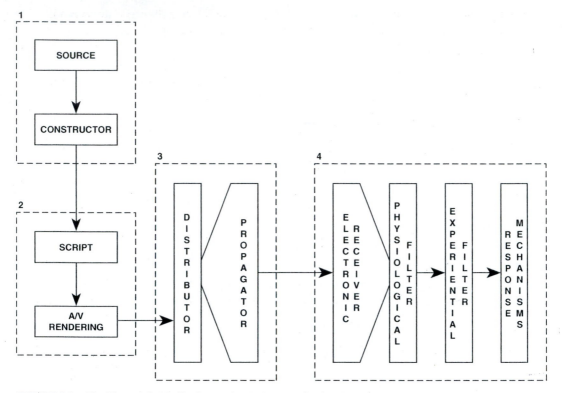

FIGURE 2.2   The Electronic Media Copywriter's Communication Process.

Preservation of Hibernating Chipmunks. It is the client source whose aims drive the process and set the agenda for what is to be communicated. Sometimes, this agenda can be a daunting one, because "clients," asserts advertising guru George Lois, "are people—who happen to be shopping for miracles."[2]

The other half of the originator function, the constructor, then strives to supply this miracle by putting together a message that is appropriate to the task and maximally adapted to take advantage of the unique capabilities of radio, television, or the Web. Presumably, you are reading this book as a means of preparing yourself to be, or collaborate with, such a constructor. Electronic media constructors work within media outlets, at advertising agencies, or in any of the other contexts discussed in Chapter 1. Whatever the environment, you must recognize that a message constructor in our industry seldom has the last (or even the first) word as to what will be communicated. To a general or specific degree, it is the source who pays the bills—the constructor's salary included—and who therefore calls the shots.

Shaller Rubin Associates' executive vice-president Paul Goldsmith illustrates this inevitability by observing that

> My ideal copywriter is fully aware of the downhill realities of the advertising process—recognizing that his work will go through more sieves, more review than any other piece of work in the agency. After it's submitted to the scrutiny of his supervisor, it goes to the creative director. On to the account group for its

suggestions and changes before it reaches the client who will surely incorporate his ideas and alterations. This tedious trip through a creative person's chamber of horrors unfortunately comes with the territory.[3]

"A good 90 percent of what I commit to paper," star British copywriter Adrian Holmes laments, "ends up being scrubbed out, abandoned halfway, completely rewritten or thrown into the bin in disgust."[4] But the client (the source) must be served. "Going into advertising is like going to Transylvania," award-winning director Frank Budgen adds. "Charming people sink their teeth into you and suck your blood and the next thing you know, you're one of them. They also stay up very late."[5]

2. Message

When people think of the electronic media message, they understandably focus on the video and/or audio form in which that message reaches them. Yet, that communication first had to be set down in more traditional written form to constitute a SCRIPT. Granted, on some occasions, the message is extemporized, entirely ad-libbed, or edited down from recorded actualities and interviews. In these instances, a script is either unnecessary or becomes an after-the-fact *transcript* for contractual or record-keeping purposes. In most copywriting situations, however, the script constitutes the motivating creative blueprint.

After approval by the appropriate sources (and supervisory constructors), this blueprint (which in video messages may have assumed storyboard form) is translated into "live" on-air readings, or digital recordings or files for easy playback by electronic outlets. As we subsequently explore in Chapters 7 and 10, the effectiveness of the script depends almost as much on its form as on its content. The best-laid concepts can be maimed, if not murdered, when the scripts that convey them are confusing or disorganized.

Assuming that the script or storyboard is cast into the industry-recognized pattern, it must then be transformed into one of the just-mentioned playback formats. This transformation (or A/V RENDERING, as it is labeled in Figure 2.2) should be as true to the original script as possible. Nevertheless, copywriters must understand that the printed word is only a partial representation of actuality. A picture, a snatch of music, or a vocal inflection can be generally indicated in the script, but their final "as-produced" rendering will have a distinct and much more specific dimension. This same principle applies to the electronic media message as a whole, which can include all of these elements. Thus although the printed script is both a creative chronicle and a contractual promise, its ultimate realization in sight and/or sound is a discrete phenomenon unto itself. This is a maddening fact of life for both sources and constructors. But it is the price gladly paid for the potential dynamism of the electronic media communication.

In the final analysis, the script is like a composer's musical score. It must set down its creator's intentions in as precise a manner as the format allows—with the realization that these intentions will be conveyed through the expressive interpretations of other people. In the following script, the concept and words the writer has chosen to convey it are clear, and the visual is a simple one. But the subsequent casting of the children and the way they are photographically captured by the production team as guided by the art director will have a great deal to do with the commercial's ultimate effectiveness.

Video	Audio
SHOTS OF KIDS AROUND THE COUNTRY; FILM IS BLACK AND WHITE	BOY 1: When I grow up, I want to file all day.
	BOY 2: I want to claw my way up to middle management.
	GIRL 1: Be replaced on a whim.
	GIRL 2: I want to have a brown nose.
	BOY 3: I want to be a yes man…
	GIRL 3: …yes woman.
	GIRL 4: (VOICE OVER) Yes sir, Coming, sir.
	BOY 4: Anything for a raise, sir.
	GIRL 5: When I grow up…
	BOY 5: When I grow up…
	BOY 6: I want to be underappreciated.
	GIRL 6: Be paid less for doing the same job.
	BOY 7: I want to be forced into early retirement.
SUPER: What do you want to be?	Monster.com
There's a better job out there.	

(Courtesy of Dylan Lee, Mullen Advertising)

3. Medium

As with the message component, the *medium* (transmission) function of electronic communication also proceeds through two stages. Even though it is often no more than clerical processing, an off-air DISTRIBUTOR operation precedes the actual airing of the pre-constructed message. If the project begins and culminates entirely within a single media outlet, this distributor function may involve nothing more than handing copies of the completed script to the appropriate colleagues for voicing and production. If the message is destined for use by other enterprises, distribution takes on more varied forms. After in-house or outside production, commercials and other continuity are regularly disseminated by satellite or fiber-optic landline to multiple stations and cable system interconnects for later insertion into their program schedules. Alternatively, ever-increasing numbers of copywriter-created messages streak via wire or wireless Internet protocols directly to their end users. In today's instantaneous world, relatively few are delivered by the post office or package express companies.

Generally speaking, the larger the number of outlets and the more major the source, the more comprehensive the distributor function becomes. Scripts engendered by the creative departments of national advertising agencies and produced by their contracted production houses result in wide dissemination of the air-ready message to scores of media outlets. Copies may also be sent to network continuity acceptance departments and to the headquarters of media groups in order to ensure that the message does not violate these organizations' self-policing standards.

After this behind-the-scenes activity, the message is finally transmitted by each participating outlet per its own schedule, or it is simultaneously aired by multiple affiliates as part of a network feed. This transmission, or PROPAGATOR function, is the factor that gives the message potential access to thousands, even millions, of people. It is not our purpose here to inventory the immense variety of digital equipment that plays a part in this broadcast or broadband dissemination operation. Nor do we have the space to isolate all the technical malfunctions beyond the writer's control that may interfere with optimal message transmission. Suffice it to say that at this point in the process, science takes over from art, and the copywriter must rely on the specialized expertise of engineers and computer programmers as well as the hoped-for reliability of their solid-state technology.

4. Receiver

This same reliance must be accorded the first (ELECTRONIC RECEIVER) stage of the overall receiver function. Electronic transmitters do not talk directly to people; they talk to people's radio/TV sets, computers, or mobile devices, which all translate the analog or digital impulses so that human beings can apprehend them. These electronic receiving sets vary widely in cost, age, and sensitivity and also in the ability of their owners to adjust them properly. Stressing the particular color of a product through the visual alone, for instance, may be a risky venture on home monitors with faulty color-adjustment circuits. Similarly, immersing your key selling point in an audio kaleidoscope may not be the wisest strategy when filtered through pocket receivers operating on depleted batteries. Despite today's digital sophistication, there are a lot of malfunctioning and misadjusted receiving sets in use by consumers. The less you, the writer, take for granted as to these units' performance, the more care you will come to exercise in safeguarding the clarity of your message's content.

The final three stages of the receiver function are internal to each human being in our audience. The first of these, the PHYSIOLOGICAL FILTER, refers to the various sensory limitations inherent in each of us. People with hearing loss obviously encounter greater difficulty in picking up the radio transmission or television soundtrack than do folks with unimpaired auditory mechanisms. Individuals with sight problems will experience trouble in perceiving certain elements of the television/Internet picture (but may acquire greater auditory sensitivity as a partial compensation).

As in the case of the electronic receiver, the copywriter cannot assume too much about the functioning level of the physiological components within our human receptors. Even people who hear or see fairly well may have problems discerning a brand name read over a "heavy" music backdrop or a video "where-to-call" graphic projected in small, indistinct numerals. This is a major consideration in fashioning messages intended for mobile phone display. Remember also that some individuals with well-functioning eyes and ears take longer to process this sensory information through their brain. Say it or show it too quickly or obscurely and they, too, will miss the main point of your message.

Assuming that these sensory barriers are successfully penetrated, our message must then encounter the much more varied and sometimes downright bizarre hurdles presented by the EXPERIENTIAL FILTER. This is the sum total of all the events, episodes, and situations through which consumers have acquired knowledge of their world and of themselves. Because no two people have experienced exactly the same things, each of us sees the world through different eyes, or, as media theorist Marshall McLuhan put it, through different "goggles." Our preconceptions, preferences, fears, and prejudices are all part of this experiential filter, which acts to guarantee that each of us behaves as a unique individual.

Fortunately for the professional communicator, even though each person is a one-of-a-kind item, individuals can be grouped into wide categories delineated by such factors as age, gender, education, geographic location, income, and national origin. Labeled *demographic* characteristics, these factors are, however, no more than broad-stroke descriptors. Much more detailed are the *psychographic* analyses used by market researchers and other social scientists to deeply probe lifestyle practices and preferences in order to predict the programs we will watch, the product gratifications we are seeking, and the political issues we might support or oppose. Many now believe it is all about psychographics. "Demography is dead," asserts Ann Mack, director of trendspotting for JWT/New York. "It's horrible to say in our industry, which has so easily sectionalized people and targeted them with advertising. But in this world, you can no longer simply target to a demographic. You also have to look at life stage versus age."[6] "For example," adds trade reporter Marilyn Moore, "a brand marketing to mothers should be looking at women who may be 24 years old— or 44. Career women could be 30—or 60. They are all going through the same life stage, but they are not the same age."[7] Because electronic media copywriters, like all mass communicators, are unable to monitor audience feedback until well after the message has been sent, they must rely on these psychographic characteristics and hypotheses in formulating the structure and content of everything from 10-second station IDs and Website pop-ups to multipart entertainment programs.

In short, the electronic media industry engages in a giant guessing game that tries to predict and target not only the demographic/psychographic composition of a likely audience, but also the words and images that best appeal to those people. Still, however the population pie is sliced, its serviceable segments are usually relatively large in order to be potentially profitable.

Somewhat standardized message construction is therefore inevitable as we strive to reach those research-targeted phantoms without boring them on the one hand or confusing and overloading them on the other. Two common expressions graphically illustrate these two undesirable communication extremes: (1) talking *down to* and (2) talking *over* the intended audience.

The dulling, oversimplified message that seems to assail us with kindergarten concepts is diagrammed in Figure 2.3. The message gets through our sensory system without difficulty. But it is so blandly basic that it seems deliberately to insult our intelligence. "They're *talking down* to me," is our reaction, and our attention either is diminished or is entirely diverted to more stimulating things. It is sobering to note that as early as 1996, a nationwide survey by *Adweek* found that 39 percent of all respondents thought that commercials talked down to them—and this figure rose to 44 percent among eighteen- to twenty-four-year-olds.[8] More recent proprietary research by several different media agencies has uncovered similar findings.

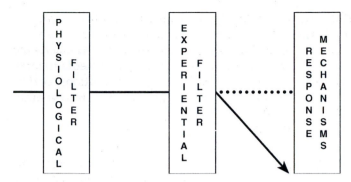

FIGURE 2.3 Talking Down.

How do you think most women would react to the following sixty-second radio spot?

ANNCR: The yucky bathroom soap dish. You've probably got one in your little home right now. That's because you don't know how to drain the water out of it. You need to realize that standing water dissolves a bar of soap. That means it turns the solid soap to liquid. In your words --- yucky. Acme's Tidy Housewife Soap Dish can help. The Tidy Housewife Soap Dish features a porous --- that means full of little holes --- top. This top lets the water drain into the dish's round-shaped bottom. With the Tidy Housewife Soap Dish, you can protect your precious soap. Get a fashionable Tidy Housewife Soap Dish today. Your husband will think you're really smart. Ask the nice people at a store near you for an Acme Tidy Housewife Soap Dish. It will brighten your life and give you more time for your favorite soaps --- the ones on TV. Write down the name so you won't forget. Acme Tidy Housewife Soap Dish.

At the other extreme is the fulsomely esoteric message that is so cabalistic or recondite that almost no one understands it. The course of such a communication is charted out in Figure 2.4. Here again, the message successfully passed through the sensory system, but then was acutely deflected by the individual's lack of experience with the terms or concepts used. "They're *talking over* my head," is the conclusion, and attempted message decoding ceases. Now, look back to the start of this paragraph and the terms *fulsomely, esoteric, cabalistic,* and *recondite.* Did these words and the sentence that contains them turn you off? If so, you've experienced this "over-my-head" conundrum (or, we should say, *problem*) first hand.

Let us assume, however, that the copywriter has fashioned a message capable of passing through both the physiological and experiential filters with minimal perceptual "bending." This means that (1) key words and concepts are easy to hear or see, and (2) the spot offers understandable and interesting rewards to the people at whom it is aimed. Now, the target consumer's RESPONSE MECHANISMS can be fully engaged. Perhaps our target consumers will buy it, vote for it, donate to it, or mix it with the cat's food once a week. At the very least, the copywriter strives to have them *remember* it so that a gradual familiarity with and favorable disposition toward the product or idea will be built up in the weeks and months ahead.

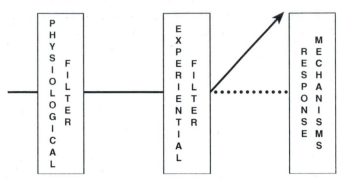

FIGURE 2.4 Talking Over.

The appropriateness or inappropriateness of audience responses in terms of the originator's expectations for the message are stringently evaluated after the fact by ratings points, sales curves, votes cast, or similar measuring devices. If possible, field trials and other test marketing have been undertaken to sample results on a limited basis as a preliminary to the costly, full-scale campaign. In any event, if the responses are found deficient in character or quantity, the message must be changed. Worse, if the responses are adjudged *negative* in nature, it may be that the constructor must be changed. For unlike the dog in Pavlov's famous psychology experiment, it is not the subject audience that is "punished" for deviant responses. Instead, punishment is administered to the experimenter/constructor—in other words, to the copywriter!

What makes all of this even more dicey is audience members' tendencies to interpret things in ways we never anticipated. Despite the misleading orderliness of our communication process diagram, message meanings accrue not only from what copywriters put into them, but also from what audience members take out of them. Meanings, in other words, are not ultimately in messages, but in the people who decode those messages. As British communication theorist John Fiske points out, an aired electronic media "text can no longer be seen as a self-sufficient entity that bears its own meaning and exerts a similar influence on all its readers. Rather, it is seen as a potential of meanings that can be activated in a number of ways."[9]

Thus the broadcast/broadband copywriter's creations are unavoidably *polysemic*—they possess multiple significances because of the contexts in which individual listeners/viewers receive and decode them. Granted, the possibilities for receiver-constructed meanings of a piece of copy are not limitless. We can narrow meaning options through what we put into our spot, what we leave out, and how we arrange the elements we *do* choose to include. Nevertheless, we can never be completely certain of what consumers will make of our message.

Even though process diagrams are helpful in freeze-framing for us the essential components of communication, we should not overestimate their applicability. Like any static model, they are incapable of accurately conveying the dynamic process of one person interacting with another, let alone the method whereby electronic media wordsmiths attempt to interact with unseen thousands of other human beings in both real and TiVo-delayed time.

If all of this unpredictability fails to diminish your interest in copywriting—congratulations! You possess two attributes essential for work on the electronic media's creative side: an uncommon appetite for stress and a thirst for constant challenge. For "if security, tranquility and peace are your goals," counsels former agency CEO Keith Reinhard, "you're in the wrong business."[10]

On the other hand, if you are up to this challenge, it can be professionally invigorating because, as McCann-Erickson deputy creative director Joyce King Thomas affirms, great consumer-respecting copy has the ability to "reflect the current culture, change popular culture. It can move people. Inspire them. Challenge them. Amuse them. It can make people be better people. But that won't happen if the creator's mind is focused on dazzling award-show judges rather than having a one-on-one conversation with their client's consumer."[11] As this chapter points out, achieving this one-on-one result is what understanding the communication process is all about.

The remaining chapters in this book strive further to analyze your commitment to copywriting. They also provide opportunities for you to probe the outer limits of your expressive talent. Even if you are pursuing some other media career role, the material that follows should help you to evaluate the contributions of the writers on whom you depend for your project's success.

3 Tools of Our Trade

Now that we have surveyed the various work environments in which electronic media copywriters operate and have explored the communication complexities to which they are subjected, let's proceed to inventory the writing implements that they typically employ. Broadcast/broadband scribes rely on many of the same devices as other wordsmiths to accomplish their tasks. We also work in situations in which clarity, conciseness, and speed are of paramount importance.

Excess is our greatest enemy—whether it is an excess of ideas that muddles a PSA, an excess of words that forces a commercial into a longer and more expensive format, or an excess of time in completing an assignment that puts an entire campaign off schedule. The writing tools most important to us, therefore, are those that replace excess with *functional frugality,* helping us communicate on target, on budget, and on time. "The thing that makes you a good copywriter is compression," affirms Ketchum Advertising creative director John Lyons. "Michelangelo had a whole ceiling. We have a matchbook cover."[1]

In achieving such compression, punctuation is a vital instrument because it provides the mechanism for grouping words into their most cogent and quickly understandable patterns. As columnist James Kilpatrick points out, "We punctuate for two reasons only—for clarity and for cadence."[2] Because of the overwhelming importance of both of these qualities to words that are written to be heard, punctuation is a major tool for achieving scripted success.

PRINT PUNCTUATION VERSUS AUDIO/VIDEO PUNCTUATION

Obviously, both print and audio/video copywriters use punctuation symbols as a means of sculpting their thoughts. But the role of these symbols varies significantly between the two media categories. In print-based vehicles (whether this print is inked onto paper or Internet reproduced on the consumer's computer screen), the writer's communication is in fundamentally the same form in which the audience will ingest it. Certainly, some editor, typesetter, or webmaster may perform minor alterations, but the message the writer affixes to the "page" uses the same punctuation symbols that the audience will apprehend from that page. Therefore, print punctuation serves as *unmodified communication* between originator and receiver. The comma symbol the writer sets down will be the same comma symbol the "reader" picks up.

For the audio/video writer, on the other hand, the printed record is only a linguistic halfway-house in the communication journey. As we see in Chapter 2, consumers of our messages do not *read* the script but *hear* and experience the translation of that script into real-time happening. Unless it is berthed on a Website, they can neither go back and reread it nor scan ahead to preview it. Thus audio/video punctuation strives to interpret the writer's message to and through announcers, actors, and technicians in order to reach the audience as natural-sounding *speech.* Ultimately, our punctuation is a set of systematic stage directions to intermediaries rather than a direct correspondence with the target audience. In fact, this was how punctuation began in the fourth century when St. Jerome, translator of the Bible, created a crude system of marking religious texts to guide the phrasing of sacred passages as they were read aloud.

Still, like St. Jerome's first attempt, our modern punctuation system remains somewhat print bound. No written symbology can ever specify completely all the nuances of a spoken message any more than a musical score is a total blueprint for a heard composition. Both the score and our script require the services of competent performers/interpreters. What composers or copywriters must do is make certain that their notation or punctuation is as systematic and standardized as possible so that, at least, it does not convey something fundamentally different from what they intended.

Even though no system of "heard" punctuation is universally accepted, the following guidelines serve to keep the various punctuation marks mutually discrete so each one fulfills its specific function as distinctly as possible. As a general rule, remember that for electronic media copy, your *ear* rather than print-oriented grammatical commandments should be the final judge of what constitutes proper punctuation. The grammatical structure of spoken prose is more fluid than that of written prose. Therefore, audio/video copywriters must write for *speech*—and must punctuate accordingly.

Period

As in print media, the period indicates that a whole thought, complete in itself, has been concluded. Moreover, the period in our copy tells the performer to insert a pause before beginning the next thought. (The duration of this pause depends on the copy's overall pacing.) At their option, electronic media writers may decide to put a period after a sentence that is *grammatically* incomplete, if the sense, flow, and memorability of the copy will thereby be enhanced:

Visit Lou's. For shoes.

Thirteen thousand sympathetic towtrucks. Your Acme Auto Club.

Radio. Red hot because it works.

Your best deserves the best. Butter. Real butter.

Notice that there are nine aurally effective idea units in these four examples, even though only the two italicized segments happen to be grammatically proper sentences.

Because the period denotes a discernible pause, it is wise to avoid its use in abbreviations, since a performer may not know whether a pause is desired after "Dept." or not. Abbreviations are undesirable anyway because announcers, reading an extended piece of copy, have been known to draw a temporary blank as to the full pronunciation of the term represented by such shortcuts as "Corp.," "Capt.," "lb.," or "GA." Imagine yourself stumbling across the following sentence in the middle of a long on-air stint:

The Brockett Corp., Capt. Foster charged, dumped its contaminants by the lb. in GA.

Even a single abbreviation can trip up voice talent on a bad day—and voice talent, like copywriters, are never immune to bad days. Take every precaution to use periods only at the end of sense-complete thought units. Whether the thought unit is also *grammatically* complete is largely irrelevant.

The only exception to this singular use of the period should be in abbreviations that are virtually never written out and that, in fact, are much more commonly used than the words they might stand for. Basically, there are six of these:

Dr.   Mr.   Mrs.   Ms.   A.M.   P.M.

As four of these words are always followed by a proper noun (Ms. Hanson), and the remaining two are preceded by numerals (11 A.M.), the use of the period with them cannot, by itself, be easily mistaken for the end of a thought unit. The acceptable indication for doctor (Dr.) does, however, make it doubly important that we never write

Lakeside Dr. or Clive Dr.

when we mean

Lakeside Drive and Clive Drive.

Comma

Just as in print, the comma generally indicates a separation of words, phrases, or clauses from others that are part of the same thought unit and of a similar or like type:

Bertha's Breakfast Grotto for the tummy yummyist waffles, pancakes, omelets, and sweet rolls.

Rain, snow, sleet, and fog. Channel 10 weather keeps track of them all.

In a like manner, commas are used to set off the name of a person addressed from the rest of the sentence, as in this historic line from a toilet tissue commercial:

But golly, Mr. Whipple, I can't help squeezing.

For electronic media performers, the comma provides a short breathing space that can be used as necessary to keep the tone round and the head clear. We thus insert commas wherever needed to facilitate announcer breathing and to gather words more clearly into effective rhythmic groupings without the period's imposed finality. As Pico Iyer observes, "A comma, by comparison, catches the general drift of the mind in thought, turning in on itself and back on itself, reversing, redoubling and returning along the course of its own sweet river music."[3]

In using commas to promote copy flow, the electronic writer may find it necessary to employ them in additional places not called for by conventional grammatical rules.

Taco Heaven, it's the place, where real sour cream, drips down, your face.

However, a single extraneous comma can wreak havoc with the sense of a message, as British writer and broadcaster Lynne Truss points out in the following example that inspired the title of her punctuation guidebook:

> A panda walks into a café. He orders a sandwich, eats it, then draws a gun and fires two shots in the air. "Why?" asks the confused waiter, as the panda makes towards the exit. The panda produces a badly punctuated wildlife manual and tosses it over his shoulder. "I'm a panda," he says, at the door. "Look it up." The waiter turns to the relevant entry and, sure enough, finds an explanation. "**Panda.** Large black-and-white bear-like mammal, native to China. Eats, shoots and leaves."[4]

Conversely, rather than adding them, aural copy sometimes omits commas where a grammar book would demand their placement if this omission improves phrasing and flow.

At the Deli and the Baker and the Ice Cream Maker. Howard Johnson's.

Two all-beef patties special sauce lettuce cheese pickles onions on a sesame seed bun.

Here again, the resultant sound of the message rather than the strictures of print-oriented grammar must be a decisive factor—as long as the intended *sense* of the passage is still taken into full consideration.

Semicolon

The semicolon, too, is a helpful tool in promoting copy rhythm. It is used between main clauses within a single thought unit and takes the place of such drab, time-wasting connectives as *and, for, but,* and *or.* Notice how the pace and forward motion of the following sentence,

Something had happened but she didn't know what.

is enhanced by replacing the connective with a semicolon:

Something had happened; she didn't know what.

To the performer, the semicolon indicates a short vocal pause between two closely related thoughts. This contrasts with the proportionately longer pause that the period deserves, coming as it does at the end of a self-sufficient thought unit. For Iyer, "A period has the unblinking finality of a red light; the comma is a flashing yellow light that asks us only to slow down; and the semicolon is a stop sign that tells us to ease gradually to a halt, before gradually starting up again."[5]

The semicolon also imparts a pleasing sense of balance to the two subparts of its thought unit while still keeping them in close temporal proximity. And semicolon patterns like the following provide more extensive breathing options for the speaker than do those ordained by a comma by also eliminating extraneous words.

(that)

Radio 93's Midday News;   serves up the action in time for lunch.

(and)

The Norseman blanket saves you cash today;   keeps you cozy tonight.

Question Mark

A question mark comes after a direct query in our copy, just as it does in printed material. The electronic media writer further must realize that, in our culture, most spoken questions end with an upward inflection. We thus must be careful to keep questions in our copy short so the performer can easily perceive that the thought unit is indeed a question and can prepare the upward inflection in a smooth and gradual manner. Otherwise, the poor talent may realize it's a question only after most of the sentence has passed. The sudden ascending inflection that results may be humorous to listen to, but hardly contributes to meaningful communication of the message. Even if the talent detects a long question early, it is almost impossible to sustain the proper rising inflection for very many words. Try reading the following copy segment aloud in such a way that it continuously sounds like a question:

Doesn't there have to be a reason why Sim's Fruit Emporium has been the best place for pears, apples, oranges, peaches and plums since Grampa Sims put up his striped awning back in the Clintondale summer of nineteen-ought-six?

For better clarity, and unstretched vocal cords, the essence of the question should be isolated like this:

Why is Sim's the best place in Clintondale for fruit? Well, since 1906 when . . .

Keep queries short and to the point so the question mark can be easily seen and accommodated by the announcer as well as easily "heard" and felt by the audience.

Exclamation Point

Both print and electronic punctuation use the exclamation point (!) after complete thought units that demand special emphasis. Comic-strip characters seem to talk in nothing but exclamation points, and this fact should not be lost on us. Because we strive for copy that sounds conversational, the constant use of this punctuation symbol is at best an irritant to the listener and at worst an indication that Daffy Duck was the writer. Novelist F. Scott Fitzgerald once said an exclamation mark was like laughing at your own jokes. In most cases, emphasis should be built naturally into the copy through your choice of words and their arrangement. A piece of continuity permeated with exclamation points can do nothing but cast doubt on your scripting ability. Wield this punctuation symbol with extreme reluctance.

Nevertheless, there are instances when the exclamation point is necessary to be certain the copy is voiced with dramatic or urgent effect. This usually occurs at the end of short idea units in which the words themselves don't unequivocally convey speaker attitude. In the sentence below, the use of the period suggests noncritical normality or even a sense of bored resignation:

The toilet's backed up.

On the other hand, punctuating the statement with an exclamation point suggests a sudden and unexpected calamity that must be dealt with quickly—perhaps by calling our plumber client:

The toilet's backed up!

Interrobang

This little-known symbol looks something like a question mark with an exclamation point over it. Since it is not available on any computer keyboard, we can only suggest the interrobang by putting these two symbols in sequence (?!) or by using a typewriter that still permits the placing of one symbol on top of another. New York advertising executive Martin Speckter proposed the interrobang symbol in the early 1960s as a punctuation mark needed to clearly convey disbelief, a grimace, or a groan:

The script is due when?!

How can I stand this pet smell any longer?!

Is this what you call pasta?!

Beginning in 1967, typeface designer Dick Isbell included the interrobang in many of his fonts, but it was not embraced by printers or other designers. Thus it still requires two keystrokes to produce.

Even if you wish to go through the trouble of using it, the cobbled-together interrobang is applicable to even fewer copy situations than is the exclamation point from which it is forged. Still, it does have a certain utility you may wish to exploit in truly special scripting occasions. Just don't expect the interrobang to appear on your keyboard any time soon, advises Professor Mark Harmon, who blames "the punctuation purists, who have killed off every new mark since they reluctantly let quotation marks in, circa 1671."[6]

Quotation Marks

For the commercial and continuity writer, the above-referenced quotation marks also are more to be avoided than embraced. Their main legitimate use is to set off direct quotations that must be read exactly as written. Occasionally, the testimonial spot or PSA will use such word-for-word statements, but it is in news copy that these punctuation symbols are primarily employed. In most cases, then, if your writing job keeps you out of the newsroom, keep away from quotation marks. As each set of quotation marks consists of four printed strokes on which eye/tongue coordination can stumble, they clutter copy appearance and inhibit smooth message delivery by announcers who are reading the copy "cold." (Notice how these just-used quotation marks caused a brief hesitation in the flow of even your silent reading.)

Apostrophe

Because this symbol makes use of only one ' instead of two ", it has only half the potential for script clutter that quotation marks entail. The apostrophe is more practical, therefore, for setting off sarcastic or ironic comments that, in print communication, depend on quotation marks.

You can't call this black gunk 'coffee' and get away with it.

Why can't my 'big, strong man' remember to pick up more Hefty Bags?

The apostrophe also identifies a part of a larger work. The apostrophe pair indicates the subunit, and underlining identifies the work as a whole:

We now hear 'Let Me Say Just One Word' from Puccini's <u>The Girl of the Golden West</u>.

That was 'Big D,' a salute to the home of the Cowboys from the hit musical revival <u>The Most Happy Fella</u>.

From Bill Cosby's hilarious album <u>To Russell, My Brother, Whom I Slept With</u>, here's a tribute to 'The Apple.'

Colon

This symbol, too, performs a task in audio/video copy that quotation marks would otherwise be called upon to serve. The colon is used to set up each line of dialogue that calls for speeches by separate characters. When combined with proper spacing, the colon ensures that the copy will be definitive and easy to read without the necessity for a jungle of quotation marks. Imagine the copy clutter in the following sixty-second spot if pairs of quotation marks had to be used in place of each colon.

> <u>Production Note</u>: No SFX. Simply two voices; the announcer --- deep, resonant, somber --- and the 'subliminal voice,' which is filtered but clearly audible.

ANNCR: No doubt you've heard about this <u>subliminal seduction</u> nonsense. You know, commercials that are supposed to have hidden messages in them. Well!

VOICE: Come to Baron's.

ANNCR: Baron's Saloon denies <u>any use</u> of this so-called mind control.

VOICE: Come to Baron's.

ANNCR: After all, Baron's is seductive enough as it is.

VOICE: Get in your car. Go there now.

ANNCR: The Baron's menu is 16 pages --- and <u>overflows</u> with fabulous lunch items: salads, sandwiches and more.

VOICE: You're starting to salivate.

ANNCR: And there are 30 dinner items under five dollars.

VOICE: Cheap out. Save big bucks.

ANNCR: Best of all, Baron's Happy Hour lasts from four until <u>eight</u> <u>P.M.</u>

VOICE: Sex.

ANNCR: Baron's has that rare combination of good food---

VOICE: Take out your wallet.

ANNCR: Good fun---

VOICE: Give us your money.

ANNCR: And good prices.

VOICE: Give us your cash.

ANNCR: So let's put this subliminal seduction nonsense to rest. <u>Nobody</u> can do your thinking for you.

VOICE: Come to Baron's.

ANNCR: You either want to come to Baron's---

VOICE: You do. You do.

ANNCR: Or you don't.

VOICE: But boy-oh-boy you do, you do.

ANNCR: Baron's. Airport and South Academy.

(© Paul & Walt Worldwide. Writer: Walt Jaschek)

In addition to dialogue clarification, the colon paves the way for any direct quotations called for in the message. It warns the performer that a distinct and generally extensive passage is to follow. (Notice that quotation marks are also required here to properly signal this direct quote.)

TV 22 is helping you. Bob Lane of the Stoltz City United Fund says: "We have exceeded our pledge goal for this year's campaign. And much of the credit goes to the folks at TV 22 in helping to publicize how the United Fund helps us all." TV 22. Serving Stoltz City; serving you.

In a similar vein, the colon can prepare the announcer for a long list of items that are to follow as component parts of the same thought unit.

Today, the Cedarville Diner and Car Wash is featuring: veal surprise, chicken over-easy, potted pork pie, and ham hock delight.

Dash

The dash serves functions similar to, but more exaggerated than, those accommodated by certain of the other punctuation symbols. Like the semicolon, it can be used to improve copy rhythm and flow by replacing drab words. It is preferred over the semicolon if more than one word is being omitted.

> (when you)
> Keep a garden in your kitchen --- keep a cupboard full of cans.

> (it has)
> Radio 97 --- the greatest tunes this side of Boston.

In both of these examples, the dash creates a longer pause than that indicated by the semicolon while still helping to convey that the phrases on either side of it are both component parts of the same thought unit.

Like paired commas, paired dashes can be called on to segregate a single word or phrase from the rest of the sentence. But whereas commas serve to underplay that isolated segment, a duo of dashes strives to heighten and emphasize it. In our previous example

But golly, Mr. Whipple, I can't help squeezing.

we want the listener to focus not on Mr. Whipple but on what you can't help doing to the product. Paired commas are thus appropriate. The following specimen, on the other hand, features the product name (always our most important information) *within* the separated segment. Because we wish to accent that product name, paired dashes are mandated.

The smoothest way --- the Finster way --- to blend the best in tea

As an experiment, let's reverse our punctuation use in these two instances. Read the two lines aloud in the manner the punctuation decrees.

But golly --- Mr. Whipple --- I can't help squeezing.

The smoothest way, the Finster way, to blend the best in tea.

Note the difference in effect and impact? So would your listener. Appropriate words must go hand in hand with appropriate punctuation.

In a more specialized way, a dash can be used to denote a sudden breaking off of a thought either because of hesitancy on the part of the speaker,

All of a sudden I want to---

or because that speaker was interrupted by another.

SAM: Florida grapefruit is---

SUE: Great fruit.

Hyphen

While the dash is the result of three key strokes, the little hyphen consists of only one. Yet, despite its diminutive size, "the humble hyphen performs heroic services," states columnist George Will, "making possible compounds that would otherwise be unsightly."[7] The hyphen also clarifies meaning. Thus, it is

                              (not deice)
Winterguard Spray will quickly de-ice   your car's windshield.

                                             (not situps)
After a few sessions at Harriet's Health Club, you'll be doing those sit-ups   with ease.

"Many words require hyphens to avoid ambiguity," Lynne Truss concludes. "A re-formed rock band is quite different from a reformed one. Likewise, a long-standing friend is different from a long standing one [who could get very fatigued]. A cross-section of the public is quite different from a cross section of the public."[8] Copywriters who allow the little hyphen to work for them will help talent make such distinctions clear and unmistakable.

Underlining

Underscoring a word is another way of requesting special emphasis from the performer. As in the case of the "great fruit" line above, or several of the words in the earlier Baron's commercial, underlining is especially helpful at directing attention to words on which we normally don't focus or that occur at a place in the sentence that prohibits the use of alternative punctuation.

I don't know why my wash is <u>grayer</u> than yours.

Any of the other means of directing attention via emphasis would only inject an unwanted pause or pauses into this thought unit and, consequently, inhibit copy flow. Note how the following punctuation marks either misdirect or hobble the thought.

I don't know why. My wash is grayer than yours.

I don't know, why my wash is grayer than yours.

I don't know why, my wash is grayer than yours.

I don't know; why my wash is grayer than yours.

I don't know why; my wash is grayer than yours.

I don't know --- why --- my wash is grayer than yours.

As discussed in conjunction with the apostrophe, underlining is also used to denote the titles of complete literary works, programs, albums, or entire musical compositions. Because we normally wish to direct attention to these titles anyway, underlining in such instances serves two mutually compatible functions.

Word processors now give copywriters access to *italics* as an alternative to <u>underlining</u>. Previously, this option was not available on a typewriter, and underlined words were converted to italics only if the copy was subsequently run through a printing press. Today, you have both functions readily available on your computer keyboard. Nevertheless, underlining is still preferable, as it makes emphasis more crisply discernible to the performer's eye.

Ellipsis

The ellipsis is <u>a series of three dots</u> that, when used more than once, can make your copy appear to have contracted the pox. It can also make for choppy copy voicing.

Use of the ellipsis . . . should therefore . . . be avoided . . . like the plague.

Lynne Truss calls the ellipsis "the black hole of the punctuation universe, surely, into which no right-minded person would willingly be sucked."[9] Its sole recognized function in audio/video writing is to indicate clearly that words have been omitted from a direct quote so that the performer can make that fact clear in how the copy is read. Yet, for some reason, lazy copywriters blissfully substitute the ellipsis for commas, dashes, semicolons, and even periods. They therefore deprive their copy of the subtle but effective shadings that the discrete and specialized use of each of these other punctuation marks helps bring to their writing. Furthermore, because each ellipsis consists of three individual dots, it causes the same kind of eye clutter we try to avoid by limiting our use of quotation marks.

Parentheses

Though often used in print media for asides and stage whispers, the parentheses have a much more singular and mechanistic task in audio/video copy. Simply stated, they are used to set off stage directions and technical instructions from the words the talent is supposed to read aloud. With the advent of computer keyboards, brackets [   ] are now readily available to serve this same function. In the following classic example, which was actually read on air, the copywriter neglected to use parentheses:

It's 8 P.M. Bulova watch time. On Christmas, say Merry Christmas. On New Year's, say Happy New Year.

The correct translation of the copywriter's intent should, of course, have been punctuated this way:

It's 8 P.M. Bulova watch time. (On Christmas, say Merry Christmas. On New Year's, say Happy New Year.)

Do not omit parentheses (or the alternative brackets) around any private communications between you and the talent who will read your copy. On the other hand, do not persist in the print-oriented approach to parentheses and put anything between them that you *do* wish the listener to hear. In the following piece of broadcast copy, parentheses have been used in a manner common to print media.

Ever been in a lumber camp? (If you had, you'd remember the meals the guys stowed away.) They needed good, hot food (and plenty of it) for all that muscle work. And no meal was as important as breakfast. They wanted a hot breakfast that stayed with them (a hot meal like Mama Gruber's Corn Mush cereal). No, her Mush isn't modern. (In fact, Mama Gruber's Corn Mush is kind of old-fashioned.) But so is hard work.

The announcer accustomed to the scripted use of parentheses would quite properly read the commercial this way:

Ever been in a lumber camp? They needed good, hot food for all that muscle work. And no meal was as important as breakfast. They wanted a hot breakfast that stayed with them. No, her Mush isn't modern. But so is hard work.

Does the spot still make sense? Not only are we left with about fifteen seconds of dead air in a thirty-second spot, we have also lost the name of our product. Restrict parentheses to their intended use. If your copy contains words and phrases that, in print, would constitute parenthetical expressions, use dashes or commas in your script to set off these expressions.

Punctuation Postscript

Parentheses and all the other punctuation tools we have discussed are indispensable if we are to communicate properly to our talent intermediaries and, through them, to our target audience. Use punctuation carefully; its abuse can change the entire meaning of your message. In the Depression-ridden 1930s, a little American girl emigrating with her work-seeking father to Canada was reported by a U.S. newspaper to have lamented at the border:

Good-bye God, I'm going to Canada.

An enterprising copywriter at the Toronto Board of Trade converted this negative implication about his homeland's remoteness into a glowing endorsement by arguing that her statement had merely been mispunctuated. The copywriter's "corrected" version?

Good! By God, I'm going to Canada.[10]

Clearly, punctuation can make a tremendous difference in how our copy is interpreted. Punctuation is also a comparatively modern tool. In his eighteenth-century *A Course of Lectures on Elocution,* English authority Thomas Sheridan reminds us that the ancients had no workable system of punctuation. They used written material merely to enable a speaker to learn the words by rote so that these words could be recited by memory in the speaker's unique style.[11] The person delivering the saga or sermon, not the script itself, was the dominant element in shaping the message. Today, the product-promoting copy is the governing force. Talent is employed to voice the script in the way we specify. So it is our responsibility to select definitive punctuation to help communicate that specificity.

As classics professor Ramsay MacMullen advises, "Our thinking about how we write should properly begin with how we speak."[12] Then use punctuation to help align the talent's performance as closely as possible to that intended speaking mode.

TOOLS TO READ/CONSULT

Punctuation is only one type of copywriter implement. Reference books comprise another. Though the following list does not attempt to be comprehensive, it does include the kinds of volumes that are an essential part of the copywriter's library. Basically, these works group themselves into three categories: dictionaries, word-finders, and style/usage aids.

Dictionaries

Any writer must be an ardent dictionary user if for no other reason than its utility as a spelling aid. Because words are our prime stock-in-trade, misspelling is inexcusable and makes the writer seem as incompetent as the physician unable to read a thermometer.

In checking for errors, the dictionary is far preferable to the spell check that came with your computer. Such software programs will approve any word that is properly spelled—but that word may not be the one intended. This is especially problematic for homonyms such as "see" and "sea," "there" and "their," "sew" and "so," as well as "no" and "know." Remember, the spell check can detect typographical mistakes, but it cannot uncover errors that are contextual in nature. Even though it may be the wrong word, if it is spelled correctly, the spell check will not call it into question. Thus the computer spell check would have been as unhelpful to the medieval monks in the following story as it is to today's copywriters:

A novice monk arrives at a monastery and is assigned to help elder monks hand-copy the book of church laws and canons. He notices that all of the monks are transcribing from copies, not from the original manuscript. The young man goes to the abbot and points out that if someone made even a small error in the first copy, that error would be repeated in all subsequent copies. The abbot recognizes that the novice's point is well taken and goes down to the vault to check the original manuscript, which has sat undisturbed for centuries. The abbot is gone for hours so the young monk goes downstairs to search for him. He finds the old man banging his now bruised and bloody forehead against the stone wall and sobbing uncontrollably. "What's wrong father abbot?" the young monk asks. In a choking voice, and pointing to the book, the abbot replies: "The word is—*celebrate.*"

In addition to monitoring the spelling of words, a dictionary is, of course, consulted to learn word *meaning*. However, as a mass communicator, the copywriter should seldom need to use this dictionary capability—at least when selecting words for a script. If you, a supposed wordsmith, do not already know the meaning of that term, how do you expect members of the mass audience to be able to understand it as the word goes flitting past their ears? Of course, if your spot is aimed at a highly specialized or technically oriented audience (auto engineers or dairy farmers, for example), words unfamiliar to you as well as to the general public may need to be used and their precise meanings sought out in the dictionary.

In most cases, a standard abridged dictionary will serve the copywriter better than a massive unabridged volume that is difficult to handle and store and that will include thousands of words, or archaic definitions for words, of which most of your audience will be totally ignorant. Since commercial and continuity copy is intended to be understandable to the audience *as it is* rather than striving to increase their vocabularies, exotic words and meanings are communication hindrances. If the word and the meaning you seek to use are in a good abridged volume, you can proceed with at least a little more confidence in considering its use in your copy.

Besides the standard dictionaries, a number of specialty ones serve the requirements of certain professions. Unless you find yourself consistently writing copy aimed at doctors, computer experts, or similarly distinct groups, such volumes will not be required. The one type of specialized dictionary that is a helpful addition to any copywriter's library is the rhyming dictionary. Even in straight copy, and especially in campaign slogans or tag lines at the end of spots, a simple rhyme can greatly enhance memorability. The rhyming dictionary can be of significant assistance in this regard as long as we never distort message meaning and clarity in pursuing some forced doggerel.

A few copywriters also find slang dictionaries useful, but such volumes can pose unacceptable dangers. Slang varies widely by era and region, and nothing kills copy credibility more quickly than a slang term your audience misunderstands or feels is outdated. If you don't naturally "speak" the slang yourself, either seek out and listen to people who do or avoid attempting to write it. Most slang usages are superseded before a book listing them can get into print.

Word-Finders

The most commonly known book in this category is *Roget's Thesaurus,* which is a complete compilation of *synonyms* (words meaning the same) and *antonyms* (words meaning the opposite) active in American and British usage. Any writer develops a preference for, or a pattern in, the selection of certain words. The *Thesaurus* helps break these patterns by giving the writer alternative choices of words that thereby avoid interest-robbing redundancy in the copy. Further, this type of volume allows you to find and select a word possessing a more precise meaning or one with a syllabic construction or phonetic makeup that better promotes sentence rhythm and rhyme. To the audio or soundtrack writer, this aural function can be of prime importance given the preeminence of sound in effective oral communication. For example, notice how the following line seems to stumble at the end:

Don't let clogged drains <u>make you mad</u>.

But by consulting a *Thesaurus,* we can find another (in this case, longer) word that concludes the thought with a stronger beat pattern:

Don't let clogged drains <u>exasperate</u> you.

Similarly, a *Thesaurus* can help us discover a shorter term if that is what we need to improve rhythmic flow. Thus we can change

Carson's Wine is <u>appropriate</u> for any occasion.

to the more cadenced

Carson's Wine is <u>well-suited</u> for any occasion.

Roget's is the classic, but by no means the only, volume in the field. Because to use it you must first look up a word category and then refer to various subcategories, some writers find the volume to be somewhat time-wasting. They prefer books like J. I. Rodale's *The Synonym Finder,* which lists the specific word and its specific alternatives in the same place. Though such works do not generally possess the scope of *Roget's* or cross-index closely associated categories of words, their ease and speed of use are important advantages in such a volatile and time-bound field as copywriting. Paul Fey of World Wide Wadio really put *The Synonym Finder* through its paces in helping him to fashion the following commercial for SmartShip.com:

<u>Production Note</u>:　FFV is 'Fast, Funny Voice' and is overlapped tightly throughout.

ANNCR:　Shipping holiday packages can be a real pain in the---

FFV:　butt, rear end, behind, buttocks.

ANNCR:	It's true. Shipping holiday packages is <u>almost always</u> a pain in the---
FFV:	tail, bottom, posterior, derriere.
ANNCR:	In fact, it's usually <u>such</u> a pain in the---
FFV:	cheeks, buns, caboose, heinie---
ANNCR:	---that you procrastinate.
FFV:	Kiester, fanny, can, tuchas.
ANNCR:	Then, the only thing that's more of a pain in the---
FFV:	rump roast---
ANNCR:	---than holiday shopping --- is <u>last minute</u> holiday shipping.
FFV:	Tush, tushie, booty, bum.
ANNCR:	Fortunately, there's SmartShip dot com.
FFV:	Gluteus maximus.
ANNCR:	SmartShip dot com helps you find the smartest, easiest, least expensive way to ship --- especially at the last minute.
FFV:	Backside, back yard, back door, kazoo.
ANNCR:	SmartShip dot com gives you free information that lets you comparison shop for the best rate---
FFV:	moon
ANNCR:	---the best delivery guarantee---
FFV:	sit-upon
ANNCR:	---and the most convenient dropoff schedule.
FFV:	Po-po.
ANNCR:	SmartShip dot com even lets you print a map to the nearest drop-off location.
FFV:	Patootie.
ANNCR:	Or tells you who can come pick up your package. Saving you a major pain in the---
FFV:	place where the sun don't sign.
ANNCR:	Don't let holiday shipping be a pain in the---
FFV:	arse, bucket, biscuits, mud flaps.
ANNCR:	Use SmartShip dot com. The way smart shipping is done.
FFV:	Pooper.

(Courtesy of Paul Fey, World Wide Wadio)

Style/Usage Ads

In general, *style aids* tell us the "correct" thing to do, and *usage guides* tell us what is actually being done out there in the world in which real people speak, write, read, listen, and watch. This is not to imply that style aids are worthless for a broadcast/broadband copywriter. Granted, in striving to mirror conversational speech, we often modify conventional print-oriented syntax. But the fundamental mechanics of good composition are common cross-media. As McCann-Erickson's John Bergin insists, "This is not a break-the-rules business. It is a know-the-rules-before-you-break-them business; there's a big difference."[13] A good stylebook such as Strunk and White's venerable *The Elements of Style* provides you with that essential appreciation of those starting-point strictures. Periodic sessions with such a book help ensure that you never become so specialized that, should the time come, you are incapable of branching out into print media, memo composition, corporate report fashioning, or the myriad of other verbal tasks that call for a wordsmith's talents.

In addition, usage guides such as Roy Copperud's *American Usage and Style: The Consensus* and H. W. Fowler's *Dictionary of Modern English Usage* can be counted on to give sensible advice and guidance on the connotations and evolving tendencies of our language.

TOOLS TO POUND ON, WRITE WITH, WRITE ON

Once we have the germ of a message, know how to spell and punctuate correctly the words it requires, and where to uncover alternative word and stylistic choices, we need some vessel in which to contain all this verbiage while we trim and refine it. Though everyone is aware of the implements serving this function, here are some special considerations that pertain to the copywriter's use of them.

Typewriter

Even though word processors (see the next section) have come to almost totally dominate what was once the typewriter's exclusive domain, some copywriters still prefer this old instrument for occasionally banging out the first drafts of brief scripts. Often, a fifteen-second spot or memorable slogan can come to life on a typewriter before we have time to fire up a computer and access its word processing program. There is an auditory dimension as well. Observing all those creative departments where the typewriter has been rendered extinct, senior copywriter Bruce McCall recollects: "The clack of typewriters, the crackling of another sheet of paper being crumpled into a ball, the howls of profanity at strikeovers or the missing bottle of white-out—all have been replaced by the dead silence of solitary communion with a glowing screen. This induces sensory deprivation and drowsiness, while lending the copy department the clammy peace of the crypt."[14]

Word Processor

McCall's comment notwithstanding, the word processor does offer its own benefits. A word processor, of course, is a microcomputer primed with the proper writing software (program) and tied to a printer that can eventually produce hard (on-paper) copy. The breakneck technological advancements in the microcomputer industry have put sophisticated word processing packages within economic reach of virtually every professional and most amateur writers.

There are several advantages to word processor use—particularly in video with its comparatively complex script formats. In conjunction with a software program such as *Final Draft*, the computer largely eliminates the tedium involved in setting up two-column (video and audio) or centered (Hollywood-style) scripts. Storyboarding software is also available, allowing you to inject your dialogue into the appropriate panels of a video layout. In the more complex programs, you can also grab clip art to create rough approximations of your visuals.

However a word processor is configured, you must be willing to train yourself to understand the instrument's capabilities and drawbacks. "Never buy a program or system," warns Gabriele Zinke of The Writer's Computer Store, "until you see it on the screen."[15] Remember, you are buying two fundamental functions. The first, the *editing* function, is the input portion of the operation. This is where you create, modify, and finalize your script. In the second or output function, called *formatting,* the finished draft is delivered in the proper arrangement and spatial style. Some software packages perform these two functions as a single operation. But in others, they are handled separately and require discrete and systematic instruction from the user (that's *you*) to create a script that looks like a script.

The ease with which you can record volumes of words on your computer does pose a qualitative danger. "Where writing is concerned, quantity and quality are in an inverse relationship," says writing professor Sven Birkerts. "The very nature of technology [the word processor] generates a vast amount of prose and discourages the next step, which would be to prune, winnow, consolidate it. Give it texture and depth. That can't be done by machine."[16] The computer can capture and beautifully format mounds of verbiage with very little physical effort from the writer. But it is the *writer,* not the machine, who must have the discipline to sculpt this precisely arranged data into meaningful human communication.

There are still copywriters—and novelists—who believe that writing must be an intensely *physical activity.* They find the word processor keyboard's prim electronic patter totally out of character with this conception and much prefer the feel of a manual typewriter beneath their fingers as it converts their verbal energy into the mechanical assault of keys against paper.

Ultimately, of course, it is not the power of your keyboard that is important, but the power of the ideas that you ask it to snare.

Pens and Pencils

Because all copy must be typed (or "processed") before it can be shown to anyone important, pens and pencils are selected for their utility in a variety of preliminary roles. Pencils are ideal for sketching out material, whether alone or with a colleague copywriter or art director. When capped by a pliable eraser, a pencil allows us to play with words, diagrams, and pictures without having to sit down in front of a keyboard to stare at its roller or monitor. "Leo Burnett used to write with a black pencil on a white pad," recounts Burnett agency executive Chuck Werle. "We're a sophisticated company, but the creative process is still associated with that black pencil."[17] With a highly portable pencil and pad, writers can brainstorm anywhere.

If you're an occasional typewriter enthusiast, soft pencils (#2) can be used to modify copy while it is still in the typewriter. Higher-numbered (harder) leads should be avoided because they can tear through the paper and mar the roller. Many copywriters also find that a small, inexpensive pencil sharpener, available in any drug or discount store, is handy to keep in their pocket to prevent disruptive trips to a wall-mounted or electric model just as the creative juices are starting to flow.

When it comes to pens, don't be taken in by the "eight for a dollar" specials some emporiums sell. Jotting down fleeting ideas is difficult enough without being harassed by a constantly clogging pen or one whose burred tip scratches across the paper like a cat clawing through the screen door. Shop around for pens that present a pleasing shape and weight in your hand. Note taking and copyediting are both much easier if you can grip the pen firmly without the scrawl that results from having to squeeze it. The pen point should be narrow enough to make a neat, clean editing incision on a piece of printed copy, though not so pointed that it pierces the paper.

In our desktop publishing era, it is easy to dismiss pens and pencils as quaint irrelevancies. But Professor Bonnie Morris argues for a balance "between the tools of professional presentation and the lives we live as writers. . . . The habit of writing . . . should not hinge on the rooted verticality of the computer screen."[18] When it becomes the only writing instrument you use, the word processor may rob you of an additional source of inspiration that the pencil or pen can stimulate. Professor Kathleen Skubikowski finds something is missing when her students completely abandon manual instruments in favor of the computer. "The real loss, students tell me, is the physical attachment to their writing—pressing down on the pen, thinking and feeling the word as your hand writes it out."[19]

Paper

Once you go to work for a station, agency, or other media institution, your stationery needs will be provided for and should not be of overt concern. You will be issued, or can ask for, pads of lined paper for note taking and doodling, plain bond paper for creating your first-draft work, and printed letterhead or other formatting manuscript for preparing subsequent drafts that will be seen and evaluated by a supervisor or client. Your only responsibilities will be to make certain that you keep your office stocked with a sufficient quantity of each variety and that you follow whatever format is mandated by preprinted letterhead and copy worksheets (format is discussed further in subsequent chapters).

If you are freelancing or otherwise self-supervised, you must provide this paper supply for yourself. You will find that having three distinct varieties of stock (lined pads, plain bond paper, and letterhead) will help you divide your tasks mentally and will put you in the proper frame of mind for idea exploration, first-draft experimentation, and final-draft polishing, respectively. When designing your own stationery on which you will prepare the actual scripts that go to clients and stations, keep these two considerations in mind:

1. Even if you are only a part-time freelancer, professional-looking, preprinted letterheads will help establish an initial impression that you know your business. A sleek letterhead won't save a bad piece of writing, but it does help open doors for a good one. Give your copy every chance for a favorable evaluation by clients and a positive treatment by performers. Showcase a solid copy painting within a suitable frame.

2. For durability, paper on which finished scripts are typed should be of at least medium weight and definitely *not* onion-skin or corrasable bond. The thin paper issued forth from some cheap word processing printers also does not pass muster in this regard. Performers need to be able to hold the script without its crackling or rustling. Such extraneous sounds will be picked up by the

station or sound studio microphone and, at best, become distractions to the listener. At worst, they resemble the old radio sound effect used to signify fire, and your message might sound like it's coming from hell.

Agency president/chief creative officer Bob Killian believes there is one more paper item you may wish to consider purchasing—a stock of cocktail napkins! As Killian explains it,

> There's something intrinsically valuable in the medium itself: the act of creating doodle layouts on cocktail napkins is necessarily an exercise in visual and verbal economy. Think about it: a felt-tip pen on a tissue surface forces you to keep your ideas and images simple, to use a single dominant visual, to stress a single selling proposition, to find the minimum number of perfect words to ignite the idea. . . . You can't fall back on production values to shore up a limp strategy. There's no color. No frenzied quick cuts. No killer soundtrack . . . No dazzling animated effects. There is, in short, nowhere to hide. . . . You're producing nothing less than a naked idea, and it has to be great to survive. . . . So when we opened our agency six years ago, one of our first investments (after the computers) was an industrial-size case of cocktail napkins. We've been using them ever since.[20]

Because the broadcast/broadband copywriter's art in particular demands a clarity of communication in a minimum of time, the low-tech napkin may be your best paper tool of all—at least in the crucial conceptual stage.

TIME—THE TOOL THAT RULES

Speaking of time, the inexorable demands of the clock on everything the commercial and continuity writer produces can create our own occupational torment. A thirty-second spot was not, is not, and will never be a thirty-five-second spot. No matter what the message and regardless of the writer's talent, all elements of electronic media communication must ultimately conform to the rigorous demands of the station program day, the network feed schedule, the Website's advertising length regulations, and the budget our client has available to spend.

Unlike a newspaper or magazine, a station cannot add "pages" onto its air schedule when advertising volume is high, or contract that schedule when volume is down. On the contrary, the radio or television outlet or cable network is on the air for a set number of hours each day, and all available program matter, commercial fare, and continuity segments must fill and compete for this time. While a Website can add pages, this does not give it license to simply fill these pages with more advertising. The amount of advertising the online consumer will accept is directly proportionate to the amount of related program content that Website has available. The Web "publisher" cannot simply increase the commercial inventory without driving viewer traffic away.

The time constraints within which the copywriter must work vary somewhat from medium to medium. Therefore, we will break down a discussion of these constraints by delivery system and discuss the radio, television, and online worlds separately.

Radio

There are general word count rules that apply to the audio medium. Copy requiring a relaxed and languid style should contain fewer words than these norms. Material meant to be more rapid and upbeat may contain slightly more. If the message contains sections in which only music or sound effects are featured, the number of words in the message must obviously be reduced.

"SIXTIES"   Though television is largely abandoning the costly one-minute message, in radio, sixty seconds remains a prominent spot type. As Kirshenbaum Bond executive creative director Rob Feakins explains, "In TV you use visuals and words so you can communicate faster. For me, you need two seconds of radio for every second in TV. I'm loath to convert from 60-second spots to :30s."[21] In addition, replacing one-minute spots with half-minute messages while keeping the length of the advertising block or "pod" the same is generally thought to increase "clutter" and audience tune-out. "If you play to a test audience a 4-minute commercial break with eight 30-second ads, and then play them a 4-minute commercial break with four 60's, the test audience will ALWAYS say the commercial break was twice as long," reports veteran radio copywriter Kevin Neathery. "Even though both breaks were exactly 4 minutes in length."[22]

A sixty-second radio script will usually contain from 135 to 145 words. As seen later, this number is proportionately less than the word count for two "thirties." Such a determination is based on the presumption that we cannot expect our audience to take in quite as much copy in one continuous minute of listening as they can in two separate messages of thirty seconds each—assuming we are not stringing too many thirties together! If a non-prerecorded radio spot exceeds 150 words, the station may charge the client an additional premium. Because PSAs depend on the station for gratuity airing in the first place, PSAs that are supposedly "sixties" but contain more than 150 words will probably not be aired at all.

"THIRTIES" AND "FIFTEENS"   A half-minute wall-to-wall radio message can accommodate from seventy to eighty words. Some radio stations, however, will levy a penalty charge for "thirties" of more than seventy-five words, since such spots, if not pre-timed and pre-produced, may therefore spill over into the station's own air space. Recent industry figures indicate that roughly 20 percent of radio spots are a half-minute in length, and the number is rising. "Asking advertisers and agencies to switch to thirty-second spots is good in my view," says Devito/Verdi president Ellis Verdi, "because it will, in many cases, force agencies to think far more conceptually and not use the medium as a dumping ground for lazy copy."[23] But as "thirties" tend to be priced at 75 percent or more of the cost of a full-minute message, the "sixty" is often the more prudent and economical buy, given radio's frequent need to establish a picture through more extended sound.

Brand recall is also higher for one-minute than half-minute messages, but not in proportion to the length differential. A recent Burke, Inc. study found that brand recall for thirties and fifteens averaged 93 percent of that for sixties.[24] However, when recall of the central selling point of the message is considered, full-minute spots seem to enjoy a larger advantage. For their part, while well-focused 15s can serve to re-register already established brands in the minds of the listener, they remain relatively rare on radio, given clutter concerns. When a quarter-minute spot is employed, it should consist of no more than forty words.

"SUPER-BRIEFS"   Especially on radio, where it can consume up to twenty-five words, the ten-second spot remains viable as a *shared ID* in which the station's call letter/city of license announcement can be married to a brief commercial pitch for a sponsor:

WMHW-FM, Mt. Pleasant, where the music is as hot as the barbeque at George's Rib Factory Restaurant; the spiciest, sauciest place in town.

"Tens" are also effectively exploited as continuity in the narrow sense—constituting liners, separators, and promos to stitch the broadcast day together. In noncommercial broadcasting, they also serve as *underwriting billboards*—the main sponsor identification allowed in the noncommercial sector.

Even shorter are the one- and two-second "blinks" and five-second "adlets" that some stations have used to stimulate new business. Fox Broadcasting, for instance, used animated anti-hero Homer Simpson's signature "D'oh!" followed by "Tonight on Fox" in radio blink promos for the TV show, and BMW featured the Mini Cooper's distinctive honking sound in a blink to promote that little car. Meanwhile, the comparative extended adlets can be used as additional listener registering devices for well known brands and as pitches for movies:

Catch *Panda the Power Dancer*—now bopping and bouncing at Cinema Five.

The beauty of such short spots is that they do not have to share commercial pods with other advertisers and can be slipped in between songs. Because of this advantage they are often priced at a premium, with a blink costing 10 percent and an adlet 20 percent of the cost of a sixty. "If your product is well known, you can probably have some fun with these things," suggests agency media executive Richard Cotter, "but they're not easy to use if you have to really communicate a sales message to listeners. You can't do that in five seconds."[25]

Television

Due to the rising cost of airtime, television has trended away from longer spots, especially on the broadcast and cable networks. Given the presence of the visual, it is felt that more compact messages are fully capable of effective communication.

"SIXTIES" AND MORE   Television Bureau of Advertising statistics demonstrate that though the one-minute spot made up virtually 100% of network advertising and 70 percent of local station commercial load in 1965, these numbers had declined to about 5 percent in each venue by the turn of the century. It is simply expected that today's copywriters should be able to use the visual tools they have available to craft effective appeals in thirty seconds or less.

However, there has been modest growth in the number of ninety-second and two-minute pitches in cable television and on local stations—particularly in overnight and other low viewership periods. These are the times when budget-scrimping direct-response (DRTV) advertisers can afford to take to the airwaves to sell their off-beat products directly to viewers through more extended demonstration spots.

Technically, the "one-twenty" is the shortest form of *Infomercial* (see Chapter 11). As the term implies, this length provides the advertiser with the time to offer in-depth information about the product/service and its range of benefits. For this reason, the format has special appeal to marketers of such things as magazine subscriptions, book and travel clubs, gold and other commodities, and special-purpose products aimed at specific occupational and life-style groups. "Nineties," "one-twenties," and even "one-eighties" (three-minute pieces) are no longer confined to television; they also show up on the screens of movie houses, where they are referred to as *sponsor trailers.* Whatever the environment, the copywriter must make certain that the infomercial (or *short-form program*, as it is alternatively labeled) features an interesting storyline to hold consumer attention over this extended time frame.

"THIRTIES" Since 1971, as a result of such factors as the escalating cost of air time and studies showing that most video messages can be as effective in half-minute as in full-minute form, the thirty-second spot has, as discussed above, vastly eclipsed the "sixty" as the most commonly used unit of broadcast television time. For example, advertising trade reporter Noreen O'Leary notes that "research says 30-second spots have 90 percent of the consumer recall of 60-second spots."[26] Such findings have had a spin-off effect on both PSAs and in-station continuity, whose lengths have had to conform to the type of schedule openings mandated by this buying pattern. In fact, the trend to "thirties" began as early as the late 1950s in the form of the *piggyback* spot: a one-minute commercial sold to a single advertiser who then broke it in half to promote two separate products.

Network-aired "thirties" were given a further boost by the 1971 ban on cigarette commercials. When the Supreme Court refused to hear a challenge to the new law, the networks turned to the half-minute length to help them replace the revenue lost from the smoking spots. As Frank Smith, then CBS sales vice president, recalls, "There had been discussions of selling :30s before, but this was now a case of supply and demand. We made :30s our unit of sale and it helped make TV more affordable to sponsors who didn't have as much money to spend. The :30s raised demand. It made TV more desirable for everyone."[27]

"FIFTEENS" The quarter-minute television commercial began through efforts by Alberto-Culver, Beecham, Gillette, and other packaged-goods advertisers to sell two separate products with a thirty-second spot. This created the "split thirty"—actually two twelve-and-a-half-second messages with a brief segue line (such as, "Here's news of another fine product from _____") between. Under intense pressure from these major advertisers, the television networks acceded to experimental acceptance of "split thirties." When station groups (companies owning multiple local outlets) refused to accept these same-length messages, Alberto-Culver brought a class action antitrust suit against them. In 1984, the group owners backed down and the "split thirty" became a fact of life. Just as important, Alberto-Culver's agreement with the groups no longer imposed on advertisers "production requirements such as opening statements identifying the message as advertising 'products from _____' or bridges between the two messages."[28] This paved the way for the entirely self-standing fifteen-second spot.

Most industry studies indicate that quarter-minute video spots are cost effective. Backer & Spielvogel Advertising's director of research, George Fabian, found that "the recall, communication, and persuasion ability of a :15 is about 75 to 85 percent of a :30" for familiar brands or strategies, although these percentages may drop dramatically for new or unfamiliar products or strategies.[29] Not surprisingly, then, in her later study of the fifteens' creative evolution, Professor Roberta Asahina discovered that agency creative directors reported communication of *product key benefit* was the objective for their "fifteens" about 54 percent of the time; publicizing *new product or use* was their intent in only 14 percent of such spots.[30]

At least for advertisers of known commodities, therefore, the quarter-minute can result in real savings because networks price it at little more than half the cost of a "thirty." (Local outlets, seeking to reduce clutter and administrative costs, charge much more: a "fifteen" sometimes is priced as high as 75 to 80 percent of the thirty-second rate.)

The principle of *recency,* embraced by many marketers by the turn of the century, further bolstered the case for "fifteens." Recency decrees that what is most important is how closely the airing of your spot comes to the moment a consumer actually makes the purchase. Thus, particularly in the case of multiple-purchase package goods like soap and cereal, "You have to be on the air more times during the week, more weeks," says media executive Kal Liebowitz. "We've got one agency, we call it Frank's Famous Fifteens. He only creates :15s because he believes in recency."[31]

For the message creator, however, the quarter-minute television spot offers special challenges. As one agency executive put it, "The creative thinking must be more focused. Discipline must be exercised so the concept focuses on one, and only one, central point. Visually, the concept must be able to quickly capture the central focal point you want to emphasize and avoid confusing the viewer."[32] From an execution standpoint, ":60s, :30s, or :15s take the same amount of pre-production, production, and post-production,"[33] another creative director adds. The copywriter's search for innovation within quarter-minute time constraints thus is still a high-stakes enterprise. Short does not mean cheap to produce.

One of the most notable of these innovations is the "interrupted thirty" or "bookend" format, in which a pair of fifteens open and close a commercial *pod*. In the Figure 3.1 pitch for Banquet's Hot Bites (which pioneered the technique), the two-and-a-half-minute pod begins with a "fifteen," in which the talent shoves the product into the microwave. The pod ends in real time two minutes later with the now-cooked treat ready to be enjoyed.

Whether book-ending a pod or self-standing, fifteen-second spots allow the copywriter no margin for error. "They reward discipline and selectivity," observes one creative director, "and punish the greedy and ambivalent."[34]

"TENS" AND "TWENTIES"   Although they are seldom logged as such, ten-second spots permeate syndicated programming in the form of PCAs (promotional consideration announcements), which publicize a product or service that has been provided free to the show's producers. Meanwhile, at the local station level, "tens" have served to limit the incursion of "fifteens" because, since 1971, when "thirties" became the prime local unit of sale, stations have been able to offer a "ten" at from 50 to 60 percent of a "thirty's" cost. Thus if the outlets were to price "fifteens" as the networks do

Banquet MICROWAVE HOT BITES

"BOOKENDS" A TRULY UNIQUE PRODUCT DEMONSTRATION COMMERCIAL.

FIRST 15: GILBERT: Ooh a commercial break. I'm so hungry, what am I gonna fix. I've got it.

New Microwave Hot Bites Chicken Nuggets

made especially for microwaves.

To taste great. Perfect.

I'll be back in 2 minutes when they're done.

(PAUSE FOR OTHER COMMERICALS)

SECOND 15: GILBERT: Ok I'm back.

Oh great six nuggets with dipping sauce.

It's too good to be true. Well, on with the show.

ANNCR: New Microwave Hot Bites from Banquet.

You could have made some in 2 minutes, too.

© 1987 CONAGRA FROZEN FOODS CO.

This spot for Microwave Hot Bites is the first commercial in history to employ the innovative media technique of being "split" in two parts (with other commercials sandwiched in between) to demonstrate product cooking time.

DMB&B Advertising, St. Louis, Missouri.

FIGURE 3.1 *(Courtesy of Stephen Nollau, DMB&B)*

(at roughly half the cost of a "thirty"), they would actually have to reduce the asking price for ten-second spots.

"Tens" frequently serve as standalone units designed for advertisers whose air-time purchases help pay for the closed-captioning of the show they adjoin. Such spots usually begin with a voiceover saying "Closed captioning brought to you by..."followed by the name of the sponsor and then that sponsor's ten-second spot.

Like the comparatively expansive "fifteen," the "dime" spot must register its selling idea and brand recognition in an immediate, high-profile vignette, as in the following spot that illuminates the lunacy of paying high prices for the lodging extras offered by Red Roof's competitors.

Video	Audio
OPEN ON MARTIN MULL HOLDING SUN REFLECTOR UNDER HIS CHIN	MULL: Okay, so I paid a little more to stay in this motel.
WIDE SHOT REVEALS MULL IN PARKA, RECLINED ON LOUNGE CHAIR. BEHIND HIM IS BRICK-SIDED, SNOW AND ICE COVERED POOL. A FROZEN DRINK SITS NEXT TO HIM.	But hey, it's got this lovely pool.
STANDARD BUMPER: RED ROOF INN AT DUSK WITH CAR PULLING IN.	VO: Next time hit the roof. Red Roof Inns.

(Courtesy of Ed Klein, Doner Advertising)

"Tens" can also be combined with twenty-second features to produce *taggable spots.* This is an especially popular practice on cable where, for example, a CNN personality might offer a twenty-second health or weather preparation tip followed by a ten-second spot for a local advertiser. As commercials, "twenties" by themselves are a very minor presence. On network air, a few multiproduct advertisers have purchased one minute and subdivided it into three "twenties" to create their own pod. But as long as most nets and stations refuse to sell "twenties" on a stand-alone basis, most time will continue to be sold in other-length units. The only other notable use of this format has been by packaged-goods sponsors who sometimes split a "thirty" into a 20/10 arrangement in which the first two thirds of the message is for one product, and the last ten seconds for another. An "and also from ——" bridge usually connects the two, with the newer or more complex product normally preceding the older or more basic one.

"ULTRA-SHORTS"   In recent years, clients and media outlets have experimented with messages that are even more brief in duration then the "ten" as they try to find new ways to reach consumers in a compelling and cost effective manner—while also circumventing commercial-skipping TiVos. "Pod punchers" are five-second spots that appear at the end of a commercial pod to increase awareness for the same product featured in a full :30 earlier in that pod. Pioneered by Fox, the pod puncher thus serves as a reminder device for the longer spot's message and is an attempt at raising awareness for a product buried in a long commercial break. "Fives" can also be standalones. Cadillac's agency recently developed one such spot to demonstrate how quickly its cars could accelerate to 60 mph. When they are placed at the end of a pod or inserted into programming by themselves, "nickel" ads have the potential to fly under the TiVo's commercial-clipping radar and successfully make contact with the viewer.

Even briefer commercials have been around since the 1970s. In 1998, Master Lock ran a one-second spot of its product surviving a gunshot as a tie-in to longer message demonstrations of this same attribute. Overseas, a Belgian ad agency developed a single-second message that showed a woman popping a One Second breath freshener in her mouth as a voiceover whispered "One second." Also known as blinks (like their one- and two-second radio cousins), such creations are usually intended—as are pod punchers—to increase awareness for brands that are frequently featured in traditional-length commercials.

An "extended" variation of the blink is the two-second "blipvert" introduced in Great Britain in 1995 to promote the cyberspace magazine *Wired*. Several executions featured different counterculture hipsters and the simple command: "Get this" or "Get *Wired*".[35] Conversely, a much shorter version of the one-second blink is the "quickie"—a 1/60th of a second promo first used by Canadian cable network MuchMusic in 2002 that included one of their veejays, the MuchMusic logo, and an audible blip.[36] Not much work for the copywriter there—and no real indication that such sensory fragments are meaningfully apprehended by viewers.

The "quickie" excluded, ultra-short television messages do seem to have a future—primarily as enhancements to longer commercial messages. "You have to [use short ads] in a way that reinforces the brand benefit," media executive John Moore points out. "You can't use them just for the sake of using them. . . . They could never stand on their own."[37]

Online Time

Because it does not always have to conform to the real-time segmentations of a broadcast schedule, the Internet can offer the copywriter more flexible message lengths. Certainly, a significant amount of the advertising carried on the Web mirrors television's typical fifteen- and thirty-second formats. But depending on each site's policies, and how actively it courts advertisers, messages of a wide variety of durations are possible. "What if I do something that is forty seconds because that's when it's perfect?" asks Arnold chief creative officer Pete Favat. "That's why the Web is gaining."[38]

Still, while self-standing ad placements are widely available online, the most common broadband commercials are the so-called "pre-rolls"—unskippable clips that precede two- or three-minute entertainment and social connection videos. Research has shown that viewers will not tolerate a wait of more than fifteen seconds to access the video's program matter, so the "fifteen" has come to be a standard. "We generally try to run fifteen second pre-rolls instead of :30s," reveals Maria Mandel, the Ogilvy agency's executive director of digital innovation. "We have also seen consumer research that shows that viewers don't want to see long pre-rolls against short-form content—for example a thirty-second ad for a two- to three-minute [clip]. There has been talk about looking into developing a ten-second format, but it is questionable if you can get a brand's message across."[39] In fact, several Websites, including those run by broadcasters like NBC Universal, refuse to accept pre-roll online video ads that are longer than fifteen seconds.

For these reasons, the quarter-minute spot has become the industry standard, for both pre-roll and self-standing executions. "Large, long files take forever to download," points out Dave Fiore, creative director at Internet agency Arc Worldwide. "Every additional second you require a Web user to wait ratchets up the expectation of the entertainment. That's why people will wait for a movie trailer, but not an ad."[40]

Still, many agencies that have produced what they believe to be effective thirty-second spots for television want to get additional mileage out of these ads via Web replay. As long as they don't insist on using 30s as pre-rolls, this practice is likely to continue. In addition, separate research studies by the Online Publishers Association and Millward Brown found that thirty-second TV spots repurposed for the Web produced far better ad likability, ad relevance, and brand awareness scores than either quarter-minute Web versions or these same 30s when shown on TV.[41]

Broadband copywriters should therefore be prepared to execute a multitude of messages in the quarter-minute format. But they should also be ready to produce spots that run thirty seconds as well as in the unconventional lengths that certain advertisers and situations may require.

Time Compression

We cannot leave the tool of time without mentioning productional techniques designed to manipulate it. The pioneering system in the field is the *Lexicon,* named after the Waltham, Massachusetts, company that introduced it in 1979. Through a computer sampling technique, this time compressor/expander allows audio material to be played back at faster or slower speed without degrading it and without attracting listener notice of this manipulation. Depending on the elements in the audio track, up to forty seconds of material can be compacted into a thirty-second spot. The *Sorensen Squeeze* from Sorenson Media was one of the first of several devices that now offer similar capability in the video field. But because video is much more complex than audio, these products can generally clip no more than two seconds from the running time of a thirty-second spot, or three seconds if the picture is no more detailed than a "talking head."

Even though the technology is proven and recently upgraded via digital iterations, the copywriter should remember that audiences are intolerant of stimulus overload. Electronics wizardry must not be used as a quick fix for bloated copy or unwieldy concept. Instead, time compression should remain primarily a tool for adding brief regional or seasonal information to complex commercials that would be prohibitively expensive to reproduce from scratch. Compression is not a fix-it for sloppy writing. It just makes it go by faster.

Keeping Time

One final thing about time. As you work, never be too quick to submit a copy solution. Because if you do, one of two bad things can happen:

1. Supervisors and clients will expect you to solve everything quickly—so will double up on your assignment load. This can soon bury you in a burn-out pit.
2. Clients will think you are being too casual about their business needs and not taking them seriously to heart. As Brazilian creative director Fabio Fernandes

confesses, "When I'm having that first meeting with the client, it's common that one of these ideas will take form in my head, and I just know that it's a good idea, maybe the best one I'll come up with. But I've learned something during my career—if you have a good idea right away, don't tell the client at that meeting. It makes it seem as if it's too easy. Clients sometimes don't understand that good ideas can happen very quickly. They like to see you work on it. So now, even if I have an idea, I pretend that I have no clue how we will solve this problem until we go back and work on it."[42]

TOOLING UP

Now that we've discussed the tools available to the broadcast/broadband copywriter, we can begin to direct these tools to the situations and problems to be encountered in the chapters and tasks ahead. But in wielding all of these implements, we must not make the mistake of thinking that our audience is breathlessly waiting for us to apply them, like some chair-encased patient alert to the dentist's next probe. For unlike that dental patient, our prospect is neither captive nor in abject need of the message we sell. As copywriters, we have to use our tools to be as relevant, as appealing, and as stylish as possible in coaxing our audience first to *attend to*, and then to *agree with* the proposition our tools have helped us construct. Three decades ago, Bernard Owett, creative director for J. Walter Thompson, New York, stated the matter well in the following comment, which, though focusing on television viewers, can be equally applied to any electronic media consumer.

> One of the great mistakes made by people in this business is to think of the viewer—our potential customer—as one who sits in front of a television set, eyes alert, mind honed to a keen edge, all interior and exterior antennae eagerly adjusted to receive the message. I think it's far better, far sager and far more realistic to think of the viewer as maybe lightly dozing—maybe semicomatose.
>
> If he's thinking at all, it's probably about his child's orthodontist bill, his wife's scrappiness, his latest problem on the job. . . . So what do we have to do to make this worthy, troubled citizen listen to our pitch? First, we have to get his attention. Then we have to be ingratiating, disarming and, above all, persuasive. And this we have to do through execution, through style.[43]

In gaining attention and being persuasive, copywriters exploit a potent arsenal of emotional and rational attractions. These appeals are examined in the following chapter.

CHAPTER

4

Rational and Emotional Attractions

Deriving successful electronic media messages involves more than choosing words and phrases that sound appealing. The process also transcends the elements of proper punctuation, tidy typing, and accurate timing. Although all of these aspects play a part in effective continuity writing, they cannot, by themselves, comprise a cohesive and purposeful communication. Such a communication can come about only by combining these ingredients within an overall structure that reflects a thorough understanding of human motivation. Especially in electronic media, where the usual absence of immediate feedback forces us to make continuous hypotheses about how the members of our audience will react, we must constantly refine our knowledge and questioning of human response patterns.

A host of authorities, both in and outside our field, see these response patterns as the result of a volatile mixture of the rational (sometimes called the intellectual or the cognitive) and the emotional (also referred to as the affective). In his *Rhetoric*, Aristotle thousands of years ago isolated the mutually supportive *pathos* (appeal to the emotions) and *logos* (reasoned consideration) ingredients of the persuasive message. Today, psychologists tie similar constructs to cranial geography in discussing the hemispheric right brain/left brain nature of people. As Patricia Einstein delineates it, the left side governs "linear, logical, analytical, critical, rational, judgmental thinking" and the right side controls "creative, intuitive, inspired, playful, symbolic thinking."[1]

Thus when an advertising message becomes more "intense linguistically" (when the words/concepts used deepen the perceiver's emotional involvement), right-brain engagement increases, report Stacks and Melson. Because the right brain can process such "qualitative" information faster than the more analytical left hemisphere, this emotionally "intense information is quickly evaluated and transferred to the left with the right's 'interpretation' attached to it."[2] This process thus suggests that use of a strong emotional appeal to grab interpretative right-brain attention will get our message noticed and will also influence the decision making of the logical/rational left. Meanwhile, a strong logical appeal provides the left brain with the vital validation of that decision. "Studies have proven that people buy for emotional reasons, and then justify their purchases with logic," points out marketing psychologist Sharon Livingston. "So when we make an emotional promise, we need to back it up with real features and benefits. Although an attractive empty promise may create trial, it won't get you repeat purchases or brand loyalty."[3]

The symbols we choose to use in our messages also influence this right brain / left brain synergy. Marketers know that *words* are processed voluntarily by the left brain. The consumer makes a calculated decision whether to apprehend them. *Graphics,* however, are immediately and involuntarily processed by the right brain— so video's pictorial element will take the lead in attracting people to the message. "The brain also registers numbers as graphics," direct-marketing newsletter *Response* advises. "That's why prospects perceive $24.95 as so much less than $25. The right brain involuntarily processes the $24.95 and whereas the left brain—the logical hemisphere—would have noodled out the difference of only 5 cents, the right brain perceives it as being less. Much less."[4]

Ultimately, as Lowe Marshalk's director of strategic planning Stuart Agres discovered in his research, commercials with combined rational/emotional benefits scored better from both message recall and persuasion standpoints with consumers than did those using only rational benefits. "It really does take two kinds of benefit promises to persuade a consumer to buy a product," Agres says. "A commercial should address product benefits such as 'Our detergent gets clothes whiter and softer' [the rational] as well as psychological [emotional] benefits such as 'Our detergent will boost your esteem in the eyes of your mother-in-law.' "[5]

The core dynamic of *product branding* is itself a rational/emotional blend. "A product occupies functional territory, while a brand occupies mental territory," asserts Bruce Nelson, McCann-Erickson's director of worldwide accounts. "Because a product seeks to persuade by its features, it is fundamentally rational. Because a brand seeks to persuade by the magnetic pull of what it stands for—in addition to its performance— it is fundamentally emotional."[6] Robyn Putter, chairman of Ogilvy & Mather's South African subsidiary, adds that, "over time, a brand develops a set of values; some of them are more rational and some are more emotional, and very often in the market it is the emotional dimension that makes the difference."[7] Thus the stewards of major brands (who are also our largest and most lucrative clients) expect that copywriters have a firm grasp of both types of attractions. As account executive Jeff Graham summarizes it, "More than making the cash register ring, brand building is about tapping into a consumer's deepest passions, beliefs and desires, striking a chord and creating a bond that can, and should, last a lifetime. Great creative makes that possible."[8]

There are several human nature–based reasons that would make someone want to buy your client's product, tune in to a program your outlet is promoting, click through for further client information, or patronize the civic function described in your PSA. But all of these reasons relate in some way to *solving a problem*—even if the problem is merely deciding how to spend a Saturday night. The difference, however, between appealing to yourself and appealing to your audience is your willingness or unwillingness to put listener/viewer rational needs and emotional values *first*. "If you want to communicate with someone in order to sell them," advises topflight radio spot creator Dick Orkin, "you better have an in-depth understanding of who they are and what they care about."[9] The unproductive salesperson uses an approach that comes across as "I'm trying to sell you something." The effective salesperson's proposition promises "Here's a difficulty (or a lack, a shortage, a quandary or complaint) I can help you with."

Whatever the problem to be solved, its resolution can be expressed as the satisfying of a fundamental want—a basic rational attraction. As mentioned earlier, it is important to encase this rational pitch in a pleasing, involving emotional package. But the emotion cannot *replace* a functional justification to buy, contribute toward, vote for, or tune in to. Thus we examine rational appeals first and then turn our attention to the collaborating emotional appeals. Many complicated systems have been devised for defining and categorizing these rational wants. However, for our purposes, and as a memory aid, just think "SIMPLE."

RATIONAL ATTRACTIONS

SIMPLE is a mnemonic (memory-building) device to help you recall the six rational appeals that people use to justify the decisions that they make. Each letter of SIMPLE is the first letter in the word that denotes one of these six attractions. Specifically, SIMPLE stands for

S afety
I ndulgence
M aintenance
P erformance
L ooks
E conomy

Let's examine each of these rational attractions in more detail. Keep in mind that every persuasive message—and that's virtually every piece of electronic media continuity—must cater to at least one of these appeals in order to trigger an appropriate solution-validating response by each member of our target audience. As will be seen, a given message can be constructed several different ways to focus on and stress a separate need than that being emphasized by competitors. If, for example, they're all pushing the *economy* of their products, your accentuating of *safety* or *performance* will help your client to stand apart from the pack and stand out more in the minds and memories of your audience. Any product or service can be promoted via any one of the six rational attractions. Sometimes, the least obvious appeal will be the source of the most stirring and powerful sell.

Safety

Though this has always been a buyer's or user's consideration, the rise of the consumer movement in the 1960s gave it much greater and continuing prominence in people's hierarchy of values. Listeners and viewers want to know if the product or service being marketed will make them sick, ruin their plumbing, or injure the psyches of their children. With the prodding of many consumer and industry action groups, the question of safety, of absence from probable harm, is being addressed in more and more pieces of copy. The banning entirely of cigarette advertising from the airwaves was an extreme example of this phenomenon; other examples include car ads stressing their steel-beamed doors, the laxative commercials focusing on the gentleness of their ingredients for people of all ages, and even the program promotion emphasizing a show's suitability for viewing by the entire family.

Given today's threatening and mistrusting environment, the prospect of assured safety is an extremely potent factor in listener/viewer decision making. Today, asserts market researcher Faith Popcorn, the tendency is "to pull a shell of safety around yourself, so you're not at the mercy of a mean, unpredictable world."[10] Particularly if the concern is central to your product or service category—as it is in the Supercuts spot in Figure 4.1—you probably heighten credibility by tackling safety head-on. Worry about hairstyling is rampant. But most salon ads ignore this fear by showing only model-perfect hair. Supercuts stands out because it dares to recognize customers' anxiety about trusting their hair to someone else's shears.

On the other hand, the safety appeal can be a dangerous one to raise—if you're only raising it in passing while putting your main focus on a different rational

WOMAN: So I went into this fancy hair salon and asked for a trim.

The stylist said that what I really needed was a "frizz."

Listen, I said, just the trim!

Then maybe a "wash of color"? he said.

Babe, I said, half an inch off the bottom, OK? "As you wish," he said.

And then he scalped me. Let me tell you, having a bad haircut is like wearing a dress you hate, every day. For months!

Next time, Supercuts.

ANNCR: Next time, Supercuts.

Because nothing grows out slower than a bad haircut.

Because nothing grows out slower than a bad haircut.

Supercuts. $8.

FIGURE 4.1   *(Courtesy of Kathy Kane and Nancy Thompson, FCB/San Francisco)*

motivation. For example, in the following thirty-second radio spot, a quick glossing over a safety issue may make consumers wonder what was (or still is) wrong that you found it necessary to sneak in the safety point at all:

ANNCR: FreeSky Airways now offers roundtrip airfare to the sunny Bahamas. Airfare that is guaranteed to be the lowest rate available from any of the Midwestern cities FreeSky serves. You deserve an escape from the tough winter weather. Let FreeSky provide that escape in the most affordable way. And even the smallest FreeSky jets are now certified as safe to fly in any operational weather condition. Treat yourself to the Bahamas for a pre-Spring thaw. Fly FreeSky and save.

"While 35 percent of consumers think safety is an issue," says airline marketing executive Beth Mack, "you may be bringing up an issue that 65 percent haven't thought about."[11] And whatever you do, don't follow the lead of the copywriter who, in promoting a group rate designed to lure passengers back to an airline that had recently suffered a deadly crash, penned the campaign slogan: "Now you can take up to three people with you."

Indulgence

We all like to be comfortable, to be self-indulgent. And we frequently are willing to sacrifice one of the other rational appeals in order to obtain this quality, which is so integral to the good life. Water beds and bean-bag chairs may be ugly—but they feel so good. Frozen dinners may not be as tasty as home-cooked—but just look at the time and dirty dishes they save. Conversely, subcompact cars are cheaper to purchase and operate—but they can jar your bones and cramp your style. Because, in the words of a classic beer campaign, we "only go around once in life," the indulgence attraction, and its comfort and convenience corollaries, are oft-used devices in a consumer-oriented society such as ours.

Extending our mention of airline advertising, the following JetBlue spot pounds home the comfort of *extra legroom* by extrapolating the meaning of that phrase. This allows the brand to move beyond its "economy carrier" positioning to show that comparatively low prices do not necessarily require physical sacrifice. The commercial also demonstrates that JetBlue's employees will treat you with a comforting courtesy no matter what the query.

(SFX: PHONE RINGS)

OPERATOR: Thank you for calling JetBlue. May I help you?

CALLER: My cousin was telling me you guys have extra legroom.

OPERATOR: Uh huh, we have extra legroom as compared to a normal coach seat.

CALLER: Okay, if I don't have an extra leg, can I use that room for something else?

OPERATOR: (Laughs) No, no, that isn't what extra leg implies. We took out one whole row of seats and that gave the rest of those rows a couple extra inches of legroom.

CALLER: Aahh.

OPERATOR: The words 'extra leg' imply that. But it has nothing to do with having an extra leg.

CALLER: I'm a pretty literal person.

OPERATOR: Uh huh, well that would be taking it very literally.

CALLER: I guess a little too literally.

OPERATOR: (Laughs) Okay, is there anything else I can help you with?

CALLER: I think that's it. You've been very helpful.

OPERATOR: Thank you for calling JetBlue.

(Courtesy of Scott Bell, JWT/NY)

Sometimes the indulgence, the convenience, arises from NOT having to do something. In the Target spot below, we learn that by shopping this retailer with its special Guest Card, we may be able to avoid frequent home interruptions by school-shilling urchins. The focus is less on what you can buy at Target and more on the comfort of not having to run to the door—while still supporting the community good. As copywriter Dick Orkin observes, "We don't so much want things for the sake of having them. But *more for the sake of our having more time to be ourselves.* More time to play, more time to socialize, more time to grow and develop, more time to find meaning in our lives, including self-understanding."[12] All of these needs come under the heading of personal indulgence.

Video	Audio
SPOT OPENS ON HAND REACHING FOR DOORBELL. REVEAL NERVOUS 8-10 YEAR OLD 'A CHRISTMAS STORY' TYPE KID WITH A BOX OF HOME-BAKED COOKIES	SFX: DOORBELL
KID READS DIRECTLY FROM FORM	KID: Good afternoon Mrs. 'Fill In the name.' Would you like to buy some bakesale cookies?
KID LOOKS UP AND SMILES	
SAME KID DRESSED IN BOY SCOUT UNIFORM.	Wanna buy some bird seed? It's for the birds.
	SFX: DOORBELL
CUT TO KID WITH MOUTHFUL OF CHOCOLATE IN BAND UNIFORM	Buy a --- mmslurp --- chocolate bar for the band?

Continued

Video	Audio
CUT TO KID IN JAPANESE GHI HOLDING OUT SPICES	Spices of the---
CUT TO KID IN SANTA HAT AS HE HOLDS ROLLS OF PAPER	Holiday wrapping paper?
KID IN SAME OUTFIT SELLING CHEESE AND THEN DIZ TO FRUITCAKE	VO: Always done your part to help schools raise money?
	KID: Cheese?
	Fruitcake?
CUT TO SERIES OF PRODUCT SHOTS REVOLVING AROUND GUEST CARD. THEN CUT TO SCHOOL ITEMS ORBITING AROUND A SCHOOL	VO: Apply for a Target Guest Card. Use it and we'll donate 1 percent of the total to your favorite school. So the schools get what they need---
CUT TO KID HOLDING TRAY OF PLASTIC TUMBLERS	KID: I'm back!
	VO: And so do you.
CUT TO PIC OF TARGET GUEST CARD	Get the Target Guest Card. Call 1-800-316-6142.
SUPER: 1-800-316-6142. See store or brochure for details	KID (VO): I know you're in there.

(Courtesy of Joan Finkbeiner, Martin/Williams Advertising)

Maintenance

If a product maintains its usefulness for a long time, or if a service has long-term benefits, we are in a much better position to justify a comparatively high cost or to overlook drawbacks in comfort/convenience. Automotive accounts such as Mercedes-Benz and Volkswagen, the lonely Maytag appliance repairman, and the entire stainless steel industry have had significant success by accenting maintenance factors over any of the other rational attractions. In what many people complain is a plastic society, the possibility that something will actually survive into downright longevity is an enticing prospect indeed. If a meaningful durability claim can be made and substantiated, it weaves aspects of performance, economy, and indulgence into a very compelling and logical strand. To function in the future, a maintenance-efficient product must certainly work now (performance). Because its life expectancy is long, it saves on replacement costs (economy) while eliminating the bother and inconvenience of having to do without while the thing is being fixed (indulgence).

In the following script, the staying power of a DieHard Battery is illustrated not by product shots of it, but by illustrations of what you can do with those jumper cables that the DieHard has made obsolete.

Video	Audio
OPENS ON ECU SHOT OF JUMPER CABLES ATTACHED TO TREE TRUNK. SHOT WIDENS TO BOAT IN POND SECURED TO TREE WITH JUMPER CABLES	MUSIC UP AND UNDER THROUGHOUT SFX: OUTDOOR AMBIANCE: BIRDS CHIRPING, WIND BLOWING THROUGHOUT
CUT TO SHOT OF SUNNY, WINDY, WIDE-OPEN PLAIN. IN FOREGROUND THERE IS FENCE WITH GATE. CUT TO CU OF FENCE AND GATE BEING HELD CLOSED BY JUMPER CABLES	VO: Know how to spot a DieHard Battery owner?
CUT TO WS OF CLOTHESLINE --- JUMPER CABLES ARE HOLDING QUILT ON CLOTHESLINE. BIRD FLYS OFF SCREEN	Look for their jumper cables.
CUT TO SHOT OF JUMPER CABLES HOLDING A TARP ON A SNOWY GROUND WITH LOGS UNDER TARP	DieHard.
CU TO SHOT OF DIEHARD GOLD BATTERY	SFX: ENGINE STARTING America's most trusted battery. With 30 years of starting power.
CUT TO SHOT OF FENCE AND GATE BEING HELD CLOSED BY JUMPER CABLES.	How much do you trust your battery?
SUPER: Sears: the good life at a great price guaranteed.	

(© Sears, Roebuck and Co.)

Sometimes the longevity of the items we own depends not on their attributes but on the attributes of other things with which they come in contact. Thus in the radio spot that follows, maintaining the prized possessions listed at the message's beginning is shown to be contingent upon the seemingly unrelated service our client provides. This innovative use of the maintenance appeal makes the Pets Inn benefit much more focused and specific.

ANNCR: 4 pairs of shoes, 3 golf club covers, a sofa cushion, 4 Barbies --- actually, 3 Barbies and a Malibu Stacy --- and the remote control to your big screen TV. All completely chewed and partially digested by 'Mister Snuggles,' your 2-year-old akida. Mister Snuggles. The kids picked that one. It's embarrassing to have to say it out loud. But it really doesn't matter what his name is, he doesn't answer to it anyway. He doesn't sit, come, stay, stop tearing up the trash bag or stop barking when you talk to him. Fortunately, there is hope. Dog Training classes at Pets Inns start May 20th. Conducted by Dog Man. Dog Man has been training dogs for over 30 years, and there's nothing he hasn't seen or corrected during that time. There are group classes, or if you prefer, he can do one-on-one sessions with Mister Snuggles at Pets Inns --- or right in your home. So come on. As long as you have to say 'Mister Snuggles' out loud, in a tone the neighbors can hear, make it accomplish something.

Like preserving your stuff. Get your dog trained the right way, with Dog Man at Pets Inns. Get the details at Pets Inns dot com.

(Courtesy of Gerry Perrett, Saga Communications)

In addition to its utilization of the maintenance appeal, the Dog Man spot also illustrates the way numbers are typically treated in our scripts. Using the numeral rather than its verbal equivalent makes it easier for the talent to read—something that is particularly important in longer copy like this Pets Inn sixty.

Performance

Even though this rational attraction often overlaps with several of the others, its essence is workability. Will the product function for me? Will my donation help solve the community problem? Will staying up late to watch TV-8's movie really "round out my weekend on a happy note"? With performance, we are not primarily concerned with what it looks like, how much it costs, how long we can maintain it, or even how safe it might be. Instead, we simply want to be convinced that the product, or service, or charity drive will meet the need at hand. *"But does it work?"* is the central question.

A straightforward problem/solution progression is a standard technique for structuring a performance appeal. But in the classic radio spot below, copywriter Jay Williams skillfully multiplies this technique. He moves from a superficial solution based on an old joke about newspapers into a whole series of solutions to problems of which the person in question wasn't initially aware. All of these needs are based on lack of prior information. All of them could have been solved simply by reading the *Globe*'s Food section. The Food section works for the consumer in a number of ways; "it all depends on how you use it." Notice also how this concept is easily expandable to additional commercials based on other food items—or to the paper's performance in the multifaceted coverage of a different subject in another of its sections or its online edition.

ANNCR: The Boston Globe presents A Practical Guide To Using The Newspaper. Use #17: Fish. Wrapping fish in a newspaper is a great idea. You take a big section of The Globe, roll it up, you can carry the fish around like a football. No scales, no slime, you look pretty smart. Until you get home. You unwrap the fish, you look down, it's the Globe's Food section. You start peelin' the pages apart, you see an ad for Captain Salty's Fish Market, he's got a special this week. Suddenly, you realize you paid too much for the fish. Then, on the next page, is a terrific recipe for fish --- only now you've bought the wrong <u>kind</u> of fish. Frustration sets in. Ya grab the fish by the gills, ya start yellin' at it, c'mon, Jacques Cousteau didn't even look that smart talkin' to fish. You wanna look smart, you read The Globe's Food section <u>before</u> you go shopping. Now you know what's on sale, what's in season, what's in vogue. You've got recipes, how to make'em, what you need to make'em. And coupons. On things like fish sticks. You'll love'em, they come already wrapped. The Globe's <u>Food</u> section, every Wednesday. The Boston Globe. It all depends on how you use it. For home delivery, Call 466-1818.

(Courtesy of Anne Daly, Hill, Holliday, Connors, Cosmopulos, Inc.)

(ITALIAN MUSIC)
WOMAN: Thank you.

MAN: I love Italian food!

(ITALIAN MUSIC)

(GREEK MUSIC)
MAN: I love Greek food!

(GREEK MUSIC)

(GERMAN MUSIC)
MAN: I love German food!

(GERMAN MUSIC)

(MUSIC)

MAN: I hate myself!

(MUSIC OF AEROBIC CLASS)

ANNCR: The Ameritech PagesPlus
Yellow Pages. How you get things done.

FIGURE 4.2 *(Courtesy of Pat Ebel, Ross Roy, Inc.)*

Using very few words, the Ameritech PagesPlus in Figure 4.2 also is built upon the performance appeal. In this instance too, the focus is on how the performance of the product enhances the consumer's performance. The *Boston Globe* pitch engaged the listener with the phrase "it all depends on how you use it." Meanwhile, the Ameritech approach shows the viewer that PagesPlus is "how you get things done."

Looks

Often the least rational of our rational attractions, the looks appeal evaluates a product based on how pleasing it is to the eye or, as in the following TV spot, how pleasing what we are using the product on thereby becomes. Here, the attained appeal is represented by the fashion model, while the search for such attainment is represented by the little girl. Milk is then twice introduced into the scene as the tool both for getting you that appearance—and for keeping that appearance once you have achieved it.

Video	Audio
OPEN ON LITTLE GIRL WEARING MAKE-UP	GIRL: Why don't I drink more milk?
SHE PUFFS OUT HER CHEEKS TRYING TO LOOK FAT	Well isn't it supposed to be --- (laughs) --- you know what they say about milk.
CAMERA PULLS BACK TO REVEAL FASHION MODEL IN BACKGROUND	I want to wear what's in and milk---
HAND APPEARS FROM OFF SCREEN AND HANDS FASHION MODEL A GLASS OF MILK. SHE SITS DOWN BESIDE GIRL AND TAKES A DRINK	Well, I know it's really good for you and all that but I want to look good. Maybe even model.
LITTLE GIRL TURNS AND NOTICES FASHION MODEL. HAND APPEARS FROM OFF SCREEN AND GIVES GIRL A GLASS OF MILK	(Heavy breath) Hi. (Quick recovery) I see you drink milk too.
SUPER: Milk. Yeah. Milk. A product of our dairy farms.	FEMALE VO: Milk. Yeah. Milk.

(Courtesy of Terrence J. O'Malley, Vickers & Benson Advertising Ltd.)

Radio as well as television can promote the appearance of the product and/or the positive influence of the product on the consumer's appearance or possessions. In fact, the looks appeal is *often even more* potent on radio because the sound medium actively involves listeners in constructing their own most pleasing mind pictures out of their own experiences. In the following spot, the natural beauty of diamonds, gold and silver is amplified by well-written copy to place the most beautiful executions of these adornments at the client's store and, subsequently, on the body of that store's customer.

ANNCR: Sparkle. Well, of course. That's what you like about diamonds. Sparkle. And not just the way they catch the light, but the way they make you sparkle when you wear them. That kind of sparkle relies just as much on the design of the setting, the style of the piece, as it does on how the diamond itself is cut. And for that kind of sparkle, you need Hanson Jewelers. Hanson is a one-of-a-kind place in Ludlow that offers unique pieces to add to your individual sparkle. You won't find jewelry like this in the mall stores because

Hanson buys from their own supplier. Carefully selecting jewelry that stands out from the rest. And of course, Hanson Jewelers would only offer first class diamonds in those first class creations. So remember. From the flashing brilliance of diamonds, to the gleaming perfection of the gold and silver artistry surrounding them, the sparkle of jewelry that only <u>you</u> are wearing is unmistakable, and makes you dazzling. Find your sparkle at Hanson Jewelers, 44 Center Street Ludlow.

(Courtesy of Gerry Perrett, Saga Communications)

Economy

Few of us, and few members of our various target audiences, can totally ignore the *cost* of the goods and services used to make our lives safer and more self-indulgent. Even the decision to devote our time to watching that program or listening to this station must often be weighed against the other more productive responsibilities to which we might better attend. Life is a constant cost/value comparison, and the disbursement of our time and of the money that is a function of that time is a more or less continuous concern. Nothing comes free, and the farther from free it is, the higher will be consumer resistance to obtaining it. "You have to stress worth," points out Ammirati & Puris research director Alan Causey. "Consumers have to know that they'll be getting what they pay for. If something is expensive, it's because it's worth it."[13] It is probably easier for most of us to decide on a brand of cereal than on what new car to buy; simpler to determine that we'll watch a thirty-minute show than a six-hour miniseries, which expends three nights' viewing. Depending on the product category, asking *how much* it costs is at least as important to consumers as asking *how safe* it is or *how long* it will last.

Sometimes, the most effective economy appeal is one that presents a comparison between doing it the way our copy suggests and the alternative. In the following radio commercial, this alternative is ludicrously misunderstood by a stubborn noncustomer who thereby makes the economy point in an even more graphic manner.

CONSUMER: You know that SEMTA bus commercial of yours?

SEMTA REP: Uh, the one where we say you can save eight dollars a day by riding the---

CONS: Hold it right there, that's the one.

REP: What about it?

CONS: Well, your figures, they just don't add up.

REP: First of all, do you live in Birmingham?

CONS: Right.

REP: Do you ride the bus to and from work?

CONS: Every day.

REP: Well, by not having to pay gas and oil and parking, we conservatively figure eight dollars a day is what you'll save.

CONS:	Save! Ha! It cost me $112 a day!
REP:	Impossible!
CONS:	Okay, you just check my math, buddy.
REP:	Go ahead.
CONS:	First, there's $72,000 for a used bus---
REP:	You bought a bus?
CONS:	Interest, gas and parking is $12,000---
REP:	He bought a bus.
CONS:	And there's $6,000 to raise the roof on my garage---
REP:	He bought a bus.
CONS:	Finally, I spent six bucks for snow chains.
REP:	Hold it! You save eight dollars a day if you ride _our_ bus.
CONS:	_Your_ bus?
REP:	SEMTA.
CONS:	SEMTA?
REP:	Yes.
CONS:	Oh, I see.
REP:	See?
CONS:	You already probably got them tall garages and everything, huh?
REP:	Exactly.
CONS:	Okay. How'd you like to buy a good used bus real cheap?
REP:	(Yelling to someone off-stage) He bought a bus!

(Courtesy of John J. Saunders, Southeastern Michigan Transportation Authority)

As we've said, time is as much a cost element in today's frenzied world as is money. The Figure 4.3 spot for an online brokerage firm sets itself apart by focusing exclusively on the conservation of the clock rather than our cash. This focus gives the audience an additional time-saving slant on a product category that usually restricts itself just to economy of the monetary kind.

Whatever rational attraction package you end up constructing, check to make certain it does not attempt too much. In spots of sixty seconds or less, it is usually unwise to try to cover more than one, or at most, two closely associated rational appeals. Some vacillating copywriters employ multiple rational pitches in the same message and think they thereby are playing it safe. "But what they end up with is not an advertisement," warns audience researcher Kevin Clancy, "but a laundry list with so many messages that none are memorable."[14]

AGENCY: OgilvyOne	CLIENT: AMERITRADE	COMMERCIAL NO.: ZOGO-1913
	TITLE: "WANNA GRAB LUNCH?/800 TO URL" :30	

AMERITRADE USER: (ON PHONE) Yeah, hi...

I just have a quick question about placing a limit order...?

ON HOLD GUY: Sure I'll continue to hold. It's only been forty-two minutes!

AMERITRADE USER: Thanks a lot!

You, uh, wanna grab lunch?

ON HOLD GUY: Lunch? No, I had lunch yesterday!

AMERITRADE USER: I'm tellin' you bud, switch to Ameritrade...
(MUSIC: UNDER THROUGHOUT)

ON HOLD GUY: Switch? And miss "Soft Hits of the Eighties"?

(LAUGHS & SINGS)
PHYSICAL...PHYSICAL.

(MUSIC)

(AVO): Go to AMERITRADE.COM.

Ameritrade.

It's how...

you can get somewhere...

on Wall Street.

FIGURE 4.3   *(Courtesy of Paul Sullivan, OgilvyOne Worldwide)*

EMOTIONAL ATTRACTIONS

The rational appeals are the underlying justifications for choices we make as to what to buy and what to spend time with. But, as mentioned earlier, it is the emotional factor that usually initiates the decision. Emotional stimuli are also key to securing initial attention to our message. Like Mary Poppins's "spoonful of sugar helping the medicine go down," the emotional appeals offer an immediate reward for stopping to listen and watch. We then try to parlay this reward into focused involvement with whatever it is we are promoting.

"Increasingly," writes DDB Worldwide marketing executive Paul Price, "science also tells us that emotion, not rational thought, is the gatekeeper to consumer behavior, rendering the most emotionally engaging experiences the most effective communications."[15] A lot of people are throwing away their money because their advertising doesn't touch you," adds BBDO chief creative officer Ted Sann. "We're always looking to make some kind of emotional connection with the consumer about the brand."[16] Further, as JWT planning executive Jeff DeJoseph points out, "Many brands have parity status and consumers are bombarded with exponentially more messages. So there's no reason to select a brand other than how you affiliate with it, how you feel about it. It's not the fact of the brand, it's the emotion you attach to the beer or the car or the jeans."[17]

It is not just that advertising executives believe emotion is an important component of successful advertising. Academic research validates the significance of this ingredient as well. Professors Esther Thorson and Jacqueline Hitchon discovered that "an execution that clearly creates a positive emotion in the viewer can be used with greater frequency without danger of damaging attitude to the commercials, brand attitude or motivation to purchase."[18] In fact, they later found that "at high levels of repetition . . . emotional messages were significantly better remembered than nonemotional messages, suggesting a further benefit of emotional commercials in a television environment in which commercial repetition is a major factor."[19] In other words, emotional attraction is important not only in the single reception of an ad,[20] but it is also a key factor in making multiple exposures to the spot palatable and more memorable. In both single and repeated encounters with our message, the emotional triggers it contains provide the incentive for audience members to stick around long enough to absorb that rational attraction designed to promote memory, belief, and action.

As we made it SIMPLE to remember those rational appeals, we can make it a PLEASURE to keep the emotional attractions in mind. PLEASURE is decoded this way:

P eople interest

L aughter

E nlightenment

A llurement

S ensation

U niqueness

R ivalry

E steem

Even though there are many ways to categorize and subdivide the various factors that solicit an emotional response, this PLEASURE approach is an uncomplicated yet reasonably comprehensive one as regards the appeals put into play in electronic copywriting. In its simplicity, PLEASURE may not have the depth to satisfy many psychologists or motivational research experts. But it has immediate utility for the preoccupied copywriter (and it is the nature of our craft for all of us to be preoccupied). PLEASURE serves constantly to remind us that human beings are emotional as well as rational creatures. And, as Bonneville Media's marketing director Jeff Hilton puts it, "People remember what they feel a lot longer than what they heard."[21]

Let's now examine, in order, each of these powerful feel-good PLEASURE vehicles.

People Interest

This attraction might be less charitably called "nosiness." We tend to have a well-developed and, occasionally, even perverse fixation on what other people are doing and how they are doing it. The testimonial spot seeks to exploit this characteristic by showing what celebrities are drinking, wearing, or shaving with. But, as seen in later chapters, we have equal interest in the doings and preferences of "real people," people we ourselves can identify with and relate to.

In a more uplifting way, a concern with the lives and problems of other people is a very warm and charitable phenomenon that motivates folks to give of their time and treasure. Many PSAs seek to tap this aspect of the audience's humanity. Whichever cause it aids, the people interest appeal works only if the characters it features and the way they are presented can compel the audience's curiosity.

The following spot heightens our attention by letting us eavesdrop on the malicious revelation of someone's adolescent past. The commercial's people interest works to support the rational attraction of performance.

(SFX: DOORBELL; DOOR OPENING)

AL: Yeah?

MARTY: Uh, Al Linkus? It's me, Martin Flink.

AL: Marty, I haven't seen you since the seventh grade. How you---

MARTY: Let me cut right to the chase here.

AL: Okay.

MARTY: August 12, '81, Saturday Matinee, The Rialto, <u>Laddie, the Farm Dog</u>. Ring a bell?

AL: No.

MARTY: You cried like a baby, said if I never told the guys, someday you'd give me anything I want.

AL: (Laughing) Oh, yeah, right!

MARTY: Well, I want your Jeep Cherokee.

AL: (Laughing again) Are you serious?

MARTY: Hey, I always wanted a Jeep Cherokee. It's a legend. You have one ---
             I want it.

AL: Marty, that was thirty years ago!

MARTY: And I've been monitoring your life. Up until now you haven't had anything
             I wanted.

AL: This is stupid!

MARTY: Your Jeep Cherokee has the available four-wheel and anti-lock braking
             system.

AL: Yeah, but I---

MARTY: I'm gonna love my new Jeep Cherokee!

AL: It's not yours!

MARTY: It has the most powerful available engine in its class.

AL: Look, I'm not giving you my new Jeep Cherokee as hush money. I was twelve
             years old. I don't care who knows I cried at <u>Laddie the Farm Dog</u>.

MARTY: You don't?

AL: No.

MARTY: Would your wife care that I have pictures of you and Gail Hellman at your
             thirteenth birthday party playing Post Office?

(SFX: DOOR SLAMS)

MARTY: (Shouting) They're in color!

ANNCR: See your California Jeep and Eagle dealer now. For the Jeep vehicle you've
             always wanted.

(Courtesy of Dick Orkin, Dick Orkin's Radio Ranch)

A copywriter's summoning of the past, as in the commercial above, is often an attempt to generate a mood of *nostalgia*. Nostalgia is really a powerful subcategory of people interest. In the act of remembering, we aren't merely recalling past times, but more especially, the people who populated those times and how we might have been back then. Copywriter Jeff Odiorne has coined the term *Peterpandemonium* to describe how brands can connect with consumers by appealing to recollections of their youth. "Even though I am on the eve of 40, my mind is still stuck at 23," Odiorne admits. "So anything that can keep me in the dreamworld is interesting to me. It's like a brand fountain of youth."[22] As researchers in a joint Duke/Penn State study discovered, ads can place a brand in a context likely to trigger "autobiographical memory" in potential customers.[23] In fact, at Dick Orkin's Radio Ranch (which produced the above Jeep commercial), they call their conceptual process *heart-storming* rather than brain-storming. "Ours is more of an intuitive and unconscious evocation of personal memories and experiences," reveals Radio Ranch creative director

Christine Coyle. "Because the memories are sometimes painful, sometimes joyful—we consider it a process more of the heart than the head."[24]

Certainly, video copywriters can employ the same process. Notice how the spot in Figure 4.4 converts a father/daughter history of product use into a glowing (even "magic") experience that goes far beyond the simple attributes of a store-bought cookie.

(MUSIC) GIRL: Dad, you don't have to wait up for me.

MAN: I wasn't, couldn't sleep. GIRL: You were waiting. MAN: I just felt like an Oreo. Want one?

GIRL: Sure. MAN: You know when you were little

I had to loosen them for you. GIRL: Really?

MAN: But now, you don't need-- don't need-- (CLEARS THROAT)

MAN: Some milk?

(MUSIC)

(MUSIC)

(MUSIC)

(MUSIC)

GIRL: Thanks, Daddy.

ANNCR: Oreo, unlock the magic. (MUSIC OUT)

FIGURE 4.4   *(Courtesy of Katie Hennicke, copywriter, FCB/Leber Katz Partners)*

Because of its primacy in the human psyche, people interest has been exploited from advertising's very beginnings. Note, for example, the following copy penned in 1840 by telegraph inventor Samuel Morse to promote his earlier portraiture business[25]:

How cold must be the heart that does not love. How fickle the heart that wishes not to keep the memory of the loved ones for after-times. Such cold and fickle hearts we do not address. But all others are advised to procure miniatures at Professor Morse's Daguerreotype Establishment.

Laughter

Human beings need to laugh, need to have the capacity to stand back and make light of the problems and conditions around them. Individuals who trudge through life taking themselves and everything else completely seriously are asking for a mental breakdown or a peptic ulcer. Laughter is a vital release mechanism for all of us—copywriters especially. That is why we seek it in our entertainment fare and try to use it to our advantage every chance we get. Comedy is disarming. It can effectively break down a reluctance to listen and at the same time build goodwill. "It's hard to be cynical about people while you are laughing with them," write agency founders Jonathan Bond and Richard Kirshenbaum. "Humor, especially the self-deprecating kind, exposes a degree of humanity. Don't you trust and believe people more if they can laugh at themselves? Contrary to many opinions, humor isn't just a device to win more creative awards, it's good marketing."[26]

A number of studies have demonstrated that "humor enhances liking," researchers Marc Weinberger and Charles Gulas point out. "In light of an increased emphasis in advertising on affect, this finding should not be underestimated."[27] As to what makes for the most compelling humor, a BBDO online poll discovered that "44 percent of the poll's participants said humor is most effective when it makes you laugh, 39 percent said it's most effective when it makes you think and 18 percent said it works best when it makes you smile."[28] According to this finding, what we have labeled the "laughter" attraction does not require that you chuckle out loud—although that may be the most preferred result. Rather, this appeal may be almost as potent when it is more subtle and cerebral.

While not every product, service, or program can be approached in a humorous vein, laughter tends to be the most coveted emotional attraction in a family-oriented, home entertainment medium. If it's appropriate, comedy can even scale attention barriers that, for some functionally disagreeable subjects, are all but insurmountable via any other emotional approach.

Lactose intolerance—in people or dogs—is not a pleasant concept. But this Joy Golden commercial deftly uses laughter to define both lactose intolerance and the product that caters to its canine variation.

Production Note: Fifi's voice that of a canine school marm.

DOGS: (RANDOM BARKING)

FIFI: Welcome to Fifi Beagle's nutrition class. Today, I have some wonderful news for you ice cream lovers.

DOGS: (RAPID PANTS)

FIFI: As you know, we dogs shouldn't eat ice cream because of our (whispers) little <u>lactose intolerance</u>. Milk products upset our tum tums.

DOGS: (DISAPPOINTED OOOOHH!)

FIFI: And so, I'd like to announce that a leading animal nutritionist has just developed new Frosty Paws Frozen Treat for dogs. With the same creamy texture as ice cream, but with almost no lactose. Isn't that a whizzer?

DOGS: (EXCITED BARKING)

FIFI: And Frosty Paws is nutritious and yummy too. Should we try some, class?

DOGS: (MORE EXCITED BARKING)

FIFI: Please wait your turn. Mr. Chihuahua --- get off my back. I <u>have</u> talked to you about that before.

ANNCR: Introducing Frosty Paws, the world's first frozen treat for dogs. It's not ice cream, but your dog will think it is.

FIFI: Oh no! Mr. Dachshund's just run off with the Frosty Paws. There he is at the hydrant. Get him, class!!

DOGS: (ANGRY SNARLING)

FIFI: Grab him by the other leg!

ANNCR: New Frosty Paws Frozen Treat for dogs. Now in your ice cream section.

DOGS: (HAPPY, EXCITED BARKING)

(Courtesy of Joy Golden, Joy Radio)

The Frosty Treat spot is also noteworthy because it successfully uses a technique known as *anthropomorphizing*—endowing a nonhuman subject with human attributes. Anthropomorphizing can be an effective copywriting tool if you remember to (1) keep the spokesthing(s) in character throughout the spot; and (2) periodically re-identify those characters for late tuners-in so they are not confused as to who (or actually, *what*) is speaking.

Of course, the antics of real people are a source of laughter, too. Human mistakes leading to humorous results are often appropriate when the miscue could have been prevented by use of our product or service, as in Figure 4.5.

Before leaving our discussion of the laughter attraction, one note of caution must be struck. Copywriters who depend on humor to substitute for a central campaign strategy or who try to stretch a pratfall into a selling proposition are doomed sometimes to spectacular failure. "I've never sold a commercial by telling the client, 'But it's really funny,' " says art director/writer C. H. Greenblatt. "It takes cold facts on how this ad meets the objectives, how clearly it communicates, what it says about the product and company."[29] "People have gotten confused between what is entertainment for entertainment's sake and what is actually smart marketing messaging," asserts Cramer-Krasselt CEO Peter Krivkovich. "The YouTube generation of advertising has forgotten that. You can have a brilliant, unique, funny ad, but if it's not coupled with insight it will be forgotten."[30] "It doesn't work when it's almost funny," *Advertising Age* critic Bob Garfield concludes. "It doesn't work when it's obviously meant to be funny, and acted as if it were funny, and cut as if it were funny, and silly or absurd or eccentric in the pursuit of funny, if it isn't actually—this is the key—funny."[31]

"Action Figures" :30

 TV ANNCR: Combat Rangers.

 They're rough.

 They're tough.

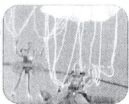 They're battle tested.

 BOY: Commence the attack!

 TV ANNCR: They're lean, mean

 fighting machines.

 BOYS: Charge!!

 TV ANNCR: When there's a battle to be won,

 (SFX: CLUNK)

 Combat Rangers

 get the job done.

 Making backyards safe for democracy.

 BOSS: Now tell me why

 they're wearing dresses?

 MANAGER 1: The commander uniforms didn't arrive from China on time.

 MANAGER 2: That's because you picked the wrong shipping company.

 ANNCR VO: Next time use the only U.S. express shipper with direct routes from China.

 FedEx, be absolutely sure.

 TV ANNCR: Matching night vision tiara sold separately.

FIGURE 4.5   *(Courtesy of Tom Darbyshire, BBDO/New York)*

You are not employed as a copywriter to sell a joke. That is for stand-up comedians to do. You are employed to promote a product, service, media outlet, or public cause.

Enlightenment

Though we often do not recognize it as such, the need for enlightenment, the need to know, is itself an emotional function. Human beings can feel more in control of themselves and their environment if they are aware of what is going on around them. If you've read *Man without a Country,* been in solitary confinement, or even survived a week in the wilderness minus radio, newspapers, and the Internet, you are aware of the real emotional ramifications that flow from a lack of information about the places, people, and institutions with which you are familiar. Our increasing reliance on near-instantaneous electronic news has deepened our information dependency. The promise that we will receive useful detail on a subject or event is often enough to initiate attention that can be sustained as long as valuable and relevant data seem to keep coming.

The Gold'n Plump commercial in Figure 4.6 not only leads with enlightenment-promising questions, but it also illustrates these questions with obvious information symbols, such as computer screen buttons and schematic cutaways. Even though the humor of the pitch later surfaces, it is benefit-relevant enlightenment that has captured and held viewer attention.

One thing about which many people feel uncomfortably ignorant is what is under their car's hood—and they fear they will be taken advantage of as a result. The following radio spot dramatizes this fear before imparting enlightening knowledge about how such a danger can be avoided.

MAN:	I'm afraid, ma'am, that since you didn't change yer blinker fluid last season, yer flange engager is gonna need replacing.
WOMAN:	Okay, sure. Uh huh.
MAN:	And yer Johnson bar's way out whack.
WOMAN:	Yes.
MAN:	And, of course, yer swaggle stick's gonna need a new moisture control separator valve gasket.
WOMAN:	Oh, my. What was that again?
MAN:	It's the chassis that separates, um, the control separator, on the um.
WOMAN:	Oh for Pete's sake. This sounds terrible.
MAN:	It ain't good.
ANNCR:	It's a matter of trust. Before someone tells you about repairs that might be a bit out of whack, come in to AAA Automotive. Experience, honesty, and good old fashioned common sense that isn't very common anymore. AAA Automotive Services at the Parkway Point Auto Center behind the Parkway Point Theater. AAA. There's a reason we're listed first in auto service.

(Courtesy of Perry Zubeck, Saga Communications)

ANNCR VO: People say, "Okay, so Gold'n Plump Chicken is plump and meaty."

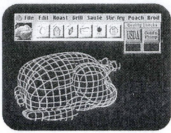

"Exactly how plump and meaty is it?

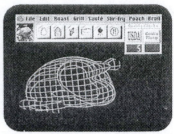

"A lot? A little?"

"Give us facts! Figures!"

"Something to compare it to!"

Lots o' MEAT
Little Bone

Okay, try *this* on for size. If Gold'n Plump Chicken were a holiday, it'd have to be the jolly one.

Here's a Gold'n Plump Chicken as a piece of furniture.

Hey, off the chicken!

And, finally, Gold'n Plump Chicken as an aircraft. Any questions?

Gold'n Plump®
(SFX: SLIDING WHISTLE)

(SFX: DRUM BEAT)

Gold'n Plump®
It's a mighty meaty chicken
It's a mighty, meaty chicken.
(SFX: CLUCK)

FIGURE 4.6   *(Martin/Williams, Minneapolis, for Gold 'n Plump Poultry. Lyle Wedemeyer, creative director; Sally Wagner, vice president and creative supervisor; Cathy Ostlie, copywriter; Karen Peterson, producer; Tim Wensmen, vice president, sales & marketing; and Deb Correll, retail marketing manager)*

Allurement

Few red-blooded copywriters require a detailed explanation of this emotional attraction, which, in a more exploitative sense, is called "sex." Actually, allurement is something of a hybrid, as it contains elements of people interest, sensation, and sometimes rivalry or esteem all rolled into one. Because the use of allurement is so widespread in several product categories, however, we tend to treat it as a distinct classification. But one definite note of caution must be raised in regard to this appeal, one that has nothing to do with taste or moral standards. Allurement has been exploited in irrelevant contexts in which it was totally foreign to the copy approach and rational appeal of the message as a whole. In such a case, sex becomes an unjustified attention-getter that makes promises the subsequent copy never fulfills. This technique has caused listeners and viewers to develop a real suspicion, if not deep distrust, of any message using the allurement appeal, even those where its solicitation is pertinent.

Allurement can be an effective emotional attraction. It also can be appropriately adapted to a wide variety of adult-oriented products and services with which it is not now paired. The copywriter must, however, make certain that the use of sex is both meaningful and helpful to the assignments at hand and is an effective vehicle for the rational appeal or appeals that are stressed. "People have been hit over the head so often with sex," complains *Victoria* editor Nancy Lindemeyer, "they don't feel the hammer anymore. We have to reach them through their sensibilities, not just their hormones."[32]

A lighthearted, almost satiric projection of allurement is accomplished in the following radio spot for Broduer Collision. The commercial illustrates the attention-heightening value of this appeal when it is used in a product category with which it is not normally associated. The trick for the writer is to find words and phrases to pull the allurement motif all the way through the copy. Otherwise, if sexiness is used only at the outset, it becomes an extraneous, cheap, and resented come-on.

	Production Note: Male voice is helpfully businesslike, female voice is warmly sexy, and on filter mic.
(SFX:	PHONE RING, PICKED UP. BACKGROUND NOISE OF BUSY BODY SHOP)
MAN:	Broduer Collision, may I help you?
LADY:	Is this the --- body shop?
MAN:	Yes, but Broduer offers a lot more than your average body shop.
LADY:	That's why I called.
MAN:	Y'know, our 20-thousand-square-foot facility here is very high-tech.
LADY:	Imaginative toys are so important.
MAN:	(Confused) Uh, and Broduer isn't greasy and grimy like other body shops.
LADY:	Nothing 'dirty' going on there, right?
MAN:	Even our waiting room is plush and comfortable---
LADY:	Mirrors on the ceiling, of course.
MAN:	Ye --- uh, no. I mean---
LADY:	I'm sure we can do business, but first, tell me about your 'special' body work.

MAN:	(Gulps) Well (Voice cracking), it's unitized repair, and we explain <u>everything</u> before we do <u>anything</u>.
LADY:	Ooooh. Talk to me.
MAN:	Broduer offers 24-hour towing, with rentals and loaners available.
LADY:	I'm always looking for a loaner.
MAN:	Then there's our European down-draft bake-spray painting that---
LADY:	Body paints! Mmmmmmmm
MAN:	And all work done with our state-of-the-art equipment comes with a year's full warranty.
LADY:	Ooooh. This 'Art' must have <u>some</u> equipment---
MAN:	(Quite unnerved at this point) Uh --- Excuse me??!!?
LADY:	I'll be right over. (PHONE CLICKS)
MAN:	M-mmaam???
ANNCR:	Broduer Collision, Groesbeck, north of 14 Mile Road. Call 296-51-hundred. 296-51-ooh-ooh.
	(SFX: DOOR OPENS. BODY SHOP NOISE HEARD)
LADY:	(NO FILTER MIC) Hello. I'm here to see Art.
MAN:	(Gulping) Oh boy---

(Courtesy of Christopher Conn. WHYT-FM)

It is <u>relatively easy to</u> keep radio's aural allurement safely suggestive. But, television's pictorial nature tends to force the allurement attraction to become much more literal and overt. This can compromise audience—and even outlet—acceptance. However, through a wonderfully sparse concept, the "Clothesline" commercial in Figure 4.7 manages to be both playfully seductive and explicitly pragmatic. As a result, the indulgence-driven difference between what men and women want is graphically yet tastefully illustrated.

Sensation

The sensation attraction requires no literacy, no social insight or broad-based experience on the part of the audience. Instead, it uses the basic senses of sight, sound, taste, smell, and touch to achieve its emotional impact. Even a very small child can respond to the taste-whetting stimulus of that rich chocolate cake or the depicted softness of that Downy-washed blanket. In fact, research conducted by marketing professor James McNeal shows that 64 percent of children's ads express the sensation appeal, making this attraction the number-one appeal in kid-aimed messages.[33] For their part, adults bring more depth to their appreciation of the beads of condensation running down that bottle of beer, but the same fundamental emotional attraction is in operation.

Sensation requires less social or scholastic background of its audiences than do any of its colleague appeals. That is why it is recruited so often to market the low-cost, mass-consumed products and services sold to such broad sections of the listening and viewing public. When properly selected and employed, the sensation appeal enables the audience to participate most rapidly in the message-building process by plugging in their own experiences almost as soon as the copywriter-stimulated image

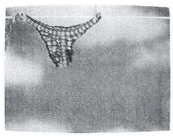

MUSIC: "HERE I AM STUCK IN THE MIDDLE WITH YOU"

MUSIC CONTINUES UNDER

FEMALE VO: What men want in women's underwear.

MUSIC CONTINUES

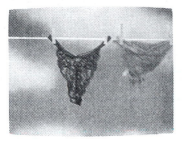

MUSIC CONTINUES

MUSIC CONTINUES UNDER

FEMALE VO: What women want in women's underwear. With more material in the seat, Fruit of the Loom underwear always stays comfortably in place.

FEMALE VO: Sorry, guys. Our bodies. Our fantasy.

FIGURE 4.7 *(Courtesy of Jeff Finkler, Leo Burnett Company, Ltd., Toronto)*

reaches them. In the thirty-second radio spot that follows, the sounds of thirst and the sounds of quenching it are amplified by a few well-chosen words that unmistakably tie the product to the pleasurable feeling it restores.

MAN: (Whistling <u>Bridge on the River Kwai</u>. After a few bars his whistle starts to go dry, and he is unable to whistle any longer.)

    (SFX: CAN OPENS --- GLUB, GLUB, GLUB, GLUB)

MAN: (Starts to whistle again.)

ANNCR: For that intense thirst, don't just wet your whistle, crush it. Crush. Available in orange, grape, lime and cream soda.

MAN: (Whistling winds up to time.)

(Courtesy of Cordelia Chhangte, Saatchi & Saatchi Compton Hayhurst Ltd.)

Because it brings us a literal visual, television's use of the sensation attraction demands even less verbal facility of the audience than does radio. Yet video sensation still can be heightened by orchestrating the counterpoint of compelling sound. In the Figure 4.8 commercial, in fact, it is the sound that dominates the initial frame and sets up surprise revelation of the product as well as off-camera sensory dramatization of its dental hygiene benefit.

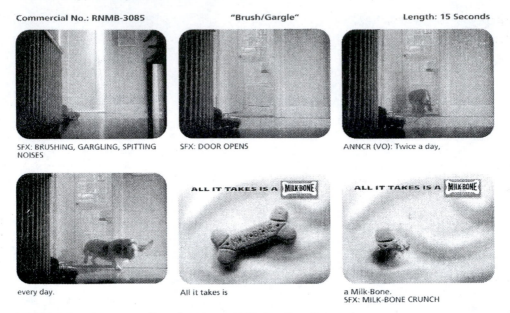

Commercial No.: RNMB-3085   "Brush/Gargle"   Length: 15 Seconds

SFX: BRUSHING, GARGLING, SPITTING NOISES

SFX: DOOR OPENS

ANNCR (VO): Twice a day,

every day.

All it takes is

a Milk-Bone.
SFX: MILK-BONE CRUNCH

FIGURE 4.8   (Courtesy of Vonda LePage, FBC/Leber Katz Partners)

Uniqueness

Alternatively referred to as "newness" or "novelty," this emotional attraction is exploited unmercifully in the marketplace as just-developed products and services try to make their mark and old established items attempt to demonstrate how up-to-date they've become. Being "where it's at" is an important concern to many consumers—especially younger ones with higher discretionary incomes. As these are the people most advertisers like to reach, not only commercials but also whole programs and the continuity that promotes them will often invoke this novelty aspect.

Because the Federal Trade Commission allows the term *new* to be applied to a product characteristic, in general, for only the first six months of national advertising, the novelty approach as attributed to the product has a severely circumscribed lifespan. But fortunately for clients and copywriters, the uniqueness appeal can also be exploited in how we write and design the message itself. Even vintage products, services, and programs can appear fresh and modern within the proper contemporary framework.

What follows is a unique way to present the benefits of radio, a way that, by implication, makes the old sound medium itself seem more novel. Clearly, the rational attractions of performance and economy are also major considerations that this spot helps spotlight.

CUSTOMER:	Your ad agency is highly recommended.
AD REP:	Oh, thanks. What do you sell?
CUST:	Fruits and vegetables. Here, I brought some along.
REP:	Great. We'll do some TV spots.
CUST:	Oh, I'd rather use radio.

REP:	Why?
CUST:	TV is too expensive.
REP:	Well, look---
CUST:	Anyway, people don't have to see my fruits and vegetables as long as they can hear them.
REP:	What?
CUST:	When we play music on them.
REP:	Are you kidding?
CUST:	No. See, I put an all-produce band together just for our radio commercial.
REP:	Oh, come on now.
CUST:	Hand me that squash there.

(MUSIC: LONG SAXOPHONE RIFF)

REP:	How did you do that?
CUST:	Practice. I'm also proficient on three leafy vegetables and two tropical fruits.
REP:	Really?
CUST:	It's economical to advertise on radio, and I can target the people who like to listen to fresh fruits and vegetables.
REP:	This, uh, band you---
CUST:	Seven rutabagas, five cucumbers, and a bass broccoli.
REP:	Uh-huh.
CUST:	So, we'll play our theme song, 'Yes, we have no bananas,' and then we'll eat our instruments. Okay?
REP:	(Laughs) Okay!
CUST:	You'll buy radio for us then?
REP:	Sure. Listen, could you teach me?
CUST:	Sure. Here, start with the celery.

(SFX: BLOWING SOUND)

You don't blow on celery. You strum it.

REP:	Oh, sorry.

(MUSIC: HARP STRUM)

CUST:	Beginners!
ANNCR:	Radio. Red hot because it works. For all the facts, call this station or the Radio Advertising Bureau.

(Courtesy of Dick Orkin, Dick Orkin's Radio Ranch)

Uniqueness can sometimes be derived from taking a standard storyline and turning it on its head—then using this new scenario to showcase the purported properties of what we have to sell. For instance, the fable the following British beer commercial borrows is a familiar one. But the product's entrance into this sappy tale is both unexpected and purposefully outlandish. Nevertheless, this novel introduction does lightheartedly suggest something about the distinctively desirable character—even beauty—of the brand.

Video	Audio
OPEN ON YOUNG FARMER'S DAUGHTER IN THE OUTBACK. SHE IS WEARING A FLORAL PRINT DRESS AS SHE SKIPS THROUGH THE FIELD DOWN TO LAKE IN FRONT OF THE FARM.	
GIRL GUSHING OVER SHEEP	GIRL: Hello, sky, hello birds, hello sheep. Isn't it a beautiful day?
SHE ARRIVES AT LAKE, LOOKS OUT ACROSS THE WATER AND SIGHS AT THE BEAUTY OF IT	Sigh.
A FROG AT HER FEET CROAKS. SHE LOOKS DOWN AND SMILES WITH DELIGHT	Hello Mr. Frog. I bet if I was to give you a kiss, you'd turn into a handsome sheep shearer.
SHE PICKS UP FROG IN BOTH HANDS AND BLOWS IT A KISS	SFX: SMALL BANG
SMALL EXPLOSION AND FROG TURNS INTO A HANDSOME MUSCULAR SHEEP SHEARER. SHE IS ONLY TEMPORARILY TAKEN ABACK.	
SHE STANDS ON TIP-TOE, CLOSES HER EYES AND PUCKERS HER LIPS TO BE KISSED	
HE DUTIFULLY KISSES HER, SOMEWHAT TENTATIVELY	
ANOTHER SMALL EXPLOSION. SHE DISAPPEARS AND HAS TURNED INTO A CAN OF XXXX AND A GLASS WHICH HE IS HOLDING	SFX: SMALL BANG
HE POURS BEER FROM CAN INTO GLASS, IT CATCHES THE SUN	VO: Castlemaine is made with golden cluster hops.
HE TAKES LONG, SATISFYING DRINK FROM GLASS	
LOOKS ADMIRINGLY AT BEER IN THE GLASS	SHEARER: You haven't got any sisters, have you?
CU PINT OF XXXX	
SUPER: Experienced hoppers wouldn't give a Castlemaine XXXX for any other lager	VO: Experienced hoppers wouldn't give a Castlemaine XXXX for any other lager.

(Courtesy of Simon Dicketts, Saatchi & Saatchi Advertising)

One caution about uniqueness must be observed. In exploiting the appeal, you must make certain that the novelty aspect is one you have established as clearly relatable to your customer's attitude and the personality of the brand. Then take it from there—like the Castlemaine commercial did. As legendary copywriter Tom McElligott reminds us, "communicating a meaningful product point of difference—assuming you're lucky enough to have one—is only half the battle. Doing it with wit, charm, intelligence and imagination is the other half."[34]

Rivalry

Dramatists and literary experts tell us that no good story can be without this element. The rivalry or conflict between two opposing entities or points of view provides the motive force for a story and constitutes a constant pull on our attention. As mini-stories, many pieces of commercial and continuity writing must use similar conflict mechanisms, but within a very reduced time frame. On several classic occasions ("Will Shell with Platformate Out-Perform Other Gasolines?"; "Can the Timex Take a Licking and Keep on Ticking?"; "Is It True Blondes Have More Fun?"), the conflict itself became the message's prime emotional attraction, with the attainment of the advocated rational appeal constituting the rivalry resolution. Yes, the Shell-fueled car did travel farther. Yes, our Timex possessed the durability to absorb that punishment. Yes, changing your looks with our hair coloring could increase your merrymaking. These and dozens of other little contests continue to be played out before listeners and viewers.

But if the rivalry is too contrived, if its results and main copy point are telegraphed from the beginning, the impact and, consequently, the emotional attraction will be seriously impaired. In order to succeed as the primary emotional appeal, the conflict must build and heighten as the message progresses. Such is the case in the following Arby's commercial, where crisis "reports" gradually escalate the tension. Also notable in this spot is its innovative point of view. We see "the revolution" not from the expected client's perspective, but from that of its unnamed competitors.

Video	Audio
LS MODERNISTIC OFFICE WITH SUNSET PANORAMA BACKDROP. OLDER EXECUTIVE (ED) FACES CAMERA AS YOUNGER EXEC (BILL) STRIDES IN	BILL: Well, Ed, burgers are *booming.*
MCU ED'S WORRIED FACE	ED: Have you seen this?
CU ARBY'S SANDWICH	BILL: Nothing to worry about.
M2S BILL AND ED	ED: These reports say otherwise.
CU ED'S WORRIED FACE	People are stepping out of our
CU ARBY'S SANDWICH	ED (VO): burger lines to go to Arby's.

Continued

Video	Audio
M2S TWO EXECS	BILL: Because Arby's roast beef with cheddar sauce is different.
CU ED	ED: Thing is --- they're not coming back to burgers.
REACTION SHOT BILL	ED (VO): They have a slogan: Beef and Cheddar's better
ED WALKS OUT OF FRAME TO FAVOR CU BILL	BILL: Come on Ed, it's still a burger world out there.
MS BOTH MEN TURN BACK TO CAMERA	ED: That may be, but it's a changing one.
LS OF ABOVE WITH SANDWICH NOW CU IN FOREGROUND	ANNCR (VO): The revolution continues. Taste the Arby's difference.

(Courtesy of David R. Sackey, Doner Advertising)

Sometimes conflicts can be made more dramatic and vivid on radio than on the tube. This is true even of little household-based disasters. The images called up by the following radio spot would be too gross to show on television, but skillful copy graphically stimulates them in the listener's imagination to position the product as much more necessary.

MOM: When you're a---

CARLY: Mooom!

MOM: ---you learn that every time you hear your name, you need to move immediately toward that---

ALEX: MOOOmmmm!

MOM: ---with your Purell Instant Hand Sanitizer. The squirtable stuff that kills germs on hands <u>wherever</u> hands are. Because following the---

CARLY: Mom!

MOM: ---is the---

ALEX: Mom. Is this bird dead?

MOM: ---or---

CARLY: Mommy look! I changed the baby.

MOM: So grab your Purell and go. The drive-thru. The diaper station. The dog drool. Purell kills 99.9 percent of germs. 'Til the next---

ALEX: Mom! Look what Billy found up his nose.

ANNCR: Purell Instant Hand Sanitizer. Go with it.

(Courtesy of Wyse Advertising. Jenny Buck, copywriter; Michael Chaney, producer)

Esteem

This final emotional attraction may be more readily recognized as self-realization, keeping up with the Joneses, becoming an envied person, or blatantly pursuing snob appeal. Goods that are among the most expensive in their product category often use this approach in an attempt to turn an unfavorable economic rationale into a positive looks or indulgence statement. Almost ninety years ago, when Cadillac Motors stopped emphasizing the technical aspects of its automobiles and began instead to position them within regal and ultra-stylish tableaus, the effectiveness of the esteem appeal became entrenched in modern advertising. The esteem appeal is even more pronounced in today's world where, as *Advertising Age* observes, "traditional luxury marketers are expanding their brands to more affordable merchandise, while at the same time the middle class is increasingly willing to, at least occasionally, buy expensive luxury goods."[35]

When combined with ego-building copy that compliments the audience member's taste, professional lifestyle, or value to the community, the esteem appeal becomes a potent generator of charity pitches in PSAs, as well as an effective means to cultivate consideration of commercial products. Even in program promos and station IDs, the esteem attraction can be used to get audience members to watch the program or listen to the station that "with-it people like you are talking about." Esteem is why you display your client's toilet tissue on a golden baroque holder instead of dangling it from a bent coat-hanger.

In the radio spot that follows, esteem is intertwined with its frequent rational partners, performance and looks. Notice how the ego-building prospect of success helps bolster the reason to buy. The copy also strengthens the case for PIP Printing by comparing its esteem gratification with a more obvious, but more wasteful, esteem-building alternative. PIP, in short, is your passage to business eminence, thereby accomplishing what former BBDO agency head Phil Dusenberry referred to as "turning the customer into a hero and the product into a catalyst."[36] This commercial also illustrates the frequent practice of *local tagging*. It is deliberately written "short" so that customized identity lines for individual client locations can be added.

(SFX:	AUDITORIUM AMBIENCE)
ROYCE:	So, there I am, strolling in to that critical sales meeting
ANNCR:	You're listening to Sixty Seconds to Success, a motivational seminar for ambitious listeners, funded by PIP Printing.
ROYCE:	Now, I know going into that meeting that I'm going to be successful because I look successful. Perhaps you've noticed this massive gold watch on my wrist. I know you're thinking, 'Royce, who cares what time it is. I could gaze at that watch for hours.' Expensive? You bet. And absolutely worthless (SFX: WATCH SLAMS DOWN) in that big sales meeting. When I leave the room, it leaves the room. My sales brochure stays behind. You say, 'Royce you destroyed your watch.' I say, 'Friend, I made my point.' It's your business printing that needs to look successful. Now you say 'Royce, good point but where do I go?' I say, 'PIP Printing.' Because at PIP Printing, they print success stories. And when you go to PIP Printing, don't say: I want to be a millionaire. They'll think you're an underachiever!

(:05 Local Tag)

(Courtesy of Maria Chaiyarachta, BBDO/Los Angeles)

Esteem is often blended with rivalry because winning is inherently an ego-building event. In the Hummer commercial below, both members of the family owning the vehicle eminently triumph over potential adversity because of it. Mom not only looks cool in the Hummer, but it has paved the way for admiration of her son by the "big kids." She need not worry about his acceptance at the new school thanks to the product's intervention. To explore the interplay between copywriter and art director, see the initial storyboard panels (thumbnails) derived from the script idea (Figure 4.9) on the facing page.

Video	Audio
MOTHER AND 3RD GRADE SON DRIVING; INTERIOR ONLY	MOM: Ready for your first day at a new school?
SON NODS HEAD SILENTLY	You nervous?
	SON: Nope.
THEY APPROACH EDGE OF SCHOOL GROUNDS	MOM: Do you want me to drop you off here so you can walk in?
	SON: No, you can pull right up.
MOM LOOKS SURPRISED. THEY PULL IN RIGHT UP FRONT. BUNCH OF OLDER KIDS STANDING THERE; LOOK LIKE 'COOL' KIDS	MOM: You sure you're gonna be alright?
	SON: (Confidently) Should be.
HE HOPS OUT AND APPROACHES PACK OF KIDS. THEY PART LIKE THE RED SEA, DROPPING, AND LET HIM PASS. AS HE PASSES BIGGEST KID, HE NODS HIS CHIN	'sup?
CAMERA SWINGS AROUND TO REVEAL CAR DROPPING HIM OFF IS A SLAMMIN' LOOKING BLACK H2 WITH LOTS OF CHROME EXTRAS. MOM ALSO LOOKS REALLY KILLER SITTING IN IT.	
PULL OUT AND SUPER: Hummer. Like nothing else.	

(Courtesy of Joyce Chen, Modernista! Ltd.)

Whichever emotional appeals are used, "the objective is to leave the audience at a higher positive emotional point at the end of the commercial than when they started," says advertising planner/researcher Elissa Moses, "and to evoke a positive emotional reaction to the product."[37] The Hummer spot illustrates this research-validated premise to a tee.

A PLAN FOR RATIONAL/EMOTIONAL PROPORTIONING

There are an infinite number of ways to pair up and combine the rational and emotional attractions in order to craft effective copy. You have been exposed to a few of these ways via the commercial examples in this chapter. You have encountered thousands more in the selling messages to which you are exposed in the course of your daily life. As a copywriter, the particular rational/emotional package you choose for

FIGURE 4.9   *(Courtesy of Joyce Chen, Modernista! Ltd.)*

a particular assignment depends on the product category, the target audience, the client's comparative position in the market, and a host of other considerations.

How do you pick the attraction package that will have the greatest chance of communicative success? What is the optimum blending of the rational and the emotional? There are no cookie-cutter answers to these questions. And the greatest single factor in deriving an effectively proportioned selling message is still the copywriter's own human intuition. "If you can't turn yourself into your customer," agency founder Leo Burnett once said, "you probably shouldn't be in the ad writing business at all."[38] Nevertheless, there are some broad classifications into which products can be grouped. These classifications, in turn, suggest (but do not dictate) certain rational/emotional mixes that would seem to increase your chance of success.

One of the simplest yet most respected classification systems is known as the FCB Grid (see Figure 4.10). Developed by Richard Vaughn, research director at Foote, Cone and Belding (FCB) in Los Angeles, the grid features four quadrants. These quadrants are fashioned from a horizontal continuum that ranges from "thinking" to "feeling" and a vertical axis stretching between "low involvement" and "high involvement." The resulting boxes "outline four potentially major goals for advertising strategy: to be informative, affective, habit-forming or to promote self-satisfaction."[39]

> Quadrant #1 is high in both thinking and involvement. Thus products falling within this quadrant are best served by the greatest focus on rational as opposed to emotional appeals. This makes sense since most products found in this box are high-price-tag items.

> Quadrant #4 is the opposite of #1. It isolates items that are high in feeling (emotion) but low in involvement. This is the arena of the impulse buy, where the greatest emphasis is likely to be on the emotional attraction.

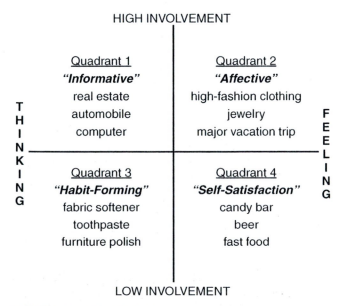

FIGURE 4.10   The FCB Grid.

Quadrant #2 is high in both involvement and feeling. Emotional attractions are important here. However, the comparatively high cost of these products and the high involvement of the consumer with them mean that rational appeals—particularly indulgence and looks—must figure prominently in the message.

Quadrant #3 contains items that are highly functional in nature, but their very practicality tends to make them less interesting (low involvement). Therefore, the rational attractions of safety, maintenance, performance, and economy have greater utility here.

The FCB Grid is not a magic blueprint for automatic copy success. But it does provide the copywriter with a long-established overview of how products can be classified, and of how this classification impacts rational/emotional appeal selection and blending. Nevertheless, keep in mind that the grid reflects the conventional approach to the categorical product task at hand. Under the right circumstances, and with the right skill, you may be able to get your product to stand out from the crowd by defying the grid's conventions. The Internet, for example, now provides much more rational information about products and services than was available to consumers when Vaughn first introduced his matrix. So television and radio spots may now need to lean more heavily on the emotional element in both: (1) driving people to the Web for further information; and (2) reinforcing positive feelings about the product *after* exposure to all that Web data. Conversely, Web copywriters should be more sensitive to the need for rational/logical content in the messages they create.

AN ATTRACTIONS ADDENDUM

This chapter demonstrates that, though our messages are brief, they still are required to engage (though not necessarily equally) both those right (affective) and left (cognitive) brain functions. The real skill comes in keeping these two spheres complementary. Communication researcher Dolf Zillman asserts that this task can best be accomplished by leading with emotional arousal to set up the rational appeal. However, he adds, "Don't make the arousal so intense that the receiver has difficulty focusing on the tandem rational product message . . . You don't want to over-arouse or the receiver will become pre-occupied with the emotional element . . . What is needed is *moderate* emotional arousal; get attention without diverting subsequent orientation from the rational point of your message."[40]

Still, cautions agency head Andy Berlin, "great advertising, really great advertising, doesn't persuade just by saying, 'Here are the features, here are the benefits, here is the rational analysis.' It also works because it becomes a little ink blot on the communal id of America."[41]

Perhaps the most ringing case for emotional/rational blending comes from Lowe/USA's chief creative officer Gary Goldsmith. In directing the copywriters who work for him, he boils the task down to nothing less than the search for the perfect appeals integration:

> My job is to send people back into the torture chamber to come up with something better, something with the right combination of logic and magic. Without the logic, no one will be persuaded. Without the magic, no one will care.[42]

CHAPTER

5   Making Sense of Our Audience

Having explored "SIMPLE PLEASURE" in the previous chapter, we now turn to the audiences at which these coupled emotional and rational attractions are directed. We begin with a look at the general attitudinal sets that audiences adopt. Then, we examine the lifestyle or *psychographic* delineations into which today's consumers are more and more narrowly segmented. Finally, we present a copy structure that is calculated to resonate with most people's behavioral patterns because it mirrors how human beings typically encounter and react to life.

AUDIENCES AND ATTITUDES

As our SIMPLE PLEASURE discussion recognizes, any electronic media audience presents the copywriter with a two-pronged communication challenge. Listeners and viewers must be approached with a balanced blend of both emotional and rational cues. This is because, although many people may be contacted simultaneously or over time by a given broadcast message or Web posting, few of these people are listening and viewing together.

Psychologically, therefore, our audience members share certain characteristics common to both large and small groupings. Because many are reached collectively over time and space, electronic consumers need an emotional stimulus to cut through the impersonality of the one-to-many communication setting. Like Marc Antony's "Friends, Romans, Countrymen" speech in Shakespeare's *Julius Caesar*, our copy must quickly strike emotional chords that each member of the audience can easily personalize, even though that audience is not actually being addressed as distinct individuals.

But since members of the electronic audience are also largely separated from one another, pure emotion alone won't compel and convince them. As solitary units of one and two, they are not prey to the sort of mob psychology that can magnify the response and dull the inhibition of individuals who find themselves part of the crowd at a rock concert, religious revival, or hockey game. This is especially true of the Internet, where the person at the computer constitutes an audience of one who can jump from one individualized experience to another with a keystroke. Even though purely emotional pitches may entertain, they lack the rational element essential to persuading the large—yet singularly isolated—electronic audiences to follow our copy's advice.

Aiming at a quantitative mass that is physically segmented into very small, often single-person units, the copywriter must not only resort to a balance of the rational and the emotional but also must be sensitive to the fundamental *attitudinal set* of the consumers being targeted. Lacking immediate audience feedback, and with a very brief time in which to engage, we must call on as much market data and raw intuition as are available. Then it becomes a matter of selecting from among the SIMPLE PLEASURE appeals those most likely to dovetail instantaneously with what we believe to be our target audience's predominant disposition.

There are four main attitudinal orientations that an audience may reflect. Each orientation must be dealt with somewhat differently in order to achieve maximum copy effectiveness. These four varieties can be identified respectively as (1) Affirmative, (2) Dissident, (3) Skeptical, and (4) Apathetic.

1. Affirmative Audience

Unfortunately, this audience is a rare commodity in the copywriter's world. It is the assemblage already favorably impressed with the fundamental thrust of your message; it is an audience that simply needs to be coaxed into tangible action or, at least, into maintaining its positive posture.

As graphically as possible, such a group must be shown why/how they should *energize* their belief. It's fine that they agree that making videos of the kids is a swell idea. But unless they are activated into buying your "handheld," you haven't sold many camcorders. It's great that they think our candidate is tops. But unless we motivate them to go to the ballot box, she's not going to win no matter how far ahead the polls put her. It's gratifying to know how highly they think of our news program or Website. But it doesn't mean much unless they develop the habit of tuning or clicking in.

With the Affirmative Audience, we don't have to sell them on the basic premise. In the Ortho spot below from BBDO/West, the belief with which all audience members can agree is stated in the very first line. The copywriter then builds on this accord with more statements that the listener can enthusiastically support before bringing in the product as the now-obvious method for taking action to sadistically "execute" this belief.

ANNCR: Fire ants are not lovable. People do not want fire-ant plush toys. They aren't cuddly; they don't do little tricks. They just bite you and leave red, stinging welts that make you want to cry. That's why they have to die. And they have to die right now. You don't want them to have a long, lingering illness. You want a death. A quick, excruciating, see-you-in-hell kind of death. You don't want to lug a bag of chemicals and a garden hose around the yard; it takes too long. And baits can take up to a week. No, my friend, what you want is Ant-Stop Orthene Fire Ant Killer from Ortho.

You put two teaspoons of Ant-Stop around the mound and you're done. You don't even water it in. The scout ants bring it back into the mound.

And this is the really good part. Everybody DIES. Even the queen; it's that fast. And that's good. Because killing fire ants shouldn't be a full-time job --- even if it is pretty fun.

Ant-Stop Orthene Fire-Ant Killer from Ortho. Kick fire-ant butt.[1]

2. Dissident Audience

These folks have a real bone to pick, either with your client's category in general or, worse, with your client in particular. There is no way you are going to sell them on anything until you first alleviate their antipathy. One way to accomplish this is to approach them with total frankness. Bring the element they don't like right up front and then show why it isn't so bad after all or why there are other factors that outweigh this disadvantage. Historically, Volkswagen pretty well neutralized the negative esteem appeal its "Beetle" had with upper-income types through a campaign called "Live Below Your Means." A & P Supermarkets put "Price and Pride" together to repair the damage done in a previous approach that had stressed economy at the expense of the company's long-time reputation for quality and integrity (performance). The copy admitted A & P had strayed, and most people forgave them. Listerine turned the "Taste People Hate Twice a Day" from an anti-indulgence debit into a positive performance credit. In the Figure 5.1 ten-second spot, Brown & Haley's agency concedes, even accentuates, the "ugliness" of its client's snack treat while revealing that the taste more than compensates for its visual unattractiveness.

   If frankness is too difficult for the client to swallow, your copy can take a more indirect approach that starts by establishing some common ground, some principles with which both the copy and the Dissident Audience can agree. That gives you some talking room before tackling the point of controversy. Nobody, for example, likes to endure the cost and potential discomfort of trips to the dentist. But if we can show people the ravages of untreated gum disease, they'll be more likely to make regular appointments. Your canned orange juice may take longer to prepare than the brand consumed right out of a carton. But if your can gives consumers more juice for less money, the inconvenience may be shown to be worth it. As in the following radio spot, the positive aspect must be both well presented and based on a premise the Dissidents support. If they don't subscribe to even your alleged common-ground principle (in this case, peace and quiet), you'll be selling two concepts and they'll buy neither.

ANNCR: We all like peace and quiet. It's nice to hear yourself think. So the noise in downtown Carrington must be driving you up the walls. Jackhammers; riveting; truck engines. When will it stop? It'll stop by the end of next year. It'll stop when our new mall is ready for your enjoyment. It'll stop when we all have a downtown mall that we can comfortably shop in; winter or summer. Your Carrington Chamber of Commerce asks that you let us continue to make some noise about the new downtown mall. Things will be peaceful again when it's done. Much more peaceful, much more relaxing than they were before we started. The new Carrington Mall. Better shopping, better business, a better city. The Carrington Mall. It'll be the quietest ever then; because we're raising the roof now.

HORROR MUSIC BUILDS
WOMAN: AHHHHHHHHHH! ! !

WOMAN: AHHHHHHHHHH! ! !

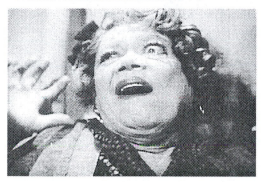

WOMAN: AHHHHHHHHHH! ! !

MUSIC STOPS

VO: They're only ugly until you taste them.

VO: Brown & Haley Mountain Bars

FIGURE 5.1   *(Courtesy of Pam Batra, McCann-Erickson/Seattle)*

3. Skeptical Audience

A target universe with this attitudinal set is certainly not hostile to your product or cause—but neither is it preconvinced. If anything, the Skeptical Audience would like to buy what you have to sell but has a nagging doubt or two that requires resolution. For them, the copywriter must present evidence and validation that the claim is true: that you *do* air more complete weather than that other station's news-cast, that your vacuum cleaner will suck up dirt others leave behind, that in the words of that old Bic commercial, "for a dollar forty-nine, it's (still) a pretty good lighter." All the common ground in the world won't satisfy the Skeptics if we don't come to grips with their objection. Ignoring weaknesses in your subject may convert them into diehard Dissidents. The Skeptical Audience, unlike the other three types, is passing through a temporary stage rather than displaying a stable condition. If you ignore them, they may lapse into indifference. If you try to mislead them, they'll be interested enough to exhibit a very active Dissident attitude. But if you can convince them with appropriate and sensible documentation, they'll be Affirmatives for a long time to come.

Red Roof Inns, for example, are known to have substantially lower prices than most other motel chains, *but*—doesn't that mean you get many more amenities at the other motels? In the following message, comedian Martin Mull quantitatively proves to the Skeptic that the "more" at the other places is not worth the premium you pay for not staying at Red Roof.

Video	Audio
OPEN MS MULL SEATED AT MOTEL ROOM TABLE NEXT TO WINDOW. ON TABLE ARE CALCULATOR AND OTHER ITEMS HE'LL MENTION.	MULL: What do 90-dollars a night
CAMERA SLOWLY TRUCKS RIGHT	motel chains offer you that you can't get at Red Roof Inns? Let's add them up and see.
HE HOLDS CAPS UP	This handy shower cap, 69 cents.
CU MULL; HOLDS UP TINY PLASTIC BOTTLE, THEN FLOSS PACKET	Shampooette, two dollars. Ah, dental floss; always a plus.
PUTS FLOSS IN SHIRT POCKET, STARTS PUNCHING CALCULATOR	Ooh.
ECU HIS FINGER PUNCHING CALCULATOR BUTTONS	We're still spending 29 dollars a night more than at Red Roof Inns.
ECU MULL'S FACE; HOLDS UP ROUND, FOIL-PACKAGED MINT	Huh, wait a minute. I forgot the mint.
LS STANDARD SHOT OF INN EXTERIOR AT DUSK WITH CAR PULLING IN	ANNCR (VO): Don't pay too much. Hit the roof. Red Roof Inns. Call 1-800-THE-ROOF.
CU MULL; TAKES BITE OUT OF MINT	MULL: It's a good mint. It's not worth 29 dollars, but it's good.

(Courtesy of Ed Klein, Doner Advertising)

Consumers are especially skeptical of car dealers. Given the shaky image of this business category, one false step on the part of an automotive copywriter easily can convert that skepticism to hardcore hostility. The following spot is fashioned to enable dealer Jim Paul to take the initiative by bringing up—and defusing—three common concerns about buying a new car. He thereby neutralizes these objections while enhancing his own image as a straightforward, credible businessman.

ANNCR: Jim Paul of Valley Chevrolet wants you to know some things you won't get at his dealership. For one thing, you won't get a curious charge for something called dealer prep.

JIM PAUL: You know what that is? That's like the grocer charging you to take the cans out of the box and putting them on the shelf.

ANNCR: You won't find yourself talking to a salesperson, agreeing on a price, and suddenly ending up in a closer's office who wants more money.

JIM PAUL: It's just an old-time psychological sales gambit, and I think it's insulting to a customer's intelligence.

ANNCR: And you won't find a separate price sticker of several hundred dollars for things the dealer decided you needed, like rustproofing, paint sealant, fabric protector.

JIM PAUL: If people want those things, fine. But we think one price sticker on the car is enough.

ANNCR: If you're finding these things at a car dealership, come find us. It's easy. We're in Apple Valley, eight miles south of the Met Center on Cedar Avenue. Jim Paul's Valley Chevrolet. A car dealer for the times.

(Courtesy of Craig Wiese, Craig Wiese and Company)

4. Apathetic Audience

This is by far the most numerous attitudinal set that the electronic media copywriter will encounter. Most mass consumable products and services do not create a strong enough impression on people to generate love, hate, or even the interest needed to be active Skeptics. Such a vast number of commercials, PSAs, and other continuity fill the airwaves and Ethernet that audiences can muster little more than profound indifference to most of them. Copywriters spend much of their lives in a constant battle against this malaise, a continuous struggle to break through to Apathetics long enough to make an impression and stick in their memory. A wordsmith's fundamental job, then, is to crack this disinterest with a compelling image that flows smoothly into a relevant problem/solution vignette.

We would be hard-pressed to find a less top-of-mind or more boring subject than a light bulb, for instance. But Figure 5.2's commercial shatters this apathy with a deliciously demented illustration of just how critical reliable Philips bulbs can be.

As another example, few listeners bolt to attention when the subject of pistachio nuts is raised. And even fewer would care about the California Pistachio Commission. Yet, in the service of this product and client, copy creator Dick Orkin

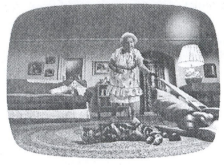

(SFX: VACUUM)

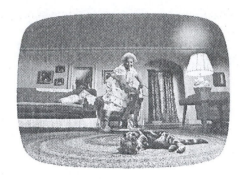

(SFX: BULB BLOWS OUT)

(SFX: CAT HOWLS, VACUUM SUCKING NOISE)

ANNCR (VO): It's time to change your light bulb.

Philips Longer Life square bulbs last 33% longer than ordinary round bulbs.

FIGURE 5.2   *(Courtesy of Arthur Bijur, DFS Dorland)*

quickly arrests such apathy via a felonious conflict that heightens awareness of the nut's "any time" attributes.

JOHN: All I know, Bernie, is I left this office to pick up a fax and returned to find that you're a common criminal.

BERNIE: What are you talking about?

JOHN: You ate a pistachio from my pistachio dish!

BERNIE: I did not!

JOHN: What is this pistachio shell doing here?

BERNIE: Okay, I had one.

JOHN: Empty your pockets, Bernie!

BERNIE: Okay, two or three.

JOHN: Two or three?

BERNIE: Okay, a handful, but the pistachios were sitting out on your desk. I love pistachios!

JOHN: These colorful new pistachios are for important new clients, Bernie, not you.

GUARD: You called for security, Mr. Cherney?

JOHN: Yes, Wendel, I did!

BERNIE: Security, for crying out loud! What's the crime?

JOHN: You ate pistachios when it wasn't a special occasion.

GUARD: Oh-oh. On your feet mister and spread 'um!

BERNIE: John, pistachios are for any time!

JOHN: Says who?

BERNIE: The California Pistachio Commission.

JOHN: Cuff him!

BERNIE: They also say --- Oww! California pistachios are high in fiber but low in fat with no cholesterol.

GUARD: You gonna go peaceful, pal, or do I have to rough you up?

JOHN: Just get him out of here.

ANNCR: That afternoon, 3 P.M. in a Los Angeles courtroom, Bernie Blindstrom was charged with nibbling pistachios out of season. Based on testimony from the California Pistachio Commission, the case was thrown out. Avoid mistaken arrests. Get the word out. Pistachios are fun anytime. A message from the California Pistachio Commission.

(Courtesy of Dick Orkin, Dick Orkin's Radio Ranch)

PROGRESSIVE MOTIVATION

As we discovered in Chapter 4, putting together a blend of rational and emotional attractions that trigger a desired response in our target audience is a formidable job. But it is not the entire copy task. As copywriters, we must also concern ourselves with how these appeals are unveiled in our messages; in other words, with the overall order and progression of the spot. To persuade consumers—particularly those attitudinally most-numerous Apathetics—it is important that the message draws them in *before* making a lunge for their wallets. What we refer to here as Progressive Motivation is a proven persuasive structure, one calculated to maximize listener/viewer involvement in what we have to say, show, and sell.

Though the study of multistep persuasion has a long history, it was most lucidly configured more than fifty years ago by speech professor Alan H. Monroe. He coined the term *Motivated Sequence* to refer to a persuasive process that he divided into five steps: attention, need, satisfaction, visualization, and action.[2] According to Monroe, a communicator must first attract the indifferent listener (attention), then identify the problem (need), provide the solution (satisfaction), project that solution into the future (visualization), and, finally, get that solution manifestly adopted (action).

Grounded as it is in interpersonal communication, Monroe's formula must be somewhat modified to conform to the needs of the electronic media. Because people are not socialized to give the same initial attention to a box of wires that they give to other people, copywriters must devote some of their already scarce time to an *attention-enlarging* step. We must strive to ensure that our unseen consumer is still with us before plunging ahead into problem-solution unveiling. Therefore, what we call *Progressive Motivation* deletes Monroe's visualization step in order to have time earlier to lock in attention. A summary comparison between Monroe's interpersonal-oriented Motivated Sequence and our electronic-media-favoring Progressive Motivation is given below:

Motivated Sequence	*Progressive Motivation*
1. Attention	1. Entice
2. Need	2. Engage
3. Satisfaction	3. Disclose
4. Visualization	4. Demonstrate
5. Action	5. Activate

In other words, we must first *entice* audience notice (1), which is usually the job of one of the PLEASURE elements. Then we must *engage* that notice (2) by providing stimuli that involve audience members' past experiences or fantasies in a way that gets them to help us construct our selling scene. Next, we apply this involvement toward the *disclosure* of a consequent need the consumer has for our product or service (3). We then *demonstrate* how our product or service can fulfill this need (4), and, finally, we encourage the audience to make some overt, *activated* response (5)—even if only to remember the name of our product, the call letters of our station, or the URL of our Website.

Initially getting and holding listener/viewer focus requires some serious labor. In formulating his *attention mechanics theory*, Ken Sacharin, president of The Media Edge, argues that the attention span is a very limited resource and must be treated as a precious commodity. "To understand how attention mechanics works," he says, "imagine entering a crowded room—a giant, noisy, unruly New Year's Eve party, say, in a city where you are alone and a stranger—and trying to get attention. The noise is deafening. There are hundreds of people milling about. Most are already clustered into tight convivial cliques. No one is waiting to say hello and welcome you. Instead, everyone else is already happily engaged in conversations."[3] That is the situation you face as a copywriter every time you strive to construct a message that will achieve admiring notice.

Beginning with a compelling image or production feature will certainly attract heed. But Professor Paul Bolls has discovered that a person's cognitive system temporarily overloads after being exposed to such a stimulus. So this stimulus must not be the central point you wish to make, because the sensory overload will cause it not to be remembered. However, some three to six seconds after that beginning feature, what he calls a *Magic Window* opens and stays open for another six seconds. It is into this "window" that you can effectively drop Progressive Motivation's Step 2; you can lock in important, audience-relevant engagement while attention is still high and cognitive overload has receded.[4] In the following spot, for example, the creaking door, howling coyote, and evil voice combine to powerfully entice the listener while the central subject of weight loss is withheld until Bolls's *Magic Window* opens around the five-second mark. The client is mentioned early on—but the Weight Watchers *solution* is not demonstrated (in this case by the announcer) until after all the problems of trying some other methods are disclosed and dramatized.

(SFX: DOOR CREAKING, COYOTE HOWLING)

EVIL VOICE: Can I help you?

LADY: Is this-uh-uh-Weight Watchers?

EVIL VOICE: No, but we're a weight loss company too. Come, let me show you--(Evil laugh)

LADY: Oh, but I have an appointment at Weight Watchers.

EVIL VOICE: We have a number of methods. In here, the starvation diet--

             (SFX: DOOR OPENS)

EVIL VOICE: (Laughs)

MAN: Food --- food --- a carrot --- a crumb.

LADY: Oh---

             (SFX: DOOR SHUTS)

EVIL VOICE: Over here, we have the work-out room.

             (SFX: HEAVY PANTING AND RUNNING FEET)

2ND MAN: Faster. Faster, I say!

             (SFX: WHIP CRACKING)

             (SFX: DOOR SHUTS)

EVIL VOICE: (Laughs)

LADY: Oh---Look, I'm going to Weight Watchers.

EVIL VOICE: Don't go---

ANNC: Instead of the horrors of the miracle diets, Weight Watchers has a balanced diet and an optimal exercise program. We'll even help you change your attitudes about food. And it's all done in a friendly, group environment. Of all the weight loss programs in the world, none have been more successful than the Weight Watchers program. We've helped more people lose more pounds than any other program.

(Courtesy of DDB Advertising)

Turning to television and the total Progressive Motivation process, examine Figure 5.3. Here, compelling concerto music paves the way for need disclosure, demonstration of the client clinic's solutions, and a phone number call to action.

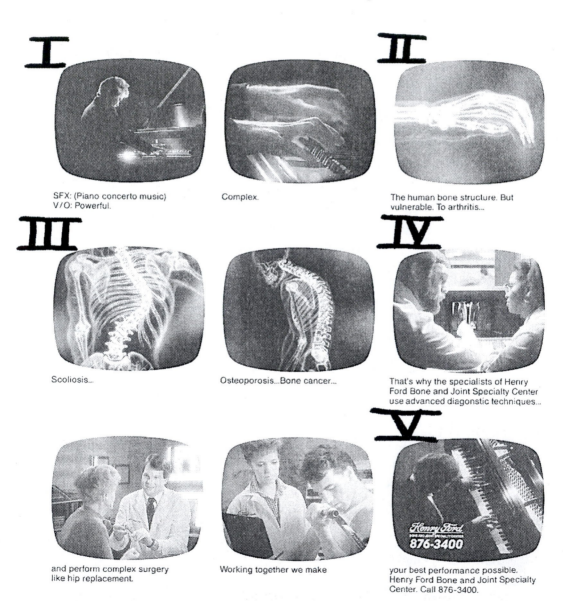

I — SFX: (Piano concerto music) V/O: Powerful.

II — Complex.

The human bone structure. But vulnerable. To arthritis...

III — Scoliosis...

Osteoporosis...Bone cancer...

IV — That's why the specialists of Henry Ford Bone and Joint Specialty Center use advanced diagonstic techniques...

and perform complex surgery like hip replacement.

Working together we make

V — your best performance possible. Henry Ford Bone and Joint Specialty Center. Call 876-3400.

FIGURE 5.3 *(Courtesy of Marcie Brogan, Brogan & Partners)*

The commercial is designed to systematically break through ingrained audience fear of "illness" subjects so that their focus can be directed to the offered remediation. The Roman numerals on the photoboard indicate where each of Progressive Motivation's five steps begins.

The following is another radio example of how Progressive Motivation can fight audience apathy. This spot enlists the emotional attractions of laughter, people interest, and a hint of allurement to carry rational economy/performance appeals. Roman numerals again have been added to highlight the commercial's structural flow.

CATHY: Our kids are three and four and [I] they're picking up on everything we say. So we decided if we were ever to mention 'making love' we needed some sort of code. [II] We came up with --- 'The Furnace kicked on.' Kinda cute. But I forgot. (Fading off) And yesterday---

STEVE: Honey, the furnace just kicked <u>on</u>.

CATHY: Well, I'm not surprised. That thing kicks on every 20 minutes. [III] I told you we should change from oil to gas. It's so much more efficient.

STEVE: Fine. But the furnace kicked on.

CATHY: I know. It's giving me a headache. I also know that [IV] Washington Natural Gas will lease us a conversion burner for $6.20 a month.

STEVE: Fine. We'll convert to a new one, but right now, the <u>old</u> furnace has kicked on.

CATHY: Exactly my point. But if we switch from oil to gas---

STEVE: Honey! This old furnace thing is not working.

CATHY: Well, it's never worked like it's supposed to.

STEVE: I'm gonna go take a shower.

CATHY: It'll probably be cold.

STEVE: (Off mic) That's what I'm thinking.

ANNCR: [V] Think about this. Washington Natural Gas will install a gas furnace or conversion burner and, if for any reason you're not satisfied after one year, they'll re-install a new electric or oil furnace at no cost. Think about it. Gas makes sense.

KID: Mommy, why is Dad kicking the furnace?

(Courtesy of Holly J. Roberts, Chuck Blore & Don Richman Inc.)

Listed in following text are eight of the spots presented in Chapter 4 and two others featured earlier in this chapter. Turn back to them now and put your own numbers on each message to indicate where each of the five Progressive Motivation steps begins:

Supercuts example of a "safety" appeal (Figure 4.1)
Pets Inn example of a "maintenance" appeal

Ameritrade example of an "economy" appeal (Figure 4.3)
Frosty Paws example of a "laughter" appeal
Federal Express example of a "laughter" appeal (Figure 4.5)
AAA Automotive example of an "enlightenment" appeal
PIP Printing example of an "esteem" appeal
Hummer example of an "esteem" appeal (Figure 4.9)
Ortho example of an Affirmative Audience approach
Philips example of an Apathetic Audience approach (Figure 5.2)

After examining these commercials, you should have discovered that the proportional length of each Progressive Motivation stage can vary widely from spot to spot. However, the basic order of step unveiling remains the same as each of the messages strives to scale the audience apathy barrier.

In the real world, people encounter problems first and then seek solutions; not the other way around. So why shouldn't our copy follow this same effective, life-reflecting sequence? *Advertising Age* critic Bob Garfield maintains that "the advantage of problem/resolution advertising is manifest; the consumer is enlightened, often in the most dramatic terms, on why to buy the product. In that sense it is among the purest forms of advertising, communicating salient information in a memorable way."[5]

Ultimately, of course, the copywriter is striving to get the audience to take some action—Progressive Motivation's culminating point. Action is not easy to achieve as we reach across the airwaves or through the wire to that often-apathetic consumer. But, as master radio copywriter Jeffrey Hedquist reminds us, "If you tell the story in an imaginative and engaging way, then taking the action won't be as foreign to the listener [or viewer], because in their mind they've already done it. If you can get the listener to take the action in their imagination, then it's a smaller leap for them to take the action in their lives."[6] Telling that imaginative story to lead up to that action is what Progressive Motivation is all about.

PSYCHOGRAPHICS

As we have discussed, Progressive Motivation is especially applicable in situations in which you face a largely apathetic audience. However, there may be many types of people within that attitudinal group. In fact, there may be many types of people within *any* attitudinal assemblage. The contemporary marketing world usually subdivides people into many more precise and sophisticated segments or *niches* than the four attitude conglomerates we earlier discussed. As Burson Marsteller's Al Schreiber observes, "If you talk about how people are selling their products and services today, you would see this whole evolution toward what we call lifestyle approach. And that is: 'I don't want to keep hitting you with just plain old ads; I want to surround you with my message.'"[7] *Psychographics* is the broad term that encompasses this lifestyle orientation, or what industry analyst Ron Gale describes as "a way of getting beyond pure demographics to get under people's skin and discover what makes them tick."[8]

The Evolution of Psychographics

In 1979, public relations executive Henry J. Kaufman explained the difference between demographics and the emerging psychographics in these terms:

> Years ago, everything was demographics. Age. Sex. Wealth. Education. Now there's a thing called psychographics that deals with lifestyles. Like cancer or the common cold, psychographics are not based on your social status or your wealth. You can have a taste for great books and be as poor as a churchmouse, and be willing to spend your last sou on them. Or you can be poor as a churchmouse and own a Leica camera, if your interest is photography.[9]

Thus people in the same demographic category may—through their preferences, self-concepts, and world views—be distributed among several separate psychographic categories. In like manner, folks from different demographic groups may cluster together in the same psychographic cell. The impoverished Leica camera owner to whom Kaufman referred may be in the same psychographic niche as people with twice the education and ten times the income. This would depend on how central the values associated with the practice of advanced photography are to the individuals in question.

These lifestyle dynamics were set in motion, says James Ogilvy, in the burgeoning affluence of the 1960s, when large numbers of middle-class young people for the first time joined upper-class youth in the quandary of having all their physical needs comfortably met. "Once the basic needs had been satisfied," says Ogilvy, "then the common denominators of material wealth no longer served as an adequate way of keeping score in the great game of life. . . . Instead of satisfying universal needs with the same universally available products of mass marketing, more and more mainstream consumers began to define themselves not as having more or less of what everybody wanted, but as having precisely what only they wanted. More of the mainstream moved from a commonly understood standard of living to an individually defined lifestyle."[10]

By the mid-1970s, a number of advertising agencies were conducting their own psychographic research, and psychologist Daniel Yankelovich had firmly established his *Yankelovich Monitor*. The *Monitor* tracked more than four dozen trends in consumer attitudes about such things as family, money, and social institutions. These and successor trends are what marketers consider when planning new campaigns and rolling out new products, thus recognizing that demographic categorizations are much too general for many of today's marketing requirements.

"Demos are sort of a metaphorical look at a target," points out McCann-Erickson senior media vice president George Hayes. "They act like this target. They look like this target. Therefore we conclude they must be in our target group. But more often than not, that's not the case. As products [reflect] marketing on a more precise basis to more segmented groups, we are beginning to discover these broad demographic descriptors just don't work anymore."[11] This realization is reflected in Nike president Charlie Denson's admission that, "At Nike we used to talk about the consumer in what we thought were specifics but today feel like generalities. We used to put an 18- and a 22-year-old in the same set of psychographic, demographic targets, but today they're living on different planets. Consumers are more multicultural and more tribal than ever."[12]

Different companies and different researchers have developed distinct methodologies for trying to slice this mysterious audience pie—and different terminologies to describe that pie's individual pieces. In psychographically profiling the age fifty and older market, for instance, Langer Associates identified four segments based on how these people deal with the effects of aging and appearance. Though wanting to be well-groomed, *Age Acceptors* "are not concerned about looking younger." *Age Modifiers* seek to look "a bit younger." *Age Reducers* pursue "more drastic steps to appear younger by coloring their hair, buying the latest skin cream, and plastic surgery." Finally, *Age Deniers* "may have hairstyles and hair colors frozen in time. Wearing styles that are too youthful, overly glamorous or too faddish."[13]

These psychographic distinctions have implications beyond the clothing, cosmetic, and health fitness industries because they shape the consumers' overall view of their world and of themselves. Examine the television spot below. With which of these four "senior consumer" psychographic groups does this commercial seem most closely aligned? Hypothetically, if the agency that created the spot were pursuing such a psychographic profile, is there something you might suggest to target this lifestyle cell even more precisely?

Video	Audio
SENIOR COUPLE IN LIVING ROOM, SURROUNDED BY FLORIDA MEMORABILIA, LOOKING AT CAMERA. Super: Florida, again?	MAN : So, we are going to Florida, again? WOMAN : Where else?
SPEEDBOAT ON LAKE	JINGLE : If you
GRAND PRIX RACE	knew Arizona---
DANCERS AT SAN XAVIER	(MUSIC, FIREWORKS SFX)
SAME AS SCENE ONE	MAN : How many years we been going to Florida? WOMAN : It's in the Guinness book.
COUPLE CAMPING BY RV IN FLAGSTAFF	JINGLE : If you
FAMILY BICYCLING IN SEDONA	*knew*
COUPLE SHOPPING	Arizona---
FOURSOME GOLFING	(GOLF SFX)
CLOSE-UP, MAN PUTS ON SEXY SUNGLASSES	MAN : I got a crazy idea---

Continued

Video	Audio
WOMAN RESPONDS, SURPRISED.	WOMAN : Animal!
RESORT SWIMMING POOL	JINGLE : If you knew
WESTERN TOWN COWBOY WITH HORSE IN HIGH COUNTRY SHOOT-OUT	If you
TENNIS MATCH	knew
WESTERN TOWN SHOOT-OUT SUPER: Free Vacation Kit 1-800-247-4000	Arizona---
INDIAN GUIDE AND TOURIST COUPLE	
COUPLE HIKING IN GRAND CANYON SUPER: SIG AND SLOGAN. Arizona Office of Tourism.	ANNCR (VO) : Arizona, If you knew it, you'd do it.

(Courtesy of Shirley S. McCalley, Taylor Advertising)

No matter what the brand category, if there is a discernible market, it is likely to have been psychographically profiled. For example, the *Yankelovich Monitor*'s polling puts 31 percent of Americans in a category it identifies as "Western Enthusiasts" and then divides this group into five cells: *Hoe-Downers* (defined by their interest in Western music and dancing); *Historians* (a primarily male group interested in Western lore); *New Pioneers* (a primarily female group enticed by contemporary Western fashion and life-style); *Art and Design Buffs* (who have an aesthetic interest in Western stylings and motifs); and *City Slickers* (demonstrating a casual rather than compelling interest in things Western).[14] Clearly, you could create several versions of that same Arizona Office of Tourism commercial to target each of these cells more precisely.

Moms can be psychographically segmented, too. But rather than being segmented by age, Leo Burnett researchers found that the eighteen- to forty-nine-year-old group was divided by a series of variables that included the involvement of dad in the family unit and the extent to which mom is looking for self-fulfillment. Four clear cells emerged: *"June Cleaver: the sequel,* mostly upscale, Caucasian women who believe in conventional, 'dad as bread winner, mom as nurturer roles'; *Tug-of-War moms,* who aspire to be Mrs. Cleaver but have to work and resent it; *Strong Shoulders,* mostly lower-income, less-educated women who get little-to-no help from dad but still make the best of it, enjoying work and child-rearing; and *Mothers of Invention,* women with super-involved husbands who have developed new systems to harmoniously attain career and family goals."[15] For further practice in psychographic targeting, try to revise the following evocative spot for clothier Lands' End so that it more definitively targets one of these "mom" categories. For which category is it easiest to make this adaptation? Why?

Video	Audio
BLACK AND WHITE FILM UNDER-CRANKED TO GIVE A 'HOME MOVIE' FEEL. MOTHER AND 12-YEAR-OLD DAUGHTER PLAYFULLY WRESTLING AND TICKLING EACH OTHER ON THE COUCH OF A WELL-APPOINTED BUT NOT LUXURIOUS LIVING ROOM	VO: What makes one child like no other? What makes one story your funniest? What makes your grandmother's biscuits better than yours? What makes that blue sweater your favorite?
GRAPHIC: landsend.com 1.800.356.4444	Lands' End. Life is in the details.
ADD LOGO AT BOTTOM OF FRAME	

(Courtesy of David Claus, DDB/Chicago)

VALS

A much more widely applicable and historic psychographic schema is VALS—the Values and Life-styles research tool developed principally by Arnold Mitchell of SRI International. VALS was cited in an *Advertising Age* poll of research executives as one of the ten top market research breakthroughs of the 1980s. SRI has continued to refine it, and VALS has consequently served as the catalyst for many other psychographic categorization systems. As in other psychographic models, writes trade reporter Betsy Sharkey, "the underlying thesis of VALS is that people and their buying habits are driven by their values and lifestyles, as well as their needs. It looks to the motivation behind the act. . . . Using values enables them [companies and agencies] to give consumers shape and texture—a face and a psychology as well as a demography."[16] In its most recent form,[17] VALS is divided into nine segments:

Innovators have abundant resources and because of this, are very active consumers with upscale tastes and interest in niche products. They are successful, sophisticated and image-conscious consumers who value their independence.

Thinkers enjoy good incomes but are more practical and conservative in their tastes. Well-educated and responsible, they are continually seeking out opportunities for learning and reflection and have a strong sense of responsibility.

Achievers are still in the process of striving for success and seek products and services that validate this success for all to see. Goal and family oriented, they respect and seek stability. Work and worship tend to be very important to them.

Experiencers value self-expression and demonstrate this via their expenditures on fashion and entertainment. Young and energetic, their enthusiasm for new, even risky things can be powerful—but also fickle.

Believers are motivated by ideals like Thinkers and are even more committed than Achievers to moral codes which they deeply hold. They are very predictable in their thinking and organize their lives around home, family, community and social or religious institutions. Therefore, they tend to be very stable in their purchases and brand loyalties.

Strivers exhibit a need to be successful and stylish—but don't have the money or skills to readily obtain the products that would win the approval of others that they so diligently seek. They therefore tend to be trendy and even impulsive.

Makers exude practicality and deeply value self-sufficiency. They take on and complete a variety of home and family projects and have little interest in the world outside their daily life. Hard-core traditionalists, they distrust both new ideas and large corporate structures.

Survivors possess the fewest resources of any VALS segment. They are preoccupied with meeting daily needs and so have no time for the pursuit of new achievements. Especially fearful of change, they are very cautious consumers.

VALS can and is used to shape the copy approach of many marketing campaigns. After research has been done to ascertain the VALS segment or segments most likely in tune with a product's or brand's characteristics, copywriters can go to work in designing a message that best taps into that segment's core motivations. Sometimes, through careful message styling and discrete media placement, the same product can be marketed to more than one VALS constituency. However, every care must be taken to insure brand character is not diluted or compromised in the process. You don't want one group to be alienated if they stumble across a pitch intended for another segment possessing a very different lifestyle focus.

For practice, examine the Figure 5.4 photoboard. With which VALS segment or segments might it especially resonate? Conversely, which of these lifestyle groupings would find no appeal in this product construct?

Now examine the following radio spot. What is the main VALS segment that it appears to target? What changes in approach would have to be made to the Ore Ida and Gordo's commercials to have them appeal to each others' VALS target?

(MUSIC: EMOTIONAL GUITAR)

MAN: As a ski instructor, I found that when a female student takes a spill, the best thing I can do is help her up. And then plant a long hard French kiss right on her mouth. I found that this helps the skier forget about the fall they just took. Sometimes I'll even say, 'Hey Sugar Britches, let's forget about this whole silly ski thing and go back to the snow lodge and snuggle up next to a couple of rum toddies.' Where upon I'll flick my tongue rapidly for 10 seconds or so. Most often these attempts to be helpful are misconstrued and I end up taking a fist in the eye. Consequently, I go through a fair amount of goggles during the winter months. Luckily, Gordo's Snowboard Store at the Maple Hill Mall in Kalamazoo has Santa Cruz goggles for only 20 dollars. So come visit Gordo at the Maple Hill Mall and see what he can do for you this winter. Because when the harsh realities of winter strike, you can never be too prepared.

(Courtesy of Dean Gemmell, Copper Advertising)

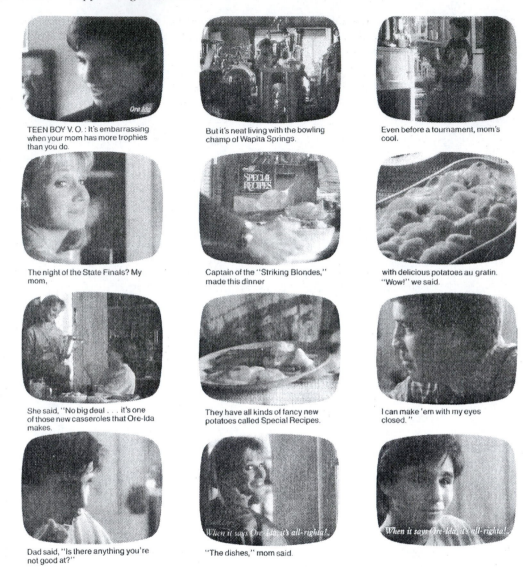

TEEN BOY V.O. : It's embarrassing when your mom has more trophies than you do.

But it's neat living with the bowling champ of Wapita Springs.

Even before a tournament, mom's cool.

The night of the State Finals? My mom,

Captain of the "Striking Blondes," made this dinner

with delicious potatoes au gratin. "Wow!" we said.

She said, "No big deal . . . it's one of those new casseroles that Ore-Ida makes.

They have all kinds of fancy new potatoes called Special Recipes.

I can make 'em with my eyes closed. "

Dad said, "Is there anything you're not good at?"

"The dishes," mom said.

FIGURE 5.4 *(Courtesy of Ore Ida)*

Sometimes, of course, much of the attraction of a product for a given psychographic group arises from the fact that it is shown to have little or no appeal to divergent groups holding much different values. (This is the "I wouldn't be caught dead using something *they'd* use" phenomenon.) If your client can be successful by serving its prime psychographic segment exclusively, you would do well to avoid fashioning messages that might be seen as enticing to other segments. As Carolyn Wall, one of the founding executives of the Fox network once put it, "If you've got a market that likes you, it doesn't matter if everyone else hates it—you'll succeed."[18]

VALS and other more specialized psychographic tools all strive to categorize and target consumers with ever greater precision. Claritas, the company that pioneered market segmentation research in the mid-1970s, now divides the population into sixty-six segmentation groups that factor in such elements as what people drive and where they vacation. In 2007, Nielsen began using the Claritas schema to provide television advertisers with ratings data broken into these more precise psychographic cells. "As we match new consumer groups (based on lifestyle and personal interests) to new sociological patterns," Optimedia CEO Mike Drexler observes, "we recognize that people not only buy different kinds of products, they have different reasons for buying the same kinds of products. So the trend toward more segment marketing and individualized media will accelerate."[19]

This has never been of greater importance than in today's interactive world, where people's expanding media choices are fragmenting audiences more than ever. "In the age after mass marketing, marketers are interested not in states, but in states of mind, which transcend geography," writes advertising critic Debra Goldman. "Their map of America is a conglomeration of archipelagos, islands of taste, habit and income that resemble similar, far-flung islands more than they resemble their geographic neighbors."[20] In fact, these forces may be moving us beyond psychographics to *technographics*. Leo Burnett/Chicago's chief creative officer Michael Conrad defines this term as comprising "the way a consumer interacts with the media and the distribution of interest across TV, radio, print, Internet, etc. [which] will influence the way they receive the message."[21] Clearly, electronic media copywriters now have much more to think about when deciding how to craft their message. They must be much more cognizant of the media in which that message will run in order to hone their pitch with greater audience targeting precision.

ACCOUNT PLANNING AND MESSAGE ENGAGEMENT

Account planners are the agency professionals engaged to assist copywriters in coping with these new methods for audience analysis. Initiated in the 1970s at British agencies Boase Massimi Politt and J. Walter Thompson/London, the practice of account planning became widely popular with major U.S. agencies by the 1990s. "Put simply, account planners represent the consumer's point of view throughout the development of an ad campaign," writes advertising reporter Noreen O'Leary.[22] This means that planners acknowledge that the real power in marketing does not reside in the advertiser but in the consumer. Because those consumers are free to do whatever they wish with our messages (including ignoring them), planners attempt to help copywriters see things from the target audience's point of view.

As David Bladwin, an executive with McKinney & Silver Advertising, observes,

> I think when creative people try to work without planning, they're sometimes more prone to come up with the kind of rational strategy that's based on a product attribute—something that comes out of sitting in a room, isolated, and just thinking about a product. The ideas become very product-based. But the good thing about planners is they tend to lead you away from that, because their focus is always on the people that use the product, not the product itself. And so they can lead you toward something less obvious, something that connects people to a brand on a deeper level.[23]

This does not mean that we shouldn't still consider rational attractions. Instead, it requires that we probe for which rational attraction is most important to the target consumer—and the emotional attitude that goes along with it. For example, milk has long been positioned as a healthy drink designed to help keep aging adult bodies fit (a maintenance rational appeal). A commercial showing active, intelligent seniors exercising and drinking milk while a voiceover explains the beverage's nutritional value would seem the logical emotional packaging (people interest and enlightenment). However, a good planner who can read what people mean in a focus group rather than only what they say, who can monitor and evaluate nonverbal as well as verbal reactions, may come up with insights justifying a significantly different approach. The Figure 5.5 Australian storyboard demonstrates such a departure. It services the discovery that what a key sector of the target really was interested in was performance—as packaged in and defined by the emotional attraction of allurement.

"A commercial," states Procter & Gamble global marketing officer Robert Wehling, "is essentially us digesting what the consumer has told us and feeding it back in a way that we think reflects what we heard."[24] Good account planning can help the copywriter accurately complete this two-part process. It can take all we know about rational and emotional attractions, all of our wordsmithing skills, and marshall these capabilities to impinge positively on the lives of those consumers we are striving to reach. Jayne Newman, who brought planning to the United States from Great Britain in the 1980s, emphasizes that the discipline's fundamental

RETIRED

A sprightly elderly couple kiss goodbye at the front door.

The man heads off down the street.

And then enters another gate. SUPER

Where he kisses an entirely different woman.

FIGURE 5.5   *(Courtesy of Tracey Russell, Clemenger BBDO/Melbourne)*

purpose is to "engage the target audience and talk to them about what they need instead of pushing your agenda on them."[25] Good planners don't bury copywriters in mounds of data. Rather, they help us to see the exciting and actionable revelation that underlies these data.

Of course, copywriters working outside the large agency sphere do not have planners with whom to partner. But we can still take whatever marketing data is available to us, together with the insights we gather in our daily lives, to envision how this product or service will impact on the worlds of our target consumers; what positive role it can play in their lifestyle existences. "By listening in on conversations and observing the way people live their lives, I find inspiration for ideas," says Palmer Jarvis DDB creative director Dean Lee. "I end up asking myself, 'Why do people think that way?' or 'What if people didn't act that way?' It's not a conscious thing that I do. It's not like I have a glass to the wall of my apartment or a telescope at my window but if you go to any restaurant, movie or bus stop, you can't help but overhear the public."[26] Account planning is simply taking such "overhearing" to a more comprehensive level.

Today, the goal of all of this is not just to reach a consumer, but to forge a true *engagement*. In an environment saturated with media exhortations, "engagement" is seen as the ultimate measure of message success. Though industry definitions vary, engagement basically involves three fundamental benchmarks: (1) how long the consumer spent with the message; (2) whether they took a specific and client-advantageous action in response to that exposure; and (3) the extent to which our brand is positively recognized and integrated into that consumer's world.

As our previous discussion of Progressive Motivation demonstrated, copywriters have long understood the need to stimulate audience action. But to get action, our message first has to be noticed—no small chore in the twenty-first century. Researchers at The Media Kitchen point out that thirty years ago, the average American came into contact with 560 advertisements per day. Today, that number is 3,500.[27] Some would argue that in this cluttered environment, online messages have an advantage because the viewer has purposefully sought out a Website and is poised at the keyboard for a more dynamic interaction with the advertising links it contains. This presupposes however, that the site itself is not muddled with too many sponsor banners or buttons that confound the consumer with too many choices. If this is the case, the message may just as well be buried in the middle of a four-minute broadcast commercial pod.

Broadcast or broadband, all of our individual and corporate planning expertise must strive to derive copy creations that are in tune with target consumers' lifestyles from the very first moment. As a result, these people actively spend time with that message, appreciate its relevance to their lives, and are persuaded to absorb it as a guide for current or future action. As engagement measurement becomes more sophisticated, copywriters, along with the media executives who decide where our creations will run, may well be held more accountable for meeting its benchmarks. "Let's engage, not enrage," advocates Saatchi & Saatchi CEO Kevin Roberts. "Enough selling by yelling. We need to stop interrupting and do what it takes to be welcomed by consumers as valuable, useful friends. That means involving them, celebrating and sharing with them, and always caring about them."[28] The following Web spot leverages middle-of-the-night placement on its parent station's stream to demonstrate it knows something about the people online at this time, cares about their particular needs, and shares friendly advice they can use.

ANNCR: So you're up at this time of the morning. Either you work third shift, you're an insomniac, or you're completely addicted to something on the Internet. No matter your reason, no matter your hours, if you're like me, you're online a lot and you want the highest possible speed at the lowest possible price. That's why I have Starnet Wireless. With Starnet Wireless I got residential high speed D-S-L service for just 19-44 per month --- every month. That's not an introductory offer. Go to the other guys if you want to be sucked in by a rate that triples after three months. Demand affordable highspeed at the best price with no long term commitments and a free 15-day trial period. Check out Starnet Wireless. High speed D-S-L for just 19-44 per month. Go to Starnet Wireless Dot-Net, 24-hours a day to get information at a time that's right for you. Hey, you're up this late --- you'll want to sleep in, right? Then get D-S-L connection information on <u>your</u> time. Connect to the future. With Starnet Wireless.

(Courtesy of Craig Allen, Citadel Communications)

AN AUDIENCE SENSE SUMMATION

As we have discovered, electronic media writing is much more than mere word assemblage. As a copywriter, you must ascertain the type of audience you are striving to reach, both in terms of its demographic and its predominant attitudinal and psychographic value sets. Then (with the help of account planners, if they are available), you develop copy goals and strategy based on these sets and execute this strategy through calculated evoking of compatible rational and emotional attractions presented in a properly persuasive order. Hopefully, the result will resonate with target consumers in a fully engaging manner.

Building on the experiences and needs of our audience requires effective electronic communication that is neither involving imagery nor stark product data—but a painstakingly tailored blend of both. Copywriters don't write for themselves. We write for the values-laden consumers we are paid to stimulate. So, suggests writer/creative director Amy Rosenthal, "instead of asking ourselves the same unanswerable questions—'Is this ad good?' 'Will it break through?' 'Will the client like it?'—maybe we should be asking, 'Is this ad a *gift*?' 'Will it change someone's life for the better?' 'Is it something I would want to receive myself?' Or is it a case of 'I sure as hell don't want this, but I think I'll wrap it up again real nice and unload it on someone else?' (As we all know, making a big production out of wrapping paper doesn't make a dumb gift any more desirable.)"[29] Copywriter Julian Koenig, who created the breakthrough Volkswagen advertising of the 1960s, once remarked that "your job is to reveal how good your product is, not how good you are."[30] Or, as German advertising executive Wolfgang Ullrich reminds us,

"Die Werbung muss dem Fisch schmecken, nicht dem Angler."
(The fish, not the fisherman, must like the advertising.)[31]

CHAPTER

6

CDVP Factors

Before proceeding in subsequent chapters to discuss the separate specifics of audio writing and video writing, we need to lay down some additional ground rules that apply to copy developed for electronic media in general. We must figure out what goal we as copywriters are striving for, how to describe and evaluate the results of this striving, and the nature of the organizational and regulatory boundaries within which the whole game must be played.

All of this is encompassed by what we refer to in this chapter as copywriting's CDVP FACTORS: **C**reation, **D**efinition, **V**alidation, and **P**rohibition.

CREATION

Creativity is probably the most often abused word in our business. Although the term didn't even appear in dictionaries until the 1970s,[1] it is used to describe what we intend to do, how we intend to do it, and what we'll have when we're through. 'Creativity' is invoked to excuse our faults and failings ("I just can't turn on creativity at will") and is cited as justification for the ignoring of client instructions ("How do *they* know what creativity is? They only make the product"). In derivative form, *creative* is also a noun that comprises the material our profession constructs. The plural *creatives,* meanwhile, refers to the copywriters and art directors who are supposed to accomplish this constructing. Most functionally, creativity is what we're paid to exercise (when feasible) and why we're paid more than somebody else to exercise it. Still, none of this addresses the question of what constitutes creativity's essence.

That question is the focal point for volumes on aesthetics. But since we cannot take time right now to read and discuss them, we will borrow the definition from legendary copywriter and agency founder Leo Burnett. He maintained that creativity is

THE ART OF ESTABLISHING NEW AND MEANINGFUL RELATIONSHIPS BETWEEN PREVIOUSLY UNRELATED THINGS IN A MANNER THAT IS RELEVANT AND IN GOOD TASTE.[2]

Burnett's is a real-world orientation that well serves the copywriter who deals in real-world products and services. Unlike some of art's more mystic extremities, the copywriter's creative product must be openly logical, must make sense, and the *same* sense, to a very large number of people on the other side of those receiving sets. Bill Bernbach, another copywriting giant, cautioned that "merely to let your imagination run riot, to dream unrelated dreams, to indulge in graphic acrobatics and verbal gymnastics is NOT being creative. The creative person has harnessed his imagination. He has disciplined it so that every thought, every idea, every word . . . makes more vivid, more believable, more persuasive the original theme or product advantage he has decided he must convey. . . . Is creativity some obscure, esoteric art form? Not on your life. It's the most practical thing a businessman can employ."[3] In short, affirms DDB Worldwide's chairman emeritus Keith Reinhard, "the definition of creativity is useful innovation."[4]

Inventor Robert Fulton (hardly a freaky artiste) brought this kind of creativity to bear when he put together a tea kettle's steam and a boat's ability to traverse water. The consequent steamboat was dubbed Fulton's Folly—until it worked, until the meaningful nature of the relationship was established. The World's Fair concessionaire who ran out of ice cream containers exercised this same sense of creativity when he bought funnel-shaped Scandinavian cookies from the booth next door and gave birth to—the ice cream cone. Even the first Western mass communicator, Johannes Gutenberg, was an undistinguished goldsmith until he fed some paper through his partner's coin punch to multiply written messages. And the copywriter who put a Bic pen on a flamenco dancer's stamping boot got a no less creative (if less historic) result in the process of proving the pen point's durability.

Here are some additional classic examples of broadcast copy creativity. The "previously unrelated things" are identified, as is the central copy point—the "new and meaningful relationship"—which ties them together in a relevant evidenced way:

The six-foot 'sub' sandwich in the Pacer automobile	=/proves	a small car need not be uncomfortable or cramped
The Jergens lotion on the dry autumn leaf	=/proves	the skin crème's softening attributes
The monk scribe using the Xerox Copier	=/proves	original-quality copies are miraculously easy with Xerox
The Ziploc bag holding a swarm of killer bees	=/proves	you can stake your life on Ziploc's leak-proof seal
The gorilla hurling the American Tourister suitcase	=/proves	even surly baggage handlers can't destroy a Tourister
The wet-suited diver eating the Wendy's burger	=/proves	the sandwich's exceptional juiciness
The diamond cutter working in the Mercury Monarch	=/proves	the luxurious smoothness of the car's ride

To fully succeed, the copywriter's "meaningful relationship" (=/proves statement) will be (1) the central copy point, (2) the entire fabric from which the message is woven, and (3) an important benefit for our target audience. Neurologist Alice

Flaherty strengthens the scientific case for this benefit necessity when she observes, "Most researchers agree that a useful definition of creative work is that it includes a combination of novelty and value."[5]

In the Figure 6.1 spot, the "previously unrelated things" are (a) the Baltimore Symphony and (b) professional baseball. The central copy point flowing from the continuous sports motif showcases the consumer benefit that Baltimore Symphony Concerts (equal) vigorous, competitive, *major league* entertainment.

A packaged-goods commercial that also demonstrates creativity in action appears in Figure 6.2. This is only a fifteen-second message. But the meaningful combination of a cough-afflicted rooster and a Walgreens remedy takes only four panels to confirm that this pharmacy can be "trusted" to provide the appropriate medication to get you up and on the job.

To make and hold an impression on the audience, radio also seeks to capitalize on the sort of creativity we've defined. That radio's creative linkage must be engendered entirely through sound increases both the challenge and the need for a clean, clear relationship that stands out and draws its conclusion in a visualizable way. The following spot juxtaposes a border-straddling house with Black Label beer to establish that buying this brand is the comparatively hassle-free way to obtain "great Canadian taste at a great American [domestic] price." As this commercial demonstrates, "creativity is about the comparison of things," British advertising executive John Hegarty points out. "Black is only black when it's shown against white."[6] So don't take the trouble to build a house on the border. In contrast, take the easy way out and just purchase our brew.

ANNCR: We're talking to a man who lives on the Canadian-American border.

MAN: If you're in my kitchen you're on the Canadian side. If you're in my living room you're on the American side.

ANNCR: What made you build a house right on the border?

MAN: Beer.

ANNCR: So you didn't mean to.

MAN: I sure did. See, I love Canadian beer. But living on the American side, I'd have to pay high imported prices.

ANNCR: So?

MAN: So now I buy my Canadian beer in Canada, walk through my Canadian kitchen---

ANNCR: Yes?

MAN: Then sneak into my American living room and drink it.

ANNCR: Why don't you just buy Black Label beer, sir?

MAN: Black Label?

ANNCR: It's the beer born in Canada but brewed in America. Black Label's got that great Canadian taste at a great American price and it costs less than imported Canadian beers.

MAN: If I woulda known about Black Label it sure woulda saved me some grief.

Continued on page 120

MAN #1: I think they're one of the best teams playing today.

SPORTSCASTER: Here's a team that can do it all: adagio, allegro, molto vivace.

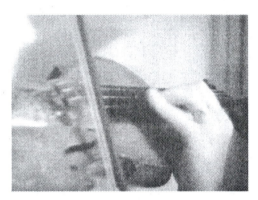

V/O: ---of any righthander I've ever seen.

FRANK ROBINSON: We could never play like that.

MAN #3: I remember Beethoven, top of the ninth. It was <u>beautiful</u>.

CHANTING CROWD: David! . . . David!

FIGURE 6.1 *(Courtesy of David R. Sackey, Doner Advertising)*

MAN #2: Great stadium, no rain delays.

VIOLINIST #1: He's got the best stuff---

VIOLINIST #2: (Heavy accent) We're feeling good, we're looking good, we're playing good.

COP: The crowds are getting bigger every year.

MUSIC: (OPENING BARS OF BETHOVEN'S 'FIFTH SYMPHONY')

ANNCR VO: The Baltimore Symphony Orchestra. Baltimore's other major league team. For tickets, call 783-8000.

MAN #1: They don't chew tobacco, they don't spit, and they're very polite.

FIGURE 6.2 *(Courtesy of Susan Rhodes, McConnaughy Stein Schmidt Brown)*

ANNCR: You wouldn't have built your house on the border?

MAN: And I wouldn't have to go through customs every time I have to use the bathroom. Excuse me.

ANNCR: Black Label Beer. G. Heileman Brewman Company, LaCrosse, Wisconsin and other cities.

(Courtesy of David R. Sackey, Doner Advertising)

Below is another example of radio's use of a "black and white" comparison to creatively visualize our product's benefits. In this case, the contrasting relationship between "rebuilt" and "new" is encased in a pairing of "previously unrelated" meat-loaf—and auto parts.

ANNCR: Plumb Auto knows there are some things you just don't want to buy rebuilt.

    (SFX: RESTAURANT SOUNDS)

MAN: I noticed on the menu you have meatloaf, and <u>rebuilt</u> meatloaf. What's the difference?

WAITRESS: Well, sometimes people don't finish their meals, sometimes your meatloaf dinner gets dropped on the way from the kitchen. But it's still good. So what we do is scrape it down, rinse off any hair, gravel, things like that. Reconstitute the meatloaf pieces --- that's <u>called</u> <u>smushing</u> in the trade --- repack it with new mashed potatoes, lay on a new coat of gravy and voila! Just as good as new. But a lot cheaper.

    (RESTAURANT EFFECTS OUT)

ANNCR: At Plumb Auto, they don't think you should have to buy a rebuilt alterna-tor or starter to save a few bucks. So they're offering brand new, fresh-from-the-factory alternators and starters at 20 to 30% less than you'd pay anywhere else. And they come with a two year warranty.

MAN: Excuse me, where do you keep the toilet paper?

CLERK: New or rebuilt?

ANNCR: Plumb Auto --- where you'll find even more of what you need. Do-it-yourselfers get all the patient, expert automotive advice people have trusted since 1929. Pros get the service and new parts availability needed to get that car back on the road fast. Plumb Auto. They've got the part, they've got the people, and no rebuilt meatloaf. Plumb Auto. Just off King Street in Northampton.

(Courtesy of Gerry Perrett, Saga Communications)

Is creativity achieved in most commercials and continuity segments being aired? Spend some time in front of a radio set, television, or computer screen with a pencil and paper. Try to detect the previously unattached subjects and the new, logical, =/proves linkage between them in each commercial message to which you are exposed. You will undoubtedly find a great many identical relationships to those being emphasized by same-category competitors. Alternately, you may also find copy that strives to construct a new relationship but ends up with a linkage that is either illogical or unrelated to the message's central copy point.

Deriving a great creative concept is a challenging and extended process. Award-winning copywriter David Johnson of Young & Rubicam maintains that this process can actually be broken down into three stages. "In the first stage, you come up with every cliché. In the second stage, you run dry and you realize you're hacks. In the third stage, you do the work you're meant to do. It would be easy to stop at the first stage—a lot of clients and a lot of agencies wouldn't know the difference. But we do good work because we demand it of ourselves."[7] Purposeful creativity is especially difficult to achieve within the electronic media's unyielding time and pixel limits. If it weren't, the manufacturers and humanitarians would be tempted to turn out their own commercials and PSAs. No one would feel they needed the special talent and expertise of the copywriter. And that could starve us!

In many assignments, a competent, straightforward description of the subject and what it will do for the prospect is all that is mandated—and difficult enough for even expert copywriters to supply. Forced, irrelevant creativity can be counterproductive and can get in the way of the selling task. "Too often, the advertising that attempts to please the viewer winds up screwing the advertiser," asserts *Advertising* Age critic Bob Garfield. "It's so busy being creative, it forgets to be advertising."[8] Creative director Mike Turner adds that "new ideas are invigorating, but we make a mistake if we think every job calls for something brand new. . . . In making ads, my goal is to grab the target's attention and hold it, and I'll do it any way I can. If it takes a never-been-done-before concept, I hope I've got what it takes. But if a 'classic' formula rendered with a fresh spin is right for the client, I am not above revisiting ad history."[9]

When the assignment opportunity does present itself, don't be afraid to probe your soul for a creative response. Creativity is not something "out there," but an impulse that derives from deep within the writer. As noted American thinker William James expressed in *The Principles of Psychology* (1890), "Genius, in truth, means little more than the faculty of perceiving in an unhabitual way." When we do derive such an "unhabitual perception," when we experience at least a moment of "genius," we must not let advertising *groupthink* inhibit us from playing out our idea to see if it makes sense. In meetings with colleagues, there is a natural tendency to play it safe, and playing it safe is the antithesis of creative thinking. Creativity workshop director Dave Dufour has compiled a list of forty phrases that "stifle any creative thinking in a group, because they destroy the part of brainstorming that allows good ideas to sprout from the offbeat or 'bad' idea." That list is reprinted below:[10]

1. We tried that before.
2. Our place is different.
3. It costs too much.
4. That's not my job.
5. They're too busy to do that.
6. We don't have the time.
7. Not enough help.
8. It's too radical a change.
9. The staff will never buy it.
10. It's against company policy.
11. The union will scream.
12. Runs up our overhead.
13. We don't have the authority.
14. Let's get back to reality.
15. That's not our problem.
16. I don't like the idea.
17. You're right, but. . . .
18. You're two years ahead of your time.
19. We're not ready for that.
20. It isn't in the budget.
21. Can't teach an old dog new tricks.
22. Good thought, but impractical.
23. Let's give it more thought.
24. We'll be the laughing stock of the industry.
25. Not that again.
26. Where'd you dig that one up?
27. We did all right without it.
28. It's never been tried before.
29. Let's put that one on the back burner.

30. Let's form a committee.
31. I don't see the connection.
32. It won't work in our plant/office.
33. The executive committee won't go for it.
34. Let's all sleep on it.

35. It can't be done.
36. It's too much trouble to change.
37. It won't pay for itself.
38. It's impossible.
39. I know a person who tried it.
40. We've always done it this way.

Some of these phrases are more likely to surface in the copywriting arena than are others. But each phrase can generate multiple negative barriers to breakthrough ideas. If we're not careful "in a world of 1,000 no's," warns radio copymaster Dick Orkin, "we suppress our ability to play, to experiment. And all truly creative acts are a form of play."[11]

So don't be afraid to *play*. Don't be afraid to keep searching, whenever the assignment permits, for that new and meaningful relationship between previously unrelated things. Award-winning illustrator Larry Moore points out that "fear kills creativity even before it begins. It creates 'fear of trying' and spawns the 'I can't syndrome.' Most people can't because they don't."[12] "Put your cynicism on hold and allow yourself to get excited about an idea," adds highly successful video game designer Cliff Bleszinski. "Let it bubble to the surface and then hang onto it like your life depends on it. Simply remember to daydream and the answers will appear. Capture that firefly in a bottle and it will turn into lightning that your peers and, ultimately, your customers will follow."[13]

Whether it is designing video games, broadcast commercials or broadband pop-ups, keep in mind that creativity can only come from within *you*—not from any electronic device or technology that may be involved in your message's production or transmission. "Creativity is a function of human ingenuity that exists independent of time and tools," observes BBDO Worldwide's chairman Allen Rosenshine. "At the end of the day, new tools and technologies do not demand or produce greater creativity. They provide creative people with new forms of expression."[14]

Play though it is, a copywriter's creativity still must always be harnessed to a business goal. "Properly practiced, creativity can make one ad do the work of ten," marvels agency president Bob Kuperman. "Properly practiced, creativity can lift your claims out of the swamp of sameness and make them accepted, believed, persuasive, urgent."[15] "Creativity at its best reveals the magic and power of a brand," adds creative director David Lubars. "It delights people and gives them something honest to consider."[16] The happiest and most successful copywriters are those who have learned how to meld this business productivity to the play. As agency chairman Joey Reiman summarizes it, "Creativity is intelligence having *fun*."[17]

DEFINITION

In the electronic media setting, creativity means very little if even a detectable minority of your target audience fails to decipher the sense of the terms you've used to achieve it. A meaningful and consumer-beneficial relationship can appear insignificant when couched in language that is vague or subject to misinterpretation. Thus copywriters must clearly define the terms and images inherent in their subject matter. At the same time, we must also beware of introducing additional elements that are more in need of definition than those with which we started.

Definitional Hazards

Five categories of terms, when used in your copy, possess the unfortunate potential to cloud comprehension. These hazards consist of (1) abstractions, (2) analogies, (3) generalities, (4) technicalities, and (5) multiplicates.

ABSTRACTIONS These are words that fail to activate the "mind's eye" because they lack tangibility. The undefined abstraction is therefore especially dangerous on radio, where successful communication requires active picture-building by the listener. Banks may prattle on about customer *service,* but to little effect without graphic descriptions of the forms that service takes. *Financial security* is a promise made by more than one insurance company, but it is impossible to picture "financial security" in your head. The *love* stressed in some PSAs exists in a vacuum unless illustrated with concrete referents of love in action. And is a *high performance engine* supposed to sing and dance? Such abstractions provide nothing on which the listener or viewer can focus.

ANALOGIES These are terms that attempt to illuminate the resemblance of two things to each other. Copywriters often encounter analogies in client/brand names. Sometimes these symbolic or figurative terms may be wonderfully appropriate, as in the computer repair shop that calls itself *Slipped Disc Inc.,* the *Grandma Had One Like That* antique store, or the *Wok & Roll* oriental fast-food stand. For other clients, however, the analogy can be ludicrously counterproductive. Reebok's marketing of its *Incubus* women's running shoe was brought to a screeching halt when an "incubus" was discovered to be a mythological devil who preys on and rapes sleeping females.

Whether brand names or referents within our copy, the analogies we select must be appropriate, understood by the audience, and understood in a way that puts the product in the most favorable light possible. *The Little Zephyr* may be a potent brand name for a fan—but only if the audience is made aware that a "zephyr" is a cooling west wind. *Barracuda* may be a sharp name for a predatory fish, but when applied to a Chrysler compact car, it dredged up a gobbling image that hinted of gas pump gluttony. *Kurl Up and Dye* may be cute as beauty shop signage, but it raises threatening prospects when voiced in a radio spot.

Copywriters often create analogies to make a product operation or benefit come alive. One radio wordsmith, for example, successfully conjured up the image of a baby's bath as an analogy for how gentle his client's car wash would treat the listener's automobile. Because most such analogies tend to be manifestations of creativity, however, they share our core creativity requirements of establishing an *obvious* meaningful and benefit-centered relationship. If you have to define your own analogy, your tool misguidedly has become your task.

GENERALITIES The third definitional hazard, generalities, are terms with such broad meaning that, unless we can stake out the particular aspect of the meaning we're invoking, our audience members will be led in several irrelevant directions. To some pharmaceutical companies, it is essential that consumers be aware of the characteristics of a *capsule* that differentiate it from the broader classification of *pills.*

Likewise, some beauty cleanser manufacturers are especially concerned that you not lump their product under the general category called *soap*.

In any case, generalities are seldom as graphic as clear copy requires and may blur the key distinction your product depends on to stand apart from the competition. Worse, if generalities in your copy are allowed to multiply, they may give the impression of deliberate vagueness, with a consequent rise in consumer mistrust. "People are so used to hearing generalities like 'lowest prices' or 'friendly sales staff' that those words have no meaning anymore," warns radio copy expert Jeff Hedquist. "Comb through your copy. Take every single phrase and make it come alive by using specifics. And where do you get those specifics? Simply tell the truth in detail."[18]

TECHNICALITIES   These are specialized terms such as those used by certain occupational groups. Unless the message is aimed at a narrow and exclusive universe (farmers, doctors, auto mechanics, software progammers), these jargon-like references can be counted on to repel the audience by either making them feel inferior (because they aren't "smart enough" to speak that language) or by irritating them because you haven't cared enough to select the plain talk they can understand. If milk is people's only referent for the term *homogenized,* telling them your peanut butter is homogenized will not, by itself, have a positive/meaningful impact. A skin creme designed to penetrate the *epidermis* had better be described in a message that shows and tells just what the epidermis is.

Sometimes, a technical word or phrase is deliberately enlisted early in the copy as a means of heightening the seeming importance of the subject being discussed. This is most often done in spots promoting products for your body, your dental work, or your car. *Eczema, iron deficiency anemia, plaque, halitosis, hydroplaning,* and *rotary power plant* are all used to document the seriousness of the communication to follow and thereby to increase consumer attention. But unless you then clearly articulate what type of malady eczema is, plaque's danger and location, and the fact that the rotary power plant in "the Mazda goes hhmmmmmmmmmmmmmmmm," the technicality alone won't hold attention long enough to accomplish your purpose.

MULTIPLICATES   Our final definitional hazard, multiplicates are terms having more than one use or application. If audience members think the Malaga *Pipe* Company turns out products for plumbers when it in fact makes the kind you smoke, your message won't sell many meerschaums. ("Meerschaums," however, is a technicality we could productively exploit to attract our real target universe.) With the capability to photographically specify from the very first frame, the visual media are able to clarify a multiplicate much more quickly than radio can, of course. But in any electronic medium, the longer you allow your audience to play mentally with their own favorite referent for *pipe, plane,* or other multiplicates (like *conductor, organ,* and *range*), the greater the probability that they will be irretrievably off on their own mental tangents. If your spot inadvertently stimulates the consumer to muse about a keyboard instrument (one type of *organ*), he or she will seldom be prepared to worry about a bodily 'organ's' excess acidity.

The Five Definitional Tools

Now that we are aware of the kinds of terms requiring definition, we can focus on the available mechanisms for accomplishing this definition. Generally speaking, a word or phrase can be clarified via any of five methods: (1) negation, (2) context, (3) correlation, (4) derivation, and (5) exemplification.

NEGATION   This is an old rhetorical technique that sets a thing apart by showing what it is NOT or by demonstrating the conditions to which it does NOT apply. Definition by negation can be a very effective copywriter device because it often lends itself to a highly developed copy rhythm in which both the sound and the sense push the message forward:

Not a roll-on, not a cream, new Mennon with Pers-stop . . .

This is NOT --- your father's Oldsmobile.

Fresca --- when you want refreshment --- not calories.

Provided we don't attempt to milk it too long, negation is also an effective suspense-builder that encourages the listener or viewer to stay tuned to discover just what the thing *is* or *does:*

If you think it's butter, but it's not; it's --- Chiffon.

It's not just for special occasions, Lancer's Rosé.

It won't improve your breath, your smile, or your love life. But a Larry's Licorice Drop will bring back the kid in your tastebuds.

Sometimes, we can use definition by negation to play off a word that is part of our product's name. In the TV spot below, the interrogators' unsuccessful attempts to persuade their thief as to what "free" isn't serve to define the benefit that "free" does entail:

Video	Audio
OPEN ON SURVEILLANCE CAMERA FOOTAGE OF MAN WALKING UP TO COOLER IN CONVENIENCE STORE, GRABS DRINK AND AS HE WALKS OUT, HE OPENS AND TAKES A DRINK — WALKING OUT FRONT DOOR WITHOUT PAYING. FOOTAGE PAUSED AND PULL BACK TO SEE TWO DETECTIVES STANDING NEXT TO TV AND LOOKING PAST CAMERA.	
CUT TO UNWITTING SUSPECT LOOKING NAIVELY BACK AT COPS	GUY: Hey, that's me.
	COP 1: We know. What were you thinking?
GUY GRABS SIERRA MIST FREE FROM TABLE, POINTS TO LABEL	GUY: It says free. I thought it was a giveaway.
	COP 2: Well, if they gave it away, how could they make a profit?

Video	Audio
	GUY: Volume. You don't know much about the retail business do you? What was I supposed to think?
COPS BOTH ROLL THEIR EYES	COP 1: (Sarcastically) Oh, I don't know. Maybe that it's free of sugar, free of carbs, free of calories, free of caffeine---
GUY FINISHES TAKING A DRINK, OBVIOUSLY THINKS IT TASTES REALLY	GUY: I don't think so.
GOOD	VO: It says free, it just doesn't taste free. Sierra Mist Free.
COP 2 GRABS SIERRA MIST FREE	GUY: Hey, get your own. They're free.
	COP 1: They're not free!!!

(Courtesy of Bill Bruce, BBDO/New York)

Negation can also be used to define what *won't* happen if one practices the behavior our spot advocates. It can encourage the audience to reevaluate a product or procedure in order to see it in its proper light, to appreciate that its attainment is easier than the audience has been led to believe. This is the brand of negation used in the PSA below to explain that eliminating litter does *not* entail immense self-sacrifice.

ANNCR: Presenting great discoveries during Stamp Out Litter Week. Three years ago, little Tommy Ferguson discovered that his arm would not fall off if he held onto his candy wrapper until he reached a wastebasket. Two years ago, Miss Edwina Perkins discovered it would not take forever to walk twenty extra feet and trashcan the newspaper she'd finished reading. Just last week, Alvin 'Big Al' Bustamonte discovered that bagging his empties, instead of drop kicking them into the lake, did not destroy his great macho image. This Stamp Out Litter Week, you <u>too</u> can discover how easy it is NOT to litter. You'll also discover how safe, simple and suave it is not to have litter around.

In employing negation on radio, remember that the listener can't picture a "not." So, negations must be wrapped in imagery that keeps audience mind's eyes filled with concrete, positive images. Notice how the following student-composed positioning lines blur the benefit that the writer is attempting to erect in the listener's imagination:

Our disinfectant's aroma is not displeasing.

(But how *does* it smell?)

The Kitchenaide Cheese Slicer prevents slices where you don't want them.

(What/where *does* it slice?)

You won't get diluted drinks or messy melting when you put Fairmont Ice Wedges in your beverage.

(What *will* I get?)

In these instances, the negation has served not to define—but only to blur—the product benefit. The same principle applies to station-positioning promos. As Miami program director Bill Stedman points out, "Stations that use a combination of 'not too hard, not too soft,' 'no silly DJ chatter' and 'no contests that you could never win' may reflect listeners' attitudes, but they don't establish a positive image. . . . The solution is for a station to tell a listener exactly what it *is* and then live up to that promise."[19]

Finally, negation is also handy to define the kind of people for whom our product is NOT intended. By so doing, we often can build up the egos of those consumers we *are* trying to sell, as in the following TV commercial:

Video	Audio
GRAPHIC: Three reasons not to buy BF Goodrich T/A Tires.	VO: Three reasons not to buy B.F. Goodrich T-A Tires.
GRAPHIC: 1. Being the center of attention makes you uncomfortable.	Being the center of attention makes you uncomfortable.
RED HOT ROADSTER ON STREET BLASTS FROM LEFT TO RIGHT. THEN MODIFIED VINTAGE PICKUP ZOOMS FROM RIGHT TO LEFT	MUSIC: PULSATING METAL GUITAR
GRAPHIC: 2. You think a little deuce coupe is a place where tiny chickens are kept.	You think a little deuce coupe is a place where tiny chickens are kept.
WHITE ROADSTER PULLS INTO DRIVE-IN. IS REFLECTED IN DARK GLASS OF CUSTOM SPORT TRUCK	GUITAR RE-FEATURED.
GRAPHIC: 3. You think lug nuts is a high fiber cereal.	You think lug nuts is a high fiber cereal.
FOUR SUCCESSIVE TIGHT SHOTS OF LEFT FRONT CHROME WHEELS OF HOT CARS IN MOTION, FEATURING T/A TIRE	GUITAR RE-FEATURED
GRAPHIC: BF Goodrich T/A Tires	B.F. Goodrich T-A Tires. For the rest of us.

(Courtesy of Dan Nelson, Doner Advertising)

CONTEXT   This is the most straightforward and least time-consuming of our Definitional Tools. With context, the meaning of the term is made clear simply by the environment in which the term is placed—by the words and phrases that immediately precede and/or follow it:

We pasteurize to purify.

Murray --- the toughest lawnmower in its class.

Prius --- Toyota's answer to the hybrid car question.

The Serta Perfect-Sleeper mattress.

In the following radio spot, for example, the copywriter makes certain to continuously position the word "cheese" immediately after the unusual "Alpine Lace" brand name. The listener thereby is given no opportunity to wander off to musings about skiing or tapestries; musings that the unqualified term might otherwise engender. Further, the product is immediately defined as a health food.

BERNIE: And how can Bernie's Better Deli help you?

LADY: My husband's cholesterol is up, his weight is up, and he's having an affair. What do you recommend?

BERNIE: Alpine Lace Cheese.

LADY: Is that the cheese that's lower in cholesterol, sodium and fat?

BERNIE: Right. Bring home an Alpine Lace American Cheese sandwich, and everything works out. His cholesterol, his pressure, his weight, even his tootsie.

LADY: You really think Alpine Lace Cheese will change Phil into the man he used to be?

BERNIE: Absolutely! He's only running around because she makes him feel healthy. If he had a good piece of cheese, he'd dump her like a bad habit.

LADY: And that's Alpine Lace Cheese, right?

BERNIE: Right.

LADY: You're so sensitive.

BERNIE: That's because we're an official Alpine Lace Cheese healthier cheese deli --- we care about you.

LADY: So what's my plan?

BERNIE: Just walk in the door with the Alpine Lace Cheese sandwich, and say, Phil---

LADY: I call him Pookins---

BERNIE: Okay, say Pookins, I'm gonna give you the greatest thing you've ever had in your life.

LADY: I'll do it!

BERNIE: How's Pookins like it?

LADY: On white, no crust, and a toothpick with a colored frill.

BERNIE: The man is an animal!

LADY: Yeah, a rabbit.

ANNCR: Ask your deli for a sandwich with Alpine Lace, the healthier cheese. If they don't carry it, they don't care.

(Courtesy of Joy Golden, Joy Radio)

(Notice also the definition by negation in the Alpine Lace commercial's last line. It stimulates additional retailers to stock the product by defining those that don't as thoughtless.)

In visual media, of course, the context in which the term is placed can be pictorial as well as verbal. Thus in Figure 6.3, the rustic setting defines Beaver Canoe as outdoor clothing long before the voiceover mentions "wearing the wilderness." This commercial also demonstrates that, even in a TV spot, sound effects can play a powerful role in constructing the relevant explanatory context.

CORRELATION   Our third Definitional Tool, correlation involves comparing the term to be defined with more familiar terms that can be shown to have a somewhat similar meaning. Through this device, we attempt to connect the less known or less vibrant term systematically and colorfully with a term possessing clearer audience image potential. Thus *unique* definitions by correlation also constitute examples of *creativity:*

Like a thousand busy fingers, Lustre Creme works to smooth wrinkles.

Wash'N Dry is like soap and water to go.

Peak Anti-Freeze is like chicken soup for your car.

The following radio commercial pushes correlation to the extreme by building one "speed" referent atop another to graphically convey just how fast Comcast internet service really is:

(MUSIC: CONTINUOUS TONE UNDER)

MALE: A rabbit. A rabbit genetically modified and bred with a panther. A rabbit genetically modified and bred with a panther --- with turbines attached --- and backed by an unusually strong tailwind --- on ice. The rabbit panther thingy with turbines and tailwind on ice --- in a zero gravity environment. Then placed securely in an industrial blender --- and set to puree. The whole Rabbit panther turbine tailwind blender scenario driven by an over-caffeinated fighter pilot --- with a lead foot. All slathered in oil. Traveling down a ski jump. In Lucerne. Under better than ideal conditions.

           (MUSIC OUT)

Beaver Canoe

Base Brown
& Partners Limited

SFX: Early morning sounds of birds, wind and rustling leaves.

SFX: Creaking Sound of chair rocking after shirt has been lifted from it.

SFX: Rustling of shirt being pulled over teen's head.

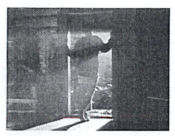

SFX: Birds, wind and rustling of leaves as teen walks to open door.
VO: When you wear beaver canoe...

SFX: Sound of waterdrop hitting water.

VO: ...you wear the wilderness.

Ripples dissolve into Beaver Canoe logo

FIGURE 6.3 *(Courtesy of Barry R. Base, Base Brown & Partners Ltd.)*

FEMALE: Fast just got faster. Comcast high speed internet. Now with up to
16 megabits of speed. So you can do even more things online --- faster.
It's Comcastic.

(Courtesy of Jamie Barrett, Goodby, Silverstein & Partners)

In a video example of definition by correlation, the Figure 6.4 television spot pictorially equates a herd of turtles with a traffic jam to embody "slow-moving" in an infuriatingly unmistakable way. Meanwhile, the audio shares information on the "comfortable" product alternative.

V.O.: Drive yourself to the airport and you could creep through traffic.

'COPTER REPORTER (V.O.): Oh, couldn't have been a worse time to have a breakdown in the center lane.

V.O.: Take the Logan Express Bus from Quincy or Framingham. It's fast, convenient and comfortable. For more information call Massport at 1-800-23-LOGAN.

FIGURE 6.4 *(Courtesy of Gary Greenberg, Rossin Greenberg Seronick and Hill Inc.)*

DERIVATION This method defines a term by expressing its semantic, geographic, or historical roots. The original meaning of the whole term can be illuminated, or we can break it down into its constituent parts and show the specific significance of each part:

In Europe, where our beer originated, Fassbeer meant draft beer.

Mata Hari : an intriguing fragrance inspired by the seductive spy.

Named for the inventor who made rubber tough: Goodyear Tires.

While a dictionary quotation can sometimes be used to present the derivation, many audiences will be turned off by such a boring and stilted approach. It is true that for a professional/technical market already interested in the field from which the term comes, the dictionary blurb may be the quickest available way to sketch the word's history. For more general consumer groups, however, a less bookish approach is needed to retain attention. In the commercial below, for instance, copywriter Joy Golden constructs an entertaining marital dialogue to define not only the product's origin for New York audiences, but also the cooking process through which it and part of its name are derived.

WIFE: Fred, do you remember when I said let's go to Hawaii?

FRED: (Disinterested) Yeah.

WIFE: And you said no.

FRED: Yeah.

WIFE: And I said why?

FRED: Yeah.

WIFE: And you said because all they've got is pineapples and coconuts.

FRED: Yeah.

WIFE: Well, do you want to hear something?

FRED: No.

WIFE: I bought new Eagle Snacks Hawaiian Kettle Potato Chips today, and guess where they came from?

FRED: Potatoes?

WIFE: No, I mean the recipe.

FRED: Columbus Avenue.

WIFE: No, Fred --- from Hawaii. Eagle Snacks slow cooks them in a great big kettle and a man stands there and gently rakes them back and forth until they're so crunchy you wouldn't believe it.

FRED: I wouldn't?

WIFE: Think of it, Fred. In this day and age, in a big American factory they actually do what they do in Hawaii.

FRED: The hula?

WIFE: No, Fred. Slow kettle cooking. Here. Taste this Eagle Snack Hawaiian Chip.

FRED: (After biting down on it with large crunch) You're right. They're terrific. What a crunch.

WIFE: See, Fred? Hawaii isn't all pineapples and coconuts. I know it's not Rockaway, but let's go sometime.

FRED: Why? We've got Eagle Snacks Hawaiian Kettle Potato Chips right here.

WIFE: But what about the glamour? The weather? The lei you get when you land?

FRED: (Suddenly interested) The what?

ANNCR: New Hawaiian Kettle Potato Chips. Nothing tastes like an Eagle Snack.

(Courtesy of Joy Golden, Joy Radio)

As in the Hawaiian Kettle commercial, there are categories in which the origin of the product can be articulated as a benefit in and of itself. Australia's image as the home of laid-back, outback masculinity is capitalized on in Figure 6.5. The spot reconfirms this image and wraps it carnivorously around the product in order to define and boast of Foster's Aussie derivation.

Sometimes, of course, it is just as important *not* to define a product by its heritage. To Americans, French beer would be about as unappealing as English wine. And that favorite toy of little girls, the Barbie Doll, "started life as 'Lilli,' a German sex doll of the 1950s, a pornographic caricature, a gag gift for men."[20] When the product sports a derivation such as this, the prudent copywriter selects a different definitional tool—at least for the broadcast media.

EXEMPLIFICATION Our final Definitional Tool, exemplification accomplishes its task either by (1) citing examples of situations to which the term best can be applied, or (2) enumerating the essential components of what the term represents.

With the first method, for instance, we help define the term/brand *Excedrin* by stating:

Excedrin is great for relief of mild headache pain. If pain persists, see your doctor.

The commercial has thereby been both truthful with the audience and respectful of the Federal Trade Commission and Food and Drug Administration in citing, in *exemplifying,* situations for which the product is and is not intended. Similarly, in the following radio promo for TV-24's Sunday evening movie, we learn that the "product" is especially applicable when you desire a flick Sunday night—but have to get up Monday morning.

(SFX: TV SET UNDER. KNOCK-KNOCK; DOOR OPENS.)

WILSON: Yes?

SANDMAN: Mr. Wilson-comma-Edgar?

WILSON: Yes?

SANDMAN: It's time, Mr. Wilson.

WILSON: Hey Edith, did you order a pizza?

SANDMAN: I'm Mr. Sandman, Mr. Wilson.

WILSON: Oh lord.

SANDMAN: You know the rules. No more TV. Tomorrow's a work day. It's beddy-time.

(SFX: TV SET CLICKS OFF)

"CAN OPENER"   :15 TV COMMERCIAL

V/O: HOW TO SPEAK AUSTRALIAN.

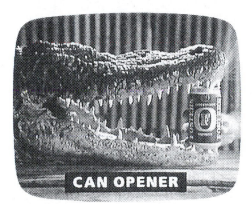

CAN OPENER

BEER

FOSTER'S. AUSTRALIAN FOR BEER.

FIGURE 6.5   *(Courtesy of Joan Pratt, Angotti, Thomas, Hedge, Inc.)*

WILSON:	Hey, I was right in the middle of that movie!
SANDMAN:	You should have been watching the <u>Over By Midnight Sunday Night Movie</u> on TV-24, Mr. Wilson. TV-24's movie starts at 10:30 and is over before 12.
WILSON:	Can't I stay up just a little longer?
SANDMAN:	Aren't you the same Wilson-comma-Edgar who always complains about being tired and/or cranky come Monday morning?
WILSON:	(Angrily) I don't get cranky!
SANDMAN:	SSH!
WILSON:	Well, I <u>don't</u>.
SANDMAN:	Next time remember: TV-24's <u>Over By Midnight Sunday Night Movie</u>.
WILSON:	You sure you're not the tooth fairy?
SANDMAN:	Do I <u>sound</u> like a fairy, Mr. Wilson?!
WILSON:	No, well it's the peach-colored pajamas that made me think---
SANDMAN:	It's the uniform, buddy.
WILSON:	Now who's cranky?
ANNCR:	Avoid the Monday morning crankies. Watch TV-24's <u>Over by Midnight Sunday Night Movie</u>.

(Courtesy of Steve Eichenbaum, Curro/Eichenbaum, Inc.)

Our second exemplification method, enumerating the term's essential components, is more of a dissection process. We can, for instance, define the performance of the Little Zephyr Fan through exposition of its namesake's effect and behavior as a gentle, cooling breeze. We identify the original zephyr's key characteristics and thereby simultaneously identify how the product itself is promised to perform. Correspondingly, as in Figure 6.6, the viewer is shown all the geographic attractions that collectively comprise and exemplify the Florida experience.

A copywriter may choose whichever Definitional Tool or Tools best fit(s) the problem at hand. There is nothing wrong in using more than one of these devices in the same spot as long as message coherence is maintained. In the Dick Orkin commercial that begins on the next page for instance, definition by *context* is applied via use of the complete brand name: Wilcox *Family Farm Dairy* Products. The vague notion of product quality is made much more tangible by *correlating* it with being 'particular,' 'picky,' or even 'obsessed.' All Wilcox foods are *derived* from an enterprise that has been in operation "just down the road" for "about 80 years" (right here in the state of) "Washington." And Wilcox products are *exemplified* by those pampered cows and chickens working to produce "the cottage cheese . . . yogurt . . . the sour cream . . . butter . . . the eggs." Orkin even uses a bit of anti-*negation* by starting to define the Wilcox establishment as "not too picky"—and then retreating from this premise to further bolster the correlated quality claim.

If I were going to create the perfect place...

I'd start with the north. I would carve out rivers...

and rolling hills. Then ride...

the moon south...

and warm the skies with a tropical sun.

I would dot the west with little hometowns...

and fill the east with excitement.

Right in the middle, I'd put a great big playground.

I would surround it all with water...

from coast...

to coast...

to coast. And I'd give it a name. Florida.

FIGURE 6.6 *(Courtesy of Tim Swies, McFarland & Drier, Inc.)*

WOMAN: Oh, we've lived just down the road from the Wilcox family our whole life.

MAN: About 80 years they've been there.

WOMAN: Nice folks.

MAN:	Very nice folks.
WOMAN:	They make all those delicious Wilcox Family Farm Dairy Products, you know.
MAN:	It's just, well, you know---
WOMAN:	Oh, go ahead, say it.
MAN:	They're just so darn particular.
WOMAN:	That's it. Particular.
MAN:	I might even say obsessed.
WOMAN:	Obsessed.
MAN:	I mean, you've never seen anything like it. Constantly fretting over those dairy cows, those egg-producing chickens---
WOMAN:	I hear that they treat those cows practically like members of the family.
MAN:	Oh, yeah. They take such pride in the Wilcox Family Farm milk, the cottage cheese---
WOMAN:	Yogurt---
MAN:	The sour cream---
WOMAN:	Butter---
MAN:	The eggs.
WOMAN:	Ahhhh.
MAN:	They're so darn particular.
WOMAN:	Very particular.
MAN:	Some might even say obsessed.
WOMAN:	Obsessed.
MAN:	Or picky.
BOTH:	Picky, picky, picky.
ANNCR:	At Wilcox Family Farms, we <u>are</u> picky about our quality dairy products, all made with pride, in Washington. Some might say too picky.
WOMAN:	Well, I wouldn't say they're too picky.
MAN:	Oh, no, they're not too, uh, they are fussy, though.
BOTH:	Fussy, fussy, fussy.
ANNCR:	Wilcox Family Farms, we're obsessed with quality.

(Courtesy of Dick Orkin, Dick Orkin's Radio Ranch)

One thing more before leaving the subject of definition. As the number of radio examples we've used in this section attest, *any* radio assignment presents the copywriter with unavoidable definitional challenges. In visual media, as long as we have enough sense to point the camera at the product-in-use, the fundamental definitional task is automatically (if not necessarily persuasively) accomplished. On radio, however, there is no product-in-use, there is no product or benefit picture, until we capture these elements with carefully chosen definitional words and supporting sounds.

VALIDATION

Let's suppose you've achieved our meaningful relationship between previously unrelated things. Let's even assume that the relationship is unbreakable. And let's further assume you've isolated the terms in need of defining and employed the appropriate Definitional Tools. You are now ready, not to relax, but to take a step back from your copy and attempt to evaluate it as a whole; to predict its overall effect on those target consumers who are definitely *not* waiting breathlessly for your next message to reach them.

This stepping back, this organized speculation about how your approach will be received, can be dubbed *Validation*. It's a process best delineated via the *Ten Guidelines for Professional Copy* developed by Stone & Adler's copy supervisor, Paul Connors.[21] When all ten of Connors's questions are brought to bear, they help ensure that copy technique has not been permitted to overshadow the ultimate marketing objective.

1. *Does the Writer Know the Product?* If you are not fully aware of the benefits of what you're selling, you are in no position to choose the advantage that has the greatest appeal to the audience you're striving to reach. And if you're blind to your subject's drawbacks, you may end up constructing a spot that only serves to publicize a client's weakness. You don't have to have personally used something to promote it. But you do need to be fully conversant with its attributes before attempting to explain them to somebody for whom the product is intended.

2. *Does the Writer Know the Market?* As we stress in Chapter 5, electronic media copywriting does not entail trying to talk to everyone. Rather, it requires targeting ever more segmented groups, each of which coalesces around distinct needs and attitudes. Account planners can provide significant assistance in helping us to understand these groups' motivations. But whether or not planners are available, copywriters must bring their own research and human sensitivity to bear in isolating and addressing the motivations most pertinent to the consumers they are attempting to impact. Marketing strategist Jay Woffington points out that "'Choosy Moms Choose Jif' isn't just a catchy peanut butter tag line. It signifies Jif's effort to identify its brand with women who want to do the best for their families. Jif has become a symbol of 'spreadable love' and an expression of good care-taking by moms."[22]

Once you have done the market research, the best way to make certain your copy reflects the results of that research is to visualize one person who epitomizes your prime prospects. Creative director Brian Dillon emphasizes that "a real weakness of advertising and marketing people today is we spend too much of our time with products and too little time with our prospects."[23] So take the time to visualize that fifteen-year-old sophomore boy, or that thirty-eight-year-old female secretary, or the retired factory worker who sat next to you on the bus. Next, forget that you're a copywriter; forget that you've written the spot; forget everything about the assignment and just go blank. (If going blank is too easy for you, get professional help.)

Now, thinking as that sophomore, secretary, or bus rider (or some other person who represents your client's prime target)—does this piece of copy make sense to you? Is it believable? Does it come across through terms and images with which you can identify? Or does the message make you want to zone out, take a coffee break, or move to another seat? And whatever your audience, as we stress at the end of Chapter 2, never talk down to them. "We'll only be in trouble," cautions agency founder Jerry Della Femina, "if we . . . give in to the cynics who say that the consumer is a boob and we should treat him like he really believes he has ring around the collar and a head filled with arrows in his nasal passages."[24]

3. *Is the Writer Talking to the Prospect?* Beyond identifying and attracting our market via concepts most likely to push these folks' "hot buttons," Validation also requires wrapping the concept in a friendly, conversational package. Arthur Godfrey, radio's first great salesman, achieved his success after a lengthy convalescence in which he had nothing to do but listen to the radio. Godfrey tried to discern why some commercials were so much more effective in convincing him than others. The explanation he formulated was that too many spots simply blabbed at "you folks out there in radio land." Although these messages were targeting a particular demographic group, there was little or no *personalization,* little or no attempt at simulating and stimulating a sense of one-to-one communication before dragging the product in by the foot. Successful commercials, conversely, took the time and trouble to establish a feeling of trust and good will before waving the product in front of the listener's ear. "I respond most strongly to messages that feel like they come from somebody, not from some organization—" states Dan Wieden, CEO of Wieden + Kennedy, "when I feel a sense of an individual voice that has conviction and passion about what they're trying to say."[25]

Prospects at either end of the age spectrum are especially difficult for copywriters to approach. For instance, a study conducted by High-Yield Marketing unveiled a key barrier to communicating with senior citizens. The consulting firm found that "agency employees are substantially younger on average than the adult population as a whole, and young adults' empathy for older generations is uncommon. Further, they don't much care about educating themselves about the older market."[26] If they're not careful, these younger copywriters create ads that are more likely to ridicule than to sell to these seniors.

At the other age extreme, comments trade reporter Ann Cooper, are the messages that "continue to speak at kids, rather than to them. In fact, advertising anything to kids is like advertising to people from another planet who occasionally speak the same language you do. You have to admit there's a lot about these people you don't know and start from there."[27] "In the past, marketers could target teens through demographics—age, income, place of residence—as key barometers of their consumer interests," says Fallon Advertising's group planning director Bruce Tait. "Now psychographic elements—such as music tastes, life aspirations, environmental and social awareness—are more telling indicators of which brands can be linked to potential purchasers."[28]

If you are writing copy aimed at either end of the age continuum, it is a good idea to begin by spending some time with members of that group. Isolate the words and preferences that resonate with that age segment and then try to weave this knowledge into messages that respect—but don't mimic—their language and attitudes.

Whatever the target audience, our copy must always establish its own credibility before it can sell the credibility of the product. Like any successful door-to-door salesperson, it must radiate enough warmth and interest to keep the door to the listener's or viewer's attention open long enough to get the product out of the sample case. "You never buy something from a salesman you don't like," warns agency creative head Allan Charles. "The spots are like having salespeople in your home. You have to like them."[29] So imagine yourself standing on an endless street of stoops mouthing the essence of your commercial. If that conjures up doors being slammed in your face, it is time to re-examine how you are really addressing that prospect. Aimed at male Ontario beer drinkers, the following radio spot gets through the door and into the mind with immediate and relevant imagery expressed in words that the target audience would be comfortable saying themselves.

ANNCR: Grown men sit petrified in front of the TV staring like deer into the headlights of an oncoming truck watching other men in strange headgear beat the living hell out of each other with sticks for the right to kiss some old guy's cup. Yep, it's the Stanley Cup playoffs --- our national right --- and the perfect occasion to enjoy an Old Milwaukee. Old Milwaukee's a good beer at a great price that tastes great with everything. Which you can really appreciate after watching them kiss some old guy's cup. Old Milwaukee. Available wherever beer is sold.

(Courtesy of Pat Rooker, Ross Roy Communications, Inc.)

4. *Does the Writer Make a Promise and Back It Up with Evidence?* Our promise, as stated in Chapter 4, is the rational attraction our copy expresses. But this attraction/promise will not be credible if we fail to support it with proof. Consumers are constantly asking "Why?" or "How?" in response to copy claims. If the message merely moves on to another unsupported assertion, as in these lines from a student-written spot, believability evaporates.

Simon's Watermelon Candy captures the nostalgia of an era gone by. [How?] And this candy is healthier for the kids than a chocolate bar. [Why?] Plus there is no better time than now to pick up a bag of Simon's. [Because?]

Conversely, the following commercial provides extensive evidence to validate Dollar General Stores' (economy appeal) promise of low prices—and even introduces this evidence *in advance of* the full articulation of the "always make it worth the trip" claim. Thus by the time the promise arrives, the listener has been pre-assured.

ANNCR: 'Well now,' you're saying to yourself, 'where in the world is one of those Dollar General Stores I've been hearing about?' Well, ask somebody. Or look us up in your phone book. It'll be the best 30 seconds you ever spent. If you don't know where a Dollar General Store is, you've been hanging around those big expensive malls too much. You won't find us there.

The rent's too high. Nope, we're right on down the road. Somewhere in a smaller, older center where you might even be able to find a parking place. Or sometimes we're in a building that somebody else deserted in order to get up there with the big boys in the new mall. Don't kid yourself. They aren't losing money when they move up. You are. And we won't let that happen to you at Dollar General Stores. You may have to look for us a little bit, but we always make it worth the trip, every time.

(Courtesy of Miller Leonard, Madden & Goodrum & Associates, Inc.)

5. *Does the Writer Get to the Point at Once?* Even in the comparative expansiveness of sixty seconds, electronic media copywriters do not have the time to wander leisurely into their subject. We must know where we are going from the very beginning. In addition, consumers tend to give us only three to four seconds before they make the decision to tune in or tune out. One technique for dealing with this condition is to imagine your target consumers with empty cartoon bubbles above their heads. Then try to fill those bubbles with a relevant and interesting image within the very first "panel" of your message. Don't draw a blank for your audience or they will quickly 'go blank' to your spot.

The radio spot below grabs us with the picture of a guy who is disappointed because his hair looks *good*! We want to find out why this makes him unhappy. The central premise of trying Kroger's 2,500 store-brand items is then immediately exposed and the listener is immersed in product amplification after only seven seconds of the message have expired.

BOBBY: (Disappointed) Oh no. My hair looks wonderful.

ANNCR: Bobby Guzinski is trying every single one of the twenty-five hundred Kroger brand products.

BOBBY: Sure, this Kroger brand tissue feels soft, but what if I blow my nose?

(SFX: NOSE BLOW)

BOBBY: (Nasal and disappointed) It still feels great.

ANNCR: He's trying to find one Kroger brand product he's not happy with. Why? The Kroger Promise. If you're not happy with a Kroger brand product, bring it back and Kroger will actually replace it with a leading national brand, free of charge.

BOBBY: This Kroger brand hand lotion says it'll help make my hands soft and (SFX: SQUIRT) --- oh, my hands have never been so soft and supple.

ANNCR: Bobby wants to take advantage of Kroger's amazing promise, but so far---

BOBBY: This Kroger brand cereal can't be as delicious as (Crunching with a mouthful) --- darn! It's delicious.

ANNCR: See, Kroger uses the same ingredients as the national brands. So Kroger brands are every bit as good. Whether it's cereal, paper products, cleaning or beauty aids.

(SFX: SQUEAKING CLEANING SOUND)

BOBBY: I'll bet this Kroger brand glass cleaner doesn't remove this smudge. (Annoyed) Heckers, the smudge is gone.

ANNCR: And Bobby is determined to try every Kroger brand product.

BOBBY: Okay, what's next? Oh yeah. These Kroger dog biscuits look tasty---

(SFX: CRUNCH)

ANNCR: The Kroger brand promise.

(SFX: CRUNCH)

BOBBY: How are they, Sparky?

(SFX: DOG BARK) That good, huh?

ANNCR: Try it, like it, or get the national brand free.

(Courtesy of Dick Orkin, Dick Orkin's Radio Ranch)

6. *Does the Writer Make Every Word Count—Is Copy Concise?* Not only must we get right to the point, but we must also direct every word we use toward that point. Unlike print writers, we can't afford a throwaway paragraph here or there because our *entire spot* is usually the equivalent of a single paragraph. So electronic media copywriting is a continuous *streamlining* process—and such streamlining is hard work. Abraham Lincoln once apologized for the length of a letter by observing, "I would have written a shorter one, but I didn't have time." Anything that doesn't directly relate to your selling picture must be eliminated. Everything that does relate must be re-examined to see if it can be expressed even more succinctly. As a training technique, some agency creative directors pay a token "bounty" on unessential words that their junior writers locate in each other's scripts.

Much of this condensation process results from ending sentences where they should end. The NewsLab's Deborah Potter points out that there is a dangerous tendency for journalists to add an extra three words to the conclusion of sentences:

The cancer victim died *of the disease.*

The tulip grower won the top award *for the flowers.*[30]

But this same tendency afflicts commercial copywriters as well:

Need cake decorations for that special occasion coming up *at your house?*

Attention all offices and businesses *around the country.*

The bag of vegetables wouldn't tear open, so you pull harder *to open it.*

When it comes to candy, everyone wants the best *they can get.*

Such excessive verbiage not only clouds your message's meaning, but it takes precious time away from words that could have enhanced your selling proposition.

Benefiting from pictures as well as words, the video media possess the capability for especially concise messages. That, of course, is what makes ten- and fifteen-second

TV and Web spots viable—if the copywriter can master the format—as did the creator of the following commercial. Through a single, compelling correlation, this spot needs no more than ten seconds to dramatize the absurdity of paying other banks to get your money from an ATM.

Video	Audio
CUT TO HOTDOG VENDER NONCHALANTLY TAKING BITE	SFX: STREET NOISE
OUT OF MAN'S HOT DOG AND HANDING IT TO HIM	ANNCR: You wouldn't put up with it here, so why let them take a bite at the ATM?
MAN STARES AT HOT DOG BEWILDERED	MUSIC: UPBEAT
GRAPHIC: With PNC, make every ATM in the world free.	
CUT TO PNC BANK LOGO. GRAPHIC: Pnc/freeatms.com Member FDIC	

(Courtesy of Dan Nelson, Doner Advertising)

7. *Is Copy Logical—Does It Flow?* Our discussion of Progressive Motivation in Chapter 5 deals directly with this requirement, of course. But whether you use Progressive Motivation or some other selling structure, it is essential that

- **a.** every phrase should drive the message forward;
- **b.** one sentence must lead directly to the next;
- **c.** no part of the message should be susceptible to cutting without breaking the idea flow.

Aristotle, who created some pretty fair copy in his own idiom, called this process *organic unity.* As he discussed in his *Poetics,* organic unity culminates in the whole being greater than the sum of its parts. Each part leads so inevitably to the next part that the conclusion (the central copy point) is itself inevitable.

Beethoven's music reflects this quality of inevitability, and so does a well-crafted legal brief or debate case. Beginning with an original concept that is compelling to the audience, we then couple together a string of little enhancements that ultimately lead to audience satisfaction with the message in its entirety. Because the parts of the pitch are so fused, the listener/viewer cannot carve it up and attack these parts piecemeal. Instead, the discourse must be either accepted or rejected in its entirety. When organic unity is employed, "Somehow, in the blend of image, words and format, there is a larger meaning that emanates from them like a bloom," advises the advertising/public relations firm of Arnell/Bickford Associates. "Each element serves the larger purpose of the advertisement: There seems to be a 'natural order' to a successful creation."[31]

The following sixty-second commercial is an example of well-executed organic unity. Beginning with its "Did I hear that right?" opening premise, it elicits both listener involvement and step-by-step acceptance of the advocated action.

ANNCR: This year, billions of bugs will lose their lives on the nation's highways. Chances are, a lot of them will end up on the front of your car. And if you don't get them off, they'll come back to haunt you.

(EERIE MUSIC: FEATURE AND UNDER)

You see, as bugs decompose, they give off a strong acid that actually eats away at your car's chrome and paint --- making it dull. The hotter the weather, the faster the acid is made. But there is a brighter side to all of this. Come to Hot Springs Auto Wash. We've developed a way to completely remove bugs before they kill your car's finish. In fact, Hot Springs is the only car wash to make this guarantee: if you find as much as one single little mosquito on your car after we've washed it, we'll give you your money back.

(MUSIC: OUT)

Next time, we'll talk to you about the problem with birds.

(SFX: BIRDS CHIRPING)

(Courtesy of Diana Monroe, Siddall, Matus & Coughter, Inc.)

8. *Is Copy Enthusiastic—Does the Writer Believe in What's Being Sold?* This is sometimes a difficult stipulation to meet. As we established earlier in this chapter, you don't have to personally use a product to promote it. But you must believe that it will do what you are claiming. Agencies have resigned accounts when they could no longer subscribe to the claims a client wanted articulated. This, of course, is a wrenching business decision that may have severe financial fallout for that agency. However, continuing to create effective advertising for a product you know to be deficient can, in the long term, hurt the client as well. As former Leo Burnett creative services vice president, Robert Noel, recalls,

> TV is the greatest way to build a brand, but it can also destroy one. We had a client in the food business that was afraid of losing share to some new competitors with new products. So the client hurriedly whomped up a product to compete. But it wasn't very good, and too little time was given to testing it. We wrote the commercials and sold a ton of first-time buyers. But the people who bought it once didn't buy it again. We advertised that product out of existence inside of a year.[32]

As an individual copywriter, you may also have to wrestle with this credibility issue. If you work for a large enough shop, you might be able to get transferred off that account. If you're stuck where you are, the most feasible strategy is to try to fashion copy that at least puts the claim in accurate perspective—while keeping your eyes open for more reputable pastures.

Functionally, most clients come to realize that you can't squeeze effective, enthusiastic copy from people who don't believe in what they are selling. That is why "the match of agency and client culture" is such an important, if illusive, quality when a company seeks out a firm to handle its advertising. As Dan Wieden, co-founder of Wieden & Kennedy Advertising, maintains, "We do what we are. If you're having fun, it shows up in your work. If you're bright and focused, that shows up. If you're trying to con somebody, that shows up."[33]

If you are truly enthusiastic about the account, you may well derive an effective approach that the client would not otherwise consider. Nick Cain, writer of the varicose vein spot that follows, coined the term "Angry Legs" that the clinic's director absolutely hated. But Cain passionately believed in the client and in this approach—which ended up generating phenomenal traffic for Vein Solutions. Women actually came in talking about their "angry legs" and the doctor couldn't have been more pleased at the results of his decision to trust the writer's zeal.

WOMAN: You know how in the movies, whenever someone gets angry they have that --- that vein that starts throbbing in their head? That's how you know they're <u>really</u> ticked off. You could call it *the angry vein*. Well, lets say you're getting ready one morning and you're not watching a movie, but there it is: *the angry vein*. But it's not on your face. It's on your leg. Maybe even both of them. Ugh. What is that?

Do you have *Angry Leg Syndrome*? No, that actually doesn't exist. What you <u>do</u> have are varicose veins, and they're definitely <u>not</u> making you happy. How did you get them? You're way too young for this, right? How are you going to get rid of them? The answer? The board certified surgeons at Vein Solutions. There are several different treatments for varicose veins or *angry legs*, and Vein Solutions will help you choose the one that's right for you. Schedule your free vein evaluation by a board certified vascular surgeon today at 866 – 301 – Vein. There's no reason to be an unhappy *person* because you have angry *legs*. Call 866 – 301 – Vein today. Vein Solutions.

(Courtesy of Craig Allen, Citadel Communications)

9. Is Copy Complete—Are All Questions Answered? Copywriters most often run into trouble with this Validation when they try to cover more than one main point in their message. Raising multiple issues/claims in a spot also means you must answer all their associated questions and doubts—an impossibility given the limitations imposed by fifteen, thirty, or even sixty seconds of time. If you follow the advice given with Validation Questions 5, 6, and 7, the danger of incomplete copy is greatly reduced.

Sometimes, it is necessary to break the concept up into two or more subthemes and pen separate ads for each. In the Hot Springs Auto Wash commercial presented earlier, for instance, the copywriter left "the problem with birds" for another spot rather than attempting to cover both bird and bug impact in a single message.

Alternatively, a sturdy central premise can provide the tree on which you efficiently and logically hang the answers to several separate questions about the client. The spot below puts a twist on the "asking Santa" motif by having the old guy contact the kid rather than the other way around. This creates a situation in which the copywriter can fill in multiple gaps that may exist in listeners' knowledge about the store.

Production Note: Timmy is about 10 years old.

(SFX: PHONE RINGS)

TIMMY: Hello?

SANTA: Ho, Ho, Ho. Hello, Timmy. Merry Christmas.

TIMMY: Oh. Hi Santa.

SANTA: You know, Timmy, I haven't received a letter from you yet, Christmas is almost here and I want to make sure you get everything you want. Ho, ho, ho.

TIMMY: Oh, I will.

SANTA: (Confused, not so jolly) Huh?

TIMMY: Yeah, Mom and Dad did all their Christmas shopping at Munn's General Store. And from the way Mom was smiling, I think she saved a ton of money.

SANTA: (A bit flustered) Well, uh, does Munn's General Store have um, bikes?

TIMMY: Yep.

SANTA: Footballs?

TIMMY: Yep.

SANTA: Electronics?

TIMMY: Uh huh. In fact, they had so much electronic stuff we nearly didn't get Dad out of there.

SANTA: But I bet Munn's won't be working Christmas Eve like some of us. (With bite) Ho, ho, ho.

TIMMY: Yes, they will.

SANTA: What?

TIMMY: They're open 'til midnight Christmas Eve in case you forgot wrapping paper, tape, or even more egg nog.

SANTA: Well, if you've already got all your gifts from Munn's General Store, can I at least stop by for milk and cookies?

TIMMY: Sure, Santa. Mom got those at Munn's General Store too.

SANTA: (Sighs) You're killing me, kid.

ANNCR: Everything you need for Christmas. At great prices. Munn's General Store. On Bay Road in Saginaw.

(Courtesy of Craig Allen, Citadel Communications)

10. *Is Copy Designed to Sell?* The ultimate function of any commercial, PSA, or promo is to convince an audience to take the course of action that your client wants them to take: to buy the product, donate to the cause, or tune in to the program. Whatever approach you decide to pursue as a copywriter, that approach must be client-serving, not writer-serving. When, as creative director Valerie Graves observes, "we just show off our hipness or entertain ourselves, we creatives evoke a predictable response in our audience. They are entertained, but the message becomes excess baggage. Consumers are reached, but they are not moved."[34]

If either the technique you've employed or its execution gets in the way of the "sell"—change it. Unlike a poem, no piece of copy can exist solely for itself or its creator. As copywriting legend David Ogilvy (who began his career selling cooking utensils door-to-door) proclaimed, "I'm a salesman. I don't care if my work wins awards in Cannes or at any other of these ridiculous festivals. I want to sell products."[35]

While seeking the sale, the Validation process strives to insure meaningful, effective and *respectful* communication with the consumer. According to Draft/ New York's chief creative officer Shelly Lanman, that consumer is ultimately asking eight things of us:

- Speak to me as you would wish to be spoken to.
- Know what you're talking about. Chances are I do.
- Tell me something I don't already know but can believe when I hear it from you.
- Respect my intelligence and engage it. Really, I'm not as ignorant as they say.
- Respect my time; tell me what matters to me.
- Don't manipulate or bully me. I don't want to be tricked into a decision.
- Make it easy for me to understand what you want me to do.
- Hear yourself, too. Basically, if you don't buy what you're saying, chances are no one else will either.[36]

PROHIBITION (REGULATORY)

Besides all of our other concerns as copywriters, we must avoid certain techniques no matter how much they might seem to enhance our marketing efforts. In the United States, several of these prohibitions are mandated by laws and regulations associated with the Federal Trade Commission (FTC), the Food and Drug Administration (FDA), the Federal Communications Commission (FCC), or a host of other national, state, and even local agencies. Other prohibitions are present in network and local outlet "standards and practices" policies, or in similar self-regulatory activities associated with the Council of Better Business Bureaus. Because this is not a legal casebook or one with only American readers, we cannot delve deeply into advertising law. However, we can point out the types of regulatory arenas of which all copywriters should be aware.

The Federal Sector

The Federal Trade Commission historically has been the prime investigator of deception in advertising. In exercising its overall oversight duties, points out business analyst Craig Stoltz, "the FTC chooses cases not just to prosecute specific offenders but to establish precedents that guide all marketers."[37] In an action brought against Listerine, for example (which was upheld by the Supreme Court in 1978), the FTC established its right to require a client to engage in *corrective advertising* to make up for past misstatements. Listerine's manufacturer, Warner-Lambert, was forced to include the following "corrective" comment in its next $10 million of advertising (an amount equal to Listerine's average annual advertising budget for 1962–1972):

Listerine will not help prevent colds or sore throats or lessen their severity.[38]

In 1984, the FTC also reaffirmed and refined its commitment to its *advertising substantiation* program, whereby advertisers and agencies must be certain they have concrete evidence in hand before disseminating product performance claims. And, in a 1992 case involving advertising for Klondike Lite dessert bars, the Commission made it clear that it is prepared not only to carefully scrutinize assertions about fat content and "lite-ness," but also to move beyond the stated facts in the copy to examine its *implications and inferences.* The FTC cited Klondike for making a "low in cholesterol" claim that, while factually accurate, implied (in the FTC's eyes) that the product was also low in fat.[39] Two years later, in 1994, the FTC issued new guidelines requiring food marketers who used terms such as "light," "lean," "reduced," and "high" in ads to satisfy the same definitions followed by the Food and Drug Administration in describing nutrients like fat, cholesterol, and fiber.[40]

Actual food labeling, as well as monitoring of advertising and promotion on behalf of pharmaceutical manufacturers, has always been the province of the Food and Drug Administration. Claims and labels permitted by the FDA will also meet Federal Trade Commission standards. Therefore, copywriters on food and drug accounts are wise to follow FDA decisions closely. Like the FTC, the Food and Drug Administration's authority allows it "in effect, to legislate by precedent," says Craig Stoltz. "Marketers making claims similar to those subjected to FDA actions must make changes or face investigations too."[41] *Adweek* editor Eleftheria Parpis adds that for pharmaceutical messages, "every product claim has to be supported by results of a drug company's clinical trials. The main side effects discovered in those trials must be mentioned, which can take up about 20 seconds of a 60-second commercial, and ads have to lead consumers to their doctors and additional sources of information."[42] (Even this may not ultimately be enough as members of Congress periodically threaten to ban over-the-air drug advertising entirely.)

In the case of the Federal Trade Commission, if its "investigators are convinced that an ad violates the law, they usually try to bring the violator into compliance through informal means," says attorney Fred Steingold. "If that doesn't work, the FTC can issue a cease-and-desist order and bring a civil lawsuit on behalf of people who have been harmed."[43] Historically, the FTC's actual enforcement efforts were primarily restricted to matters of outright *deception.* But in 1994, the Commission acquired additional clout when, after fourteen years of wrangling, Congress finally passed a law allowing it to police *unfairness* by finally providing a legal definition for that term:

> Acts or practices that cause or are likely to cause substantial injury to consumers, which is not reasonably avoidable by consumers themselves and not outweighed by countervailing benefits to consumers or competition.[44]

Additional federal oversight has come about as a result of the Trademark Law Revision Act of 1988. Under prior law, advertisers' main concern was to avoid misrepresenting their *own* products. But the new act enlarged this concern by holding companies liable for misrepresenting the qualities or characteristics of *competing* products as well.

Trademark law also covers *misappropriation.* In 1995, a Supreme Court decision decreed that even a color can act as a protectable trademark provided it (a) serves no utilitarian function and (b) has attained "secondary meaning" in consumers' minds. Owens-Corning was thus able to prevent competitors from using its pink hue because the color does not impact the insulation's performance (is nonutilitarian). In addition, through the product's packaging, the use of the animated Pink Panther as spokesthing, and the slogan ("put your house in the pink"), the company has invested its color with strong secondary meaning.[45] Similarly, Tootsie Roll Industries was able to stop a novelty toilet paper manufacturer from wrapping its product in a brown paper with a thin red stripe and white panels and marketing it as Tushie Roll.[46] Even when it does not involve direct competitors, such parody is out of bounds. To be permissible, advises attorney Rick Kurnit, the parody must "comment on or criticize the underlying work—what doesn't work is to simply do an homage—replicating someone's copyrighted work."[47]

As our discussion so far suggests, commercial speech historically has enjoyed less Constitutional protection than have other forms of expression. Thus the creators of advertising need to be much more careful than are journalists in what they say and how they say it. However, commercial speech acquired greater legitimacy through the 1996 *44 Liquormart Inc. et al.* v. *Rhode Island et al.* Supreme Court decision. Though ignited by Rhode Island's ban on advertising liquor prices, this case acquired much broader ramifications. In his principal opinion for the Court majority overturning the ban, Justice John Paul Stevens wrote:

> It is the state's interest in protecting consumers from "commercial harms" that provides "the typical reason why commercial speech can be subject to greater regulation than non-commercial speech." . . . Yet, bans that target truthful, non-misleading commercial messages rarely protect consumers from such harms. Instead, such bans often serve only to obscure an "underlying government policy" that could be implemented without regulating speech.[48]

As trade reporter Ira Teinowitz points out, this ruling thereby "reversed the high court's previous decision saying if a state legislature had the authority to ban a product but didn't, the lawmakers could instead choose to ban its advertising."[49]

Instead, through *44 Liquormart,* the Supreme Court established that, except for matters of fairness and accuracy, our commercial speech should have much the same First Amendment protection as noncommercial speech. If government wishes to restrict a product, it should do so directly rather than indirectly via the quashing of its advertising. This doctrine was further advanced in the 1999 case *Greater New Orleans Broadcasting Association* v. *United States.* Here, the U.S. Supreme Court overturned a Federal Communications Commission regulation that had barred broadcasters from accepting commercials promoting slot machines and games of chance sited on Indian reservations. The Court ruled that the federal government could not make exceptions in advertising. Thus it could not restrict casino ads to air only on tribal land. "The speaker and the audience, not the Government, should be left to assess the value of accurate and nonmisleading information about lawful conduct," wrote the Court.[50] Admittedly, these two decisions do not overtly impact the day-to-day job of the copywriter. Nonetheless, they constitute significant steps toward affording greater protection to the commercial speech we create.

This does not mean copywriters must not still be vigilant as to the numerous and sometimes obscure Federal regulations that govern our use of words and images. Title 47, Chapter 8, Subchapter 1, Sec. 906 of the *U.S. Code*, for example, makes it a criminal offense to air an Olympics-themed ad that doesn't have Olympians in it within thirty days of the Olympic Games.[51]

The State Sector

As evidenced by Rhode Island's involvement in the *44 Liquormart* litigation, advertisers must worry not just about federal oversight, but about more aggressive state regulation as well. During the 1980s, when Reagan administration deregulatory and budget-paring tendencies substantially reduced FTC activities, state law enforcers took notice. "When the FTC wasn't doing anything, we saw dynamic growth of the National Association of Attorneys General because the state ag's saw themselves filling a void in regulation," advertising law attorney Felix Kent points out. "NAAG has grown in power and influence and, even though the FTC is back in business, NAAG isn't necessarily resigning."[52]

Although it has no statutory legal standing in its own right, NAAG's membership uses its collective resources to approach advertisers with a united voice and, implicitly, with the threat of lawsuits if its recommendations are ignored by the advertising community. Beginning with actions against airline ticket and rental car price advertising, NAAG members have moved on to additional battlegrounds. In 1990, pressure from the Minnesota attorney general forced General Mills to pull an ad that showed psyllium (an ingredient in Benefit cereal) as a PacMan-like cholesterol-eater. The company also agreed to pay $7,000 to each state in which the ad ran in order to cover legal costs incurred by those states in bringing the action.

The following year, acting on a tip, the Texas attorney general's office discovered that a Volvo commercial shot in Texas featured client cars in which roof supports had been reinforced with steel girders and lumber to prevent collapse when a monster truck rolled over them. Once the ads ran, the AG went after Volvo and extracted a $316,250 fine plus corrective advertising. (Volvo later fired its long-standing advertising agency in retribution for the deception.) Still later, the same state attorney general threatened suit against Pfizer *as well as its advertising agency* for alleged deception in regard to the plaque-reducing qualities of Plax mouthwash. To varying degrees (depending on the political make-up of their administrations), attorneys general continue to scrutinize the content of advertising aired in their states. Media agencies as well as their clients face state legal hassles if their claims appear deceptive or unsubstantiated. (At the national level, the FTC also has served notice that it will hold agencies co-responsible for problem ads.)

The Self-Policing Sector

For their own legal protection, broadcast/cable networks and outlet owners have devised a number of guidelines governing what they will and will not permit in their commercials and other pieces of continuity.

Every year, the typical broadcast television network performs preliminary reviews on up to 40,000 spots. This is done by executives in its standards and practices department. "I know of no way to remove some degree of subjectivity from the process," admits CBS executive vice president Martin Franks. "However, our decisions on any ad are the product of a review by more than one person, and we do our best to be guided by precedent, consistency, and a desire to serve the sometimes competing interests of our three constituencies: our audience, our affiliates, and our advertisers."[53] Because post-production changes are expensive, many agencies bring in their commercials at the storyboard stage, in which modifications are relatively easy to accomplish. Once the broadcast nets give their approval, odds are a spot will be able to air in other venues.

Some cable nets have their own standards departments, but many do not. Because cable content is not sent over the open airwaves by stations relying on the FCC for a license, commercials aired on cable often are more edgy or "adventurous" than those carried by broadcasters. This is particularly true of wired content providers (both cable and Internet) that cater exclusively to adult audiences. Still, for both broadcast and broadband electronic media, the substantiation of claims made in commercials is an important consideration. A copy claim that cannot be supported may mean that an expensively produced message is never transmitted—or, if it is run, may attract expensive lawsuits from competitors or aggrieved special interests.

Another self-regulatory apparatus is maintained by the National Advertising Review Council (NARC), an alliance between the advertising industry and the Council of Better Business Bureaus (CBBB). Funding for NARC comes from CBBB. Policies and procedures emanate from the NARC board, which is composed of the heads of the key advertising trade associations and the CBBB. NARC is comprised of three entities: the National Advertising Division (NAD), the Children's Advertising Review Unit (CARU), and the National Advertising Review Board (NARB).

NAD's staff responds to consumer and competitor complaints and arbitrates unresolved cases that originate with local Better Business Bureaus. It expanded its scrutiny to Internet advertising in 1995. In 2008, NAD handled 214 cases. As a means of industry preventive education, the group also publishes policy papers about key advertising issues. At the regional level, approximately three dozen Local Advertising Review Programs (LARPs) operate in major cities as joint ventures of the Better Business Bureau and chapters of the American Advertising Federation (AAF).

CARU focuses exclusively on children's advertising. Unlike the NAD, CARU does not wait to act until a complaint is filed. Instead, the great majority of its cases arise from complaints it files itself as a result of its own monitoring of spots aimed at children via all electronic media, including the Web. For example, as a result of such monitoring, CARU recently ruled that commercials promoting mealtime foods to kids must place the products within "the framework of a balanced meal," which was defined as showing four out of the five food groups in the advertising.[54]

When the NAD or CARU cannot persuade an advertiser to accept its decision on a complaint, a case is referred for arbitration to the National Advertising Review Board. Founded in 1971 by three advertising associations and the Council of Better Business Bureaus, the NARB consists of a peer-review group of seventy advertising professionals and public-interest members. Cases are heard by five-person panels whose composition changes from case to case. Since its birth, the NARB has heard three or four cases per year. One of the most important decisions made in establishing the procedure was that "there would not be a single advertising code," says American Advertising Federation president emeritus Howard Bell. "It was agreed that the standard would be truth and accuracy and the need for adequate substantiation of claims, and each case would be considered on its individual merits."[55]

If advertisers refuse to take part in the voluntary process, a case can be referred directly to the Federal Trade Commission. Nobody wins when matters go this far. Voluntary and self-regulatory activities are certainly preferable (and considerably less punitive) than the actions of government overseers. "Our job is to protect the integrity of the advertising industry so it won't be regulated," states NAD director Andrea Levine, "but also to give consumers the confidence that what they see is true and accurate."[56] Having to defend your message even in industry forums is stressful, time consuming, and client infuriating. The most efficient self-regulation is accomplished by the copywriter at the moment of the spot's conception. Making certain the copy is clear and accurate before it leaves your desk is the best way to prevent later catastrophes.

In addition to carefully weighing the words you use, Attorney Rick Kurnit suggests four cautions designed to keep you and your spot out of potential legal quagmires:

1. Early in the creative process, get written permission from the appropriate people if an ad carries the potential to violate copyright and/or privacy laws.
2. During production, make sure no one hires someone to sound like, look like, or otherwise represent a celebrity.
3. Before the shoot, get producers' affidavits signed to substantiate that demonstrations are not mockups.
4. Have regular seminars with a lawyer to update staff on how to specifically stay within the limits of advertising law.[57]

PROHIBITION (STYLISTIC)

Even though they are largely outside the scope of governmental and industry regulation, four audience-offending stylistic crimes do so much damage to the client that they merit special attention here. With a little self-policing, you should be able to respect these stylistic prohibitions against (1) fraudulent attention-getters, (2) disparagement, (3) repulsiveness, and (4) superlatives.

Fraudulent Attention-Getters

Some people will do anything to attract attention to themselves—or to their copy. As we've seen previously, a good attention-getter is vital if your message is to grab the audience's eyes and ears. But an attention-getter that has nothing to do with the copy's main point, or a main point that has nothing to do with the offered product or service, is both a lie and a theft. It promises prospects something your message is never prepared to give and robs them of the time each expended in taking the whole message in. Loud noises, screams, and other "now that I've got your attention" ripoffs resurrect the specter of the huckster copywriter. Spots like this may show imagination, but such imagination is both unprincipled and undisciplined:

(SFX: WAILING SIREN UP AND UNDER)

ANNCR: (In a panic) Fire! Fire! What a tragedy! What a disaster! All those poor
           people and what it does to them. Makes you sick right down to your
           stomach. Yes, the tragedy of heartburn, of excess acidity that comes from
           eating all that 'fast food,' is a national calamity. But all the flaming agony
           can be prevented. Stop burning yourself out at those plastic food palaces
           and start enjoying how 'cool' a good meal can be at Barney's Beefsteak
           Bistro. Barney's Beefsteak Bistro, corner of Fulton and Business Route 9,

> takes the time and care to prepare a meal that stays with you; but stays
> with you the right way. A lunch or dinner at Barney's leaves you cool and
> collected; not hot and bothered. Plan now for a relaxing noon or evening
> at Barney's Beefsteak Bistro, Fulton and Business Route 9. Barney fires up his
> trusty grill; not your tender stomach.

(SFX: WAILING SIREN UP AND OUT TO TIME)

Barney's deserves to burn in hell, most listeners would conclude. And so does the
copywriter who wrote such fraudulent trash.

Disparagement

People do not enjoy having their egos bruised—especially by some jerk on the airwaves or the Internet. Thus copy that tries to bludgeon the audience into accepting
your point of view through sarcasm and ridicule is bound to go down in flames, just
like Barney's steaks. Few writers deliberately attempt to disparage their audience, but
ill-considered lines like the following do no less harm just because they are oversights.

Even you can operate a Sharkfin outboard on the very first try.

Well, Mom, are you about to bake another batch of those drab, dull, everyday cookies?

It's time the Hades Oil and Gas Company taught you a few things about home heating.

Banking is simpler than ever at Fidelity. So even you can understand it.

Nor is it wise to disparage people outside your target audience. A Mercedes-Benz
SUV spot once referenced "mean old truckers out hogging the street." Within hours
of the message's first airing, angry truck drivers were burning up the phones to
Freightliner—the largest big-rig manufacturer in the United States and a company
that was also owned by Mercedes' parent company. The commercial was pulled
immediately, to the mutual embarrassment of Mercedes and its advertising agency.[58]

Disparagement is also a problem when directed at the competition. Until 1971,
both CBS and ABC refused to accept advertising that "named names," and their stance
helped keep both fair and unscrupulous product comparisons off most of the airwaves.
If two of the networks wouldn't accept the copy, it was just too difficult to get proper
penetration for it. Then the Federal Trade Commission ruled that euphemisms such as
"Brand X" and "our larger competitor" were confusing the public and depriving them
of meaningful consumer information. The two networks got the message and joined
NBC in permitting the specification of which "Brand X" the copy was talking about.
This resulted in a significant upswing in what are officially known as "comparative"
commercials and in the consequent rise in advertiser-versus-advertiser litigation.

It must be clarified that comparison, by itself, is neither evil nor disparaging. As
long as the focus of the message is on the positive aspect of your product (comparison)
and not on the alleged negative attributes of the competition (disparagement), the practice can play a beneficial role for both the advertiser and the cause of public
enlightenment. A study by Research Systems Corporation found that TV spots taking a
brand-differentiating comparative approach somewhat improved their odds of achieving superior persuasion scores. More to the point, observed *Adweek,* the study seemed

to indicate that "the main virtue of doing a comparative commercial may be that it compels you to define the 'point of difference' that characterizes your own brand."[59]

However, "what a brand gains from comparative advertising depends on your position in the marketplace," says JWT/New York director of planning David Lamb. "The best use of comparative advertising is to challenge an established brand leader . . . Consumers like small, scrappy brands taking on the big guy . . . If you poke the tiger long enough, you might draw him into unfamiliar territory."[60]

Still, comparative spots may present special risks for new brands, states Mark Gleason, Research Systems' executive vice president. "New brands that compare themselves to well-established brands add confusion to what is being advertised, so people tend to remember the established brands [identified in the comparative ads] and not remember the new brands."[61] As marketing consultant Joe Marconi summarizes,

> Ads in which one brand attacks another often backfire by giving the competitor a higher level of attention, name recognition, interest, and perhaps even sympathy. The best ads emphasize the benefits of the product advertised. If the best you can say about your product is something negative about your competitor's, your product doesn't have much going for it. Take the high road. Be positive.[62]

Nevertheless, even though "people may say that they hate mean-spirited (comparative) ads," reports marketing consultant Al Ries, "that doesn't mean that they won't buy the product if the commercial presents a compelling argument."[63] If you feel you can make such an argument in your copy, it is a good idea to check that copy against the following ten guidelines for comparative commercials advanced by the American Association of Advertising Agencies:

1. The intent and connotation of the ad should be to inform and never discredit or unfairly attack competitors, competing products, or services.
2. When a competitive product is named, it should be one that exists in the marketplace as significant competition.
3. The competition should be fairly and properly identified, but never in a manner or tone of voice that degrades the competitive product or service.
4. The advertising should compare related or similar properties or ingredients of the product, dimension to dimension, feature to feature.
5. The identification should be for honest comparison purposes and not simply to upgrade by association.
6. If a competitive test is conducted, it should be done by an objective testing service, preferably an independent one, so there will be no doubt about the veracity of the test.
7. In all cases the test should be supportive of all claims made in the advertising that's based on the test.
8. The advertising should never use partial results or stress insignificant differences to cause the consumer to draw an improper conclusion.
9. The property being compared should be significant in terms of value or usefulness of the product to the consumer.
10. Comparisons delivered through the use of testimonials should not imply that the testimonial is more than one individual's thought unless that individual represents a sample of the majority viewpoint.[64]

In short, any honest, comparative message should concentrate on placing your client in the best verifiable light—not on placing the competitor under some unsubstantiated cloud (a cloud that could all too likely rain on your own parade).

The following radio commercial illustrates a *positive* comparison. The competing Ajax candles aren't disparaged—in fact, they're conceded to look the same and be less expensive. But the Re-lites advantage is described in such a manner that a key superiority shines through—a superiority that comes from concentrating on an honest Re-lites *attribute* rather than a competitor *flaw*.

ANNCR: If you're searching for something to brighten up your next birthday party, then you're searching for Re-lites. Re-lites look just like ordinary Ajax birthday candles. And Ajax candles are a lot cheaper. But unlike ordinary Ajax candles, when you blow Re-lites out, they re-light. By themselves. Magically. And they'll keep on relighting as long as you have the breath to keep blowing them out. Don't miss out on the laughs that Re-lites can bring to your next birthday party. Re-lites. The more you blow, the more they glow.

A more aggressive but still fair and truthful comparative approach is set forth in the following TV spot. Here, the focus is on space, and the commercial concedes that each truck could be said to have the same cargo capacity. But it is *where* that space is located that becomes the humorously depicted point of difference.

Video	Audio
ESTAB. SHOT BUSY CEMENT/GRAVEL YARD. REAR VIEW OF F-150 AND C-1500 TRUCKS. BED OF EACH IS FILLED WITH CEMENT FROM A CHUTE. SPOKESMAN IN HARD HAT AND WHITE COAT STANDS BETWEEN TRUCKS	MAN: The Ford F-150 spacious cargo box will hold 75.6 cubic feet of
ZOOM OUT TO REVEAL CEMENT TRUCKS AT END OF EACH CHUTE, STILL FILLING PICKUP BEDS	whatever you choose to put in it. But to be perfectly fair,
CU OF SPOKESMAN MOVING CHUTE FEEDING CHEVY FROM NOW FULL TRUCK BED TO TRUCK CAB'S OPEN PASSENGER'S WINDOW	the Chevy C-1500 will also hold 75.6 cubic feet of cargo.
CEMENT FLOWS DOWN CHUTE TO START FILLING PASSENGER COMPARTMENT	Of course, only 60.5 of it will fit in the back.
BEAUTY SHOT OF F-150 WITH MOUNTAIN OF GRAVEL BEHIND IT. KEY PRICING INFO SUPERED	VO: Right now, get 500 dollars cash back on a new F-150 regular or super cab.
FORD TEXAS DEALERS LOGO	At your Texas Ford dealers.
MS SPOKESMAN UNSUCCESSFULLY TRYING TO OPEN DOOR OF CEMENT-FILLED CHEVY CAB	SFX: THREE FUTILE CLICKS OF DOOR LATCH BUTTON

(Courtesy of Dan Nelson, Doner Advertising)

Repulsiveness

This third stylistic prohibition addresses the issue of offensive or unpleasant words and pictures. Particularly on a broadcast or broadband entertainment medium, people will be patently unwilling to expose themselves voluntarily to extended periods of agony. Gone is that poor suffering mortal with the hammers pounding and the lightning flashing through his skull. Gone, too, are the people bent over with the torment of constipation and unrelentingly assailed by the torture of skin itch. Spots that dwell on such images can appeal only to masochists—and there aren't enough of them to bolster many sales curves. If you must depict a discomforting image in your commercial, don't wait too long before introducing relief. And in order to avoid violating our first stylistic prohibition, that relief had better be a *relevant* result of using our product. As *Modern Maturity* magazine's advertising standards appropriately suggest, "Instead of a message that says, 'I feel terrible, give me product X,' we welcome ads that say, 'I feel great with product X.'"[65]

Public service announcements may be tempted to ignore this prohibition more than do their commercial counterparts. How many PSAs expend virtually their entire time in showing us starving orphans or ravaged wildlife? Certainly these are vital concerns. But the message that illuminates nothing but the grotesque effects of this or that calamity will cause listener/viewer tune-out before folks learn how they can help. It does the starving orphans or endangered species little good if the people who could have lessened their plight were driven away prematurely.

Don't remain repulsive. If you must use a disagreeable image, get through it as soon as possible to make way for the relief. And make certain such relief is a tangible and logical outgrowth of the product or service for which you have drawn the assignment. The Figure 6.7 television PSA adheres fully to this principle. Frame 2 starkly illustrates a child abuse setting—without exploitatively placing a child in it. The spot then cuts to a series of graphics that present not just relief—but strategies for prevention of this grotesque torture.

Superlatives

Inexperienced copywriters tend to try too hard; they tend to oversell the product or service to such a degree that the listener or viewer may conclude it is just too good to be true. If the product, service, or program sounds so unbelievably divine that we expect the Three Wise Men to come over the hill, the copy needs total rethinking. Superlatives (words of overpraise) will not be credible to an audience that is bombarded daily by hundreds of spots and promotion pieces. Our jaded consumer is well aware that heaven is not "just around the corner from where you live" or "yours by mail for only twelve ninety-eight." Copy that attempts to say different is begging to be scorned. Imagine how you would react to the following pitch:

ANNCR: Spectacular! Stupendous! Those are just some of the words used to describe Gramma Hubbard's Hominy Bread. Gramma Hubbard's Hominy is the best thing ever to come out of an American oven. Its texture is unsurpassed. Its taste is incredibly delicious. And Gramma Hubbard's Hominy Bread makes the most tremendous toast your taste buds have ever experienced. Try a loaf of this fantastic bread breakthrough. Witness the marvel of real milled hominy. Gramma Hubbard's Hominy Bread.

"STOVE" :30 CNCA-2330

(SFX: WATER BUBBLING)
ANNCR: To you, this is a place to make macaroni and cheese.

To someone else, it's a way to make a kid sorry for what he did.

Preventing child abuse and neglect doesn't just mean reporting it.

It means stopping it before it starts.

Find out how at preventchildabuse.org or 1-800-children.

A child is helpless. You are not.

Volunteer Advertising Agency: Lowe   402

FIGURE 6.7   *(Courtesy of The Ad Council)*

A copywriter compounds the superlative sin when the highly questionable claim is also of questionable taste. The Connecticut state lottery's Powerball game was promoted in an ad that promised, "You could get even luckier than you did on prom night." Public outcry forced the message to be quickly pulled by a state official who admitted he hadn't read the copy before approving it.

Even if your product is as good as you claim (and its claimed 'goodness' is not in poor taste), depicting that meritorious quality too enthusiastically may still be counterproductive. Decades ago, a spot for Dupont's Xerex antifreeze showed a hole being punched into a can of the stuff and the product package then resealing itself. The claim seemed so incredible that many viewers thought it was phoney. So did the Federal Trade Commission. It required Dupont to substantiate the claim that Xerex would work in a similar way to seal small holes in a car's cooling system. Dupont did substantiate it, and the FTC backed off. But some viewers still could not believe a coolant could perform so amazingly well.

As one advertising executive on an aspirin account observes, "When you have a superior product claim, it's difficult creatively because we're all used to parity in this business. Everybody is already out there trying to position their product as a superior one, and it's an even more difficult assignment to do that right when the claim is true. . . . And every time you have a real superiority, you face the risk of unbelievability."[66] Moral: sometimes even a truly spectacular product requires more humility than it deserves.

Don't canonize your product or service. Don't make a saint out of every account to which you're assigned. Superlatives cause mistrust to mushroom and may prevent the audience from accepting suggestions that would otherwise have been truly beneficial for them. And whatever you do, avoid the words *guarantee* or *offer* unless your client really intends to extend a guarantee or an offer. "Such wording," Professor George Stevens points out, "has been used to support findings for plaintiffs"[67] that an oral contract thereby had been made.

A CDVP REASSURANCE

If it seems as though everyone—government, industry, client, and consumer—is looking over your shoulder, you have acquired a healthfully paranoid view of copywriting today. By its very nature, the electronic media's power and potency attract the close scrutiny of a wide variety of groups with both legitimate and self-serving axes to grind. Creative Director Tom Darbyshire recalls a few examples from his own experience:

> We recently created a radio spot with a gag suggesting that listening to three days of accordion music might be tiresome. Our client promptly received a complaint from the Accordion Players Association.
>
> We did a TV spot featuring a live chicken sporting a large pair of human ears. . . . A distraught woman phoned to tell us it was undoing her years in therapy for bird-phobia.
>
> We did a TV spot set at the Pearly Gates to make the point that our fast-food client served heavenly fare while flame-broiling was something done at the "other place." We got diatribes from zealots who wanted us to know that "hell is a place of eternal torment and no laughing matter."[68]

It is not easy to fend off the extremists, anticipate and compensate for legitimate questions of taste and sensitivity, while still fashioning a message that attracts positive notice in today's cluttered media world. As SS+K partner Marty Cooke laments, "On one hand you have marketers pushing to be outrageous, and on the other you have the tyranny of political correctness that is coming from the boardroom."[69] But things will usually work out if you keep your focus on the core needs of your client and core preferences of your primary universe. Conversely, warns Darbyshire, "If you write with the hypersensitive fringe in mind, they become your *de facto* target audience. The result is advertising so bland it gets no reaction of any sort from your real target."[70]

Try to see the humor in even a pressure-cooker situation. For along with the four "CDVP Factors," a sense of humor must also accompany copywriters as part of the toolbox they bring to each new assignment. Recognizing the incongruity, if not the downright ludicrousness, of some work situations will do a lot to keep your blood pressure down and your enthusiasm up. The resilient ability to find humor in all things—even in occasional failure—is what preserves a copywriter's vitality. It is exactly in this spirit that creative director John Lyons counsels, "Don't worry about rejection. There isn't a profession anywhere that pays you more for revising your own stupidity."[71]

Granted, the "establishing of new and meaningful relationships" that make sense to regulators as well as to target audiences may not be an easy task—and often is simply not feasible. But even if it doesn't meet our criteria for true CREATIVITY, copy that is properly DEFINED and VALIDATED and respects the PROHIBITIONS we've just outlined is well positioned for success.

Forty years ago, radio commentator Earl Nightingale put the whole struggle in reassuring perspective when he reminded his contemporaries that

> Most products advertised and sold in this country are good products. A lot of hard work, research and brains have gone into them, and there's a market for them. So all we have to do is tell the truth about them, in a straightforward, interesting and even creative way. There's an interesting story lurking in every product or service. It is the job of the advertising people, and especially the copywriter, to ferret it out and present it in an interesting and believable way to the consumer.[72]

In undertaking the "ferreting" of which Nightingale spoke, the copywriter's main governor is not some external regulator, but a sense of professional *responsibility.* As described by advertising veteran Whit Hobbs, this means that

> When I sit down to write, I feel a strong sense of responsibility to a lot of people—to my client, to my associates, to my customer/reader/viewer. This is what creative people in advertising are *supposed* to feel, and I wish all of them did. . . . I keep seeing advertising that seems to be designed by creative people in agencies primarily to impress *other* creative people in other agencies—inside jokes that leave the customers out there relatively unmoved. It is very nice to win praise from one's peers, but it's far more important to win *customers.*[73]

The *responsible* winning of customers is the ultimate COPYWRITING DIMENSION, the central and candid goal that motivates everything we write. In the next three chapters, we turn our attention to how this goal can be achieved in the audio world.

7

Key Elements of Audio Writing

For years, many people thought radio to be a second-class medium, a kind of "television with the picture tube burned out," as master radio humorist Stan Freberg once protested. Copywriters saw the building of their "TV reel" as the way to fame and glory and looked on radio assignments as hardship duty. So they (along with a number of national sponsors) abandoned the medium in droves, leaving it to the tender mercies of cookie-cutter hacks. As former N. W. Ayer chairman Jerry Siano recalls,

> When television came along people started watching that. Radio didn't change. But our perception of it did. We forgot a quarter of a century of people watching their radio sets. And this might be what led to the development of the "secret" to bad radio advertising . . . . Just stuffing the commercial full of twaddle, wall-to-wall words, endlines and some cheap music is the sure-fire formula for ineffective radio advertising.[1]

Happily, things have changed; partly, it is true, as a result of television rate-card increases that have priced many advertisers out of that medium. But the rehabilitation of radio is also due, argued then-president of the Radio Advertising Bureau, Bill Stakelin, to the renewed realization that "Radio *is* visual. It is one of the most visual if not the most visual medium in existence today. Where else can you see 5,000 albino rhinos stampeding down Pennsylvania Avenue? Only on the radio. Radio is visual, and as you plan for it, as you create for it, as you write for it, think of it visually."[2] Award-winning radio copywriter Bert Berdis adds, "Radio is a low budget ticket to places you could never afford to take a TV crew. Think about it; a few screeching birds—you're in a jungle. Want to go back in history? Forward in time? We can take you there."[3]

This visual imagery via sounds alone is not, however, easy for a writer to capture. Everything you want to say and show must be conveyed through words, sound effects, music, and the ultimate punctuator—silence. There is no camera lens to convey automatically what the product looks like and how it works; the audio copywriter must explain these things through sound-only sensations. "There is no place to hide in radio," observes creative director Tom Monahan. "Weak copy can't hide behind great design . . . . In radio there's simply no place to hide anything. No place for the mistakes, the poor judgment, the weaknesses. Everything is right out there in front for all thirty or sixty seconds. Everything must be good for the spot to be good. The concept, copy, casting, acting, production—everything. One of them goes wrong and sorry, but tune-out time."[4] For the audio wordsmith, "there are few crutches," concludes copywriter Steve Dildarian. "There's a lot more demand on the writing. It's a harder discipline."[5]

This and the next two chapters are designed to assist you to master this discipline. Along the way, you will discover the audio medium to manifest a respect for language like that print accords—but a respect that must be rationed into segments of a minute or less. Also unlike print, the radio message cannot be "re-read" by our audience. Nor can they slow down the speed with which they consume it. An audio spot exists in real time, at one predetermined velocity, and then disappears until the next occasion it airs or the consumer again stumbles across it on the Web. If the listener doesn't comprehend it the first time, there may not be another chance.

Yet, despite all these drawbacks, the audio communication can become more integral to our consumer's life than messages on any other medium. This is because the appropriate sound cues from us force the perceivers to recall specifics from their own past experiences in order to complete the picture. "Unlike TV, which is at the mercy of the size of the screen," points out Stan Freberg, "the monitor of our head is limitless."[6] As award-winning copywriter Jay Williams puts it, "The thing that's nice about radio is that you can get the audience to fill in the blanks. The best radio ads tend to be interactive that way."[7]

The visually compelling audio message thus becomes a part of the listener, and the listener becomes a part of the spot. Tom O'Keefe of Foote, Cone & Belding deftly exploits radio's participatory eye-filling attribute in this colorful commercial:

MAN: We spent the day in blue waters off the Gulf near Turquoise Bay. My neon-orange wet-suited buddies and I --- fifty feet down in an aqua world of Yellowtails and Green Moray eels until a Great White chased us --- yellow-bellied --- back to our boat, <u>Blackbeard's Revenge</u>. There, on deck, we seized a golden opportunity and asked for the Red. 'Killian's Red,' said the leather-skinned cook, named Tanner, who pointed to a cedar sea chest full of sand-frosted white amber bottles. Grabbing one, I quickly popped its orange-rimmed, horse-of-a-different-color-labeled top off, poured the crisp, scarlet lager into a tall ivory stein and then tasted the smooth flowing difference of Red. And there, on <u>Blackbeard's Revenge</u>, we slowly sailed on blue waters back to the shore near Turquoise Bay drinking our cold Killian's while the leather-skinned cook prepared the Red Snapper.

ANNCR: Killian's Red. Ask for it by color. Coors Brewing Company, Golden, Colorado.[8]

When you pen an audio spot, says copywriter Kevin O'Donoghue, "You are the one creating the mood, the environment, and you are reaching the person one-on-one in ways no other medium can."[9] Copywriters who feel abused because they have been dealt a radio rather than a television or online assignment would do well to recall master communicator Garrison Keillor's observation that "the spoken word, not pictures, is the doorway to memory . . . . If I tell stories on radio, I will run into people months and years later who can repeat back to me what I said, word for word."[10] The reason for this message persistence is rooted in radio's heritage. "We proudly trace our lineage clear back to the primitive campfire, the tribal storyteller," points out legendary radio dramatist Himan Brown. "As those passers-on of tribal legend, of heroic adventure, of the mysteries of nature told their stories by word of mouth, so do we! We do not show you—we tell you! We leave the trappings to your imagination."[11]

STANDARD AUDIO FORMAT

In order to properly prepare that memorable audio concept for distribution, we must construct a clear script blueprint. As we mention in Chapter 2, even the most innovative message must first be set down in standard script format.

The body of the copy, the script's working section, is our focus here. It is in the body that we must indicate our precise structuring and manipulation of any or all of the parts of audio's sound element quartet: words, music, sound effects, and silence. The commercial in Figure 7.1 has been constructed not as a "hall of fame" spot but to demonstrate a useful and cogent pattern for script organization. It features all of the key ingredients that might need to be scripted. Reference numbers have been added to facilitate dissection. **(As with all of our scripts in this book, what is *single*-spaced here would be *double*-spaced on actual copysheets, and what is *double*-spaced here would be *triple*-spaced.)**

As[1] shows, an indented production note may precede the actual copy and is used to give a general casting or stage direction that will pertain throughout the script. This keeps clutter within the copy to a minimum and segregates continuing script elements from those relevant only to limited passages.

Specific talent movement and stage directions, such as the one marked by [2], exist in parentheses, with the first letter capitalized. These directions are placed in the copy at exactly the point when they're to become operative.

Sound effects are likewise in parentheses and, unlike stage directions, are entirely in CAPS. They may or may not be preceded by the designator SFX. When they occur between character speeches but within the same scene, sound effect directions are indented at least three spaces more than are lines of dialogue. The [3] marks such a situation. When sound effects occur within a speech they, like stage directions, are placed at the actual point of occurrence, as [4] demonstrates. Sound effects' FULL CAPS format is the prime means by which actors can distinguish such technician-activated devices from the lower-case stage directions for which these actors themselves are responsible. Finally, when sound effects comprise the bridge between scenes or are the prime means of initial scene establishment, their cue begins at the far left margin, as [5] points out.

Music cues are also in parentheses and are also in CAPS. They are further distinguished from sound effects by being fully underlined but may or may not begin with the term MUSIC. As reference numbers [6], [7], and [8] illustrate, the location of music cues within speeches, between speeches, and as scene-bridging devices, respectively, follows the same rules as do sound effects serving similar functions.

[1]Production Note: All talent should convey lines like actors in an early 1930s movie.

ANNCR: Motion sickness; that queasy feeling. And it's hard to imagine a better place for it than this choppy cruise. Doesn't seem to bother that guy out on deck though. [2](Fading off) Let's try to find out why---

[3](FADE IN: CREAKING TIMBERS, SPLASHING WAVES)

BILL: (Fading on) What? No, I'm no sailor. I'm Bill the Bookie from Davenport. [4](TIMBERS/WAVES OUT) Motion sick? Not me. Not since that day (Fading off) back at George's Drug Store---

[5](STORE SOUNDS UP QUICKLY AND GRADUALLY OUT)

GEORGE: Hey, Bill. [6](MUSIC: OFF-KEY WHISTLING OF 'CAMPTOWN RACES' FIRST FOUR BARS) Know this tune?

BILL: Give it some hay, George. Oh, that bumpy flight from Vegas. Like riding a swayback steer.

[7](TWO MORE WHISTLED BARS OF 'CAMPTOWN RACES')

GEORGE: Then saddle up to this. It's Owen's Elixir.

BILL: Owen's what?

GEORGE: Owen's Elixir. Makes you feel like it's post time.

[8](TRADITIONAL 'AT THE POST' TRUMPET CALL)

[9](CROSSFADE TO SHIP SOUNDS UP AND UNDER)

BILL: From then on, it was Owen's for me. You can bet your calm stomach on it. It's Owen's Elixir to win, every time.

FIGURE 7.1   Audio Copy Format Template.

When separate music and sound effect cues assist each other to shift the scene, both directions are normally placed at the left margin with a separate line for each, as [8] and [9] designate.

The spacing of each subsequent line of copy is also important in providing both talent and audio engineer with the clearest possible blueprint of what the copywriter has in mind. As mentioned earlier, this book compresses format and script examples to single and double spacing in order to save pages. However, it is important to reemphasize that typical professional practice in a production script is to **DOUBLE SPACE WITHIN SPEECHES and TRIPLE SPACE BETWEEN THEM.** In addition, never break a line over a page turn, as this causes awkwardness for the talent in attempting a smooth reading of your message.

Triple-spacing is further utilized between a speech and a sound effect or music cue that completely separates that speech from another character's line to follow (see [3] and [7]). Triple-spacing also precedes and follows music and/or sound-effect bridges between separate scenes (such as [5] and [8-9]). All of this helps to create white space and, as radio copy expert Jeff Hedquest reminds us, "White space is essential . . . Give your voice talent room to make notes, draw arrows, underline, doodle, write in copy changes—anything that will give them a clear road map through the script. Why should a voice actor struggle, even a little, with your copy? Make it easy for them so you both can concentrate on making the delivery natural, compelling and interesting."[12]

A commercial announcement or piece of continuity will seldom be extensive enough to require the use of even half the specialized cues called for in Figure 7.1's Elixir script. In fact, such a cluttered productional orgy would be a technical and cognitive nightmare. The Owen's Elixir presentation does, however, demonstrate a standardized plan for message typography, a plan that promotes consistent script layout and ungarbled communication with the skilled voices and technicians who must mold your copy into sound-propelled images.

In reaching that communication goal, here is one last format fundamental: Copy should always be written using both upper and lower case. Some writers persist in setting their message in ALL CAPS because they think this is easier for talent to read. In fact, many perceptual studies have found exactly the opposite to be the case.

AUDIO PRODUCTIONAL TERMINOLOGY

The copywriter's adaptability to audio's technical requirements is more than a matter of proper format. It also encompasses an understanding of those basic terms that, for the writer, translate into sound capabilities. For our purposes, we separate terminology into three categories: (1) talent instructions, (2) control booth instructions, and (3) other writer-used technical terms. It is not our intent here to cover all of audio production's specialized vocabulary. Instead, we call attention only to words you are most likely to need in preparing the actual script.

Talent Instructions

This category can be thought of as traffic- or stage-directing devices, several of which are included in the above Owen's Elixir commercial. In essence, they tell talent where they should be in relationship to the microphone—and whether they should stay there. Because talent are expected to be *on mic* unless told otherwise, this instruction requires writing out only when needed to indicate the desired completion point of a long move toward the microphone. Walking toward the microphone is called *fading on*, as Bill's portrayer does in his first Elixir spot speech. The reverse effect is called, not surprisingly, *fading off*. The Elixir announcer does this to give the impression that he is walking away from the listener and out on deck to Bill. Bill does the same thing at the end of his first speech to suggest the feeling of a gradual flashback in time. If we instead want the talent to stay "in the distance" for any significant portion of their dialogue, we use the term *off mic* at the beginning of the first line to be delivered in that mode.

Moving talent in and out creates a much more realistic sound picture than the mere adjusting of volume in the control room. When someone walks away from us in real life, for example, our ears do not suddenly pick up less sound from our total environment. Instead, quieter but closer sounds grow more prominent as the receding person's voice grows less distinct in the distance. The total sense of presence is what radio seeks, and we therefore move people accordingly. As a slightly more sophisticated application of this principle, we sometimes use the terms *behind barrier* or *thru soundscreen* when we want the effect of someone talking behind a closed door, from the depths of a cellar, or locked in a trunk, to name just a few possibilities. A special acoustical panel is placed between the talent and the microphone to suggest this condition. When the fictional door is opened or the trunk is unlocked, the talent can simply move quickly around the barrier to be instantaneously *on mic*. Alternatively, if our aural scene depicts a climb from a deep hole or pictures a door that is supposed to be some distance from the listener's central vantage point, the talent can be instructed to *fade on* (either *quickly* or *slowly*) *from behind barrier*.

Control Booth Instructions

As mentioned above, volume is the most obvious productional function to be manipulated by the control booth engineer. Sound effects and music are commanded to FADE IN or FADE OUT when respectively introduced and removed from the scene. Sound effects and music that are *already present* in the scene may be requested to FADE UP or FADE DOWN in order to enlarge or diminish their part in that total sound picture. We can also use refinements to these general directions, such as ESTABLISH, SNEAK IN/SNEAK OUT, FEATURE/FEATURE BRIEFLY, or construct hybrids, such as FADE UP AND OUT, FADE DOWN AND UNDER, FADE UP AND UNDER, and FADE DOWN AND OUT. As the conclusion to the Elixir spot in Figure 7.1 demonstrates, we can, in addition, CROSSFADE one music or sound effect cue to another by overlapping the receding element with the sound source just taking the stage. Especially when both elements are musical in nature, the CROSSFADE is also known as a SEGUE.

You may occasionally need certain more rarefied control booth instructions, too. The FILTER MIC effect historically was accomplished by having the talent talk into a tin can --- but is now often accommodated through a more sophisticated microphone or control room modification of the input line that carries the talent's voice. A FILTER MIC mechanism is used to give the effect of a voice coming over a telephone, through a public address system, or to denote unspoken thoughts and musings in a character's mind. As these musings get more and more unreal or frenzied, we may also want to bring REVERB—electromechanical echo—to the sound source. Varying amounts of REVERB are also effective in denoting such specialized locations as an empty warehouse, the Grand Canyon floor, or the inside of your refrigerator. (In a precise engineering sense, "echo" is *delayed* sound whereas "reverb" is *deflected* sound that is then "bounced back" to the listener's ear.)

In distinguishing control booth instructions from talent instructions, remember that people fade *on* and *off*, whereas control booth–originated sounds fade *IN* and *OUT,* and *UP* and *DOWN.* In addition, as the Elixir commercial shows, stage ("talent") directions are not in full caps. Control booth directions and music and sound effects cues, on the other hand, are entirely set IN CAPS, even in those rare instances when sound is created "live" in the studio rather than in the control booth.

Other Writer-Used Technical Terms

The following miscellany is comprised of additional productional designations commonly understood in the audio industry. These terms might find their way into, or border, the actual body of our script.

ACTUALITY: *production that seems to be originating live from some scene external to the studio.*

AD LIB: *impromptu dialogue not written out in the script. We might, for example, ask background "crowd" to ad-lib reactions to what is being said or portrayed by the characters on mic.*

AMBIENT SOUNDS: *sounds that are a normal and expected part of the scene/environment being presented (train station, jungle, cocktail lounge, etc.).*

ANNCR: *the standard abbreviation for "announcer."*

AS RECORDED: *final script that reflects all changes made in copy when it was actually produced.*

BACK TIMING: *timing a spot from the end in order to allow for insertion of music or dialogue occurring earlier.*

BG: *abbreviation for "background"; normally referring to sound that will not be at full volume.*

BRIDGE: *aural transition (usually via music or sound effects) between two separate scenes or vignettes.*

BUTTON: *a brief musical signature, often at the end of a commercial.*

CONTINUITY BOOK: *loose-leaf collection of spots and promos in the order they are to be read or played over the air; also called copy book.*

CUT: *a particular band on a disc recording from which a specific music bed or sound effect is retrieved.*

DEAD AIR: *period of time when no discernible sound is being transmitted.*

DRY: *a recording made without the introduction of any echo or reverberation.*

FLIGHT: *a series of announcements for the same product or service that are usually done in the same style and format as part of a single campaign.*

GAIN: *the radio sound term for "volume."*

KILL DATE: *last day on which a particular piece of copy is authorized to be aired.*

LIVE TAG: *a line at the end of a recorded message that is added by a local announcer to help adapt the copy to local/seasonal programming, personalities, and conditions.*

LOGO: *the visual or auditory/musical corporate symbol used by a station or client to identify itself.*

MASTER: *the "original" recording of a disc or taped message from which duplicates can be dubbed.*

MIX: *two or more separate signals brought into a desired collective balance.*

MONOTONE: *a line to be vocalized without any expression.*

MUSIC BED: *piece of music over which a spot is written to create the geographic or mood environment in which the action takes place.*

OUT CUE: *last word of a message and the signal for the next message/program to begin.*

OUT TAKE: *recorded segment not used in creating the final production.*

PAD: *material added at the end of a message to bring it to the exact time specified; also referred to as* fill.

SFX: *the standard abbreviation for "sound effects."*

SITTING MIC: *a microphone placed on a table rather than mounted on a floor-length stand* (stand mic) *or from an overhead boom* (boom mic).

SOTTO VOCE: *stage whisper; often used to comment on an off-mic event without disturbing it.*

SOUNDER: *short musical/copy identification of a particular programmatic element.*

STAB: *musical or sound exclamation used at the beginning of or within a spot.*

STING: *a stab used at the end of a spot.*

STOP SET: *series of copy messages read between songs on a music-formatted radio station; a string of commercials within a stop set is sometimes referred to as a POD.*

SWEETEN: *adding some acoustical element or process to a segment to make it sound richer or fuller.*

SYNTHESIZER: *audio signal processor that can manipulate conventional sounds (including music) or create entirely new sounds.*

TAG: *line at the end of the spot added by a voice outside the spot's main action.*

TIMBRE: *the tonal makeup and quality of any sound that is the sum of its frequencies and overtones.*

VOICE OVER (VO): *an announcer reading over a music segment.*

WET: *a recording to which reverberation or echo has been added.*

USING SOUND EFFECTS

Today, few effects need to be "custom made" during the production of the audio message. Readily available sound effects libraries like those provided by the Groove Addicts, FirstCom, or Sound Ideas companies contain virtually every effect piece a copywriter might need to specify. But whether an SFX is "canned" or custom produced, the vital thing to keep in mind is that it should be used to further the message rather than as an end in itself. The spot or PSA that becomes "that pitch with the jackhammer" instead of "that pitch *for*" whoever the client might be is a waste of everybody's effort (unless you really are selling jackhammers).

In his study *The Grammar of Radio Advertising*, British audio authority Chris Wilson observes that sound effects have two kinds of expressive capabilities: denotative and connotative.

DENOTATIVE: *furnishing the unseen environment with identifiable sounds, such as phones, crowds, traffic, and cash-tills, to provide acoustic images that enable listeners to imagine or identify location.*

CONNOTATIVE: *offering wider cultural associations. The throaty exhaust of a sports car, for example, implies affluence. The loud closing of doors suggests a decisive moment or imprisonment or the end of a phrase.*

Whether used denotatively, connotatively, or even to give substance to something that is silent in real life (such as a zipper noise to signify a tangerine's unpeeling), a sound effect must appropriately serve four functions:

1. Promote the progression of the selling tale
2. Enhance the main copy point
3. Integrate well with the copy's style and form
4. Accomplish these tasks without creating aural clutter

Sound effects should not be used in an attempt to slavishly duplicate reality. The only result will be a muddled jumble of noise. Instead, the writer should select, as the human ear selects, the most prominent or more relevant sounds in a given situation, use these with discretion, and forget about the rest. "Don't go sound effects crazy," advises the Radio Ranch's Dick Orkin. "The truth is a sound effect (real-sounding, novel or funny) will not save a bad spot . . . . When sound effects are used properly, they are organic to the situation and are there to clarify location, move a story forward or to explain action. Not every moment or action needs a sound effect."[13] In the spot below, the phone SFX is both "organic to the situation" and "moves the story forward" because it represents the escalating frustration of dealing with some other HMOs.

(SFX: PHONE RINGING)

OPERATOR: Presto HMO. If you'd like a membership card, please punch in your age.

       (SFX: TWO PUNCHES)

OPERATOR: Please punch in your age in dog years.

       (SFX: TWO PUNCHES)

OPERATOR: Please punch in the last year Toronto won the Stanley Cup.

       (SFX: FOUR PUNCHES)

OPERATOR: By how many goals in the final game?

       (SFX: ONE PUNCH)

OPERATOR: Lucky? Please punch in tonight's six winning lottery numbers.

ANNCR: Does your health plan make getting a membership card more difficult than it has to be? At TakeCare Health Plan, even the littlest things get the attention they deserve. Which is why we'll answer most calls on our toll-free number in ten seconds. That kind of service has made us one of the largest, most trusted health plans in California. So, if you're part of an employer group of ten or more, call TakeCare at 1-800-635-CARE. That's 1-800-635-CARE. We'll give you the service you deserve, no question about it.

OPERATOR: If you still want a membership card, please punch in Beethoven's Fifth.

       (SFX: PUNCHES OF FAMILIAR OPENING FOUR NOTES
OF SYMPHONY --- DA DA DA DUMMMMMM)

OPERATOR: Now in D minor.

(SFX: PHONE SLAMS DOWN IN HANG UP)

ANNCR: TakeCare. The cure for the common health plan.[14]

Sometimes, sound effects are most effective when contrasted with a much quieter or nearly silent condition. In a classic commercial, Farrell Lines, a large shipping firm, once used this principle to undercut some executives' stereotypes about Australia by dramatizing the vitality of its business climate. Against a cacophony of bustling, industrial SFX, the voice-over copy pointed out that

Australia is so booming that you can't hear the sheep being sheared. You can't hear tennis balls pinging off rackets. You can't hear koala bears eating leaves off eucalyptus trees. Listen to the sounds of booming Australia.[15]

One caution: sound effects should never be expected to accomplish identifications beyond their intrinsically recognizable aural capabilities. Examples like the following are impossible to portray adequately without the assistance of spoken copy.

(SFX: WATER BEING POURED INTO CAR RADIATOR)

How does listener know the receptacle is a *radiator*? How does the listener know it's *water* and not some other liquid?

(SFX: HORSE CHOMPING ON APPLE)

How does listener know it's a *horse,* not a slovenly human? How does listener know it's an *apple*?

(SFX: 10-YEAR-OLD GIRL GOING UP STAIRS)

How does listener know she's *10*? How does listener know she's a "she"? How does listener know she's going *up* and not *down* stairs—or on stairs at all? Conversely, when properly deployed and identified, sound effects can play a significant communicative role and a role that goes beyond their short-term aural resonance. As researchers Robert Potter, Annie Lang, and Paul Bolls discovered, the addition of sound effects "appear to increase attention and memory" on behalf of the message in which they appear.[16] That is no small contribution to the ultimate success of our spot. And if you still think a sound effect doesn't matter that much, the auto industry has something to teach you. As marketing executive Martin Lindstrom found in a brand-sense study, "44% of all consumers stated that the sound of a new car is more important than the design. This includes the door. It's serious business. So serious that Mercedes-Benz has 12 engineers dedicated to the sound of opening and closing doors! Does it work? Check out the competing Acura TSX and you'll notice the perfect sound of an opening and closing door . . . No wonder—the sound is artificially generated and even the vibrations in the door generated by electric impulses."[17]

USING MUSIC

Like sound effects, music is readily available to the commercial and continuity writer in conveniently prepackaged form from a wide variety of sources, such as Stephen Arnold Music, Network Production Music, Omnimusic, and Manhattan Production Music. This availability is especially helpful to the writer working at a station, cable system, or Website. If your outlet has purchased the library or service from any of these or several other firms, all relevant copyright fees have already been paid, and the often formidable task of obtaining copyright clearances is thereby avoided. Although this text is not a casebook on copyright law, it must be emphasized that music virtually never comes "free." Mechanical/ recording, synchronization, performance, and grand dramatic rights may all be involved in your using even a brief musical cut, and these rights may often be held by several different firms or individuals. The fact that a station has ASCAP, BMI, and SESAC performance rights licenses does *not* give automatic prerogative to turn popular compositions licensed by them into background music for continuity. In fact, such unauthorized appropriation usually constitutes overt copyright infringement.

Especially if you're a freelancer, or an outlet writer directly involved in the production of your message, make certain the music you've selected has been properly cleared—and for more than just performance rights. Advertising agencies and other larger organizations will normally have specific employees who assist with these clearance concerns.

Wherever the music comes from, take special care that it is of professional quality in styling and sound reproduction. As more and more sources of production music come on the scene, there is a natural tendency on the part of some companies to underprice the competition by offering an underproduced product. If the music bed sounds like it emanated from the group shown in Figure 7.2, don't use it to accompany your copy. Bargain-basement music is a cellar, not a stellar commodity. If it is cheap, it will sound cheap—and so will your client.

As the third of radio's quartet of potential sound elements, music has unsurpassed utility in quickly and comprehensively constructing an environment for the message it complements. William Stakelin, former president of the Radio Advertising Bureau, observes that "music is the most natural way to stimulate thought and action . . . . Music sets up our expectations—brings a pastoral scene into focus, swells up feelings of love or affection, hints at troubles to come, establishes movement and, using a basic sound motif, heralds an important idea or event. Music plays to the moods and desires of customers. The right music, in the right format, on the right stations establishes an unspoken bond with your target audience."[18] In addition, G.J. Gorn discovered in his experiments that when a spot's music bed engenders a positive emotion in the listener, it can produce a carryover effect in which the listener is conditioned to have a positive attitude toward the

FIGURE 7.2 Have you ever wondered where some production music is recorded?

(Courtesy of Michael Anderson, Network Production Music, Inc.)

product promoted in that spot.[19] Music possesses this potential power, says Leo Burnett group creative director Greg Taubeneck, because it "is a below-the-radar element in advertising. You can't quantify it or be logical about how it works. It becomes the personality of the brand."[20]

Selecting the music that is appropriate to the brand and the message is not a simple task, however. The copy style, the product or service category, the situation being conveyed in the spot, and the outlet(s) on which the spot will be run must all be considered in music specification. Because, for the audio copywriter,

M U S I C
e s e o
a i n n
n n t t
s g i e
    m x
    e t
    n
    t
    s

Intrinsically, music *does* mean using sentiments in context. Even a very short musical passage can simulate and stimulate a wide variety of feelings. "Music can be more powerful than words and pictures," argues commercial music producer Martain Pazzani, "and it can achieve deep levels of communication and connection that words and pictures cannot. Music is also a powerful mnemonic device. And music can be endlessly refreshed with different arrangements, styles and tempos, and it crosses cultures, borders and language barriers."[21] Your job as a copywriter is to make certain that the passage and arrangement you have chosen will call up sentiments appropriate to your selling context. Notice how, in the spot below, a single musical effect harmonizes with the spot's premise that personal, local attention from a bank must be more than just 'lip service':

Production Note: Male has put-on folksy down-home voice

MALE: Howdy there, I'm a folksy announcer type. Big banks hire me to make them sound all local and friendly. And how do I do it? I just drop the letter 'g' from fancy bankin' words. Like investin', checkin', savin's. Take off the 'g' and it's right neighborly. I can even pretend I'm strummin' a little guitar.

(MUSIC: ACOUSTIC DOWN HOME GUITAR, FEATURE AND UNDER)

MALE: So even though the bank I'm talkin' 'bout --- see that, I dropped the 'g' and the 'a' --- is headquartered in New York, you know their heart is right here, in whatever city this ad's runnin' in. (MUSIC OUT) Now that's what I call a friendly, local bank.

ANNCR: HomeStreet Bank has been family and employee-owned right here in the Pacific Northwest since 1921. We've been here so long, we don't have to tell people we're local. We let our friendly, personal attention speak for itself.

MALE: I'd say speakin' if I was you.

ANNCR: HomeStreet Bank. Great neighbors. Great bankers. Member FDIC. Visit HomeStreet.com.

(Courtesy of Patti Emery, Copacino + Fujikado)

If, on the other hand, your music implies one thing and your copy says something else, it will probably be the music's point of view that predominates in both the listener's short- and long-term recollection. Never start off with a musical "bed" just because you like it and then try to construct a message around it. You may end up with a nice commercial for the tune but only at crippling expense to your central copy point.

How do you select the most appropriate music—particularly if you are not a trained musician yourself? Leading commercial composer Elizabeth Myers offers this advice: "Can you put into words what you would like the music to do? If not, you are already in trouble. It doesn't have to be more than two words—adjectives like *mysterious* or *heroic* are much more useful to composers than words like *quirky* or *simple*." When you get a selection to consider, she adds, "If you can turn your head and simply listen to the music track alone and get those feelings, then the music is right."[22]

Keep in mind that you are not selling the tune but the product. "Music is not the whole campaign," states Leo Burnett music director Ira Antelis. "It's got to fit what they're trying to say. What kind of audience are you talking to? If you're doing Coors Light, you're not going to do big-band music."[23] This doesn't mean you are always restricted to the most obvious choice. At first glance, a classical Chopin piece would not at all seem in keeping with a bowling alley spot aimed at the 18- to 34-year-old demographic. However, in the following spot, this unexpected pairing sets up a comedic irony that supports the client's attempt to position itself as a fun place for young people rather than a senior citizen hang-out.

(MUSIC: ROMANTIC CHOPINESQUE PIANO UNDER)

WOMAN: David had everything I ever dreamed of --- cute, good-looking, and handsome. He had it all. He used to say the sweetest things.

DAVID: God, you look great with me!

WOMAN: If we'd fight, I couldn't stay mad at him, because he'd call me and say---

DAVID: Don't hate me because I'm beautiful.

WOMAN: I couldn't help but love him. Okay, so he could have been a littler brighter. A little wittier. Employed. But we didn't need money. Besides, David could always find someone to lend him a-dollar-ninety-nine. He'd take the two bucks, borrow his mom's car, and we'd both go to Fairlane's Bowling Center. David loves Fairlane's automatic scoring because, well, he couldn't. So we'd go to Fairlane's anytime, all the time, seven times a week for just a- dollar-ninety-nine a game. That's where I met Larry. I was showing David how to make bunny ears with his shoelaces when---

LARRY: (Sexy, movie-heart-throb voice) Can I help?

WOMAN: He was a vision. Spoke in complete sentences. I'd forgotten stuff, you know, like conversations. I haven't seen David since. Now I only date guys like Larry. And we go to Fairlane's; they tie their own shoes.

(Courtesy of Craig Wiese, Craig Wiese and Company)

Whatever you choose, think of music in your message as set designer rather than lead actor. Thus, asserts creative director Tom Monahan, "I happen to think the best music in broadcast is music you don't hear. Not unless you listen for it. It's like great music in a film. It adds texture, but if it owns the scene, it's usually gone too far; if the music leads, it usually means the conceptual or verbal message doesn't."[24]

On the other hand, don't be afraid *not* to include music in your spot. In fact, if surrounding or competing commercials tend to make heavy use of music, a solid piece of straight copy will project very well by comparison. This is especially true when your client's main rivals have all awkwardly tripped down Melody Lane and you want your campaign to be distinct.

In the following chapter, we'll have much more to say about music's various applications.

USING SILENCE

The absence of sound sometimes can be the most potent of all audio tools. Silence is the aural equivalent of print's white space. It provides the important elements of our message with a neutral or anticipatory buffer to give our central statement some breathing space and to help direct audience attention. As researcher Paul Bolls discovered, "People engage in orienting response to anything that can be novel. And silence can be novel."[25] Conversely, a message stuffed end-to-end with words, music, and sound effects is as tiring to listen to as a page covered in unbroken print is to read. Just because your client is paying for thirty or sixty seconds of airtime doesn't mean you must fill every one of those seconds with racket.

The following PSA by Jay Williams orchestrates only one pause. But it is this single cell of silence that requires the listener to reflect on the horror of the just-described scene—and that sets up that listener for the tale's surprise twist. The spot thereby affirms what Deborah Potter of the NewsLab preaches: "Silence is a great storytelling tool."[26]

KING: The rats seemed to pour out of the pipe and run down the alley.

ANNCR: Stephen King, author of <u>Carrie,</u> <u>The Shining,</u> and <u>Pet Cemetery.</u>

KING: His legs were too bad to let him move with any speed. He shifted frantically, trying to get up as he watched them come in a seemingly endless wave, past the dumpsters and the barrels. But he couldn't move. And so he sat, against the bags of trash, his face frozen in horror, as they raced toward him, past him, around him, over him and finally settled on him. Diving into his pockets, shredding the bags behind him, ripping at the shopping bag he held, nipping at the exposed skin at his ankles and his wrists. The squealing seemed to fill the sky---

          (PAUSE)

KING: The most horrifying part of this story, is that I didn't write it. It's the true account of what happened to a homeless man in an alley in Boston's Back Bay. Please. Support The Pine Street Inn. You can't imagine what the homeless go through. Even I can't.

ANNCR: The Pine Street Inn. 444 Harrison Avenue. 482-4944.

(Courtesy of Wendy Becker; Hill, Holliday, Connors, Cosmopulos, Inc.)

Silence can also be used to suggest a complex condition the listener needs help comprehending:

ANNCR: Listen closely to this sound --- machinery in a Southwest Asian paper plant, pounding away to fill orders for export.

          (PAUSE)

          Now listen to this --- the sound of trading in Eurobonds in the London market.

          (PAUSE)

          And now this --- the construction of a new auto parts factory in South America.

          (PAUSE)

> If you can't hear these sounds, don't worry. Because we can. We're G. T. Global and we manage global mutual funds from offices all over the world. So we can hear the sounds of economic activity --- and investment opportunity --- on six continents. Ask your financial advisor for our Special Report. Or call 1-800-G.T. Global for a prospectus with more complete information including the funds' current holdings, as well as charges, expenses, and the risks associated with global investing. When you invest for your future, think global. G.T. Global. 1-800-G.T. Global.[27]

And silence can even be enlisted to focus sympathetic attention toward things that will always be mute:

> ANNCR: Here is the sound of animals protesting cruel conditions imposed upon them.
>
>   (A FEW SECONDS OF SILENCE)
>
>   Here is the sound of animals requesting compassion in a language people understand.
>
>   (A FEW SECONDS OF SILENCE)
>
>   Here is the <u>only</u> understandable sound animals could make---
>
>   (A FEW SECONDS OF SILENCE)
>
>   ---if we didn't make sounds on their behalf. A public service of the <u>Animals' Voice Magazine</u>.

(© Paul & Walt Worldwide. Writer: Walt Jaschek)

Too many copywriters think they are paid to gather words rather than to create communication. They pack their copy with as much linguistic baggage as possible and then wonder why listeners stop listening. As audio producer Eric Larson tells his clients, "If you make a good point, sometimes . . . the best thing to do is just give a break to the copy right there, so that strikingly convincing sales point can be absorbed."[28]

If you can learn to follow Larson's suggestion, you will get a lot closer to becoming a "real writer." This is the accolade that art director Don Easdon ascribes to his counterpart, Bill Heater, when Easdon acclaims:

> He's a real writer, and a real writer is a student of the way people talk, what they say, phrases they use. And more importantly, what they *don't* say. The little pause in between the sentences. He's the first [copywriter] who ever talked to me about that. He said we really don't have to fill up the 30 or 60 seconds with copy. It's what he doesn't say that makes the work so powerful.[29]

Silence can be created by punctuation, by the natural separation in time of one thought unit from the next, and even, if necessary, by the stage direction: (PAUSE) --- generally placed in ALL CAPS to emphasize its importance. Whatever the indication, silence allows us to isolate what comes on either side of it for easier and more focused contemplation by the listener.

THE AUDIO COPYWRITER AS POET

Whether they realize it or not, successful copywriters are much like musicians and poets. "Anytime you write words for performance, they have the exact same properties as music," says *The West Wing's* Emmy award–winning writer Aaron Sorkin. "There's rhythm, tone, pitch, volume. You'd be silly to ignore the sound of the music."[30] As to poetry, *Webster's New Collegiate Dictionary* describes a poet as "one endowed with great imaginative, emotional or intuitive power and capable of expressing his conceptions, passions or intuitions in appropriate language." In fact, the radio copywriter's job is to find and select words and other sound elements that are *so appropriate* to our message that the listener will not only comprehend but also remember them as the means of recalling the workings of our product and service. Thus through the years, we recall what will "double our pleasure, double our fun," where to go for a "sandwich that's a manwich," whom to call "when it absolutely, positively has to be there overnight," and maybe even how to feel "the heartbeat of America" or "quench that deep down body thirst."

These electronic slogans are simply commercial manifestations of an age-old tradition. Before the age of print (and, consequently, before the age of widespread literacy), fables, sagas, and folklore in general were passed down orally. From the ancient Greek rhapsodes and Biblical psalmists to the medieval minstrels and their successors, poets seeking to communicate with significant numbers of preliterate "common folk" did so by casting their messages into concise yet colorful verses that could be understood easily by all and remembered, at least in part, by many.

Like these earlier poets, the sound copywriter performs in a totally oral and fundamentally nonliterary environment. Our listeners, like those of our historic predecessors, have no concrete, permanent record of the subject being communicated. Everything the aural audience carries away with them must not only be visualized but also implanted in the mind through an unusually harmonious juxtaposition of sounds and ideas. In a process with which any past or present minstrel can identify, the audio writer continually struggles to attain the perfect marriage between *sound* and *sense,* a marriage that will enable the message to spring to life and stay alive in the listeners' memories during the days and weeks to follow.

As eighteenth-century poet Alexander Pope once wrote:

True ease in writing comes from art, not chance,
As those move easiest who have learned to dance.
'Tis not enough no harshness gives offense,
The sound must seem an echo to the sense.

Much more recently, semanticist S.I. Hayakawa observed that the "copywriter, like the poet, must invest the product with significance so that it becomes something beyond itself . . . . The task of the copywriter is the poeticizing of consumer goods."[31] "It is almost like poetry," agrees Young & Rubicam copywriter Kevin O'Donoghue, "because each word is creating a meaning or a feeling in people. Each word is important."[32]

Yet in many ways, the audio copywriter's task is even more difficult than that faced by most other poets. Conventional poets can usually choose their own subject, the attitude they will take toward that subject, the form to be employed, and the length to which that form will extend. Audio copywriters, conversely, virtually always have the subject assigned to them together with a compulsory subject attitude, which is nearly always positive (unless it is something like an *anti*-litter PSA). The specified form is certain to be budget- and time-bound. If there is no time or money for a dialogue spot to be produced, for example, the copywriter must proceed with a univoice approach regardless of personal or professional preference. And the dictated length is precisely the length decreed by the campaign managers and the broadcast and broadband media selection plan they have adopted—no longer and no shorter.

The conventional poet can decide to write in praise of a solitary stalk of corn. The copywriter is told to pen a corn flakes spot. The literary poet may decide this particular cornstalk represents man's parched thirst for independence. The audio poet is instructed to demonstrate how the one brand of corn flakes meets the whole family's breakfast requirements. The traditional poet decides to discuss the corn stalk in Italian sonnet form: fourteen lines in iambic pentameter grouped into two subsections of eight and six lines. The copywriter has thirty seconds of airtime to devote to a univoice maternal testimonial. The remarkable aspect of all this is that, despite the comparatively cramped boundaries within which they have to maneuver, audio wordsmiths must still construct a message that is just as meaningful and memorable to the mass audience as the traditional poet's message is to his or her far fewer and initially more attentive constituents.

Just for a moment, let's see how a conventional poet and a "copywriter poet" might approach and describe the identical subject. In this case, the topic is the same small-town cafe. Certainly, the literary writer's imagery is more descriptive and extended. But does the poet make Bannerman's *benefit* as 'significant' and discernible as the copywriter's thirty-second spot?

DINER

A new day's procrastination
Lets night's veil still opaque the sun.
The silky mist floats on the highway
And the dew embosoms the grass,

While sleepy truckers and travelers,
Draped in coats, soon discarded,
Gather in bleary-eyed company,
Sipping the heavy-mugged coffee.

The morning's high tide arrives;
Rays of sunshine put neon to shame.
The grey road crawls toward tomorrow
And the ground is a mottled pastel.
A carpet which grade school children
Imprint with rubber-ribbed sneakers
In their jumbled, vibrant rush
To the charm-filled gum machine.

Exhausted, a spent afternoon
Plods by in thankful surrender,

Leaving a dusked thoroughfare
Flanked by the darkening earth
Where the bachelors and creased businessmen
Stretch out their day-piled stiffness
While stumbling from autos and vans
In pursuit of the house specialty.

An eve with a moon for lapel pin
The ebony mystery of midnight
Makes the highway a concrete river,
Gives each blade of grass a new boldness
To the starry-eyed couples,
As linked pairs of feet
Drift through the door
To prolong their beguilement..

ANNCR: A place to start the day off right; a place to stop before saying good-night. Tempting food, relaxing atmosphere, and an always-here-to-please-you attitude. That's what you'll find every day, twenty-four hours a day, at Bannerman's Diner. From that first up-and-at-em cup of coffee, to a late-night, home-cooked snack, Bannerman's Diner serves you the food you like --- whenever you like it. Bannerman's Diner on Route 23. Your any-time, every-time eaterie.

In comparison with the poem, the copywriter's radio-tailored effort may seem somewhat humdrum. But our words must be instantaneously accessible to an audience likely to be paying only partial attention. The commercial must sell Bannerman's. The poem need only promote itself.

Occasionally, product positioning may be right for a copywriter to pen "real" poetry. A few years ago, Campbell-Ewald Advertising's Patrick O'Leary was inspired to write the following lines as the thematic expression for radio and television spots on behalf of the Chevy Tahoe:

There's a place that I travel when I want to roam
And nobody knows it but me.
The roads don't go there and the signs stay home
And nobody knows it but me.
It's far far away, and way, way afar
It's over the moon and the sea
And wherever you're going
That's wherever you are
And nobody knows it but me.

English teachers wrote to Chevrolet for the text of the poem, and people debated as to which famous poet had penned it.[33] Many were surprised that it came from the keyboard of an advertising scribe. Yet, the piece was true marketing communication, a lyrical description of where this SUV could take you and a powerful piece of imagery to bolster the more direct selling elements that accompanied it.

POETIC PACKAGING

Both poets and audio copywriters are required to energize and activate audience members' visual and other senses via media that are not, in and of themselves, pictorial. Rather than being a drawback, this is a 'memorable' advantage for both types of wordsmiths. For, as award-winning copywriter Robert Pritikin once noted, "When you write a radio commercial for the eye, instead of for the ear, you can expect to achieve enormous recall value. The most elementary memory course will teach you that to remember something, you must visualize it."[34] Pritikin himself created one of modern radio's most poetic illustrations of this principle in a series of spots that illuminated a paint's very visual essence via the supposedly "blind" radio medium:

ANNCR: The Fuller Paint Company invites you to stare with your ears at --- yellow. Yellow is more than just a color. Yellow is a way of life. Ask any taxi driver about yellow. Or a banana salesman. Or a coward. They'll tell you about yellow. (PHONE RINGS) Oh, excuse me. Yello!! Yes, I'll take your order. Dandelions, a dozen; a pound of melted butter; lemondrops and a drop of lemon; and one canary that sings a yellow song. Anything else? Yello? Yello? Yello? Oh, disconnected. Well, she'll call back. If you want yellow that's yellow-yellow, remember to remember the Fuller Paint Company, a century of leadership in the chemistry of color. For the Fuller color center nearest you, check your phone directory. The yellow pages, of course.[35]

This Fuller Paint spot is a perfect example of audio using its own unique advantages to capitalize on video's disadvantages. Every member of the audience was enticed into poetically painting, in his or her own mind, what was most appealing about yellow. There was no forced dependence on the film processor's yellow, the kind of yellow the video engineer admired, or even the brand of yellow the home receiver was adjusted to reproduce. Instead, it was everyone's perfect yellow displayed in everyone's most perfect showcase—the individual mind.

Like any successful aural copywriter, Pritikin engaged in a little *Poetic Packaging*—he isolated the element of the subject on which he wanted to focus and then derived some picture-potent symbols to bring that element to mind's-eye life. Broken down, the development of the above commercial, like the development of any image-filled piece of *Poetically Packaged* audio, results from a unified process that springs from three successive questions:

1. What is my subject? (Yellow Fuller Paint)
2. What is its key element or quality that I want the listener to appreciate? (the vibrancy of its yellow color)
3. How can I *poetically package* this quality? (relate it to other prominent examples of the color yellow: taxis, bananas, dandelions, melted butter, lemon drops, a canary, even the yellow pages and cowards)

What we are doing is nothing more than taking the product and the specific characteristic of that product we want to stress, and then substituting a more vibrant and familiar image that possesses the same characteristic.

Many aspiring writers realize they must use imagery to make their message come alive, but they neglect the vital second step. They mistakenly try to describe, to

Package Poetically, the product or service as a *whole* rather than first selecting its key attribute and the central copy idea that must be fashioned to display that key attribute. Since no short piece of copy can ever be expected to make more than one memorable point, the adopted *Poetic Package* must likewise work in undistracted service to that point instead of attempting to characterize the product's totality.

For practice, take the following items and try to pull out what the key element or quality of each might be:

a ball-point pen	a watchband
a pizza pie	an automobile shock absorber
a life insurance policy	an underarm deodorant

Do you and, given your subject's specific advantages, *should* you focus on the pen's shape, the pizza's convenience, the policy's low monthly cost, the watchband's strength, the shock absorber's gentle ride, and the deodorant's aroma? Or do you stress the pizza's shape, the deodorant's convenience, and the policy's strength? Whatever you decide, you must then as a radio writer encase that central concept in the most vivid and meaningful wrapping you can derive. Does the pen fit your hand like an extra finger? Does the watchband's strength come from "tank-track" weave? Does the deodorant go on "gentle as a goldfish's kiss"? And what about that pizza with its shape or convenience? Keep digging until you find your subject's most appropriate element and a convincing *Poetic Package* to match. It's not easy, and a lot of seemingly unproductive "think time" may be expended before you ever start setting your copy to paper. But hang in there. "Because," as agency chairman George Lois exhorts, "a big campaign idea can only be expressed in words that absolutely bristle with visual possibilities."[36] Once you have successfully dealt with all three of *Poetic Packaging's* questions as they apply to the assignment at hand, you'll have a message that involvingly 'bristles' because it engages the listener's pictorial experience and imagination. "Listeners have to become collaborators," says New York radio writer/producer Joy Golden. "If they don't click into the scenario, if there's no visual coming into their minds, then the commercial sucks. You want to leave a little permanent dent in the listener's brain."[37]

Poetic Packaging can be effective in creating PSAs as well as commercials. In fact, the process may be even more helpful in the public service arena, where we must promote an intangible belief or selfless dedication instead of a product that offers the listener an imminent benefit. Isolate how *Poetic Packaging's* trio of queries was answered in formulating the PSA below:

(MUSIC: FEATURE DRAMATIC, OMINOUS MOTIF. THEN UNDER)

WOMAN: Imagine you're at a lake---

(SFX: FAINT CRY FOR HELP, OBSCURED BY MUSIC)

WOMAN: ---and a man has fallen in.

MAN: Right now, thousands of people are dying, waiting for organ and tissue transplants.

WOMAN: You throw a rope---

MAN: If you've decided to be a donor, you must tell your family now so they can carry out your decision later.

WOMAN: The rope --- the man can't reach it.

MAN: Otherwise, it's like throwing a 12-foot rope to someone who's 15 feet away. Organ and tissue donation. Share your life. Share your decision. To learn more call 1-800-355-SHARE. This message brought to you by the Coalition on Donation and the Ad Council.

(Courtesy of The Advertising Council)

1. What is the subject?	organ/tissue donation
2. What the key element/quality?	need to register as a donor now
3. How to poetically package the element?	compare delaying registration to a rope too short to save a life

The imagery on which Poetic Packaging depends can do much to enhance communication with your audience. Research conducted by Professor Paul Bolls found that listener heart rate actually increases for about the first thirty-five seconds of a high-imagery one-minute spot. In addition, such imagery leads to active "visual" processing of the message on the part of the listener, as well as to increased attention, better message retention, and better attitudes toward the spot and the client, with claims being perceived as more believable and trustworthy.[38]

OTHER TECHNIQUES FOR THE AUDIO POET

In addition to the umbrella concept of *Poetic Packaging*, there are six precise writing techniques for improving your message's sound and sense potency. Specifically, skilled "audio poets": (1) vary length, (2) erect fulcrum phrases, (3) exercise evocative phonetics, (4) lighten up on alliteration, (5) explore onomatopoeia, and (6) paint a backdrop.

1. Vary Length

Compelling copy projects a sense of flow. And flow is enhanced best by a progression of related thought units that vary in length. If all of its sentences expend about the same number of metric beats, a spoken message will develop a lock-step character that is enjoyable as a music lyric, but monotony incarnate as unaccompanied copy. In a jingle like the Spangles' spot below, for example, the pulsating, *uniform* stanzas propel the flow in an ear-pleasing, foot-tapping progression that is totally appropriate for musically depicting a lively nightspot.

Spangles is where the fun begins.
Party times that never end.
Great food, great prices, great service too.
It's all waiting here for you.

Call all your friends in the neighborhood.
You don't have to settle just for good.
For a sit-down dinner, or a quick bite,
Make it Spangles; Spangles tonight.

When you feel like relaxin',
You know that we're gonna treat you just right.
When you feel like some action---
Make it Spangles, make it Spangles,
Make it Spangles; Spangles tonight.

Spangles is where the fun begins.
Party times that never end.
Great food, great prices, great service too.
It's all waiting here for you.

Make it Spangles; Spangles tonight.
Make it Spangles; Spangles tonight.

(Courtesy of Fran Sax, FirstCom)

But in the case of straight copy, there is no melody to add interest to a uniform beat. So the ear demands *flow variety*. And this variety is totally dependent on the words and sentences themselves, which should proceed in contrasting short and medium units. After all, flow is best appreciated when balanced by ebb. The shorter units help hold the thought up momentarily before the medium ones propel it ahead again.

The copywriter should be enough of an artist that the listener will not notice the means by which flow is regulated—but only experiences its pleasing effect. The tedium of unaccompanied same-length sentences, on the other hand, is a dulling distraction for audience attentiveness. Often, listeners may not be able to identify consciously what caused their attention to wander. But the lack of contrast inherent in uniform-length thought units takes its toll no matter how glowing the word choices that make up those units. Read the following spot for a school supply product aloud:

ANNCR: Paper's cheap but your time and effort aren't. Ripped binder holes result in losing your homework. Now's the time to put a stop to this problem. Surround those holes with Talbot Gummed Reinforcements. A round Talbot circle will keep the hole from tearing. So keep that valuable work right there in your notebook. Don't waste the time and effort you put in that essay. Get Talbot Gummed Reinforcements before it's too late.

Did you notice the sluggish sameness of the sentences? Each succeeding line has the same five beats, which pound relentlessly on without regard to copy meaning or aural flow. It's like the maddening uniformity of a dripping water faucet. If you didn't quite catch this deadening pattern, the beats are scanned below.

1   2   3   4   5
Paper's cheap but your time and effort aren't. Ripped

1   2   3   4   5   1   2   3   4
binder holes result in losing your homework. Now's the time to put a stop

       5   1   2   3   4
to this problem. Surround those holes with Talbot Gummed

```
        5               1       2       3       4
Reinforcements. A round Talbot circle will keep the hole

        5           1       2       3       4
from tearing. So keep that valuable work right there in

        5               1       2       3       4
your notebook. Don't waste the time and effort you put in

        5       1       2       3           4
that essay. Get Talbot Gummed Reinforcements before

            5
it's too late.
```

Length, then, is measured in *beats,* which combine to create copy *rhythm.* It is not the number of words but the number and arrangement of beats that comprise the framework for copy flow. Take the measure of some of your own material in the way we've just scanned the Talbot spot. That should help you detect metrical monotony in the making.

Contrast the mechanical effect of the Talbot commercial with the nonrepetitive progression in this restaurant spot. Compute the beats in each thought unit. Here, the sentence lengths are varied and conversational enough to retain rhythmic interest without eclipsing copy comprehension.

<u>Production Note</u>: Gravelly private-eye voice

ANNCR: The case I was on had sounded easy. Just find the best food around. But I'd been slapping shoe leather on concrete all day long. And the only thing I had to show for it was a stomach full of a whole lotta empty. And that told the tale. I was beginning to think it would be easier to find Osama Bin Laden at an FBI picnic than come up with a burger worth laying a taste bud on. Then, I saw something that grabbed me like a Velcro tee-shirt. Guido's Drive-In. I yanked the door open and entered a world where the 50's were alive and kicking. A place where the burgers were as big and fresh as the potholes on 91. The fries were seasoned. The grinders were as perfect as a three hundred game. The shakes came in 17 flavors and the waitresses are on wheels. And as my teeth sank like Enron stock into my fresh, made-to-order burger, I knew I'd cracked the case. The best fast food going was waiting at Guido's Drive-In. A place where they still care about quality. Guido's. The service is as fast and easy as a two-dollar scratch ticket. The food --- is worth a million bucks.

(Courtesy of Gerry Perrett, Saga Communications)

In his book *My Life as Author and Editor,* the eminent writer H. L. Mencken stated his firm belief "that writing verse is the best of all preparations for writing prose. It makes the neophyte look sharply to his words, and improve the sense of rhythm and tone-color—in brief, that sense of music—which is at the bottom of all sound prose, just as it is at the bottom of all sound verse."[39] Varying sense unit length is a critical part of this poetic sensitivity. So, as Mencken suggested, try your hand at creating some poetry—to train for writing copy that waxes poetic.

2. Erect Fulcrum Phrases

The most potent device for achieving verbal rhythm is the fulcrum phrase. A *fulcrum* can be described as the brace point of a seesaw. When positioned exactly halfway between the board's two ends, it holds the board perfectly horizontal once the weights on the ends are in balance. Linguistically, the *fulcrum phrase* possesses this same capability. It is a thought unit constructed in such a way that its midpoint is obvious because there is an equal metrically balanced load on each end. Such a line is intrinsically pleasing to the ear and, therefore, like any pleasing rhythm, makes it easier to remember the message being carried. True, listeners may not be able to define just what a fulcrum phrase *is*, but, to paraphrase Justice Stewart's comment on obscenity, they'll "know [and appreciate] it when they hear it."

A landmark series of spots for the Fuller Paint Company employed an excellent example of the fulcrum phrase. Not coincidentally, that phrase was also the company's identity line:

A century of leadership in the chemistry of color

Where is the fulcrum? Between the words *leadership* and *in*. This balance point, as shown in Figure 7.3, is literally *composed* into the line to give it the appealing sense of proportion, of stability, so important in aiding and stimulating recall.

Other classic commercial phrases that have served to enhance brand identify over the years include:

Ivory Soap.   ^   So pure it floats.

The best thing that happened to corn   ^   since the Indians discovered it. (Post Toasties)

Our L'Eggs   ^   fit your legs.

From the valley of the jolly   ^   ho-ho-ho, Green Giant.

Got   ^   milk?

Every woman alive   ^   loves Chanel Number 5.

Melts in your mouth   ^   not in your hands. (M&Ms)

Relief is just   ^   a swallow away. (Alka-Seltzer)

Just wait 'till we get   ^   our Hanes on you.

They plump   ^   when you cook 'em. (Hygrade Ballpark Franks)

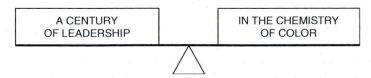

FIGURE 7.3   The Fulcrum Phrase Visualized.

K-Mart is ^ your savings place.

You can't do better ^ than all A's.

The proud bird ^ with the golden tail. (Continental Airlines)

Best of all ^ it's a Cadillac.

McDonald's ^ and you.

You're in the Pepsi ^ generation.

We sell no wine ^ before its time. (Paul Masson)

Like a good neighbor ^ State Farm is there.

With a name like Smucker's ^ it has to be good.

Bandini is the word ^ for potting soil.

Chock Full 'O Nuts ^ is the heavenly coffee.

Like the refrain of a recited poem, a well-crafted fulcrum phrase endows the audio writer's central idea with a propelling clarity that is especially important in aural-only communication. Over the next few days, listen for fulcrum phrases in the spots you encounter. Which of these are the 'stickiest' in recalling their brand's true essence?

If the fulcrum phrase is a valuable asset to a spot, it can be downright vital to the comparatively abbreviated program promo that often has a *total* of only one or two isolated lines in which to accomplish its objective. Notice how even these short promos seem confident and complete in themselves because they are conscientiously balanced:

The hits roll on with Mel St. John ^ and they never stop 'til ten.

Let <u>Dialing for Dollars</u> ^ give your purse a silver lining.

Here are four more fulcrum program promos. Plot the balance point in each for yourself.

Take the pressure out of rush hour with <u>The Rick Sykes Show.</u>

Jeff Smith has better weather 'cause he helps you understand it.

Cool, mellow sounds for a warm Akron night as Trey Stohlman grooves jazz just for you.

Play-by-play baseball with Kenny Jay sticks the bat and ball in your ear.

3. Exercise Evocative Phonetics

As a true soundsmith, an electronic media copywriter will choose words not only for the precision of their meanings and the feel of their rhythm and balance, but also for the appropriateness of their phonetic makeups.

Audiences as a whole tend to respond in different ways to different sounds. They are conditioned by certain quirks of the language to perceive some words as much for their aural composition as for their denotative meaning.

The '*short i*' sound as in the word *little,* for example, very often occurs in words that depict something little: *bit, kid, mitten, chick, tiff, whiff, pill, kilt, thin, pin, inch, lint, snip, wisp,* even *witticism.* Similarly, a crisp, decisive effect is auditorily suggested by words that end emphatically, such as *pep, jet, swept, attack, act, clap, clout,* and *catapult.* Or, a rapid, lightning-like impression can often be conveyed more fully by words that begin with the *fl* sound, such as *flash, flurry, fling, flay, flag, flaunt, flail, flare, flee, flame,* and *fluorescent.*

Want your phonetics to suggest humor? Then, Ira Schloss advocates choosing words that start with or contain *k* and *p* sounds—words like *chicken, cookie, popcorn, cupcake, pickles, cucumber, porcupine, car keys,* and *petticoat.*[40] Even place names with this phonetic makeup can be funny. Which is probably why there are more jokes about Cleveland and Peoria than about Boston and Baltimore. Conversely, words featuring the syllable *-ain* can help to paint a generally listless or unpleasant image, as evidenced in *pain, bane, rain, drain, stain, strain, wane, abstain, complain, inane, mundane,* and *profane.* Thus a sensitivity to evocative phonetics would cause you to take care that the *-ain* sound is enlisted to describe the condition your product or service is designed to alleviate and not the product or service itself.

Meanwhile, the letters *c, s,* and *b* "are perceived as much more traditional or classic," according to research done by William Lozito, the president of Strategic Name Development, "and what could be more classic than Coca-Cola, Sears and Budweiser?" He also found that the letter *q* (like in Quicken or QuickBooks) suggests innovation in people's minds, while *v* is distinctly feminine (Victoria's Secret, Venus) and *x* resonates well with men (Jaguar's X-Type, Gatorade X-Factor, and Nissan Xterra).[41] Although none of these relationships is unequivocal, they further support the contention that sounds do suggest properties over and above the literal meanings of the words they comprise.

Examine the following program promo. How are evocative phonetics used to further its pitch and portray program character?

If talk is a pain and country's a drag, flip your dial to rockin' 98 and The <u>Kevin Corbett Show.</u> Join the jump to Denver's fast track.

Contrast that characterization of Kevin's show with the way evocative phonetics help to depict this one:

The mystery of moonlight on Lake Erie shorelines. Midnight in Buffalo with the mellow melodies of Larry Patrick's <u>Sonatas 'til Sunrise.</u>

Lyrics, of course, are especially effective evocative tools when instrumental and copy sounds combine to further the same overall mood. The mellow music that bedded the following "Here with You Tonight" song was complemented by euphonious long vowel sounds as in *radio, low, know, go,* and *you.* This last word possesses special utility because, other than his or her own name, *you* is the most pleasing sound in the world to any listener.

Sitting here with you
The lights and the radio way down low

We listen to a song or two
And I know it's gonna be awhile before I go.

Here with you tonight.

Everything is just exactly right
Here with you tonight.
Chicago 101 is our special friend
WKQK playing our song again
Here with you tonight.
WKQK Chicago 101
We hear it with you tonight.
Here with you tonight.

(Courtesy of Jim West, FairWest)

At the opposite end of the day and format spectrum, this morning drivetime promo for an adult rock outlet used a much more uptempo music bed (*Movin' on Up*—the theme from the old *Jeffersons* TV show) to accompany short, percussive phrases containing plenty of consonants and *'short i'* sounds. The aim here, of course, is to crank up a feeling of morning energy and fun.

Yeah, we're wakin' on up, wakin' on up
In the morning, wakin' on up
With Kidd Kraddick on my radio.

Yeah, we're wakin' on up, wakin' on up
Get me going, wakin' on up
With the KISS FM morning show.

Coffee's brewin, in the kitchen
My body feels like lead
Took a whole lot of trying
Just to get out of that bed.
Radio gets me movin'
Playing my favorite songs
They keep me laughing
Give me information
They ain't gonna steer me wrong.

Yeah, we're wakin' on up, wakin' on up
In the morning, wakin' on up
With Kidd Kraddick on my radio.

Yeah, we're wakin' on up, wakin' on up
Hear the warning, wakin' on up
The inmates have their own morning show.

(Courtesy of TM Century, Inc., Dallas, Texas)

Whether radio promo, PSA, or commercial, read your copy aloud to see if its phonetics are appropriate to the ultimate meaning you want to convey. Your choice of sounds begins without boundaries. As Gary Provost tells us, "In writing, there are no intrinsically good or bad sounds, just as there are no good or bad notes in music. Just as giggling is a 'good' sound during recess and a 'bad' sound during a geography test, the sound of your words must be considered in the context of what you have written."[42] Analyze the following commercial by copywriter Wally Wawro. Observe how he manipulates the phonetic makeup of succeeding thought units to give his copy just the right pace, mood, and character.

ANNCR: For your pleasure --- a daydream from Southwest Marine Sales. The sails are full. The vessel glides quietly and gracefully through the water. White, foaming waves cascade over the deck. The refreshing spray a coolant from the mid-day sun's warming rays. Seagulls soar overhead --- specs of white against a backdrop of blue. Gentle gusts of a salt-scented breeze and you. The strain of muscles conquering wind and wave. The thrill of motion. <u>This</u> is sailing. Man and the elements. Willful. Strong. Exciting. This passage a thought from Southwest Marine Sales --- Texas' largest sailboat dealer. See Texas' finest sailing vessels at Southwest Marine Sales, today, on Highway 146 at Seabrook Shipyard. Once sailing's in your blood, you may never be a land-lubber again. Southwest Marine. Number One at making daydreams reality.

(Courtesy of Wally Wawro, WFAA)

In audio copywriting, as in poetry, we employ evocative phonetics to achieve *descriptive* rather than merely *declarative* writing. In penning a spot for Gold Dragees (small, beadlike confections used to decorate cakes), one student wordsmith, for example, wrote that they provided a "great decorating touch." This is declarative writing only. It asserts product benefit but paints no picture to visualize it. Another student more deftly praised the "glistening crunchy sparkle" that the product brought to the cake. This is descriptive writing. The words evaluate the product by conveying a specific and positive *image* of that product in use. And the very sound of those words suggests their flashy appearance and tactile firmness.

In pursuit of evocative phonetics, "It is the word alive the writer wishes to capture," points out Judson Jerome. "Its vowels pure and unfaded, its consonants brittle, unchipped, its sinews tough. The syllables of the word should articulate for you with all the give and spring of a rattlesnake's jointed spine. Sniff the word for its sweat-and-leather smell. Does it ring on the counter like silver or clang like brass or chink as dully as lead? When you squeeze it, does it squirt?"[43]

4. Lighten Up on Alliteration

Unlike poetry, audio copy tends more to avoid alliteration (the repetition of the same initial sound in succeeding words) than to embrace it. The listener may marvel at the announcer's ability to enunciate the *"pervasive Peruvian poverty that the penniless peasants personify in patient passivity"* but, in the process, will undoubtedly miss the appeal's main point. Thus, the peasants persist in their penury.

Our job is not to trip up the performers of our copy with lines like *"It's August Brothers for the best bread and buns you can buy."* (Try articulating that line five times.) Nor is it to distract the listener by favoring sound *over* sense. Reading your copy aloud will immediately flush out unintended tongue-twisters. If it trips you up—change it. There is no sound poetry in a sprung tongue.

5. Explore Onomatopoeia

Onomatopoeia is the ultimate extension of evocative phonetics. It results from using words that sound the same as the subject/action to which they refer. A copywriter spelled his beer client's name BUSSSSSCH rather than BUSCH as a means of portraying its can's sound when opened. The Mazda rotary engine went "hmmmmmmmm" in a sung spot to convey how smoothly the motor purred without pistons. And the Weed *Whacker* actually spits out that sound while it works.

These and many other such phonetically imitative devices help us reach through the radio to the listener's other senses. If there's no word to describe the sound of your subject, don't be afraid to invent one:

ANNCR: Listen to your car. Properly inflated tires should purrrr down the road. But under-inflated tires foo-wapp, foo-wapp, foo-wapp. So check your tires for proper air pressure with the Accu-Test tire gauge. Just a quick psssst with the Accu-Test lets you know if your tires need more air. Prevent tire-wearing foo-wapps with a tire-saving psssst. Use the instant tire checker from Accu-Test. The quick psssst that keeps the purrrr in your driving.

If nothing else, onomatopoeia (and evocative phonetics in general) should serve as constant reminders of the importance of *sound* in successful audio communication. Certainly, our copy must make linguistic sense. But it must move beyond this sense into the realm of auditory sensation. This latter requirement sometimes takes real labor to satisfy. "A lot of times, I'll do something again and again, and it still won't be right," admits Massachusetts copywriter Paul Silverman. "You feel sour notes. It isn't right inside your ear; it bumps and thumps all over the place. It's gotta go bdlmp, bdlmp, and if it breaks that speed, it's no good."[44]

6. Paint a Backdrop

Finally, the copywriter/poet must recognize that audio presentations should reflect a locale, should seem to arise from some specific setting. TV or Webcams, with their opening shot, can easily show the viewer the context of the message to follow. Audio vehicles have no such automatic establishing device. Unless special care is taken, the listener is immediately disoriented. Therefore, like a curtain that rises on a carefully dressed stage, the opening seconds of your sound presentation should frame and spatially locate the action to follow. Granted, you don't want the listener to come away "whistling the scenery." But you do want to construct a mind's-eye habitat that heightens *visual* memorability while housing your central copy point. In the following spot, for instance, the locale and the problem situation it contains are both swiftly established by the first few lines of dialogue.

Production Note: Man is a normal guy; Gordo a stoner

(SFX: DOOR OPENS)

MAN: Hey, Gordo. I just thought I'd stop in and check out your new --- pellet --- stove.

GORDO: What do you think?

MAN: Um, dude? That's not a pellet stove---

GORDO: It's a snowmobile.

MAN: In your living room.

GORDO: In my living room.

MAN: You were supposed to buy a pellet stove to cut your heating bills this winter!

GORDO: I went to the place, to get the stove, but you know, they also had snowmobiles, the dealer was real nice, and it was so shiney---

MAN: Didn't I tell you to go to Fireside Designs? They only sell hearths, so they know more about 'em than anyone else around. They offer safe installation. And remember how I told you to buy a pellet stove now so there'd be time to get it installed before the heating season?

GORDO: The headlight works and everything.

MAN: How is a snowmobile going to help cut your heating bills?

GORDO: Well, I been running it for a few minutes every hour. The heat from the engine makes it pretty toasty in here---

MAN: How about carbon monoxide?

GORDO: No thanks, I'm not hungry. In fact, I'm kind of woozy.

MAN: Come on. We're gonna get you some fresh air, then we're going to Fireside Designs.

(Courtesy of Gerry Perrett, Saga Communications)

Despite its brevity, even station continuity can create a sense of locale. That may, in fact, be a core mission in encouraging local listener identification with the program or station being plugged. The following three snippets illustrate how time and place can be quickly communicated and capitalized on in your continuity:

Don't you just love coming back to work on Monday? Well, I do. This is <u>The Bill Robinson Show</u> and I'm ready to go with Big Lake Country music on KJCK.

It's springtime where the hills meet the plains. What a great place to be, in 102 country and <u>The Bill Robinson Show.</u>

(Courtesy of Jon R. Potter, The Musicworks, Inc.)

The maples are scarlet and the cider is flowing. A beautiful time to harvest the golden oldies here on the valley's WMHW.

An experienced audio copywriter never forgets to paint a backdrop—and to sketch it immediately in order to engage the listener's mental picture-making. Whether it's a sixty-second commercial or brief promo piece, if all you give your audience is a vague or blurry scene, they'll tune out. Notice how your mind's eye draws a blank with this copy opening:

Service is something we'd all like to expect from those we do business with.

Far better to give the listener's pictorial imagination something tangible to *play with* as an incentive to *stay with* our developing story:

The old corner gas station. Where they'd wash your windshield and check under the hood without you having to ask.

Likewise, if you try to begin your scene with a question that can be answered negatively,

Can you see yourself on a Caribbean cruise?

those listeners who answer "no" will decide the rest of the spot must not pertain to them and summarily depart. As any good salesperson knows, it's much more productive to elicit initial agreement from which to build a persuasive pitch:

Wouldn't it be great to get out of the snow for awhile?

This is a line that promises localized pertinence to the listeners' life (assuming they live in the frost belt). So they're tempted to listen a little longer.

As star radio copywriter Joy Golden concludes, "In television, a commercial writer works with the art director to create the picture. In radio, the listener is the art director, because you're giving him the material from which he has to create his own visual image. The reason a lot of radio commercials don't work, is that they give the listener bad pictures."[45]

AUDIO'S ESSENCE

Poetic Packaging and the audio poet's other techniques, together with the proper use of format, terminology, sound effects, music, and silence, are all essential elements in the styling of sound messages that truly engage the "theater of the mind." Certainly, audio-only media present a writer with an immense challenge. But they also give you unrivaled opportunity. What creative director Ed Butler observed decades ago about radio remains true today for any broadcast or broadband aural message. "Radio is all yours. You create it. You select the talent. You may even get the chance to direct your brainchild. And, more often that not, radio is 60 seconds. Epic proportions in a world that seems to be measured in 10- and 30-second segments. It's my opinion that if you can write good radio, you can write great television."[46] Besides, audio doesn't have the hobbling blinders of a TV or computer monitor frame, a cell phone's screen or print's column inch. Audio, when professionally written, is as expansive and unbounded a medium as you can induce yourself and your listener to make it.

8 Audio Commercials

Having survived the previous chapter, you should now be able and perhaps even *willing* to really home in on the creation of audio commercials. Writing effective aural advertising can be a gratifying and potentially lucrative enterprise. It can deepen your insight into the beauty of language and heighten your sensitivity to the power of sound. It can acquaint you with music and sharpen your diction. Besides all of this, as compared with composing print ads, devising audio commercials is more ecologically responsible. Why? Well, as F. Joan Roger of Berkshire Broadcasting points out,

> Radio advertising is clean. Radio messages are crisp and to the point. Radio advertising doesn't require growing trees, manufacturing paper, printing and distributing, carrying it home, shifting and sorting through it and then carrying it out to the trash. There's no depletion of national and natural resources with radio advertising.[1]

Whether or not you accept Roger's argument, you should discover that an audio medium—whether on our radio, our computer, or our mobile phone—allows us to convey richly colored mind pictures at frugal black-and-white prices.

COMMERCIAL DATA BLOCK

As with most commercial/continuity scripts, an audio spot begins not with copy, but with a *data block* or *header.* This block serves as a standardized memorandum that helps writers, media outlets, and clients keep track of the scripted message and its scheduling. The skeleton of the data block is set forth as preprinted stationery. The specifics pertaining to the particular commercial are then typed in on the appropriate lines. A typical example of an audio commercial block appears as Figure 8.1.

The series of dates in the upper-left portion of the copy head pertain, respectively, to when the commercial was originally submitted for review to a supervising

```
                        AIMED-WRITE ADVERTISING
                          (broadcast division)

2/20/10                 client:      B & E Chemicals
3/9/10 rev.             product:     Dynamite Drain Opener
3/13/10 rev. apprvd.    title:       Plunger Parade
4/2/10 prod.            length:      60 seconds
                        script no:   BE-167-10R (as recorded)


. . . . . . . . . . . . . . . . . . . . . . . . . . . . . . . . . . . . . . . . . . . . .

        Production Note: ANNCR is middle-aged female.

ANNCR:    I've got five sinks in my house. All different sizes. With different size
          drains. But they had one thing in common. They all clogged. So I owned
          five different size plungers. Which all worked --- sometimes. Then
          I found out about . . .
```

FIGURE 8.1   Audio Commercial Data Block.

officer, when the resulting revision was prepared, the date on which that revision was approved, and, for a message released in recorded rather than script-only form, the date of sound studio production. The complete chronology of the spot is thus available at a glance, and any unusual time lag between stages can be noted. If this same lag begins to appear in the development of other commercials, management can conduct an appropriate investigation to ascertain whether there is an organizational bottleneck that needs attention.

Moving to the block's right column, and below your agency's centered name, the client line contains the contracting firm's official corporate designation. On the next line, the specific product being advertised is identified. For small, one-product companies, these client/product lines may carry identical entries.

Next, the spot title is the name that illuminates the copy's central concept and provides a quick means of identification for those who will be cooperating in its creation and production. Forcing the writer to set down a spot title is also a good quality-control device. If the writer has difficulty evolving a title, or if the title does not relate well to the script as a whole, it is a good indication that the central concept is vague, irrelevant, or missing altogether. In the following commercial, the title "Long Lost Lovers" encapsulates both the plot line and what will be the title characters' continuing dilemma if they don't *find* our bank.

(SFX: FOOTSTEPS, STREET AMBIENCE)

WOMAN: (With a start) Oh, excuse me.

MAN: That's alright.

WOMAN: Wait --- Roger? Is that you?

MAN: (Pause/Surprised) Gail?

WOMAN:	(Gushing) Roger! It _is_ you!
MAN:	Gail!!! Oh, Gail.

(ROMANTIC MUSIC SWELLS. THEN UNDER)

WOMAN:	When you left town for that big job in Iowa, I didn't know what to think.
MAN:	(Melodramatically) I had to leave. They had free dental.
WOMAN:	What has it been? Ten years?
MAN:	It seemed like an eternity!
WOMAN:	So, have you married?
MAN:	No, I could never give my heart to another.
WOMAN:	My darling!
MAN:	My love! (Smooch)

(MUSIC SWELLS/KISSING NOISES)

WOMAN:	(Blissful sigh) Finally, we're together.
MAN:	Together 'till the end of time.
WOMAN:	Time. Oh my. What time is it?
MAN:	Oh, it's, uh, 4:45 my love.
WOMAN:	4:45! Oh no!

(MUSIC STOPS WITH A RECORD SCRATCH)

(SFX: FEET RUNNING AWAY)

ANNCR:	Gotta get to the bank?
MAN:	Wait! Honey-bunny! Come back!
ANNCR:	Maybe you should bank at TCF. We're open earlier. Later. And every day at Cub Stores. With totally free checking and the free TCF check card. TCF. Member FDIC. We're open more.

(Courtesy of David Alm, BBDO/Minneapolis)

A script number, such as BE-167-10R in our Dynamite Drain Opener format sample (Figure 8.1), is a more objective and necessarily bureaucratic means for designating a given spot. It is used in intra-agency correspondence as well as in communication with the outlets whose facilities have been contracted to air the commercial. With a numerical designation, the outlet does not have to take the time to audition the entire spot in order to ascertain whether it is actually this version of the "Plunger Parade" or "Long Lost Lovers" treatment for which time has been purchased. The number makes such a chancy subjective judgment unnecessary. Further, a numerical designator serves to identify the commercial as it wends its way through the various continuity acceptance offices at networks and stations. Everyone concerned will therefore have an accurate record of which spots have been previewed by the outlet and cleared for airing. (Review the 'prohibition' section in Chapter 6 for a discussion of industry clearance processes.)

Script numbers may be constructed in several different ways, but usually with an eye toward identifying any or several of the following:

    a. the originating agency
    b. the client or company for which the spot is written
    c. the spot's location in the total sequence of advertisements produced by the agency for that client
    d. the year in which the spot is produced or in which it is intended for first airing
    e. the medium for which the spot is intended
    f. the spot length

In our sample, "BE-167-10R" indicates that the client is B & E Chemicals (BE), that the spot is the one-hundred-sixty-seventh treatment for that client that this particular agency created, and that it is a *2010* commercial for use on Radio. Alternatively, we might use a number like AW-5-167-60r in referring to this same spot. In this case, the script number first reflects the agency name (AW for Aimed-Write), and then uses a client number (5) rather than a letter abbreviation. Everything Aimed-Write creates for B & E Chemicals would thus be identified via symbols beginning AW-5. The specific spot sequence number then follows (167), as does the designation that this is a sixty-second radio spot.

GENERIC CLASSIFICATION OF AUDIO COMMERCIALS

The audio spots that these data blocks identify can be divided into four main categories based on the general technique each spot employs: (1) univoice, (2) multivoice, (3) dialogue, and (4) musical.

1. Univoice (Straight) Commercial

In this category, which is alternatively known as the "straight" commercial, a single voice delivers the selling message without support from any other sound elements. Most spots sent to outlets in script form for live on-air reading by an announcer or disc jockey are therefore, by necessity, univoice treatments. Because it cannot depend on music, sound effects, or the energizing interaction of different voices, this spot type requires an especially clear and cogent use of the language. On the plus side, a straight commercial is also very inexpensive to produce, since only the script need be sent to the stations or at most, a single voiceover talent be employed. It also means that revised versions of the spot can be created very rapidly in order to take advantage of a local condition or seasonal event. An April blizzard can sell a lot of leftover snow shovels if appropriate copy can be quickly marshalled.

Of course, the univoice commercial also lends itself to prerecorded rendering by a corporate spokesperson who may be a prominent personality. The copywriter must be careful, however, that the words themselves do the selling job and don't become dependent on the personality for the announcement's impact. The spot below, for example, could be voiced by a nationally famous athlete or anonymous local announcer without compromising its concept-centered imagery:

ANNCR: Okay, here's how it works. If you've got this itsy bitsy teeny weeny little thirst, drink some water or something fizzy or what the heck, suck some nectar out of a flower. On the other hand, if your sweat shirt looks like it just came out of the washer and pronouncing your name requires major effort, reach for the Gatorade. Then if you want to suck nectar out of a flower --- hey, we've done our job. Gatorade Thirst Quencher. It's absorbed up to 30 percent faster than water for your deep down body thirst. Don't you just love science?

(Courtesy of Terrence J. O'Malley, Vickers & Benson Advertising Ltd.)

Because of their productional sparseness, univoice radio spots present the copywriter's greatest challenge. If appropriate to the product and campaign, one response to this challenge is to use *synesthesia.* Fundamentally, synesthesia ("joined perception") is the conversion of a stimulus received via one sense into an alternative sense experience. Synesthesia was first explored in the seventeenth century by Jesuit music theorist and mathematician Athanasius Kircher in an attempt to explain "colored hearing"—how some people perceive musical timbres as particular hues. Provided that the synesthetic reference is exclusively imaginative and not a literal property of the product, researchers Michelle Nelson and Jacqueline Hitchon found that ads employing synesthetic linkages "are perceived to be pleasanter and more novel than literal ads; cross-sensory ads were also preferred over literal ads when subjects were asked to suggest the better ad."[2]

"Taste the Rainbow," the slogan for Skittles candy, is an example of a synesthetic metaphor in its translation of a gustatory sensation into a visual one, while Doritos' "The loudest taste on earth" converts sound into tasted crispness. "The most deafening orange on the planet," a line from a teen-marketed lipstick ad, uses its audio referent to achieve a saturated visual image. And a house paint's description as "a mint green that breathes" changes a visual stimulus into a respiratory response. The univoice spot below sets up a soup-selling scene by using synethesia to convert the kinesthetic sense of temperature into 'colorful' sound. It then 'shows' how the sound of the product is the melodious remedy.

ANNCR: Sometimes it's so cold around here you can hear it. It's a muffling blue drone that gets deeper and darker the colder you get. That's the time for a bowl of Kettle Hearth Tomato Soup. Kettle Hearth Tomato Soup breaks through the blue drone with a bouncy red flavor that whistles warmth and nutrition in every steamy spoonful. Next time you hear the cold, listen to your stomach. Stir yourself up a sunny song of flavor. With Kettle Hearth Soup. Now in cozy single-serve cans.

Nelson and Hitchon argue "that a synesthetic claim (such as bright sounds) can be more persuasive than a literal claim in the context of products whose usage does not literally require both senses."[3] But with or without synesthesia, if you can create sensory-triggering 'univoices,' you will be much more facile in writing other spot genres that provide more varied auditory tools.

2. Multivoice Commercial

This is a derivative of the univoice commercial since, in both types, the voices talk directly to the listener. In the multivoice, *two or more* characters who are *not* in conversation with each other are used to deliver the selling message. The employment of more than one talent is a means of bringing vocal variety to the spot and/or helps suggest universality. Especially in a commercial that is required to impart a significant amount of specific information, the multivoiced approach can keep jogging the listener's attention more than would a straight spot. Still, don't make the multivoiced method a crutch on which to lean swollen writing. Like any audio technique, it cannot do the selling job without well-sculpted copy. In the following multivoiced application, three mutually supportive testimonials all speak directly to the listener in a persuasively interlocked fashion:

FRAT LEADER: The fraternity of 'Alpha Pizza PI' welcomes this year's pledges to our noble brotherhood of pizza pie lovers. The pledges have successfully completed the most difficult of initiations. It was tough --- eating all those inferior pizzas that---

PLEDGE #1:   Yeah, it wasn't too funny when the guys made me scarf those soggy things from Pizza Pit.

PLEDGE #2:   And me? I hadta choke down all those greasy pizzas from Mr. Joey's. I missed a whole day of classes trying to recover.

FRAT LEADER: Sure. They've all been there. They know what it's like. But it was worth it. Because now the guys can really respect the excellence of Uncle Mario's Pizza. Now they're ready to discover what real pizza is. I'm going to open this box and---

PLEDGE #1:   Look at all the cheese!

PLEDGE #2:   And Uncle Mario's whole wheat crust. Really something to sink your teeth into.

FRAT LEADER: If you're a pizza freak, like the brothers of 'Alpha Pizza PI,'---

PLEDGE #1:   You can skip our initiation.

PLEDGE #2:   And initiate <u>yourself</u> to real deep-dish pizza from Uncle Mario's.

FRAT LEADER: That's Uncle Mario's on South Jefferson. Or check the white pages for Uncle Mario's free delivery phone number.

ALL: All right, Mario!

As the Uncle Mario's treatment demonstrates, universality is implied when we have several voices all saying similar things about the product, service, or condition. Another way for a multivoice message to accomplish this is to have the characters separately echo or overlap each other's words. In this way, we get two seemingly distinct points of view—but both reinforce the same selling story:

<u>Production Note</u>: Voices overlap with identical words at the end of each speech.

HE: Well, you know, it's the era of casual acquaintance. No one really wants to make a commitment. That's why I was surprised that she committed to meeting---

SHE: ---committed to meeting me at the Brass Cafe downtown. I thought he was going to say: 'I couldn't find it; I got lost, sorry.' And I'd know that wouldn't be true, because I told him it's right on the corner of Main and Michigan---

HE: ---corner of Main and Michigan. 'Just look for the green awning,' she said. I got there before she did, so I got a booth for us and had the waitress bring out a candle---

SHE: ---waitress bring out a candle, just for effect. How sweet. But he didn't have to do that, because that secluded booth was so cozy and romantic. He even ordered wine and Chicken Hibachi---

HE: ---Chicken Hibachi for her. Hey, it was just a lucky guess that she'd go for the Brass Cafe's grilled chicken, mushrooms, and veggies served up shiskabob style. It's one of the things the Brass Cafe does best. Just like the Philly Beef and Swiss---

SHE: ---Philly Beef and Swiss he ordered. I mean there was more meat, onions, mushrooms and cheese than the bun could hold. Some of it dripped on his shirt. I think he needs me.

HE: I think she wants me.

TAG: The Brass Cafe. Main at Michigan. Fine food. Soft lights. The rest is up to you.

(Courtesy of Anthony Clark)

Sometimes, a multivoice is built from comments gathered through telephone or on-the-street interviews, which are recorded and later edited into an audio montage. In such semiscript cases, the copywriter sets down the interviewer's questions and the desired direction in which the responses should be led by that off-mic interrogator. Provided a large number of answers can be collected from which to choose, the results are often more effective than if writers try to script out all the lines themselves. For example, when copywriter Mike Sullivan created a series of ads for BF Goodrich in which an announcer calls people named Goodrich in search of the real "BF," his team phoned more than 200 Goodrichs to get enough usable material.[4] Of course, release forms had to be signed by each of those Goodriches used in the final commercial.

3. Dialogue Commercial

With this technique, rather than talking to the audience, the multiple voices used are in conversation, in *continuous* conversation, with each other. Usually, one voice is a salesperson surrogate and the other voice or voices represent the prospect by asking the kinds of questions and expressing the kinds of doubts we believe our listeners would vocalize. The salesperson and prospect surrogates need not be actual clerk and customer. They might just be neighbors talking over the back fence. The salesperson substitute can be the neighbor who owns/uses the product and is testifying to its effectiveness in answer to the friend's queries. Even though radio lacks the immediate feedback of the actual point-of-of-purchase setting, the dialogue spot allows us to simulate that environment. In convincing our commercial's surrogate buyer, we are striving to simultaneously persuade the real listener at the other end of the airwaves or Ethernet.

To be effective, the dialogue must seem natural, feature distinctive characters, and possess dramatic tension. "When characters have words put in their mouths, the conversation sounds phoney," radio creative director Chris Coyle points out. "But when the writer steps back and allows the characters to interact as they wish, what results is far more dramatic and real."[5] Inept dialogue, conversely, sounds as though the characters are either delivering soliloquies to no one in particular or are attempting to pitch directly to the audience like a uni- or multivoice message. Remember, if it's believably juicy dialogue, the listener will want to eavesdrop on it. But no eavesdropper wants suddenly to be addressed directly by the parties she's spying on. This is why it is risky to intermix both multivoice and dialogue methods in a single spot. The disoriented audience will not know whether they are intended to be in the conversation or simply to overhear it.

Therefore, if you want your listener to be approached directly, stick to a straight or multivoice technique. Similarly, when a direct-sell line is mandatory at the end of overheard dialogue, don't compromise your characters by making one of them deliver it. After all, observes agency creative chief Virgil Shutze, "God created announcers to say the poison stuff."[6]

Natural dialogue also requires that character commentary—especially product exposition—be delivered in brief snippets rather than in big chunks of information. "If you can say something in three words instead of six, do it," directs radio master Dick Orkin. "Notice that normal conversation involves people interrupting one another, overlapping, even with short 'uh-huhs' or grunts or other sounds. And don't forget a dramatic space here and there."[7] To acquire an enhanced sensitivity to the qualities of realistic dialogue, radio creative consultant Jeffrey Hedquist suggests you secretly tape a one-minute conversation two people are having. On playback, "Note the incomplete sentences, the interruptions, the tiny attitude revelations."[8] Then capture these stylistics in your own scripting.

We often hear a dialogue spot that begins interestingly enough, with short, alternating exchanges between the characters. But then, right in the middle of the commercial (and usually about the time the product first appears), the "seller" mouths twenty to twenty-five seconds worth of uninterrupted details that drone on like a blurb from a mail-order catalog:

LOU: I hate my grass.

MAC: What's wrong with it?

LOU: It keeps growing and growing. My old lawnmower just can't keep up with it.

MAC: I remember those days.

LOU: So how do you keep your grass under control?

MAC: With my new Pasture Master. The Pasture Master is that great riding mower from Beasley Products. It features a tilt steering wheel, adjustable cutting heights in 10, accurate-to-the-millimeter settings, and accelerates from zero to 15 miles-per-hour in just 45 seconds. And the XKE Pasture Master even comes with roll bars, racing stripes, and a 30-db horn. Right now, you can put yourself behind the wheel of a brand-new Beasley Pasture Master for no more than the price of a small luxury sedan.

LOU: Sorry I asked.

Don't abandon your sense of dialogue halfway through the spot. Instead, permit your characters to volley back and forth briskly rather than laboriously pushing bowling balls at each other.

Dialogue characters should also be thoroughly distinguishable, one from the other. If taking a line from Character A and giving it to Character B makes no difference, that line should not have been included in the first place. One good way to foster distinctiveness is to maintain that buyer/seller demarcation mentioned earlier. One voice can be knowledgeable about the product while the other voice (along with the listener) has the problem or question that the product can address. Be careful, however, never to let seller and buyer switch roles. For instance, if the *buyer* suddenly starts spouting torrents of product information, the situation's believability is crippled. An additional means of enhancing character separation is to create contrasting types: a man and a woman; a senior citizen and a youngster; a stock/normal voice and a colloquial one.

Whatever delineation method you choose, it should help promote *tension* between the two conversants. Author Gary Provost describes this tension as "that quality of 'something else going on' during the dialogue."[9] It doesn't have to be two people slugging it out, just an issue or quandary in which they, and our listener, can become immersed. This quandary, of course, should be solvable by our product or service in a way that drives home the central copy point. Then make certain that each line in the spot advances our march from problem introduction to solution exposition. Remember that every phrase you write should be a vehicle for advancing the sale. If the speech serves *only* as characterization or gag-carrier, lose it. The client is not paying you to write sixty seconds of entertainment.

And whatever you do, don't lock up the sale (get buyer concurrence) too soon. If you do, the tension will evaporate before the end of the commercial and your listener will be irritated by the anticlimax.

The dialogue spot below introduces two conversational characters for whom a tension-fueled problem is quickly identified and a solution naturally unveiled. Note that all speeches are short and mutually responsive. We don't get the feeling that the lines are predetermined. Instead, we are led to believe that each little comment is a spontaneous reaction to the line that preceded it. Finally, an announcer is brought in for the product tag rather than forcing one of the characters to suddenly spin and pitch it to the audience.

SHE: Hi. Uh --- I have the window seat.

HE: Well, I can't move. Just crawl over me.

SHE: Okay --- uh---

HE: That's a handsome carry-on bag you have.

SHE: Thanks. Got it at The Luggage Center.

HE: Yeah, if I bothered with luggage I'd probably pick one up myself.

SHE: Well, you have a suitcase though.

HE;   No. Everything I'd put into a suitcase, I'm wearing.

SHE: What?

HE: I have on socks and underwear for a week, seven shirts, three slacks, P.J.'s, a blazer, a robe, this pair of shoes tied around my neck and the pair of shoes I'm wearing.

SHE: Aren't you uncomfortable?

HE: Excruciatingly. But I never have to worry about packing a suitcase again.

SHE: See, The Luggage Center has free how-to-pack seminars. Everything you're wearing is packed nice and neat in this carry-on bag.

HE: Wow. Say, could you hold my coffee up to my lips? I can't bend my arm---

SHE: And The Luggage Center offers a huge selection of brand names at the lowest guaranteed prices --- and you're really, really sweating.

HE: Yeah. I lose about 7 pounds a trip.

SHE: You should try The Luggage Center. They promise to make your next trip better.

HE: Uh-huh. Oh, listen. In an emergency, I can be used as a flotation device.

ANNCR: The Luggage Center. We'll make your next trip better.

HE: Wanna see how long I can hold my breath? (Short inhale) That's it.

(Courtesy of Dick Orkin & Chris Coyle, The Famous Radio Ranch)

Dick Orkin, co-creator of the above spot, believes an engaging dialogue can overcome the seeming pictorial advantage a screen medium has over radio. "With TV you . . . plop yourself down on the couch and just look at it," Orkin says. "In radio we have to attract the attention of listeners who are actively involved in other things at the time. In order to grab their attention you have to do something at the top . . . so the listener gets the idea that he's eavesdropping on a personal, private conversation. It's this eavesdropping quality that makes radio work so well."[10]

To summarize, when you check over a draft of your dialogue spot, apply the following five questions. If you have to answer "no" to any one of them, the commercial needs reworking:

1. Is there a buyer and a seller? (If there are two sellers, the spot becomes a psuedo-multivoice.)
2. Is there role consistency? Does the buyer stay the buyer and the seller stay the seller?
3. Does each line advance the *selling* (not merely the entertainment)?
4. Is there frequent speaker alternation, especially once the product is introduced?
5. Is the sale the climax (or are characters left with nothing meaningful to say for the last several seconds)?

The following classic Dick Orkin spot passes all of these tests—and with a couple of innovative twists. For one thing, the fearful seller is trying to *unsell* the buyer on the merits of the amusement ride. But his increasingly frenzied anti-sell only makes the ride more appealing to Gramma—and therefore to the listener. Second, Gramma doesn't ultimately buy what he wants her to—NOT going on the ride. His failure to sell thereby validates the real sell for which the commercial has been constructed. Notice too that this message doesn't fragment by attempting to promote "everything in the store" (a laundry list of Disneyland attractions). Instead, it concentrates on *one* product and pounds its merits home.

Production Note: Gramma has thick Eastern European accent.

MAN: Well Gramma, here we are at Disneyland.

GRAMMA: Beautiful.

MAN: So what ride would you like to go on?

GRAMMA: That one.

MAN: Oh. Ha, ha, ha! That's a new one, Splash Mountain. Very scary.

GRAMMA: Scary?

MAN: Yeah, you wouldn't like that Gramma, so pick any other ride.

GRAMMA: That one.

MAN: No, Splash Mountain is too scary for you Gramma, okay?

GRAMMA: Okay.

MAN: But they have lots of other rides, okay?

GRAMMA: Okay.

MAN: So, which one would you like?

GRAMMA: That one.

MAN: (Clearing his throat) Hmmmhhh. Gramma, see Splash Mountain has five steep water falls---

GRAMMA: Yah.

MAN: ---and they drop into swamps and stuff with alligators.

GRAMMA: Alligators.

MAN: Pretend ones, but very real-like. And then Gramma,---

GRAMMA: Yah.

MAN: ---are you listening?

GRAMMA: Yah.

MAN: At the very end of Splash Mountain, you fly off the world's highest water drop, five stories high. Very, very scary---

GRAMMA: Scary.

MAN: ---Not a ride for Grammas, okay?

GRAMMA: Okay. I want to go on---

MAN: Yes?

GRAMMA: That one.

MAN:	Gr-Gramma, the truth is, I won't let you go alone on Splash Mountain. I'm not, I can't, I won't.
GRAMMA:	It's okay, Gramma take care of you.
MAN:	No, that's not the point.
GRAMMA:	Take my hand.
MAN:	No. I don't want---
GRAMMA:	Take my hand,
MAN:	I don't, I don't, I don't---
ANNCR:	Splash Mountain. (ROLLER COASTER SOUNDS AND SCREAMS). The only way out is a long way down!

(Courtesy of Dick Orkin & Chris Coyle, The Famous Radio Ranch)

This "Gramma" spot also illustrates an additional attribute of effective dialogue writing: it leaves some things about the Splash Mountain experience up to the listener's imagination. As DDB/Chicago's chief strategic officer Jim Crimmins explains,

> research in linguistics has found that the most effective conversations are those in which everything the listeners can supply themselves is left implicit. . . . What's left out establishes a degree of complicity, a level of emotional closeness. . . . The danger lies in creating a lecture that alienates rather than a conversation that leaves enough up to the audience to involve them.[11]

4. Musical Commercial

As we suggest in Chapter 7, music can establish itself more rapidly and more powerfully than can any other sound element. Provided the music matches the product category and blends well with your product's personality and your campaign style, it can bring unparalleled staying power to your selling message. Music "tattoos a permanent resonance in your brain," says Grey Advertising VP-director of music Josh Rabinowitz. "We learn our alphabet through music... Song is permanence. That's what branding should be—permanent resonance."[12] Like Rabinowitz, commercial music producer Stephen Arnold refers to this process as *sonic branding.* "It implants a memory in the aural pathways of your brain that is so powerful it is virtually impossible to forget (and just as difficult to ignore.)"[13]

Before we examine the four main types of musical commercials that, to varying degrees, possess the potential to engender this effect, we should briefly discuss how best to specify musical effects in our copy. Much of the music a copywriter might choose will be of the straight instrumental variety and so will have no lyric cues to be used as script referents. In such instances, there are several possible methods for indicating how you wish music to be handled:

A. In the case of many music services and libraries, you can identify the music you want via the catalogue number and/or the musical segment title that the packaging firm has assigned to it. Thus your music cue might look like this:

(MUSIC: FADE IN 'COUNTRY TWANG,' EZQ 634-R2)

B. Similarly, a particular passage within a larger work that exists independently of a sound library can be specified as follows:

(MUSIC: ESTABLISH SECOND THEME FROM BEETHOVEN'S 'EGMONT OVERTURE')

(MUSIC: SNEAK IN FLUTE SOLO FROM RIFKIN'S 'THREE JAZZ NIGHT'–SOLO IS 2:40 INTO THE PIECE)

C. Alternatively, for the copywriter who does not have direct access to a music library, or whose client can afford the services of a custom music composer, it is sufficient to construct a phrase that specifically describes the musical effect sought. The tempo, the style, and, if possible, the instrumentation of the desired passage should be indicated to guide your spot's producer. If the particular musical effect is important and precise enough to enhance your copy, you as a writer should have little trouble finding the proper adjectives to describe it:

(MUSIC: FADE UP LANGUID OBOE DAYDREAM)

Or, for an entirely different effect:

(MUSIC: FEATURE FRANTIC PERCUSSION EXPLOSION)

In this classic Spam commercial, copywriter Steve Kahn sets down the essential requirements for the music, but without locking in to any one song or recording that might be unclearable or prohibitively priced. This is generally the most feasible practice. Identify the musical specifications you desire but try not to make them so inflexible that the whole spot must be junked if a single tune or cut is unobtainable.

(MUSIC: IMPRESSIVE DRUM ROLL)

ANNCR: In 1985, an old American soft drink changed its formula.

        (MUSIC: BRASSY FANFARE STARTS; WINDS DOWN TO A PITIFUL STOP)

ANNCR: People were not amused.

        (MUSIC: DRUM ROLL AGAIN)

ANNCR: Now, another American favorite has changed its formula.

        (MUSIC: REINVIGORATED FANFARE; THEN FEATURE DRUM ROLL AND UNDER)

ANNCR: Introducing Less Salt Spam, with twenty-five percent less salt, twenty-five percent less sodium. Taste tests prove that Less Salt Spam Luncheon Meat tastes great. But just in case you're not amused---

        (MUSIC: FEATURE ABRUPT STOP OF DRUM ROLL)

ANNCR: ---we still have classic Spam.

        (MUSIC: RAUCOUS PARTY HORN BLEAT)[14]

You may be constructing music-related script cues for any of the four distinct forms that the musical commercial can assume:

1. The pseudo-sound-effect
2. The slogan/sales point enhancer
3. The backdrop
4. The end-to-end lyric vehicle

Music as *pseudo-sound-effect* is epitomized in the above Spam spot. In such an approach, we are not using music for its emotive, melodious qualities, but rather for its ability to punctuate and characterize our copy statements quickly in a humorous or attention-riveting way. As long as it is relevant to our context, music can focus the product-in-use scene more quickly and sharply than any sound effect. This is because music, unlike SFX, also reflects an attitude. Reread the Spam spot to see just how unequivocally those musical 'opinions' come through.

Musical attitude also comes through strongly in the Bud Light commercial that follows. Here it is lyric rather than instrumental punctuation that heightens the humor and contributes to the brand's edgy, tongue-in-cheek persona.

(MUSIC: HEROIC UPTEMPO CONTEMPORARY STATEMENT FEATURE AND UNDER

ANNCR: Bud Light presents --- Real Men of Genius.

SINGER: Real Men of Genius.

ANNCR: Today we salute you --- Mr. Supermarket Free Sample Guy.

SINGER: Mr. Supermarket Free Sample Guy!

ANNCR: Though man dreads few things more than a trip to the supermarket, you offer us hope and sometimes a free mini-weenie.

SINGER: Love that freebie weenie!

ANNCR: What exactly do you have? Aerosol cheese products, deep-fried morsels? Who cares? If it's on a toothpick and it's free, it could be plutonium and we'd eat it.

SINGER: It's all good baby!

ANNCR: For a guy wearing oven mitts and an apron, you're alright.

SINGER: You're a star!

ANNCR: So crack open an ice cold Bud Light, titan of the toothpick. (SFX: BOTTLE OPENING) Because you put the free in freedom.

SINGER: Let it be free---

ANNCR: Bud Light Beer. Anheuser-Busch. St. Louis, Missouri.

(Courtesy of E. J. Militti, DDB/Chicago)

In our second category, music as slogan/sales point enhancer, a musical tag line is linked to what is otherwise a completely nonmusical production. Over the years, lyric tags such as "From the Valley of the Jolly—ho ho ho—Green Giant," "Ace is the Place with the Helpful Hardware Man," "You're Looking Smarter Than Ever—J. C. Penney," "I Am Stuck On Band-Aid, And Band-Aid's Stuck on Me," "And Like a Good Neighbor, State Farm Is There" all epitomize this brief but nonetheless incisive enlisting of music's recall power. To get such simplicity yet memorability into a musical sell line takes real talent on the part of the composer. (The last two examples, for instance, were both penned by super-star composer/singer Barry Manilow.[15]) In the following eatery commercial, singers punch out the product-in-use slogan as a bumper between brief dialogue vignettes:

MAN: Every once in a while, I --- get lonesome. So I just --- go there.

DOCTOR: To Munchie's Delicatessen?

MAN: Yeah, I know I should feel guilty, but just one little order, that's all. One for my baby and --- maybe --- one more for the road, but that's all. I can take it or leave it alone really.

DOCTOR: Can you <u>really</u> leave Munchie's alone?

MAN: Well, except when I see all of that great food. Then I think --- one quickie can't hurt. I mean, one teensey-weensey bite? It --- (CROSSFADE TO SINGERS) --- oh --- ohhhh---

SINGERS: <u>Oh, Oh, open your mouth; and put Munchie's great food in.</u>

WOMAN: Well, for a woman to function properly, she needs emotional escape.

DOCTOR: And Munchie's Delicatessen offers these escapes?

WOMAN: It's awesome. Of course, it's a very personal thing. Just one little bite. (CROSSFADE TO SINGERS) Oh --- ohhhh---

SINGERS: <u>Oh, Oh, open your mouth; and put Munchie's great food in.</u>

ANNCR: Others make promises. Munchie's delivers.

(Courtesy of Fran Sax, FirstCom)

Sometimes, the musically heightened slogan has been extracted from a complete spot-length lyric and used as a tie-in to other commercials that are primarily straight copy. Such a practice helps keep an entire campaign integrated while, at the same time, avoiding the cost and copy limitations of having every message fully scored.

The third musical commercial form, music as the *backdrop*, is exemplified by the Chanel spot below. There is no lyric in whole or part in such an approach. Instead, instrumental music provides the complete mood/motif frame within which the product and situation can more graphically be set. As in all good commercials of this type, the copy here is not *dependent on* the music in achieving its objective but rather *works with* the music to acquire an extended and more vibrant dimension. To enhance the copy/music integration, note that the script is set down as a series of lyric-like phrases rather than a single paragraph "block." In this way, the copywriter conveys a sense of the length of the melodic sub-elements that the selected music bed should contain.

As an exercise, we have deleted the script's specific music description. What precise musical backdrop would *you* select in order to complement this product and copy texture? What words would you use to describe this music?

(MUSIC: UNDER)

MAN: Why do you give a woman Chanel Number Nineteen?
Because she called one evening, and asked if you'd like to go out and grab a hamburger.
You said sure, why not?
She said she'd be by in an hour.
And she was. In a hired limousine, complete with a uniformed chauffeur and a bar stocked with chilled French champagne. Hamburgers to go were never like this.
You drove slowly around the city, looking at the lights.
And at her.
Finally, she closed the window between the front and back seats so the chauffeur couldn't hear the conversation.
She smiled slightly, and gave you a conversation you'll never forget.

WOMAN: There's a single fragrance to give that woman --- Chanel Number Nineteen. Witty. Confident. Devastatingly feminine. Inspire her today, and pick up some Chanel Number Nineteen to go.

(MUSIC: BRIEF FEATURE TO TIME)

(Courtesy of Melissa Wohltman, DDB/Needham Advertising)

In selecting appropriate backdrop music, you must be sure that the musical bed will sound appealing as low-volume scenery. If it has to be placed at 'full gain' (engineer talk for high volume) in order to register, the music will control center stage. Your talent—as well as your copy—will have to shout from the wings. "Possibly the most stupid thing advertisers do," complains Robert Snodell, "is allow their agency to have background music, usually loud, rock-type music, played while the person is trying to explain the features of the product. Frequently the music is louder than the voice, so the commercial goes down the drain."[16] Even if the volume is kept under control, backdrop music does not work well with a male announcer who sounds "down-in-the-mud"—whose vocalized pitch range is so low that you can't get solid music under him. Voice-over artists who function effectively with music know they have to get their voices "up and out in front" of the music bed.

Music as a carrier of copy that is entirely or mainly cast in lyric form, our fourth and final category, goes back to the earliest days of commercial radio. Historically called *jingles*, these end-to-end lyrics have evolved a great deal from the banal mantras of the thirties and forties. Today's jingles or musical images are carefully sculpted and orchestrated to bring together a particular target universe and a particular product.

A few years ago, some people prematurely labeled the jingle as dead. However, something quite different has happened because of changes in the music business. Formerly, few popular artists agreed to have their tunes used in commercials. But with the traditional record industry buffeted by Internet download competition, more and more music publishers have been seeking out commercial placements for their tracks. "As record sales and revenue sources for artists decline," observes music promotion executive Jon Cohen, "relationships with brands help fill that void."[17] In the profession, such placements are known as *licensed music* and may or may not feature the performer who originally made the tune famous. Unfortunately, the resulting glut of popular songs in spots has taken the novelty out of the practice and made commercials that use them stand out far less. In addition to this disadvantage, there are two further reasons to avoid using licensed music, according to media consultant Marvin Waldman:

> No.1. They really do get in the way of memories and special moments that make up the richness of our lives. Not only is that a crappy thing to do, but do it often enough and I bet the consumer will end up disliking you. And if they don't like you, they're not going to buy.
>
> For those who couldn't care less about robbing memory banks, we give you reason No. 2: The connection between the original meaning of the song and the product is often so thin and off-base that the client ends up looking stupid.[18]

Agency head Linda Kaplan Thaler agrees. "There's such a massive use of [licensed music] that it runs the risk of people not remembering the product but the songs. They don't buy the car, they buy the CD."[19] (This drawback applies not only to songs with lyrics, but to instrumental-only beds of popular tunes as well.)

As a consequence, the custom produced commercial jingle has staged a comeback. "The death of the jingle is only the death of the jingle as we have known it in the past," observes commercial composer Steve Ford.[20] Today's jingles strive to sound as contemporary as regular pop tunes. They lighten up on multiple mentions of the product name and instead, focus more on adjectives that suggest the product or its benefits. Thus the lyrics in the Figure 8.2 *lead sheet* for Ford articulate the "possibilities" flowing from driving a Ford while leaving specification of the brand and vehicle to the surrounding copy. (A *lead*—as in leader—*sheet* is the basic fabric of the tune on which full-fledged orchestrations and variations can be based.)

Contemporary musical treatments are usually selected for jingles because most clients want to appear in tune with the times and because a modern sound blends well with the formats of the greater number of radio stations. A large client trying to reach several complementary universes thus may commission multiple stylings of the same campaign theme to blend in seamlessly with the station format environment.

What follows are three different executions of a Pepsi summer campaign called "Sweating." Each uses the same basic imagery. However, the music *and copy* character in each is distinct so as better to appeal to each outlet category's audience. Soft drink consumption spans many demographic and psychographic groups. But these format-specific lyric stylings allow Pepsi to talk to each format's audience individually. "We presume it's a different problem reaching urban, country, and teen (rock) listeners," reports David Fowler, the campaign's creative director. "We're aggressive about being fresh to each target, not just rehashing . . . a jingle."[21] Each of these copy lyrics was, of course, backdropped by a music bed appropriate to, and reflective of, the format within which it was placed.

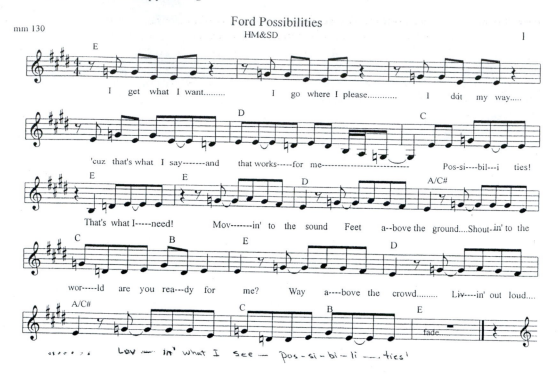

FIGURE 8.2   © *Copyright Harvest Music + Sound Design (Courtesy of Steve Curran)*

Urban Version

RAPPER 1:   Sweatin' on the sidewalk, drippin' in the street.
                   'Bout to drown in sweat from the sticky summer heat.

RAPPERS 1 & 2:   I need a Pepsi. Gotta have it, Jack. Cold. Wet. Now.

RAPPER 1:   Do a Pepsi.

POSSE: Don't sweat the heat.

RAPPER 1:   Do a Pepsi.

POSSE: Don't sweat the heat.

RAPPERS 1 & 2:   Stick a finger in the ring, rip the pop-top open.
                   Don't sweat the heat, G, we ain't jokin'.

RAPPER 1:   Do a Pepsi.

POSSE: Don't sweat the heat.

RAPPER 1:   Do a Pepsi.

POSSE: Don't sweat the heat.

RAPPER 2:   Hey, homey, you sweatin' like a pig, you'd melt her
             If you got too close. It's the steam heat swelter.
             That's a pity 'cause the lady is sizzlin', don't doubt it.

RAPPERS 1 & 2:   But it's just too hot to do anything about it.

RAPPER 1:   Do a Pepsi.

POSSE: Don't sweat the heat.

RAPPER 1:   Do a Pepsi.

POSSE: Don't sweat the heat.

RAPPER 1:   Grab it by the neck and give it a twiggity, twiggity twist.
             Don't sweat the heat, G, it's all in the wrist.

POSSE: Do a Pepsi. Don't sweat the heat. (Fade to time)
             Do a Pepsi. Don't sweat---

Country Version

HIM: You got me hotter than a tin roof.
        I'm sweatin', baby, over you.

HER: You got me sizzlin' like a fry pan.
        I sure could use a Pepsi; how 'bout you?

BOTH: Yeah, babe, we're sweatin'.

HIM: Well, it's tricklin' down your nose.

BOTH: We're sweatin'.

HER: It's seepin' through your clothes.

BOTH: Get the Pepsi, haul it over, it's icy and wet.
        Aw Pepsi --- nothin's better for breakin' a sweat.

HER: I'm like a wet dishrag in the hot summer sun.

HIM: Well, I'm sweatin' like a hound dog out on the run.

HER: You got me hotter than a pistol. Here's a Pepsi, my treat.
        'Cause it's not the humidity, it's the heat.

BOTH: Yeah, babe, we're sweatin'.

HIM: Well, it's tricklin' down your nose.

BOTH: We're sweatin'.

HER: And it's hotter than hell-o.

BOTH: Pepsi, good to see ya, so icy and wet.
        Aw Pepsi --- nothin's better for breakin' a sweat.

Teen Rock Version

LEAD: Rolling down across my chin
             Dripping down and wetting
             My chest hairs and the skull painted on my shirt.
             This heat has got me --- sweating.
             Chill the cool elixir.

GROUP: Sweating. Sweating.

LEAD: Just let that Pepsi touch my lips.
             Cool me, quench me, Pepsi.

GROUP: Sweating, Sweating.

LEAD: Save me from all this --- sweating.
             Sweat is rusting my guitar strings
             And my earring is covered with corrosion.
             This sweat could short out an amp,
             Causing an explosion.
             Chill the cool elixir.

GROUP: Pepsi. Pepsi.

LEAD: Just let that Pepsi touch my lips.
             Cool me, quench me, Pepsi.

GROUP: Pepsi. Pepsi.

LEAD: Save me from all this --- sweating.

GROUP: Cool me, quench me, Pepsi. (Fade) Cool me---

(Courtesy of Lou Allison, Copywriter, Tracy-Locke)

As all three of these versions indicate, a jingle's musical/verbal syntax is kept uncomplicated for easy listener absorption and inadvertent recall.

     The copywriter usually creates the lyric before the tune is composed. It thus is especially important that the rhythm and sound of your words (those Audio Poet Techniques discussed in Chapter 7) accurately convey the personality of your product. If your copy is rotund and relaxed, permeated with long vowel sounds, there's not much a composer can do to give the message (and the product) more zip. However, if your words and phrases are short and percussively consonant-filled, the music bed is enabled to be briskly up-tempo too—as in this spot promoting attendance at major league baseball parks. The aim here is to make going to the game a dynamic experience. Therefore the words are short and crackling.

SINGERS: It's a bat, it's a ball
              It's a mitt, it's a call

              It's a sacrifice bunt down the line

              It's a catch at first base

              It's the sun in your face

It's a flame thrower shaking a sign

It's a time with your friends
Hoping it never ends.

'Cause it's still tied after nine---

Get up and go for all the action

Get up and go for all the fun

It's major league satisfaction

It's a family homerun

Get up and go.

ANNCR: A message from Major League Baseball.

(Courtesy of Laurie Rhame, Bonneville Media Communications)

Conversely, Kraft wanted to focus on "warm nurturing images" of Moms using their products to prepare family meals. So the copywriter made extensive use of mellow, extended "ooh" words in the lyric:

SINGERS: Look what you've made
With your own two hands
What you've made
With your own two hands
It's something good.

You shape each day
With your own two hands
Point out the way
With your own two hands
Let's make something good.

ANNCR: We make it taste good, but you make it feel good. Kraft.
Let's make something good.

SINGERS: You hold each moment
In your own two hands
Let's make something good.

(Courtesy of Dain Blair, Groove Addicts)

One further musical device, though not a category unto itself, must be mentioned. Termed the *doughnut* technique, it is a means of customizing a preproduced national or regional spot to meet local needs and situations. The doughnut normally uses a lyric and an instrumental accompaniment. At a point clearly specified in the script, the lyric stops while the accompaniment continues. This allows the local announcer a "hole" over which can be read information exactly tailored to a particular store, special, or time of year.

Figure 8.3 indicates how a doughnut hole is shown on a singer's lead sheet. On the fifth line of the music you can see an "11." This signifies that there are eleven bars

FIGURE 8.3   *(Courtesy of Cathy Madison, Carmichael-Lynch)*

(measures) with no vocal, thereby marking where the hole/announcer read occurs. Notice also that this hole is preceded by another bar without lyrics and followed by an additional almost completely singer-less measure. This means the copywriter has virtually thirteen full bars (fifty-two beats in a four-beats-per-bar tune such as this) in which to give specific time/place details about the visit of the Jostens class ring salesperson to each particular high school.

There are two main types of doughnuts—"open" and "closed." In the "open" variety, the hole runs from the point of its introduction to the very end of the message without the lyric ever being reintroduced. In the "closed" doughnut (see Figure 8.3), the preproduced lyric is featured again after the hole copy to conclude the spot. Because timing is especially crucial in achieving a smooth "closed" doughnut effect, a safety valve is sometimes added in the form of a brief hummed or "la-la" phrase by the singers. If the announcer runs over the actual hole, the "la-la" lets him or her know that fact and provides a bit more time to wrap up the live copy without stepping on the lyric.

Even if the specific copy in the hole does not *demand* content localization, its reading by each station's own air personality helps blend the message much more effectively with the program on which it appears. The following closed donut for a franchise food establishment, for instance, sets up a hole that can be voiced by a local deejay to promote a currently featured "fresh and fast" item and/or stress the location of the Whistle Stop Deli in this particular town.

SINGERS: There's something about that special place
     That brings you back, yeah brings you back
     The food's so good it brings you back
     There's nothing quite like that deli taste
     It brings you back, yeah brings you back
     The Whistle Stop is the kind of place
     You simply can't ignore
     So fresh and fast, it brings you back
     The Whistle Stop Deli
     Brings you back!

ANNCR: (:23 hole copy)

SINGER: So fresh and fast, it brings you back
     The Whistle Stop Deli
     Brings you back

(Courtesy of FirstCom Broadcast Services)

That 23-second hole could be filled with copy like this:

ANNCR: Come back to your Mapleville Whistle Stop this week for our March corned beef special. Yes, just in time for Saint Patrick's Day, the Whistle Stop features custom-sliced corned beef brisket for only three-thirty-five a pound. Perfect on rye or a bed of cooked cabbage. Celebrate Saint Paddy's Day with a quick corned beef trip back to Brookshire at Third Street. The Mapleville Whistle Stop.

When you write a doughnut, don't think of the lyric as something separate and discrete from the spoken copy. This is, after all, a single commercial. So try to make the *sense* of the message flow smoothly from lyric copy to spoken copy and back again. In other words, if the entire spot was sung, or if the entire spot was spoken, would the progression of ideas still be cohesive? If not, you have some rewriting to do.

The same principle applies to donut spots that are entirely verbal, with pre-produced words coming before and (if a closed donut) after the "hole" copy. In the spot below, each disc jockey can insert material pertaining to a particular product to be pushed that week. This not only allows the client to easily shift from one product promotion to the next, but also serves to better blend the spot into each deejay's own show and patter. Here again, it is important that the first words in the hole form a natural flow from the last line of the donut's opening, and the hole's final words lead seamlessly into the donut's end copy.

ANNCR: Carnivores near and far. Rejoice! Because today is a happy day. A day to exercise those God-given choppers. After all, you've got teeth, why not use them? And if you're gonna sink your teeth into anything, it's gotta be Detroit's own Winter Sausage. Lengthy Links, Sultry Sausage, and Proud to Be Polish Kielbasa. It's a bun-loven, meat lover's heaven. Heck, it'll make your teeth smile.

HOLE: (15-SECOND PRODUCT FOCUS INSERT)

ANNCR: It's easy to exercise your incisors, because you'll find Detroit's own Winter Sausage brand in your better local deli's, including Farmer Jack. Tell 'em it's gotta be Detroit's own Winter Sausage. You've got teeth for a reason. Sink into Winter Sausage --- so tasty it'll make your teeth smile.

(Courtesy of Terry Phillips, WYCD)

Returning to the subject of music, whatever form your tonal spot takes, you need to be clear in describing the effect that you want. You may not be a musician, but you should still be in charge of how music is employed. Producer Stephen Ford provides these helpful suggestions:

When dealing with orchestration, communicate in terms of mood. A nice method . . . is to use visual color descriptives [recall our earlier *synesthesia* discussion]. Red could be a trumpet or a screaming electric guitar. Woodwinds are earth tones, clarinets yellow, oboes orange, bass clarinets dark brown, French horns a deep blue, and flutes a light green. This technique works especially well when creating sounds electronically on a synthesizer. . . .

Who is the announcer? Male? Female? The tonal range and attitude of a voice will determine the selection of instruments in orchestrating an underscore. . . .

If you don't have an idea of what sort of musical treatment would be suitable, that's what music houses are for—to offer creative input that could enhance your concept. Maybe put an Addy on your wall.

However, be wary of those producers who talk above you and hide behind a technical bush with words like "echo tweaks," "digital delay" or "square waves." They're probably technicians, not musicians.[22]

In short, when it comes to music, don't be afraid to trust your own instincts and don't be mesmerized by technicalities. Advertising music and its production are a communicative tool, not a secret cult. Sometimes the simplest musical styling of all is what's needed to get the job done. A recent *Washington Post* item noted that in today's frantic and sound-congested world, people don't whistle much anymore. So the spot that features a whistling motif could stand out well in its sparse and old-fashioned cheeriness.[23]

PUTTING 'PUNCH' IN THE AUDIO SPOT

Whatever its generic form, *any* audio spot of a half-minute or more can and should accomplish five product-related tasks. While, at first glance, this seems a huge assignment to complete in thirty or sixty seconds, the message that in some way encompasses all five will possess real marketplace PUNCH. Specifically, this PUNCH consists of

P   roduct specification(s)
U   ser experience(s)
N   otable competitive advantage(s)
C   ost/value ratio
H   eightened listener benefit

What follows is a classic one-minute univoice pitch for Motel 6. Let's see if it possesses PUNCH:

TOM: Hi. Tom Bodett for Motel 6 with some relief for the business traveler, or anyone on the road tryin' like the dickens to make a buck. Well, money doesn't grow on trees and I'm probably not the first person who's told you that, but maybe I can help anyway. Why not stay at Motel 6 and save some of that money. 'Cause for around 69 bucks, the lowest prices of any national chain, you'll get a clean comfortable room, free TV, movies and local calls. And long distance ones without a motel service charge. No, we don't have a swingin' nightclub or a mood lounge with maroon leather chairs and an aquarium where you can entertain clients, but that's OK. I got a better idea. Take the money you save and meet that client in town. Besides they probably know all the best places to go anyway. So let them tell you what they know best and you do what's best for business. Call 505-891-6161 for reservations at Motel 6. I'm Tom Bodett for Motel 6 and we'll leave the light on for you.

(Courtesy of John Beitter, The Richards Group)

Product Specifications

Even from this single commercial, listeners learn a great deal about Motel 6. They know that it's a national chain, offering clean rooms as well as free TV, movies, and local calls plus long distance calls without a service charge tacked on.

User Experience

The spot shows that the spokesperson (and, by extension, the management of Motel 6) is aware of the needs of the average business traveler and how best to meet those needs. When you're "on the road tryin' like the dickens to make a buck," it is clear Motel 6 can and has helped—not with extraneous luxuries, but with services and suggestions to conserve those hard-earned dollars. Motel 6, in short, helps you "do what's best for business."

Notable Competitive Advantages

The central and overriding advantage is, of course, the low price—in fact, "the lowest prices of any national chain." Still, Motel 6 doesn't neglect any of the things you require to be comfortable, including the homey promise to "leave the light on for you."

Cost/Value Ratio

In this spot, as is often the case when the rational appeal of economy is used, Cost/Value Ratio and Notable Competitive Advantage become the same thing—as long as the *cost* doesn't come at the expense of customarily perceived *value*. Therefore, this Motel 6 commercial indicates that the low price does *not* result from cutting corners in value-significant areas. Credibility is then enhanced by specifying exactly what *has* been trimmed to keep the price low—and then demonstrating why the absence of these items ("swingin' nightclub or a mood lounge with maroon leather chairs and an aquarium") is probably all for the best. You can "take the money you save and meet the client in town" because "they probably know all the best places to go anyway."

Heightened Listener Benefit

If you're a business traveler, and you want to obtain comfortable lodging without inflated prices, Motel 6 is your place. If it's an economical motel you need rather than a pricey resort, Motel 6 has "got a better idea." As in most effective commercials, Heightened Listener Benefit thus constitutes the cumulative and persuasive sum of all the other PUNCH factors.

Here is a dialogue approach for a different product category. Let's examine its PUNCH factors:

(SFX: DOOR OPENS, LIGHT OFFICE SOUNDS IN BG)

MARG: May I help you?

GEOG: Marge, it's me, George.

MARG: George Kryzynski?

GEOG: Yep.

MARG: *The* George Kryzynksi who left two years ago to buy office furniture and never came back?

GEOG: Hey, to get professional grade office furnishings I had to go to so many places --- the desk store, the carpet store, the tall filing cabinet store, the short filing cabinet store---

MARG: George, why, didn't you just go to Target Commercial Interiors?

GEOG: Like I could do it all in just one place.

MARG: You can at Target Commercial Interiors. You can get everything you need, the quality is first rate---

GEOG: This place looks different.

MARG: We got furniture.

GEOG: You couldn't wait?

MARG: We went to Target Commercial Interiors. The staff helped us with design and layout. And it's the Target company. Great prices, great service.

GEOG: I see.

MARG: We got professional grade furnishings. Everything an office like ours needs! Floor coverings, desks---

GEOG: I get it. Fine.

MARG: But welcome back. George Kryzynski is a real legend around here.

GEOG: Well, I was a great assistant junior vice president.

MARG: No, because you left two years ago to buy office furniture and never came back.

GEOG: Oh.

MARG: You've got 9,452 phone messages. Would you like to start returning?

GEOG: Guess I better.

ANNCR: Target Commercial Interiors. For all your professional-grade office needs. At 494 Penn. Expect more, pay less.

(Courtesy of Dick Orkin and Chris Coyle, Dick Orkin's Radio Ranch)

Product Specifications

The eavesdropper on this little vignette knows that Target Commercial Interiors carries desks, carpets, and everything else a modern office needs (including both tall and short file cabinets.)

User Experience

George is the ultimate non-user loser, spending two years of his life on a mission that could have been completed in a day at TCI. Meanwhile, his colleagues went to Target and have quickly and effortlessly moved on—without him.

Notable Competitive Advantages

Unlike a multitude of limited-inventory competitors, Target Commercial lets you "do it all in just one place." You can get "professional grade furnishings" as well as a staff to help "with design and layout."

Cost/Value Ratio

In addition to saving two years of your life, TCI offers "first rate" quality, "great prices, and great service." Although the cost of individual items is not mentioned, the clear implication is that there is a lot to be saved in both time and money by going to a single store that will also assist with overall office configuration.

Heightened Listener Benefit

Target therefore offers the business purchaser efficiency, economy, and the esteem that comes from "professional grade furnishings" in a custom-designed arrangement.

In attempting to achieve PUNCH in your own copy, two considerations are especially important. First, make certain that a product specification *is always converted into a listener benefit.* (For example, Target's comprehensive inventory *saves you time.*) The product attribute alone will be meaningless to the consumer unless it is shown to make a difference in that consumer's life. Inept copywriters restrict themselves to mere characteristic listing and then wonder why prospects aren't motivated:

Clean Gene detergent's filled with sparkling blue granules. And because of their unique molecular structure, these granules are more tightly compacted than any powdered competitor.

So What? Who Cares? What difference do "sparkling blue granules" and "unique molecular structure" make in the listener's washing machine? Far better to write it this way:

Clean Gene. The detergent with the sparkling blue granules that are easy to pour because they don't clump up. And Clean Gene's granule form packs more cleaning power into each ounce. That means a box of Clean Gene goes farther than other laundry powders so it's gentler on your budget.

Here the product specifications make sense because the writer has empowered them with customer benefits of "easy to pour" and "gentler on your budget."

Second, do not require your product to share the benefit acclaim with other props or its desirability will be overshadowed. For example:

The elegant china, the vintage wine, and your new hairstyle from Cut 'N Run. Everything you need to make your dinner a triumph.

Is the triumph due to the client's beauticians? The china? The wine? Or all three? Will my Cut 'N Run coiffeur bring me success even in the absence of these other commodities? Change the line so the benefit spotlight shines on your product *exclusively:*

You've worked hard on your dinner. And the table looks beautiful. But what makes you most confident about the evening is your new hairstyle from Cut 'N Run.

Through this revision, those other props still help dress the scene, but your client is clearly the star.

No matter who the client, and regardless of whether you are working in a univoice, multivoice, dialogue, or musical mode, the PUNCH analysis forces you to take a step back from the specifics of product data and copy technique to ask the ultimate question:

IS MY SPOT DOING THE JOB MY CLIENT IS PAYING ME TO ACCOMPLISH?

As David Fowler (creative director for both the Motel 6 and Pepsi "Sweating" flights) reminds us, "Good radio . . . needs to start with an idea and deliver it in a way that will get the listener to do something. When all else fails, great radio just needs to be clear. It needs to be the truth well told. It doesn't have to be art. Or theater. You can make better radio by making radio simple again. It's the lightening that strikes, not the thunder."[24] The PUNCH analysis lets us separate copy that makes an illuminating impact from a spot that's only a lumbering sequence of purposeless sounds.

THE TEN AUDIO COMMANDMENTS

In addition to putting PUNCH in their spots, successful audio copywriters follow these ten tenets to keep their commercials on the right selling track:

1. Stay conversational.
2. Voice and time the copy.
3. Remain present and active.
4. Beware uncertain pronouns.
5. Avoid TV soundtracks.

6. Keep humor in bounds.
7. Stress sponsor identification.
8. Concentrate the attack.
9. Conclude with energy.
10. Ask for the order.

1. Stay Conversational

Radio copy must be conversational, not only because that quality helps simulate an essential feeling of one-to-one communication, but also because conversation is the style in which we are most conditioned to pick up aural meaning and to pick it up the first, and often the only, time the message is delivered.

The sentence above is a good example of *print* rather than *audio* writing. It is an extended thought unit that pulls several related elements together into one package. If necessary, the meaning can be garnered by rereading or simply reading more slowly the first time. But for audio communication, we have to sacrifice the unity of one extended "lead" idea for shorter thought units that will cumulatively give us the same information in a more "aurally digestible" serving. Rewriting this paragraph's lead sentence to meet radio's requirements might give us something like this:

Radio copy has to be conversational. A conversational quality helps simulate the involving feel of one-to-one communication. Besides, we're used to picking up aural meaning when it's delivered in a conversational style. And we realize conversation won't often be repeated. So we work harder to understand conversation, the first time.

Sometimes, as this example shows, audio must use just as many if not more words than print to cover the same ground. That's why on radio, where real-time communication is so brief, we can seldom afford to deal with more than one main point in any commercial or piece of continuity.

Yet too many writers still try to send out the same piece of copy to both print and electronic media. This practice results either in print copy that does not offer enough information to hold a reader's focus or, more often, in aural copy that is just too congested for most listeners to decipher. Here is a newspaper ad that also was sent to radio stations without rewriting. Is it styled conversationally? Does it make one main point? Does that point come through clearly?

Honest Abe is the wood burner for big jobs. For $769 you can heat your entire home with this amazing model 35GX wood-burning stove and save one half or more in fuel costs. Clean and safe burning, it's free of smoke and fireplace odor. Minimum maintenance with easily emptied ash drawer. Roomy 24 by 20 firebox allows one fire to burn for hours. And the Honest Abe 35GX is easy to install. Call Harry's Heating at 320-8865.

Though the copy conforms to the word limit inherent in a thirty-second spot, there is little else about it that shows adaptation to the audio medium. In reaching the *listener* as opposed to the *reader,* some of the technical data would have to be omitted so that the main copy point can be allowed to surface and the "how to contact" information amplified.

It's been a cold winter, with more to come. And those high heating bills have probably given your budget a real chill, too. Harry's Heating offers the solution. The Honest Abe woodburning stove --- to cut those fuel costs in half. The easily installed, Honest Abe wood-burner is the clean, safe, economical way to bring cheery warmth to you and your budget. Call Harry's Heating at 320-8865. Get Honest Abe warming for you. Call 320-8865.

Aural copy obviously cannot depend on typeface alterations, layout patterns, and the other graphic implements through which print can present and arrange a comparatively vast quantity of information. And unless they are composed into the very essence of the copy, paragraphing and headlining are undetectable to the listener, who receives the message only one word at a time in the order in which the announcer's voice is unveiling it. On the other hand, audio can paint pictures in the mind—pictures that can be much more involving and multidimensional than the pen-and-ink starkness on which print must so often depend. If our aural copy can escape "printese," it can attain what Richard Mercer long ago recognized as the "freedom from print's static vulnerability. Radio doesn't just stand there like a four-color proof begging to be nit-picked into appalling mediocrity."[25]

Contractions are especially helpful in promoting conversationality while avoiding printese. Contractions shorten time-wasting helping verbs while mirroring the way most people talk in real life. To illustrate the importance of contractions, we have removed all of them from the following spot and substituted complete helping verbs (underlined for easy recognition). Read the commercial aloud and note how stilted and unnatural the absence of contractions makes it.

DICK: What is wrong with the way I sell cars?

BOSS: Go ahead. Sell me a car.

DICK: You say you would like a good deal on a car. Tell you what I am gonna---

BOSS: Hold it. That is enough. At J. K. Chevrolet we are very low key. There is no pressure, no hype.

DICK: Who is hypin'?

BOSS: No shouting.

DICK: Who is shoutin'?

BOSS: We are all very relaxed.

DICK: That is why I wear this pink coat and white shoes. It relaxes me.

BOSS: It is very nice.

DICK: You would like to buy it? Tell you what I am gonna---

BOSS: No. No. At J. K. Chevrolet we believe in selection, value, service.

DICK: All right. I get it. I am just a fast talkin', slicky car salesman.

BOSS: Why do you not try our competition?

DICK: They fired me.

BOSS: How come?

DICK: They did not think I was aggressive enough.

BOSS: I will see you around.

　　　　(SFX: DOOR SLAM)

ANNCR: J. K. Chevrolet. 3901 North Broadway at the bypass.

(Courtesy of Fran Sax, FirstCom)

Unless you really want to portray a character as pompous or verbose, let that character communicate in the conversational contractions of oral speech.

2. Voice and Time the Copy

As we've just seen, words and sentences that look fine on paper can sound stilted, awkward, or even incomprehensible when launched into the ether. Great writing is not necessarily great *audio* writing. Actually voicing the copy is the only way to test your words in a manner comparable to the way your listeners will encounter them. Here is a piece of great writing from novelist William Faulkner's *Light in August*. Can it also be used as great *radio* writing? Try reading it aloud to find out:

> All the men in the village worked in the mill or for it. It was cutting pine. It had been there seven years and in seven years more it would destroy all the timber within its reach. Then some of the machinery and most of the men who ran it and existed because and for it would be loaded onto freight cars and moved away. But some of the machinery would be left, since new pieces could always be bought on the installment plan—gaunt, staring, motionless wheels rising from mounds of brick rubble and ragged weeds with a quality profoundly astonishing, and gutted boilers lifting their rusting and unsmoking stacks with an air stubborn, baffled and bemused upon a stumppocked scene of profound and peaceful desolation, unplowed, untilled, gutting slowly into red and choked ravines beneath the long quiet rains of autumn and the galloping fury of vernal equinoxes.[26]

Your copy may not approximate classic literature but, as we've just demonstrated, classic literature will often not succeed as digestible aural copy. So vocalize everything you write for audio as you write it. Perform the message you've created exactly the way you would want a voiceover artist to read it. If something trips you up, change it. That same imperfection is likely to cause similar problems later for both talent and listeners.

If you neglect to voice your copy, you're likely to be deaf to its true tonality. This deafness is especially likely on copy you've revised several times. As writing authority Gary Provost points out, "Often when you write and rewrite and constantly rearrange information, your ear for the sound of the writing becomes corrupted. Reading out loud will return to you the true sound of your story. You will hear the sour note of the word that's 'just not right,' and the drastic changes in tone will cry out to you for editing. You'll notice that you are breathless at the end of one long sentence and you know that you must break it up into two or three. Read out loud. Listen for the music, the variety, the emphasis."[27]

While reading aloud, you should also obtain the actual running time of the copy. Word count, as noted in Chapter 3, is only a general indication of the number of seconds a given piece of material will expend. The only exact method is to put a stopwatch to the copy as you are voicing it. And make sure you do *really* voice it. Some copywriters invariably come up with material that is over-time because they whisper the message to themselves. Since it takes longer actually to vocalize a word than it does simply to form it with the mouth, lip-read copy will always time out shorter than when fully articulated by a performer. The result is a forced accelerating at the end of the copy as the talent strives to fit it into the allotted time. Nothing can be more detrimental to listener attention than this involuntary speeding up. Avoid it via careful timing of several fully articulated run-throughs paced at the tempo at which you wish the performers to read. In this way, your message will be as succinct in form as it should be in content.

3. Remain Present and Active

With its extreme availability and portability, radio is a "right-now" medium. Thus good aural copy is normally expected to convey a sense of immediate, present-tense vibrancy. It is easier for any of us to become involved mentally in something happening *now* than to meditate on the past or speculate on the future. Audio copywriters, therefore, usually keep verbs in the present tense. This not only makes it easier for listeners to visualize the action our copy depicts, it also cuts down on the drab, time-wasting helping verbs that can destroy copy conciseness. In case you slept through junior high English, here is a list of these always dull and often extraneous helping or linking verbs. They are divided into five sets to facilitate heightened familiarity if not downright memorization:

1. be, am, is, are, was, were, been
2. have, has, had
3. do, does, did
4. may, might, must
5. can, could, will, would, shall, should

Thus, it's:

We play it for you on 93 KHJ.

Not:

We WILL play it for you . . .

The first set of helping verbs (all forms of the verb *to be*) should be avoided for another reason as well. Because they all convey only state of being rather than action, they put your ideas into the dreaded *passive* voice, which destroys the sense of dynamism so important to vibrant copy. In the *active* voice, the subject performs the verb's action:

Comet cleans all kitchen surfaces.

But in the time- and energy-depleting *passive* voice, the subject merely seems affected by the verb's action:

All kitchen surfaces are cleaned by Comet.

Sometimes the passive voice is grammatically unavoidable. But the less we use it, the less the danger that we are projecting static stills to our listener's mind's eye rather than compelling motion pictures.

For a comparison, here are two versions of the same spot. The first version (the commercial that actually aired) stays in the present tense and active voice by holding helping verbs to a minimum:

ANNCR: Say, teen, let's celebrate Premiere style. Get your Easter vacation off to a really great start. Grab a partner or a group of friends and come on down to Premiere Center for a night of fun you won't want to miss. This Saturday, April the second, dance on the area's largest dance floor to today's hot tunes. Played by the area's most talked-about deejay. The fun happens from 6:30 p.m. until 11:30 p.m. That's this Saturday, April second. Dress up in your favorite fashions and come on down to where it's happening. The Premiere Center. Three-three-970 Van Dyke Avenue in Sterling Heights.

(Courtesy of Christopher Conn, WHYT-FM)

Though most of the words are the same, the second version below illustrates how energy drains from a spot when helping verbs and the passive voice are allowed to predominate:

ANNCR: Say teen, you can be celebrating Premiere style. You'll soon be on Easter vacation so you will want to have that vacation start off great. All your friends should be coming on down to Premiere Center for a night of fun you will not want to miss. This Saturday, April the second, you could be dancing on the area's largest dance floor as today's hottest tunes will be featured. They'll be played by the area deejay who is the most talked-about. The fun will happen from 6:30 p.m. until 11:30 p.m. That will be this Saturday, April second. So you should be dressed up in your favorite fashions and come on down to where it will happen. The Premiere Center. It's located at three-three-970 Van Dyke Avenue in Sterling Heights.

The second set of helping verbs (*have/has/had*) also deserves disdain. Too many writers allow them to solo as a thought's only verb. Because these words are so color-less both in their own phonetic makeup and in what they contribute to their subjects, *have/has/had* should not be permitted to stand alone. Compare this copy line,

The Vistacruiser <u>has</u> a European-style grille.

with these possibilities:

The Vistacruiser <u>sports</u> a European-style grille.
The Vistacruiser <u>displays</u> a European-style grille.
The Vistacruiser <u>flaunts</u> a European-style grille.
The Vistacruiser <u>boasts</u> a European-style grille.
The Vistacruiser <u>brandishes</u> a European-style grille.
The Vistacruiser <u>projects</u> a European-style grille.
The Vistacruiser <u>features</u> a European-style grille.
The Vistacruiser <u>accentuates</u> a European-style grille.
The Vistacruiser <u>exalts</u> a European-style grille.
The Vistacruiser <u>emboldens</u> a European-style grille.

Certainly, some of these images may be "overripe" (depending on your target universe). But all of them are more dynamic, and more vibrant, than the lackluster *has*.

Finally, action and flow are also affected by how you use prepositions. There are two key issues here. First, you can save time and improve focus and pacing by converting prepositional phrases to adjectives. Thus:

the flakes with the frosting

becomes

the frosted flakes

and

the unveiling of the dessert

is changed to

the dessert's unveiling

Second (and related to our earlier conversationality discussion), do not be afraid to conclude an idea unit with a preposition if that wording improves copy flow and understanding. As Professor Michael Spear reminds us, "many sentences end pleasantly, effectively and forcefully with prepositions, and most of the great writers of English have known this for 600 years. Who would quibble with the Shakespeare line? 'And do such bitter business as the day Would quake to look on.'"[28]

4. Beware Uncertain Pronouns

We have previously established that, unlike readers, listeners cannot go back to pick up ideas missed the first time. By the same token, these listeners cannot regress to find the referent for pronouns such as *he, she, it, they, them,* or *that.* Because pronouns have such a high potential for listener confusion and diversion, they should be used sparingly in aural copy. Particularly to be avoided is the use of the relative pronouns *this* and *that* to refer to a complex idea. Listeners will certainly tire of mentally retracing their auditory steps and may overlook the entire point of the spot in the process.

This trainee-written commercial for Sanford's Mucilage illustrates how pronoun proliferation can clog continuous auditory revelation. Even if listeners remain tuned in, they become so preoccupied with determining which nouns the pronouns replace that there is little time left to focus on the product-in-use situation.

ANNCR: Many of you may not know what Sanford's Mint-Flavored Mucilage is. Some may say it's a new kind of dessert, or maybe it's an after-dinner drink. Well, it's not. It's an adhesive that's used like licking a stamp. Just apply it to what you want bonded. Then lick it and hold its two surfaces together. It bonds in seconds. And with Christmas getting close, children can use it to make more tree decorations. Yes, it can make it even more fun for them because it's mint flavored. Its rubber top regulates the mucilage flow so they get out only what is needed. The bottle is unbreakable too so you won't have to worry about their mess. Try Sanford's Mint-Flavored Mucilage. It's great fun for them because it tastes like mint.

Count the number of pronouns that have been inflicted on this poor, harmless product and on the poor, harmless listener at whom this spot is aimed. Not only must time be taken to locate the referent for all of these pronouns, but at several points the identity of this referent also may be in considerable doubt. *What* "bonds in seconds?" *Who* will "it" be even more fun for, and what is the "it?" *What* has a rubber top and *who* makes that mess? Little wonder if listeners get bored with the guessing game and turn their minds to other things.

Keep pronouns to a minimum in your copy. If a pronoun has been used to avoid the redundant use of the same term, either find an appropriate synonym or try rearranging the sentences so that term does not appear at the same place in succeeding thought units. In an aural-only medium, most pronouns are confusing stumbling blocks to listener comprehension.

The main exception to this rule is the pronoun *you*, which represents each individual listener's name in simulating a sense of one-to-one communion. As master radio copywriter Jeffrey Hedquist reminds us, "Using the second person perspective allows the listener to make the commercial theirs."[29] Notice, for example, how the following commercial propels the listener into The Fifth Season Lounge through the copywriter's discrete exploitation of *you* and *your*:

ANNCR: Where do you go for live music? Free hors d'oeuvres? All right in the middle of one of the state's most luxurious night spots. You go no further than Greensboro to The Fifth Season Lounge in the Holiday Inn Four Seasons. The music? Your favorite classic rock. Free hors d'oeuvres Monday through Friday from 5 to 7. The company you find is the cream-of-the-crop in the triad. And the dancing is outrageous. Dance to your heart's delight --- and meet the people you want to meet. At The Fifth Season Lounge. In the Holiday Inn, Greensboro. Your kind of fun.

(Courtesy of Bernard Mann, Mann Media)

With a menu much like other fast-food feeders, McDonald's broke away from the competition in the 1970's largely due to consistent advertising whose second person tags and treatments always put consumers front and center in the scene:

You deserve a break today (1971)

We do it all for you (1975)

You, you're the one (1976)

What you want is what you get at McDonald's today (1992)

Have you had your break today? (1995)

We love to see you smile (2000)

5. Avoid TV Soundtracks

Having been continuously exposed to so many video commercials from the virtual moment of birth, it is easy for today's copywriters to create defective audio messages that are nothing more than *television soundtracks*. This occurs because the copy fails to answer two fundamental questions: (1) What does the product look like? (2) How does the product work? In a video context, both of these questions are automatically addressed simply by pointing the camera at the product. True, the commercial may be poorly executed and unpersuasively styled, but the viewer has at least been given a picture of the product in operation.

Unfortunately, writers whose audio spots are really TV soundtracks forget they do not have a camera at their disposal. So they do what most visual media do. They leave appearance description to the lens, while the copy amplifies the problem being shown—and then jumps ahead to discuss the glowing product-in-use benefit/result the camera is documenting. But radio has no camera. An audio spot cannot convey that essential *product-in-use* unless that use is translated into aural pictorialization via words, music, and sound effects. These auditory elements must overtly and specifically describe what the product looks like and how it works.

Note how the following thirty-second commercial for Baker's Guild Gold Dragees sets up the problem, but then leaps directly to "use aftermath" without ever touching upon the dragees' defining appearance or the process of applying them. So listeners are unsure of how the "All-Occasion Cake's" transformation was achieved, uncertain as to whether they have the ability to obtain this positive result themselves.

ANNCR: I'm the All-Occasion Cake. Being in the cake family hasn't been easy for me. Especially with a popular big brother like the Birthday Cake. I was a plain, ordinary pastry. A ho-hum experience about as exciting as a saltine cracker. But now I'm a star too. Thanks to Baker's Guild Gold Dragees, I'm the sparkling All-Occasion Cake that turns everyone's head. Nobody takes me --- or the person who baked me --- for granted anymore. For your own creative cake decorating, use Baker's Guild Gold Dragees. Baker's Guild Gold Dragees make both you and your All-Occasion Cake a star.

What does a gold dragee look like in shape and size? How exactly does it work? The listener has only product claims and no product pictures—so will neither be involved in, nor persuaded by, this copy.

You don't need a lot of time or a battery of sophisticated sound effects to aurally demonstrate product-in-use. Even thirty seconds of straight copy can do the job if the words are well chosen and well arranged, as in the following univoice depiction of the Lintaway. How (with what words) is product-in-use articulation accomplished in this commercial?

ANNCR: Going out? Chances are, you're taking more than you need. Chances are you're carrying lint. There --- on your favorite sweater. On your new suit. Or on that expensive wool jacket. But now, you can eliminate lint with the Lintaway. The Lintaway's 6-inch adhesive surface actually peels lint off in smooth, easy strokes. Shaped liked a mini-paint-roller, the Lintaway is fun and easy to use. Just roll the Lintaway up that sleeve and watch as the Lintaway's hungry adhesive tape eats up lint, hair, and other unsightly particles. Next time, leave lint at home. With the Lintaway adhesive roller.

6. Keep Humor in Bounds

Particularly on radio, the trend has been toward more and more humor as a means of promoting an ever-widening range of products and services. The proponents of comedic commercials observe that you can't reason with people if you don't have their attention. And radio research by Duncan and Nelson suggests that "humor appears to increase attention paid to the commercial, improve liking of the commercial, reduce irritation experienced from the commercial, and increase liking of the product."[30] These findings are in line with legendary radio humorist Stan Freberg's belief that, "At the end of any commercial that I've ever created, you have the feeling, whether you can articulate it or not, subliminally even, you have the idea 'This must be a pretty good company because they don't take themselves too seriously.'"[31]

On the other hand, as Duncan and Nelson also discovered, "Humor does not appear to reduce mental arguing of the advertised message, improve product-related beliefs, increase intention to buy . . . or increase recall of the commercial's selling points."[32] In short, even though a comedic approach will help attract your listener's ear and set up a presumption of agreeableness for your message, humor cannot consummate the sale or compensate for the absence of a clearly articulated consumer benefit.

It must be recognized that you can't use comedy to promote everything. As a general rule, the more expensive an advertised product or service is, the less appropriate a humorous appeal becomes. When is the last time you chuckled at a Lincoln or Lexus spot? Guffawed at an ad for a $180-an-ounce perfume? Giggled at a luxury jeweler's commercial? Things seem to become less humorous the more money they will siphon from our wallets or bank accounts. If for this or any other more rarefied reason, humor does not seem appropriate to your client and/or your client's product category, don't use it.

You must also beware of the extraneous humor that ad man Robert J. Wanamaker long ago labeled *parasite advertising* because it feeds off, chews away at whatever positive image the product or service previously possessed. If listeners remember the joke but not the product that joke was supposed to promote, the quip has sustained itself entirely at the expense of the client, with no beneficial return in either brand recall or product knowledge.

Because humor is so prevalent on radio, and because when radio humor fails, it fails so abjectly, copywriters for the aural medium must be especially suspicious and wary of giving birth to anything that might translate itself into parasite advertising. To keep your humor in bounds, and to ferret out parasite advertising before it feeds off *you*, stand your proposed comedic treatment up against these "don't's and do's" fashioned by agency president Anthony Chevins:

1. Don't tell a joke. Jokes wear out fast.
2. Never make fun of the product. Have fun with the product, but not at the expense of it.
3. Don't have a surprise ending. Surprise endings are only a surprise one time.
4. Don't make it difficult for the listener/viewer to figure out whether you're laughing at him or with him.
5. Don't ever let the humor get out of hand and get in the way of selling your product. Don't pull the chair from under the listener/viewer.
6. Don't use humor because you can't figure out anything else to do.

Now the do's:

1. Way out front and number one by far is make the humor relevant—relevant to the product—relevant to its benefits—relevant—relevant—relevant.
2. Involve the listener/viewer in the humor in the first ten seconds of the commercial.
3. Use humor to point out the product's strong selling points.

4. Be charming rather than funny. It is better to get a smile than a belly laugh.
5. Make your humor simple and clear. Make it basic and broad. (Give it a chance to appeal to everybody.)
6. Make sure that the humor is so tightly integrated with the product and its sales message that there would be no way that one could survive without the other. A humorous approach that could be used to sell any number of products by simply picking out one and putting in another is usually worthless—as with all borrowed interest.[33]

The spot below is a typical piece of parasite advertising in which the attempted humor tramples all over the client. Pay particular attention to how the most potent imagery focuses not on the product but on the allegedly funny condition that product is supposed to alleviate:

WIFE: (Syrupy) Good morning, dear. How's my little pigeon?

HUBBY: Awful. My mouth feels like the bottom of a bird cage.

WIFE: That's terrible. Here. Stick your little beak into this.

HUBBY: What is it?

WIFE: It's Apri-Grape. A juice to wake-up crowing about!

HUBBY: Apri-Grape? With a bunch of starlings molting in my mouth?

WIFE: Just try it, ducky. This apricot and grapefruit blend will really get you flying.

HUBBY: (Tasting) Hey! This stuff sure plucks up my ruffled spirits!

WIFE: (Sexily) Anything for my little rooster.

In contrast, below is a comedically appropriate commercial. Rather than feeding off the product, this spot meets every one of Chevins's criteria for humor that sells effectively. The concept quickly establishes and then builds on a scene that evolves to communicate how the product is the long-lasting, less "uncomfortable," and now, even more convenient way to muscle pain relief.

JANE: Sir, I'm a little uncomfortable with the way we've been having our Monday morning meetings.

BOSS;   A little uncomfortable?

JANE: Extremely uncomfortable with meeting in your bathroom, sir, while you're in the tub.

BOSS: Well, I'm wearing a tie---

JANE: I can see that sir.

BOSS;   Over the weekend I play ball with the kids, do yard work, and get in some tennis. So by Monday my muscles are very sore. Spending all day in a hot tub is the only thing that helps.

JANE: Have your tried---

BOSS: Wrapping myself in cabbage leaves. Yes, I have.

JANE: Actually, sir, I was thinking of Tiger Balm Pain Relieving Patches.

BOSS: Tiger Balm? The little jar with the tiger on it?

JANE: Yeah, right. Tiger Balm. It's been around for about a hundred years.

BOSS: Jinkies.

JANE: And now Tiger Balm comes in these neat pain relief patches.

BOSS: Hmm --- could you hand me that duck there?

       (SFX: RUBBER DUCK SQUEAK)

JANE: You just stick the patch on where it hurts.

BOSS: Uh huh.

JANE: And Tiger Balm's Pain Relief Patches are very fast acting and long lasting. So, we wouldn't have to meet in your bathroom every Monday.

BOSS: And I would be less pruney and your report wouldn't be in the microwave.

JANE: What?

BOSS: I dropped your report in the tub. So I put it in the dryer, but it caught fire, so my wife doused it with water and put it in the microwave. Let me just go grab it.

JANE: No, no, don't get up, sir!

BOSS: Oops. Sorry. Sitting back down.

ANNCR: Long lasting, fast acting, pain relieving Tiger Balm Patch. Works where it hurts.

(Courtesy of Dick Orkin and Chris Coyle, Dick Orkin's Radio Ranch)

In summing up humor's justification and deployment, British actor/writer John Cleese reminds us that "As the old Chinese proverb has it, 'Tell me and I'll forget, show me and I may remember, involve me and I'll understand.' The point of comedy is that it involves the audience."[34] And Fallon Advertising's Bob Barrie concludes, "People like to be charmed by advertising, and it has a better effect on them if you can deliver a message with some humor. We like to do things that attract attention, but our ads are always based on strategy—an understanding of marketing, the media, how the tone of the ad represents the client."[35]

7. Stress Sponsor Identification

The world's most colorful and comedic piece of audio writing won't justify itself if the listener fails to discern the brand name being promoted. It used to be that clients and/or agencies would translate this commandment into a mathematical formula that decreed how many mentions of the brand name must be included in given length spots. Today, it is recognized that you do not have to mention the product a dozen times or in every other sentence. The particular *placement* of the mentions within the spot and how the spot as a whole hooks the listener are much more important considerations. In the univoice rant below, the client name naturally appears as a "what we didn't have" referent for comparing 'back then' with benefits now available—and available from this particular eaterie.

<u>Production Note: Guy is a crotchety 60-ish</u>

GUY: When I was your age --- we didn't have The Break Room Cyber Café. All we had was greasy spoons that served overcooked, stale coffee with old milk, and sugar substitute. And we *liked* it. We didn't have any fancy gourmet coffees like they have at The Break Room Cyber Café. And we didn't have any Internet. All we had was dirty cups and old letters from our draft board telling us it was time for our physicals. The only servers we had were wrinkled up old ladies who wore enough perfume to kill the smell of gas leaking from the space heater in the corner. And if we wanted breakfast, we had to go out and kill our own pigs and steal some eggs from Old Man Baker's chickens --- and cook them over a fire we made from that pile of last week's newspapers. And we *liked* it. And when I was your age, we never had homemade soups and sandwiches and cookies and muffins like they have at The Break Room Cyber Café. Shoot --- I wish I was *your* age.

ANNCR: The Break Room Cyber Café. For today's age. The best gourmet coffee in town --- and a lot more. 30-15 Merle Hay Road. Open Monday through Saturday 6:30 in the morning. The Break Room Cyber Café.

(Courtesy of Brian Whitaker, Saga Communications)

A prime device for sponsor identification is often the *identity line*, the short but swingy slogan that enhances rapid recognition of the brand or corporate name. When this line comes at the end of spots, it is called the *tag*. According to marketer Robert Sawyer, "The test for a 'savvy slogan' is whether or not it completes the intended communication in a compelling way, one that helps eliminate the anxiety of choice in the consumer's mind."[36] Therefore, the identity line should exhibit a categorical thrust—it should showcase the brand name *and* the product category of which that brand is a member. Brand names in isolation do not exist in the listener's mind for long. So if the identity line also designates the product category (and this particular product's benefit), the line will enjoy a longer and much more functional life. A line "should, best case, be the advertiser's unique selling proposition—the core benefit that comes from using the product or service" marketing consultant Steve Cone advises. "Powerful taglines are inspired phrases created by great copywriters who see clear and compelling brand promises and make them come to life to inspire, entertain and enlighten the rest of us."[37] Here are some past and present lines that establish both the brand name and its categorical promise:

When you're out of Schlitz, you're out of beer.

Diet Delight. If it wasn't in cans you'd swear it was fresh fruit.

Tigner Waste Management's got what it takes to take what you've got.

Molson Beer and Ale --- with the taste as big as Canada.

You've got an uncle in the furniture business --- Joshua Doore.

When it comes to pizza, who knows? Jenos.

You don't have to be Jewish to love Levy's Rye Bread.

Red Lobster for the seafood lover in you.

We put eight great tomatoes in that little bitty can --- Contadina.

Shasta Root Beer --- the foam that you feel.

Trojans --- they're a matter of condom sense.

Piccadilly Circles. The English muffin with the meal on top.

Larry's Radiator Shop; the best place in town to take a leak.

Coca-Cola: the pause that refreshes.

Federal Express --- when it absolutely, positively has to be there overnight.

Jenkins Optical. If you don't see what you're looking for --- you've come to the right place.

Ace is the place with the helpful hardware man.

Whether or not their spots make use of an identity line, some copywriters like to substitute the pronoun *we* in contexts that would otherwise call for the brand name. This is generally an unwise practice for two reasons. First, each use of *we* is one less mention of the client's name in a place in which it would be just as easy to be specific. Second, unless the client has one voice under contract on an exclusive basis, the listener is fully aware that this announcer is not, really, the *we* down at Joe's Service Station any more than he was the *we* at the Astro Appliance Mart whose message he delivered earlier. Multiple *we's* cut down on message credibility and do nothing to facilitate sponsor identification.

8. Concentrate Your Attack

Given all the potential perils of the real-time message that reaches its audience solely via sound, one audio commercial cannot cover everything there is to say about the product or service. Nevertheless, declares creative director Martin Bihl, "A lot of clients use it as a repository for all the stuff they can't jam into the TV spot. Mind-numbing litanies about product features are routinely shoe-horned into the radio spot and trundled out with all the grim determination of a stage mother shoving an untalented brat into the unforgiving maw of public scrutiny."[38] An audio spot is neither a video commercial brimming with digital detail nor a print or Webpage layout with its variety of typefaces and graphics. So even sixty seconds of audio maximizes its chance for success when it selects a single need or problem and zeros in on the product attribute designed to fix it. In the Southwest Eyecare spot that follows, the problem is aurally epitomized in a way that cries out for the client's immediate intervention.

MALE: At Southwest Eyecare, we want to remind you that the holidays are a great time to think about improving your vision. Being able to she this lime of ear is impotent. Just margarine you're singing a cheese mess carol and can't read the worlds. So you just fart baking them cup. You would probaby sound bike an idiot. Or maybe you're strangling to see the in graduates in a pump win fly recipe. You put two cups of floor and the recipe called for two cups of slugger. I beet that would be one nasty pump win fly. So it seems preppy clear. Wind you can she, everything is just butter.

(MUSIC: LIGHT HOLIDAY INSTRUMENTAL UP AND UNDER)

FEMALE: Waiting until after the holidays to think about improving your vision with LASIK just doesn't make sense. Especially if you have a flex spending account. If you need to plan your vision health expenses for the coming year, have a balance to spend before the end of this year, or just want to give someone you love the gift of better sight, call Southwest Eyecare at 3-4-6-oh-five hundred. For a free LASIK consultation. Southwest Eyecare. 3-4-6-oh-five hundred. Total vision health.

(Courtesy of Jeremy Spencer & Adam Greenhood, copywriters, Esparza Advertising)

If you *must* make more than one major point, resort to separate spots, similarly styled, that together can constitute a cohesive *flight* of commercials. In this way, the listener will become acquainted not only with each aspect, but also with the fact that all of them relate to the same brand or company.

Varying the product appeal in different spots or flights is often the best mechanism for telling a complete story about the product while avoiding individual message fragmentation. With proper spot rotation (a big concern of agency media planners) and consistent copy styling, listeners will get an in-depth picture of your client's wares over the weeks and months of the campaign without sacrificing the individual commercial's integrity and precision.

Whether you use the same appeal in different situations or vary the appeal from spot to spot or flight to flight, make certain that any and every appeal selected is calculated to aim your copy directly at your target audience. Your entire approach, the appeals used as well as the words that convey them, should show the listeners in your universe that you (and, by implication, your client) know something about them and their needs. A teen-oriented message that tries to use slang, for example, may only imply that the client knows little about young folks. "Teen slang," writes Julie Schwartzman, "is a precise code that obscures meaning and prevents an unwelcome outsider from comprehending an insider's meaning, such as Cockney slang does. A commercial that misuses slang and renders an adolescent way of talking inane and vacuous is more likely to alienate teenagers than impress them."[39]

A similar problem occurs when ethnic audiences are clumsily targeted in copy styling. As Caroline Jones of Mingo-Jones Advertising warns, "slanguage has never worked, and probably never will. Especially if it comes from general advertisers. We still call that 'patronizing' advertising, not ethnic."[40] Ethnic markets should be addressed via the same process as any demographic/psychographic cluster—through careful research into their wants and lifestyles rather than by superficial parroting of alleged ethnic verbal patterns. Like any group, "we [African Americans] are turned off by corporations that don't take the time to get to know us," adds public relations executive Faith Griffin Morris. "We feel they've taken advantage of us if they don't."[41] Consequently, the use of contrived ethnic slang as a substitute for in-depth understanding of any racial group will not result in reputable copy or successful communication. It will deflect, rather than concentrate, your pitch.

9. Conclude with Energy

Whatever your target universe and main copy point, your message won't make a solid impact unless each thought unit within that message ends in a crisp, forward-leaning finish. To bring a sense of impending climax to a commercial, performers need something to *read up to*. They can experience the copy's natural impact and, through their voices, their listeners experience it also. Both talent and listener need to feel that each succeeding sentence was worth their time and trouble. This helps ensure and heighten further attention as the spot progresses.

Conversely, the anticlimactic sentence or message ending that lets the audience down rather than conferring a reward for listening is like Aunt Eleanor's bright-tinseled Christmas packages—with the perennially boring fruitcake inside. The result never lives up to how it was wrapped or the time expended in opening it.

Don't be an "Aunt Eleanor Copywriter." Make sure your audio messages reveal engaging discoveries as the sentence-by-sentence unwrapping proceeds:

MAN: I don't know. Maybe I'm a freak of nature. Guys are supposed to know about cars. Not me. I was frightened of mechanical things. I'd go into a crying jag if I had to use the self-service pump. A friend suggested I confront my problem. Visit a Bumper-to-Bumper Store, he said. They're helpful, and nice. Won't laugh at dumb questions. Still, I was petrified. I had visions of a brute with a tattoo slurping thick coffee into a toothless grin. Well, to my relief, the Bumper-to-Bumper man was a real member of the human race. He actually liked answering my questions, told me whenever I needed an auto part, he'd have it for a low price. Really boosted my confidence. I started to shake his massive hand, but instead I was so happy, well, I kissed him full on the lips. Okay, now that was wrong. I know a guy is not supposed to---

ANNCR: He's got low prices, free answers and dirty hands. Your Bumper-to-Bumper man. If he can't help you, nobody can.

(Courtesy of Craig Wiese, Craig Wiese and Company)

10. Ask for the Order

Some copywriters get so preoccupied with appeals selection, benefit description, and entertaining imagery that they forget to write a call for action. They fail to close the sale. Agency CEO Ron Bliwas observes that "too many commercials focus on being clever and conceptual rather than creatively communicating reasons to buy. Commercials today seem almost embarrassed to ask for the order . . . Too many spots focus on being provocative, funny or emotional, but fail to make a sale."[42] KMEO general sales manager J. D. Freeman adds, "It's not enough to say, 'Oh, by the way, here we are.' It's important for your commercial to ask somebody to do something. 'Come into our business today.'"[43] In this stereo shop pitch, for instance, Santa asks for the order on three separate occasions when he urges his petitioners to "go to Dixie Sound Gallery."

SANTA: Hi. This is Santa Claus with a special message for you car stereo enthusiasts: Get off my back! And that goes for you nimrods who write asking me for remote car starters and alarms and stuff like that too. What'd'ya think --- we got oil wells at the North Pole? I'm Santa Claus, for cryin' out loud. I do choo-choos and dollies and wagons. I don't do five band graphic equalizers. If you want car stereo equipment for Christmas, go to Dixie Sound Gallery or Sound Gallery 59. They specialize in auto sound, alarms, and remote starters by the top names like Pioneer, Sansui, Jensen and more. And at Dixie Sound Gallery and Sound Gallery 59 they do professional installation.

And they're the area's only authorized Alpine dealers. I don't do installation, and as far as I'm concerned, Alpine is Mr. and Mrs. Pine's little boy. Get the idea? I am not the guy to ask for car stereo. Go to Dixie Sound Gallery on Dixie Highway in Drayton Plains or Sound Gallery 59 on M-59 in Pontiac. You want a candy cane, I can take care of ya. Car stereo? Go to Dixie Sound Gallery or Sound Gallery 59. I'm Santa Claus. I'm old. Give me a break---

(Courtesy of Rick Wiggins, WDFX)

With some clients, "asking for the order" may be enhanced by using a "radio coupon." As broadcast researcher Gerry Hartshorn suggests, "Why not design your commercial copy to instruct the listener to ask for a special deal or limited offer at the sponsoring merchant? If the offer is only available through your radio coupon, it gives the retailer a direct means of assessing the effectiveness of advertising on your station.[44]

As in the spot below, such coupons can easily be localized to reference a particular store or time of year.

(SFX: KNOCK ON DOOR AND DOOR OPENING)

CURT:	(Instantly terrified) Rocco!
ROCCO:	(Calm, yet firm and ominous) Yeah, Rocco the Decorator. You strayed from our arrangements.
CURT:	I-I---
ROCCO:	I hate to be crossed
CURT:	(Groveling) --- Well, it's this La-Z-Boy Motion-Modular Furniture, Rocco. It can be a corner unit, a long sofa --- I can't stop rearranging. (Pleading) You gotta understand!
ROCCO:	Put it back the way I like it---
CURT:	Sure, Rocco, sure.
ROCCO:	---or next time I'll rearrange more than your furniture.
LOCALIZED WRAP:	La-Z-Boy Motion Modulars. So many great combinations and all on sale. See them at Conroy's Furniture, 862 North Cherry. And from now until May 31, say 'Rocco sent me' and receive twenty dollars off the sale price on a La-Z-Boy Modular at Conroy's.

(Courtesy of Ross Roy Inc. and La-Z-Boy Chair Company)

AN AUDIO ASSURANCE

Whether it's a lean univoice treatment or a fully dramatized dialogue spot, well-executed audio remains the medium in which writers and their words can conjure up the most vivid and most audience-participatory scenes. With wise selection of vehicle (univoice, multivoice, dialogue, or music), the injection of PUNCH, and a commitment to the ten Audio Commandments, sound *will* sell. It will sell because it most directly and most intensely thrusts the audience into the picture-determination process. Guided by your well-wrought words, listeners can fantasize product benefits in use—and in use within the immediate intimacy and specifics of their own lives.

CHAPTER

9

Additional Audio Endeavors

The previous chapter covers the basics of radio commercial construction. In this chapter, we explore a variety of outlet-based audio writing challenges and also examine the special copy challenges posed by retail, co-op, classified, and direct-response advertising. As with Chapter 8, we begin by setting forth the appropriate data block that, in this case, services many in-house script assignments.

IN-HOUSE DATA BLOCK

When you are creating material that your outlet itself commissions, produces, and airs, the data block can be less formal than the standard commercial version. This is because your script is a piece of internal communication (like a memo) rather than something that must be sent to outside organizations. Nevertheless, for all but the smallest operations, the block should be detailed enough to facilitate production and tracking of the message by staffers other than those who wrote or requested it. Figure 9.1 presents a sample arrangement that accommodates a significant amount of helpful information within a compact space.

In this particular example, a *maintenance* promo is one intended to sustain the current audience for the show by reminding listeners of the benefits of staying with us. The completed items in this data block indicate that the promo has been ordered by Sid, the program director, and written by Thelma, the in-station copywriter. The blank items signify that it has not yet been produced (recorded) or given final approval by management. These dates, and the *Accepted By* line, will be inked-in later to monitor and document announcement completion.

This data block format should *not* be used if the assignment is a commercial for an outside client. Even though such an advertisement may be produced and written in-house, it is still being generated for an external entity that requires additional tracking information. In these cases, the conventional commercial data block presented in Chapter 8 should be used, with the station name/call letters occupying the heading that would otherwise identify an advertising agency.

```
┌─────────────────────────────────────────────────────────────────────┐
│               WAAD CONTINUITY PRODUCTION ORDER                      │
│                                                                     │
│   Subject: Bruce/Lucy Fall Maintenance        Order #: 1383         │
│   Date Ordered: 8/20/10                        Length: :30          │
│   Format: Univoice                             Start Date: 9/15/10  │
│   Ordered By: Sid Sharepoint                   End Date: 10/13/10   │
│   Written By: Thelma Thesaurus                 Scripted: 8/26/10    │
│                                                Produced:            │
│   Accepted By:                                 Approved:            │
│   . . . . . . . . . . . . . . . . . . . . . . . . . . . . . . . .   │
│                                                                     │
│   ANNCR:   Days are getting shorter and those mornings getting      │
│            darker. But you can keep your pre-dawn bright with        │
│            WAAD's very own early-A.M. toast-burners, Bruce and       │
│            Lucy . . .                                                │
└─────────────────────────────────────────────────────────────────────┘
```

FIGURE 9.1   Radio In-House Data Block.

IDS AND TRANSITIONS

Turning to actual copy construction, a station identification may just give the information required by FCC regulations—the call letters immediately followed by the community to which the station is licensed. (The only material that can be inserted between these two items is the station frequency.) Often, however, this legal ID is followed by a brief promo or client billboard (*shared ID*) in order to fill a standard ten seconds of time.

An example of the shared ID, with two seconds for the government and eight seconds for the station's sales department, would typically be fashioned like this:

This is KTRE, Cedarton. Enrich your day with Nestor's Ice Cream in fifteen dairy-delicious flavors. Nestor's Ice Cream makes any meal a party.

For variety, the two parts of the ID can also be reversed:

Gas for your outboard and bait for the fish. Duke's Store-on-the-Shore gets you on the lake quick. This is KTRE, Cedarton.

A legal ID can also be pressed into service for station or program promotion. As the following example demonstrates, FCC-required information can also be put in the middle of the line.

It's where rock n' roll legends live. 1350 KRNT, Des Moines --- and Dic Young's Original Saturday Night Oldies Show

(Courtesy of Jim Brown, Saga Communications)

Or, a mini-PSA can be thrown in as a public relations gesture:

Your hits-happy radio station doesn't want trees to be only a thing of the past. Be careful with campfires. This is hits-happy radio, KTRE --- Cedarton.

Beyond the legal IDs mandated to air as close to the top of the hour as possible and at sign-on and sign-off, stations are free to signify themselves as often, and in any manner, that they see fit. In fact, most outlets schedule many more IDs than required by law as a means of reasserting their identity for the listener. Because these additional (*optional ID*) announcements are not compulsory, they need not even contain the name of the station's home city. Instead, optional IDs can be devoted exclusively to outlet image-building. They may therefore be shorter, or a good deal longer, than the traditional 10-second identification. Most often, optional IDs consist of straight copy that ties into a particular format, show, or personality while always making certain that the station is clearly positioned in the speaker's mind:

Telling the stories of your life --- one song at a time. We're number one for today's country and the legends. One-oh-four point one. The Wolf.

One-oh-four point one. The Wolf. With the blond leading the blind in the morning --- Scott and Jamie. Proving once and for all that the inmates can indeed run the asylum.

(Courtesy of Dee Davis, Saga Communications)

The Zoo Crew from the Nut Hut. All yours from Z-100.

The music you remember from the station that never forgot. 68 WCBM.

(Courtesy of Julie Sizemore, JAM Creative Productions, Inc.)

Drive home, New York, with Rocky Allen, 95.5. WPLJ.

He's the Czar of your car, the Commute Galoot, Rocky Allen, 95.5. WPLJ.

(Courtesy of Janie Autz, TM Century, Inc.)

At home, at work, in the car, online or anywhere you want to be. It's the Steve Harvey Show on ninety-five seven, R and B.

(Courtesy of Don London, WVKL)

93 WFLS. Virginia's best country. And home of the no-talk triple play. Custom-designed to keep the music rollin'. 93 WFLS.

93 WFLS. With the music you love and the artists that make it. Song after song, it's Virginia's best country, 93 WFLS.

(Courtesy of Bill Poole, WFLS)

ANNCR: WLOL. (HEAVY LASER SFX) Now playin' more music.

JOAN RIVERS: Can we talk?

ANNCR: No! (LASER TRAILS OUT)

(Courtesy of Tom Gowan, Emmis Broadcasting's WLOL)

Optional IDs, like those above, are also known as *separators* or *liners* and should be regularly rewritten, updated, personalized, and localized for maximum listener impact. Outlets strive to rotate these separators throughout various parts of the day and on a week-to-week basis in order to have well-established identity without listener-boring redundancy. Thus many such separators are usually required from the copywriter.

Some program directors will have you prepare distinct stylings for more precise segue tasks:

1. *Backsell* liners are for use at the end of a 'music set' (back-to-back records) and just before a 'stop set' (series of commercials and other announcements). Ideally, they should be perceived as a natural extension of the music:

That's another classic on WAAD. Your station for soft music and more of it. Be sure to listen all day at work. Even your boss will like the music on WAAD.

2. *Return* or *re-entry* liners segue from the end of the stop set back into the next music set. They should reiterate the station's promise/benefit to reinforce overall image:

The songs you know --- and the information you can use all week long. You're listening to the John Tesh Radio Show on thirteen fifty KRNT; where the legends live.

(Courtesy of Jim Brown, Saga Communications)

3. *Sweep/transition* liners are quick reidentifiers in the middle of a music set (also known as a 'sweep'):

The Southside is waking up with the Steve Harvey Morning Show on ninety-five seven, R and B.

(Courtesy of Don London, WVKL)

4. *Recaps* are backsell liners in which the copy restates the titles of the tunes just played. For maximum station recognition, recaps should begin with the call sign or dial position:

WMHW, Oldies 92, just cruised through: 'Runaway' by Del Shannon; The Association's 'Along Comes Mary'; and sweetened the set with 'Sugar Shack' from Jimmy Gillmer.

5. Especially important for automated stations, *location* liners "personalize your station and involve listeners outside of your immediate city of license," instructs programming executive Dennis Soapes. "Location liners can also be used to target listeners in key neighborhoods."[1]

Virginia Beach, we've got you covered with the Steve Harvey Morning Show on ninety-five seven, R and B.

(Courtesy of Don London, WVKL)

A tightly formatted station will even commission sets of liners geared to time of day, day of the week, and season of the year:

Starting your day in the very best way, WAAD.

Middleburg's afternoons move to the sound of WAAD.

Another night of favorites, just for you on WAAD.

(Courtesy of Bill Wolkey, Broadcast Programming)

We keep you going on a Monday, at WAAD.

Clutter-free on a Thursday. This is WAAD.

You bring your radio and WAAD will bring the best music this weekend.

(Courtesy of Renee Fleming, Century 21 Programming, Inc.)

Celebrating the birthday of our great nation, we're WAAD.

A whisper of sweet somethings on Valentine's Day from WAAD.

WAAD; putting on our Sunday's best. Have a pleasant Easter.

(Courtesy of Billy Wolkey, Broadcast Programming)

One-oh-four point one The Wolf loves everything about Halloween. Popcorn balls, candy corn and, of course, anything chocolate. But what The Wolf loves most about Halloween --- is scaring small children. (SFX: GUTTERAL 'Raahhhhhhhhhh' FOLLOWED BY KID SCREAMS). One-oh-four point one The Wolf.

Thanksgiving roll call! Scott and Jamie (SFX: GOBBLE GOBBLE), Erin (GOBBLE), Matt (GOBBLE). And let's not forget about Dee (GOBBLE). You're going to find the biggest turkeys --- right here on one-oh-four point one The Wolf.

(SUNG) Dashing through the snow --- with a great big (WOLF HOWL) ho ho hooooo. Merry Christmas from one-oh-four point one The Wolf.

(Courtesy of Dee Davis, Saga Communications)

To create liners that make a consistent statement while still providing variety, you can write a common 'bed' into which different inserts can be dropped:

93 WFLS. This is Brian and Sheila. (INSERT FUNNY KICKER FROM SHOW). This is Virginia's Best Country. (UP-TEMPO CURRENT SONG HOOKS). And this is the station with both --- 93 WFLS.

(Courtesy of Bill Poole, WFLS)

Optional ID material can also be cast in lyric form, usually by a writer at a specialty ("jingle") production house. In most cases today, these lyrics are short *signatures* that tie station recognition to a clear listener life-style benefit. Here are six examples:

I'm getting up with Lite
It's another Houston dawn
Start the morning with a song on 93.7 FM --- K-Lite.

Bumper to bumper, miles to go
I don't mind
I've got Lite Rock playin' on the radio

93.7 FM --- K-Lite.
Meetings, reports, a million things to do
Everyday you play the songs that help me make it through
93.7 --- K-Lite.

I could never leave you
I listen all day long
You understand my feelings
You play my favorite songs
93.7 FM --- K-Lite.

(Courtesy of Century 21 Programming, Inc.)

Turn that alarm, off for me
Waking early is misery
Come on Kraddick, you know it's true
Waking up is hard to do.
Remember when, I switched to KISS
Now my mornings are filled with bliss
When I hear Kraddick I'm not so blue
But, waking up is hard to do.

The sun is starting to rise
And the music helps you open your eyes
Well we're having some fun, with 106.1
Put some coffee in your cup
And let Kidd Kraddick wake you up.

(Courtesy of Janie Autz, TM Century, Inc.)

Tom Cusic, TM Century's studio manager, reports that stations typically order from ten to fifteen versions of a jingle so the styling does not "burn out" through constant repetition of the same cut. Thus a variety of lengths and instrumental mixes are prepared to 'sweeten' the package.[2]

Of course, jingle ID copy usually will expend fewer words for the time allotted than would straight copy. You can't pack a music bed full of verbiage and still expect that bed to play a balanced role in the ID's total impact. It is also important that the style of the music and the swing of the writing tightly mesh, not only with each other, but also with the overall image the outlet is striving to project.

IDs constitute a station's most available and most important continuing public relations device. It is therefore vital that, whether lyric or straight copy, they be well written, well produced, and carefully oriented in consultation with station programming executives. More than any other type of material a copywriter creates, the ID reflects on the character and identity of the outlet for which it is constructed. Consequently, it is essential that copy and program personnel be operating on exactly the same wavelength when it comes to aural definition of what the station is and of what it is striving to say about itself. In today's radio, *format* is everything. It imbues everything the station airs and everything the station sells or fails to sell. Continuity/programming clash makes for a disjointed, schizophrenic outlet personality that disrupts format and design integrity. The format will *never* be changed to fit the style of your continuity, so your continuity had better be a mirror image of that format from its inception. This rule applies to all continuity but especially to the ID material, which is supposed to promote and epitomize the format's essence.

Even the shortest ID should reflect the heart of your station image line—the one overriding statement that must adhere like glue to the listener's entertainment-seeking consciousness. This may be expressed in straight copy, a musical statement, or a combination of the two. But whatever its form, the line must embody the outlet and be almost infinitely expandable from both length and seasonal standpoints. Stations are consumer products, radio group owner Lew Dickey reminds us, and "must compete as brands as well."[3]

It is generally an efficient practice to ascertain the length of the longest ID requested by the programming department. Then, write this lyric or straight copy first so it can be the fountainhead out of which the shorter IDs flow. These comparatively brief, derivative announcements are known as *lift-outs*. Such a procedure not only saves on production costs but also ensures a tight consistency of outlet image throughout all day parts and ID applications.

In articulating that image, "don't assume listeners know what your slogan means; tell them what it means," concludes radio consultant Rob Balon. "Simply put, the most eloquent station positioning liners are those that educate and translate for the listener. . . . Communicate with the listeners in *their* words, not in yours. . . . Save the broadcaster jargon for your next guest piece in the trades, and *concentrate on finding out how your listeners describe the things that your radio station does.*"[4] Thus, it's

Five eighties hits in a row. Neon 92's morning guarantee to you.

rather than

Tune to Neon 92 for the market's longest classic rock sweeps in morning drive.

As indicated earlier in this chapter, backsell and re-entry ID liners often do double duty as transitional devices between major programmatic elements. But these are not the only transitions that the radio copywriter may be called on to create. Frequently, sports coverage requires an extensive inventory of linking material. The aim here is not literary elegance but cogent, hard-working traffic-directing that 'takes care of business' while propelling the program forward, as in the following hockey continuity:

The Herb Boxer Pre-Game Show --- brought to you by your friends at Copper Country Ford-Lincoln-Mercury. Your volume price dealer with reliable service; located next to the Mall in Houghton.

. . . .

The first period is brought to you by Superior National Bank and Trust, with offices in Hancock, Hubbell, Baraga, and the Copper Country Mall. And by Aurora Cable Communication --- providing Houghton-Hancock with a better picture. The switch is on --- to Aurora.

. . . .

The second period comes courtesy of Maki Oil of Ripley, offering you 24-hour emergency fuel oil delivery and furnace repair. And by Thomas Ford-Mercury of L'Anse --- where you can drive a little and save a lot.

. . . .

Coming up --- the third period --- through the courtesy of D and N Savings Bank with offices in Hancock and Calumet and the new Bank-Mart now open in K-Mart at the Copper Country Mall.

. . . .

Stay tuned for <u>The State Farm Three-Star Show</u> brought your way by your local State Farm agents: Ted Gast in Houghton, Gary Sands in Ontonagon and L'Anse, Art Vasold in Calumet, and Mike Lahti in Hancock. Like a good neighbor, State Farm is there.

(Courtesy of Jeffrey Olsen, WMPL and WZRK-FM)

Sports and other live, out-of-studio events are not, of course, entirely predictable. So, sometimes, a copywriter must prepare *contingency continuity,* which announcers can use in a variety of possible situations. Here is a set of such lines designed to help the sportscasters get into the sponsor's commercials with as little disruption as possible. Like all professional transition copy, it does not call attention to itself but instead, helps conserve and direct that attention to the important event to follow:

(POSSIBLE USE: AT THE START OF THE GAME OR DURING THE PRE-GAME SHOW)

Hey, what a nice crowd out there today! Looks like about (ESTIMATE NUMBER) fans came out to watch the stars shine. To all of them and to all you fans listening to the game --- this Bud's for you!

. . . .

(POSSIBLE USE: AFTER AN INJURY OR WHEN A DOUBTFUL PLAYER ENTERS THE LINE-UP.)

Do you believe that? It takes a lot of courage to be playing in such pain. But you've gotta hand it to the trainers, right? Yeah, for all you guys who help keep the players playing --- this Bud's for you!

. . . .

POSSIBLE USE: WHEN A PLAYER MAKES A KEY PLAY ROUTINELY --- LIKE KICKING A FIELD GOAL OR SINKING FREE THROW.)

What a play! Just like in practice! Now that's what makes these guys so good. They perform under pressure just like it was routine. So for everyone who looks as good during the game as they did in practice --- this Bud's for you!

. . . .

(POSSIBLE USE: IN A TIGHT GAME SITUATION.)

Talk about tense situations! Boy, I'd hate to be in the coaches' shoes right now. But win or lose, they know how to handle the pressure --- just like Budweiser knows how to handle thirst. So for all you coaches pacing the sidelines --- this Bud's for you!

. . . .

(POSSIBLE USE: LATE IN THE GAME WHEN THE TEAM IS HOPELESSLY LOSING.)

This Bud's for all the fans who are still here and to all of you still listening. Yes, to everyone who supports the (TEAM NICKNAME) win, lose or draw. For all you do --- this Bud's for you!

(Courtesy of Annette Abercombie, Mutual Broadcasting)

PROGRAM PROMOS

Many of the ID construction principles we've just discussed pertain to promotional continuity for individual programs, station personalities, or program series. Like IDs, program promos must mirror the station's overall sound. They also frequently serve transitional purposes:

Gary Havens playing the country hits in KIOV Country. And by the way, there's more great country music with your favorite stars on <u>Live from the Lone Star Cafe</u> every Sunday night at 10:05 here on KIOV.

Big Lake Country Radio and Bill Robinson here on KJCK. Listen to <u>Swap Shop</u> Monday through Saturday from 9:30 to 10:00 in the morning. If you have anything to buy, sell, or trade, call us during <u>Swap Shop</u> at 2-3-8, zero-one, fifty-one.

(Courtesy of Jon Potter, The Musicworks, Inc.)

Wherever possible, program promos should also exploit seasonal subjects in order to tie the feature more closely to what is in the listener's mind (and environment) at the time:

Look outside. It's finally Spring in New England. The daffodils, the tulips, the azaleas, the dogwoods. The black flies! It's finally time to get outside. Work the flowerbeds, put in the vegetable garden. Your lawn needs mowing <u>already</u>! And time to check in with WOKQ twice every hour for the radar weather. Jim Witt and his staff don't get to go outside --- they're glued to their radar screens watching the weather for you. On 97 point 5, WOKQ.

(Courtesy of Ramsey Elliot, Fuller-Jeffrey Broadcasting Companies, Inc.)

Many times, a radio program promo is really a promo for the personality around which a show or airshift is built. So the copywriter's job is to give that personality something to say that characterizes them in a way that will be attractive to target listeners. Listen carefully to the talent's way of speaking and then craft a script that is comfortably in keeping with their delivery. This is especially important when the person is new to the market.

MITZI: Hi. I'm Mitzi Miles. Yep, that's me, on Magic everyday from 10:30 to 3. Although I was raised in Pennsylvania, I feel at home here. In fact, Detroit and Pittsburgh are a lot alike. In both cities people work hard, enjoy their down time, and often cheer for sports teams that don't always win. Of course, I love music. But the opportunity to meet members of the Magic family, and take part in community events, makes this job one I wouldn't trade. Let's spend some time together. Weekdays from 10:30 to 3, and Saturdays from 10 to 3. Here on Magic radio, WMGC.

(Courtesy of Lisa Drummond, Greater Media Detroit)

A special challenge arises when the program being promoted by the local outlet originates at a network or syndicator. In such case, the best solution lies in copy prepared by the station's writer that is then sent for voicing by that outside talent. Following is a promo that makes the most of such a situation by having the syndicated personality plug not only his show, but also the local outlet's key deejays.

TESH: Hi, this is John Tesh. Did you know that if you combined all the time that Steve Gibbons, Mary Day and Jim Brown have been on the air --- it would add up to over one-hundred-and-ten years? And that's not even counting Cal Beermin. I'm really excited to join the KRNT line-up every Sunday night at 7 with the John Tesh Radio Show. It's your favorite KRNT music, combined with intelligence for your life. If it doesn't make you better, happier and more interesting, you won't find it on the John Tesh Radio Show. Sunday night at 7 --- on 13-50 KRNT. Where the legends live.

(Courtesy of Jim Brown, Saga Communications)

A pre-recorded program provides additional options. By taking sound 'bites' from the feature and combining them with announcer commentary, you can create a multi-voice promo with –the impact of a movie preview:

Production Note: Paul's lines SOT.

(MUSIC: MELLOW SAX FEATURE AND UNDER)

PAUL: It's the same as when anyone dies, really.

ANNCR: Paul McCartney.

PAUL: You wish you told him all the stuff you really want to tell him. But you don't.

ANNCR: One half of one of songwriting's most influential duos.

PAUL: The last phone call I had with John was just very warm. We talked all about his kids. And about his cats. And about this and that.

ANNCR: On WLOL. To talk about it. And he does.

PAUL: I really don't want to come out as any kind of preacher for pot.

ANNCR: Tonight on Phil Houston's Countdown Show. Hear a living legend talk about his music, his new movie, his old friend. An exclusive in-person WLOL interview with Paul McCartney. Beginning at four this afternoon.

(MUSIC: FEATURE TO TIME)

(Courtesy of Tom Gowan, Emmis Broadcasting's WLOL)

The same technique applies if it's a radio plug for a video program or news story. In that case, your script's 'bites' are simply pulled --- as SOT --- from that package's soundtrack. ("SOT" stands for "sound on tape" --- a designation that survives even though magnetic tape has largely been replaced by digital media.).

SOT: It's so easy and it just makes you feel so good.

ANNCR: Thursday on Fox Two News at Ten. A problem solver investigation. Most parents know G-H-B as a dangerous date rape drug. Kids say --- it's also an easy high.

SOT: You get a lot of people in the same room doing it together --- and everybody has a good time.

ANNCR: Highly addictive, incredibly destructive, and what's worse? We bought it right off a drug store shelf. Problem solver Amy Lange goes to work. Thursday on Fox Two News at Ten.

(Courtesy of Nisa Phelps, Fox 2/Detroit)

Of course, video program promos conceived for radio can be entirely copywriter-generated without the use of soundtrack 'grabs.' What is important is that the benefit for watching is clearly established as an engaging scene in the listener's mind's eye.

WOMAN: I brought you out a plate of cheeseballs.

MAN: Class reunion looks like fun in there.

WOMAN: You wouldn't be sitting here in the car---

MAN: ---if I would've watched the news on BC-TV with Tony Parsons with you tonight. I know. Can I come in for five minutes?

WOMAN: No.

MAN: Two minutes?

WOMAN: No. Do you want to come off as an uninformed clod, with no idea of what happened today in the country?

MAN: In the province.

WOMAN: Or Vancouver?

MAN: I'd look like a dope.

WOMAN: Besides, I told everyone you're dead.

MAN: Dead?

WOMAN: You don't expect me to admit I married someone who doesn't watch The News Hour?

MAN: Good point. I'll stay in the car. Can I play with the blinkers?

WOMAN: No.

(SFX: CAR DOOR SLAM)

ANNCR: The BC-TV News Hour makes everything interesting; especially you.

(Courtesy of Dick Orkin & Chris Coyle, Dick Orkin's Radio Ranch)

OUTLET PROMOS

Sometimes the assignment is to plug the station or network as a whole rather than a single personality or program on it. One way this task can be performed is by an image song's lyric copy. Because we discussed music earlier in this and the previous two chapters, little more need be said here. When both lyric and the tune that transports it combine to (1) mirror the essence of the outlet's format, (2) repeat the "what we do for you" promise, and (3) lock in station location, the resulting promo will prove a marketing plus:

SUNG: Move right on Q
        Go right to the top
        On Q-1-oh-7 the hits never stop.
        Yeah, 1-oh-7 --- it's right on Q
        Less talk --- more music
        comin' to you.
        So slide to the right '
        bout as far as you can
        the hits are just waitin'
        for a twist of your hand.
        Hits happening right on Q
        Q-1-oh-7.
        Q-1-oh-7
        Hits happening right on Q
        Riiiii-ght!

(Courtesy of WRQX Radio)

More often today, the outlet promo is spoken rather than sung and uses ID liner-type techniques in a more extended form. "Liners alone are not enough to get the [station positioning] idea across," maintains promotion veteran Jim Teeson. "Use your creative copywriting skills to embellish your basic positioning statement."[5] "The foundation of every station image," adds promotion executive John Follmer, "is its personality. It is what makes it indigenous to its locale, yet different from the other stations it competes with. A station's defined personality is what is used to focus an image campaign and, an image campaign, in turn, helps build on that personality."[6] This thirty-second New England outlet promo wraps its image statement around a clear expression of specific listener benefits:

What makes country music great? People the world over, people in New Hampshire, Southern Maine and Northern Mass agree: country songs talk about real life. Real people. You can understand the words. Above all, country songs are fun. And out of all the conceivable songs we could play, the WOKQ personalities are workin' hard to select just the best songs --- and put them together just right. On Country Favorites --- 97 point five, WOKQ.

(Courtesy of Ramsey Elliot, Fuller-Jeffrey Broadcasting Companies, Inc.)

Even when trumpeting station awards, an efficient outlet promo still presents a clear listener benefit filtered through the station's distinct personality:

(SFX: CHEERING CROWD FEATURE AND OUT)

ANNCR: After hearing from the Michigan Association of Broadcasters that our news team had just won another load of awards, we'll be honest. We'd love to take the day off, head over to the local watering hole and throw back a few cold ones. But we'll resist the temptation.

(SFX: NEWSROOM SOUNDS FEATURE AND UNDER TO END)

ANNCR: You can be sure, we're very proud of those first place awards for best newscast, and best breaking news and sports coverage. But right now, we're too busy working on the next newscast. NewsRadio WOOD 13-hundred. We're always here.

(Courtesy of Phil Tower, Clear Channel Radio)

Outlet promos can also take the form of dialogues. Most often, the conversation is between two station or network personalities. However, the danger with this approach is that you will not involve the public, because this technique results in two seller surrogates and *no* buyer who could ask the key questions. (Review the section on dialogue writing in Chapter 8.) An alternative is to cast both voices as listeners—one who knows your station and the other who has yet to discover it:

JACK: Yes, I've tried to choose the best all my life. In food, friends, leisure, et cetera.

DICK: Really?

JACK: Oh, yes. Nothing mainstream about me. I trickle down my <u>own</u> river and so forth.

DICK: What radio station do you listen to?

JACK: Hmmmm?

DICK: They say the best programming is on KCRW.

JACK: Oh, yes. K-C- uh, yes. Love it!

DICK: Do you listen to KCRW?

JACK: I wouldn't go to any other place on the dial.

DICK: What program?

JACK: Well --- I don't have a fav---, Everything!

DICK: Do you listen to <u>Morning Edition</u>?

JACK: Oh, yes. I --- yes, I do.

DICK: <u>All Things Considered</u>?

JACK: All things concerned, yes.

DICK: <u>Considered</u>!

JACK: Right, Love it.

DICK: How about <u>Phil's Polka Parade</u>?

JACK: Very fond of it, never miss it.

DICK: You big phony! There isn't such a show on KCRW!

JACK: I don't know that? I know that! I sensed you were joshing me, you scamp you!

DICK: You don't listen to KCRW at all!

JACK: What?

DICK: Not the great music, the exciting drama, the commentary, the news---

JACK: I do too!

DICK: What do they do on <u>Morning Becomes Eclectic</u>?

JACK: They talk about --- electricity.

DICK: What?

JACK: The plugs, the bulbs, the wires, and that's wrong, right?

DICK: Right, wrong!

JACK: So, you found me out for the phony fool I am. Well, I deserve a good smack!

       (SFX: SMACK)

JACK: Thank you.

ANNCR: If you're not a regular KCRW listener, you deserve a good smack too!

       (SFX: SMACK)

JACK: Thank you again.

(Courtesy of Dick Orkin & Chris Coyle, Dick Orkin's Radio Ranch)

Lyric, univoice, or dialogue, an outlet promo must be conceived with one overriding principle in mind. As radio consultant Ed Shane puts it, "a station has to market itself not from how it perceives itself, but how it best can serve the listener."[7]

ENHANCERS AND FEATURES

In striving to solidify their position in an ever-more fragmenting marketplace, stations, syndicators, and networks are constantly developing new copy-driven format embellishments. Some of these offerings are straight news or commentary—outside the scope of this book. But in many other cases, these devices consist of comedic entertainment bits injected on a regularly scheduled (feature) or occasional drop-in (enhancer) basis. These enhancers and features are designed to brighten the listener's day and encourage that listener's continued loyalty to our audio service.

A typical example is this sixty-second bit from The American Comedy Network, one of a number of specialty syndicators whose copywriters generate such short-form materials:

ANNCR: Hey, middle-aged guy. Here's a message for you before you waste money on an over-priced foreign car to capture your lost youth.

       (<u>MUSIC: PULSATING UP-TEMPO BRASS --- FEATURE AND UNDER</u>)

ANNCR: Introducing the new 'Mid-Life Delusion' and fuel-injected 'Responsibility'; high-performance cars made in America for the man who doesn't know who he is!

       (SFX: CAR IGNITION, BIG START-UP, REVVING)

ANNCR: These babies are as sleek and sexy as that new secretary you just hired, but not quite as fast.

    (SFX: LOUD HUM OF SUNROOM OPENING)

ANNCR: Open up the sunroof and let the wind race through your thinning hair---

    (SFX: CAR SQUEALING THROUGH STREET)

ANNCR: Settle into an extra-wide seat for <u>your</u> extra-wide seat.

    (SFX: MORE TIRE SQUEAL)

ANNCR: And look into a brilliantly designed rear-view mirror that lets you see everything you've just left behind, <u>except</u> your wife and children---

    (SFX: WOMAN'S VOICE CALLING IN DISTANCE: 'Honey!!!')

ANNCR: All this, plus a fool-injected engine that lets you accelerate away from all your obligations in under six seconds.

    (SFX: SCREECHING STOP, LOUD IDLING)

ANNCR: And both cars have our standard 7-year-itch, 70 thousand mile warranty!

    (SFX: CAR DOOR SLAM)

ANNCR: So, test drive the all-new 'Mid-Life Delusion' and fuel-injected 'Responsibility'. Cars that take you where you want to go --- even if you have no idea where that is.

(Courtesy of Andrew J. Goodman. The American Comedy Network)

One advantage of such spoof commercials is that they tend to increase attention paid to the 'real' commercials being aired. Because listeners never know when an entertaining put-on is coming, they give more heed to the entire spot pod.

Among the most numerous features offered by contemporary audio services are personal enrichment and helpful hints series. These brief segments are styled and selected with the needs of each station's target universe in mind. When brightly written, as in the following car-care module, they provide easily digestible and informative entertainment—perfect for the listener-friendly requirements of today's audio formats. As with any continuity, the copywriter must keep the message focused, interesting, and unequivocally understandable without talking down to the audience.

BRO. #1:   If you've ever been stuck steaming by the side of the road, then you've probably asked yourself the question we've all asked.

BRO. #2:   Why me?

BRO. #1:   We'll tell you because---

BOTH: We're the Rhodes Brothers, with a minute about your car!

BRO. #1:   Now, the reason you're boiling over maybe is because you didn't check your fanbelt.

BRO. #2:   (Singing) Fan belt's connected to the water pump---

BRO. #1:   Which pumps cooled water from your radiator right back into your---

BRO. #2:	Engine.
BRO. #1:	That's it!
BRO. #2:	What're we doing here?
BRO. #1:	Talking about checking maybe two or three belts under the hood, is all.
BRO. #2:	And a serious warning---
BRO. #1:	Yeah, the engine must be off when you're checking.
BRO. #2:	Well, if you'd like future use of your fingers.
BRO. #1:	Now, the belt must be tight to do its job, so press your thumb down on the middle of the belt---
BRO. #2:	Just like this.
BRO. #1:	No, your thumb. If it yields more than a quarter of an inch, it should be adjusted.
BRO. #2:	You can do it, or ask your mechanic.
BRO. #1:	Your favorite auto supply can give you some advice, and show you the tools you need.
BRO. #2:	Tools? I use my teeth.
BRO. #1:	Which explains a lot about your face. Now the other thing you're checking for is cracks and frays.
BRO. #2:	That's right!
BRO. #1:	Now do this, because you remember how lonely it gets at the side of the road.
BRO. #2:	That's it! A minute about your car.

(Courtesy of Rene Crapo, RJ Programming)

ON-/OFF-AIR LISTENER PARTICIPATIONS

Another means of hooking audience ears is the outlet-promoting contest. Some of these games take place on air, some off air, and some combine both on- and off-air activities. The copywriter's job in these matters is to (1) build listener enthusiasm; (2) clearly explain the rules and prizes; (3) link the contest unmistakably with the station and its image; and (4) accomplish all of this within thirty or, at most, sixty seconds.

Off-air participation promotions are usually tie-ins with one or more retail outlets. Thus the contest copy assumes the additional burden of identifying who the retailers are. If, as in the following WWWY promo, a large number of client stores are participating, it is best to prepare a number of interchangeable tags or pieces of hole copy. In this way, all retailers receive equal mention without forcing your announcement to sound like a recitation of the Chamber of Commerce membership roster.

	<u>Production note</u>: She speaks in a nursery-tale voice; He in a not-too-bright, cynical voice.
SHE:	Once upon a time, there were thirty-three little bears.

HE: Excuse me, that should be <u>three</u> little bears.

SHE: No, it's <u>thirty</u>-three little bears and they're really not so little. In fact, they're almost 4 feet tall.

HE: Wow! So there's about 11 Momma Bears, 11 Papa Bears, and---

SHE: No, you see, they're <u>all</u> Christmas Bears and they're <u>all</u> super-soft, cuddly, and down-right adorable.

HE: Can I see one?

SHE: You can see all thirty-three. They're at stores all over the Y-one-oh-5 listening area.

HE: You say they're almost 4 feet tall?

SHE: Yep, and each store will give its bear away on December 21st. No purchase is necessary. <u>You</u> could win one of these giant, super-plush Christmas Bears and---

HE: Live happily ever after, right?

SHE: Actually, I was gonna say, 'And have a Merry Christmas.'

ANNCR: Register to win one of the Y-1-oh-5 giant plush Christmas Bears at:

    (TAG #1)   Lincoln Center, Ketchum's Kornucopia, Tovey Shoes, The Big Blue Store, and Folger's Four-Season Florist.

    (TAG #2)   Gary Davis Music Makers, Elsberry's Greenhouse, The Fourth Street Bar, The Cosco Shop, and Steve's Taxidermy and Bass Shop.

    (TAG #3)   National Video, Tom Pickett Music, Ray's Marathon, Bradbury's Christmas Wonderland, Hull's Office Supply, and Dag's on 46-West.

(Courtesy of James Ganley, WWWY)

When a continuing off-air promotion garners a winner, a little advance preparation can enable you to turn the triumphant moment into an excitement builder for other listeners. By bringing an audio recorder and a release form along, WKHQ's Prize Patrol staffer captured a live actuality from which the station's writer could later harvest 'people-interest' excerpts to be bumpered with announcer copy:

ANNCR: 106 KHQ's Prize Patrol takes you to the streets every week to find you listening to 106 FM at work.

VOICE: (Screaming) Randy---

ANNCR: We searched high and low for Randy Weeter at Boze Wood Products in Harbor Springs.

VOICE: (Still screaming) We won for 'Take Your Radio to Work!'

ANNCR: We tracked him down---

VOICE: (Still screaming, now even louder) Randy!!!

ROB: I'm Rob Hazelton, 'Take Your Radio to Work Day' --- What do you do here?

RANDY: I'm foreman over next door.

ROB: What are you doing over here? We almost couldn't find you.

RANDY:	Just helping out.
ANNCR:	If it's 'Take Your Radio to Work Day', it's KHQ-Cash on the spot.
ROB:	Hey! One hundred --- one, two, three, four, five and six. One hundred and six bucks!
ANNCR:	And that's not all---
ROB:	You've just won an on-the-spot massage for one hour, good for up to three people in your work place.
ANNCR:	Three certificates --- three people --- three one-hour massages.
RANDY:	We sure can use that.
ROB:	And the money comes in handy, too.
RANDY:	It sure does, I'm getting married in 4 months, it's going to help out a lot.
ANNCR:	Each week brings a new 'Take Your Radio to Work Day' from the Fun and Games Department of 106 KHQ.

(Courtesy of Tim Moore, WKHQ)

Figure 9.2 is a print layout from an off-air event that is a joint project of a station group and a local newspaper. The event brings together a large number of businesses in a job fair likely to attract thousands of local residents. Notice that the on-air spot not only promotes the Expo to jobseekers, but also establishes the broadcaster as the place for businesses to call in order to participate. This copy approach thereby enhances the station group's community image while also initiating contact with a number of potential prospects for its advertising services.

ANNCR:	The Clear Channel Radio Mega Employment Expo is back at the DeltaPlex on Saturday, May 5th. And this one is going to be bigger than ever. Clear Channel Radio stations have partnered with the Grand Rapids Press to bring you the biggest, the best, and the greatest job fair in the history of West Michigan. We'll have representatives from dozens of West Michigan companies, anxious to employ hundreds of workers right away. When you come to the Mega Employment Expo, you'll find employers anxious to set up

FIGURE 9.2 *(Courtesy of Rich Berry, Clear Channel Radio)*

appointments for interviews --- sometimes right on the spot. Best of all, the Mega Employment Expo has found jobs for literally thousands of people over the past three years. If your business is in need of quality employees, then your business needs to be represented at the Clear Channel Radio/ Grand Rapids Press Mega Employment Expo. Saturday, May 5th at the DeltaPlex. Call us right now at 4-5-9, one-nine, one-nine, and we'll provide you the information you need right away. That's 4-5-9, one-nine, one-nine. The Clear Channel Radio Mega Employment Expo is the largest job fair in West Michigan. See you on May 5th at the DeltaPlex.

(Courtesy of Rich Berry, Clear Channel Radio)

Combination on/off-air participation announcements persuade listeners to take some action (usually at one or more of the station's advertisers) that qualifies them for involvement in later on-air activities. Such *value-added* campaigns give sponsors more customer traffic for their advertising buck and enhance the station's sales efforts. However, the copy must be listener-oriented. It must depict the ease of taking part, as well as establish the relationship of the off-air errand to the on-air fun:

VOICE: A crossword puzzle on the radio?

RICH: You bet! And you can win free groceries for one year from P&C and Radio 57/WSYR, when you play along. Pick up your crossword puzzle entry form at your local P&C Store and listen for the on-air clues. Only on Radio 57/WSYR.

VOICE: I'm sharpening my pencil!

RICH: The fun starts on March 17th with the last word in crossword puzzles from P&C, the Prize Champion, and Radio 57/WSYR.

For this particular contest, the on-air copy clues were set up in this manner:

ANNCR: Sharpen your pencil. It's time for another clue in the Radio 57/WSYR and P&C crossword puzzle---

           ONE ACROSS --- Radio 57/WSYR is the blank Weather Station; you can depend on it.

           Keep listening for the next crossword puzzle clue on Radio 57/WSYR.

(Courtesy of Yvonne Sacripant, WSYR)

In contrast, the *on-air* participation event depends on the telephone to achieve its goal—often in conjunction with the station's Website. This promotes both vehicles simultaneously. It used to be that stations would call out to potential players at random. However, this practice often resulted in listener-boring busy signals, no answers, and other unusable reactions. You're assured of a player, however, if the game is designed so that willing, pre-registered participants call *in*. As in the script below, it is also important to emphasize how easy it is for anyone to sign up and win. This spot also illustrates how a sponsor/donor can be brought into the contest and copy to lessen station costs.

ANNCR: Here at Rock one-oh-two we strive to keep you happy by providing the best classic rock every day, all day. But I gotta tell you, that's just too hard.

Recently, however, we learned something that made our jobs a whole lot easier --- you people can be bribed! And while, yes, we were a little disappointed in you, we decided we like it easy. So here you go --- it's Rock one-oh-two's Great Gas Giveaway. Join the workforce at Rock one-oh-two dot-com, then listen weekdays 9 to 5. Keeping in mind that it's even easier now that we're streaming 24-7. We'll call a name out every hour. If it's yours, call us within 10 minutes and you get one-hundred-and-two dollars worth of free gas. And you'll keep getting *another* one-hundred-two dollars in gas *every hour* --- until the next winner calls in. The Great Gas Giveaway, brought to you by F. L. Roberts, whose golden nozzles have free self-serve vacuums, and the shameless hucksters at Rock one-oh-two, Springfield's classic rock.

(Courtesy of Gerry Perrett, Saga Communications)

Whatever kind of listener participation project is developed, The Radio Store's Maureen Bulley stresses that, to be maximally involving, the copy promoting it should "project the listener ahead as though they had already won the contest."[8]

INTERVIEWS AND SEMISCRIPTS

In order to survive, today's audio outlet must project a sense of active involvement in the lives of listeners. As we've discussed, participation contests contribute to this goal through concise continuity bursts. Audio interview programs, meanwhile, address this task in more lengthy segments, depending on a format's design and target listeners. The community discussion show, consisting primarily of conversations between a station personality and pertinent guests, is a common mechanism for catering to audience interests. To service a local (or, for that matter, national) interview show, a copywriter must perform several duties. First, as in the creation of program promos, the writer must set up a vibrant sense of expectation.

Therefore, the interview introduction, although brief, entails three distinct functions: (1) arouse listener interest, (2) provide a tight capsule of information that puts the guest and host in perspective, and (3) make the guest feel comfortable and at home. The same attention-getting devices discussed in previous chapters can be used to accomplish the first objective. The writer might need to structure these opening lines in such a way that they can also be used as lift-outs that serve periodically to promo the interview for several days before its airing.

Second, the interview intro needs to trace the essential parameters of the subject without being deliberately evasive on the one hand, or giving away the discussion's main revelation on the other. To open a drug abuse segment by saying, "Here is a man who was hooked on cocaine but after ten months of the new megatherapy is healthy and drug-free," would leave the listener with little reason to stay tuned.

Finally, because many guests are not professional communicators, the interview introduction must strive to put the individual at ease. In this context, overpraise is just as dangerous as unabashed derision. Too many guests have suffered through introductions that were so overzealous that they hardly dared open their mouths for fear of destroying that just-concocted image. Write a deserved compliment or two for the guest, but refrain from using intimidating superlatives.

The interview's closing or "outro" also has three intertwined purposes: (1) re-identify the guest and his or her topic/qualifications for late tuners-in, (2) also re-identify the host and program, as well as (3) briefly promo today's next guest or the guest on the series' next show. As in the intro, the third function is fraught with the greatest dangers. The audience must be sufficiently intrigued about the next guest that they will tune in or stay tuned. But at the same time, you cannot demean the contribution just made by the current guest. The outro that seems to imply, "Once we get this turkey out of here, there's a really interesting person we want you to meet," is an unintentional but unforgivable disservice to the guest who's just finished. The opposite extreme, which might be accidentally conveyed as, "Wish we could bring you back but we've already scheduled some city sewage guy," serves the future guest no better.

The body of the interview might also require the copywriter's attention. You may be asked to prepare a list of key questions that can be put to the guest and that are guaranteed to elicit more than one-word responses. Many program hosts do not have the time, and some do not have the brainpower, to read up on the topic on which the guest is going to expound. Carefully worded and pre-checked questions make the host look suitably knowledgeable, keep the guest comfortable and self-assured, and allow the interview to harvest the expertise or point of view for which the guest was invited in the first place.

Particularly if accompanied by commercial and continuity inserts, this list of questions, together with the fully scripted intro and outro, could be said to constitute a *semiscript*—a skeletal framework that allows the show to be extemporaneous while still adhering to an established announcement schedule and preordained set of objectives. The continuity writer must therefore sketch in the essential subject, pace, and tone of the show while allowing the on-air personalities to flesh out the program within those guidelines. In semiscripting, the writer succeeds when the show displays a structured spontaneity that keeps the listener unaware it was preplanned at all.

A more limited derivation of the standard semiscript entirely omits the questions as well as most outros. It concentrates almost exclusively on carefully fashioned intros and tight transitions between the program and the commercial messages that punctuate it. Normally, this version of the semiscript is used when the interviewer is an experienced communicator/interrogator adept at drawing out guests without major reliance on a set of preplanned queries. *FOCUS*, a much-copied and long-running daily talk/discussion show aired by Detroit's WJR, had just such a host. A composite *FOCUS* script is reproduced below:

        <u>Production Note</u>: ANNCR is pre-recorded

ANNCR: From Studio D, this is J. P. McCarthy's <u>Focus</u>.

(MUSIC: <u>THEME UP, UNDER AND OUT</u>)

ANNCR: WJR presents an active view of life and living in the Great Lakes Area,
               a lively look at people, places, events and attitudes. Put into focus
               by --- J. P. McCarthy.

J. P.:   Paul, thank you very much. In <u>Focus</u> today, the senior managing editor for
               the Detroit Free Press, Neal Shine, to give a postmortem on last year --- what
               was interesting, what was significant. Also, an update on one of the major
               Detroit riverfront projects, Harbortown --- how it's going this chilly Monday
               in January. All of that, in <u>Focus</u>, in just a minute.

ANNCR: Today's <u>Focus</u> program is being brought to you in part by the Oreck Excel --- the famous 8-pound upright hotel vacuum.

POS. #1 --- ORECK SPOT

POS. #2 --- DETROIT AUTO SHOW SPOT

J. P.: Our first guest in <u>Focus</u> today is a familiar face from the back page of the Free Press --- Neal Shine. I'm told he's the father confessor to about 90% of the writers at the Detroit Free Press; probably because he hired most of them. They come to him with their problems, for his suggestions. Neal's been a chronicler of Detroit and Southeast Michigan for over three decades. He's making his annual visit with us to take a look at the year just past: the good, the bad, and the awful. Good afternoon, Neal---

(INTERVIEW #1)

The Detroit Free Presses Neal Shine. One of the big downtown riverfront projects that we referred to --- Harbortown --- discussed with two principals in just a moment.

POS. #3 --- JOE MUER RESTAURANT SPOT

POS. #4 --- FORD COMMUNITY COLLEGE SPOT

ANNCR: You're in tune with the interesting interviews of J. P. McCarthy's <u>Focus</u> show. On WJR, Radio 76.

J. P.: My next guests in <u>Focus</u> are involved in one of the most ambitious of the Detroit riverfront projects --- Harbortown. So for an update on how it's gone, how it's going, and where it's going, it's a pleasure to welcome the president of American National Resources, Larry Marantette, and the president of MichCon Development Corporation, Dan Kern. These two companies are joint owners of this enterprise. Are your two firms connected in any other way?

(INTERVIEW #2)

Danny Kern from MichCon Development Corporation and Larry Marantette from A-N-R. We'll see you on <u>The Morning Show</u> from 6:15 to 10:00 tomorrow. And in <u>Focus</u> tomorrow, our special guest will be Detroit Free Press columnist Robin Abcarian, who will show us her tattoo right here on the radio!

(MUSIC: <u>SNEAK IN THEME UNDER</u>)

ANNCR: Today's <u>Focus</u> program has been brought to you in part by the Oreck Excel, the famous 8-pound upright hotel vacuum.

(MUSIC: <u>FEATURE TO TIME</u>)

(Courtesy of Marilyn Gordon, WJR)

Unlike those for live interview shows, semiscripts for *preproduced* entertainment programs tend to have more segments because written continuity must be interjected between each of the multiple musical and/or prerecorded verbal features. Each copy segment, however, is usually quite brief. People want to listen to the actual tunes and personalities—not to long stretches of announcer/host copy about them. The writer's job is to concisely establish essential flow and identifications and then get out of the way, as in the following syndicated show. (Here again, the SOT's are the "sound on tape" segments lifted from prior recorded interviews.)

BUZZ: Welcome to Country Music Month Salute! I'm Buzz Bowman and today, we salute one of country music's most honored groups --- Alabama!

SOT: (RANDY) I think when people come to a concert that they really don't pay for the music, they pay to experience the feeling and that's what Alabama has to offer that I'm so proud of.

BUZZ: We'll be back with that Alabama feeling after this.

SPOTS: (:30 National/:Local)

BUZZ: It's hard to think about the group Alabama without thinking of harmony --- the harmony among the group members, with their audience, and of course, in their music. As Jeff Cook says:

SOT: (JEFF) We look for lines that have a harmony and that, ah, sounds like our style.

SOT: (Randy) We have no ego problem when it comes to sayin' --- ahh, I wrote this song or we didn't write that song. I think we'd rather have songs that people say: 'Yeah, boy that sounds great.'

(MUSIC: 'DIXIELAND DELIGHT' --- CHORUS)

BUZZ: Jeff Cook gives another example.

SOT: (JEFF) 'Love in the First Degree' is a song that no one in the group wrote. We felt it was a good song --- a song that Alabama could do real well.

(MUSIC: 'LOVE IN THE FIRST DEGREE')

Buzz: Though some of their biggest hits were written by other people, Randy Owen says:

SOT: (Randy) We write good songs together. I enjoy writing a song --- there's a special feeling goes with writing a hit. When you know you've written one, that is the biggest high you'll ever experience in your life.

(MUSIC: 'MOUNTAIN MUSIC' --- CHORUS)

BUZZ: And what about the future? According to Mark Herndon:

SOT: (MARK) If the, ah, public still wants to hear Alabama music, I hope we're still putting out another album, you know. If not, ah, I'll be home with the family and spending some time thinking about all the good times I've had on the road.

(MUSIC: 'WHEN WE MAKE LOVE')

BUZZ: Alabama, we salute you as we celebrate Country Music Month. Join us tomorrow for Ronnie Milsap on another Country Music Month Salute.

(Courtesy of Denise Oliver, United Stations Programming Network)

A station buying the above presentation would receive an entirely produced program, including the host's (Buzz Bowman's) recorded segments. Often, however, stations like to showcase one of their own local personalities. In such a case, the production would come with a script and prerecorded music and guest modules. The station's own talent would then use the script to do the host voicers instead of Buzz In the trade, this practice is known as a BYO (Build Your Own) property; it gives the finished product a customized and station-enhancing flair.

One further variety of the semiscript is the *cheat sheet* prepared for air talent to assist them in conducting a client remote. Such assistance from us is critical. Veteran station copywriter Kevin Neathery points out that, "It is not a DJ's job to 'make up' the script as he goes. It is *your* job to provide your DJs with a complete script. It's not the DJ's job to analyze the store's marketing mix, determine appeals, quantify solution value and develop a hot campaign. It's not the DJ's job to tour the inventory with the client and determine copy points at the remote . . . It's your job."[9] Here are some of the lines from the cheat sheet Neathery created for a February restaurant remote. These can be aired in any order that the deejay finds workable:

We are live, where dinner is always special: Corky's Ribs and Barbecue on Caraway Road in Jonesboro.

At Corky's the choices are many and delicious including their 'Sweetheart' Smoked Prime Rib Dinner for two available tonight, Wednesday --- that's Valentine's Day --- and Thursday night.

Wait 'til you try Corky's all new Fried Green Beans. They're fried, they're green, they're beans. Trust me --- you'll love 'em.

Steak eaters love Corky's certified Black Angus beef. I'm talkin' big, juicy ribeye and top sirloin steaks grilled to perfection with hearty baked potato and garden fresh salad. Mmmmm.

At Corky's, there's something for everyone: burgers, sandwiches and wraps, Italian spaghetti, Cajun shrimp, southern fried catfish, chicken tenders, barbeque nachos and so much more.

Bring your sweetie for the best prime rib dinner you've ever had, cooked the old-fashioned way --- slow and delicious with a distinctive hickory flavor that's pure Corky's.

Corky's ribs and barbecue on Caraway Road in Jonesboro.

(Courtesy of Kevin Neathery, Saga Communications)

In constructing a cheat sheet, begin with the commercials currently running on behalf of that client. Harvest the key lines and benefit statements from these spots and work them into the patter you have scripted for the live remote. In this way, deejay live commentary and the ongoing ad campaign will be mutually reinforcing.

SPECIAL COMMERCIAL CHALLENGES

Before closing this chapter on additional audio endeavors—and our entire three-chapter section about writing for sound—we need to examine four kinds of advertising that present unique difficulties. We are talking here about retail, co-op, classified, and direct-response assignments. To an extent, these problem categories overlap. But each category is discussed separately as a means of revealing its critical requirements.

Retail Advertising

This category embraces all the copy generated for local outlets (both locally and nationally owned) that sell a variety of consumer goods and services directly to the general public. Traditionally wedded to newspaper advertising, these retailers were one of the most overlooked—but are now one of the most important—targets for radio sales departments. Unlike other clients, retailers are looking for *results today*—not just for general image building or brand awareness. They tend to measure these results in terms of: (1) traffic and inquiries generated, and (2) orders taken/goods moved out the door. Most successful retailers are skilled pitchmen—they know their products well and know how to describe them in order to consummate sales.

Radio copywriters are therefore well advised to gain a working knowledge of their respective retailing communities. This knowledge-gathering should include conversations with retailers, noting the specific expressions that flow most glibly from their mouths as they talk about their services and products. The retailer has probably used these phrases on customers for years—and used them successfully or they would not be a continuing part of his or her persuasive arsenal. The copywriter who can encapsulate those proven statements is thus not only profiting from a consumer-oriented approach, but is also making the spot more appealing to the retailer, who will have a preference for audio messages that use those favored pitches. In the following commercial, client-tested phrases such as "deep down cleaning," "superficial scrubbings," "remove the toxins" and "get rid of the grit and grime" personalize the selling scenario for both audience and advertiser.

ANNCR: Next time you come in from going to the mall, or tramping around outside, take a towel and vigorously wipe the bottoms of your shoes. If your dog is with you, be sure to wipe his paws off as well. Next, take that towel and rub it all over your baby's face and hands. (Short pause) What? You don't think that's a good idea? Well it's what happens every time your baby crawls around on your carpet. Or it <u>would</u> be, if you hadn't had Superior Rug Cleaning keep your carpets clean and fresh. Superior comes and delivers a deep down cleansing. This isn't one of those quick fix or superficial scrubbings. Your carpets are sanitized, freshened and <u>really</u> clean. So if you want to keep the outside from getting all over the inside of your home, come clean. Kill the germs, remove the toxins, get rid of the grit and grime. Contact Superior Rug Cleaning. Progress Street in Springfield and Granby Street in Bloomfield.

(Courtesy of Gerry Perrett, Saga Communications)

Sometimes, retailers will want to voice the copy themselves. But most of them lack an affecting and effective "audio personality." If possible, you can keep them happy by having the client do just the opening or closing line of the spot. In this way, they have gotten on the air but do not have to carry the whole message themselves. One method for coming up with these lines is to record an extended conversation with the retailer. Get them talking about their business and what excites them about it. Chances are, you will be able to harvest several potent comments from which to choose. If you have recorded this conversation in the studio, you might even be able to pull the lines from this informal chat without the stiltedness that often results when the client is asked to later tape the statement in isolation.

In spots for multiple-product retailers, such as grocery and department or discount stores, the audio copywriter encounters an additional difficulty. Comfortable with and accustomed to newspapers, these merchants will want you to compress all the product pictures and price balloons from a half- or even full-page print ad into one grossly overloaded minute. The resulting laundry-list commercial makes little or no impact on the listener because not enough time can be devoted to any one item to have it properly situated on the stage of the listener's "mind's eye." The alternative is to find a strong central concept on which the listener can focus and from which individual products can be hung like ornaments on a well-proportioned Christmas tree. The following "what else is in the K-Mart bag" idea embraces dozens of back-to-school items that aren't even mentioned. Yet, through this heartwarming father/son scenario, the copywriter has managed to condense a multi-paged K-Mart advertising circular (known as an *FSI*, or *free-standing insert*) into a compelling and retailer-centered sixty-second drama.

Production Note: Kid is 6 years old.

KID: Dad?

DAD: Yeah, what's up?

KID: I think I'll drop out of school.

DAD: Oh? Why?

KID: I think it will be too hard.

DAD: First grade?

KID: Yeah.

DAD: Who says?

KID: Tim's sister says it's real hard. You've gotta read. I can't read.

DAD: Well, you'll learn, son.

KID: I can't learn!

DAD: Gosh! What are you gonna do? Get a job?

KID: Yeah, I can work with you, Dad. Okay?

DAD: Well, maybe. Gee, guess we'll have to take this back.

KID: What?

DAD:	This bag from K-Mart.
KID:	What's in it?
DAD:	All your school stuff. Let's see --- these go back.
KID:	New gym shoes?
DAD:	Yeah, you don't need gym shoes at the office.
KID:	Yeah, but---
DAD:	Look at these crayons. Wow! A lot of colors---.
KID:	Can we keep those, Dad?
DAD:	Nope.
KID:	Dad!
DAD:	Hey, look at this --- your own pencil case. So long, pencil case.
KID:	Maybe I will try it, Dad.
DAD:	Maybe you should. Let's face it, you aced kindergarten.
KID:	Yeah! What else is in the K-Mart bag?
<u>SINGERS</u>:	<u>Back to school at K-Mart, America's favorite store.</u>

(Courtesy of Craig Wiese, Craig Wiese and Company)

It is vital that, no matter what (or how many) goods and services the local merchant is pushing, a distinct and stable personality is maintained in your copy. "Typically," chides station KHAT general manager Dan Charleston, "local retailers run four different spots, written and voiced four different ways on four stations. There's no consistency. Their image is a jumble, and awareness plummets."[10] Whether you're an outlet or an agency writer, you cannot allow this to happen. If radio doesn't establish clear marketplace identity for the retailer, stations as well as agencies will lose that retailer's patronage.

Make certain that your copy sells as consistently and as hard on the air as do those retailers back at their stores. Construct copy that is sales-oriented—copy that speaks directly, conversationally, and cohesively to the wants of both prospect and retailer. Good point-of-purchase salespeople don't push a product, they solve a problem. They don't just persuade, they explain. And they seem to empathize as much as they talk:

ANNCR:	All right, so you were hoping for some silky, sensuous lingerie for Valentine's Day --- and he got you a subscription to <u>The Betty Crocker Newsletter</u>. So what are you gonna do? Bake a cake? NO! You're gonna go to Manhattan Unmentionables and treat yourself to an 'After Valentine's Day' present. And you're gonna save money. Because this Thursday, Friday and Saturday only it's Manhattan Unmentionable's big 'After Valentine's Day Sale.' Prices are already reduced at Manhattan Unmentionables --- but this Thursday, Friday and Saturday only, they'll be knocking an additional

five to twenty percent off everything in the store. Save on stockings, baby dolls, negligees, camisoles, teddys --- by all the best names. All five to twenty percent off the already reduced prices. So go to Manhattan Unmentionables this Thursday, Friday and Saturday, on Kelly Road four blocks south of Nine Mile. And get yourself something really sexy. Then, when he asks you to model it, you tell him thanks for <u>The Betty Crocker Newsletter</u> --- but he can't have his cake and eat it too. Manhattan Unmentionables.

(Courtesy of Rick Wiggins, WDFX)

Co-op Advertising

In a cooperative (co-op) enterprise, the manufacturer shares the cost of advertising its product with the local retailer. Co-op spots force the copywriter to do double-duty. All the pitfalls associated with conventional retail advertising apply to co-op as well. But in addition, you must wrestle with the problem of two simultaneous clients who share a contractual right to co-star status. It is essential that the listener be able to discern which is the brand (manufacturer) name and which the retailer (store) name. If, for example, Gladstone's Shoe Store is featured in a co-op spot with manufacturer Dexter Shoes, and the listeners are led by the copy to look for the Dexter Shoe Store, they might pass right by Gladstone's, to the long-term detriment of both clients.

As a general rule, it is less confusing for the listener if you don't alternate between brand and retailer name. Instead, follow a clustering strategy in which you concentrate on one identity at a time. This can be accomplished by any of four patterns:

1. Emphasize brand in the spot's first part, retailer in the second part.
2. Emphasize brand for most of spot, followed by retailer tagging.
3. Emphasize brand at beginning and end, retailer in the middle.
4. Emphasize retailer at beginning and end, brand in the middle.

We briefly discuss these four options in order.

The "first part brand/second part retailer" approach is a very logical one. Consumers initially perceive a need for a product or service and then focus on where to get it. They do not normally feel a need for a store—and then worry about what they might buy there. In the following spot, the "product" is a trademarked medical procedure and the "store" a clinic authorized to provide that procedure.

(MUSIC: <u>GAME SHOW THEME UP AND UNDER</u>)

ANNCR: (Vigorously) It's *Look Good Naked!* The game where contestants discover the best way to retain their youthful looks. Now, here's your host, Beau Tocks.

BEAU: Today's category is 'Great Legs.' This new procedure is the only complete, non-surgical alternative to liposuction approved by the FDA for all skin types and colors. (SFX: CONTESTANT BUZZER) Yes, Contestant Two?

TWO: Velashape!

BEAU: That's right! Velashape reduces the volume and appearance of fat tissue to reveal smoother, firmer thighs in as little as 4 visits. Next question: what about time and discomfort?

(CONTESTANT BUZZER)

TWO: None! Velashape feels like a warm, deep tissue massage.

BEAU: Right again. What other areas can Velashape help? (CONTESTANT BUZZER) Contestant One?

ONE: (Unsure) Abdomen and --- booty?

BEAU: Yes! Now for the triple point question. Who is metro Detroit's Velashape Expert?

(CONTESTANT BUZZER)

ONE: (Excited) Oh, oh, I know this! Skin and Vein Center of Michigan! They're board-certified dermatologists with more than 20 years experience.

BEAU: Correct! Tune in tomorrow for another chance to play *Look Good Naked.*

(APPLAUSE AND GAME SHOW MUSIC UP AND UNDER)

ANNCR: Sponsored by Skin and Vein Center of Michigan. To learn how you can look more youthful and self-confident, visit Skin and Vein dot com. Or call 800-400-VEIN. 800-400 V-E-I-N.

(Courtesy of Lisa Drummond, Greater Media Detroit)

Retailer tagging involves devoting most of the co-op commercial to the brand and then ending with identification of where that brand can be obtained. This technique is common when the manufacturer's co-op plan is paying a greater percentage of the airtime fee and/or when two or more retailers are getting together to split the local portion of the time buy's cost.

ANNCR: Wisconsin's got Summerfest, and Winterfest. Now the biggest fest of all --- Recyclerfest. And you don't even have to wait until summer. It's going on now at every Toro dealer in town. During Toro's Recyclerfest, you'll save on every single Toro Recycler mower in stock. Get behind the wheels of a Toro Recycler and mow your way through the summer with ease. Now, during Recyclerfest, the Toro Recycler mower is more affordable than ever before. Toro Recyclers start at just 299 dollars. With a Toro Recycler, your lawn can have that just-manicured look without bagging. So don't just mulch. Recycle with a Toro during Toro's Recyclerfest. This is the one fest you can't afford to miss. Sensational sale prices and no payments 'til October make owning a Toro Recycler mower easier than ever. Visit one of these Toro dealers today:

TAG #1:   In Depere, see Ambrosius Sales and Service or VanEvenhoven Hardware.

TAG #2:   In Green Bay, see Mathu's Appliance and Power, Pamp's Outboard, or Paulson Hardware.

(Courtesy of WNFL/WKFX)

Emphasizing the brand at the beginning and the end of the spot is standard practice in manufacturer-supplied doughnut commercials. At the same time, the local business acquires greater visibility by essentially having the 'hole' all to itself. The spot is provided to the station pre-produced with the hole left empty for local insertion.

SINGER: Come home to quality. Come home to Andersen.
                Come home to quality. Come home to Andersen.

ANNC/SOT: Andersen introduces a double-pane insulating glass more energy efficient than triple pane. It's their new High-Performance insulating glass --- optional in Andersen windows and gliding patio doors.

HOLE: And available from Miller-Zeilstra Lumber. It's good news for homeowners here in Western Michigan because Andersen's special transparent coating keeps radiant heat indoors --- where it belongs in winter. Reduces heating costs while keeping you comfortable in the coldest weather, even next to windows. For specific details about High-Performance insulating glass, talk to the experts at Miller-Zeilstra. They've been serving Grand Rapids area homeowners for over fifty years. Miller-Zeilstra is at 8-33 Michigan Northeast, just east of the beltway. Open daily 'til 6, and Saturdays 'til 4.

SINGER: Come home to quality. Come home to Andersen.

(Courtesy of Paul Boscarino, Clear Channel Radio)

Conversely, wrapping dealer discussion around the brand mention is especially appropriate when the manufacturer is paying a lesser amount in co-op reimbursement. The dealer can later use the same commercial as a hammock in which to drop alternate products and brand identifications, thereby securing co-op dollars from other manufacturers whose line this retailer carries.

ANNCR: The freedom to choose. That's what makes America great. And when it comes to tires, Freedom is your best choice. Freedom Tire with 11 Central Iowa locations is your best choice for tires, service, and great deals. Freedom Tire guarantees they will not be undersold on comparable tires.

HOLE: And right now, the Goodyear Pit Stop Tire Sale is going on at all Freedom Tire stores. Through August 28th, you can save on popular Goodyear tires, like the Goodyear Integrity, Eagle GT-HR, and Wrangler A-T-S. And when you buy four selected Goodyear tires at Freedom Tire, you get up to 75 dollars on a cash card. Hurry, this pit stop is flying by.

ANNCR: Plus stop in for great Gemini Automotive Care. The A-S-E Certified Technicians at Freedom Tire can keep your vehicle running in tip-top shape. You have the freedom to choose. So choose Freedom. Freedom Tire. Choose your location too. Freedom Tire, with 11 Central Iowa stores. Remember, Freedom Tire will not be undersold on comparable tires. For details, check on-line at Freedom Tire dot com.

(Courtesy of Jim Brown, Saga Communications)

Whatever technique is used, the co-op copywriter must recognize that the manufacturer plays a determining role in the copy approval process. Often, stations obtain approval by delivering the copy directly to the manufacturer via fax or email. Such precautions are essential. If the manufacturer does not believe its wares and name have been adequately showcased in the commercial, it will not reimburse the local merchant for a portion of the airtime. Because the merchant counts on such reimbursement, the copywriter had better make certain that the script fully justifies this payment—or risk losing a local client.

Everything discussed so far in this section is known as a *vertical co-op*—the joint marketing of the product/service creator and the local store that actually conveys that product/service to the consumer. *Horizontal co-op,* also known as *tie-in advertising,* is a little different. In this type of enterprise, two or more manufacturers or two or more retailers come together for a joint promotion. Thus a cereal company and an orange juice producer may use spots extolling the merits of a nutritious breakfast—defined as a blend of cornflakes and o.j. In an example of the other breed of horizontal co-op, several stores may join forces to get folks through their doors in a shared on-air campaign. As in any retail copy, the trick is to find a central concept strong and flexible enough to showcase multiple products presented in multiple combinations.

ANNCR: Finally, after all that snow, it's outdoor barbeque time here in the North Country. But why waste your short summer on 'everybody does it' grocery store food? Warm weather time is special. So make those barbeques special with:

HOLE #1:   Fresh, hand-packed bratwurst from Kleinhofer's Meat Boutique on Quincy Street. Kleinhofer brats on your grill turn a picnic into a banquet.

[or]

HOLE #2:   Corn for roasting and buns for toasting purchased from Edna's Farm Market. Edna's produce is all locally grown, and her breads and rolls are baked from scratch right in the store on Route 23.

ANNCR: Summer's also the best time to take advantage of all the fun our lakes have to offer. Make your day on the beach or the boat more pleasurable.

HOLE #1:   Prevent sunburn and bug bites with tanning lotions and insect repellants from Dirkman's Drugs, corner of Lakeview and Pine. Dirkman's carries everything made to protect your skin in the sun and shade.

[or]

HOLE #2:   Take along a cooler filled with your favorite sodas from The Pop Shop --- where you'll find the area's bubbly-best selection of specialty soft drinks. Pop on in to The Pop Shop, right next to the fire hall.

ANNCR: While the blizzards are away, it's time to play. Visit these North Country stores to help you make the most of your short but precious summer.

Classified Advertising

As newspaper readership has declined, and audio media search for new revenue streams, classified advertising has changed from a print-only vehicle to a viable electronic commercial category. In creating an audio 'want ad', the copywriter must develop a scenario. A print classified can simply set down data for the reader to scan at will. But its audio counterpart, like any good commercial, needs to fashion a situation that attracts active listening—and active listening by the type of job candidates we are striving to reach. The following dialogue, for example, spins out a recruitment storyline on behalf of the station itself.

(SFX: SIREN WINDING DOWN)

DRIVER: Hello, officer, what's up? Why did you pull me over?

COP: I'm taking you in.

DRIVER: But officer, I haven't done anything wrong.

COP: Are you dependable?

DRIVER: Yes.

COP: Do you like to meet new people?

DRIVER: Yeah, but what---

COP: Sir, are you a self-starter with high self esteem, unstoppable confidence, tons of energy and a natural passion for sales?

DRIVER: Well, yeah. But there's nothing wrong with that, is there?

COP: Then out of the car. I'm takin' you in.

DRIVER: Officer, what have I done wrong?

COP: Nothing. You're Mister Right. I'm taking you in to WHTC. They're looking for people just like you to sell advertising on 14-50, WHTC. Holland's hometown station.

ANNCR: At WHTC, we're looking for a few good people who are ready for an exciting and satisfying career in radio sales. E-mail your resume to Kevin-at-WHTC-dot-com. Midwest radio group station WHTC is an equal opportunity employer. That's Kevin-at-WHTC-dot-com.

(Courtesy of Kevin Oswald, WHTC)

To be gender neutral, the same spot can be re-recorded with a woman as the driver, simply by changing 'sir' to 'ma'am' in the cop's fourth line and 'Mister' to 'Miz' Right in his last speech.

It is important that the audio classified compliments target listeners as a reward for them to *keep* listening. Just be certain this compliment is related to the job qualifications the employer is seeking. The 'traffic stop' commercial does this, and so does the following music-assisted ad for an air handling technician.

Production Note: 'Klopf' rhymes with 'off' – 'p' is silent

(MUSIC: MAJESTIC, GRANDIOSE ORCHESTRAL SWELL – FEATURE AND UNDER)

ANNCR: (Dramatically) You have the power. When it's cold, you make everyone warm. When the summer heat is unbearable, you see that there's a cool breeze. You make it possible --- because *you* are a professional heating and cooling service technician.

(MUSIC: CROSSFADE TO SUNNY, UPBEAT CONTEMPORARY TRACK AND UNDER)

ANNCR: (Normal read) A-C Klopf Heating and Air Conditioning of Saginaw is looking for qualified service techs like you. If you're self-motivated, dependable, and can deliver on a deadline with minimal supervision, send your resume to A-C Klopf today. Earn union scale wages and a full benefit package, all while enjoying a great working atmosphere, stable employment, and advancement opportunities. You could make up to 72-thousand dollars, based on experience. A-C Klopf Heating and Air Conditioning is looking for professional service techs to repair commercial and residential heating and air conditioning units, as well as refrigeration. You have the power to bring comfort in whatever weather Michigan can dish out. Send your resume to A-C Klopf, 5-24 Franklin Street, Saginaw, 4-8-6-0-7. That's A-C Klopf, 5-24 Franklin Street, Saginaw, forty-eight, 6-0-7. A-C Klopf Heating and Air Conditioning; an equal opportunity employer.

(Courtesy of Craig Allen, Citadel Communications)

Direct-Response Advertising

Classified spots are actually a specialized form of direct-response advertising. In DR (also known as *per inquiry*) advertising, it is not a matter of just sending people to a place of business where the merchant is expected to complete the sale. Instead, *the commercial itself* must consummate the sale by having the listener call, email, or snail mail an order (or job application). Thus the direct-response spot must not only create the desire to own but also secure a commitment. While it is said that advertising in general is the process of "diverting the consumer past the merchant's door," the DR message must work as the functional substitute for that door and the point-of-purchase sales-people who normally stand behind it. This means, says Ketchum Direct's president, Maryalice Fuller, that "direct response has to be incredibly clear, incredibly precise. Far more so than with all other forms of advertising. And you don't just get that kind of clarity and precision without the highest attention to creativity."[11]

Because of the selling and delivery burdens imposed on it, direct-response copy does not have the time to be artsy or allegorical. Every word must be directed not just to the sell, but also to the activation of the purchasing decision through dialing, logging, or writing in. What is more, with DR, it soon becomes unequivocally apparent whether you have succeeded or failed based on how many units of the product your copy has actually moved, how many service orders have been written, or how many qualified job applications have been received. "Everything we and our agencies do," reveals direct marketer Thomas McAlevey, "is designed, executed, placed and measured in terms of cost per lead, appointment, and finally, sale. I found out quickly that creative egos and Clio-seeking writers . . . had no place in the direct business, where communication is only judged to be successful if the target prospect acts, *in a measurable way,* in favor of the product."[12] The discipline taught in such an arena is why advertising legend David Ogilvy maintained that "Every copywriter should start his career by spending two years in direct response."[13]

One can't blame poor store location or limited shelf space for a failed direct-response campaign because the commercial *itself* is that store and that shelf as well as the emotional/rational selling appeal. Direct response "is a real challenge for creative people because it's a test of their skills," points out agency owner Martin Puris. "There's a direct relation between what you're doing and how the product is doing. You know immediately whether the commercial you wrote is or isn't working. That's scary for a lot of creative people."[14]

To cope with DR fear, familiarize yourself with the following seven DR-mastering principles. They, along with what we've already discussed about effective audio writing in general, should outfit you with the confidence you need to make the direct-response landscape less foreboding.

1. *Prepare Them for Action at the Top of the Copy.* Because listeners are going to be urged to call, write, or email, provide advance notice for them to "get pencil and paper ready," or to "listen for our toll-free number (or Web address) at the end of this message."

2. *Show How the Product Can Impinge on the Listener's Life.* Like any effective piece of salesmanship, the DR spot involves solving problems for people. But because these people can't check the product out in the store first, the DR commercial must be a *demonstrated* problem-solver before a listener is willing to part with some money or make some other sort of commitment.

3. *Make Product Exclusivity Unmistakable.* Lines like "This product is not available in any store" inform the listener there is no alternative to patronizing our client. Direct response will never be direct if the audience feels they have the option to shop around.

4. *Take Listener Objections into Account.* You don't want to replace one prospect doubt with another. "You pay nothing now," "try it with no risk for 30 days," or "certified safe by Underwriter's Labs" are lines that show the listener you have nothing to hide and make the buying decision less apprehensive.

5. *Clearly and Repeatedly State Product Cost.* Listeners know there is a price to everything. So don't arouse suspicion by attempting to conceal it. If the initial mailing is "free," *free* becomes the price and should also be repeated. This does not, however, mean you can obscure the cost of succeeding installments.

6. *Stress the Need for Immediate Action—but Don't Make the Deadline Too Near.* Just as we don't want our prospects to assume that there are in-store alternatives to our client, we also don't want them to postpone their purchase or reply into the indefinite future. Furthermore, an audio DR commercial leaves nothing behind as does a newspaper coupon or a direct-mail piece. So even if the audience has written down our number or Web address, delayed action probably results in *no* action—because there remains no printed reminder that details just what that number/address could bring. Sometimes, immediate response is facilitated through setting of a deadline for ordering or

applying. If possible, make the deadline the same month in which the spot is airing. In this way, listeners will realize they only have until the end of *this* month and thus are less likely to put it off. However, if the deadline comes too quickly, you may be shutting the door on some prospect procrastinators, as well as allowing insufficient time for the spot to generate a profitable return. The way around this is to offer an "act now" bonus such as "a second bottle" or "a special ten percent discount." You thereby keep the product availability window open indefinitely but still provide an additional stimulus to "act now."

7. *Communicate the Specific Purchase Process.* Whether it's the repetition of a mailing or email address, or a toll-free number, you must clearly state the "how-to-get-it" part of the message at least twice. Creating the desire to own and getting the decision to buy will be worthless achievements if you do not set the customer on the path to client contact.

The commercial below includes all seven of these ingredients required for a hard-working DR pitch. Try to detect each ingredient in analyzing this sixty-second spot.

DEEP VOICE: Twelve ninety-five. Twelve ninety-five.

MARY: Hello. We've asked a man with a <u>very deep voice</u> to say:

DEEP VOICE: Twelve ninety-five.

MARY: Over and over again. Because now you can get cable hook-up for---

DEEP VOICE: Twelve ninety-five.

MARY: That would normally cost you---

DEEP VOICE: Twelve ninety-five.

MARY: No, cable installation is normally about <u>fifty bucks</u>. Plus, you can get a <u>second</u> TV hooked up for---

DEEP VOICE: Twelve ninety-five.

MARY: Wrong! The second cable TV hook-up is <u>free</u>. We guarantee that in writing. And, when you order a <u>premium channel package</u>, we'll give you <u>grocery coupons</u> for Ralph's worth---

DEEP VOICE: Twelve ninety-five.

MARY: No! The coupons are worth <u>forty bucks</u>, the installation is---

DEEP VOICE: Twelve ninety-five.

MARY: Right. Now try it <u>lower</u>.

DEEP VOICE: <u>Ten</u> ninety-five.

MARY: No, I mean the <u>voice</u> lower.

DEEP VOICE: (Lower) <u>Twelve ninety-five</u>.

MARY: Good. And the only phone number to call?

DEEP VOICE:	1-800-Cable Up.
MARY:	Beautiful. Okay, one last time, make me feel it. Cable installation for---
DEEP VOICE:	(BIGGER, REVERBED) <u>Twelve ninety-five</u>.
MARY:	---just by calling that one-and-only-number---
DEEP VOICE:	(BIGGER, REVERBED) <u>1-800-Cable Up!</u>
MARY:	Offer ends September 30th! You know, that's a very deep voice.
DEEP VOICE:	(Even deeper voice) Thank you.

(© Paul & Walt Worldwide. Writer: Walt Jaschek)

Due to the explosion of talk formats and dial-in promotional contests, listeners are becoming increasingly accustomed to the DR marriage of the radio and their phone or computer. This, together with the precise demographic slivering engaged in by each station, makes audio an increasingly potent selling vehicle. In addition, the growth of *integrated marketing*—created by companies' desires for greater message consistency and cost efficiencies—has resulted in fewer investments in 'brick and mortar' and more reliance on direct marketing communication and order fulfillment.

The Web's *audio banners* are the latest extension of radio DR. In this medium, a conventional banner ad is combined with a streamed audio message that strives to entice the prospect toward the purchase in much the same way as a radio spot—but with one important advantage. "Because," says Internet marketer Dave Bialek, "as opposed to a traditional radio ad where somebody hears the ad in the car and then has to remember the Web site to go to…they can hear the ad right there and click on the banner and go directly to the Web site."[15]

Whether on-air or online, DR is a powerful marketing vehicle—provided the copywriter is able to handle direct response's double-duty job. "When working on a spot," reveals Ron Bliwas, president of DR agency A. Eicoff & Company, "the creative staff is constantly trying to balance two requirements: producing something that is personally satisfying, and producing something that sells. While these requirements aren't mutually exclusive, they are tough to reconcile at times."[16]

Though Bliwas was referring to DR assignments, he has, in fact, sketched a pretty good description of the balancing act you face on *every* electronic media copy assignment. We begin exploring the video challenge in the next chapter.

10 Key Elements of Video Writing

Because many of the communicative writing principles discussed in the previous chapters on audio also pertain to video, they will not be reintroduced in this section. Instead, the next three chapters concentrate on concepts that apply mainly to the *visual* components of continuity and commercial creation or to the particular problems encountered in the interlocking of video and audio. Thus if you have not already done so, the entire section on audio writing should be read before proceeding into the additional complexities of the video dimension.

VIDEO CONCEPTUAL VEHICLES

Three main instruments are used to capture and refine a visual idea: the script, the storyboard, and the photoboard. A given project may progress through all three as it wends its way onto the air.

The Script

As the following 7-Eleven treatment demonstrates, video scripts are usually fashioned in the conventional two-column format, with pictorial directions on the left and the corresponding audio directions on the right.

Video	Audio
OPEN ON SUNNY, PEACEFUL PARK AT PICNIC TABLE. LITTLE BOY RUNS DOWN TOWARD WATER CARRYING SLICE OF BREAD	SFX: NATURAL PARK NOISES, BIRDS, RIPPLING WATER
FATHER AND SON AT EDGE OF WATER ABOUT TO FEED A DUCK	VO: (Deep, serious) Fresh bread can mean the difference between a safe day at the park---

Continued

Video	Audio
BOY TOSSES SLICE OF BREAD TOWARD DUCK	
HARD, STALE BREAD HITS DUCK ON TOP OF HEAD, KNOCKING HIM UPSIDE DOWN. OTHER DUCKS SWIM AWAY. MAIN DUCK'S WIGGLING FEET THE ONLY THING ABOVE WATER LINE	SFX: BONK OF HARD BREAD HITTING DUCK'S HEAD
SURPRISED DAD LOOKING BACK AT DISTRAUGHT SON	---and an emotional scar. So be safe.
QUICK CUT TO 7-ELEVEN LOGO, AND SUPER: Thank Heaven for 7-Eleven. PULLBACK REVEALS FRESH LOAF OF BREAD	<u>MUSIC: BURST OF UPBEAT NOTES</u>
	7-Eleven. Fresh bread and milk delivered daily. Oh Thank Heaven!

(Courtesy of Rob Baker, The Richards Group)

Care is taken in spacing so that the audio indication is always directly opposite the visual it is intended to complement. To do otherwise would make the script very difficult to comprehend and would force the director or editor to read slantwise in trying to synchronize sound and picture properly. Video directions are in ALL CAPS, with the exception of copy on supered graphics, which is usually set lower case (such as 'Thank Heaven for 7-Eleven'.) Capitalization is also used on the audio side for character names (or VO for "announcer voice-over") and also for sound effect and music cues. Music cues are underlined as well. Thus the video script's sound side follows the same uppercase/lowercase conventions as its audio counterpart.

An alternative script format ignores the left side/right side (dual column) separation in favor of a centered (single-column) approach. This format often uses the right two-thirds of the page for the actual script, leaving the left one-third blank to accommodate notes by the director and other production people. As in the dual-column arrangement, all entries except dialogue are in CAPS. Hollywood writers have used the single-column format for years. It has the advantage of being clearer to read—especially by clients. With a two-column script, the temptation is to read the entire audio side first—thereby distorting the spot's progression as well as underestimating the visual's importance. No such problem is encountered in the single-column format's chronological layout:

OPEN ON HERO LEANING ON MODERN CAR.
'BRIDGEMAN' RESTAURANT SIGN IN
BACKGROUND,

HERO: I'm going back to my favorite
        Bridgeman's, 1968.

<u>MUSIC: TEEN PSYCHEDELIC</u>

HERO NOW BACK IN TIME, SEES FRIENDS

    HERO: Rejects!

    GUYS: Dirtball!

    HERO: My old girlfriend---

SHE TWISTS HIS NOSE. THEN BULLY
GIVES HIM SLOW NOOGIE WHILE HE
SAVORS FOOD

    HERO: M-mm; just like I remember it---

FRAME WIDENS TO REVEAL DESSERT

    HERO: And now, the Lallapallooza.

AS HE REACHES FOR DESSERT, A HAND STOPS HIM

    HERO: Mom!

    <u>MUSIC OUT</u>

HE SNAPS BACK TO PRESENT, NOTING
WITH SOME GLEE THAT HE STILL HAS
THE LALLAPALLOOZA

    <u>MUSIC: MORE MODERN BACK IN</u>

    VO: Bridgeman's. Stir up some memories.

    SUPER: 'Stir up some memories'

(Courtesy of John Olson, Kruskopf Olson Advertising)

A slight variation on the single-column format is sometimes used in corporate/industrial scripts when extensive narration occurs. To distinguish what happens on camera from what will be added later as narrative voice-over, the narrator's words are set in CAPS and moved to the right margin:

CLOSE-UP OF CHAIR LEG BEING FASHIONED
ON LATHE

             NARR: MAPLE-RICH
                     FURNITURE
                     COMPONENTS
                     ARE
                     CUSTOM-MILLED
                     FOR SUPERIOR
                     FIT AND
                     FINISH.

STEVE IN HARDHAT STANDING IN PLANT

> STEVE: Maple-Rich has never
> compromised on workmanship
> by forcing production
> speed-ups. My dad taught
> me that---

The professionally structured video script gives the copywriter the opportunity to probe visual concepts without having to draw the illustrations. Because many copywriters are somewhat the other side of stick figures in their artistic abilities, the video script is a blessing for all concerned. It is used as one of the bases of consultation when the copywriter gets together with an art director for the actual sketching of the proposed visual segments. Between these conferences, the script allows the writer to work alone in refining the treatment so that valuable artistic time is not wasted before the message concept has really jelled in the writer's mind.

The evolution of one commercial's script is distinctly focused in the following four drafts from Doner Advertising. Though several more fine-tuning stages occurred between the creation of each version, the major copy refinements, which extended over eleven months, are well represented here. Clearly, video script maturation is neither a slap-dash nor an approximate business. Every word and every pictorial aspect must be scrupulously examined and evaluated in deriving the most cohesive and incisive treatment possible.

Read over these four scripts carefully. Note the progressive modifications made in both audio and video and try to figure out what made these changes necessary and what they helped to accomplish in message clarification. As a video copywriter, you will soon have to make these same determinations about your own commercial and continuity material.

DRAFT #1

Video	Audio
SPOT OPENS ON A PACKAGE OF AMERICAN TUBORG.	ANNCR V/O: This is Tuborg, the world famous beer of Denmark.
CAMERA GOES IN CLOSE TO LABEL TO SHOW THAT IT IS BREWED IN THE U.S.A.	As you can see, Tuborg is now brewed in America.
DISSOLVE TO WIDER SHOT AS HAND COMES INTO FRAME AND EXECUTES A LONG SLOW POUR. THERE IS AN UNUSUAL SIGNET RING ON ONE OF THE FINGERS.	Imported Tuborg used to be a very expensive beer. But now that Tuborg is also brewed in America --- it is affordable by anyone who
THE DESIGN IS A COAT-OF-ARMS.	loves the flavor of good light Danish beer.
GLASS COMES BACK INTO FRAME.	(PAUSE)
CAMERA PANS TO COPY ON LABEL THAT READS "BY APPOINTMENT OF THE ROYAL DANISH COURT."	It is the only beer in America brewed by special appointment for the personal enjoyment of the kings of Denmark and Sweden.

Continued

Video	Audio
CUT TO REGAL-LOOKING SPOKESMAN AS HE SMILES, REPOURS AND TOASTS THE VIEWER WITH A TONGUE-IN-CHEEK SMILE.	Now, if Tuborg is good enough to be a beer for Kings, shouldn't it be good enough for your next Saturday night beer bash?
SUPER POPS ON TUBORG.	
MANDATORY: Tuborg of Copenhagen, Ltd., Natick, Mass.	

DRAFT #2

Video	Audio
OPEN ON MEDIUM SHOT OF BOTTLE OF TUBORG BESIDE RICHLY DESIGNED GOBLET.	ANNCR V/O: This is Tuborg, the famous beer of Denmark.
START ZOOM TO CLOSE-UP OF LABEL THAT IDENTIFIES THE BEER AS BEING BREWED IN THE U.S.A.	Now brewed in America
DIZ TO PART OF LABEL THAT IDENTIFIES APPOINTMENT TO DANISH COURT.	by special appointment to The Royal Courts of Denmark
BOTTLE ROTATES TO ALLOW VIEWER TO READ LABEL COPY THAT IDENTIFIES APPOINTMENT TO SWEDISH COURT.	and Sweden.
DIZ TO WIDER SHOT OF PACKAGE AND GOBLET.	Now you may think a beer brewed for Kings would be expensive.
HAND ENTERS FRAME AND GRASPS BOTTLE FOR POUR.	It was.
AS BEER IS POURED INTO THE GOBLET, ONE CAN SEE THAT ON THE MIDDLE FINGER THERE IS A RICHLY CARVED RING BEARING THE ROYAL COAT OF ARMS OR THE SEAL OF STATE OF DENMARK.	But now Tuborg is affordable by anyone who loves the authentic taste of good light Danish beer.
THE FILLED GOBLET IS HOISTED OUT OF FRAME AND CAMERA STARTS SLOW ZOOM INTO THE PACKAGE.	And for about the same money you've been paying for the king of beers---
THE DRAINED GOBLET IS THUNKED DOWN BESIDE PACKAGE AND CONTINUES TO ZOOM TO THE CROWN ON THE LABEL. TUBORG LOGO AND MANDATORY POP ON.	now you can get Tuborg, the beer of kings.

DRAFT #3

Video	Audio
OPEN ON CLOSE-UP OF BOTTLE NECK, READING "Tuborg Gold."	ANNCR V/O: This is Tuborg Gold---
CAMERA TILTS DOWN ON BOTTLE, PICKS UP CROWN ON MAIN LABEL,	the golden beer of Danish kings---
AND PANS ACROSS TO READ:	
"By appointment to the Royal Danish Court/the Royal Swedish Court."	by appointment to the Royal Courts of Denmark and Sweden.
DISSOLVE TO CU OF LABEL ON BOTTLE BEING TILTED BY HAND FOR A POUR, AND READ, "Product of USA."	Tuborg Gold is now brewed in America---
DISSOLVE TO BEER BEING POURED INTO DANISH GLASS WITH RAISED IMPRIMATUR OF CROWN ON ITS FRONT.	and affordable to anyone
DISSOLVE TO HAND WEARING REGAL RING LIFTING GLASS UP AND OUT OF FRAME.	who loves the authentic taste of light, golden Danish beer.
DISSOLVE TO BEAUTY "STILL LIFE" OF BOTTLE AND FOOD ON A TABLE BEFORE BEAUTIFUL STAINED GLASS WINDOW, MOVING IN AS THE DRAINED GLASS IS SET DOWN BY HAND INTO THE FRAME, ENDING ON CU OF LABEL, FINALLY READING LARGE, "Tuborg Gold."	So, for about what you'd pay for the king of beers --- now you can have Tuborg Gold, the beer of kings.
SUPER MANDATORY: Tuborg of Copenhagen, Ltd., Baltimore, MD.	

DRAFT #4

Video	Audio
OPEN ON CLOSE UP OF BOTTLE NECK, READING "Tuborg Gold."	ANNCR V/O: This is our Tuborg Gold---
CAMERA TILTS DOWN BOTTLE, PICKS UP CROWN ON MAIN LABEL,	the golden beer of Danish kings---
AND PANS ACROSS TO READ:	
"By appointment to the Royal Danish Court/the Royal Swedish Court."	now affordable to anyone who loves the pure taste of light, golden Danish beer.

Continued

Video	Audio
DISSOLVE TO BEER BEING POURED INTO DANISH GLASS WITH RAISED IMPRIMATUR OF CROWN ON ITS FRONT.	For Tuborg Gold is now brewed in America.
DISSOLVE TO HAND WEARING REGAL RING LIFTING GLASS UP AND OUT OF FRAME.	By appointment to the Royal Danish Court.
DISSOLVE TO BEAUTY "STILL LIFE" OF BOTTLE AND FOOD ON A TABLE BEFORE BEAUTIFUL STAINED GLASS WINDOW, MOVING IN AS THE DRAINED GLASS IS SET DOWN BY HAND INTO THE FRAME, ENDING ON CU OF LABEL, FINALLY READING LARGE, "Tuborg Gold."	So, for about what you'd pay for the king of beers --- you can now have Tuborg Gold, the golden beer of Danish Kings.
SUPER MANDATORY: Carling National Breweries, Inc., Baltimore, MD.	

(Courtesy of David R. Sackey, Doner Advertising)

The Storyboard

This sequence of selected sketched stills in a proposed video treatment helps keep concept creation and evaluation pictorially oriented. In some situations, even the first attempt at an assignment is done in storyboard form by a copywriter/art director team. At other times, it is the copywriter who comes up with an initial script draft and perhaps even refines it before bringing the draft to the artist for visual workup. For reasons of economy and efficiency in conserving valuable artist time, several script rewrites may occur between each storyboard. This is particularly true if freelance storyboard artists, who command from $750 to $1,000 per day or more, are employed.[1]

As video producer Peter Putman points out, a central reason for using a storyboard "is to ensure consistency on your part when it comes to delivering what you promised to your client in the first place! Other than on birthdays and holidays, most people are apprehensive about big surprises—especially after several thousand dollars of their money have already been spent. Showing a client what you'll give him or her and then delivering it is a sure-fire recipe for follow-up business."[2]

Traditional storyboard format features a series of panels with a visual block on the top and an audio block below it. Together, these panels (or 'frames') strive to illustrate the sequence of visual action, the camera angles, transitions and optical effects desired, and also the dialogue, music, and sound effects being considered. Pads of blank storyboard sheets, with multiple panels per sheet, accommodate this task. Each panel is perforated for easy separation and rearrangement. Obtainable from a number of suppliers, these pads provide ready-to-use storyboard layouts at a very low cost. Computer storyboard programs are also available for artists who prefer to work electronically. These programs have the additional advantage of being able to be emailed instantaneously to other agency and client offices for quick feedback and approval.

As it is being prepared, the storyboard also provides the opportunity for good interplay between copy and art people, a practice pioneered by advertising legend

Bill Bernbach who created the writer/artist team concept well over a half-century ago. "No longer would a copywriter slip a headline and copy under an art director's door with an order for a layout, like ordering a pizza," recalls BBDO Vice-Chairman Brett Shevack. "Working as a team, each gave up individual control to create better ideas. The team concept forever changed the way agencies solve problems."[3] This interplay can be most effective when the two people involved are not afraid to make suggestions about the other's area and to accept suggestions about their own. Art directors *have* been known occasionally to come up with a better word or phrase than the copywriter had originally captured. And copywriters, in their own scattered moments of pictorial brilliance, do stumble upon more compelling visual ideas than the artist at first had in mind. Because the professional well-being of both depends on their *collective* ability to derive a successful audio/visual communication, the copywriter and the art director each have something to gain from pooling rather than departmentalizing their knowledge and insight.

To be cohesively productive, the relationship between the two creatives should be a simultaneous rather than a consecutive enterprise, or the original concept may be lost. "Traditionally," laments commercial artist Alexander Molinello, "art directors or illustrators take copy and run with it and then come back with something that the writer never saw that way."[4] When artist and wordsmith physically work together on the board, however, you are much more likely to end up with one unified concept rather than with two mutually exclusive ones. Creating a unified concept takes active collaboration and the willingness to modify by both parties. Only partly in jest, copywriter Peter Kellogg warns, "If you walk into an art director's office with an idea and say, 'Here it is!' you're just asking to get your head chewed off. Art directors, you see, like to think that they have some part in the creative process, and you've got to convince them they do . . . Besides, sniffing spray mount and magic markers all day seems to affect their brains. So it's always wise to proceed with caution."[5]

The result of truly effective copywriter/art director partnership, the two storyboards that follow (Figures 10.1 and 10.2) illustrate intermediate stages in the maturation of the same Tuborg spot to which the four scripts pertain. From this pair of layouts, it is relatively easy to see how the script modifications determined and were themselves determined by refinements in the storyboard. With its self-contained audio/visual segments, the storyboard format also facilitates quick rearrangement of frames in the pursuit of more effective idea flow.

Some agencies have replaced the traditional "comic strip" storyboard arrangement with a vertical or "stacking" format. In a vertical 'board, the pictures run down the center of the page, with verbal descriptions of the video to the left and audio elements specified to the right. Figure 10.3 is an example of such a layout. Users of this stacking format believe it better conveys the flow of the spot than does the down/up/down eye scan required to read successive panels in the conventional storyboard layout. The choice remains largely a matter of organizational preference and should not impact the conceptual process. Both formats contain the same information, notated in the same basic manner. It is only the spatial arrangement of complementary words and pictures that changes.

Technically, the first quick sketches, suitable only for showing to co-creators, constitute a *rough* or *loose* storyboard. Later versions (like Figures 10.1 and 10.2 of the Tuborg treatment), which may be polished enough to exhibit to the client and more precisely delineate each frame, are known as *refined, tight,* or *comprehensive* boards. In short-deadline or low-budget projects, however, it is not uncommon to proceed directly from a *rough* into actual production—provided that the rough is definitive enough to motivate executive approval.

With greater use of computer technology, the distinction between rough and refined boards is narrowing. Desktops now allow art directors to expand, contract, shift, and otherwise modify their frames on a video monitor before printing out their best effort as hard copy. Software programs like StoryBoard Artist and FrameForge 3D include pre-built locations, props, and poseable characters. All can be shown from various angles and additional images can be imported from other clip libraries or the artist's own digital files. In computer-derived storyboards, type style and size can be experimented with as well. When the client wants changes, the stored image can be quickly retrieved, adjusted, and reshaped accordingly. Such capabilities can cut the artist's time by one-third or more, with a much greater proportional saving in art materials and photoprocessing. At the same time, the availability of software-derived storyboards permits artist and copywriter to sit down at the screen and manipulate images together—before anything gets locked into uncompromising ink.

A decade ago, it looked as if computer-drawn boards would totally replace those sketched on paper. But even though hand-drawn comps have become scarce in preparing material for print media, video storyboarding is often still done in a paper/pencil format. This is because the older method offers an originality impossible on the computer, where everyone is working from the same stock images. "Hopefully, what you're going to present to clients is something that hasn't been seen before," says storyboard artist Matt Myers. "If it's something new, you have to draw it."[6]

There are two other drawbacks to relying too heavily on computers in storyboard generation. First, there is a tendency to become so preoccupied with the software tools that more time is spent on executing a slick digital board than on developing the conceptual idea that should be the foundation of the message. Second, because digital picture-building can be done faster than manual renderings, clients think they can speed up the conceptual stage as well. But the time required for good idea generation is independent of the process used to set those ideas into storyboard form. Good ideas take significant time to gestate—whether the creative team is using a Ram-rich computer or pencil sketches on paper pads.

The Photoboard

After the last-stage storyboards are prepared and approved, and footage shot, but before final editing, dubbing, and distribution of spot copies is authorized, a photoboard traditionally has been constructed to give those people who have the final decision the clearest possible idea of the actual creative and production values present in the project. Sometimes the photoboard consists of selected stills lifted from already shot footage. In other situations, where reviewers want to evaluate spot styling and casting earlier, photoboards replace the later (refined) storyboards. In such instances, still pictures are shot and pasted up as board panels for scrutiny *before* final shooting commences. Increasingly, however, since everything is available digitally, agencies are avoiding the expense of reproducing hard-copy photoboards.

(continued on page 283)

ANNOUNCER V/O: This is Tuborg Gold the famous Beer of Denmark...

that is now brewed here in America.

that is brewed by special appointment

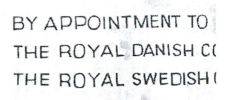

to the Royal Danish Court

for kings would be expensive.
It was.

But now that Tuborg Gold is brewed here...it is affordable to anyone who loves the authentic taste

FIGURE 10.1   *(Courtesy of David R. Sackey, Doner Advertising)*

It is the only beer

in the U.S.A.

APPOINTMENT TO
ROYAL DANISH COURT
ROYAL SWEDISH COURT

and the Royal Swedish Court.

Now you may think a beer
brewed

FIGURE 10.1 *(Continued)*

Instead, they rely on computers to reference the digital sequences or stills from the production or preproduction shoot and grab and review individual frames as needed.

A conventional photoboard—Figure 10.4—was produced for the Tuborg "Label" commercial we have been studying and represents the spot's culmination. You can see that it matches the copy called for in script draft #4 but that the visuals

OPEN ON CLOSE UP OF BOTTLE NECK, READING
"Tuborg Gold."

- -

ANNCR V/O: This is Tuborg Gold --

CAMERA TILTS DOWN BOTTLE,

- -

the golden beer

"By appointment to the Royal Danish Court/
the Royal Swedish Court."

- -

of Denmark and Sweden.

DISSOLVE TO CU OF LABEL ON BOTTLE BEING
TILTED BY HAND FOR A POUR,

- -

Tuborg Gold

DISSOLVE TO HAND WEARING REGAL RING
LIFTING GLASS UP AND OUT OF FRAME,

- -

who loves the authentic taste of light,
golden Danish beer.

DISSOLVE TO BEAUTY "STILL LIFE" OF BOTTLE
AND FOOD ON A TABLE BEFORE BEAUTIFUL
STAINED GLASS WINDOW,

- -

So, for about what you'd pay for the king
of beers...

FIGURE 10.2 *(Courtesy of David R. Sackey, Doner Advertising)*

284

PICKS UP CROWN ON MAIN LABEL,

- - - - - - - - - - - - - - - - - - - -

of Danish kings --

AND READ, "Product of USA."

- - - - - - - - - - - - - - - - - - - -

is now brewed in America...

MOVING IN AS THE DRAINED GLASS IS SET DOWN
BY HAND INTO THE FRAME,

- - - - - - - - - - - - - - - - - - - -

now you can have

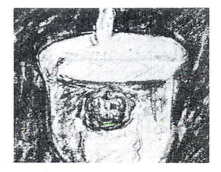

AND PANS ACROSS TO READ...

- - - - - - - - - - - - - - - - - - - -

by appointment to the Royal Courts

DISSOLVE TO BEER BEING POURED INTO DANISH
GLASS WITH RAISED IMPRIMATUR OF CROWN ON
ITS FRONT.

- - - - - - - - - - - - - - - - - - - -

and affordable to anyone

ENDING ON CU OF LABEL, FINALLY READING
LARGE, "TUBORG GOLD."
SUPER MANDATORY: Tuborg of Copenhagen,
                 Ltd., Baltimore, Md.

- - - - - - - - - - - - - - - - - - - -

Tuborg Gold, the beer of kings.

FIGURE 10.2 *(Continued)*

TITLE CARD -
DYNAMICS

MUSIC THROUGHOUT
MARIONETTE

DISSOLVE THROUGH
TO PEOPLE IN RED
UNIFORMS CARRYING
AIRLINE SEATS AND
DEPOSITING THEM.

OTHER PEOPLE (IN
GREEN, BLUE & YEL-
LOW UNIFORMS) ARE
COMING IN AND PICK-
ING UP THE DIS-
CARDED SEATS AND
CARRYING THEM OFF.

GRIFF RHYS JONES
VOICE OVER: There's an
interesting dynamic
developing here.

While Virgin has been
removing seats to make
more room.

FIGURE 10.3   *(Courtesy of Robbie Fink, Korey, Kay & Partners)*

have been further refined. This photoboard is also a good deal more polished than either of the stages marked by the two storyboards. In addition, because the visual component has already been shot as actual production *rushes* (total captured footage from which the final version will be edited), a photoboard such as this does not require the storyboard's verbal description of the pictures. (Revisit Figures 10.2 and 10.3 to see how such ALL CAPS pictorial description is handled at the storyboard stage.)

After final approval, the photoboard, or the digital file that replaced it, can also be used to provide stations and networks with a specific document they can review for continuity acceptance purposes. Hard copy or digital, photoboards can also be

other airlines have been adding seats.

One's got to wonder...

are they using our seats?

SUPER: VIRGIN
ATLANTIC AIRWAYS.
NON-STOP 747's TO
LONDON.

Virgin Atlantic Airways
Non-stop 747's to London

Virgin Atlantic
Airways. The
entertainment capital of
the sky.

FIGURE 10.3   *(Continued)*

sent to distributors of the product as a means of highlighting the marketing efforts that the manufacturer is exerting on this commodity's behalf.

Additional Vehicles

Animatics are a way of bringing motion to a storyboard so that the concept can be presented to clients or tested on consumers before a commitment is made to full-scale production. In the past, animatics were constructed almost like inexpensive cartoons, with individual illustrated panels shot several times and then spliced together.

ANNCR V/O: This is our Tuborg Gold . . .

the golden beer of Danish kings . . .

now affordable to anyone who loves the true taste of light, golden Danish beer.

For Tuborg Gold is now brewed in America.

By appointment to the Royal Danish Court.

So, for about what you'd pay for the king of beer . . .

you can now have Tuborg Gold, the the golden beer of Danish kings . . .

Carling National Breweries, Inc.
Baltimore, Md.

FIGURE 10.4   *(Courtesy of David R. Sackey, Doner Advertising)*

Nowadays, computers have given the process much more fluidity while lowering the price of these 'movie storyboards.' Art directors can now create moving pictures on the computer screen, add sound, and then email the result to the client for reaction. Many digital animatics now produce characters with natural-looking hair and skin and accommodate sophisticated three-dimensional effects. There is, however, a conceptual downside to these ever-advancing digital capabilities. "Once you give those tools to creative people," warns creative director Peter Farago, "they get lost in the abyss of decisions. It's like giving an art director 10,000 typefaces."[7]

Photomatics also have been in use for some time and, like animatics, are being reinvigorated by the computer. The photomatic differs from the animatic only in that it uses photographs instead of an artist's illustrations. Any of several software programs can then invest these photos with flow and motion. When these photos are of real people rather than of graphically created characters, the result is sometimes known as a *live-o-matic*. Much less innovatively, *steal-* or *rip-o-matics* are made up of sequences pulled from other commercials that are quickly computer-assembled to suggest how the spot under development might look when completed. There is, however, a major danger in relying on such techniques. "Instead of storyboards, we can now work on the Avid and create a rip-o-matic that pulls together the best scenes from 15 award-winning, million dollar commercials shot by star directors and jam them into a rough cut for one ad," admits veteran art director and creative director Rick Boyko. "Once you've shown this to the client and he's signed off on it, you've set yourself up for a fall. To actually replicate all the great stuff in the rip-o-matic would probably cost you $15 million to shoot, and your budget is $500,000."[8]

A BUBBLE ABOUT ANIMATION

As our discussion above suggests, the rapid development of visual computer technology has increased the use and diversity of animated material in video spots and continuity. Certainly, through its ability to vivify concepts and events impossible in real life, the animated commercial provides the maximum in creative freedom and flexibility. In addition, the specially customized cartoon "spokesthing" can be an almost priceless long-term asset to brand recall and a ready-made tie-in between the video message and such nonelectronic media as print layouts, billboards, display cards, and direct-mail pieces. McGruff (see Figure 10.5) demonstrates that this phenomenon can work for both PSAs and commercials.

Sometimes, if a creative linkage with the product can be defined, and if the rights can be obtained, an *already popular* animated character may be recruited to promote your client. Such a character combines the elements of the celebrity testimonial with the inherent charm of cartoon characters who, unlike real people, are difficult for viewers to dislike. Animated characters also are able to demonstrate the product in ways real people can't, as in the Figure 10.6 Uniroyal spot that enlists a prominent inhabitant of the comic strip "B.C." The spot's effectiveness is further heightened by the appropriateness of using a caveman to demonstrate the fundamental necessity of the Uniroyal steel-belted radial, a snow tire seemingly second in importance only to the invention of the wheel itself.

Care must be taken in choosing an animated 'spokesthing.' It is not enough that the character possess visual appeal and have a tie-in to the product benefit. The entity must also be interesting in its own right. "Effective brand icons are characters with a story line," advises Leo Burnett chief creative officer Cheryl Berman, "including friends, limitations, and fears."[9] Veteran advertising mascot developer David Altschul adds that some fundamental strategic questions need to be addressed before any such character is recruited for your campaign: "What is the story about? What are the flaws, vulnerabilities and sources of conflict that connect the character to the brand in a deep, intrinsic way? What human truth is revealed through the story that audiences can relate to? Every effective brand character is built on this kind of story framework."[10]

If the above questions can be satisfactorily answered, there is still the question of cost. Even if you can avoid licensing fees for a popular animated character by creating your own, animation is still expensive. And if cartooning action must be matted (overlaid) onto footage of real-life scenes and characters, as in the kid-targeting Cookie Crisp spot in Figure 10.7, costs can skyrocket. If your account is on a small

"SCRUFF ADVENTURES II" CNCP-6160   (Also available in :30 length, CNCP-6130)

McGRUFF: Here's my nephew Scruff

about to run into trouble again.

SCRUFF: Hey, Bobo, where's your videogame?
BOBO: In here. But look at this!

SCRUFF: Uh, oh!
BOBO: It's my dad's. Wanna hold it?

SCRUFF: What'll I do?

McGRUFF: You'll see, but that's not the only problem he has.

SCRUFF: Hey, here's a short cut.
LEANDER: Not down there, Square.

INEZ: I don't think it's safe.

SCRUFF: C'mon. The coast is clear. LEANDER: I'm not taking a chance, Lance.

SCRUFF: Oh, no.

BULLY: Well, well. Hello, dog face. Come to give us your sneakers?

McGRUFF: Uh, oh, Trouble again, Scruff. What are you gonna do now
SCRUFF: I–I–dunno.

McGRUFF: If you get my new comic activity book "More Adventures with Scruff"

you'll find out what you can do... about bullies...

drugs...

and guns.
SCRUFF: Am I the hero again?

McGRUFF: You'll see... and you'll see lots of games.
SCRUFF: Cool!

McGRUFF: For your free copy of my new comic activity book, write...

ScRUFF-McGRUFF
CHICAGO, IL
60652
ONE BOOK PER REQUEST

SCRUFF-MCGRUFF, Chicago, Illinois 60652.
SCRUFF-MCGRUFF, Chicago, Illinois 60652.

And you'll be helping take a bite out of crime.
SCRUFF: I want it! I want it!

Volunteer Advertising Agency: Saatchi & Saatchi Advertising
Campaign Director: Richard Bodge, ADT Security Systems, Inc.

Sponsors: National Crime Prevention Coalition
and the U.S. Department Of Justice

FIGURE 10.5   *(Courtesy of Sarah Humm, The Advertising Council)*

UNIROYAL

UNIROYAL
SNOW RADIALS
:30 Seconds T.V.
"Snows"

ORSON WELLES: "When man invented the wheel, he soon realized . . .

. . . that wheels have an enemy.

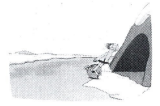

The enemy is winter.

So to cope with winter, man invented . . .

. . . the Uniroyal Steel Belted Radial Snow Tire.

On ice and snow, Uniroyal M&S Plus Steel Radials . . .

. . . have proven they can turn the trick . . .

. . . in man's annual contest with winter.

Uniroyal.

From the first man . . .

. . . the last word . . .

. . . in Steel Belted Radial Snow Tires!

FIGURE 10.6   *(Courtesy of Barry Base, Base Brown Partners Ltd., Copyright Field Syndication Inc.)*

Cookie-Crisp®

RALSTON PURINA
Cookie-Crisp
Cereal

:30 TV
Commercial
"Cookie Crook: Intro"

SFX: (CROOK WHISTLING NONCHALANTLY.)
KIDS: Hey, Cookie Crook, whataya doing?

CROOK: Uh...scratching my back!

GIRL: He's trying to steal our Cookie-Crisp!

BOY: Where's the Cookie Cop!
SFX: (SIREN)

COP: Cookie Crook, you'll do anything

to get the real cookie taste of Cookie-Crisp Cereal.

CROOK: I know. I know.

It even looks like little chocolate chip cookies!

COP: But it stays (Tap! Tap!) crispy in milk!

COP: (VO) And it's part of this complete breakfast.

COP: Well, Cookie Crook, whataya have to say for yourself?
CROOK: I guess I'm not such a smart cookie, after all.

ANNCR: If you like cookies, you'll love Cookie-Crisp.

© Ralston Purina Company 1984

FIGURE 10.7   *(Reprinted with permission of Ralston Purina Company)*

budget but an animated scene or spokesthing is considered essential, don't hire some art school dropout to animate the whole sequence simply because the price is right. Better to hire a top-notch artist to execute a few, well-rendered, single pics between which you can intercut and that lend themselves to use in several different messages or contexts.

In the spot for Ocean Spray Cranberry Sauce (Figure 10.8), a simple but concept-encompassing piece of cartooning is used to attract attention and set up the "cut-away"

Hi. I'm a turkey,...gobble,...gobble...

...You don't believe I'm a turkey, right?...

...That's why I can't get cranberry sauce. The turkeys get it all...

How about a cranberry glazed pork roast?...

The recipe's now on the Ocean Spray can...

Melt the cranberry sauce, stir in orange juice and brown sugar...

...and your pork gets cranberry excitement!

...Or, serve Cranberry Sauce with pork chops...

...With chicken? Go ahead...

...Serve it as a glaze...or in slices...

...Just don't forget me.

...Check the recipes on the Ocean Spray can...and gobble, gobble.
(SUPER) CHECK THE RECIPES.

FIGURE 10.8   *(Courtesy of Irene Taffel, Kelly-Nason Inc.)*

to the actual demonstration. All of animation's advantages are accrued without the necessity for cartoon/real-life matting and without expensive end-to-end animation.

If you just *must* secure a completely animated treatment, recognize that a thirty-second film spot contains 720 frames (twenty-four frames per second). Full, Disney-quality cel animation would thus require the artist to produce 720 separate drawings. In practice, of course, this is rarely done. The eye will easily tolerate the same drawing in two consecutive frames—which cuts the number in half to 360. For really "limited" animation, one can reduce the number to as few as six drawings per frame (180 per thirty-second spot), but this few will be disturbingly obvious unless the actions and characters are extremely simple.

There are, of course, an increasing number of computer-video alternatives to paying an artist to draw hundreds of acetate cel overlays. Through use of a computer-driven 'paint box,' a given cel can be *electronically* replicated and changes made only to the parts of the picture that move. Each perfected frame is then digitally recorded as the process continues. In a related technique, design director Ron Pearl reveals, "You can transfer a film source digitally, using it as a background, then animate other objects on top, which interact with that background. Because of this evolution, rendering has been really simplified."[11]

Even the most sophisticated computers cannot replicate everything that is attainable via an artist's hand-painted cels. "Cel offers a softness and an artistic control that can only be obtained through a human touch," points out video production chief Tom Stefani. So today, "the video and film industries borrow from both worlds of animation to produce the desired effects in the most practical manner. . . . Even film directors are calling upon the computer to generate 3-D backdrops for primarily cel-animation productions."[12]

Rotoscoping is another process that combines cel and computer techniques and offers video as well as film applications. With rotoscoping, either frames of live-action film are projected onto a table and traced by hand to make cels, or a digital recorder feeds one frame at a time into the computer, allowing the artist's electronic tracings to customize it before recording the image and moving on to the next. In both media, rotoscoping permits the designer to (1) position animated characters in relation to live actors or (2) actually replace the frame space occupied by a 'real' person with an animated character to match. The effect can be dazzling, but only if it is carried through every one of film's twenty-four or video's thirty frames per second. This used to be extremely laborious. Back in 1992, Digital F/X chairman Steve Mayer pointed out that, "In a typical application, such as one commercial where the bags under an actress's eyes had to be painted out, the artist had to grab, paint and record 1,800 pictures."[13] Fortunately, thanks to digital technology, this is no longer a monumental task. "As an animation technique, rotoscoping is flourishing, writes trade journalist Jim Hanas, "now that digital film and computer graphics have made it more efficient and accessible than ever."[14]

Three additional animation-style procedures that have come to the fore are *morphing, motion capture,* and *claymation. Morphing* is the sophisticated computer-generated effect through which one object becomes another in a seamless and liquid-looking transformation. You have seen morphing, new media expert Michael Schrage points out, "in Schick Tracer commercials, in which ethnically diverse faces morph in and out while the razor remains the same." Such image progressions were impossible before a new generation of computers entered the production process. "Before the arrival of high-powered computer graphics processors and the digital algorithms to run them, you simply could not transform images of moving automobiles into leaping tigers," Schrage adds. "The analog technologies of composites and mattes were completely inadequate for the task. Digital media, by contrast, are ideally suited for the sort of intense mathematical manipulations required to generate such effects."[15] The beginning and climax of one of the pioneer morphing sequences is shown in the three opening frames of the Figure 10.9 LeSabre commercial. Here, the morph makes it appear that the new model is emerging from beneath the tarp-like skin of the old.

In *motion capture* animation the intent is not transformation but the investing of inanimate objects with realistic human movement. The "mo-cap" process begins with sensors that are attached to a human body to chart the subtleties of its motion. A computer then interprets this information and applies it to the movements of the object the designers wish to manipulate. Ogilvy & Mather used this technique early on to create its dancing Shell gas pumps, on which seven animators worked for three months to create a trio of spots.[16] By utilizing motion capture, the pumps don't seem to gyrate uniformly like typical cartoon characters but instead, danced with the awkward imperfections of partying human beings.

Claymation is even more labor-intensive. In it, actual clay figures are physically positioned and a single frame is shot. The figures are reset and another frame is exposed. Figure repositioning is modeled after "reference footage" on which live humans perform the movements that the clay dolls are being manipulated to replicate. As epitomized by the characters in the Figure 10.10 PSA, "claymation resembles live action more than it resembles any form of animation," says claymation expert David Altschul. "We're shooting and lighting in three dimensions, we're blocking and editing sequences exactly as you would a live action piece of filmmaking."[17] Because of the painstaking nature of the process, it can take from ten to fourteen hours to complete a two-second sequence according to producer Moyra Rodger. "If the project calls for characters to lip sync to a song or dialogue track," she continues, "the animators create bar sheets. Each frame of sound is broken down and recorded. For example, it may take 25 frames [25 clay doll repositionings] to say 'hello.'"[18] Consequently, even with the assist of improved digital technology, claymation, --- like motion capture and morphing --- are not viable options when you are creating for low-budget accounts.

In considering any form of animation, the copywriter should ascertain whether it is really needed for the project at hand. Ultimately, there are six capabilities that

AVO: Once again, Buick is raising the banner for quality in America.

Introducing the 1992 LeSabre.

With a higher level of power . . .

FIGURE 10.9   *(Courtesy of Marie Ialapi, McCann Erickson)*

OBESITY--WATCH OUT, ARNOLD Television Public Service Announcement :60 & :30

MUSIC...

DOCTOR: Listen to yourself, Arnold. You're totally out of breath because you're much too heavy. I'll give it to you straight.

DOCTOR V.O.: At this rate, you could be eating yourself into an early grave. But it's not too late to do something about it.

DOCTOR: Now first we give you a check up and work out a program of diet and exercise.

DOCTOR V.O.: And remember, Arnold, eat right and exercise. A healthy life is up to you.

FIGURE 10.10   *(Courtesy of Holly Holmes, Will Rogers Institute)*

justify animation's use. Stephen Wershing and Tanya Weinberger of Telesis Productions isolate four of these:

1. Such graphics can convey complex ideas in concise fashion.
2. You can portray processes not normally observable.
3. Dull subjects become initially more attractive.
4. A cartoon character, particularly a humorous one, can serve as a less intimidating spokesperson when addressing unpleasant subjects or possibilities.[19] (See Figure 10.10.)

As a further illustration of point #4, director/animator J. J. Sedelmaier recalls, "We did an animated ad for the Episcopal Church that showed a kid walking out into the middle of traffic—that would be disturbing if you saw it in live action. Because animation is fantasy, almost anything is accepted."[20] "In Shakespeare's comedies, the person that says the harsh truth is the jester," adds Cartoon Network's creative director Michael Ouweleen. "I think animation can be like the jester. Somehow there's a layer of removed-ness; you can come off softer, more playful."[21]

Computer consultants Bob Bennett and John Javetski provide two further rationales for animation's deployment:

5. Given the attention span of the video game generation, animation is more memorable than reality.
6. Animation is an ideal way to illustrate processes that flow over time and space, such as how to build a perfect hamburger.[22]

If none of these reasons demonstrably apply to your concept, it may be that animation, of whatever variety, is not right for the assignment at hand—even if you *can* afford it.

When some form of animation *is* to be pursued, agreement on an initial storyboard is essential so that art director, copywriter, graphic artists/designers, and client all understand the message's destination and what it will cost to get there. Then, as production begins, the first thing to reach final form must NOT be the visuals, but rather the talent's voicing of the copy and laying down of any music track that may be called for. From a synchronization standpoint, it is much easier for the cel or computer artist to fit the action to prerecorded dialogue and music than for performer and composer to fit their contributions to finished animation. Once voice track and music bed have been captured, it is a comparatively straightforward job for the animator to refine the finalized 'cartoon' movements that will match verbal and musical accents.

Above all, remember that animation is never a substitute for a central concept. "A lot of unimaginative people try to mask their lack of skill with lots of effects," argues producer Randy Field. "You see everything spinning and twirling ad nauseam. It can become visual cotton candy. You wind up saying, 'What was that?' I don't know, but it cost them $100,000."[23]

BASIC VIDEO PRODUCTION METHODS

Besides animation (which is a contributing agent to some of these more fundamental techniques) there are four basic processes from which the video commercial, PSA, or piece of continuity is begotten.

Live

This is the quickest, cheapest, and also the most risky technique for producing anything for television. The annals of video are filled with sagas of refrigerator doors that refused to open, frying pans that wouldn't scour clean, and puppies who not only refused to eat the sponsor's dog food but also directed a defecative comment at the dish that contained it. Given these dangers, and the ease and availability of digital recording, the live spot was thought close to extinction. Recently, however, some late night talk shows have brought the "live" spot back to create a greater sense of spontaneity and combat commercial-skipping TiVos. Live spots "feel urgent and fresh, not like another canned thing," says Spike TV marketing executive Niels Schuurmans.[24] Particularly when delivered by a popular talk show host, "to have someone who is a great talent like that make the ad a part of the content will help get our messaging across," adds Havas advertising executive David Barrington, "and help break through the clutter."[25]

These same advantages may accrue at local outlet talk shows. If kept simple, the live message does provide the most rapid turnaround time for copy changes and the greatest adaptability to specific events and conditions. Like program promos and other forms of similar continuity, uncomplicated commercials can viably exploit live copy—especially when delivered on camera by a personality who is already well-established on the individual show or outlet.

Electronic Recording

Following its industry debut in the late 1950s, videotape gradually replaced much of television's live fare and came to challenge film as the most-used medium for programs, commercials, and continuity. Tape provided live picture quality, but with a safety net—you could reshoot/re-edit the demonstration until it came out right. Though pre-recorded, the taped production's visual quality made it seem to the viewer as immediate as if it were being performed live. Now, digital recorders and hard drives have largely replaced tape by providing even better pictorial resolution and ease of storage and retrieval.

If not included as a service by the outlet on which you are placing commercials, video studio time or remote shooting can be expensive. Still, if your spokesperson does not talk on camera, even this cost can be mitigated by preproducing the audio track at a much cheaper cost-per-hour sound studio. Then you can use your rented video facilities for only as long as you need to "lay down" a good visual with which the previously finished audio can easily be meshed. If motion is not required, expenses can be further reduced by shooting high-resolution digital stills and then marrying these to voice-overs and music beds.

Film Voice-Over

This same basic technique can be applied to film as well. If no one talks on camera, still or motion picture film can be quickly shot anywhere, stock footage can be rented as needed, and a nicely fashioned audio added and interlocked at the editing/assembly stage. Many producers still prefer the softer "look, tone, and mood" of film. So it will remain a viable if not a preferred medium for many PSA and commercial assignments into the foreseeable future. Because stations no longer have a control room film chain, the spot is converted to digital form prior to distribution.

Film Lip-Sync

Especially if outdoor location shooting is involved, this can be the most time-consuming and therefore expensive approach to visual message creation. Because the characters in the presentation talk on camera, great care must be taken to record their dialogue properly and synchronize it with the visual being captured at the same time. This process can become especially complex as the scene is consecutively reshot from several angles—each with its own sound bed—that must later be edited into a matching whole without visual or audio "glitches." Sometimes, later sound stage dubbing, in which the characters repeat their lines to match the previously filmed lip movements, must be scheduled in order to achieve acceptable audio quality and synchronization. Indoor shooting normally allows for greater control of the sound environment than when filming outdoors. Therefore subsequent sound stage work can usually be avoided in the case of interior scenes, at least for the dialogue. Other sound sources like music may also have to be layered in, however, and unlike electronic production, this can seldom be done when the film cameras are rolling.

Choosing the Right Methodology

It is possible, of course, to mix and match elements from several productional methods in order to achieve your objectives within the available budget. Just keep in mind that whatever techniques are employed, they should not call attention to themselves, but rather should help to articulate the central point of your spot, PSA, or continuity segment. "Too many people are in the business because it is their mini Hollywood or their chance to work with a certain director," Campbell-Ewald creative director Brent Bouchez observes, "and they forget that this is about selling stuff."[26]

In pursuit of this selling goal, don't try to adapt a production method that the budget really can't afford by cutting time and picture-value corners. The result will look shoddy and so, by implication, will whatever it is that your message is striving to promote. It is much better to use a less expensive productional methodology that can be optimally exploited.

VIDEO PRODUCTIONAL TERMINOLOGY

As in the case of audio writers, wordsmiths working in video must know and use the proper lingo if words and sketches are to be translated into desired moving and talking images. Directions for audio in the visual media are fundamentally the same as for radio so need not be reintroduced here. They are found in their entirety in Chapter 7. What does require cataloging at this point is the *visual* terminology writers must use in communicating their concepts to production crews. One cautionary note: Some copywriters, once they acquire a working knowledge of video jargon, tend to *overuse* it, to overspecify every visual detail so that the production personnel are entirely locked into what might not be the best visual treatment of the sequence in question. Give as many directions as needed to convey the main intent of your shot progressions, but don't become so detailed that the hands of your video or film production experts are totally tied. Allow them some leeway to take advantage of opportunities that might present themselves on set or on location.

In this Montana Power Company message, the copywriter has clearly described overall effect and visual progression required while leaving subsidiary details to the best professional judgment of the director and other people responsible for creating the footage.

Video	Audio
WIDE ESTABLISHING SHOT OF WOMAN STANDING LOOKING OUT WINDOW, HER BACK TO CAMERA	WOMAN: (Despondently) Empty promises! That's all I get! You promised to keep me warm. You don't. You made me think I'd live in comfort. I don't.
WOMAN TURNS SLOWLY AWAY FROM WINDOW	Instead, I spend all my time cleaning up after you. You just take, take, take.
SHE BEGINS TO SMILE	Well, enough is enough! (Proudly) Today, I bought a natural gas furnace.
SHOT WIDENS TO REVEAL HER OLD WOODSTOVE	That's right! (Triumphantly) You're through!
SUPERS: Montana Power Company 4.9% APR financing. You may qualify. Call for details.	VO: Get more than you expect with clean, comfortable natural gas heat. It's the smart choice. SFX: WOODSTOVE COUGHS, SIGHS

(Courtesy of Pam Lemelin, Wendt Advertising)

This Montana Power spot also exemplifies what distinguished cinematographer William Fraker calls "the power of *imperfect imagery*."[27] Until shot #4, the copywriter has deliberately restrained the audience from seeing who/what the soundtrack makes them want to see, thereby intensifying their attention.

We now turn to the specific pieces of visual terminology with which the video copywriter should be familiar. These designations can most easily be divided into four categories: (1) camera movements, (2) shot lengths and angles, (3) control room transitions and devices, and (4) other writer-used technical terms. As in our audio terminology discussion, it is not the intent here to cover the entire vocabulary of video and film production. Instead, attention is limited to words the copywriter is most likely to need in preparing the actual script.

Camera Movements

This category consists of directions that call for maneuvering of the camera and its base or some manipulation of the camera "head" alone—while the base on which it is mounted remains stationary.

DOLLY IN/DOLLY OUT   When this movement is specified, the entire camera is pushed toward or away from the subject of the shot, who or which usually stays immobile.

TRUCK LEFT/TRUCK RIGHT   This term specifies a lateral movement of the entire camera parallel to the scene being shot. Alternatively, trucking left or trucking right may be referred to as *tracking.*

CRANE/ARC/BOOM   These designations, which have become more or less interchangeable, require that the camera be mounted on a long manual, hydraulic, or electric arm that allows for shots that demand smooth, flowing changes in height and/or semicircular sweeps toward and away from the scene. A much more restricted derivation of this type of movement is the *ped up/ped down,* where the camera is raised or lowered on its base without changing its angular relationship to or distance from the scene.

PAN LEFT/PAN RIGHT   This is a more limited version of the truck since only the camera head turns to follow the action as that action modulates to one side of the set or the other. Because the camera's base does not move, the panning procedure also more graphically changes the shot's angle on the scene than does the *truck,* which keeps a constant parallel relationship with the locale and its elements. In the case of character movement, for example, a trucking shot would give the feeling of *walking with* an actor, whereas the *pan* would have the effect of following his approach to or departure from the viewer's psychological location at scene center.

TILT UP/TILT DOWN   If you stand in place and change the subject of your visual attention by the simple raising or lowering of your head, you will achieve the same effect created by the *tilt* as the camera head tips up or down on its base. The tilt allows us to change the altitude of the viewer's gaze without changing the perceived distances from the perimeter of the scene.

Shot Lengths and Angles

These designations refer to how close or how far the subject of the shot will seem to be in terms of the viewer's perspective as well as to the angular relationship between viewer and subject. The effects of shot lengths and angles are achieved by manipulation of available lens components and/or by the actual movement of the camera in any of the ways just discussed. The basic shot length continuum extends from the full shot (FS) to the extreme close-up (ECU). (See Figure 10.11.)

FULL SHOT (FS) OR COVER SHOT (CS)   The entire scene is encompassed by this shot, which may thus include the whole set or even an outdoor epic's entire horizon. Because it often occurs at the opening of the message in order to acquaint the viewer with the total visual environment, the full shot/cover shot is also known as an *establishing shot.*

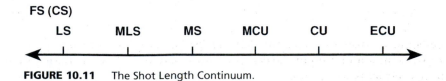

FIGURE 10.11   The Shot Length Continuum.

LONG SHOT (LS) OR WIDE SHOT (CS)   Long shots may or may not reveal the entire scene; if they do, they can be interchangeably referred to as *full shots*. In any event, long shots do encompass a comparatively wide angle of vision and would, in the case of the talent, show a character from head to toe. The term *wide shot* is also used to denote this same orientation.

MEDIUM SHOT (MS)   This very broad category includes all visual fields too close or "narrow" to be called long shots and, on the other hand, perspectives too wide to be referred to as close-ups. Though medium shots can thus vary widely depending on the scope of the scene in question, we generally think of them as framing only the upper two-thirds of a character and with minimal additional revelation of the set behind that character. When two or three characters are featured, a *medium two-shot (M2S)* or *medium three-shot (M3S)* can be requested. (Any more than three persons would require so wide an angle as to be called a long shot.) For more definitive designation, the terms *medium long shot (MLS)* and *medium close-up (MCU)* refer to each end of the medium-shot spectrum.

CLOSE-UP (CU)   In the close-up, the specific character or prop fills most of the viewing screen. For example, only the head and shoulders of a person would be seen, and thus the CU may also be referred to as a *tight shot*. The *extreme close-up (ECU or XCU)* is the ultimate extension of this principle so that a pianist's hands or a single leaf on a tree can fill most of the picture area and engage the viewer's total focus.

For pictorial examples of the basic shot lengths, examine the Figure 10.12 photoboard. Here, the teacher is framed with a long shot in panel 1, medium shots in panels 3 and 9, close-ups in panels 5, 7, and 11, and an extreme close-up (part of her hand and the product) in panel 8.

ZOOM IN/ZOOM OUT   Though it is technically a lens function to be treated under this section, the zoom in or out is functionally a technological replacement for the physical and comparatively awkward *dollying* of the entire camera. Through either manual or electronic changes in the lens's optics, a good zoom lens can smoothly bring viewer orientation from a full shot to an ECU and, if desired, back again without moving the camera base at all. In the case of outdoor productions, a zoom could traverse hundreds of feet—a much greater distance than the camera itself would be capable of moving within the spot's time confines.

In our discussion of shot lengths, we have tended to use the word *angle* to refer to the width of the resulting picture. This is because the closer we focus on a single object, the narrower our peripheral vision becomes. Thus, as already implied, long shots are also *wide* shots and close-ups are also *tight*. Writers of video commercial and continuity copy tend to use either or both of these descriptive sets, depending on what seems to depict most clearly the pictorial effect they have in mind.

Camera angles can also be designated another way in order to describe more graphically the spatial and psychological relationship between shot subject and viewer. A *point-of-view (POV)* shot, for example, looks at the scene through the eyes of a character or implement within it. In Figure 10.13, the POV might be referred to as that of the gridiron's turf or (if you wanted to inject tragedy), POV DOWNED QUARTERBACK.

TEACHER: Sometimes I wonder if I'm getting through to them.

Brian, am I getting through to you?

The only things that matter to them are Godzilla, basketball and chocolate.

BOYS: ARRRR!!

TEACHER: Not that I have anything against Godzilla or basketball.

(BOY SHOOTS BANANA PEEL INTO TRASHCAN)
BOY: Yes!

TEACHER: Or chocolate. I drink Yoo-Hoo.

It's a delicious chocolate snack

with vitamins and minerals.

BOY: Ready? Go.

TEACHER: It's the one thing we have in common. The only thing.

VO: Yoo-Hoo. The cool way to do chocolate.

FIGURE 10.12   *(Courtesy of Rodney Underwood, Geer Dubois, Inc.)*

A similar effect is obtained with the writer calls for a SUBJECTIVE CAMERA, in which the on-camera (OC) talent addresses the lens as though it were a participating character. The PSA in Figure 10.14 uses this technique (SUBJECTIVE CAMERA: BABY IN CRIB) to demonstrate the infant's helplessness in protecting itself from secondhand smoke.

FIGURE 10.13 *(Courtesy of Carole McGill, Camp Associates Advertising Ltd.)*

MUSIC: BABY MUSIC

MOM: She has your eyes.

DAD: Oh, but she has your chin.

MOM: And she definitely has your smile.

SFX: BABY COUGHS UNCONTROLLABLY.

BOTH: (ADMIRINGLY): And she has your smoker's cough.

ANNCR: If you smoke, the kids around you smoke secondhand. Which can mean lifelong health problems like asthma, pneumonia, ear infections and others.

Call 1-800-537-5666 for information on how to quit.

FIGURE 10.14 *(Courtesy of Marcie Brogan, Brogan & Partners)*

Over-the-shoulder shots are another derivation in which one character is viewed by looking over the shoulder of the other. A *reverse angle* shot can then be used to give the viewer the scene from 180° away—looking "over the shoulder" of that second character back at the first. Either separately or in conjunction with any of these other techniques, *high angle* and *low angle* shots can draw special relationships or promote unique vantage points in order to illustrate more powerfully the message's main tenet. Notice how a variety of carefully linked shot lengths and angles helps convey the central concept and psychological involvement exploited for Paul Masson Champagne in Figure 10.15 and featuring legendary British actor Sir John Gielgud. In this classic photoboard, numbered frame 7 is an OS PLAYER (over-the-shoulder shot, with the shoulder being that of the football player). The following numbered frame 8 is then a reverse angle to complete the exchange. (Technically, frame 8 is a ¾ REV ANGLE since we see the player from Gielgud's *side* rather than from directly behind his head. This is done here to enhance viewer participation by using the audience's rather than the product spokesman's frame of reference.) Notice too how a high angle shot such as frame 7's seems to diminish the subject's (Gielgud's) size in relationship to the athlete and how frame 8's low angle shot makes that athlete seem even more giantlike.

As a general rule, tighter (closer) shots tend to be more common in video scripting than do a preponderance of wider (longer) framings. Big-screen sets notwithstanding, the in-home TV or computer screen viewing experience is still much more intimate than is taking in a film at the movie house. Wide vistas are not only more indirect as rapid focusers of meaning, but they also fail to blend in with the coziness of the living room, family room, study, or bedroom. This is not to say that we should use nothing but close-ups in our broadcast or broadband spots, for the result would be visual monotony. It does mean, however, that tighter shots are generally of greater perceptual utility in quickly reaching people "where they live." A common finding in several shot-length studies reviewed by researchers Maria Grabe, Shuhua Zhou, and Brooke Barnett was that "the close-up shot commands attention and establishes emotional closeness between television content and viewers, whereas the long shot encourages a certain level of distance and detachment between content and viewers."[28] Messages created for mobile phone delivery, of course, require a special type of "closeness" because of the proximity of the device to the viewer and the small screen size, which makes longer shots indecipherable.

Control Room Transitions and Devices

In video production, switchers and editing keyboards control the routing and assemblage of shots. This can be done either live (in real time) or by manipulating a number of prerecorded sources. The lower the budget for the project, the more we strive for instant editing via a video switcher instead of extensive post-production work in editing bays. Either way, video production uses a basic grammar of shot transitions. This grammar was borrowed from film—a medium that today is also edited electronically after transfer of its production rushes to a digital medium.

FADE IN/FADE OUT   Virtually all video messages "fade in" from "black" at the beginning and fade out or "fade to black" at their conclusion. Due to the abbreviated nature of commercials and continuity, these fades are very rapid and not normally specified in the script. For longer messages such as dramatic programs, varying the

COMM'L NO.: DSPM 2053

LENGTH: 30 SECONDS

(PLAYERS CHEER)

(PLAYERS CHEER)

JOHN GIELGUD: Gentlemen,

this is Paul Masson Champagne.
Supremely elegant

because it's made with the greatest
care.

And each bottle is vintage dated.

Can you read? **7.**

PLAYER: Vintage 1980. **8.**

JOHN GIELGUD: Remarkable.

Paul Masson Champagne.
(PLAYERS CHEER)

The civilized way to celebrate

Paul Masson will sell no wine before its
time.

FIGURE 10.15   *(Courtesy of Melissa Wohltman, DDB Advertising)*

length of a fade can help to raise or lower more definitively video's version of the theatrical curtain.

CUT   This is the quickest and simplest method for changing from one shot to another. Today's visually literate audiences are so accustomed to this instantaneous transition that it often does not even impinge on their consciousness. Properly punctuated cuts can do a great deal to help the pacing of even very brief visual messages, and *intercutting* (rapid switching back and forth between two or more shots) has proven of significant utility when the creative concept requires an intense, pulsating delivery. *Cutaways* are a further variation on the term; they are especially prominent in certain types of commercials when we briefly replace the main scene with some laboratory or animated demonstration of a specific property the product possesses.

Because cuts are by far the most commonly used transition, a cut, or "take," is assumed whenever any other scene or angle shift device is not specified in the script or at the top of the storyboard's audio block.

DISSOLVE   In this transition, one picture source seems gradually to "bleed through" and then finally replace another. A dissolve (abbreviated as DIZ) may be slow or fast and, in either case, provides a more fluid and gentle transition than the comparative punchiness of the cut. Visualize how the dissolves in the following KitchenAid spot facilitate the smooth unveiling of this extended pictorial and benefit-focusing analogy:

Video	Audio
OPEN ON WS DESERT MOUNTAINS	MUSIC: WESTERN PASTORAL UNDER THROUGHOUT
DIZ PAN-IN ON OVEN	VO: Timeless forms.
DIZ MOUNTAINS AND RIVER	Golden warmth.
REVOLVING SUPER: KitchenAid	
DIZ BREAD BAKING IN OVEN	
DIZ OVERHEAD PAN OF ROCK WALL	Strength that
DIZ OVEN DOOR CLOSING	endures.
DIZ DESERT FLOWERS OPENING	A mystery that
DIZ SOUFFLE RISING IN OVEN	unfolds.
DIZ SUN IN SKY	The fire
DIZ CU OF STOVETOP	of creation.
DIZ VEGETABLE STIR FRYING	All

Continued

Video	Audio
DIZ DESERT LANDSCAPE	someplace a little
REVOLVING SUPER: KitchenAid	closer to home.
DIZ WOMAN AND FRIENDS IN KITCHEN	KitchenAid free-standing ranges, built- in ovens, and cooktops. Because
DIZ DESERT LANDSCAPE	we took a cooking lesson from Mother Nature.
SUPER: KitchenAid. For the way it's made.	KitchenAid. For the way it's made.

(Courtesy of Susan McFeatters, NW Ayer Inc.)

When the progress of the dissolve is stopped so that both picture sources remain discernible to the viewer, the result is a *superimposition,* or SUPER for short. *Matched dissolves* are hybrids in which we obtain a cumulative effect by dissolving from one similar or like thing to another. The clock-face matched dissolves that indicate the passage of time or the series of dissolves that make the pile of dirty dishes get smaller and the stack of clean ones get taller are both common (even trite) applications of this technique.

Contemporary solid-state electronics also makes possible a virtually infinite number of customized transitions. Many of these effects are made possible by a *chroma-key*—the generic name for an apparatus that allows the removal of a given color (usually green) from the original scene so a visual element from another source can be inserted in its place. Special effects terms, such as "split screen," "sunburst dissolve," and "checkerboard transition," are quite descriptive of the function each provides.

A standard cluster of special effects devices are known as *wipes.* Instead of one picture "bleeding through" the other, as in the dissolve/superimposition, a *wipe* allows one picture visually to push the other off the screen. Common direction-denoting varieties are *vertical, horizontal, diagonal, corner,* and *iris* (circular) wipes. A *split-screen* is simply the midpoint of a vertical, horizontal, or diagonal wipe. *Squeeze-zoom,* meanwhile, is a manufacturer-derived term referring to the namesake device's ability to compress, expand, and manipulate individual elements within a frame.

Squeeze-zoom and other proliferating electronic special effects phenomena use auxiliary terminology that is much more obscure because many of these state-of-the-art effects owe their existence to a computer. This marriage of television switching apparatus and computer hardware/software systems begets an almost bewildering array of tools from which to choose and an equally bewildering jargon of its own. *Flashes* insert about five frames of video white between two shots to create a camera flash effect. *Slide and peel* is a specialized wipe that approximates the turning of a book page, and *rotations* and *bounces* cause images to flip or tumble.[29] The copywriter, however, is wise to stick to a commonly understood phrase when attempting to specify some rarefied piece of special effects wizardry. The production and graphics people can put in their own parlance later, but they will at least start out with an accurate conception of the result you want.

One overriding admonition must be heeded about special effects. Keep in mind that you are not selling, promoting, or identifying the transition or effect itself. Any technique that calls attention to itself at the expense of your subject is to be studiously avoided. If you should find yourself concentrating on what jazzy digital explosion you can shoehorn into your next spot or promo, it's time to stop and reexamine your priorities. "Special *defect* is my term," says Grey Advertising's executive vice-president Richard Kiernan, "for a totally inappropriate use of special effects. Things like using a laser beam to create an apple pie when the strategy calls for old-fashioned-like-Grandma-used-to-bake. That kind of special effect not only doesn't reinforce the strategy; it undermines it. Or the bank that uses computer graphics in the attempt to dramatize warm, friendly, personalized service. . . . The magic, I maintain, is in how organic the solution is to the selling proposition. If you lose sight of the objective, then special effects can become special defects."[30]

Any truly appropriate visual device will evolve naturally out of whatever you are trying to say in your message. The message's selling concept, not the effect, must come first. Leave the extraneous kaleidoscopes to the entertainment programs, which have thirty or sixty *minutes* to play with and can afford to be occasionally irrelevant.

"Clients give us money to make sure that customers give them money," declares agency CEO Tim O'Leary. "They are not artistic patrons sent to subsidize our film-making fantasies, and they don't have limitless resources. If we squander their advertising dollars on 'overproduction,' they will go out of business."[31] Or, as creative director Pat Burnham more bluntly reminds commercial creators:

1. The production budget can't buy you an idea.
2. The director can't give you an idea.
3. You can't polish a turd.[32]

Other Writer-Used Technical Terms

Here are a variety of additional visual production designations often used on a script or storyboard to communicate the writer's intent to those people who will pick up the project from there:

A/B ROLL: *editing procedure in which scenes/sounds on two decks (recorder A and recorder B) are intermixed onto a third machine (recorder C).*

ABSTRACT SET: *a plain and neutral background that uses only a few scattered implements to suggest the message environment. A single gas pump might represent a complete service station or a few framing tree branches simulate an entire forest. Though the abstract set is certainly not realistic, there is also less visual clutter in which the viewer might lose the product or central point of your message.*

ASPECT RATIO: *the constant three units high by four units wide that used to be the standard dimensions of the television screen and are still standard for the computer monitor. Meanwhile, emerging High Definition Television (HDTV) uses a ratio of nine units high by sixteen units wide. Today's copywriters and art directors have to keep both protocols in mind when planning their messages, since aspect ratio will circumscribe every visual idea funneled through the screen or monitor.*

BACKGROUND PROJECTION OR REAR PROJECTION (RP): *throwing a still frame or moving image from behind a translucent screen so performers can use the result as scenery and stand in front of it without blocking the projector's illumination beam.*

BACKGROUND WASH: *a visual effect in which the matte color gradually changes in darkness/lightness or from one color to another.*

BACKLIGHT: *illumination from behind a subject in order to distinguish it more clearly from the background area.*

BEAUTY SHOT: *still picture of the product set in an environment that heightens its appeal, prestige, or appearance.*

BG: *commonly used abbreviation for the background of a scene.*

BLACK: *the condition of a video screen when it is processing no video information.*

BORDER: *electronically produced edges that provide visual separation between pictorial elements, such as split screens or wipes.*

B-ROLL: *reel of video segments to be interspersed within the spot bed.*

BUMPER: *a graphic, picture, or brief animation used before or after a program or commercial segment.*

BUST SHOT OR CHEST SHOT: *a more specific designation for the Medium Close-Up (MCU) calling for a picture of a talent from the chest to just above the head.*

CAMEO: *lighting a foreground subject against a completely black background.*

CAPTION: *words/titles that are inserted onto other pictorial information.*

CHARACTER GENERATOR (CG): *computer keyboard apparatus that can electronically produce letters, symbols, lines and backgrounds on the screen. Also permits these elements to move horizontally (crawl) or vertically (roll). Sometimes referred to as Chyron, after one of the original manufacturers of the device—although Chyron-type machines now can manipulate all sorts of graphic images.*

CROSSFADE: *a pictorial transition in which the first scene dissolves to black and the next scene then dissolves from black.*

CUCALORUS: *metal design inserted in front of a spotlight's beam to produce a shadow pattern against the set backdrop. Also known as a cookie.*

CYC (CYCLORAMA): *a U-shaped, stretched curtain that provides a neutral background for a set.*

DEFOCUS: *a purposeful blurring of the picture.*

DEPTH OF FIELD: *that swath of territory in front of the camera lens in which all objects and subjects are in focus.*

DIGITAL VIDEO EFFECTS (DVE): *blanket term encompassing all the specialized computer techniques that allow images to expand, contract, spin, stretch, contort, or be otherwise manipulated.*

DOWNSTAGE: *the area nearest the camera lens; seemingly closest to the viewing audience.*

DROP: *a piece of scenic background, normally painted or electronically rendered on canvas.*

EDGE WIPE: *wipe in which picture fringes are manipulated to give the central subject more prominence.*

FG: *commonly used abbreviation for the foreground of a scene.*

FISHEYE LENS: *lens that delivers an extremely wide angle picture to provide a field of view of up to 180°.*

FOLLOW SHOT: *use of a single, stationary camera to follow the action of a moving subject or object.*

FOLLOW SPOT: *high-intensity, narrow-beam light used to illuminate subjects in motion.*

FREEZE FRAME: *stopping the motion of a sequence so a single frame can be viewed as a still picture. Also called STOP ACTION and, particularly when it occurs at the end of a spot, may result in a BEAUTY SHOT (see above).*

HARD LIGHT: *a strong directional beam from a spotlight that produces sharply defined shadows.*

HEADROOM: *area between the top of a subject's head and the upper edge of the viewing screen.*

HIGH KEY: *relatively even illumination with few discernible shadows.*

IN MORTISE: *literally, "in a box"; placing the subject within a graphically rendered frame--often to set it off from "supered" titles that appear on the border this frame creates.*

JUMP CUT: *a disturbing or unnaturally abrupt transition between two pictures.*

KEYING: *use of a chroma-key to electronically insert elements into a scene.*

LIMBO: *a perfectly neutral and empty background.*

LOWER THIRD: *supered graphic appearing in the bottom portion of the frame to identify the subject featured above it or present additional information.*

MATTE SHOT: *a portion of the image is blanked out and replaced by a separate picture or pictures of any of a variety of sizes; often accomplished via chroma-keying.*

MONOCHROME: *a picture consisting solely of shades of gray.*

MONTAGE: *composite picture generated from many separate images or a series of rapidly intercut visuals designed to create a certain association of ideas.*

OC: *abbreviation for "on-camera"; person speaking is shown in the shot. Generally used to cancel a previous "voice-over" direction (see VO).*

PIXILLATION: *frame-by-frame animation technique using live actors or actual props rather than cartoon characters. When projected up to standard speed, pixillation makes talent/subject movements comedically jerky and abrupt.*

QUAD SPLIT: *four separate images appearing in different corners of the frame simultaneously.*

REACTION SHOT: *any picture designed to reveal the emotional response of a character to some previously shown, or about to be revealed, event.*

SHARED ID: *in television, commercial material that is placed in the frame together with some graphic representation of the station identification.*

SOF: *abbreviation for "sound on film"; a motion picture sequence with its own synchronized sound track.*

SOFT FOCUS: *a slight defocusing of the picture resulting in a hazy effect indicative of dreams or semi-consciousness.*

SOT: *same as SOF when the medium is electronic rather than film. Formerly stood for "Sound on Tape," and the designation survives even though tape has largely been replaced by digital vehicles.*

SPECIFIC ILLUMINATION: *lighting of highly localized and discrete areas.*

STOCK SHOT/STOCK FOOTAGE: *still or motion pictures of subjects that can be used in many different messages. An urban street scene, picture of a jet-liner taking off, or view of a charming old castle can all constitute stock footage.*

SWEETENING: *adding elements to a signal such as captions, pictorial inserts, and enhancing sound information.*

SWISHPAN: *an extremely rapid camera pan that is perceived on the screen as a blur.*

TEASE: *very brief promo for an upcoming program segment or the opening "grabber" in a long-form commercial.*

TIGHT CLOSE-UP (TCU): *more precise delineation of a close-up in which we deliver a forehead-to-chin view of the talent.*

UNDERCUT: *changing the background of a scene without modifying foreground subjects—usually accomplished via matte or chroma-keying.*

UPSTAGE: *the area farthest from the camera lens; seemingly the most distant from the viewing audience.*

VO: *abbreviation for "voice-over"; words spoken by someone not shown in the shot.*

VTR: *abbreviation for "videotape recorder" or for the recording it makes.*

X/S: *abbreviation sometimes used to designate an over-the-shoulder shot.*

THE AUDIO–VIDEO COALITION

All of these video techniques and terms must not be allowed to obscure the importance of audio in general—and copy in particular—to the successful pictorial communication. What Associated Press Broadcast Division President Jim Williams says about TV news stories is equally true of most visual spots: "Pictures are great; they help tell the story. The sound is great; it helps tell the story. But getting the words right—copy—is the critical component of the story."[33] Many novice copywriters find it difficult to grasp the fundamental principle that their words must enhance, not merely be an afterthought echo of, the picture. They fail to understand that effective copy neither distracts from nor duplicates what the picture is striving to present.

Some writers rebel at this concept. Either they don't believe audio is that important or they have never learned to write effective audio in the first place. That is why a solid grounding in radio copy creation is so valuable for the video writer. Given a large shooting budget and high-priced production personnel, a lot of visually adept copywriters can come up with a fairly interesting, even relevant piece of pictorial continuity or advertising. But let an assignment come along that for budgetary or conceptual reasons demands a relatively basic and unadorned picture, then many of these same visual artists will fall flat on their eyeballs because their audio is only good enough to stash behind the scenery. Associate creative director Martha Holmes maintains that "there isn't any reason to think that words are less interesting in commercials—as long as the words are not advertisingese, and don't have a list of client strategies in there. People's interest is not necessarily visual . . . what's important is a synergy between what's spoken and the film [or video] technique."[34]

Certainly, television and the Web are visual media. But they are also frantically competitive ones in which every possible advantage must be exploited to break through the clutter of the screen and into the listener's consciousness. If the audio in your message is only "no worse than anybody else's," you are throwing away an immense opportunity to stand out from the crowd. Think the soundtrack of a video communication really doesn't matter? Then imagine:

shots of various mouth-watering delicacies available at your local ice cream emporium—and a soundtrack consisting of a bunch of pig snorts.

or

action footage of a new pick-up truck bounding across rough terrain—with an audio that features a tinkling music-box rendition of 'Twinkle, Twinkle, Little Star.'

Just now, even with the imperfect conveyance of print, were you able to keep concentrating on the tempting ice cream after the audio barnyard was called up in your mind? Could you maintain your focus on the ruggedness of the pick-up truck once its delicate little aural counterpoint impinged on your consciousness? Obviously, most television sound tracks are not this incongruous. But the power of the audio portion of the video message to confuse as well as to complement must always be respected—because that power is present in every video assignment you face.

In the mid-'90s, students at the Massachusetts Institute of Technology conducted an experiment to see if the quality of a TV audio track impacted perceived quality of the picture. Participants sitting at monitors were instructed to indicate when picture quality began to degrade. The responses were surprisingly uniform. When the researchers degraded the audio signal, the subjects would say that the video was getting worse. In fact, the video signal was never altered.[35] This is yet another indication that inattention to what you are doing with your soundtrack can clearly hobble even the most brilliantly shot and edited footage. Conversely, if you treat your audio with respect, your message has a much better chance of standing out. Advertising critic Barbara Lippert points out that, "As quick-cut visuals start looking like so much video-game wallpaper, the power of sound—of music and human voice—will be more important in breaking through."[36]

The South African script that follows demonstrates how well-selected audio can complement and embellish the visual without making that visual a slave to it. This is very important because the basic point of a good pictorial message should be understandable from the visual alone. The audio then serves to amplify that point. An enticing visual naturally arouses audience attention toward the audio that augments it. It is then audio's task to help fulfill the expectations that the visual has set up. In this headache-reliever spot, the picture conveys a clear if conventional problem/ solution progression. But it is the audio that provides us with much of the sexy surprise and manipulative twist that the husband brings to product-in-use.

This commercial won the top prize at the prestigious Cannes international commercial festival and garnered the highest recall scores of any analgesic spot in South African history. "It worked because analgesic spots are so boring all over the world," says its creating agency's managing director, Reg Lascaris.[37] This treatment, conversely, capitalized on this boredom-prone product category by skillfully employing its soundtrack to give 'preventive medicine' a whole new meaning.

Video	Audio
NIGHT-TIME IN A BEDROOM. WE CAN JUST MAKE OUT SHAPES OF THE FURNITURE	SFX: NIGHT-TIME SOUNDS
BEDSIDE LAMP SWITCHED ON BY PAUL, WEARING STRIPED FLANNEL PAJAMAS	PAUL: Alison, wake up.
	ALI: Hmmmmmmmhhhh?
CU BEDSIDE TABLE. WE SEE A GLASS OF WATER AND THE ASPRO CLEAR PACK	PAUL: Darling, I'm making you some Aspro Clear.
CU ALI LOOKING CONFUSED	ALI: What?
PAUL DROPS TABLET INTO GLASS	PAUL: Aspro Clear. The effervescent painkiller.
ECU TABLET FIZZING AND DISSOLVING INTO CLEAR LIQUID	PAUL (VO): Because it's fizzy, it dissolves to a clear liquid.
CU ALI MORE CONFUSED	ALI: Aspro Clear?
ECU GLASS OF CLEAR LIQUID NEXT TO THE PACK	PAUL: Yes. It's absorbed faster to relieve aches, pains, fever, headaches.
CU ALI TOTALLY CONFUSED	ALI: But --- I don't have a headache.
CU PAUL WITH DEVILISH LEER	PAUL (OC): Excellent!!
MCU HORRIFIED ALI AS PAUL SWITCHES OFF LAMP	<u>MUSIC: TORRID ROMANTIC EFFECT FEATURE AND UNDER</u>
SCREEN GOES TO BLACK. SUPER: All you need is Aspro.	ANNCR (VO): All you need is Aspro.

(Courtesy of copywriter Stefania Ianigro, Hunt Lascaris TWBA)

To review, the visual alone should be capable of attracting viewer interest and conveying a basic understanding of what the message is about. In fact, a good test of a video spot is to view it, or imagine it, with the sound off. Does the fundamental point of the message—including brand ID—still come through? Does it make us *want* to turn up that audio so we learn more? *Do we learn more* once the audio is provided?

Because a visual message must *be* visual to grab attention, it is general practice to write your pictorial descriptions first. Let the sense of sight carry as much of the basic revelation task as possible and then enhance as needed with spoken words, SFX, and music. In creating visual impressions, your most extensive writing will not *be heard* by the audience, but instead will be *seen* by them through the produced result of your script's verbal video-side phraseology.

This necessity of determining pictures before words is as true in electronic copywriting as it is in electronic news. Both journalists and copywriters are inherently storytellers. "In doing a television story," declared CBS News Correspondent Charles Kuralt, "you must always know what picture it is you're writing to. That is, you never write a sentence without knowing exactly what the picture is going to be. I will say that again. My philosophy is that you must always know what picture accompanies the words you write. You cannot write for television without knowing what the picture is."[38]

Tonight, try turning off the sound on the video announcements and news stories to which you are exposed. How many of these messages convey the main point with the visual alone? And of these, how many tempt you to turn up the audio to get more information? Finally, did the audio actually deliver that information? Was that aural material relevant and meaningful? The results of this experiment should give you a general idea of the percentage of messages that really exploit the audio–video coalition to its full potential.

It is through this coalition that video communication becomes a cohesive rather than a fragmentary discourse. Scripts, storyboards, camera movements, shot lengths, shot transitions, and the other devices introduced in this chapter are all complementary or alternative means to the same end. Use them as needed to produce the most effective copy concepts possible. Don't let them use you lest you become a purveyor of *technology* instead of *ideas*.

No matter how state-of-the-art or costly the technique, it is irrelevant when not motivated by the strong, central selling concept that you, the copywriter, must sculpt. As creative director Jim Dale cautions, "It all keeps coming back to the idea. Being forced to have one. And having everything riding on the idea being great. When you have it, there's always a way to bring it off. When you don't have it, all the techniques and tricks and hot songs and New Wave and blah blah blah aren't enough. And the funny thing is, when you do have a strong idea, finding a way to pull it off isn't even as hard as you thought anyway. Because people *want* to work on a great idea. They can smell it on a storyboard or a script and they start pulling rabbits out of hats from the beginning."[39]

CASTING AND VOICEOVER CONSIDERATIONS

Whatever the environment for which you are preparing a video message, the people who deliver that message will significantly impact its appeal and palatability. Because video announcements that show people tend to be more interesting *to* people, casting is an important issue most of the time. Although the copywriter might not make the final casting decisions, the writer's specifications, often translated via the art director's sketches, form the blueprint from which the producers choose their talent. This selection process deserves as much of your input as possible because if the audience does not like the people who appear in your message, they will apply this distaste to the message itself. Take some time to write a vivid and compelling production note that clearly delineates the type of person you had in mind during script creation. Then, read over that description to make certain it describes the sort of individual who would most likely be found in the environment in which your vignette transpires. (Or, if you want comedic incongruity, specify just the opposite.) When multiple roles are required, particularly to suggest our message's universal relevance, well-chosen, differentiated casting can be effective in the same way the multivoice technique functions on radio.

A fundamental casting decision involves whether to use (1) real people, (2) pseudo-real people, or (3) celebrity people. Real people possess a charm all their own. If you have the time and budget to shoot and edit their random activities and unpolished commentaries, real people help keep the spotlight squarely on your message because viewers have no distracting prior association with them. The people-interest emotional pull is thus exerted without the people becoming the central point of our message. Instead, they are tools for the spot's goal attainment and can sometimes bring extemporaneous touches to our message that a professional actor would never have devised.

This same principle applies to the use of clients in your audio or video spots. "Client as talent" can be an especially appropriate strategy where a bond of trust needs to be created. This is especially true in categories where consumers have high levels of *dis*trust, such as auto dealers, jewelers, discount appliance stores, and medical procedure providers. Because they typically don't sound or look like they should be 'on the air,' clients can add an important sense of genuineness and candor to the pitch that lessens consumer misgivings. However, before you write a single line of copy for the client, take some time to listen to the rhythm and flow of their speech pattern as well as the phrases they like to use in describing their product or service. Then sculpt your copy accordingly. Mistrust will only be heightened if it sounds like the client is reading from a script or TelePrompTer. When you do place the client in the spot, ten things will happen, according to Roy Williams, president of Wizard of Ads Inc. While his observations relate to local radio advertising, they are just as applicable to any electronic media spot, whether local, regional, or national.

1. You'll be accused of pandering to the ego of the client.
2. The client won't want to read it the way you wrote it.
3. You'll have to keep the client from watering down your message.
4. You'll have to coach the client into sounding relaxed.
5. The Program Director [or someone at the agency] will beg, 'Let us record it with professional voices.'
6. It will be five times more work than it ought to be.
7. The client's competitors will accuse him or her of 'going negative.'
8. Those same competitors will complain to the station.
9. Several of the client's friends will tell them they heard [or saw] the ad. Some won't like it.
10. The client will tell you they never knew advertising could work like this.[40]

Alternatively, *psuedo-real people*, like the 'Mom' cast in Figure 10.16, are professional but anonymous talent. They should be able to convince the viewer that they're

VIDEO

Open on a woman and her family in front of the Shark Aquarium as the camera slowly pushes in.

Cut to an underwater shot as the Adventure Aquarium logo plunges into water and is then quickly devoured by a shark.

Tagline is revealed as the shark wipes across the screen.

AUDIO

SFX: Ominous strings

Mom: We, the Jaeger family, hereby accept the fact that when we enter the Adventure Aquarium,

we forfeit our position at the top of the food chain. We realize that at times we will be completely surrounded by large, toothy, meat-eating fish.

And we acknowledge this with the full understanding that we, in fact, are made almost entirely (pause) of meat.

VO: The all-new Adventure Aquarium on the Camden waterfront.

You're in their world now.

FIGURE 10.16 *(Courtesy of Caroline Debrot, Red Tettemer agency)*

'just folks' without expending the shooting/editing time required to make authentic real people palatable. These unknown actors or actresses need not be imported from New York or Los Angeles. They are available throughout the country and can deliver compelling performances at no more than scale rates. Youngsters, oldsters, and people at every age in between, these professionals can bring a polished credibility to your message without making it too glitzy, on the one hand, or too untutored on the other.

Celebrities are individuals already well known to viewers. Celebrity pitches work best where there is a natural tie-in between what is being discussed and the reason for the celebrity's fame. A NASCAR winner can talk about automobiles because we know his professional and physical survival depends on this car expertise. A famous scrambling quarterback can visually attest to the fit and flexibility of a pair of slacks by demonstrating his continued dexterity while wearing them. But a teenage rock idol lauding a detergent's power or an insurance company's dividend record savages credibility because that idol is in no position personally to authenticate either. "The mistake that some advertisers make," says Sprint's consumer services president Tom Weigman, "is borrowing the identity of a celebrity rather than building on one that is intrinsically related to the brand."[41] "Increasingly, adds public relations executive Cathy Yingling, "trying to get my client's products to bask in the glow of a celebrity's 'borrowed cool' feels, frankly, a little bit lazy. With a celebrity seal of approval, you don't have to take the time to craft a real story about a product or even ensure that it lives up to its promise. And there seems to be an 'any celebrity is a good celebrity' mentality, particularly when you see something like Louis Vuitton featuring Mikhail Gorbachev in an ad . . . He helped end communism in the old Soviet Union, but will he make somebody want to buy a luxury tote?"[42]

In their study of consumer perception, persuasion, and processing of celebrity advertising, Professors Abhilasha Mehta and Clive Davis found that "Celebrities trigger past connection in viewers' minds, so use celebrities that would evoke positive connections. Thoughts related to the celebrity dominate the processing. Thus it appears that if the celebrity in the ad is well-matched with the product and highly involved with the product in the ad, thoughts about the celebrity may evoke product-related thoughts, which may help promote favorable attitudes."[43] An example of affirmative and effective celebrity employment is found in the vintage Figure 10.15 spot for Paul Masson Champagne presented earlier. Here, Sir John Gielgud's status as an actor of elegance and culture helps confer these same qualities on a relatively low-cost brand of bubbly—even while placing that brand within a less than high-culture scene. This spot also follows advertising legend George Lois's advice that you've got to fashion a celebrity message in such a way that "they're enjoying themselves. There's no one way to do it. In most cases, it's witty, it's fun and the advertising always makes the man or woman look good. You look at them and you like them for it."[44]

Whether using real, pseudo or celebrity people, *voice-overs* present the option of casting a video message without worrying about the subject's physical appearance, mannerisms, or the prior associations these might conjure up in the mind of the viewer. Unless you want the voice to be recognized as someone specific, it can remain anonymous because audiences have long ago become accustomed to the unidentified aural being. Use of the voice-over even allows you to cast a role two ways. In the Figure 10.17 commercial, for example, our young tuba player never speaks on camera.

"TUBA"

CAMPAIGN: "HOME RUN FAMILY"
COMM'L. NO.: HZOG 7120

LENGTH: 30 SECONDS

VO: Mom teaches the violin . . .

. . . but the tuba is my instrument.

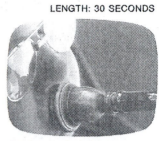

I think it sounds great . . .

. . . when I practice outside.

The bird's don't.

Playing the tuba takes lots of energy.

So does carrying it.

When I get home, I'm *hungry*.

So mom makes me great dinners with lots of crinkly Ore-Ida fries.

I told her that if every tuba player had Ore-Ida fries after practice . . .

. . . there'd be a lot more tuba players.

Mom said, let's just keep this to ourselves.

FIGURE 10.17 *(Courtesy of Ore-Ida and DDB Advertising)*

Thus you could cast one child based on his visual appeal and use another child to portray that same character's voice. In fact, because we never have to show the articulator of the copy, you might recruit a young female or even an adult talent for the voicer if the delivery better matched your conception of what this bespeckled munchkin should sound like.

On the other hand, in selecting voice-over talent that is supposed to sound adult, there has been a change in stylistic emphasis. "In the past, it has been the voice of God or authority," comments creative director Robbi Auftin. "Now it's toward authenticity. What you want is an honest quality."[45] "The use of naturalistic, pleasant-sounding, warm and energetic voices furthers an effort to make the corporation appear more human—and accessible—to its audiences," writes industry observer Stephen Barr.[46] "An effective narrator," adds producer Ken French, "conveys the *attitude* behind the information. He or she must be versatile enough to infuse the appropriate personality into your words, yet still be sincere and accurate."[47]

Barr's recognition of the "he/she" option is important. For decades, clients and copywriters assumed that male voices were more authoritative and effective. Then, in 1986, the Women's Voice-Over Committee of the Screen Actors Guild's New York branch commissioned a McCollum-Spielman study of the subject. The research results indicated that "those consumers tested found commercials equally persuasive when they had a female voice-over as when they had a male voice-over."[48]

When you have the opportunity to indicate the kind of narration you want for your spot or script, give careful consideration to both female and male options. Research studies have consistently found that women buy more than fifty percent of automobiles, more than fifty percent of household cleaning supplies, and more than fifty percent of items such as cereals, pet foods, soap, cameras, household cleaning supplies, and movie tickets. Therefore, shouldn't a female voice be at least as persuasive as a male in describing and validating the merits of these and related products?

One final casting caution. Whether on-camera or voice-over, male or female, don't employ a look- or sound-alike substitute for a celebrity whom you can't afford. If the imitation is inept, it will make your sponsor look cheap or shady. If the imitation is skillful, it invites an infringement suit from the celebrity being mimicked.

11 The Business of Television Commercials

In proportion to the number of words expended, television commercial writers probably get more money per word than do scribes for any other medium --- even when the vital but unspoken words on the script's left side are included in the computation. These high-priced words are also key to career advancement.

Just as important, from a psychological standpoint, video spot writers experience the fun of dealing with a communications vehicle that is becoming more flexible and more pervasive all the time. Professor Thomas Cooper points out, for example, that "the primary information stored by individuals in Western society is advertising; before learning to read, a pre-school child sees over 5,000 TV ads."[1] But in serving our advertising-saturated TV audience with the latest digital techniques, we must not assume too much of our target or those tools.

The danger for copywriters is that we become so captivated by video's technological possibilities that the ads we create become too complicated. As researchers Jacqueline Hitchon, Peter Duckler, and Esther Thorson remind us, "Most important from an advertising perspective, viewers' initial reactions to complex stimuli produce unfavorable evaluations, which translate in an advertising context into unfavorable attitudes toward the ad and toward the brand."[2] All of our efforts, therefore, must be directed to focusing our message and to employing only those tools that are essential to that message's realization in the minds of our target viewers.

TV COMMERCIAL DATA BLOCK

In television, message focusing is typographically initiated, as it is on radio, with a well-organized data block such as the one Figure 11.1 illustrates.

Because the television script must direct simultaneous attention to both audio and visual elements, and because of the high expense of television as compared with most radio production, the TV data block requires a specific articulation of the commercial's objective. This precise goal statement is a constant reminder of the project's reason for being. It provides an unblinking quality-control mechanism for the copy and pictorial

AIMED-WRITE ADVERTISING
(video copy)

CLIENT	Simmons Gum Company	SUBMIT DATE	Oct. 30, 2010
JOB #	V-SG-31	ISCI # SIGC-1411	LENGTH :30
PRODUCT	Tooth-Treat Gum	TITLE Tooth-Treat Troll	
REVISION #	3	AS PRODUCED Nov. 26, 2010	
CLIENT APPRV DATE	Nov. 9, 2010		

OBJECTIVE: To demonstrate to subteens that the blackberry taste of Simmons Tooth-Treat Gum is so stimulating that it brightens the disposition of almost anyone.

PRODUCTION NOTE: The locale is a picturesque though sinister-looking bridge spanning a forest ravine. A sharp-featured, scowling troll appears from under the bridge. Young (7–10 year-old) boy and girl who encounter him are of contrasting types --- one a dark brunette, the other a light blond.

Video	Audio
OPEN ON ESTABLISHING SHOT OF RAVINE	MUSIC: LONELY, EERIE 'STORY-BOOK TYPE' THEME
TROLL APPEARS STAGE LEFT	TROLL: I hate people--

FIGURE 11.1 TV Commercial Data Block.

elements that follow this objective on the page. Thus in the Figure 11.1 spot, the objective is not "to sell gum." That any spot is supposed to "sell" its product goes without saying. Rather, this commercial's written objective specifies (1) a universe (subteens), (2) the precise product characteristic being promoted (blackberry taste), and (3) the viewer benefit flowing from the characteristic (the brightening of a person's mood/disposition). Every well-honed objective statement must cover all three of these elements.

In addition to the objective's prominent display, the data block features several other noteworthy items. Working from the top, the block sets forth the client's corporate name and the SUBMIT DATE of this particular script to them. The JOB # (V-SG-31) is the agency's own filing designation for this project. In this case, 'V' means it's a video assignment for (SG) Simmons Gum and is the 31st television spot created for that client.

The ISCI # is an abbreviation for the Industry Standard Commercial Identification System. ISCI (pronounced 'iss-key') was created in 1970 to, in the words of its chief administrator David Dole, "answer the need for a standard-length, standard-format, computer-compatible identity code for television commercials."[3] ISCI prefixes are assigned without charge to qualifying agencies and advertisers because the system is underwritten by the major networks, as well as by broadcast and advertising trade associations. If you look carefully, you will find ISCI numbers on some of the photoboards appearing in this book.

Reading on, the data block also tells us that this is a thirty-second spot in LENGTH, and that the script to follow is its third major REVISION. The treatment's TITLE is Tooth-Treat Troll (recall the importance of title development in our Chapter 8 audio discussion), and it was given final approval by the client on November 9. Actual videotape production was then completed on November 26.

Below the OBJECTIVE, to which we already have referred, the PRODUCTION NOTE sets forth the commercial's major scene and casting requirements so these are prominently called to the reader's attention while not cluttering the body of the actual shooting script.

SHOW IT, USE IT—THE D.D.Q.

In constructing the actual body of the commercial script, focusing the television message means centering on the product/service demonstration. Through its simultaneously moving audio and video discourses, television is the real "show and tell" vehicle. Your viewers have come to expect a demonstration from the products they see on the tube, and your client is paying big money to put it there. So as a copywriter, it is incumbent on you to use this costly capability to the fullest. The television commercial that does not demonstrate does not belong on television.

Can all products or services be demonstrated? Yes. Provided you are willing TO FULLY ANALYZE the assignment in front of you. The best way to structure this analysis is via the following five-step question/answer process that we label *The Demo-Deriving Quintet (D.D.Q.):*

1. What is the subject's key attribute?
2. What benefit flows from that attribute?
3. What implement(s) make(s) the benefit most tangible?
4. What scene best showcases the implement(s)?
5. What happens in that scene? (What's the pictorial progression?)

1. What Is the Subject's Key Attribute?

You may recall our previous focus on "key attributes" in conjunction with the Chapter 7 discussion of *Poetic Packaging.* There, the emphasis is on isolating the prime component of our product so the proper *sounds* can be enlisted to describe it. Here, we are seeking to cull out the same key attribute as the first step in determining which *pictures* will best delineate the entity we are selling. Most often this key attribute is, by itself, intangible, as in the "best comfort" core of this Serta commercial:

PRODUCTION NOTE: Sheep are animated and identified by numbers on their sides.

Video	Audio
OPEN ON SERTA DELIVERY GUY WITH JOAN AT BEDROOM DOOR. WE SEE A BRAND NEW SERTA MATTRESS	GUY: Enjoy your new Serta. JOAN: Thanks.
JOAN TURNS INTO ROOM TO SEE THE FLOCK OF COUNTING SHEEP	ONE: A Serta? Does this mean you won't count us anymore?

Continued

Video	Audio
JOAN SITS ON EDGE OF BED, PATS MATTRESS. #1 REFUSES TO CLIMB UP	JOAN: One, come here. Feel that comfort. ONE: Never.
OTHER SHEEP START TO CLIMB ON	TWENTY: Uh --- I'd like to try. EIGHT: Me too. VOICES: (FLOCK MUMBLES IN AGREEMENT) ONE: Hey guys --- no --- this is unprofessional.
CUT TO DELIVERY GUY WALKING BACK IN ROOM; LOOKS UP WITH SURPRISE	GUY: I forgot to get---
CUT TO HIS POV. ENTIRE FLOCK PILED ON BED, RIGHT TO CEILING. THEY'RE ALL BLISSFULLY ASLEEP EXCEPT #1 WHO IS NEXT TO BED	SFX: GROUP SNORING ONE: Happy now, mattress man?
LOGO AND SUPER THEME: Dare to compare. #1 WALKS INTO FRAME AND GRIMACES	VO: We make the world's best mattress.
SUPER: Incredible savings.	Come in now for incredible savings on a great selection of comfortable Serta mattresses.
SUPER: ADD LOCAL RETAILER LOGO	Hurry in to your retailer today.

(Courtesy of Dan Nelson, Doner Advertising)

2. What Benefit Flows from That Attribute?

The important word in this second-level question is, of course, *benefit*—benefit in relation to the viewers at whom the commercial is directed. We need to answer what direct marketers call the WSGAT (pronounced WIZ-gat) query: "What's so good about that?" It is one thing, for example, to use slow motion and freeze frame to show tennis players that your client's ball stays on the racket longer. But unless this attribute is unequivocally translated into the greater *control* that is thereby brought to your game, the viewer will be unimpressed. Similarly, we can expend sixty seconds or more in illuminating the coarse texture of our breakfast cereal. This will be wasted effort, however, if our geriatric universe isn't able to comprehend the bowel advantages this texture provides. In Serta's 'Sheep' spot, the isolated benefit is the mattress's ability to surely and quickly put you to sleep.

3. What Implement(s) Make(s) the Benefit Most Tangible?

Now, with the frustratingly nonvisual initial two steps decided, and with the indispensable framework they provide in place, we can proceed to carve out the concept at which a camera can point. We can choose a pictorial referent for that product-derived and consumer-related benefit. In the Serta script, the flock of counting sheep represents the imperfect alternative to the client's mattress; an alternative that is itself "put to rest" by the product's power. Meanwhile, in the Kendall Oil script below, an unmarred ring of gold is used to substantiate the product's impressive maintenance benefit.

Video	Audio
KENDALL CAN AND GOLD RINGS IN FOREGROUND	ANNCR (VO): Kendall Motor Oil protects engines from friction.
HAND PICKS UP RING	To prove how well.
MCU ANNCR AND RINGS	ANNCR (OC): we plated ordinary piston rings with pure gold.
CUT TO MS ANNCR AND ENGINE	and ran them inside this engine for 5,000 miles.
HOLDS UP CAN	Kendall friction fighters are better than car makers demand.
CU HAND REMOVING RIM RINGS	but can Kendall protect even soft gold?
ECU ANNCR HOLDING UP RINGS	Look --- no visible wear! That's protection.
BEAUTY SHOT CAN AND RINGS. SUPER: Protection worth its weight in gold.	VO: Friction-fighting Kendall Motor Oil. For protection worth its weight in gold.

(Courtesy of Ken Merritt, Al Paul Lefton Company, Inc.)

The range of benefit-illustrating implements from which you, as a copywriter, can select is as broad as ever-widening computer-based technology can provide. Today, small, local accounts can obtain productional services that, until recently, were available only to the costly, nationally distributed commercials of the largest companies in the land. But this does not mean you select a pictorial implement simply because it's now within budgetary reach or because a lot of other commercials are using it. That is nothing more than "me-too" advertising; a dangerous tactic because it only invites more imitation with consequent loss of identity. And "in those cases where 'me-too' advertising has led to 'me-three' look-alikes," reports commercial testing expert Dave Vadehra, "anything short of innovative will surely be as boring to the viewer as it is confining to the advertiser."[4] If, on the other hand, your chosen benefit implement is a natural and inevitable outgrowth of the conclusions reached in the Demo-Deriving Quintet's first two levels, that implement's intrinsic relationship to your product will make others' copying attempts counterproductive.

4. What Scene Best Showcases the Implement(s)?

In some assignments, this aspect is decided almost simultaneously with the third step above. To endanger a gold piston ring, for instance, it immediately follows that we need an engine in a service garage. To frame sleep-inducing power, a bedroom

326 Part III • Video Copywriting

makes obvious sense. Whatever the scene, it must form a backdrop that enhances the benefit-illustrating implement without diverting attention to itself. As in musical theater, we don't want the audience to leave 'whistling the scenery.'

Alternatively, if a certain venue is common to an entire product category (such as laundry rooms in detergent commercials), it might be possible to come up with an innovative alternative that still sets an appropriate stage for the benefit. Most casino ads illustrate "winning luck" with in-house shots of slot machines and gaming tables. But the following spot breaks from this convention by showcasing "lucky" through different implements and setting:

Video	Audio
OPEN BACKSTAGE BEHIND CURTAIN. TWO BEAUTY CONTESTANTS ARE IN BG ANXIOUSLY WAITING TO BE CALLED	SFX: CROWD CHEERS/<u>TYPICAL PAGEANT MUSIC</u> AND ANNCR VOICE
'MISS NORTHSIDE --- BLOND, TAN AND FAKE AS A HIGH SCHOOL KID'S ID --- PRACTICING HER 'SURPRISED WIN' LOOK IN MIRROR. 'MISS SOUTHSIDE --- MORE GENUINE AND WHOLESOME --- WATCHES SHYLY	MISS N: Me? --- no --- Meeee!! MISS S: You are so beautiful.
NORTHSIDE CAN HARDLY KEEP FROM ADMIRING HERSELF IN MIRROR AS SHE ANSWERS	MISS N: (Put-on sweetness) Well, you are too --- in your own special way. (False consoling tone) But no matter what happens out there, there are no losers.
NORTHSIDE HEARS HER NAME, STRAIGHTENS UP AND AFFECTS A GIANT, PHONEY SMILE	ANNCR (VO): Next up, Miss Northside.
AS NORTHSIDE TURNS TO WALK ON STAGE, WE SEE THAT SHE HAS ACCIDENTLY TUCKED HER GOWN INTO HER PANYHOSE AND HER BUTT IS HANGING OUT IN VERY EMBARRASSING FASHION	SFX: CROWD APPLAUSE, THEN GASPS AND LAUGHS
CUT TO SOUTHSIDE, WHOSE NERVOUS FACE NOW CHANGED TO ONE OF CONFIDENCE	
CUT TO SUPER; Feeling lucky?	
ADD SUPERED ID: Cherokee Casino	

(Courtesy of David Lipson, Ackerman McQueen Advertising)

5. What Happens in That Scene? (What's the Pictorial Progression?)

Finally, after carefully thinking through the first four levels of D.D.Q. analysis, we are in a position to determine the scenario, the actual storyline of our commercial. "Stories attract memories," points out Saatchi & Saatchi CEO Kevin Roberts.

"Seventy-seven percent of Americans can name at least two of Snow White's dwarves. Only 24% of them can name two Supreme Court Justices. The difference? The dwarves have better stories than the Justices."[5]

It is important that the tales we are spinning unfold in a manner that continues to hold viewer attention while, at the same time, keeping the product benefit at center stage. The story that is so dominant that the mission it serves gets lost is a story that should never have been told. Fortunately, if the first four levels of *Demo-Deriving* have been scrupulously and honestly dealt with, the resulting scenario should be so product/benefit actuated that it is difficult to separate the story from the client's wares. After the Serta mattress is delivered, the flock's debate and ultimate validation of its benefits naturally follows. Similarly, the prospect of 'nice' people encountering good luck encourages the viewer to try Cherokee Casino for an equally pleasurable experience. And in the Australian story below, a climactic twist comedically affirms the benefit claim that the Honda Odyssey is more than just "a family car."

<u>PRODUCTION NOTE:</u> Male around forty, female in mid-thirties.

Video	Audio
LATE EVENING. ODYSSEY COMING AT US, LIGHTS ABLAZE ON SUBURBAN STREET	<u>MUSIC: FUNKY TRACK POUNDING FROM CAR' S SOUND SYSTEM</u>
CUT TO ODYSSEY INTERIOR, POV DRIVER TO FEATURE ILLUMINATED INSTRUMENT PANEL	
ODYSSEY PULLS INTO DRIVEWAY. DRIVER SWITCHES OFF LIGHTS, ENGINE, TURNS DOWN MUSIC	<u>MUSIC: FADE UNDER</u>
M2S INTERIOR TO SHOW MALE DRIVER AND FEMALE PASSENGER	WOMAN: I had a wonderful evening, thank you.
MAN RUNS HIS FINGERS THROUGH HAIR ON NAPE OF HER NECK	MAN: So did I.
HE MOVES IN AND TONGUES ENTWINE IN VERY PASSIONATE KISS.	
AFTER SEVERAL MOMENTS, THEY PART	WOMAN: Shall we go inside, for a coffee?
	MAN: What a good idea.
MS COUPLE OPENING DOORS AND EXITING CAR	<u>MUSIC: SNEAK OUT</u>
PULL BACK TO SEE WHOLE CAR AS THEY FEATURE AND WALK AWAY FROM IT, TOWARD HOUSE	SFX: NIGHT EXTERIOR – UNDER

Continued

Video	Audio
WOMAN SUDDENLY REMEMBERS SOMETHING, TURNS ON HER HEEL TOWARDS THE ODYSSEY	VO: The new Honda Odyssey.
CUT TO HER OPENING DOOR, LEANING IN CUT TO CU OF 4 KIDS' FACES, IN BACK SEAT FROZEN IN SHOCK AT WHAT THEY'VE SEEN	WOMAN: Come on then, kids!
PULL BACK AS KIDS EXIT CAR HOLD ON FS OF CAR AS THEY MAKE THEIR WAY TO THE HOUSE. SUPER: From $36,990	VO: It doesn't feel like a family car.

(Courtesy of Kay Brabham, FCB/Melbourne)

This Odyssey spot also conforms to what advertising industry legend John O'Toole long ago isolated as the need for *commercial tension,* which in the Honda commercial is further propelled by sexual tension.

> It seems to me that something has to happen very quickly in a commercial, much as in a print ad, to engage and hold the prospect. I suspect it must occur in the first five seconds.
>
> It also seems to me (and again, this is not dissimilar to the print experience) that the commercial must establish a tension, a sort of magnetic field compelling enough to overcome the viewer's natural tendency to discuss the preceding program material, to listen to someone else do so, to go to the bathroom or to simply disengage his mind.
>
> In addition, it seems to me that the tension must center on, or lead quickly to, some question the viewer might want answered, some need or want or problem he suddenly recognizes or acknowledges, some insight into the reality of his life. Whichever, it must relate logically to the product or service that is being advertised.[6]

A spot need not depict a life-threatening situation to achieve a storyline that both demonstrates a benefit and possesses the O'Toole-advocated tension. Nor must it feature a wealth of special effects and shot changes. Sometimes, the simplest environment and scenario project tension best. As evidence of this truth, consult the historic Broxodent Automatic Toothbrush message featured in Figure 11.2. This is a highly-charged duel and story *dramatization* that additional props and characters would only have cluttered.

Despite the obvious differences among the clients and treatments presented in the preceding pages, they all share and exhibit a persuasive demonstrability that flows unstoppably from the central attribute of each product being advertised. Notice that nowhere in the *Demo-Deriving Quintet* have we mentioned camera angles, special effects banks, or fancy superimpositions. Instead, applying the D.D.Q. allows the subject itself to determine what should be done and the visual components that most naturally should be called on to do it. There is plenty of time to worry about specific

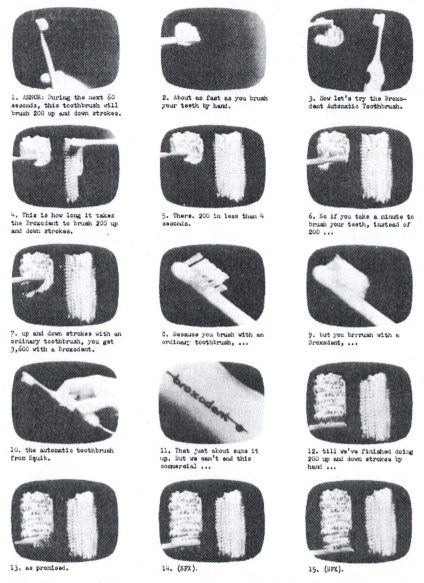

1. ANNCR: During the next 60 seconds, this toothbrush will brush 200 up and down strokes.

2. About as fast as you brush your teeth by hand.

3. Now let's try the Broxodent Automatic Toothbrush.

4. This is how long it takes the Broxodent to brush 200 up and down strokes.

5. There. 200 in less than 4 seconds.

6. So if you take a minute to brush your teeth, instead of 200 ...

7. up and down strokes with an ordinary toothbrush, you get 3,600 with a Broxodent.

8. Because you brush with an ordinary toothbrush, ...

9. but you brrrush with a Broxodent, ...

10. the automatic toothbrush from Squibb.

11. That just about sums it up. But we can't end this commercial ...

12. till we've finished doing 200 up and down strokes by hand ...

13. as promised.

14. (SFX).

15. (SFX).

FIGURE 11.2 *(Courtesy of Robert Levenson, Doyle Dane Bernbach Advertising)*

production techniques once each of *Demo-Deriving's* five questions has been success-fully met and, in order, perceptively answered. To "think production" any earlier is to sell a video technique rather than digging for a client-centered story. Research Systems Executive Vice-President Mark Gleason has found in his study of commer-cials that "In many cases, people have been trying to use heavy production values to compensate for not having anything to say."[7] "The problem," adds agency founder Jeff Goodby, "is that a lot of people go into things now without an idea. They just ex-pect the thing is going to get all the bells and whistles in post-production that will somehow pull people into it. You have to have an idea [a story] that is compelling."[8]

The reason that wordsmiths with no experience in video production often make better television copywriters than those who come out of the television industry is that people such as Humanities majors lack the background to concentrate on anything but the *message concept* and the stories inherent in it. The video production veteran, on the other hand, has spent so much time with the machinery of the medium that questions of execution keep getting in the way of much more central questions of storyline content. "I see a lot of commercials where there is a good idea, but it's buried in production values or too many benefits," observes star TV copywriter Bruce Bildsten. "The spot can still be beautiful and richly produced, but it's more the simplicity of the idea itself. You have to make it work so that the idea comes through."[9]

If you possess, or are acquiring, a production background --- fine. That knowledge will help you polish your finished scripts and boards so that they will more easily jump the gap between the creation and production phases of a commercial's development. Just don't let your technical expertise clutter up your mind and your advertisement any earlier in the process. Don't, whatever you do, let the production run away with the message in the conceptual stage or it will invariably run away with the message once it gets "on the screen."

Keep structuring your commercial development process via the *Demo-Deriving Quintet*. The D.D.Q. will not only keep your television creations "on track" but will also make you a more focused and disciplined visual writer. And just to review the Quintet's five steps, and the progressive interaction of each of those steps on the others, let's follow the labors of one trainee group who was given the exercise of evolving a spot for a particularly dull and initially uninspiring product:

The Terry Cuff Ring (an actual though largely unadvertised device) is an oval-shaped and open-ended, flexible metal band, imported from England. Cyclists clamp it above their ankles to keep pants cuffs from snagging in the bicycle chain.

What is the Terry Cuff Ring's key attribute? After unproductive forays into aspects of "protection" and "safety"—forays that broke down in later steps—the trainees (in some unjustified panic) clutched at the idea of *convenience*.

What benefit flows from convenience? Most obviously, quickness of use. The Terry Cuff Ring can be slipped onto one's leg in far less time than it takes to position and tie a lace or small piece of rope.

What implement(s) make(s) the benefit most tangible? This too is very obvious in this case, and, with a little fine-tuning, the trainees decided on a trouser leg that sported a substantial cuff.

What scene best showcases the implement? To determine this answer took some time and seemed to present several possible ways to go until one of the trainees perceptively pointed out that (1) the product was English-made; (2) English-made goods have a positive reputation for quality; and (3) there were American-made versions of the Terry Cuff Ring from which it must be distinguished. An English motif seemed to be the natural response to these factors, and what is more English than a bobby (English policeman)? Whose trouser leg more appropriate than his?

What happens in that scene? Whatever the event, it was crucial that it set up an episode in which the previously selected "quickness of use" benefit could prominently be showcased and that it be the bobby who derived this benefit. After more trainee discussion, the scenario took shape.

A stereotypical British crook (complete with little tweed cap, black eye mask, and turtle-neck sweater) bursts out of a village thatched-roof bank carrying a bag of money. He runs toward his bicycle but, en route, sees and is seen by our stalwart bobby who is standing down the street near his own bicycle that sports a "Constable" sign on the handlebars. The nervous robber, after some obvious disconcertion, jumps on his bike but his heavy trouser leg is already enmeshed in the chain. Frantically, he pulls the string off the bag of money and attempts to lace it around his cuff. A view of the bobby then displays his exquisite poise and confidence as he pulls a Terry Cuff Ring out of his pocket and effortlessly places it on his trouser leg. The robber is still tying his lace with money falling out of the now-open bag as the bobby rides up and arrests him. The Terry Cuff Ring triumphs again.

Visual technology and, in fact, the determination of the entire soundtrack, could come later. What the trainee group had succeeded in doing was to shape a compelling demonstration that possessed flow and tension, held interest, and clearly defined both the specific product and the benefit that the viewer would accrue from using it. If you want to write television that *is* truly television, go ye and do likewise. Provide your video treatments with benefit-centered demonstrations that are so intrinsic, so relevant, that you never need to call on some overexposed announcer to scream those viewer-alienating words: "Here's proof."

Ultimately, queries Leo Burnett's chief creative officer Cheryl Berman, "Is it a good story? Does it stay with you? As opposed to just a good joke, which you laugh about and don't remember the next day, I look at how it affects consumers, not just advertising aficionados."[10]

GETTING RECOGNIZED AND REMEMBERED

As you concentrate on demonstration display, don't forget that the product name must come through loud and clear. The viewer has to be made aware (and be able to *recall*) that the *Terry Cuff Ring* kept the bobby unencumbered, that the *Broxodent* beat the ordinary toothbrush by fifty-six seconds, and that the *Honda Odyssey* is the sexy vehicle that can also haul the kids around. Brand recall is as important in television as it is in any other electronic medium and should be promoted as part and parcel of the benefit-depicting demonstration.

The same *identity line* formulation principles that were presented in the chapter on audio commercials can also be applied to television *themelines*—but with the additional requirement that the lines have conspicuous *visual* relevance to the demonstrations being featured. Thus, to succeed on television, the commercial must let the viewer *see* that Kendall Motor Oil's protection is "worth its weight in gold"; *see* that you brush with an ordinary toothbrush but you "brrrush with a Broxodent"; *see* that the Serta can put anyone or anything comfortably to sleep.

As in radio, the television line that is also *categorical*—that signifies its product classification—usually has a longer and more functional life expectancy. Here are some classic and contemporary video themelines that helped the spots demonstrating them to drive home category/brand benefit recall:

Gatorade for that deep-down body thirst.

Nothing runs like a Deere.

Timex takes a licking and keeps on ticking.

You'll wonder where the yellow went when you brush your teeth with Pepsodent.

Krylon Paint. No runs, no drips, no errors.

Head and Shoulders hates your dandruff but loves your hair.

Miracle Whip: the bread spread from Kraft.

Raise your hand if you're Sure.

Joy cleans down to the shine, and that's a nice reflection on you.

Southwest Airlines. You are now free to move about the country.

Michelin. Because so much is riding on your tires.

Arm and Hammer --- a nice little secret for your refrigerator.

Red Lobster for the seafood lover in you.

Such visualizable slogans are not easy to create. That is why esteemed copywriter and agency head Phil Dusenberry has said that "the people who become valuable are people who write great themelines. Commercials are often forgotten, but a great themeline lives on for a long time."[11]

Slogans can't do the selling job by themselves, of course. Getting recognized and remembered requires writing a total commercial that gives that themeline a positive and memorable context. This is becoming increasingly difficult as more and shorter spots crowd the airwaves and the DVR becomes even more lethal than was the VCR.

As far back as the 1990s, astute marketers, like Buick's Jay Qualman, used fast-forward viewing as a test to make sure that spots provided by his agency projected a clear and straightforward storyline, a scenario that could be appreciated even at high speed. Roger Sarotte, Qualman's counterpart at Chrysler, took a similar approach. "We try to make sure people can catch the key things, so they grab the idea of the ad," said Sarotte.[12] In a zipping environment, the graphic demonstration—enhanced by a verbal and visual themeline—can be the copywriter's best chance of engineering a recall breakthrough.

DVR technology may even *benefit* well-focused TV spots. In a recent study, NBC Universal research head Alan Wurtzel found that viewers speeding through ads are actually paying closer attention to the screen than live TV consumers.[13] "Viewers will pay attention to the speeded-up ad more than they do to the 'live' ad, "agrees marketing analyst Anne Marie Fink, "because (1) they have to find out when the ad ends and the program restarts; (2) with a short break there is no incentive to change channels or run to the kitchen; and (3) they want to know if the advertised product is of interest to them . . . This interest in commercial content is why recall of commercials in DVR homes is as good as in non-DVR homes."[14] Such corroborating research "shows that simple, traditional plotlines perform best in fast-forward," the Wall Street Journal's Stephanie Kang reports.[15] So the DDQ progression we discussed earlier may well be even more important to employ in the DVR era.

Our resulting storylines may not necessarily require spoken copy. Experienced video wordsmiths realize that, with some assignments, a strong visual story can register more effectively without a verbal narrative. The spot in Figure 11.3, for instance, grabs attention to an elderly lady driving an ice-surfacing machine. The viewer next

FIGURE 11.3   *(Courtesy of Terry Schneider, Borders Perrin Norrander)*

sees something protruding from the ice. The only sounds are those of the machine plus muffled ice rink–typical organ music. Subsequent shots reveal a soda straw attached to a man layered under that ice for the purpose of testing the Columbia jacket's durability. Other parts of the campaign establish that the woman is Columbia CEO Gert Boyle and the unfortunate fall guy for this rigorous product testing is her son. But in this commercial, such identifications are unnecessary. Brand identity and benefit are registered through the visual story progression alone—even when the spot is fast-forwarded.

Ultimately, good writing may be the best antidote of all to spot fast-forwarding. "Viewers don't fast-forward through great commercials," proclaims DDB chairman Lee Garfinkel. They skip crappy ones. This is not a new phenomenon. Don't blame new technology and all the new media. Blame bad ideas."[16]

VIDEO DR, INFOMERCIALS, AND Co-op

Television direct response (DR) commercials require an additional recall element, of course --- registration of the contact phone number or e-mail address. In fact, all the tenets of audio DR introduced in Chapter 9 also apply to its television execution. That is, the TV direct response ad should (1) prepare viewers for action at the top of the message, (2) show how the product can impinge on the viewer's life, (3) make product exclusivity unmistakable, (4) take viewer objections into account, (5) clearly and repeatedly state product cost, (6) stress the need for immediate action, and (7) communicate the specific purchase process.

Because television has both sound and picture available to accomplish these objectives, the copywriter enjoys greater message design flexibility than on radio. Phone numbers and website addresses can be supered on the screen, for example, thus freeing the soundtrack for other information. But whatever they carry, the DR spot's audio and video tracks must both, in the words of direct marketer Freeman Gosden, work toward

> selling the offer, not your product. This is especially true in lead generation pro-
> grams where you are trying to get people to identify themselves as someone
> who might be interested. Once you have enticed them with the offer, you can
> sell them in person, by phone or by mail much more easily. . . . State your offer
> prominently. If you bury your offer, you might as well not even use one. People
> are used to seeing offers prominently displayed. They also want to learn all
> they can about the offer—because that is what they are responding to. . . . State
> your offer's benefit clearly. People are not buying your product and they are
> not really buying your offer. They are buying the benefits of your offer. Offers
> are not perceived to be good unless you tell the audience they are good.
> Benefits, benefits, benefits.[17]

In fashioning a benefit statement, the copywriter must decide whether to strive for a *maximum* response or a *qualified* response. A maximum response may generate a significant number of leads --- but are all of these leads in a position to obtain the product? A qualified response will result in fewer inquiries --- but virtually all of these inquiries will be from prospects whose financial and lifestyle attributes makes product purchase feasible. In either case, if your offer includes a premium, make certain it is a 'freebie' that will appeal to your client's prospects. Potential customers of a discount brokerage house probably already own a pocket calculator. Holding it out as a gift will be insufficient motivation to call.

The following maximum response spot, built around the popular cartoon character Cathy, promotes a "special trial offer" as its premium. It is built around the universal need to 'be sure' in our chosen options --- in this case, to be sure of the quality of the water we select. Anyone who wants the benefit of good water is a potential responder to this clearly communicated proposal.

Video	Audio
CATHY IN ANDREA'S LIVING ROOM BABYSITTING HER CHILDREN GUS AND ZENITH	ANDREA: Nothing like a night with my little angels to make you want your own.
CHILDREN DESTROYING LIVING ROOM AFTER ANDREA LEAVES	CATHY: Are you sure?
CUT TO CATHY AT BEAUTY SALON	STYLIST: It's just a body wave, won't damage your hair at all.
CATHY'S HAIR PEELS OFF TOP OF HER HEAD	CATHY: (Scowling) Are you sure?
CUT TO CU OF HAND FILLING GLASS WITH TAP WATER	VO: There's a lot to worry about in life --- maybe even your tap water.
ECU HAND HOLDING UP GLASS	With everything in the news today, who knows?
MCU 5-GAL BOTTLE, ZOOM TO LABEL	One way to be sure is to use Hinckley and Schmitt bottled water. Hinckley and Schmitt
CU HAND HOLDING UP BEAKER OF WATER IN LAB	tests three ways every hour, for lead and chlorine-free great tasting water.
SHOTS OF VARIOUS SIZE BOTTLES	You'll find lots of sizes and varieties at your store.
MS CHILD IN KITCHEN FILLING GLASS FROM H&S COOLER	And for friendly, reliable home or office delivery, just call 1-800-44-WATER for our special trial offer.
CU CATHY IN KITCHEN, 800-NUMBER AT TOP OF FRAME	CATHY: I may never find a swim suit that fits both halves of my body.
WIDEN OUT	And I wonder why men don't come with instructions. But it's nice to be sure of something.
H&S DELIVERY MAN ENTERS WITH 5-GAL BOTTLE	JIM: Hi, Cathy. CATHY: Hi, Jim.

Continued

Video	Audio
CATHY AT COOLER	VO: Just call 1-800-44-WATER. For your special trial offer.
CATHY HUGS COOLER	CATHY: Mmmmm. At least one relationship in life can be a sure thing.
SUPER H&S LOGO AND PHONE	VO: Hinckley and Schmitt.
NUMBER WITH WATER LEVEL IN COOLER GOING DOWN	1-800-44-WATER.
	SFX: BLUB, BLUB, BLUB

(Courtesy of Doyle Albee, Sterling-Rice Group)

The spot below, conversely, is seeking only qualified respondents—in this case, amateur tennis players who take their game very seriously. Here again, the premium is a natural extension of the main product's benefit with frequent how-to-get-it mentions in both video and audio.

Video	Audio
QUICK SHOTS AND CUTS IN FAST AND NORMAL SPEED OF MAN PLAYING TENNIS	MAN (VO): No way this guy's gonna beat me. Not today.
CUT TO VARIOUS *TENNIS MAGAZINE* COVERS FEATURING CURRENT STARS	My serve is booming.
	A forehand --- like a first seed.
	C'mon backhand.
	I read all about psyching out guys like this. And it works, It's really a pretty easy game --- when you get the right help. This guy's gonna be lucky to get more than two games off me.
ACTION SHOT SAME MAN PLAYING TENNIS, CAPTURED IN MAGAZINE-LIKE BORDER	ANNCR (VO): Get a year of *Tennis* for only $19.95. Less than half the newsstand price.
SUPER: One year. Only $19.95.	Call 800-000-0000.
SUPER: 800-000-0000. Free tips booklet.	You also get our free booklet with tips to improve your game. Call 800-000-0000.

(Courtesy of Lawrence Butner, Lawrence Butner Advertising, Inc.)

Formerly the exclusive province of small companies with unconventional products, DRTV is now being utilized by even blue chip corporations. As trade reporter Steve McClellan explains, "In a business environment where marketers are obsessed with return on investment [ROI], direct response is a tailor-made device, as marketers can track phone calls and Website hits generated by the ads. Direct TV ads are also cheaper to air, usually 40 to 60% of the cost of traditional network ads, which have come under fire for being too pricey, as network audiences get smaller every year."[18] In addition, the Web offers DR advertisers an alternative to maintaining expensive operator phone banks. Their sites can process transactions 24-hours-a-day with money saved on operators diverted to more advertising. The resulting growth of DRTV means there will be many more direct response assignments coming television copywriters' way.

Infomercials

Especially when they provide a substantial amount of instruction, DR spots of two minutes or more also qualify as *infomercials*. Extending up to a half hour in length, these descendants of the old newsreels and PR films provide significantly more time to register the subject and specifics of your message. DR experts often enlist the shorter infomercial lengths mainly to reinforce "how-to-get-it" directions. A one-minute spot, for example, usually allows only ten to twelve seconds for such information, whereas the two-minute infomercial usually permits twenty to twenty-two seconds.[19]

As its name implies, however, the true *info*mercial requires that more than just offer/benefit/purchase process be discussed. The viewer must also be given tangible and detailed *information* that can be of interest and value *in its own right*. "A good infomercial establishes a long-term relationship with a customer," asserts veteran infomercial creator Tim O'Leary. "It explains a product, positions the product and company to make the sale, and then attempts to keep the customer positioned for subsequent sales."[20] The following Grocerama message, for example, provides enlightenment on nutrition as well as on the economics of food distribution. It also has time to dramatize much more extensively how Grocerama can impinge on the viewer's life. Spots of this length (and, indeed, all infomercials) owe much of their increasing popularity and exposure to cable television networks, which have the scheduling flexibility, available time, and more specific "narrow-cast" audience to accommodate the infomercial's needs and the sponsor's market requirements.

Video	Audio
OPEN MLS WOMAN W/SHOPPING CART AND STOCKBOY	WOMAN: Excuse me, where do you keep your olives?
	BOY: Huh?
	WOMAN: Your olives.
	BOY: I don't work on *that* side of the store, lady.

Continued

Video	Audio
DIS M2S WOMAN AND CASHIER; CASHIER HOLDS 4-PACK OF BATHROOM TISSUE	CASHIER: There's no price on this. WOMAN: It's two-forty-nine. CASHIER: (Yelling into mic) Toilet paper price check on 11, Al.
WIPE TO MS SPOKESMAN STANDING IN FRONT OF HOME FREEZER	SPOKES: You don't have to put up with supermarket hassles any longer. Not with Grocerama in your corner.
SPOKESMAN STEPS ASIDE TO REVEAL GROCERAMA LOGO ON FREEZER DOOR	Grocerama is the new shop-at-home food plan that lets you order all your grocery needs online.
PULLS FREEZER DOOR OPEN TO REVEAL NEAT, WELL-STOCKED SHELVES	Yes, steaks, chops, vegetables, frozen fruit, ice cream.
DIZ TO HIM STANDING NEXT TO KITCHEN CUPBOARD WHICH HE OPENS TO REVEAL ITEMS	Plus all kinds of canned and bottled items for your cupboard.
ZOOM IN, PAN ACROSS SHELVES	SPOKES (VO): You name it, Grocerama gets it for you. And delivers it to your home twice a month.
DIZ SPOKES IN BOOK-LINED OFFICE, HOLDING UP CHECKLIST BOOK	SPOKES (OC): And to help you stay healthy, this exclusive Grocerama Food Analysis Checklist was prepared by certified nutritionists to insure that what you buy is not only what you'll enjoy, but what you need for healthy living.
DIZ 'NUTRI-8 CHART'	SPOKES (VO): We've all heard of the Basic 4 food groups: dairy products, meat, fish and eggs, vegetable and fruits, and bread and cereals.
PAN SLOWLY ACROSS CHART	But new research has refined these categories. Grocerama's exclusive 'Nutri-8' chart lets you see the new groupings at a glance as a help for menu planning.
DIZ MS SPOKES	SPOKES (OC): And how about the sources of calories? Fats, carbohydrates and protein? Do you know how each of these contributes to your health?
SPOKES MOVES TO BLACKBOARD ON WHICH SOURCES OF CALORIES ARE WRITTEN	Well, Grocerama's food packaging plans take all of these dietary needs into consideration in helping you create the tastiest, healthiest meals imaginable.
MLS WOMAN IN HER OWN KITCHEN	WOMAN: But I can't afford all of this.
SPOKES WALKS INTO FRAME	SPOKES: Not only can you afford it, but you'll probably *save* money over what you're spending at the supermarket now. WOMAN: How can that be?

Video	Audio
PAN TO FEATURE SPOKES	SPOKES: Because Grocerama buys in bulk from distributors and delivers the groceries direct to you. Grocerama eliminates the middle-man's profits to put more money in your pocket.
WIDEN TO M2S	And think of the gas you'll save by eliminating those trips to the store.
	WOMAN: Can I check this out?
PAN BACK TO SPOKES	SPOKES: You sure can. Just visit our website at www.grocerama dot com for further information.
SQUEEZEZOOM SPOKES IN MORTISE SUPER BELOW: www.grocerama.com	And you can sign up to receive free nutritional pamphlets in the mail. Discover just how easy it is to eat healthier for less.
CUT TO GROCERAMA LOGO ON BLUE	SPOKES (VO): Why waste time and money shopping the old way.?
ADD SUPER: www.grocerama.com	Visit our Website now to learn how Grocerama can start working for you. Grocerama. Better service, Better nutrition. Better prices.

Because of space limitations, we have used a relatively short script as an informercial example. Most infomercials are considerably longer, with thirty minutes a common length. A half-hour package is easy for programmers to schedule and provides much more time to develop the product storyline and the characters who are presenting it. Given the multiplicity of channels in a digital world, and the sales successes that many infomercials have historically posted, these long-form commercials are likely to remain a significant part of the TV commercial landscape. Well-conceived 'long-forms' have worked for decades—and in a cost-effective manner. For example, a thirty-minute ad back in 1990 for a Kitchenmate handmixer cost just $125,000 to produce, but is said to have generated $55 million in sales.[21]

Given its extended length, however, an infomercial must be more than the waving of the product in front of the viewer's face. "A successful infomercial is a unique blend of entertainment and selling," says Steve Dworman, publisher of *Infomercial Marketing Report*. "[Viewers] must find the show so compelling, so entertaining, that they watch 'till the very end. . . . Yet, as soon as it becomes too entertaining, as soon as a viewer cares more about a character than the product being sold—you lose the sale."[22] No matter how the infomercial is dramatized, therefore, you should analyze what is being shown and talked about to be certain the emphasis remains on the *character of the brand* rather than on the characters presenting it. If you can accomplish this, the sales results (not just the story) can be dramatic. "What better way to inform consumers about the character of a brand . . . than with a 30-minute program?" asks creative director Don Easdon. "In two hours with a good movie, you get to know the main character pretty well. It can work the same way with a brand. Infomercials allow you to give people a feeling about the product."[23]

TV Co-Op

Although television *co-op* efforts occasionally assume infomercial form, they most often consist of conventional thirty-second efforts. The essence of co-op, after all, is to divert customers to a local point-of-purchase. This element is absent in most infomercial situations, where there is no 'store' and the sale must be consummated on a DR basis. In addition, a co-op 'thirty' is a much more affordable length for local retailer budgets. The basic structure and function of effective co-op commercials are covered in our Chapter 9 audio discussion. By adding the visual, television makes it easier to find more ways to register manufacturer and local store names.

Most of the time, the manufacturer is featured in the body of the spot, with retailer audio and video tagging occurring in the thirty's last few seconds—as shown in Figure 11.4. (Note that this Oshkosh photoboard is also part of the co-op verification form that the station must complete and return to the manufacturer to obtain reimbursement on behalf of the local client/store.)

In more fully integrated (*co-equity*) co-op messages, such as the Champion commercial below, dealer referents can be sprinkled throughout the ad. Here, four different hole-copy options are provided for Frame 4 from which the local dealer can choose and into which that dealer's name can be inserted. Because co-equity treatments are more involved and expensive to produce than a simple concluding tag, however, the local merchant must usually make a greater budgetary commitment to the spot's media placement. Note, for example, that the Champion script begins with a production note warning retailers that they must purchase enough airtime to accumulate 100 gross rating points (GRPs) before the manufacturer will pay to customize the spot for them.

<u>PRODUCTION NOTE</u>: A minimum 100 G.R.P. schedule must be purchased to qualify for FREE spot customization.

Video	Audio
MCU THRU WINDSHIELD OF MAN AT WHEEL OF CAR – VERY DARK NIGHT	VO: Why get Champion Spark Plugs from (local dealer name)?
SUPER: Local dealer name	
LOSE SUPER. MAN NOW LOOKING AHEAD WITH SCARED EXPRESSION	Imagine you're on a dark and lonely road.
AS SNOW BLOWS TOWARD HIM ACROSS BARELY-SEEN HOOD	SFX: OWLS
	At midnight in a blizzard.
	SFX: WIND HOWLS
SNOW NOW BUILDS UP AND WAVE OF WATER POUNDS WINDSHIELD; MAN IS PETRIFIED	And your car --- won't start. Then the dam breaks.
	SFX: CRASHING WATER
	MAN: Help!!!

Video	Audio
CUT TO PIC OF SPARK PLUG AT LEFT SUPER AT RIGHT: "Copper Plus". (Local dealer name) $ (price) each. This week only thru Sunday	(SEE CUSTOM-COPY CHOICES BELOW)
SAME AS FRAME 1, MAN HAS NO SNOW, RAIN OR PANIC	MAN: I'll just spend winter in a warm place.
	VO: You're in a desert.
SAME AS PREVIOUS BUT NOW WITH HOT DAYLIGHT SUN AND MAN GASPING FOR AIR SUPER UPPER LEFT: (Local dealer name)	SFX: HOT WIND
	Miles from home.
	SFX: CAR ENGINE GRINDING
	MAN: Okay, I'll get 'em.
	VO: Nothing sparks like a Champion from (local dealer name).

FRAME 4 COPY OPTIONS

<u>Price</u> Help is at (local dealer name). Where Champion's Copper Plus Spark Plugs, uniquely designed for performance in winter, are just (price) each.

<u>Non-Price</u> Help is at (local dealer name). Where right now, you can get Champion's Copper Plus Spark plugs at a special low price.

<u>Tune-Up</u> Help is at (local dealer name). Where you can get a complete tune-up with Champion's Copper Plus Spark plugs for just (price).

<u>Dual</u> Help is at (local dealer name). Where Champion's Copper Plus Spark Plugs are just (price) each, or (price) with a tune-up.

(Courtesy of Dan Nelson, Doner Advertising)

RETAIL AND BUSINESS-TO-BUSINESS PITCHES

In so-called 'pure' retail advertising, the dealers are on their own, with no manufacturer dollars to create the spots or to help underwrite the cost of airing them. Some retail outlets are, of course, mammoth enterprises fully capable of mounting major national and regional television campaigns. Other retailers and service providers, however, are one-store operations. Attracted by local cable's low rate-card prices, such businesses are now at least considering the idea of television exposure.

Since the early eighties, the broadcast television industry, led by its sales promotion arm, the Television Bureau of Advertising (TVB), has attempted to show local and regional retailers that television is an effective and affordable advertising vehicle for them. TVB's Retail TV Commercials Workshops and its various sales clinics strive to provide industry copywriters and salespersons with extensive assistance in courting

VO: Is there anyplace where
kids *don't* wear
OshKosh B'Gosh clothes?
Sure, they got 'em in Brazil.

VO: So, who invented
OshKosh B'Gosh?
KID: George Washington.
VO: No wonder he's so famous.

VO: Oui, Oui ...

VO: They love them in
France, too.

VO: How do you spell
Mississippi? ... Timbuktu?
KID: I don't know.

VO: What's it say on your chest?
KID: B'Gosh!

VO: Smart kid.

(CLAPPING)
VO: OshKosh B'Gosh

VO: Small world isn't it?

(5-second retailer message)

The "Small World" OshKosh B'Gosh television commercial qualifies for co-op reimbursement.
To place your claim, have the following ANA/TVB statement completed by the television station and submit with a copy of the station invoice to:

OshKosh B'Gosh Co-op, The Advertising Checking Bureau, Inc.
P.O. Box 981, Memphis, TN 38101-0981

Announcement #QOAO 1473 was broadcast _____ times as entered
in the station's program log. This client was billed on our invoice(s)
numbered/dated _____ at the earned rate of: Signature of Station Official

$_____ each for _____ announcements for a total of $_____.
$_____ each for _____ announcements for a total of $_____.   Typed Name and Title
$_____ each for _____ announcements for a total of $_____.

                                                                 Station Name

(Notary Seal here)

FIGURE 11.4   *(Courtesy of Steve Laughlin, Laughlin/Constable Inc.)*

retail clients. The Cabletelevision Advertising Bureau (CAB), the Internet Advertising Bureau (IAB), and the Radio Advertising Bureau (RAB) provide similar services to their industries. But even though local dealers have long been accustomed to the fact that radio is at least an option one of their marketing tools, the idea of television still appears somewhat daunting—obscured in the ominous fog of the super-production mystique.

As a copywriter, you may not be directly involved in the television salesperson's task of persuading that restaurant, beauty parlor, or lumberyard to use video. You probably will, however, be called on to assist in the pitch by designing a sample (spec) commercial that showcases the prospective client in an effective, yet frugally produced manner. And, should the retailer make an initial commitment to try television, you, as an in-station or agency wordsmith, must be the prime person to satisfy the local business's expectations for a penetrating and cost-efficient production --- expectations that the station, system, or agency sales folks may have inflated to a disturbingly high level.

Fortunately, one inherently persuasive charm of local television advertising accrues when it *looks* local. As Louisville Productions' President Richard Gordon long ago told a convention of the National Retail Merchants Association:

> Whether you are Bloomingdale's or Bacon's, May Company or Belk, you are still local and should appear that way. Your spots should stand out from the impersonal national spots. This does not mean a sacrifice of image or quality, but they should be different. . . . The spot should say that here's a local store with the fashion and items the customers want. Don't try to be national when being local is an advantage.[24]

In the following spot for a local grocery, home-town customer values are well articulated by both the audio and video. Just as important, the commercial has been constructed to have a long life and yet still be seasonally, even weekly, adaptable. Try to figure out how this adaptation could most simply be accomplished.

OBJECTIVE: To demonstrate that Donovan's produce is so fresh that mothers can let their children shop for it and still be certain of good quality.

PRODUCTION NOTE: Johnny is 7-9 years old. Mom's voice featured exclusively throughout.

Video	Audio
M2S IN KITCHEN. MOM GIVES LIST AND SMALL CHANGE PURSE TO SON AND SENDS HIM OFF	MOM: Run down to Donovan's and get what's on this list, please.
AS SON EXITS FRAME, SHE FACES CAMERA	I send Johnny to Donovan's Market because---
MLS DONOVAN EXTERIOR. FEATURE 'DONOVAN'S MARKET' SIGN ON STOREFRONT	MOM (VO): at Donovan's I'm sure of getting only the best produce for my money.
MCU STILL OF LARGE, SHINY RED APPLE DISPLAY IN FG, WITH JOHNNY'S FACE LOOKING UP AT IT	Donovan's apples, like all their fruits and vegetables, are the freshest in town.
DIZ MCU JOHNNY AT CHECK-OUT COUNTER. CASHIER'S HANDS GIVE HIM GROCERY BAG OF UNDISCLOSED CONTENTS; DROP CHANGE BACK IN COIN PURSE HE HOLDS OUT.	And this week, they're at especially low prices.

Continued

Video	Audio
DIZ LS DONOVAN'S EXTERIOR TO INCLUDE ENTIRE STREET CORNER	Donovan's Market at Kane and Columbia is nice and close too. In our neighborhood, for our neighborhood.
DIZ M2S AS JOHNNY ENTERS KITCHEN AND IS GREETED BY MOM	MOM (OC): My, that was quick.
MOM LOOKS DOWN INTO BAG AND SMILES	Donovan's Market --- mmmmmmmm.

If you weren't able to ascertain the modular nature of this script, re-examine segment 4. In this particular ad, Donovan's is using apples to generate next day (or even *same day*) traffic. But merely by substituting a pic of a different display, and changing the fruit-specifying module 4 voiceover, the treatment can become a promotion for Donovan's oranges, tomatoes, bananas, or any other produce item. The spot thus has the capability of an almost unlimited number of modifications --- and at virtually no additional cost beyond that required to produce the initial commercial "bed." Expenditures can be further reduced by using stills rather than video footage for segments 3, 5, and 6. And, if Donovan's is in a four-season climate zone, these photographic or digital stills could even be shot to reflect the different times of the year. Because we never see Johnny outdoors, the footage of him and his mother at home (segments 1, 2, 7, and 8) could be used year-round as long as telltale costuming like a snowsuit or shorts was not used in the kitchen scene.

For a retailer with a somewhat larger budget, another way to vary the product pitch is to produce a series of ten- or fifteen-second spots, each of which features a different product category. It is important, however, that the same basic concept and retailer identity be maintained in all commercials making up the campaign. Each of the three Snyder's commercials in Figure 11.5, for instance, begins with a categorical question, follows this with a comedic illustration of the resulting problem, and concludes with the client logo and promise. These and other tens- could also be cut together into 'twenties' or 'thirties' if air times of such lengths are more readily available and/or more reasonably priced.

Remember that retailers measure advertising success by how many customers come through the door. Long-term image building is fine --- but not if it gets in the way of stimulating same- or next-day traffic. Placing items on sale is a long-standing retail practice to lure people to the store. Yet a sale is hardly a breakthrough idea on which to center your copy. In their work for Bayless Markets, however, Rubin Postaer and Associates prove that a sale --- even on very prosaic items --- can stand out in the viewer's mind if you give it a neat little twist. And the twist need not require super-production expenditures.

Video	Audio
SHOT OF HAND SETTING DOWN BATHROOM TISSUE ROLL	VO: Ladies and gentlemen:
TISSUE ROLL JUST STANDING THERE, LIMBO BACKGROUND	Bathroom tissue. Right now for a limited time only, on sale at Bayless.

Video	Audio
HAND REACHES TOWARD INSIDE OF TISSUE	And inside every roll of bathroom tissue---
HAND PULLS OUT TUBE, SETS IT DOWN---	you'll get a cardboard tube.
FOCUS ON TISSUE AND TUBE NEXT TO IT	Absolutely free.
SUPER: Bayless	The new Bayless.

(Courtesy of Robert Coburn and Gary Yoshida. Rubin Postaer and Associates)

Convenience stores can be an important client category—but their spots often make it difficult to distinguish one from the other as they all strive to push multiple products in a single message. However, the Figure 11.6 storyboard for the am/pm chain elevates the client by the tongue-in-cheek positioning of it as the 'birthright' triumph of civilization. The spot's progression thereby puts am/pm 'convenience' in a whole new customer-empowering light. It ends with a tag that suggests bountiful selection—without being compelled to list bunches of items.

AVO: Out of diapers?

Snyder's has 4 top brands of diapers.

AVO: Out of hairspray?

Snyder's has 28 brands of hairspray.

AVO: Out of mosquito repellent?

Snyder's has 11 different kinds of protective sprays and lotions.

FIGURE 11.5   *(Martin/Williams Advertising. Creative Director: Lyle Wedemeyer)*

VO: I am a carnivore.

VO: Millions of years ago my ancestors crawled from the ocean.

VO: They fought volcanoes, dinosaurs and great woolly mammoths.

VO: Without fur, fangs, claws or wings, we battled our way...

VO: to the top of the food chain—naked—

VO: and emerged victorious.

VO: This is my birthright...This is my legacy.

Logo
VO: Too much good stuff.

FIGURE 11.6 *(Courtesy of Grant Holland, Ogilvy & Mather/Los Angeles)*

Customer *service* is an important attribute for a lot of retailers. But the copywriter needs to find a way of illustrating 'service' without relying on that vague and hackneyed word. You will not find a single use of the term in the Target spot below. But the extent to which Target goes to accommodate customers comes through loud and clear. The VO tag at the end can also be changed for use in other locations --- and to promote preexisting as well as new stores.

Video	Audio
MAN APPROACHES TARGET SERVICE COUNTER WITH SON IN TOW. UNIFORMED TARGET EMPLOYEE CHEERFULLY GREETS HIM	MAN: I want to return this bat. It's De-Fec-Tive.
	MALE EMPLOYEE: Okay.
FEATURE MAN HOLDING BAT IN FRONT OF HIM	MAN: No, you don't understand. Every time my son swings this bat he never hits the ball.
MCU EMPLOYEE	EMPLOY: Well, that sounds defective to me.
CU SNARLING MAN	MAN: Are you calling me a liar?
CU EMPLOYEE	EMPLOY: Not at all. In fact, I could give you a store credit if you'd like.
WIDEN TO M3S	MAN: Nobody calls me a liar.
	SON: (Embarrassed) Dad, I think he believes you.
	ANNCR (VO): We've got an easy return policy.
TIGHTEN TO M2S MAN AND EMPLOYEE	MAN: You're lucky you changed your mind.
	EMPLOY: Yes, sir.
DIZ TARGET LOGO. SUPER: Target.	VO: The New York area's first Target. Are you ready for a store like this?

(Courtesy of Lia Abady, kirshenbaum bond & partners)

Though we don't stop to think about it, sports franchises also are local retailers with an irrevocable need to get traffic through the stadium door *all at once.* Unfortunately, that door opens a limited number of times, so prospects must be channeled to take very specific action. Finding a concept that will convert a 'coming event' newspaper layout into a true television scenario is not easy, but it is nonetheless vital in motivating a viewer. The BVK/McDonald agency created just such a concept in this spot promoting the "smashing good time" to be had at a Milwaukee Admirals minor league hockey game.

Video	Audio
ADMIRAL PLAYER STANDING OUTSIDE PENALTY BOX	PLAYER: Yeah, you could say I spend a lot of time in the penalty box.
PLAYER ENTERS BOX, TAKES OFF HELMET, WIDEN TO REVEAL BOX IS DECORATED LIKE A SECOND HOME INCLUDING TV AND PHONE	SFX: TV SOUNDS. PHONE RINGS
PLAYER PICKS UP PHONE	PLAYER: Hi mom. Yeah, I'm in the penalty box again.
SUPER: Milwaukee Admirals Hockey	VO: Admiral's Hockey. A smashing good time.
MASCOT SLAMS INTO BOARDS, THROWS PLAYER A NEWSPAPER	
SUPER: Admirals take on (specific team and game date)	SFX: UNSEEN BODIES CRASHING INTO BOARDS, CROWD CHEERS WILDLY

(BVK/McDonald, Milwaukee, Writer: Gary Mueller. Art Director: Scott Krahn)

With the loosening of restrictions by their professional associations, legal and medical service providers are also now in the same local commercial mainstream as other small businesses. And like other retailers, because the concept of service is an intangible, television commercials written for such clients must always demonstrate specific *executions* of that service on behalf of people with whom target viewers can identify. Once again, as in all video spots, clear and relevant scenario construction is the key. Notice the dramatic progression in this message created by a copywriter at a local cable system.

VIDEO	Audio
MAN ON CELL PHONE, SMASHED UP CAR IN BG	SFX: ENVIRONMENT NOISE
WOMAN AT HOME ENTERS FRAME TO ANSWER PHONE	SFX: PHONE RING
MAN AT ACCIDENT SCENE	MAN: Marge, this is Tony. Listen: I've been stopped by the police. And I need the number for Lee Steinberg, the lawyer.
WOMAN SEARCHING FOR NUMBER	WOMAN: Oh, Tony --- Here it is. Lee Steinberg. 3-5-6- sixty-two, fifty.
DIZ MAN NOW IN POLICE STATION ON PHONE	MAN:---I don't know. But I need a lawyer, and fast!
LAWYER ON PHONE IN OFFICE, SLEEVES ROLLED UP, EXUDES BUSINESS-LIKE CONFIDENCE	LAWYER: Are you okay? We'll send legal counsel right away. So rest a little --- we'll take care of you.

VIDEO	Audio
DIZ POV LAWYER, MAN LOOKS UP FROM JAIL CELL COT THROUGH BARS	LAWYER (VO): Tony?
	MAN: Hi. Boy, am I glad to see you.
SUPER: Lee Steinberg, 356-6250	ANNCR (VO): For 24-hour legal help, call Lee Steinberg. 3-5-6- sixty-two, fifty.

(Courtesy of David Clements, United Cable Television of Oakland County)

Just like professional services advertising, *business-to-business* messages have also been attracted to cable due to the medium's low costs and well-delineated audience slivers. This activity, in turn, has further stimulated business-to-business use of broadcast television, too. Corporations once content to communicate to each other via trade magazine and financial newspaper layouts are now trying new marketing options. "In this age of instantaneous communications," argues A. Scott Hults, president of Infomedia, "there's got to be a better way for a b-to-b advertiser to get its messages across than being stuck on page 44 of a newspaper."[25] "Now," adds Martin/Williams Advertising's creative director, Tom Weyl, "[advertisers] realize that business consumers are people, too. They see TV like anyone else and still need to be talked to."[26]

But writing business-to-business television does not mean merely committing a print layout to video. Everything we emphasized in regard to the D.D.Q. and the importance of Getting Recognized and Remembered also applies in business-to-business activities. "We're moving away from the old get-the-name-out-there approach," reports National Business Network director Walter Johnson, "to very bright, user-oriented, user-benefit advertising that reaches out with the same tools formerly exclusively used in consumer advertising."[27] The following American Standard commercial, addressed to the building and automotive trades, features a demonstration of quality that parallels what we strive to document in spots aimed at segments of the general public.

Video	Audio
OPEN ON MAN IN SUIT WALKING DOWN PICTURESQUE EUROPEAN COUNTRY LANE	MAN: I'd like to tell you about a company you may have heard of. American Standard.
CUT TO MLS LARGE DIESEL TRUCK	SFX: ENGINE STARTS
CUT BACK TO MAN ON LANE	Oh, sure, I know what you're thinking. American Standard, they're the guys who make toilets. True, but that's only part of the picture.
CUT TO TRUCK GETTING UNDERWAY	SFX: GEARS SHIFTING
CUT BACK TO MAN	They're actually a global company, In fact, they're the leading foreign producer of plumbing products in China.

Continued

VIDEO	Audio
CUT TO TRUCK AS IT PICKS UP SPEED, SCREAMS PAST EUROPEAN SCENERY	SFX: ENGINE ROARING
CUT BACK TO MAN	And if you've ever heard of Trace air conditioners, well, that's an American Standard company, too. They're one of the largest makers of commercial air conditioning systems in the world.
CUT TO WS MAN. IN THE DISTANCE, TRUCK ROUNDS CURVE BEHIND HIM AND STEAMS TOWARD HIM AT HIGH SPEED	So, American Standard does a lot more than just make toilets.
TRUCK NOW RIGHT ON TOP OF HIM	Oh yes. Their WABCO division created the anti-lock braking system found on half the heavy commercial vehicles built in Europe today.
INTERCUT QUICK CLOSE-UPS OF TRUCK TIRES, BRAKING TO A HALT. AND MAN WHO NEVER FLINCHES	SFX: TRUCK SQUEALS TO STOP BEHIND HIM
CUT TO LOGO	MAN(VO): American Standard. More than you ever expected.

(Courtesy of Mike Bales, The Richards Group)

Unfortunately, a number of business-to-business spots are still "too rational," observes advertising commentator Mark Dolliver. "They're written as though they'll be read [or viewed] by corporations, not by flesh-and-blood individuals who have their own ambitions and anxieties. Those readers would respond to a more emotional approach than many b-to-b ads dare to take."[28] The following spot dramatically plays to these anxieties in promoting this business system supplier's antidote for them.

Video	Audio
OPEN ON CEO AND SIX VP'S AT CONFERENCE TABLE. TENSION IN THE AIR	CEO: Let's start with lead generation and conversion rates for the past seven days. Jim?
CEO LOOKS AT JIM, PANIC IN JIM'S EYES	JIM: Well, that's difficult to---
CUT TO JIM IN DARK CAVE-LIKE PLACE, BEING LOWERED INTO LARGE, RAGING FIRE PIT	
BACK TO CONFERENCE TABLE	CEO: Nancy? Steve?
M2S OF PANIC IN THEIR EYES	STEVE: Well---
CUT TO NANCY AND STEVE IN MIDDLE OF OCEAN, TREADING WATER	---that's an interesting qu-
STEVE SLOWLY GOES UNDER WATER; NANCY PULLS HIM BACK UP	NANCY: We're still working on that.

Video	Audio
BACK TO TABLE. FRUSTRATED CEO LOOKS AT VP ON HIS LEFT WHO'S NON-VERBALS INDICATE HE DOESN'T HAVE THE ANSWER	
CUT TO VP IN DESERT, HIS ARMS AND LEGS TIED TO TWO HORSES RUNNING IN OPPOSITE DIRECTIONS. EYES DART AROUND AS HE REALIZES HIS FATE.	
CUT TO SUPER CARD: Say goodbye to That awkward, uninformed feeling.	
CUT BACK TO TABLE; VP'S NOW ENERGIZED	JIM: We have 981 new leads---
	NANCY: ---thanks to a more productive call center---
	STEVE: ---which increased conversion rates by 17 percent.
MCU CEO LOOKING PLEASED SUPER: Siebel.	Sales, Marketing, Service

(Courtesy of Tavia Holmes, Venables Bell and Partners)

Business-to-business advertising is expanding in all media, including television. With broadcast, cable and the Web all hungry for new ad dollars, b-to-b is an attractive field and will remain attractive as long as video copywriters apply the same proven communicative principles to its execution as they use in fashioning advertising for traditional consumer accounts.

THE STORYBOARD PRESENTATION

No matter what category of video commercial we're composing, a major hurdle is the securing of our concept's acceptance. For most major clients and production budgets, getting approval for a television spot is not, like radio, simply reading copy to someone in an office or over the phone. Rather, whole teams of people with the diffuse power of group decision making will want to see your video concept early, and in detail. Under these circumstances, the storyboard is most often the central focus of attention and main creative battleground. Since both writer and art director sink or swim by what is on that 'board as well as by how well they *present* what is on it, you must know how to handle yourself and your multi-frame offspring in the review sessions, where its fate is ruthlessly determined. "The art of advertising," asserts agency founder George Lois, "is profoundly dependent on the art of selling and the 'sale' begins by stirring up a sense of expectation in the bosom of the client that a giant idea will soon be released from the genie's bottle."[29]

At the outset, it must be made unequivocally clear that a good presentation (imposing bottle) won't sell a conceptless storyboard (powerless genie). Unfortunately, a powerless presentation *will* kill a potent 'board! If you are as glib of tongue as you are of pen, the fates have smiled kindly on you. But don't come to rely on your gift of gab as a substitute for a disciplined and well-ordered idea. Water-cooler mythology notwithstanding, client representatives, creative directors, and account supervisors have not earned their seats in storyboard review sessions by being easily duped.

Nevertheless, the best 'board still needs some well-fashioned oral promotion to transform it from a static piece of cardboard or series of Powerpoint stills into a dynamic, breathing story. Even walking in with an approach in which you are supremely confident, you must be aware that the storyboard review session requires you to perform three simultaneous selling jobs on its behalf:

1. You are selling yourself as an articulate, knowledgeable, product-wise copywriter. Your art director is normally there to help you with the presentation, but your message's judges expect the most precise treatment defense to come out of your mouth. You, after all, are supposed to be the duo's wordsmith.
2. You are selling your 'board as an appropriate, even heaven-sent answer to the client's marketing needs. Once you've shown yourself to be a competent professional, you must then prove that you've fully applied this competence to the 'board at hand.
3. You are selling the product or service being featured on that 'board. This, of course, is the ultimate task of advertising, but your approach will never get a chance to accomplish it if you have not surmounted the previous two selling barriers.

Assuming that, as a backdrop, you understand the tri-leveled, persuasive role you are expected to play, let's proceed with the five-step unveiling that constitutes the review session's usual liturgy:

1. State the specific purpose, the defined objective, that the spot is intended to achieve. Depending on the situation, this may also involve an explanation of *why* television is required to meet the objective, why (if television commercials for the product are already being run) this additional treatment is needed, and how it will fit in with the style and orientation of all other advertising the client is currently running or planning to run on behalf of this product. This may include a discussion of print as well as of other electronic campaign material and strategies.

    Don't slight this first step just because it appears more a marketing than a creative concern. Copywriters today are as involved in writing copy platforms and strategies as they are in penning commercials. Modern competitive forces no longer permit writers to be oblivious to the dynamics of the marketplace. The evolution of VALS and subsequent psychographic targeting systems discussed in Chapter 5 indicates just how extensively copy styling and market delineation must now intermesh. Only after you have justified your proposed orientation in terms of business realities can your storyboard presentation proceed to the selling of creative values.
2. Unveil your treatment's video properties slowly. Do this via a frame-by-frame progression that serves to put the picture in your reviewers' minds. Explain any technical terms and effects quickly and simply. You don't want your presentation to become a video production seminar any more than you want your finished commercial to submerge the message in the medium.

    Even in an informal review session, a pointer is helpful in directing attention to the proper frame without blocking anyone's view. A collapsible metal or laser pointer is easy to carry around in your pocket or folder and is another indication that you're in well-prepared command of the situation. If possible, stand to the left of your board—or the screen on which it is electronically projected—as you point. "Western society is used to reading information left to right," communication consultant Mark Dominiak reminds us. "Speaker(s) should be on the left acting as the conduit into ideas presented at their left hand. Positioned in this way, the speaker guides the audience into the information. Audience (client) eyes will focus on the speaker and move left to right from speaker to the information and creating an anchor point from which to build chemistry."[30]

3. Next, with pointer at the ready, go through the entire commercial again, now articulating the audio as you direct attention to each succeeding picture. Read dialogue in a style as similar as possible to the way in which you expect the talent to deliver it. If the music background is important, you may also want your art director to hum along or, especially if your partner is tone deaf, a cassette or CD player can be called on to suggest the general musical effect you have in mind. Above all, keep your portrayal of the audio clear so everyone knows exactly what the soundtrack is saying.

4. Now present the entire storyboard again, combining both audio and video descriptions. This is your chance to make that whole greater than the sum of its parts --- and your audience's opportunity to put the complete communication into interlocked perspective. If the reviewers (who are handsomely paid to pay close attention to your proposed spot) don't understand the concept by this time, the bored and listless consumers on the other side of the tube will never get it. Step 4 should pull everything together with all the assurance of a steel trap springing shut.

5. Last, close with a solid and meticulously prepared summary statement that reemphasizes the storyboard's objective, the mechanism by which it meets that objective, and the indispensable way in which the video medium is enlisted to serve the project's needs. At this juncture, the meeting is normally opened for questions and follow-up discussion. You answer these questions in a confident and non-defensive manner that spotlights the 'board rather than your proprietary interest in it.

In short, "To advance in this business, has a lot to do with how you come off to clients, how you present ideas," one creative told a group of advertising professors. "Presentation is everything. . . . You can very well be standing in front of a bunch of people wearing suits and looking at you with stone faces and you're presenting a storyboard and acting out the part of a dog. And you better be a damn good dog."[31]

For practice, take the Figure 11.7 storyboard and stage your own five-step exposition of it to your favorite full-length mirror. This drill should familiarize you with the presentation process without the additional confounding variable that comes from ego-involvement with a 'board that you have created yourself. The exercise will also force you to dig out and articulate the spot's central objective and the manner in which it's portrayed. Once you're satisfied with your handling of "Bumpy Road," you should be ready to attempt a storyboard demonstration of one of your own creative concepts.

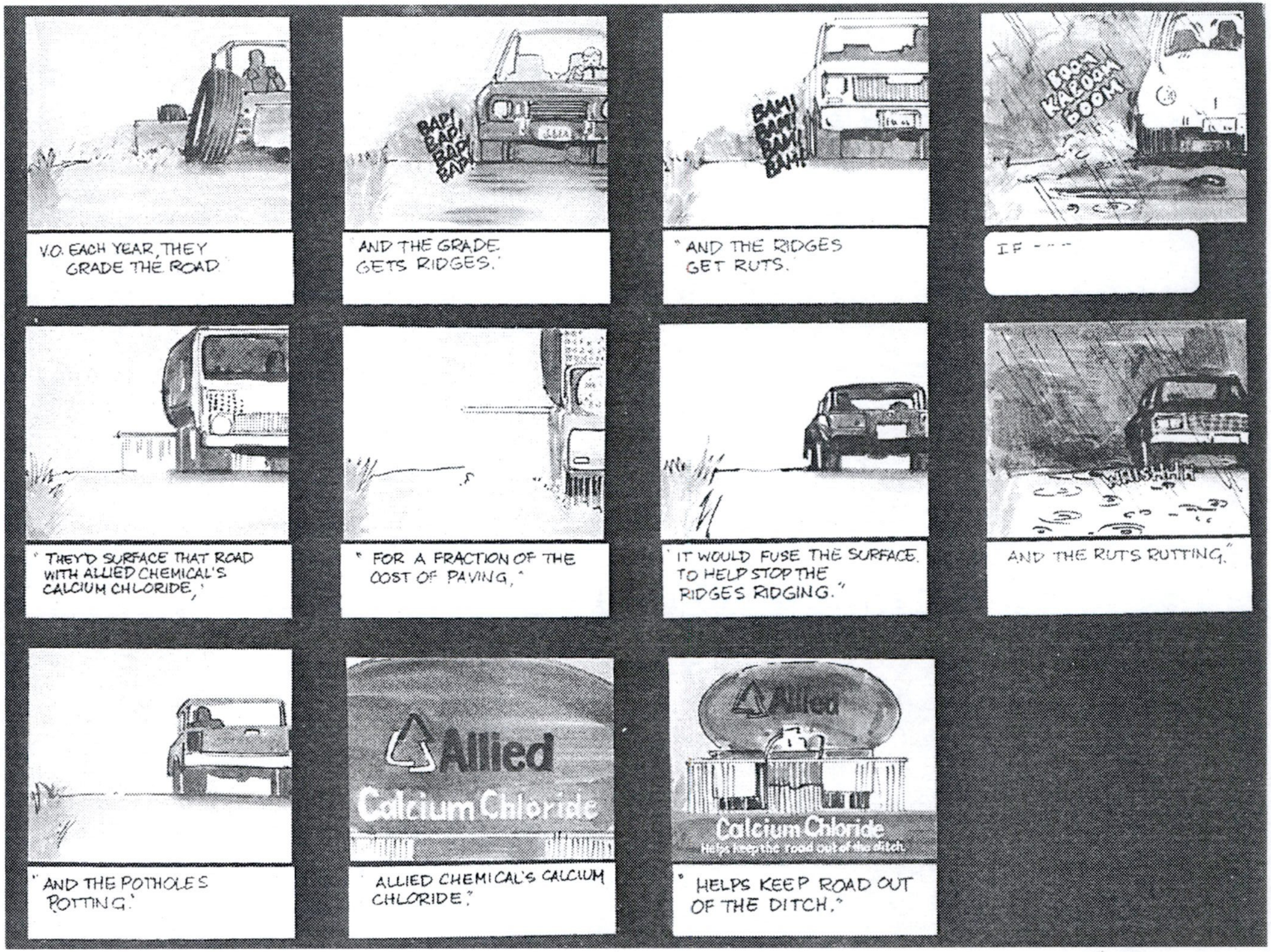

FIGURE 11.7 (Courtesy of Barry Base, Barry Base & Associates)

No matter how experienced you become, intensive practice sessions are an essential prelude to successful storyboard pitches. As advertising consultant Helene Kalmanson warns, "Lack of rehearsal is painfully obvious to clients. It results in a visible lack of teamwork (such as presenters contradicting each other) and produces presentations that run too long. Few of us can afford the luxury of looking unprepared, uncoordinated or out of sync with our co-workers. Rehearsal allows you to fill in the holes, enliven the boring bits, clean up the logic flow, turn stilted tech-ese into memorable sound bites and focus on the client instead of your next line."[32]

Once you enter the actual presentation, corporate communications expert Phillip Stella urges adherence to what he labels his ten Fast Tips:

1. Stay calm. You're the boss on stage.
2. Smile and the whole world smiles with you.
3. Be aware of on whom and what to focus your line of sight.
4. Gesture clearly at the audience members or visual media.
5. Don't pace the floor.
6. Don't jingle change.
7. Don't answer questions too quickly.
8. Be patient with the audience asking questions.
9. Don't drink too much coffee before a presentation.
10. Watch the clock.[33]

In addition, here are the *Nine Deadly Sins* that copy trainees are especially tempted to commit in the zealous fostering of their own 'boards. Mending your ways now will prevent your concepts' damnation later:

1. The objective is clearly stated --- but is never really linked to the treatment being proposed. Reviewers are thereby left to wonder whether they misunderstood the objective or whether your approach is at all compatible with it.
2. The consumer benefit is stated in negative terms ("this spot for the Futzmobile is intended to keep people from buying an imported car"). Audiences seldom remember what they *shouldn't* do—especially if you haven't really bannered what they are *supposed* to do.
3. The overall presentation lacks flow. Instead of each step smoothly segueing into the next, reviewers are assailed with such clumsy stop/start lines as: "Now that we've gotten step two out of the way, let's move on to the audio." Your oral transitions, in short, should be as fluid and graceful as your written and pictorial ones.
4. The presentation is projected into the storyboard/screen rather than out to the reviewers. This gives the impression that you are self-conscious about the approach being proposed --- and sets up a reviewer suspicion that you may have a right to be. Use the aforementioned pointer and a few inconspicuous note cards so you can talk to the people rather than the props. This avoids blocking the line of sight and doesn't force you into the awkward contortions required to read audio blocks off the storyboard itself.
5. Production costs are totally ignored. Saying, "I don't care what this costs because it's a zowie approach" will never stretch a ten thousand dollar budget

to thirty thousand --- or a seventy thousand limit to ninety. Do some prior research to obtain at least an approximation of your 'board's shooting price tag. And, if no one bothered to tell you, find out the budgetary range that the particular account has devoted to video production in the past.

6. Brand recall is advanced as the commercial's objective. Yet, as you should be aware by now, brand recall is useful and feasible only when it is tied to a specific, consumer-related benefit. It is the articulation of this benefit that constitutes the core of your spot's objective and through which brand recall can be implemented. People don't remember names that mean nothing to them.

7. Inadvertently, or out of an acute sense of frustration, the client or assignment is belittled in an attempt to make the treatment look more praiseworthy: "This is a terrible product to try to do anything with on television but—." To paraphrase a famous theatrical truism, there are no terrible TV products, only unimaginative copywriters.

8. Reviewers are told upfront that the spot is comedic. As copywriter George Rike warns, "When describing your hilarious work to clients, don't ever describe it as funny or humorous. They're spending huge sums of big serious money and, to them, funny may well mean zany or strange or bizarre or even eccentric. Just say you've tried to make it lighthearted and entertaining, and let them discover for themselves that it is truly sidesplitting and hilarious."[34]

9. You attempt to close the sale by overpraising your 'board's brilliance. But as British advertising consultants Martin Jones and Paul Phillips point out, "The more hyperbole you have, the more desperate and unconfident you look. The most confident agencies don't need to exaggerate. Understatement is far more powerful and believable than overstatement."[35]

Finally, for your own self-preservation, don't assume your 'board is yourself. Put some distance between you and it—not physical distance, or professional distance, but *psychological* distance. All advertising review sessions, and storyboard presentations in particular, can generate a lot of sometimes heated discussion and often pointed criticism. If you see your 'board as a total projection of your psyche --- if you can't separate attacks on it from attacks on you --- real psychological damage can result. Serena Deutsch of Riverside Psychotherapy Associates, who treats a number of patients from the advertising community, warns that a creative person's strong identification with his or her work can be dangerous. "If they so identify with their work and the work is attacked, then they feel attacked," Deutsch observes. "Sometimes they have trouble seeing the difference."[36]

Identifying too closely with your work can create mental anguish even after a *successful* storyboard pitch—when other people are let loose to produce it. For, as copywriter April Winchell laments:

> The truth is, once you sell an ad, you've really sold it. It doesn't belong to you anymore. It's like putting your baby up for adoption. Perhaps people will care about him. He'll win awards. Make you proud. On the other hand, he might get stolen by baboons. Years later, you'll see him in a freak show, covered with hair and eating bananas with his feet. And as he picks up a handful of excrement to throw at you, you'll realize he has your eyes.[37]

AVOIDING THE STORYBOARD

Now that you've absorbed all the whys and wherefores of storyboard presentations, let it be said that there are people in the industry who would circumvent their use altogether—not the use of presentation sessions, but the use of poster or Powerpoint storyboards *in* them. Such a situation makes the review arena all the more rigorous for the copywriter because there is now nothing to capture that judgment panel's attention except your words on paper and in the air. It is as though you are back pushing a radio concept but, due to the cost factor, with stakes that are much, much higher.

Four decades ago, advertising veteran Alfred L. Goldman made one of the strongest cases on record for *not* using storyboards, a case that revolves around these key points and that is still used as anti-board ammunition today:

> We discovered that beyond the selling of words, pictures, and ideas, there was a "fourth" dimension: a kind of total impression that not only underscored the words, pictures and ideas, but which turned out to be an experience in itself, a kind of "cathedral effect" (thank you Mr. McLuhan) that spread its wings over the entire commercial and helped win friends and influence sales.
>
> Second only to the basic selling idea, and far more vital than isolated words and pictures, this total impression is something that no storyboard can deliver.
>
> In fact, the storyboard tends to kill it. We are looking at a print interpretation of a motion picture idea. And we are looking at it in a logical series of pictures with captions on a frame-by-frame basis. What's more, we are forced to accept what a talented artist can do with a drawing pencil in the suffocating confines of a little box measuring a few inches wide by a few inches deep.
>
> Neither the artist nor the still camera can capture the essence of the idea as it will emerge on a fluid piece of film. There is a distortion of values, too, because we illustrate "pretty girl goes here" and "pretty package goes there" and it has nothing to do with the true dimensions of time and space as they will occur in the finished commercial. . . .
>
> So how can you beat the storyboard booby trap? . . .
>
> Go to the client with a script. Let your creative people play it out by creating a movie in the client's mind. They can explain, describe, act out, flash pictures, use sound effects and do whatever they must to set the stage and position the players just as if they were describing a feature film they had seen. Then, read the script against this background and the whole reel will unwind in the client's mind and he'll get the full "cathedral effect" of your commercial. When he "buys" the idea, he is buying a *tour de force* rather than meaningless isolated pictures and words as they appear in a storyboard.[38]

Much more recently, top creative director Steve Dworin bolstered the anti-'board argument with this observation:

> The worst mistake you can make is to come into the first meeting with finished storyboards containing every single copy point. Because that forces the client to focus on every little thing that's likely to cause him anxiety, like how many times the brand name is mentioned or how long the demo is instead of seeing the Big Idea. You've got to bring them to the Big Idea and let them take ownership of it,

because when the client and agency agree on the Big Idea, the actual ads are practically already sold.[39]

Producer Linda Tesa argues that the storyboard can present problems at the later production stage as well. "Sometimes," she has found, "a storyboard is just too stiff and it's better to let the spot evolve through discussions between the creative team and the director. However, I want to say that there is a big distinction between an arrangement like this out of choice versus being forced into it by the client. One way is productive, but the other way is scary and out of control."[40]

In the event that you someday find yourself in a "no storyboard" ballpark, prepare now to erect the "cathedral effect" of which Goldman spoke. And even if you never have to face a video review session without your trusty 'board, the communication dexterity that comes from successfully presenting pictures without pictures will stand you in good stead in describing radio treatments, too. Words are words whether scrawled on paper or gliding through your dentures. Particularly in the advertising arena, you must learn to string them together effectively in both contexts.

As an exercise to hone your oral abilities, take the following script for British cell phone manufacturer Phones 4U and "play it out" for a friend. Then evaluate your effectiveness by having that friend tell it back to you. Did the commercial's objective survive the retelling? If so, you're on your way. If not, if the point of the spot got lost between A and B, you really didn't comprehend the objective yourself or you lost sight of it in your efforts to convey pictorial humor and snippets of soundtrack. Strive to make your oral presentation as much a cohesive, *demonstrative* totality as is the commercial concept on which that presentation is based.

<u>PRODUCTION NOTE</u>: Late-30's woman is well-preserved but heavily made-up with wild-patterned blouse and pleather slacks. Slightly older neighbor has far less make-up and conservative one-color pant suit.

Video	Audio
OPEN MLS WOMAN IN HER LAUNDRY ROOM, PERCHED ON EDGE OF WASHING MACHINE WHICH IS GENTLY HUMMING AWAY. HER FACIAL EXPRESSION SAYS SHE IS ENJOYING THE EXPERIENCE	SFX: GENTLE HUM/THROB OF MACHINE
THROUGH WINDOW BEHIND HER WE SEE NEIGHBOR COMING UP THE PATH	NEIGHBOR: (SHOUTING) Yoo-hoo . . . only me.
LOOK OF HORROR ON WOMAN'S FACE. REACTS INSTANTLY TO COVER HER EMBARRASSMENT BY PICKING UP OLD CLUNKY-LOOKING MOBILE PHONE ON NEARBY WORK SURFACE AND THROWING IT INTO DRYER NEXT TO WASHER.	SFX: THUDDING OF PHONE INSIDE SPINNING DRYER MALE (VO): Ashamed of your mobile?
CUT TO FULL SCREEN OF PHONE WITH BROWN PAPER BAG OVER IT --- TWISTS TO BECOME FEATURED PRODUCT	Right now, get a sleek, slim Go-Phone 2X for half its normal cost.

Video	**Audio**
CUT TO LOGO AND SUPER CARD: We'll find the right Phones 4U.	We'll find the right phones for you.
CUT TO WOMAN STILL PERCHED ON WASHER, ENJOYING THE MOTION. HER NEIGHBOR IS PERCHED NEXT TO HER ON DRYER WHICH IS HUMMING AWAY AT HIGH SPEED, MUCH TO HER DELIGHT	SFX: HUMMING OF DRYER NEIGHBOR: (Shrieks loudly and happily)

(Ian White, Copywriter; and Stewart Critch, Copywriter, Cheetham Bell/JWT Manchester)

You may wish to ask yourself whether the trial presentation of the Phones 4U script was easier or more laborious than your practice pitch for the Allied Chemical 'board. The answer to this question will help reveal the differences between script and storyboard "selling" as well as how radically different product categories and commercial 'tones' impact your presentation's style and tempo.

If you found both exercises difficult, remember that this difficulty will be ego-compounded when it's your own creations that have to be pitched. Nevertheless, whether boosting a 'board or selling a script, you must strive to make your approach stand out --- and stand out in a credible, relevant way. If it can't attract favorable attention in a session called specifically to debut it, you can't expect your message to survive in the wilderness of television air schedules.

Agency consultant Chuck Phillips urges that your review presentations, like your video spots, "must get the prospect: (a) to like you; (b) to think you're smart; (c) to feel you're enthusiastic about their business (or life); (d) to believe you do terrific ads!"[41] This task is not insurmountable. You can count on the fact that your client or consumer audience "carries around in its dustbin of a mind just about every reference you're capable of dredging up," emphasizes creative director Barry Day. "TV sees to it that nothing gets thrown away and everything is in a constant present tense. All that matters is that you treat the references with reverence, style and wit."[42]

CHAPTER

12 Additional Video and Broadband Endeavors

The previous section focused on the television commercial, which is still the mainstay of our industry and serves as the launchpad for an ever-expanding array of video short-form messages. This chapter explores the copywriter's role in a number of these additional applications --- from conventional program and outlet promos to the newer variations being repurposed or created from scratch for broadband and hybrid delivery systems. While each of these content types and media venues possess their own special writing challenges, all are grounded in communicative principles and practices pioneered for the television medium and the commercials that have fueled so much of its development.

IN-HOUSE DATA BLOCK

When a video script for an outside client is written in-house, the conventional commercial data block is used. (See Figure 11.1 in the previous chapter.) For video outlet self-promotional scripts, however, a heading very similar to that used for audio in-house projects is adopted, as modeled in Figure 12.1.

The only significant departure from audio's in-house block is the addition of a line (*Air Sked*) that permits insertion of the times in which the piece is slated to air. Because video outlet time is expensive and generally less flexible than radio availabilities, scheduling decisions require documented executive approval. This and other items left blank in Figure 12.1 are usually inked in after the spot's production. Depending on the number of staffers involved and the complexity of the project, the OBJECTIVE and PRODUCTION NOTE may or may not be employed.

OUTLET IDS AND PROMOS

IDs and promos are just as important in the visual media as they are on radio. And, as in radio, each ID or outlet promo must compete with a lot of other continuity. The growth of new video services and delivery systems via cable, satellite, home video,

---

TV-34 CONTINUITY PRODUCTION ORDER

Subject: Al Slick Intro Promo   Order #: 1621–10
Date Ordered: 5/29/10   Length: 15
Ordered By: Jerry Gazette   Start Date: 7/1/10
Written By: Paula Prompter   End Date: 7/15/10
Accepted By: Scripted: 6/8/10
Air Sked: Produced:
                                                  Approved:

OBJECTIVE: Position Al as the weatherman who can make meteorology enjoyably concise.

PRODUCTION NOTE: All pics must center on Al with plenty of head room for weather scene registration.

FIGURE 12.1   Video In-House Data Block.

Internet, and mobile phone has propelled both mature and fledgling vehicles to unprecedented efforts in establishing an identity with the viewer. Emerging multi-channel entities are seeking ways and means to achieve recognition in an arena that used to be dominated by single-channel broadcasters.

This outlet identity is comprised of two parts: (1) the image of the transmitting entity (station, network, or cable service) itself and (2) the sum of the programmatic appeals encompassed in that entity's offerings. In short, today's viewers need to be constantly reminded of who you are, what you did for them yesterday (*proof of performance* promotion), and what you *will do* for them both today and tomorrow.

Given the ever-increasing number of video competitors, broadcast stations can no longer take outlet identity for granted. Veteran promoter Tony Quin warned years ago that:

> In order to remain a primary choice, stations will have to develop a clear, credible identity that transcends their programming, yet, at the same time, encompasses all of it—both local and network. . . . Why not position programs and forget about the station? Because, by relying solely on the vagaries of programming, stations will be less able to motivate sampling of new programs; they will be less likely to be a first-look in the planning of an evening's viewing; and they will be less able to command viewing for marginal programs and flow-through. In short, stations with no identity will not be able to compete with narrowcasters with clear identities.[1]

Similar to sound-medium procedures, video IDs and outlet promos can occur separately or as a single thing. A station identification may simply give the governmentally mandated information in audio and video form and then apply the remaining eight seconds to a commercial pitch (see the "Shared ID" definition in the "other technical terms" section of Chapter 10). In this case, the audio copy is not much different from that found on a radio billboard spot with the graphics accentuating the station call letters, channel number logo, and corporate symbol for the parent company or participating sponsor.

But as the competition for viewers and the dollars they bring has everywhere intensified, more and more facilities are preferring to reserve this ID entirely for self-promotional purposes. Many outlets now boast their own "signature slogans" that come complete with moving graphic and music bed over which the announcer can read customized and timely promotion copy for the outlet or one of its exclusive programs. Frequently, these ID enhancement devices are prepared by an outside production or design firm. This firm sees to it that the comprehensive graphic elements will work equally well in Web and off-air media, such as print ads, billboards, letterhead stationery, and even the paint job on outlet mobile units.

The music beds that sometimes back up these graphics exhibit many of the same style and copy characteristics used to showcase IDs on radio. But because television stations do not have a single well-delineated music format they must project, most TV identification music and lyrics tend to reflect a "safe" though up-tempo, middle-of-the-road orientation. The average broadcast channel's viewing audience is comprised of a more heterogeneous mass than the niches to which most radio stations strive to appeal. Thus although the ID stylings may vary somewhat from one part of the outlet's viewing day to another, the music and the copy are seldom allowed to wander too far from mainstream acceptability. However, cable networks—particularly those appealing to younger audience segments—can afford to use more edgy musical IDs.

Lyric copy for video promotional IDs is not markedly different from that used in the counterpart continuity on radio. (Turn back to Chapter 9 to review radio samples.) We simply must make sure that the picture is appropriate to the lyric and the audience with which both are striving to connect. The musical spot below seeks to further CW-50's positioning as a station that younger viewers will find to be "contagious."

Video	Audio
FS APARTMENT LIVING ROOM. THREE 20-SOMETHING MALE FRIENDS SITTING ON DECREPIT COUCH. ONE IN MIDDLE PLAYS ACOUSTIC GUITAR AND STARTS SINGING. SPOT SHOT FROM TV SET'S POV.	GUY: (sung) Well I was looking for a show On TV. A cool comedy Or reality.
FEATURE FRIEND AT LEFT PLAYING SMALL KEYBOARD	Too bad I didn't know the choices are whack. Now I know what I shoulda been lookin' at.
FEATURE FRIEND AT RIGHT HOLDING DRUMSTICKS AND USING LEGS IN PLACE Of DRUMS	CW-50, Detroit TV. That's contagious watching, baby!
M3S FRIENDS INCREASINGLY GETTING INTO THE BEAT AND PREMISE	Saw their shows on my big screen Thought about switching, that would be crazy. Instead of being bored and takin' naps --- My eyes are glued to the set a TV dinner on my lap
SUPER: CW-50. Contagious watching.	CW-50, Detroit TV. That's contagious watching, baby!

(Courtesy of Todd Van Cleve, CW-50. Writer: Tim Sargent)

Promo writers at local affiliates must be careful that their spots don't clash with network image elements. "The challenge," points out promotions consultant John Chavez, "is how to effectively integrate the network theme into the station's overall promotion effort to create a single, unifying on-air look."[2] Unfortunately, adds WQAD-TV Creative Services Manager Stan Teater, "Networks and locals are like two people in a donkey costume. We're not always going in the same direction, but we're both trying to get to the same place."[3] For their owned-and-operated stations, several networks have gone to a strategy of dropping their call letters for all but legal IDs in favor of a network/channel number designation. Thus WJRT-TV in Flint, Michigan, is promoted as ABC-12, visually featuring the ABC logo and channel numeral. The approach was pioneered by marketer Alan Cohen on NBC and then transplanted to ABC when he moved to that network.[4] Although it simplifies the identity problem, some stations not owned by the network they carry have been slower to adopt the practice, feeling it excessively subordinates their image. Further, if the station is carried on different channels by different cable systems, the channel number has less significance and might prompt a clarifying line such as "Wherever you see us on cable, we're TV-34."

Should the local outlet writer always emphasize network-derived identity packages? Promotions packager Bob Klein argues that "It's best to be selective. If there is a question, go it on your own. If your promotion is strong, it will do a lot more for you and the network than the network can do for you."[5] If you decide on a separate and distinct local campaign, then, as a general rule, use network-derived image builders solely around network shows and your own image package at times that are locally programmed. If a logical link cannot be found between the network thematic package and your own, then keep them mutually isolated to avoid confusing your own viewers on your own air. At the least, you should be able to design or acquire some ID graphics from your net that bridge the gap between the two themes at times in the program day when network and local features abut.

Just like its radio cousin, the video ID/promo package must reflect how your outlet's sales, promotion, and programming departments view the operation of which they are all a part. Any continuity, no matter how brilliant, that does not mesh with the organization's overall programming promise and sales orientation is only worth its weight in ulcers. Creative director Karl Sjodahl advocates asking yourself ten key questions to test the viability of your ID/promo concept. If these questions cannot be answered unequivocally, or if different people in the outlet answer them differently, it's time to rethink the whole project.

1. So what? Who cares? Is it clear *why* you are doing the piece at all?
2. What's in it for the viewer? Is there a specific viewer benefit?
3. What *results* do you expect from the campaign? (Short *and* long term?)
4. How do you want the viewers to *feel* about the station after the campaign? And how is that feeling *different* from the way they feel *now?*
5. Is "impact" important to achieving your objective? If it is, does the statement reflect that?
6. Is it do-able? Given staff capabilities, time, and budget, is the objective within your reach?
7. Is the objective *specific* to the strengths of your station and your current position in the market?

8. Will it set you apart from your competition --- or could anybody run it with equal success?
9. Does everyone involved with the project *agree* that it is possible to meet the objectives and the statement is accurate and complete?
10. Is everybody involved willing to *actively support* the achievement of the objectives?[6]

Ultimately, points out marketing agency president Bruce Bloom, "Audiences tend to be more comfortable spending their time with stations they know and trust. Stations they perceive as better able to meet their viewing needs."[7] Successful IDs and promos make those acquaintances, isolate those needs, and build that trust by showing how their video service's benefit statement has taken those needs to heart.

The following Emmy-winning promo for WNEM-5 built trust and audience involvement by promoting *The Talk Spot Show,* a video kiosk placed at area malls where viewers could record comments on any subject they wished. These "real people" remarks were then edited into brief vignettes dropped into newscasts and sculpted via copywriter-continuity as self-standing outlet promos. The campaign not only gave the audience a simulated interactive experience but, more importantly, also established WNEM as a friendly and community-attuned station.

Video	Audio
DIZ FROM BLACK TO RED CURTAIN THAT OPENS TO REVEAL PEOPLE TALKING TO CAMERA --- MCU'S	VO: Whether you're busy, or tired, or don't know what to do, take a break for a TV show that cares about you.
MAN AND WOMAN KISS, 'TALK SPOT' BUG ROTATES IN TOP LEFT CORNER UNTIL END GRAPHIC	Lovers show their affection,
ANOTHER WOMAN PLAYFULLY PUNCHES MAN ON THE ARM	the sexes will battle.
YOUNG MAN	Some guy talks about---
	SOT: ---cream cheese.
OLDER MAN IN COWBOY HAT	VO: Still others will tattle.
MAN/WOMAN IN FRONT OF U.S. FLAG	Some show their pride.
WOMAN WAVES ARMS IN DISGUST	Others voice their pet peeves.
MAN IN WHITE HAT/LARGE	SOT: ---Bahama Mamas.
SUNGLASSES	VO: Now, what does he mean?
THREE MEN RAPPING	A little song.
TEEN GIRL SINGING	A little dance.

Video	Audio
TWO WOMEN SOUNDING OFF	Then some raves and some rants.
MOMS/BABIES WAVING AT CAMERA	We'll bounce some babies.
ORANGE-HAIRED TEEN, TEEN WITH SPIKED HAIR	We'll stare at some frocks.
PERSON IN SKELETON COSTUME	We'll hear some complaints.
ELDERLY MAN	SOT: ---and I think it's a crock!
ROW OF MONITORS ACROSS TOP THIRD VO: OF SCREEN WITH VARIOUS PEOPLE ON CAMERA. 'The Talk Spot Show' GRAPHIC FILLS REST OF SCREEN OVER STATIC BG	The Talk Spot Show's coming. It's sure to arrive.
CUT TO WNEM-5 LOGO	Watch for it here. WNEM-5.

(Courtesy of Brad Maki, WNEM-5)

Network IDs and promos exhibit most of the same characteristics as do those for local outlets --- but with the advantages of bigger budgets and larger in-house staffs. They too, should use words that speak to audience benefit rather than outlet attribute. "No viewer uses words like 'resources' when they're telling a friend why they watch CNN," admits that network's marketing vice president Scot Safon.[8] So CNN has moved away from that term and others like "coverage," "perspective," and "insight" to instead concentrate on examples of what these qualities achieve.

Copy generated for a network also must pay just as much attention to brand benefit and theme-bolstering repetition as do local outlet promos. This is true for broadcast and cable networks alike. In the following promo for cable net TBS, the writer takes us behind the scenes to document how TBS is the expert arbiter of "funny"—the central tenet of its benefit positioning.

Video	Audio
OPEN EXT TBS HEADQUARTERS --- EPICENTER OF FUNNY. COLOSSAL SOARING TOWER OF STEEL AND GLASS, WISPS OF CLOUDS DRIFTING PAST UPPER FLOORS; BIG LOGO ON OUTSIDE OF BUILDING	
CUT TO HUGE CONTROL ROOM, PEOPLE WORKING FEVERISHLY EVERYWHERE LIKE HOUSTON MISSION CONTROL. BIG SCREEN SHOWS TBS LOGO AND CLIPS FROM CLASSIC SIT COMS.	SFX: DIN OF HUNDREDS OF VOICES

Continued

Video	Audio
PAN ACROSS ROOM TO HEAR SNATCHES OF OPERATOR CALL RESPONSES	VOICES: Sir, we are taking a hard line on 'slapstick' --- well, an octopus will grab things --- there was a woodpecker on his prosthetic leg?
SLOW ZOOM INTO ONE OPERATOR AS HIS PHONE RINGS, HE PICKS UP	OP: Operator eighteen-hundred. TBS Funny?
CUT TO FEMALE FACTORY WORKER TALKING INTO CELL PHONE ON FACTORY FLOOR	WORKER: My foreman's here and he's all misbuttoned. Is this funny?
CUT TO OPERATOR	OP: Which buttons are they, ma'am?
CUT TO WORKER	WORKER: Two button in the four hole.
CUT TO OP'S MONITOR SHOWING DIAGRAM OF COAT WITH VARIOUS BUTTON/HOLE CONFIGURATIONS	OP: Double-miss. Is your boss well-liked?
CUT TO WORKER	WORKER: He's a (drowned out by factory sound)
CUT TO OPERATOR	OP: Not well liked. Okay, what's he doing?
SPLITSCREEN OP AND WORKER	WORKER: He's berating someone.
	OP: Hands waving?
	WORKER: No, high on his hips.
	OP: Magnifying how lopsided his coat is!
	WORKER: Exactly.
	OP: Overall posture?
	WORKER: Like a rooster.
	OP: Any skin showing?
	WORKER: Big belly hair.
	OP: (Shudders) Has he done this before?
	WORKER: Never. He's all about appearance.
WIPE TO FEATURE OP	OP: Does he get respect?
CUT TO WORKER	WORKER: He gets his tires let out.
CUT TO OP	OP: Say he fell in the machinery, you would---?
CUT TO WORKER	WORKER: (laughs)

Video	Audio
SPLITSCREEN OP AND WORKER	OP: Okay, good, we've got a double-button miss, foreman, posturing, hatred, prissy dresser --- yep, that's a go ahead. You've just witnesses something funny. Laugh it up. WORKER: I knew it!
CUT TO TBS LOGO: Very funny.	WORKER (VO): Hey, Lenny, we got a really quite funny.

(Courtesy of Eric Quennoy, Publicis/NY)

Because television can deliver pictorial analogies for an outlet's character, radio stations increasingly are turning to video to promote their own unique identities. The same visualizable stylings that are applied to distinguish a video outlet or network from its competitors can also be used to register a radio operation in the eyes of its target audience. Examining the Figure 12.2 photoboard, what kind of personality does WJLB project? To what prime audience is the projection designed to appeal?

Meanwhile, New York's WNEW-FM (102.7 Blink) uses satire to establish how immediately and continuously it delivers its female target listeners the three-part promise of "Music. Gossip. Entertainment." As good promos should, the spot moves beyond the claim to show its actualization.

Video	Audio
BACKSTAGE OF LUXURIOUS DRESSING ROOM WITH AMENITIES FIT FOR DIVA.	MUSIC: SONG PLAYING ON BLINK
DIVA SITTING IN CHAIR , HAVING HAIR DONE. SHE IS WEARING SUNGLASSES AND LOOKING IN MIRROR	DIVA: It's just very jarring to feel your fingers on my head. STYLIST: Okay, I don't know how else to do your hair. DIVA: It's all wrong anyway. It's too dark. STY: Okay, you know, you're wearing those sunglasses--- DIVA: Anger! Anger! This is why your husband left you, sweetie.
CUT TO WARDROBE STYLIST TALKING TO HIS ASSISTANT WHO IS IN TEARS.	WA: She said she wanted me to die.
SEATED DIVA IN BG	WS: That's just her sense of humor. DIVA: Where's my wittle doggie? My wittle woof woof!

Continued

Video	Audio
BODYGUARD QUICKLY BRINGS LAP DOG OVER. SHE GIVES DOG BIG, NASTY KISS	<u>MUSIC: SONG ENDS</u> DJ: Next, a 102 point 7 Blink update. A diva's concert is suddenly cancelled, after a suspicious accident with a curling iron.
PEOPLE IN DRESSING ROOM IN SILENT DISBELIEF. SOME BEGIN TO SMILE.	
DIVA STILL CLUELESS.	DIVA: What's that smell? STY: Just makin' you beautiful.
SUPER: Music. Gossip. Entertainment.	DJ: Before it's news, it's here on 102 point 7 Blink.
SUPER: 102.7 Blink. Or you'll miss it.	

(Courtesy of Jacques Tortoroli, Infinity Broadcasting)

TELEVISION PROGRAM PROMOS ON RADIO

Just as radio stations can use television to promote their essence, so television can exploit radio as a "barker" for its programs. Often, this can best be accomplished by writing radio spots that lift compelling sound bites out of the TV program you're pushing. When properly selected and showcased, these bites make the listener want to watch in order to experience the visual scene they have just overheard. This technique works especially well in freshening interest in off-network syndication shows.

Block promos, in which a whole daypart's programming must be marketed, require some sort of coordinating element to tie the various shows together. On television, a block promo can use overarching visual effects such as *in mortise* or *quad split* (see Chapter 10's technical terms list) to help package the daypart's segments. The TV block promo conveyed by radio, however, demands a *conceptual* frame that efficiently displays each program unit and the contribution it makes to the overall viewing experience:

ANNCR:	WXIN-TV recently conducted a test to find out which was more fun --- our new weeknight lineup, or a barrel of monkeys.
WOMAN A:	We're family A.
MAN A:	We chose the TV shows.
MAN B:	We're family B.
WOMAN B:	We chose the monkeys.
ANNCR:	Family A---
WOMAN A:	Well, at 6, we watched <u>Home Improvement</u> and <u>Seinfeld</u>.
MAN A:	A solid hour of laughs.

V/O: WJLB FM 98.

Pumping out strong songs.

WJLB FM 98.

Working out

strong songs.

WJLB FM 98.

Detroit's strongest songs.

WOMAN: Now is that strong enough for you?

FIGURE 12.2   *(Courtesy of Marcie Brogan, Brogan & Partners)*

BOTH A:	Ha, ha, ha!
ANNCR:	Family B---
MAN B:	At 6, the monkeys crawled out of the barrel.
WOMAN B:	It was fun for about two minutes.
BOTH B:	(Sarcastically) Ha, ha.
ANNCR:	Family A---
WOMAN A:	From 7 to 8 we enjoyed <u>Everybody Loves Raymond</u> and <u>Frasier</u>.

MAN A:	Another WXIN hour of hilarious family fun.
ANNCR:	Family B---
WOMAN B:	From 7 to 8 those filthy little beasts ate all my house plants.
MAN B:	Yeah, and frisbee'd my Elvis records out the window.
WOMAN A:	At 8 o'clock we saw <u>Voyager</u>.
BOTH A:	What a show! Yayy!
WOMAN B:	At 8 o'clock we saw monkey see monkey do all over the carpet.
BOTH B:	What a mess! Yech!
WOMAN A:	We were delighted with the WXIN weeknight lineup.
MAN B:	We were sorry and disgusted with the monkeys.

(Courtesy of Kelly Cory, Sarley, Bigg & Bedder)

Even sports telecasts can be effectively promoted on radio when the copy, as in the WXIN promo, allows the listener to conjure up and anticipate pictures that are more self-involving than any highlights (or lowlights) film:

ANNCR:	To the uninitiated it's a swirling mass of confusion.
	Anarchy on ice.
	Impossible to follow.
	But for anyone who has ever put a deke on an opponent
	or a puck in a net,
	hockey is not only easy to follow,
	it's easy to love.
	And when such a person watches the professionals play,
	he may groan at their clumsiness
	and boo at their mistakes.
	But deep down he knows how much skill and
	how much courage is needed---
	to play the world's fastest game
	in the world's toughest league.
	<u>Hockey Night in Canada</u> on CBC.

(Courtesy of Stephen Creet, MacLaren: Lintas Advertising Ltd.)

Notice, too, that because the above promo strives to be like a poem in its imagery, it is typed on the page as a poetry stanza. Such clearly modularized copy imagery also would make it easy to convert this into a video spot by overlaying matching visuals.

TELEVISION PROGRAM PROMOS ON VIDEO

Most television program promos, of course, are written to appear *on television* and to air on the outlets actually carrying the show. Promos for network and syndicated series are usually prepared by their network or syndicator source with provision made for local channel tagging at the end. Series promos can either be *generic* (in support of the show as a whole) or *topical* (selling a particular episode). CBS promotion executive Joe Passarella believes that the generic or "image" ads create "a receptivity to your show which you then follow up with the more 'retail' [topical] ads geared toward a program's specific episodes."[9]

In choosing the exact elements to spotlight, Warner Television's Jim Moloshok reveals that "Our goal is to define what we call a show's 'hot spots' and 'cold spots.' The 'hot spots' are those areas that attract potential viewers to the program, and conversely, as you can easily guess, 'cold spots' are those points that may turn off an audience if not properly treated in all advertising."[10] The "hot spot" for syndicated *Judge Mathis*, for instance, is the droll way in which he handles the domestic disputants who come before him. This show attribute is mirrored in the style of the following generic promo that can be easily customized on a market-by-market basis simply by changing the phrases that have been placed in parentheses as well as the final video graphic.

Video	Audio
GRAPHIC: Tales in Contagious Watching	VO: And now, tales in contagious watching.
MS YOUNG WOMAN SEATED IN BLACK VOID. SHE SPEAKS TO OFF-CAMERA INTERVIEWER	WOMAN: Me and my boyfriend were fighting a lot. I just didn't know how to communicate with him. But while watching *Judge Mathis* weekdays at (9 A.M. on CW-50), I learned that you just have to be honest and direct. My boyfriend was so happy to hear I felt this way because it gave him the courage to tell me he's in love with my sister and is running away to Costa Rica with her.
SHE TURNS TO CAMERA	(Sarcastically) Thanks a lot, (CW-50).
CUT TO GRAPHIC: Judge Mathis	VO: Contagious watching with (CW-50).
ADD SUPER: 9 A.M. Weekdays, CW-50___	

(Courtesy of Tadd Van Cleve, CW-50)

This same focus on hot spots carries over to topicals. "With so much competition, every promo counts and each one needs to hit the nail (i.e. target audience) right on the head," asserts King/World creative services director Frank Brooks. "Creative needs to grab a viewer's attention in the first few seconds and hold their attention over and over again. Even daily topical spots deserve some 'kick.'"[11]

Promos created by local outlet copywriters also make use of both generic and topical approaches. The following TV-21 generic, for instance, establishes that the outlet's edgy, youth-oriented character extends to its news shows. Unlike other morning newscasts in the market, TV-21's *Daily Buzz* is anything but pretentious.

Video	Audio
BEHIND-THE-SCENES MONTAGE OF BUSY NEWSROOM.	VO: (serious; campy) *The Daily Buzz* on TV-21.
CLAYTON LEANS TOWARD COMPUTER WITH PURPOSE. SUPER: Heart of the Story	Getting to the heart of the story.
CLAYTON'S HEAD SNAPS TO CAMERA	CLAYTON: You can tell I'm a serious journalist because my jacket is off and my sleeves are rolled up.
CUT TO KIA TYPING SUPER: Digging Deeper	VO: Digging deeper. KIA: If I sit here and pretend to type, you might think I write my own copy.
CUT TO MITCH AT WEATHER WALL, VIOLENT STORM RADAR IMAGE RAGES BEHIND HIM SUPER: Saving Lives	VO: Saving lives when weather strikes! MITCH (gesturing broadly) I gesture broadly to make the weather look as severe as possible.
CUT TO ANDREA WALKING THROUGH NEWSROOM CARRYING PAPERS SUPER: Extra Mile	VO: And going the extra mile! ANDREA: I complained to my agent when they said I wouldn't be in this promo. Well, here I am!
DIZ TO GRAPHIC: The Daily Buzz. 5 to 8 AM. On TV-21. ADD STATION LOGO	VO: Wake up and smell the news! Weekday mornings from five to eight on TV-21.

(Courtesy of Tadd Van Cleve, TV-21)

Newscasts are certainly the main, and often the *only*, programming produced by a local outlet. Thus news promos become the chief way of distinguishing your facility from the competition. And because a person is more tangible than a program, some of the most successful news generics are built around the people who comprise the local news team. In creating these *personality promos*, the copywriter must make certain that each spot answers four questions for the audience: (1) Who is this person? (2) What makes this person unique? (3) What viewer benefit flows from this uniqueness? and (4) On what channel is this person to be found? Note how all four of these questions are covered in the following personality promo for a station meteorologist:

Video	Audio
BOYS COME OVER CREST OF HILL CARRYING KITE	MUSIC: LIGHT WOODWIND AND STRINGS UNDER
	VO: Even when Eric Nefstead was a kid, his head was in the clouds.
M2S BOYS LOOKING SKYWARD	BOY ERIC: You know what kind of clouds those are, Tommy?
	TOMMY: (sarcastically) White ones!
CU BOY ERIC POINTING AT SKY	BOY ERIC: They're fair-weather cumulus clouds. That means it's great kite flying weather.
M2S FROM BEHIND BOYS, SHOWING KITE IN TREE	TOMMY: If we ever get it out of the tree.
CU KITE IN TREE	MUSIC: STINGER, THEN SNEAK IN EYEWITNESS NEWS THEME UNDER
DIZ TO KITE; ZOOM OUT TO SEE IT IS UNDER WEATHER DESK WITH MAN ERIC SITTING AT DESK. HE TURNS TO CAMERA AND SMILES	VO: Meteorologist Eric Nefstead. Down-to-earth weather reporting from a forecaster who's always known what he is talking about.
SHOT FREEZES, SUPER EYE-NEWS LOGO	Weeknights at 5:30 and ten on 19 Eyewitness News.

(Courtesy of Charles E. Sherman, WHOI-TV)

Topical news promos are often accomplished by blending an inventory of past specific successes (proof of performance) with a spotlighting of at least one current story or series. In this KTVN topical, three past scoops help give credence to this week's bannered live coverage from San Diego. At the same time, viewers are also reminded of the uniqueness of the station's hourly voice-over updates:

Video	Audio
GRAPHIC: News Doesn't Wait	VO: News doesn't wait.
FEMALE REPORTER IN DESERT MIDDAY	That's why News Source 2 instituted news updates.
REPORTER; DAWN OUTDOOR BKG	On the hour, seven days a week.
OTHER REPORTER AT NEWSDESK	Since then, News Source 2 has brought you:
WIPE TO OAKLAND FIRE PIC WITH REPORTER IN FG	the first live coverage of the Oakland fire;
CRASH PIC	breaking coverage of the Thanksgiving Day CareFlight tragedy;

Continued

Video	Audio
GAMING NEWS CONFERENCE	the first coverage of the Gaming Commission probe;
CHRIS AULT ON SCENE	and this week, live coverage of Chris Ault in San Diego.
PLANE LANDING MINUS NOSEWHEEL; SPARKS FLYING	You heard these stories before you saw them on our newscasts. On our *Updates*.
REPORTER IN MORTICE; COP CARS BY SIDE OF HIGHWAY	For live, up-to-the-minute coverage, wherever, whenever news happens.
CAR SPEEDS PAST ACCIDENT SCENE	Count on News Source 2.
SLOGAN GRAPHIC ABOVE LOGO	Because breaking news doesn't wait.

(Courtesy of Ruth Whitmore, KTVN)

Topicals can also be combined with personality promos. This hybrid form exploits a distinctive aspect of the talent's personality to frame a current story or series. In the promo below, meteorologist Bradley's self-deprecating humor shines through while the viewer learns of a weekly show feature and the tip it will cover today.

Video	Audio
GREEN LETTERBOX. KURT WATERING PLANTS. GRAPHIC: Kurt Batscheke; Greenhouse Owner, Gardening Expert	VO: Kurt Batschke. Greenhouse owner. Gardening expert.
DARRIN READING GARDENING FOR DUMMIES. PULLS UP PLANT.	Darrin Bradley.
GRAPHIC: Darrin Bradley; Meteorologist. Gardener wannabe. LOSE LETTERBOX	Meteorologist. Gardener wannabe.
KURT RAKING	One works *in* the weather.
PULL BACK TO REVEAL DARRIN IN LOUNGE CHAIR, W/SUNGLASSES, ICED TEA, UMBRELLA, COMIC BOOK	One works *with* the weather.
KURT PLANTS SEED; DARRIN LOOKS ON	One plants a seed.
DARRIN PULLS FLOWER, KURT SHAKES HEAD. LETTERBOX REAPPEARS	One pulls a weed.
BOTH HOEING GARDEN; DARRIN USING WRONG END OF HOE	Thursdays they work together in
GRAPHIC: Thursdays at 5 and 6 ADD WEATHER GARDEN LOGO	the WNEM-5 Weather Garden.
DIZ BETWEEN THREE SHOTS OF KURT ASSISTING DARRIN. DIFFERENT LOWER-THIRD TITLE UNDER EACH: Tips, Tricks, and Time-Savers	Tips, Tricks, and Time-Savers to help *you* relieve your growing pains.

Video	Audio
LS KURT AND DARRIN IN GREENHOUSE, ZOOM OUT AND LOSE FOCUS	The WNEM-5 Weather Garden.
ADD GARDEN LOGO, BATSCHKE LOGO	Brought to you by Batschke Flowers and gifts.
TITLES: Thursdays, Take 5 at 5:00; News at 6:00	Thursdays on <u>Take Five at 5</u> and WNEM <u>News at 6</u>.
ADD WNEM-5 LOGO	VARIABLE TAG: This week, Kurt gives Darrin some 'iris ideas' on WNEM-5.

(Courtesy of copywriter Brad Maki, WNEM-5)

END-CREDIT VOICERS, SNYPES AND TRAILERS

One additional topical device that can be exploited by both networks and individual outlets is the end-credit voicer. With this continuity technique, an audio-only promo for the next program is read over the visual credits of the show that has just concluded. Networks and local outlets may use this technique at the conclusion of their own or each other's shows in an attempt to hold their audience for the subsequent event and thereby inhibit channel switching.

Because the video is unrelated, however, the voicer itself must be especially compelling to break through this pictorial irrelevancy and entice the audience into sticking around. Attention-getting skills learned in radio copywriting thus are put to good use in end-credit voicer exploitation. Notice how the following ABC voicer leads with a powerful hook calculated to attract female demographics to the upcoming program.

LEA: So, Deana, have you found a man yet?

DEANA: No, they're all so <u>boring</u>.

LEA: (Teasing) I know where to find funny men.

DEANA: Really? Funny men! Where? How? When?

LEA: I'm not telling.

ANNCR: But I am. You'll find lots of funny men and women on the Fifteenth Annual American Comedy Awards. Next.

DEANA: He sounds funny.

LEA: Yeah, for an announcer.

(Courtesy of ABC Affiliate Marketing Services and Andrew Orgel, Video Jukebox Network, Inc.)

Beginning in the fall of 1994, NBC took the concept of end-credit voicers one step further with the introduction of "seamless programming." Using digital editors, the technique squeezed a show's closing credits into the right one-third of the screen. The other two-thirds were devoted to humorous outtakes, classic scenes from earlier

NBC shows, trivia questions, or a riveting moment from the upcoming program. Other networks have long since adopted similar strategies. In this situation, the copywriter's role becomes more one of visual package selector than verbal script author. But the goal remains the same—the creation of that inescapable audience-retaining segue. As NBC promotions head John Miller comments, "We can't guarantee that the new show will keep the audience, but seamless programming can get them in the door. It can actually accelerate the process of building a new hit."[12] Recently, this practice has been augmented by the use of "snypes"—an animation that flies into the corner of the screen to plug an upcoming show. This "hooks the viewer who might be leaving," says Paul Lines, president of Spencer Technologies whose products facilitate snype insertion. "Then you fly in another snype to hook the viewers who are surfing through the channels. So you hook them on the way into the break and then out of the break."[13] Snypes can accommodate no more than a single graphic and short phrase of copy, of course, so it is vital that this phrase resonate its appeal quickly:

Eggplant ecstasy --- next (promo for a cooking show)

Coming up. Roller coaster homicide. (promo for a crime show)

Will Janie keep dancing? (promo for a talent contest)

The saucer men are coming. (promo for a science fiction movie)

Trailers

These promos for long-form programs traditionally use both voice-over narration and audio/video clips from the show being pitched. The term *trailer* comes from the old movie house practice of having the teaser for the next week's serial episode follow or "trail" the current week's installment. Thus today's television trailers mirror this "come-back-into-the-tent" heritage. They exploit several short, attention-riveting cuts to overcome home distractions and register the appealing essence of an offered movie-length feature.

Trailers continue to be used in movie houses and on television to preview upcoming films, and the form has been diversified to cross-promote video and motion picture industry releases on each other's screens. Trailers can also be used on the Web to direct people to broadcast or movie house offerings, or over-the-air to entice people to view broadband offerings. Many purchased DVD's are also bumpered with trailers for separate projects being distributed by the same media company. Even though trailer technique hasn't changed much over the years, the form's multiplying promotional applications now offer the copywriter a variety of assignments. The following trailer script, for example, was penned by an agency writer for in-theater display as part of client Cineplex Odeon's campaign to improve audience deportment. It follows the same form used in constructing trailers that promote entertainment features.

OPEN ON WRITER SITTING BY PHONE.
HE STARTS TO STARE AT TABLE WITH
COMPUTER ON IT.

      SUPER: To Complete a Single Screenplay

CU LINE BEING TYPED ON COMPUTER SCREEN.
TILT DOWN TO WRITER'S HANDS ON KEYBOARD

    SUPER: The Average Writer Will Go Through

CU TYPED SHEET OF PAPER COMING OUT
OF PRINTER. CU WRITER'S ANGUISHED FACE.
MS OF WRITER PACING THE FLOOR

    SUPER: One Square Mile of Carpet

WRITER PACING FLOOR, MUMBLING TO HIMSELF.
CUT TO WRITER RIPPING OUT SHEET OF PAPER
FROM PRINTER AND CRUSHING IT INTO A BALL

    SUPER: 22 Reams of Paper

WRITER SITTING ON BED CRYING

    SUPER: 512 Dangling Participles

WRITER SITTING DISCONSOLATELY ON
BATHROOM FLOOR

    SUPER: And a Crate of Pepto-Bismol

WRITER SITTING AT DESK WITH ONE HAND
ON KEYBOARD. CUT TO CU WRITER'S FACE

    SUPER: The Least You Can Do

CUT TO MCU OF WRITER TYPING

    SUPER: Is Be Quiet and Listen to Every Precious Word.

WRITER PUTTING COMPLETE SCRIPT TOGETHER
ON TABLE TOP. CUT TO WRITER ROCKING BACK
ON CHAIR LOOKING VERY RELIEVED THAT JOB
IS DONE

    SUPER: Thank You.

FEATURE CINEPLEX ODEON LOGO

(Courtesy of Debbie Ramsingh, Chiat/Day, Toronto)

    Theaters are also exhibiting *commercial trailers* that promote a product, service, or media vehicle in lengths of from fifteen to ninety seconds. In fashioning the message, however, "You have to be careful what you recommend for cinema," says creative director Andrew Christou. "You can't confuse production value with entertainment value."[14] Consumers have paid money to enter the movie house and will react most unkindly to complex or unengaging messages. Sometimes this means creating a treatment specifically for movie house display in which 'the point' (the client) is not immediately discernible. "You have to lead the audience," advises trailer creator Chuck McBride. "Let them follow you a bit, just like a movie does."[15]

But at other times, a spot created for television will work equally as well on the big screen. "A good ad is a good ad," argues Cinema Advertising Council president Matthew Kearney, "so it will work anywhere."[16] As long as the spot is entertaining, a recent Arbitron Cinema Study found that two out of three adults and 70% of teens did not mind pre-movie ads.[17] Nevertheless, cautions advertising agency executive Larry Postaer, keep in mind that "you really are interrupting. You'd better be entertaining so people don't throw popcorn at the screen."[18]

Wise copywriters exploit every possible avenue --- movie trailers and Web streams included --- in order to define and register their outlet's or network's brand or sell their client's product. Sometimes the same message will work cross-media. At other times, different scripts must be created to more exactly conform to the viewing experience presented by a big screen, TV screen, computer screen, or even mobile screen environment. Examine the Figure 12.3 photoboard for a brewer's 'public service' commercial originally designed for television. What if any changes would need to be made in this fifteen-second treatment to make it appropriate as a commercial trailer? As an online spot? As a mobile phone message?

INTERVIEWS AND SEMISCRIPTS

While most commercial assignments require the copywriter to specify every word contained in the message, certain jobs, such as interview servicing, require that we create a conceptual framework into which the conversations and contributions from other people can be dropped. Interview programs, particularly at the local level, can be an important part of the "public interest" responsibility that the FCC expects stations to meet. From a structural standpoint, the television interview's intro and outro each should accomplish the same three purposes as their radio cousins (see Chapter 9), but with some added dimensions that must be taken into consideration.

Arousing audience interest about the television interview may prove more difficult given the comparatively undynamic but nevertheless prominent visual of two or more people sitting and looking at each other. Film/digital clips or selected still pics that relate to the guest's subject can help overcome the initial talking-head doldrums. If this is not possible, the opening of the program itself should be visually scripted and produced in such a way that viewers' attention is grabbed long enough for a compelling statement of the topic to sink in and, hopefully, keep them watching.

Making the guest feel at home is even more difficult on television, where bright lights and moving cameras can cause nonmedia visitors to feel especially isolated and uncomfortable. Thus the continuity writer's well-chosen words of welcome are probably even more crucial in this environment than they were on radio, where the guest had only to contend with a blind and stationary microphone.

Other aspects of the television interview in particular, and of video semiscripts in general, tend to follow much the same procedures and possess much the same requirements that these forms entail on radio. The one unblinking overlay, however, is the presence of the visual dimension that the continuity writer may need to embellish subtly via suggested props or graphic bumpers. The following continuity bed for the opening

<u>SFX</u>: PHONE RINGS.
<u>WOMAN</u>: Hello? There's no one here by that name.

The breakfast special?

Where am I? Speak to my who?

<u>CALLER</u>: Mrs. Williams...?

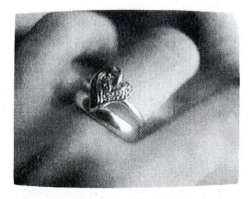

Is your husband there? Can he talk to me?

<u>SFX</u>. WEDDING MARCH MUSIC.

FIGURE 12.3 *(Courtesy of Brian Howlett, Axmith McIntyre Wicht. Ltd.)*

portion of a *Street Beat* program from WKBD-TV is indicative of the semiscripts used by many successful interview and magazine shows. In this script, the term *homebase* refers to the host's position just to the left of the standard in-studio conversation set.

Video	Audio
STUDIO TEASE HOMEBASE	TIM: I'm Tim Lawlis for *Street Beat*. Are you interested in signing? I mean, not like me signing an autograph for a *Street Beat* fan. --- Though no one has ever asked me for my autograph. --- But using sign language to talk to your baby? Find out more about this in just a few itty bitty minutes. Stay with us.
SHOW TITLE SEQUENCE FIRST SPOT BREAK	
HOMEBASE SUPER: Kenya Lowe	Today's community correspondent, Kenya Lowe, is a native of Port Huron and received a Bachelor of Arts in Deaf Education from Michigan State University. Lowe was crowned Miss Deaf Michigan in 1999 and was the first African-American to hold this title.
LOSE SUPER	Join Kenya and her guest as they discuss the advantages of using sign language to communicate with your baby. Personally, I like all the screaming and yelling, but that's just me. Kenya?
PAN TO CONVERSATION SET	KENYA: Thanks, Tim. Did you know that it's easy to communicate with your baby? You can communicate with your little one through sign language. Joining me now is Kid Black, Deaf Education
SUPER: Kid Black	Consultant for Bloomfield Hills Schools, to talk about the importance of language development for both hearing and deaf babies --- and how sign language can help this process. Kid, thank you for joining us this morning.
LOSE SUPER	(Kenya/Kid Interview)
	Thank you, Kid, for this insight into sign language and its role in improving infant communication.
KENYA TURNS TO CAMERA SUPER: Kenya Lowe	And thank *you* for joining me today on *Street Beat*. If you have any questions for me about deaf education, just write to *Street-Beat* at WKBD-TV dot com.
SUPER streetbeat@wkbdtv.com	Now, back to Tim.
LOSE Lowe SUPER; HOMEBASE	TIM: Time for a break. But I'll be back sooner than you think. When I return, we've got some cool community events you can participate in. After this!
(OTHER SEGMENTS WERE SCRIPTED HERE – OUTRO FOLLOWS)	
HOMEBASE	That's it for this week's edition of *Street Beat*. If you have any questions, comments or know why people always ask me for directions --- they do, I don't know why --- email us at *Street-Beat* at WKBD-TV dot com. I'm Tim Lawlis, and thanks for watching.

Although a show's open and close are important, the interview scripter should not neglect the show's body. Like an effective commercial, an interview should be based on a specific and achievable objective. And like any engaging story, the interview must possess a beginning, a middle, and an end. The beginning stakes out the nature of our subject by unveiling interesting facts about the guide (the guest) who will help viewers explore it while the end summarizes why this exploration has been worth pursuing. The middle, meanwhile, coaxes the guest and host through the investigation --- via questions designed to reveal the guest and enlighten the viewer. Here are the queries the copywriter helped prepare for the above sign language segment:

1. There are many hearing parents teaching their hearing babies sign language. Why is that?
2. Why do you think it's trendy to teach hearing children sign language, yet it's still looked upon unfavorably to teach deaf babies to sign?
3. If teaching sign to hearing children fosters the development of language, why wouldn't it do the same for deaf children?
4. How important is language development for infants?
5. At what age is it best to begin teaching baby signs?
6. Do you have any tips for teaching baby signs?
7. Where can parents get more information on baby signs?

(Above courtesy of Kris Kelly and Tadd Van Cleve, WKBD-TV)

Obviously, most interview scripts are semiscripts. And, as we point out in the Chapter 9 discussion of radio, we can also use semiscripts to develop commercials. In video media, a semiscript sometimes takes the form of a rough storyboard, as shown in Figure 12.4. In this commercial concept for Toronto's Ontario Place amusement park, suggested dialogue has been written for Dad in frame 1, Mom in frame 3, Girl in frame 4, Boy in frame 6, Grandma in frame 7, Boy in frame 9, and Dad in frame 10. The actual comments to appear in the final spot, however, will depend on what real people extemporaneously say when asked leading questions on-camera at the park. Semiscripted spots like this have become more and more common as the explosion of reality programming demonstrates that viewers enjoy messages in which real people say and do authentically 'real people' things. And subjects are much more willing to express themselves on camera now then in previous decades. "People will talk about most anything because of reality and talk shows like *Dr. Phil* and *Oprah*," reports Laura Slutsky who runs a real-people casting agency. "Television has become a confessional."[19]

Whether in storyboard or exclusively verbal form, the preplanned semiscript avoids squandering time while still accommodating the spontaneity of what happens during the production's sequence gathering. It is a blueprint that keeps the project on-target and in-budget. "In any situation, there's any number of things you could be shooting, or in an interview, any number of things you could ask," says producer Christina Crowley of the Kenwood Group. A semiscript "narrows your focus, so you don't ask unnecessary questions. You come back with what you need, rather than what you need plus another 10,000 feet [of footage]."[20]

In the following commercial, the prescripting was all on the visual side—meaning no wasted footage at all. Every visual was specifically pre-planned. The final voiceovers, on the other hand, resulted from unrehearsed and spontaneous responses by the real

SINGER: Ontario Place!

MUSIC   Upbeat,   percussive,
continue under

Cut to a Dad with his family
outside the Cinesphere

DAD: Ontario Place is one place
where we can all have fun together.

Cut to MCU Mom with the lake
behind her.

MOM: We love the Cinesphere, the
Waterfall Showplace...

Cut to little girl at Children's
Village

GIRL: moon bounce...

Cut to boy in same position

BOY: waterplay...

Cut to Grandma sitting on a bench
at Children's Village

GRANDMA: I love just watching the
kids play

Cut to family playing together at
Mini Greens.

Cut back to boy

BOY: Dad won't play Mini-golf
'cause I always win!

Cut back to Dad.

3   DAD And it doesn't cost that much
at all

Cut to signature Graphic

ANNCR: Come to the place where
the whole family can have fun
together, Ontario Place.

SINGER: Ontario Place. It's more
fun every day!

FIGURE 12.4   *(Courtesy of Barry Base, Base Brown & Partners)*

customers named in the final as-produced script (but not identified to the viewer). The comments came in casual audio interviews about what these folks found important in their lives and in their relationships with other people as well as their perceptions of the BOM's (Bank of Montreal's) promise to "pay attention." This strategy of gathering audio-only segments has four advantages: (1) people are more relaxed and natural in front of a microphone than many of them would be looking into a camera; (2) it doesn't matter if their facial reactions or other nonverbal behaviors are photogenically flawed or distracting; (3) their distinct vocal qualities allow the audience to participate by visualizing (as in radio) each of these people any way they choose; and (4) the economy of audio-only recording means that many more respondents can be interviewed, and at a more leisurely pace, than is possible if a camera crew has to be retained. As a result of these factors and a carefully preplanned pictorial progression, this commercial projects a warm, human, and engaging quality that establishes that the bank really is "determined to see ourselves through the eyes of our customers."

Video	Audio
OPEN ON BLUE BG WITH BMO 'M' BAR SUPER IN WHITE: What grabs your attention?	MUSIC: BMO THEME UP AND UNDER
CUT TO CHILD SLEEPING; CUT TO ASIAN MAN AND LITTLE ASIAN GIRL	BELINDA METZE (VO): Dreams. Not just for yourself but for your kids.
CUT TO MOM TEACHING CHILD TO RIDE BIKE; CUT TO PORTRAIT OF GIRL LAUGHING	ROGER BARTON (VO): Yeah, hoping the future'll be okay. And they'll be happy.
CUT TO WHITE SUPER ON BLUE BG: What else?	
CUT TO BRIDE AND GROOM; CUT TO GRAMMA HOLDING CHILD'S PICTURE; CUT TO CU OF POTTER'S HANDS SPINNING A CLAY POT	WENDY LANDS (VO): Sharing. You know, not seeing everything the same old way.
CUT TO VET AND PUPPY; CUT TO MAN IN FISH MARKET	LIAM BULL (VO): Yeah, like having an appreciation of how other people live.
CUT TO WHITE SUPER ON BLUE BG: BMO 'M' BAR UNDERNEATH We're determined to see ourselves through the eyes of our customers.	
CUT TO PORTRAIT OF FARMER; CUT TO STUDENT IN LIBRARY; CUT TO LITTLE GIRL ON STREET	GIULIO KUKURUGYA (VO): Saying that is one thing. Meaning it --- well, that's another.
CUT TO WHITE BMO 'M' BAR WITH LOGO: Bank of Montreal ABOVE WHITE SUPER ON BLUE BG	ANNCR (VO): We're bank of Montreal. We're paying attention.
CUT TO TELLER ON PHONE IN BANK; CUT TO MOM AND DAUGHTER AT BANK COUNTER	MAUREEN MCRAE (VO): Great. But as customers --- we'll be watching.

(Courtesy of Terrence J. O'Malley, Vickers & Benson Advertising Ltd.)

SPECIALIZED VENUES

The continued proliferation of script-driven events in both on-site and video environments has provided us with new writing options and opportunities outside the conventional broadcast/cable television arena. Although this book lacks the space to explore all these situations in detail, it is encouraging to note that their scripting challenges all can be met by applying the basic principles for effective audio/visual communication that we have introduced in this and the previous two chapters.

Corporate and Trade Presentation Events

Though primarily for conference room, exhibition hall, or closed-circuit delivery, the presentation event (or *dog and pony show,* as it is sometimes known) is really an extended and fully fleshed-out cousin of the TV semiscript. In writing a project aimed at employees, other businesspersons, or on-site consumers, you may be integrating still pics into a live speech or preparing narrator/presenter wraparounds to relevant pieces of film or video footage. You may even be developing a minidrama designed to vivify the subject you have been commissioned to convey. In fact, today's corporate presentations are frequently referred to by their professional scripters as *business theater.*

Because the presentation event thus draws on the same components as conventional television continuity writing, and since presentations are vital aspects of decision making in our own and our client's businesses (recall Chapter 11's discussion of the storyboard presentation), dog-and-pony-show design should be well within the video copywriter's area of expertise. In fact, corporate communications experts Chris Petersen and Guillermo Real argue that in all presentation event writing, "The mission must be to stop creating lengthy, laborious industrial sales, corporate image and training programs. Instead, we must produce 'cluster of-commercials' films which utilize the thinking and creative style that govern the production of advertisers' TV announcements."[21] John Seely Brown, chief scientist at Xerox Corporation, argues that today's business meeting writers must "structure an experience" rather than just "render a presentation." "Artistic skills are becoming important again," he adds, making today's presenters and the writers who assist them "knowledge artists."[22]

As in any electronic media writing, the aim is to keep the copy conversational so the presenter seems to be *talking with* rather than *lecturing to* the audience. In his seminars, Texas producer Mark Bernthal refers to this as 'EDUTAINMENT' or 'teaching through entertainment.' It all boils down to what veteran corporate video executive Larry Eder identifies as "Knowing your audience, sending your message to them, and showing them what they want to see when they want to see it."[23]

In preparing the presentation script, first make certain you and the client know and agree on the objective for the piece. Scriptwriter Ed Neal urges that you "develop a theme word or phrase that can encompass your subject and develop a theme visual. Think of your theme visual as a computer click-on icon that visually describes your program in one concise image."[24] Get client agreement on this central and pictorial theme before moving on. Next, develop a *treatment,* a summary overview of the piece that describes how the presentation will unfold and how the audience will be led to feel at each stage of this unfolding. Once this treatment is agreed to, you can begin the actual scripting process.

Neal advocates a three-draft writing procedure. The *first draft* is circulated to the appropriate reviewers of the script for their comments. These comments are then incorporated as feasible into a *final draft* for the eyes of only the senior decision makers. The rework of this final draft then becomes the *final for production script,* which the top executive at the client should sign. From the first draft on, says Neal, you need to write your script in six- to nine-second units. This is a procedure with which television copywriters, experienced as they are in creating fifteen- and thirty-second spots, should feel very comfortable. "Every six to nine seconds" Neal advises, "bring something new to the viewer: a new shot, new information or new development."[25]

As we discussed in Chapter 10, you should write the visuals for each unit first, and then use the soundtrack to supplement as necessary. Clean, clear interlock between visual segments and their amplifying narration or dialogue is of preeminent importance. Nothing short-circuits a dog and pony show faster than when the dogs and ponies get out of sync: when the pics and event modules are scripted in such a way that they come too fast or too slow for the presenter's aural delivery and/or audience comprehension.

By the first two minutes of the program, the audience should know in general terms what your piece is about. But don't place the heart of your message there. At the top of the presentation, people are still settling into the room or exhibit area and may not apprehend the first moments of your material. Provide rewards for early listening and viewing, but don't make immediate attention a prerequisite to later understanding.

In planning the overall format of your presentation, consider equipment needs carefully. Electronic media copywriters are especially tempted to recruit a more sophisticated delivery system, or more glitzy production effects, than the project's objective requires or can profit from. In the process, they devalue their own currency—the script itself. "It doesn't matter what the latest trend, technology or toy is in corporate media," affirms multimedia wordsmith Eric Paulsen. "We will always need good writing and communication design as the foundation of the media we produce. In the end, it's all about convincing people, with images and words and sounds and about telling a compelling story."[26]

In short, don't become a technology junkie and overindulge in hardware any more than you should overindulge in excess verbiage. "No amount of beautiful footage, special effects, impassioned delivery, exquisite editing or dramatic music will save a bad script," Paulsen concludes. "It's like giving a starving dog a rubber bone: It might look real, but the audience quickly realizes there's nothing there."[27]

Speaking of music, moderation is important in its use as well. If it is selected and planned for early in the project, music can create real impact and stimulate audience involvement. But "too often," declares Omni Music's Sam White, "music is tacked on after everything else is done. This tends to force the music into the background of the track, eliminating interaction of the music with the visuals to create the desired effect."[28] As White also points out, the style of the music must be dependent, not on the copywriter's or client's personal taste, but on the intended audience:

> A corporate image video with a score that's heavy on big orchestral themes may do well among potential investors because the music tells the audience that the company is solid as a rock. However, it may not fare as well among young potential recruits, who will hear the music as old and stuffy. And that guitar and harmonica theme that makes a big agricultural company seem friendly to the farming community may foster a negative company image to a Wall Street audience.[29]

Finally, never surrender the power and responsibility that as a copywriter you are paid to exercise. "When copywriters get the feeling that they're doing nothing but transcribing what the client has told them then they should take a vacation," producer Eric Larson advises. "When they're fresh they have a little more fight. And they realize that what they do is an art and is crucial."[30] Eric Paulsen seconds this attitude when he asserts, "Your biggest responsibility is to your audience, sometimes to the exclusion of your client, because sometimes clients are too close to the subject, or they're not in tune with their audience, inexperienced about what good video is or just so happy to get their ideas or product on video that they're blind to the effectiveness of the delivery."[31]

What follows is the opening of an Auto Show presentation that Visual Services, Inc., prepared on behalf of the Chrysler Corporation and thematically tied to the upcoming Winter Olympics. Note that in more complex stage presentations such as this, the actual script is preceded by a Scenario Summary that concisely yet graphically sets forth the essential set details and general flow of the pitch. In this way, the client gets a clear idea of the overall presentational environment before examining the actual words and actions that the copywriter has employed.

<u>Scenario Summary</u>

A Dodge Grand Caravan is positioned onstage opposite a 4-ft.-tall Olympic Gold Medal, leaning back slightly as if resting on its ribbon, which is coiled behind it.

The show begins when the model/narrator takes the stage. The Grand Caravan and the gold medal are elevated on their rotating circular stages. The Grand Caravan then descends to eye-level where noted in the script.

As the narrator moves onto the stage, midway between the Grand Caravan and the Olympic gold medal, special lighting and a <u>musical fanfare</u> (on the show's pre-recorded soundtrack) draws the attention of passers-by, alerting them to the fact that a show is about to begin. This happens for approximately 18 seconds.

Special lighting enhances the luster of the gold medal and highlights the van --- and the narrator, whenever appropriate.

During the show, the "live" narrator's presentation is augmented by video on monitors suspended above the stage, showing the features or components the narrator is describing.

Throughout the show, the circular stage on which the Grand Caravan is positioned will be lowered, for better viewing of its interior and components. The Grand Caravan will be programmed to slowly revolve, or to remain stationary during the presentation, in keeping with the requirements of the script. The Olympic Gold Medal will revolve slowly throughout the presentation.

:18 FANFARE & SPOTLIGHTS AS NARRATOR/MODEL ASCENDS STAGE

:00 LIVE NARRATOR (OVER FOOTAGE OF 1984 CARAVAN):

When it was introduced in 1984, the Dodge Caravan set a new standard by giving birth to the mini-van market! Caravan quickly became a leader in resale value and owner loyalty, often imitated but never duplicated.

:14 "GOLD STANDARD" TITLE SLIDE W/OLYMPIC RINGS AND GOLD MEDAL

Today, Chrysler is a proud sponsor of the U.S. Olympic Team, as American athletes compete for the ultimate honor:

NARRATOR SWEEPS HER ARM TOWARD, WALKS TOWARD, GOLD MEDAL

the gold medal. At the Olympics, athletes from all over the world strive to reach the performance standards set by previous gold medal winners and record-holders. In much the same way, mini-vans the world over are trying to reach the standard set by Dodge

Caravan. But today's Grand Caravan continues to set a gold medal pace the competition just can't match.

NARRATOR SWEEPS HER ARM TOWARD CARAVAN, AS IF "INTRODUCING" IT

Ladies and gentlemen, Dodge proudly presents the 'Gold Standard of Mini-Vans!' Witness the evolution of the mini-van!

:54 'METAMORPHOSIS' COMMERCIAL RUNS, IN ITS ENTIRETY, WITH FULL SOUND. FOLLOWING COMMERCIAL, THE MONITORS GO BLACK FOR 9 SECONDS AS NARRATOR SAYS:

(1:24) Now, ladies and gentlemen, let's take a closer look at the new Dodge Grand Caravan, and see why it continues to set standards.

1:32 FRONT OF THE VAN IS ANGLED TOWARD THE NARRATOR, AND THE MALE V/O NARRATOR (PRE-RECORDED ON THE VIDEO'S SOUNDTRACK), TAKES OVER.

(Courtesy of Jerry Downey, Visual Services, Inc.)

Although the full Grand Caravan presentation runs 7:28, it nonetheless, like any effective thirty-second spot, projects and develops a single theme. In this case, the theme exploits an Olympic tie-in of "being first/getting (winner's) gold." When you write your own dog-and-pony scripts, make sure that they are grounded in a single-concept base as well. Even in a full-length presentation, scattered ideas and techniques make for fragmentary audience impact.

Video News Releases

Usually referred to as VNRs, these electronic handouts combine the techniques of journalism and public relations to promote events and developments that are of substantial interest to a corporate client. The VNR gives television news directors a press release in a format adapted to their needs --- just as the printed handout has met the needs of newspaper editors for over a century. "When I was a television news reporter, the assignment editor had a stack of newsletters," recalls VNR production house owner Nancy Herr. "He'd have to have a reporter like me turn it into a form we can use. That's what a video news release is: a press release in a form that's *usable*."[32] The VNR writer has "got to think in terms of news producers looking for pictures, features, and angles," adds Medialink senior editor Nick Peters. "If it's a good story, with a good hook, *somebody* will use it."[33]

This hook, and the story as a whole, must be honest and accurate --- the same ethical burden that a copywriter bears when preparing a commercial. But because the VNR is not a paid spot, extra care must be taken to ensure that the piece provides audience-helpful information first, and client-serving impact second. Otherwise, news outlets have no incentive to run it. "I have an ethical problem of taking a lightweight story and going to the trouble and expense of producing it," states Hill & Knowlton's George Glazer. "If the story doesn't justify it, we don't do it. We've got our name on it. We don't want stations saying 'Here comes more Hill & Knowltons -- '."[34]

The following pioneering VNR for GM Hughes Electronics was topical because it tied into the upcoming Indianapolis 500 auto race. It presents interesting information both visually and via the soundtrack and possesses highway safety implications as well. The fact that it also promotes the technological expertise of its corporate sponsor does not detract from these positives because the device being profiled was, in fact, a GM/Hughes innovation. Like many VNRs, the piece is packaged in such a way that each station's own talent can voice the intro and subsequent narration.

(Suggested On-Camera Introduction)

Even before the green flag waves, starting the running of the Indianapolis 500 race, one driver will be using technology that was originally developed for use in military aircraft---

Video	Audio
MS DRIVER IN PACE CAR	SUGGESTED VO NARRATION: The driver will be behind the wheel of the GM-built pace car and he'll be seeing
LS HEAD-UP DISPLAY	a projected image of his speed which will appear to be floating out over the front bumper of the car. It's called a Head-Up Display and it's designed to keep the driver's eyes on the road ahead.
LS TWO FIGHTERS IN FORMATION	Because of the complicated instruments and controls in a modern jet fighter, the original Head-Up Displays have been a boon to fighter pilots who can't afford to take their eyes off the instruments for even a split second.
LS HEAD-UP DISPLAY, INDY TRACK	Developed by GM Hughes Electronics, the down-to-earth model is expected to make a positive contribution to driving safety.
MS HARRY KING SUPER: Dr. Harry King, GM Hughes Electronics	KING SOT: Particularly in collision avoidance situations where you may be looking down at the dashboard,
PROFILE DRIVER, PAN TO WINDSHIELD	if an emergency occurs and you're looking up through the windshield instead, you're certainly
HEAD-UP DISPLAY, TURN SIGNAL	going to pick that up more quickly in your field of view and respond to it more quickly.
CONTINUE HEAD-UP DISPLAY SCENE	SUGGESTED VO: In addition to speed, the Head-Up display in the pace car shows low fuel, high beam headlights and turn signals.
LS FOLLOW PACE CAR ON PIT ROAD	KING SOT: We can also put other displays there, possibly allow you to tune your radio or set heater controls or have other
LS ¾ FRONT RUNNING SHOT	temporary displays that you could use to make the drivers' lives easier as they drive the car.
CONTINUE RUNNING SHOT	SUGGESTED VO: Although the Head-Up Display is now only in the limited production replica pace
LS PAN PACE CAR DOWN PIT ROAD	cars, it is expected to be available in a number of General Motors cars in the future.

TOTAL RUNNING TIME: 1 MINUTE 24 SECONDS

(Courtesy of Jim O'Donnell, NTN Film & Video Productions)

Remember that, unlike a standard news story, a VNR is designed to promote a corporate entity. Brand identity and recall must be advanced in the script but without seeming so overt that news directors will be turned off to the piece. As the GM/Hughes message illustrates, the potential that the VNR will be run increases when the script makes it easy for local station talent to perform the narration.

Direct-Marketing Videos

Like the VNR, the direct-marketing (DM) video is a promotional message distributed on DVD. But it can also be made available to consumers online who are targeted by marketing databases as being prime prospects for the product in question. Thus most of what we learned in Chapter 11 about infomercial writing also pertains to the DM video. It is primarily the distribution mechanism, rather than the format or content, that is different. As the price of disks has declined, direct-marketing videos are becoming more and more cost effective. Putting the message online is even cheaper than mailing disks, of course, but with less chance that it will be noticed by the intended consumers.

Direct-marketing videos are also much more likely to get consumer attention than are printed mail pieces. "Video has high perceived value while print mail is still stigmatized by the characterization 'junk mail,'" argues direct-marketing expert Hugh Aoki. "While print pieces are often met with negative response, video can generate excitement and elicit a positive response even before it is opened. . . . Videos are sometimes perceived as an invitation to something special, because consumers know that businesses aren't sending tapes out to everyone --- people actually feel special or 'singled out' when they receive a video."[35] And because DM videos are not being aired by a mass-media outlet, they are particularly appropriate for promoting controversial products, services, or issues. As political consultant Tom Edmonds points out, "Videos eliminate [audience] waste, allow for personalized, targeted messages --- and keep the media from critiquing the message."[36]

Unfortunately, many DM videos are hobbled by faulty 'bookend' structure. Typically, this involves a company executive introducing the piece who often reappears at the end. As producer Barry Hampe maintains, "Having the CEO tell about the video before it's shown can make the video itself an anticlimax. The CEO's comments almost never make the program more interesting. . . . A bookend structure means the video has two openings and two closings—and that's one too many of each."[37] As discreetly as possible, the writer needs to fashion and champion a script in which the product or service tells its own story from fade-in to fade-out. Similarly, despite the fact that it costs almost nothing additional to send out or stream a twelve-minute video instead of a ten-minute one, don't stretch the ending just because you have the disk or server space to do so. Whether it's a movie or a DM video, viewers respond best to tight stories with strong climaxes.

Cable Vehicles

Eager to increase their share of local advertising dollars, cable systems have recruited two tools to make it easier for these smaller clients to employ cable spots. The first of these tools is called *photo-advertising*. Photo-advertising uses spots created from a series of still pics accompanied by copywriter-created voice-overs. These are carried on a dedicated cable channel and are particularly appropriate for clients such as auto dealers, real estate agents, and restaurants—local businesses with a number of individual and frequently changing items to promote. "Photo-advertising is one of the easiest ways to produce spots at the local level," says the Cable Advertising Bureau's president Thom McKinney. "You can put together a decent spot inexpensively, thereby competing with newspaper and local radio."[38]

But because the visuals all are static, the effectiveness of the photo-ad depends more heavily on the copy than do most conventional television spots. The voice-over narration must create a logical progression out of several separate pictures that may be changed frequently as the products being featured by the business change. So we need to create a strong and flexible narrative within which individual photos/items can easily be substituted:

Video	Audio
ESTAB SHOT EXTERIOR OF AGNES'S	VO: In 1978, Agnes McDonald decided to open a restaurant called Agnes's Wonderland Diner.
MS AGNES STANDING AT CASH REGISTER	Her aim was to serve everyday working people a satisfying meal at a reasonable price.
CU OMLET WITH HASHBROWNS, BACON, AND CINNAMON TOAST	Breakfast starts at 6 A.M. and supplies everything you need to give you strength for the working day ahead.
CU BOWL OF CHILI AND GIANT SLICE OF LEMON MERINGUE PIE	Lunches break up your labor with homemade specials, soups, chili, and Agnes's own fresh pies.
MCU MALE CUSTOMER AT SALAD BAR	And every Friday evening, you can reward yourself for a hard week's work with Agnes's fish fry and accompanying salad bar.
M3S AGNES SERVING TWO MEN IN WORK OVERALLS	Agnes's Wonderland Diner. Friendly staff, good cooks, and fast service to keep you on schedule.
MS EXTERIOR SIGN SUPER: Mission and Bennett	Agnes's Wonderland Diner. Mission and Bennett in Mount Pleasant. We work hard to serve you, because you work hard for a living.

Each copy module in this photo-ad ties into the "food for working people" theme. Every visual is a simple still pic. And segments 3, 4, and 5 can easily be replaced with other entrees or specials that the client might wish to emphasize from time to time.

The second cable tool, *digital insertion*, now makes it even easier for clients to change their cable spots. Digital ad insertion systems encode commercials as computer files that can be sent to any individual cable system tied into the regional network. This procedure allows for specialized tags and copy that can be adapted electronically to each individual system's consumer base. You could use a standard ad bed for a car dealer client, for instance, and digitally select different modules to promote luxury cars in upper-class areas and economy autos on systems serving lower-income residents.

This same technology can also be exploited by larger advertisers to direct different Web ads to different zip codes and even individual households depending on how marketing databases categorize these destinations.

Digital insertion thus makes it possible to meet the needs of retailers who heretofore have had to depend on print or radio. "In the past, if grocers had too many bananas, they depended on newspapers because of the quick turnaround," points out digital equipment executive John Coulbourn. "Now grocers can use cable to advertise a sale in markets where customers live."[39] Digital insertion makes the same two basic demands on the copywriter as does the photo-ad. You must create (1) solid, single-concept spots that (2) can easily be modified via a library of several interchangeable modules to which you are constantly adding.

Place-Based Media

The industry defines a place-based medium as "one where the demographics of the reader, viewer or listener are controlled by the location in which the message is delivered."[40] The in-school *Channel One* is among the oldest and most well-known of such operations, but there are now many others in stores, gas stations, restaurants, doctors' offices, elevators, ATM machines, cabs, airports, and airplanes. Placed-based media now even extend beyond the grave. Forever Enterprises, a St. Louis-based cemetery conglomerate, has installed video kiosks in which 'videographies' of the deceased in nearby plots can be accessed. Prices range from $295 for a simple six-minute video scrapbook to $7,500 for a full hour tribute.[41]

While this may not be the case for the graveyard kiosks, the key advantage to most place-based enterprises is that they can touch highly desirable consumer target groups who are not easily reachable via conventional television. Tweens (eleven- to fifteen-year-olds) are infrequent and fickle watchers of "regular TV." But they were captive audiences for the school-based *Channel One* and are readily available viewers at amusement parks, video game parlors, and fast-food palaces. Similarly, upscale viewers, who rarely tune to traditional network programming, are sitting (or standing) targets in high-rise elevators, doctors' offices, taxis, and airplanes.

In fact, several major advertisers make a concerted effort to reach business prospects via the highly targeted avenue of airline programming. Airlines sell in-flight commercials as wrap-around material to the movies and news shows featured on longer flights. Initially these *sky spots* were used mainly by travel-related companies such as hotels, luggage manufacturers, and car-rental firms. Later, computer companies, credit card services, and auto makers joined the mix. From a copywriting standpoint, in-flight messages tend to be shorter, more sophisticated, and less reliant on voice-overs than are their grounded counterparts. "I don't think you are going to sell them [business travelers] with someone barking at them like in a carnival," asserts airline in-flight entertainment manager Judy Oldham. "This kind of person doesn't want to be hammered at that way."[42] And when the visual rather than the voice-over carries the essential information, even those passengers who don't rent headsets are likely to be exposed to the essence of your pitch.

Retail stores began to make significant use of place-based video in 1990, when Sears placed monitors in the activewear, seasonal, and young men's fashion departments of more than 500 of its outlets. By 2006, Premier Retail Networks (PRN), the largest retail media network in the United States, was operating a network that included more than 6,000 retail locations, encompassing chains such as Wal-Mart, Best Buy, Sears, K-Mart, Circuit City, and Foot Action and reaching 225 million viewers a month.[43] Such enterprises offer tremendous opportunities in merchandising control. For example, explains trade reporter Claudia Kienzle, "If the merchandising manager at a retail chain's corporate office sees that there's too much inventory in the Northwest region, a promotion to move that inventory can quickly be created and delivered to the relevant stores from the corporate office. Also, if a blizzard hits one particular market, corporate managers can capitalize on the opportunity by sending those stores commercial programming that promotes snow-related merchandise, like shovels, rock salt, and sleds."[44]

Through application of Internet Protocol Television (IPTV), some chains like Wal-Mart are customizing further by airing videos tailored to individual aisles—so that products are being promoted near the shelves on which they are stocked. All of this activity provides copywriters with a wealth of new assignments. However, many of these venues do not conform to the conventional thirty- and sixty-second formats common to television. Instead, our place-based creations are often shorter than typical video spots and may require multiple and interchangeable executions. These videos might all be for the same product line, or (as in the aisle-specific project just mentioned) they may put the focus on store image while promoting various products that the store sells. Sometimes a place-based spot does both. Recently, Unilever ran a message for Dove body cleanser only in Wal-Mart stores that extended its "real beauty" campaign by featuring an elderly Wal-Mart employee talking about how pretty the product made her feel, wrinkles and all.[45]

The fundamental tenets of effective television writing still apply in place-based executions. But the distractions and viewer mobility in many of these venues require that we pare down our concepts even more to their most graphic and unmistakable essence. This is certainly true in the commercials featured on Gas Station TV, which utilizes video monitors built into gas pumps (see Figure 12.5) that deliver snippets of broadcast and cable network programming interspersed with ten- or fifteen-second commercials like the one below:

Video	Audio
BEGIN ROTATION OF HIGH-ANGLE MCU OF TOP OF ICED COFFEE GLASS. 'Iced-Coffee' BANNER TO LEFT	VO: Thirsty? Come in now for an
ADD 'Thirsty?' BANNER TO RIGHT	Island Coffee Chiller. An iced drink that keeps you going.

(Courtesy of Mike Feltz, Gas Station TV)

"We create a very specific one-on-one relationship with the consumer, who's tied to a company's ad with an eight-foot rubber hose," states Gas Station TV CEO David Leider.[46] Similarly captive audiences are now also being targeted by place-based

FIGURE 12.5 *(Courtesy of Mike Feltz, Gas Station TV)*

installations in taxis, and elevators—and with comparable mixes of brief informational content and short spots like the GSTV treatment above. "Our competition isn't that tough," asserts Mike DiFranza, president of the elevator-specializing Captivate Network. Viewers "are in a metal box with five other people. Their options are to look at the backs of the heads of the people in front of them, look at the numbers of floors on the display or look at Captivate's screen."[47]

Nevertheless, such captive situations do not excuse sloppy, boring, or insensitive spots. If anything, we must be even more respectful of our viewers because they know there is no escape from our message and therefore expect to be appropriately and beneficially engaged by what we have to show them.

Quips and Quiz Shows

Before concluding our discussion of Specialized Venues to which electronic media copywriters can apply their craft, let's take a moment to explore two especially offbeat opportunities.

"Quips" are one-liners that copywriters are sometimes called upon to produce for client on-air 'billboards,' Websites, digital outdoor installations, on-hold messaging, or point-of-purchase activities. Usually, the assignment to produce such copy is an 'add-on' to the work you do in more conventional media for your client. It becomes part of the overall branding of that client and the consistent brand personality you are paid to build and project. Sometimes these quips impart essential nuggets of product benefit information, as in these on-air billboard announcements for participating sponsor KFC:

KCRA 3's local coverage of the Winter Olympic Games is brought to you in part by KFC. Your dollar goes further at KFC, Chicken Capital USA.

KCRA 3's local coverage of the Winter Olympic Games is brought to you in part by KFC. Get Sunday Dinner seven days a week from KFC, Chicken Capital USA.

or in these same-sponsor billboards to accompany televised fireworks coverage:

KFC. For more than 50 years, providing the food to go with the fun and fireworks of the 4th.

KFC. Our buckets proudly wear the red, white and blue all year long.

KFC: That's some Yankee Doodle *Dandy* Chicken.

In slightly more extended form, informational quips can frame on-site activities or contests, as in the following stadium announcer copy during a National Basketball Association game. Notice that this is scripted very much like a video message, with "live action" replacing video directions in the copy's left column:

Live Action	Stadium Announcer
MASCOT THUNDER RACES THROUGH ONE OF THE TUNNELS AND ONTO THE FLOOR DURING TIME-OUT, ALONG WITH THE HOOP TROOP GIRLS, CREATING QUITE A COMMOTION SO FANS LOOK THEIR WAY	Yo! Thunder is in da house. And he's gonna give a freshly prepared
THUNDER RACES INTO STANDS TO DISTRIBUTE MEALS	8-Piece Meal from Kentucky Fried Chicken to two lucky families
HOOP TROOP SPREADS OUT, DISTRIBUTING COUPONS IN OTHER STADIUM SECTIONS	while The Hoop Troop passes out valuable KFC coupons. (Calling out) Who wants Free KFC Chicken?!

In other on-site applications, quips are designed as humorous enhancers to the venue's mood. Rather than mention the brand, they simply enhance the brand experience. The 'Cheers' airport bar/grilles feature an animatronic wall-mounted moose head which periodically voices insult lines like the following that are prepared by the chain's copywriter:

You think you're drunk --- there's a guy on the other side of this wall lookin' for the rest of me.

Hey buddy, love your aftershave! Reminds me of a cousin of mine.

You think you've got hang-ups? At least you're never mistaken for a hat rack.

(All of the above quips courtesy of Jerry Downey, Alan Frank & Associates)

Because the client is paying us to create involving and entertaining commercials, it is expected we have the expertise to handle 'quip' and similar off-beat scripting duties as well. Quips force us to be even more concise and focused than we are in our broadcast copy. While it can sometimes be aggravating to accrue these additional duties, they do provide us with the chance to stretch our skill-set.

A still more unconventional test of our talent is the writing of quiz show questions. This opportunity has increased even below the national level as some local stations try to bolster their community involvement through production of knowledge contests between area schools. Like any copywriting assignment, we can be content to pen prosaic (even trite) contributions --- or we can dig a bit deeper for a more innovative response. Ryan Hopak, writer for such shows as *Hollywood Squares* and *Win Ben Stein's Money*, offers these guidelines:

A dry question would read:

What World War II general famously said "I shall return"?

- a. General Douglas MacArthur
- b. General Dwight D. Eisenhower
- c. General George Patton

That type of writing is fine for a history test, but a little wordplay and some new information can yield a much more entertaining piece of material:

"I shall return" is not the motto of December 26th shoppers. It's the statement that what general made upon leaving the Philippines during World War II?

Let's say the game show gives clues to decipher words. Compare these clues for Tiger Woods. The second clue is clever, entertaining and more challenging to the viewer.

Famous golfer	TIRGE SWOOD
Successful club owner	TIRGE SWOOD

Even category titles can become more witty with a little forethought.

Instead of 'Science': YOU CAN CONTACT THE AMOEBA ON HIS CELL PHONE

Rather than 'Geometry': TO PICK UP THAT HOT MATHEMATICIAN, YOU'LL NEED THE RIGHT ANGLE.

(Above commentary written by, and courtesy of, Ryan Hopak)

ONLINE AND MOBILE APPLICATIONS

As our extended discussion of Specialized Venues just illustrated, versatility is a valuable trait for the video copywriter to possess. And this versatility is certainly in demand when it comes to writing continuity for the online world of the Internet and the even newer mobile phone medium.

Online

To a significant degree, the online/broadband world is the diametric opposite of the world of place-based media. Place-based media exploit a captive environment in which the viewer has a 'non-choice' of only one message delivered in one predetermined form. Online media simultaneously offer the viewer uncountable subject choices as well as several interactive ways to examine many of them.

The scripting rules for this mushrooming environment are slow to evolve because this hybrid medium itself is anything but stabilized. At this point, online copywriting is a mutating blend of creating for print and creating for broadcast. It is electronically delivered, like radio and television, but many of its verbal patterns are conveyed in the print-like world of consumer-read sentences, blurbs, and paragraphs. Some online copy is cast in concise spoken snippets to accompany still and moving graphics --- similar to a television spot. But other broadband-delivered copy is considerably more extensive --- particularly in destinations to which the consumer has opted to click.

If there is one general tenet of online copywriting that emerges from all of these contradictions, it is that the writer needs to be prepared to craft messages that can be consumed in consecutive stages and that lead in different directions. Unlike the one-way broadcast situation, the *interactivity* of the online world gives people the power to digest your communication in a variety of ways. "This is not about TV," advertising analyst Jim Nail reminds us. "This is a consumer-controlled medium."[48] For the viewer, adds agency founder Jeff Goodby, there is "no reason to actively seek out a message that isn't entertaining or informative. Those who rely on appealing to the lowest common denominator will be outta here."[49]

Securing favorable attention is only the beginning of the task. When the attractiveness of your initial banner or page motivates the consumer to click and move further into product description, you will need to have written a variety of messages that enable prospects to view various parts of your product line, often from different psychographically defined perspectives. Every broadband ad project, in short, can become the equivalent of a multi-flight broadcast campaign consisting of dozens of 'spots.'

Despite this great interactive potential, online media are not replacing conventional television any more than conventional television has been able to retard online's expansion. Instead, these and other delivery systems can all be teamed because each has different capabilities from which our clients can choose. "Now, TV spots are not just TV spots," says Deutsch/LA's Director of Integrated Production Tom Dunlap. "The films we shoot, or rather 'assets' as they are now commonly referred to, are leveraged across many uses."[50]

Thus there is a significant degree of similarity between writing for online and writing for broadcast. In their conceptual stage, many broadband messages continue to utilize conventional audio and video script formats --- both because media professionals are comfortable working in these familiar patterns and because this makes it easier to shape and adapt our messages for cross-media exploitation. Therefore, the scripting vehicles we have discussed in previous chapters are often adaptable to Web work as well. People do not consume online content as print --- even though it appears print-based. Instead, they see it as an electronic experience to be easily sampled rather than comprehensively read. The reason that some 'print-trained' wordsmiths fail in the online world is that they conceive of the broadband display as a newspaper or brochure layout. Experienced electronic media copywriters, on the other hand, understand that screen-based messaging for the Web requires the same conciseness, clarity, and conversational quality they are used to bringing to their broadcast treatments.

Still, there are some specific online techniques to which we must be sensitive and which can even help us become better broadcast copywriters because they reinforce what constitutes any effective electronic message.

First and foremost, Marketing Evolution's CEO Mark Briggs emphasizes, "Use a simple, iconic message and make sure the image and copy work together."[51] The computer screen's size militates against excessive pictorial detail and background busyness, while dimly lit scenes, as dramatic as they might be on television, cause only dislikable squinting. "Divide graphics by four," advises MSNBC's Michael Silberman. "Take whatever you learned about presenting information on a TV screen and cut it to one fourth of that."[52] Similarly, although broadband speeds have vastly increased, rapid movements can still appear jumpy or disjointed in the online environment. And like excessive motion, dissolves degrade image quality because of all the pixels they are processing at one time. Use straight cuts instead.

Michelle Eule of Dynamic Logic advocates sticking to a limited amount of text and enticing product shots because Web ads "are competing with a lot of other elements."[53] Notice how the Figure 12.6 online storyboard conforms to these visual tenets. The objective of these particular banners is to draw the eye, generate awareness, and shift brand opinion while driving incremental traffic to Saturn.com via the "learn more" button in the lower right hand corner of the frame—the eyescan's ultimate destination.

Eyescan is important in planning your copy elements as well. Web viewers are more likely than print readers to scan for keywords --- a tendency that the Search industry has served to encourage. Therefore, eye-grabbing phrases like the ones in the Saturn message are of critical importance, as are easy-to-digest short sentences. People read from a computer screen about 25 percent more slowly than they do from a page of hard copy, so don't make intake of your message too time-consuming. All our previously discussed techniques for copy condensation and dynamism that are so important in the construction of broadcast spots come fully into play in writing for the Web. Again, this is what makes it easier for broadcast than print copywriters to jump to the online world.

The Web's interactivity results in a very personal environment in which the use of pronouns like "you" and "we" is a key to encouraging this two-way communication. These pronouns help establish a bond with the consumer that retains their

FIGURE 12.6 *(Courtesy of Tom Else, Deutsch/LA)*

FIGURE 12.7 The Sympathetic Tow Truck.

attention and encourages them to click your links for more. This bond can easily be broken, however, if you resort to cumbersome headlines and extraneous sub-heads that remind the viewer of the lock-step print experience. Certainly, headlines can be helpful to divide thought units into digestible sizes. Go ahead and replace introductory sentences with headlines. But then see if you can eliminate some of these headlines altogether --- particularly in messages using spoken copy. You just may discover your copy is more involving and palatable as a result.

Here is a 'Web spot' for an auto club, including the art director's conceptual sketch of what the 'star' of the commercial would look like (Figure 12.7). In reading the script, notice that the ad's main point comes through clearly and visually --- even when casually scanned. As is frequently the case in broadband commercials, this script is cast in a slightly modified version of the "Hollywood single-column format" that we discussed back in Chapter 10.

MID-STATE AUTO CLUB --- "Sympathetic Towtruck"

Production Note: All pics feature simple but bright-colored animations of vehicles set against sparse outdoor backgrounds.

FADE IN:

EXT. NONDESCRIPT COUNTRY ROADSIDE

¾ view front of little coupe by side of the road with hood up. We can see by coupe's expression ('sad' headlights, bumper curved down) that it is distressed.

ANNCR (VO)

Sometimes, your car can get in a funk. And for no apparent reason.

SUPER: GIANT QUESTION MARK OVER SCENE

CUT TO EMPTY PARKING LOT

Side view of minivan with obviously flat rear tire causing entire rear to sag badly. Front of van is twisted around to look in dismay at the flat.

ANNCR (VO)

Other times, we know why your vehicle's feeling down. But that doesn't make things any less upsetting.

SUPER: !!#&//##!! (TO SUGGEST EXTREME IRRITATION)

CUT TO

FRONT OF MID-STATE GARAGE

Door raises with a powerful, reassuring hum to reveal front of towtruck whose grille is smiling confidently.

ANNCR (VO)

Mid-State Auto Club understands. Our three-hundred-and-eighty Sympathetic Towtrucks are ready anytime you need them.

Trucks roar out of garage, one after another, driving off in all directions.

SUPER: 380 SYMPATHETIC TOWTRUCKS

CUT TO ORIGINAL ROADSIDE SCENE

Truck races up to coupe which is still looking sad. Truck peers under the hood.

ANNCR (VO)

Mid-State's sympathetic tow trucks listen to how it happened. And can tell you why.

Truck closes coupe's hood with its front wheel. Coupe is now smiling.

CUT TO PREVIOUS PARKING LOT SCENE

Another Mid-State truck at rear of van which it has jacked up to complete tire change.

ANNCR (VO)

Our trucks are trained to prop you back up, put things on an even keel, and help you get on with your life.

Jack now removed, smiling minivan heads off screen. Mid-State truck 'waves' good-bye with its front wheel. Truck then turns to fully face camera.

ANNCR (VO)

And that's just part of Mid-State's assistance. A sympathetic service provided to Mid-State families for only 145 dollars a year.

SUPER: $145

CUT TO NEUTRAL BG

Icons for an insurance document, a gas card, and a small sail boat perched atop trailer cumulatively pop onto the screen with "find out more" button underneath each.

ANNCR (VO)

Mid-State also offers compassionate deals on auto insurance, discount gas cards, and extended protection for your boat and trailer. You deserve more sympathy. And Mid-State is ready.

Tow truck zooms to bottom center of screen, faces camera, and smiles warmly.

ANNCR (VO)

With three-hundred-and-eighty sympathetic tow trucks—and more.

SUPER: MID-STATE AUTO CLUB

Viewer accessibility is the key to successful online messaging, and this includes the 'typography' of the screen. Make certain that your art director uses a 12-point or larger font size and restricts her/himself to san-serif fonts unless the chosen size is considerably larger than 12. Text color should be as readable as possible against the selected background, with darker backgrounds and lighter text hues normally pre-ferred --- although without such extreme contrast that the words irritatingly glow. For your part, keep your writing as digestible as possible. If significant on-screen copy is necessary, try to use bullet points that are both easily scannable and lure con-sumers to proceed from one point to the next.

Even though online writing requires certain specialized considerations, do not assume that it is completely distinct from other forms of video creation. As producer Stan Ferguson told a meeting of broadcast educators, "Fundamental principles of writ-ing and storytelling do not change in the new media. If it does not work well off the Internet, it won't work well on."[54] In focusing on what they now call "screen-based delivery systems" (television, computer, and cell phone), today's communication exec-utives are amalgamating all video vehicles into mutually supportive marketing arse-nals. As copywriters, we need to know which video weapons to select, and how best to use them on any mission to which we're assigned.

We do not here have time to examine the broader issue of complete Website design—any more than it was our objective in earlier portions of this book to dis-cuss the building of radio formats and writing of entire video programs. However, because Website ownership is possible for even the smallest of clients, copywriters are sometimes called upon to service site development. Therefore, here are four guiding principles to assist in that task:

1. Focus the site on the consumer, not the company. Too many Web presences are set up as monuments to corporate pride. They demonstrate that the company is contemporary enough to be on the 'Net—but they show little regard for what the consumer might be seeking by visiting the site.
2. Make the site fun to visit. Despite some obvious similarities, Web sites are not newspaper or magazine layouts. Many people click on and click in, looking for enjoyment and to fuel their imagination. Online material that takes itself too seriously clashes with the freewheeling nature of this medium.
3. Convert browsers to users. When consumers reach your home page, you have their active attention. Write copy that makes them glad they have found you --- and entices them to explore your site more fully. In the online world, no one will linger in environments to which he or she is indifferent.
4. Make client contact easy. A core advantage of the online medium is its ability to immediately link company and consumer. If your copy seems to discourage such contact—or makes it too stiff and convoluted—people won't participate. Clients will miss out on valuable audience feedback and the chance to forge advantageous acquaintanceships with the public. And prospects will stop visiting the site.

Mobile Phone

Everything we have said about clarity, simplicity, and condensation in online scripting applies even more to writing of messages for viewing on a cell phone. But despite the smaller screen, "When it comes to mobile creative work, we need to apply the same litmus test that we have for the Web," argues Richard Ting, new media creative director for agency R/GA. "Is there compelling narrative? Is the campaign designed well? Does it provide real utility for the user? All these questions must be answered before a mobile marketing campaign can be executed."[55] Above all, we must keep in mind, writes branding consultant Allen Adamson, that "Unlike TV's and PC's, which may be shared with other family members, a cell phone is personal space. As such, tolerance of unwanted content is nil . . . Brands that are invited in will provide consumers with what they want, not interrupt them with content they don't want."[56]

Once we have isolated what the consumer would want from our message, successful creators for 'mobile' suggest taking no more than 25 percent of what would be conveyed in a Web ad and then adapting it for this personal medium. For example, here is a mobile message that could be harvested from the Mid-State Auto Club online message presented earlier:

FADE IN:

¾ view of animated coupe against neutral background with hood up and dismayed expression shown via 'sad' headlights and curved-down front bumper

DIZ TO GRAPHIC: NEED ROAD SERVICE SYMPATHY?

DIZ TO FRONT VIEW ANIMATED TOW TRUCK

Truck's friendly headlights and grill smile warmly.

ANNCR (VO)

Mid-State Auto Club's three-hundred-and-eighty sympathetic tow trucks can help.

ADD SUPER BELOW: 380 SYMPATHETIC TOW TRUCKS

DIZ BACK TO COUPE

Smiling coupe with hood now down faces camera; tow truck beside it also faces camera with satisfied expression.

ANNCR (VO)

Road service compassion for you and your car. Call 1-800-555-2600

DIZ TO GRAPHIC: MID-STATE AUTO CLUB, 1-800-555-2600

REPLACE MID-STATE AUTO CLUB PHRASE WITH: 380 SYMPATHETIC TOW TRUCKS;

Retain supered phone number

In composing a message for mobile phone distribution, here are several specific principles to keep in mind.

1. Use as few people/characters as possible. If you only use one, it can be advantageous to position that character off to the side so that key background or supered titles can easily share the screen.
2. Close up shots are essential for clarity. Wide shots lose focus and make your character(s) hard to distinguish.
3. Make background as simple as possible while still setting the essential scene.
4. Character/graphic movement is difficult to watch on the small screen. Keep it to a minimum and avoid rapid movement at all costs. Most mobile phones can display video at only fifteen frames per second, while broadcast television transmits twice this number. You don't want smearing of your picture.
5. Similarly, quick cuts are disorienting, so rely on more gradual transitions unless the new visual is very simple (such as a short text slogan) and you really want it punched in.
6. Keep any required visual text extremely short. Use the audio to repeat and, if necessary, add explanation. It takes viewers 50 percent longer to read text on a phone screen compared with a television screen.
7. Use soft, non-fluorescent lighting and sharp contrast between the background and the character(s).
8. Because of its small size, the phone's speaker will distort bass-heavy audio. Plan your audio mix accordingly and avoid talent with "down in the mud" voices. Talent must also have especially clear diction for the mobile medium and know how to emphasize words. Radio announcers tend to be your most appropriate hires.
9. Rely on primary colors for your graphics (blue rather than aqua, red instead of pink). This permits viewing of the picture in a variety of illumination settings in which the phone's users may find themselves.

10. Sixty seconds is the maximum length that we can expect viewer attention—and this may be too long in distracting settings. Fifteen seconds is usually much more preferable.

Cell phone copywriting may be the most challenging assignment of all. But that is the price we pay for acquiring the chance to move so closely into our target consumer's personal space.

THE JOY OF VISUAL SELLING

In the last three chapters, we have dissected a number of video formats and tasks. The technology available is often mind boggling, and the marketing job it must accomplish can be equally formidable. But despite the mass of pictorial options and client demands, you need to keep in mind that the resulting video should be *fun*—for copywriter and consumer alike.

As Donald Gunn, worldwide director of creative resources for Leo Burnett, reminds us about the television spot,

> A lot of people believe they need to put all the sales points they can muster into a 30-second commercial. They think anything that smacks of fun or is not related directly to the process of selling --- those seconds are wasted. And that's a shame, because what seems to work is to be able to come up with the one single, right thing to say --- and then to say it with charm and intelligence and reward people for the time they spend with your message.[57]

Even though newer delivery systems have emerged, many would argue that all of these options are still grounded in the principles of effective television commercial creation. "The television commercial is alive and well," argues Jamie Barrett, creative director at Goody/Silverstein & Partners. "It's hanging out on the Internet. It's tunneling its way into your inbox. It's filling the big screen at your local theater. It's in your left front pocket on your fancy new cell phone. The TV commercial is nothing more than words and pictures. It's sight and sound and motion. It's ideas. And ideas will never die."[58]

13

Public Service Assignments

S everal examples of successful public service announcements (PSAs) in previous chapters illustrate various copy-creation principles. As these spots amply demonstrate, public service messages need not be any less skillful or appealing than their commercial counterparts. Yet too many writers approach the PSA assignment with self-imposed blinders. Because the client is a church, a charity, or a governmental institution, these scribes construct dignified, straitlaced, and totally boring messages that are too bland to enlist anyone's interest or attention.

"It's easy to tug on the heartstrings," asserts Jeff Goodby of the Goodby, Silverstein agency. "But most public service stuff is terrible, and you just can't go with what's expected. Besides, having good stuff isn't enough. You're dealing with huge bureaucracies, and people continually want you to soften the message. Maybe if they weren't so afraid, they'd save more people."[1] "The agencies that are really good at PSAs use the same discipline towards it as they do their day-to-day clients," adds McCann-Erickson's chief creative officer Nina DiSesa. "The biggest mistake they can make is not doing it that same way. You can't throw logic to the wind just because you are doing a PSA. You still have to use your God-given talent and the skills you've learned growing up in the business."[2]

If anything, PSAs must be even more creative, more vibrant than commercial copy because:

1. the "product" is often an intangible (safety, love, patriotism), which must be made concrete for the audience;
2. this "product" often asks more of the audience (give, join, call) with a less immediate or less specific benefit to be gained in return;
3. because they receive no money for airing them, outlets are free to select for airing whichever PSAs they wish.

The importance of this last point cannot be overstressed. As long as a *commercial* is not libelous, obscene, or in violation of continuity acceptance policies, we know it will be transmitted because the outlet is being paid to do just that. Thereafter, it is a matter of

405

whether the advertisement is appealing enough for consumers to give it heed. In the case of public service announcements, however, we cannot even take airing for granted. Instead, the PSAs we write must contend with those prepared by scores of other copywriters and organizations equally dependent on making a favorable impression on outlet personnel before they will even have the opportunity to make a favorable impression on that outlet's audience. "Many PSA directors are finding it increasingly tough to choose among the many well-intentioned public-service campaigns," reports *Adweek's* Joe Mandese. "And for every national campaign vying for time and space, 'you have to figure that there are tens of thousands of little local groups out there doing something,' [the Advertising Council's Eleanor] Hangley says."[3]

The Ad Council itself, which annually coordinates approximately fifty national nonprofit campaigns through volunteer advertising agencies, is inundated with 300 to 400 requests for assistance each year. In light of this "good cause glut," and the formidable resources that the Ad Council is putting behind the campaigns it is able to handle, don't expect that a dull or format-incompatible PSA you produce will have much of a chance of being aired. Therefore, all the copy techniques and appeals we've previously mentioned should be considered and, as appropriate, exploited when it comes to fashioning a PSA campaign. Local, regional, or national, your announcement must be distinctive enough to successfully compete for airtime exposure with those hundreds of other worthy causes.

THE PSA DEFINED

Before going further, let's review just what a PSA *is*. According to Ruth Wooden, former president of the Advertising Council, there are three different types of messages that try to fit the public service announcement label:

1. Messages created for nonprofit organizations to educate audiences about important social issues
2. Network promos that feature their own program stars discussing such issues. Sometimes, these spots have no tie to a nonprofit entity and may even be sponsored by a corporation.
3. 'Cause-related marketing' in which corporations actually purchase the time for the spot, such as a beer company's advocacy of responsible drinking (review Figure 12.3 in the previous chapter) or a cereal brand's focus on nutrition tips.

While she applauds all three categories, Wooden (and most other public service advocates) believe that only the first properly fits the networks' traditional definition of a PSA as a spot that is "non-sectarian, noncommercial and non-partisan."[4] The other two categories have, at least in part, a commercial purpose. They attempt to build up a network's or profit-making sponsor's image by associating these corporations with a good cause. Cause marketing may actually be narrowing corporate support for authentic PSAs, because, as advertising reporter Paul Bloom observes, "companies are thinking strategically, looking for consistency between their corporate missions and their donations."[5] Consequently, they are abandoning general PSAs for advocacy messages directly related to their business interests.

We therefore devote this chapter exclusively to the fashioning of traditionally defined PSAs (category one). No matter how noble, at their core, categories two and three are just further extensions of the promos and commercials on which we have focused in our earlier discussions.

True PSAs can come from copywriters working in a variety of venues. The large advertising agencies that volunteer their services to the Ad Council are the most obvious but hardly the only contributors. Local "ad clubs" create PSAs too. Nonprofits themselves often self-generate messages using in-house or outside writers and place these spots on their Websites in addition to sending them to stations and cable systems. For their part, broadcasters produce and air their own local PSAs because such messages have special relevance to their communities --- a quality that the nationally focused Ad Council campaigns cannot be expected to fully reflect.

By fashioning messages tied to the specific issues and problems of its region, a station enhances its public service image. Just as important, local PSAs more unequivocally demonstrate to the Federal Communications Commission that the outlet has ascertained --- and is doing its part to address --- local community needs. As a recent study of station public affairs directors conducted by Professor Ronald Bishop found: "The chances that a PSA will run are drastically improved if the cause is local. . . . Local groups are more important, one respondent said, because they're the ones 'more likely to have something that relates to our listeners.' "[6] Similarly, among stations responding to a 2006 Advertising Council Media Panel survey, the results of which were widely circulated, 56 percent of the PSAs they ran were local and only 44 percent were national.

THE THREE HALLMARKS OF SUCCESSFUL PSAs

In whatever venue you write them, you should evaluate your messages via these three key questions:

1. Do the PSAs break the intangibility barrier?
2. Do the PSAs appeal to *enlightened self-interest?*
3. Do the PSAs make an outlet want to air them?

Breaking the intangibility barrier means coming up with a pictorial concept that encapsulates the essence of your message in a manner that can easily be visualized. Many people have difficulty dealing with subjects that lack a concrete dimension. By providing them with an easily comprehendible symbol for what we are talking about, we make our PSA much more accessible. This, after all, is why Jesus used parables. By building his lessons around mustard seeds, stray sheep, and lost coins, he was able to communicate complex philosophical principles to a largely uneducated populace. Even for modern and well-schooled media audiences, a central, concrete referent (like the following spot's rope analogy) helps the PSA 'lesson' break through to memorability.

> Production Note: DRAMATIC STRING MUSIC throughout, but dropped out during all male announcer lines.

(MUSIC: FEATURE AND UNDER)

WOMAN: Imagine it's night, you're standing at the edge of an ice-covered lake --- alone.

(SFX: FAINT CRY FOR HELP, OBSCURED BY MUSIC)

WOMAN:	You see a man --- he's fallen through --- and he desperately needs your help.
MAN:	Right now, there are well over a hundred thousand people waiting for organ and tissue transplants. Thousands of them will die needlessly --- still waiting --- because there aren't enough donors.
WOMAN:	The ice is too thin, so you quickly grab a rope. You throw the rope with all your might to the drowning man. You desperately want to save him.
MAN:	You want to save lives. You've decided to be a donor, maybe you've even signed something. But there's something else you must do. You must tell your family now, so they can carry out your decision later.
WOMAN:	Suddenly, to your horror, the rope snaps taut. Just out of reach of the drowning man's hand.
MAN:	Because if you don't tell someone, it's like throwing a 12-foot rope --- to someone who's 15 feet away. Organ and tissue donation. Share your life. Share your decision. To learn more about organ and tissue donation, call 1-800-355-SHARE. That's 1-800-355-SHARE. This message brought to you by the Coalition on Donation and the Ad Council.

(Courtesy of Sarah Humm, The Advertising Council)

Appealing to 'enlightened self-interest' is a two-part process. As they move through life, most people like to think of themselves as reasonably "good"—as doing the right thing when confronted by choices and temptations. That is the 'enlightened' part of human nature. At the same time, however, it is also human nature, when faced with a task or an option, to ask 'What's in it for me?' That is the less noble but no less common component of the human equation. "After all," writes psychology professor David Barash, "*Homo sapiens* includes not only its nasty 'animal' aspects of violence and selfishness, but also those positive, equally animal components of benevolence and even self-sacrifice."[7] By appealing to enlightened self-interest, therefore, we try to cast our spot in such a way that both laudable virtue and audience benefit flow from the action or belief that our PSA is advocating. Try never to make a "we need your help" appeal without also demonstrating what the listener or viewer will obtain by providing that assistance. Thus this multivoice PSA showcases the "right" thing to do by testifying that such enlightened action is simultaneously good for business:

	Production Note: Owner is casual, voice is matter-of-fact, without emotion.
OWNER:	I'll be honest with ya. At first, I wasn't really enthused with the idea of hiring a disabled person.
VOICE:	Mid-Michigan Industries is a private, non-profit corporation for training handicapped adults.
OWNER:	I guess I didn't think they could handle the work.
VOICE:	An M-M-I job coach helps the client to completely master the job.
OWNER:	I mean, I'm a businessman. I didn't want to jeopardize my place. And I also didn't want to put someone in over their head.

VOICE:	Clients are entered into the job placement program only when their skills completely meet job needs.
OWNER:	But ya know? Everything turned out great. Ted's one of my best workers. And he gets along really well with everybody.
VOICE:	If you want trained workers for your business, call Mid-Michigan Industries at 773-6918. That's Mid-Michigan Industries. 773-6918.
OWNER:	Looking back at it, I'm glad I called Mid-Michigan Industries. Come to think of it, so is Ted.

(Courtesy of John Schroeder and Mid-Michigan Industries, Inc.)

Making an outlet want to air your PSA involves careful handling of two elements: content and form. The content of the message must be entertaining and compelling enough that it will keep the audience tuned and attentive to the channel presenting it. The nonprofit organization wants people to perceive its spot actively, and the station wants its audience to stay rather than leave. Therefore, both the organization and the outlet depend on the copywriter to make the PSA an interesting "tune-in" rather than a boring or repulsive "tune-out" program segment. The following spot, for instance, uses an involving "quiz show" format to engage the listener, plus a humorous style that proves its point without preaching.

(SFX: HIGH SCHOOL HALLWAY SOUNDS)	
ANNCR:	The question is: Who is Rodolph Nureyev?
KIDS:	(Various hemming and hawings)
BOY 1:	Rudoph Nureyev --- okay, I know this one --- wasn't he the dude --- wasn't he the dude --- Nureyev --- wasn't he a defenseman for the Red Wings?
ANNCR:	You sure about that?
BOY:	It could have been the Maple Leafs.
ANNCR:	Can you tell me who Louie Armstrong was?
BOY 2:	Easy! He was the first guy on the moon. You know, 'One small step for man---'
ANNCR:	You there. Does the name 'Caravaggio' mean anything to you?
GIRL:	Wasn't he the guy that went out with Tony Soprano's sister until he got whacked?
ANNCR:	No.
ANNCR 2:	Are your kids as well-rounded as they could be? Kids who participate in the arts do better in school and in life. To learn more about the value of arts education, visit Americans For The Arts dot org. Because all kids should get to appreciate Nureyev's dancing, Armstrong's horn and Caravaggio's brush. Art. Ask for more. A public service message brought to you by Americans for the Arts.

(Courtesy of Nicole Sparks, Americans for the Arts)

BUILDING ON AUDIENCE WANTS

A public service announcement is actually selling virtue. But no spot can hope to promote a particular virtue if that virtue is incompatible with the audience's pre-existing beliefs and needs. So the PSA must (1) affiliate itself with what the consumer already feels; (2) demonstrate how *the action* it advocates will respect that feeling; and (3) help satisfy the feeling's associated needs. In her extensive review of PSA research, Professor Virginia Roark isolated two fundamental ways in which public service advertising can build on previously present audience wants:

1. Make the promoted action as easy to perform as possible and as relevant as possible to the audience's environment.
2. Through transformational advertising, tap into the emotional responses of the target audience.[8]

In the radon detection message that follows, taking action is no more complicated than calling an 800 number or picking up a test kit. Just as important, the PSA demonstrates that this action will help adult children in the worrisome task of protecting their parents --- while sympathetically recognizing the sometimes maddening behavior that these parents can exhibit.

VO: So last week, I'm over at my parents' house, the shrine to cleanliness, the ICU ward gone condo. There by the plastic covered sofa, I say, 'Ma, dad, have you had the house tested for radon?' I heard that you can't see or smell radon gas, but lots of homes have it and it can cause lung cancer, so I figured they should get a test, right? Well, Mom starts crying about how she works her fingers to the bone cleaning this house and if there's radon, it's all your father's fault and I'm trying to explain that it isn't anybody's fault, it's just that certain homes have radon regardless of how new, old or well kept they are. Geez, you'd think she said I found a roach or something.

ANNCR: It doesn't matter how or where you live, radon could be living with you. For more information, call 1-800-RADON GAS.

VO: So anyway, I said I would pick them up a radon test kit on the way home. Mom said I was a good son, and liked how clean I was keeping my nails.

ANNCR: Learn more about how easy it is to test for radon at 1-800-RADON GAS. A message from the Michigan Department of Public Health.

(Courtesy of Marcie Brogan, Brogan & Partners)

Transformational advertising, to which Roark referred in her second point, is defined by Edell and Burke as communication that "connects the experience of the advertisement so tightly with the experience of using the brand that consumers cannot remember the brand without recalling the experience generated by the advertisement."[9] In the case of PSAs, this means projecting a situation that cannot be recollected without also calling to mind the action or belief we are advocating. Thus the locally customizable Ad Council spot below establishes a clean water concern that might be triggered each time the listener fills the bathtub.

ANNCR: Imagine you're drawing a bath. But before getting in, pour in motor oil and
weed killer. Sadly, that's what we're doing to (A BODY OF WATER IN YOUR
AREA, I.E. LAKE HURON). So practice natural lawn care by composting and
using fewer chemicals. And take your used motor oil to a gas station to be
recycled. Clean water. For bathing and for life. If we all do a little, we can do
a lot. To find out more, call 1-800-504-8484. That's 1-800-504-8484. Brought to
you by (YOUR STATION), the Natural Resources Defense Council, and the EPA.

(Courtesy of Sarah Humm, The Advertising Council, Inc.)

If transformational advertising strikes you as being too manipulative for PSA
(as opposed to commercial) endeavors, keep in mind that public service messages
ask more of the consumer than do commercials --- and with a much less immediate
return. Just because we are writing for a "good cause" doesn't mean we can ignore
the realities of human nature and expect that the worth of our charity will sell itself.
As James Webb Young, one of the founders of the Advertising Council, observed, "it
takes more cunning to do good than to do evil."[10]

A key reason that PSA writing requires such cunning is because it is attempting
to move audiences in the reverse mental direction of our other copy assignments. In
fact, advertising critic Debra Goldman labels the PSA process *unselling*. As she
observes, "Unselling is its own art, demanding from the consumer the opposite of
what most ads ask. Stop and think, anti-drug ads urge the audience. Don't be influenced. Don't be stupid. Exercise independent judgment. Don't give in to immediate
pleasure. Look at the big picture. In other words, they say the opposite of what all
other ads say."[11] For PSA copywriters, the trick is to somehow ultimately craft the
'unselling' negative into a positive consumer-enticing benefit.

PSA FORMAT CONVENTIONS

While the content of the PSA must be capable of striking a responsive chord in the
audience and must be appealing to the outlets we want to air it, that is not enough.
The spot must also be cast in a *format* that makes it as easy as possible for the broad-
caster/cablecaster to move it out of the mailbag and onto the air. Here are several
guidelines to secure the best possible reception for your free airtime–requesting
message. In the case of submitted radio scripts:

1. Double-space all copy on standard 8½ × 11-inch paper, leaving ample margins
   at the sides and bottom. Copy should start one third of the way down the page,
   preceded by the proper data block (discussed in the next section of this chapter).
   Remember, because PSAs are freebies, those that enter a station's copy book in
   script form will probably be read 'cold' without talent rehearsal. So give this
   talent every typographical assistance to pick it up easily.
2. For this same reason, make sure the copy is cleanly imprinted on reasonably
   heavy, noncrackly paper. A clean, well-inked impression on the page is a must.
3. Type (MORE) at the bottom of a page when another page follows and '30' or the
   symbols # # # at the end of your copy. The reader should not have to guess
   whether a second page exists. Also, never break a spoken line over a page turn.
4. If your PSA is not being provided in prerecorded form (and most radio stations
   prefer recordings to scripts they would have to produce themselves), always give

the station an ample number of script copies to meet its legal and productional requirements. The outlet will want at least one file copy of the script and one copy for each of what might be several continuity books used in its on-air studios. Anywhere from five to ten copies may be required. If your PSA is being prepared for recorded distribution, provide the production studio with several scripts so costly time is not wasted when some minor functionary demands a personal copy. And even if you are sending recordings to the stations, be certain to include at least two copies of the script for their previewing and record-keeping purposes.

The engineering and productional functions required in creating and transmitting *video* content are considerably more complex than those demanded by radio. Consequently, the personnel and equipment at the television station or cable system can seldom accommodate material that does not come ready for airing. Normally, this means that PSAs should arrive as broadcast quality (not home camcorder) video. Each disk should be accompanied by a script and a postage-paid reply/evaluation card that can be mailed back as a record of when the spot was aired or why it was rejected.

For the moment, let's assume that your copy is communicating a local message the station/system is so interested in addressing that it will accept still pics in lieu of a finished digital recording. In that case, the following procedures should be used to avoid the channel's having to go any farther out of its way to serve the needs of the community and your client organization:

1. Take the visuals that have been selected for the PSA and have them all made into disk-stored digital files. The minimal expense that disk creation entails is an investment that any PSA organization user should be prepared to absorb in order to make everyone's life easier.

2. Provide one 'picture' for approximately every six seconds of running time (two pics for a 'ten,' three for a 'fifteen,' six for a 'thirty'). This is, if not a happy medium, at least a workable one that promotes some visual interest on the one hand, but does not demand rehearsed and split-second intercutting on the other. No station has the time to produce a technical extravaganza that comes disguised as a thirty-second "freebie" kit.

3. Keep the copy "spacious"—don't pack the message so tightly that the technicians have trouble catching each pic's cue line or don't have time to check the monitor for proper word/picture matching. This means, of course, that multiple copies of your PSA script must be provided along with the preproduced audio. If it likes your message, the channel will probably transfer it to disk or place it in a server and then simply replay the recording whenever the PSA is scheduled. Thus it is especially important that your copy and script allow for a "clean" and trouble-free assembly the first time so as not to antagonize any of the technicians who may be involved in its replay.

4. Make certain that the visuals selected are intrinsically related to the central point of your PSA and are necessary to the realization of that point. Too many low-budget public-service announcements try to use pictures that are conveniently lying around rather than ones specifically appropriate to the message itself. If highly relevant and meaningful illustrations are not available, and if resources don't permit their procurement, then fashion the communication for radio, where it can have positive rather than negative impact.

If your PSA has been cast in sixty-second form, be sure to prepare and distribute a half-minute version as well. Only this shorter length has a chance to be aired during a broadcast television station's more lucrative hours, but the sixty is potentially playable at low-viewership times and in local cable inserts anytime. To provide stations with maximum flexibility, radio PSAs should be submitted in thirty- and sixty-second lengths, too. Television ten- and fifteen-second messages may also be appropriate, but many stations like to reserve such slots for paying customers exclusively.

PSA DATA BLOCKS

The other component of an outlet-friendly format is use of the proper data block to identify your creation. Figure 13.1 sets forth a standard radio PSA heading. Even though some of this information might be rearranged into other patterns, it should all be included somewhere in the block. Of course, if the PSA source generates a good deal of radio copy, much of these data will be cast as preprinted letterhead or logohead.

This format sample in Figure 13.1 clearly provides the outlet with information as to the source of this material, a code number in order to identify unmistakably this particular message, an indication of how contemporary this announcement is, and a specification of total message length. Particularly when PSAs arrive from small or relatively obscure organizations, the word count/length data let the station know that this thirty-second message will, in fact, fit into thirty seconds. Thus the outlet has the assurance that it will not end up giving more free time to the announcement than it will be able to get credit for.

A slightly different data arrangement is used when the subject of the radio PSA is a limited-duration event. In such a case, it is vital that neither the outlet nor the copywriter be embarrassed by the airing of event promotion *after* that event is over! Consequently, the use dates will begin before the actual start of the observance and will end on, if not slightly before, the event's conclusion. Event PSA scripts also begin

---

From:
Committee for Field Mouse
Preservation
George Doorstop, Director,
Public Relations
613 Kane Street
Meritorious, Maine 04651
(207) 339-6085
Time: 30 seconds
Words: 72

For release:
Wednesday, November 18, 2010

Message No.: CFP-64R-04

. . . .

ANNCR: As cities annex more farmland, and developers put up new subdivisions,
a little one's rights . . .

FIGURE 13.1   Radio PSA 'Release' Data Block.

BANTAM HOCKEY LEAGUE WEEK

From: For Use: September 10, 2010
Eddie Shack, Coordinator,   to
Sudbury Bantam Hockey League   September 23, 2010
65 Imlach Lane
Sudbury, Ontario L9G 2K1
(705) 774-7279

BANTAM HOCKEY LEAGUE WEEK
September 18 to September 24, 2010

Time: 60 seconds
Words: 148

. . . .

ANNCR: As pucks hit the ice all over Ontario, it's time to pay tribute to the
         leagues that give our children a start in the noble sport of hockey. Here
         in Sudbury, this means skating into the Bantam League fundraiser at
         full speed . . .

FIGURE 13.2   Radio PSA 'Event' Data Block.

with a "headline" to further highlight the name of the activity and its time frame. Figure 13.2 provides an example of such a data block.

Because many television PSAs are produced by advertising agencies, they use the same data block as in their commercial scripts. An ISCI number (see Chapter 11) might even be assigned if the PSA is promoting a national organization. On the other hand, if the nonprofit group itself is supplying the script, the standard heading is often preceded and modified by additional entries in order to reflect more clearly the noncommercial source and nature of the communication to follow. Figure 13.3 illustrates such a situation.

PSAs, of course, are aired free. Therefore, no written contract specifies the running schedule, and the data block must clearly indicate any time-frame limitations to the message's usability. In addition, radio and television PSA copy arrives at the outlet totally unsolicited and from people who may be completely unknown to the outlet's staff. Public service scripts thus must sell *themselves* every step of the way --- beginning with their professional introduction at the top of the page and following through with well-crafted copy. "If it is horribly written," declared one public affairs director, "it goes right in the trash, because if I can't read it, I'm not going to waste my time trying to have other people try and understand what it says."[12]

TEN PUBLIC SERVICE POSTULATES

In constructing what comes below the data block, try to be as fluid in your PSA conceptions as you are in writing your commercial assignments. Far too many other-wise uninhibited copywriters seem mentally to put on black suits and high starched collars when given a public service task. Their resulting scripts sound like somber sermons rather than engaging conversations --- and somber sermons are the last

A PUBLIC SERVICE MESSAGE FROM:
The League of Community Orchestras
1291 Cadenza Avenue
Rosin, Rhode Island 03212
(401) 598-6763

FOR RELEASE: August 13, 2010
         (or)
FOR USE: September 1, 2010 to September 15, 2010

JOB/ISCI #	SYMP-8816		
SUBJECT	Composition Contest	LENGTH	:30
REVISION	4	TITLE	The Winning Chart
APPRV DATE	5/30/10	AS PRODUCED	6/21/10

OBJECTIVE: To encourage college-age composers to submit overtures that are playable by volunteer/community orchestras throughout the country.

PRODUCTION NOTE: The entire scene takes place in the lobby of a nondescript bus station. STUDENT is young (19–22-year-old) woman. Three PASSENGERS she encounters are all over 50; two males and one female.

Video	Audio
OPEN ON ESTAB. SHOT OF STATION LOBBY	ATMOSPHERE SFX
SLOW ZOOM INTO STUDENT ON BENCH, SCRIBBLING ON MANUSCRIPT PAPER	VO: Inspiration can strike at any time---

FIGURE 13.3 TV 'In-House' PSA Data Block.

thing most people want when they turn on their TV or radio. All the successes and techniques that you've established in the writing of commercials and promos should be brought to bear on the PSA pitch. In addition, there are ten postulates to keep in mind in order to maximize your PSA's chances of being aired by the media outlet and profitably attended to by your target audience:

1. Cultivate Bizarre Thinking
2. One Concept to a Cause, Please
3. Bolster Believability
4. Liberate the Visual
5. Tag with Discretion
6. Localize to Your Advantage
7. Instruct --- Don't Intimidate
8. Don't Re-wage the Crusades
9. Remember That Stodginess Stinks
10. Banish Commercialism

We now examine each of these postulates in order.

1. Cultivate Bizarre Thinking

One way to prevent "good-cause dullness" and PSA predictability is to draw relationships that are out of the ordinary --- if not downright creative. Veteran PSA producer Jim O'Donnell gives this example of what he means by bizarre thinking:

> An insurance industry client wants a PSA that urges car owners to lock their vehicles to make it tougher for car thieves. Conventional thinking would produce pictures of people locking their cars and pocketing the keys, etc., accompanied by a droning narrative about the importance of locking your car. Bizarre thinking would open with a shot of a briefcase lying in a parking space in a crowded parking lot. A suspicious character would approach, open the unlocked briefcase stuffed with $100 bills, close it and disappear. The viewer's first question is likely to be: "How absurd --- who in his right mind would leave fifteen grand in cold cash lying unprotected in such a place?" Here, straightforward narration would remind the viewer that people do it every day by not locking their cars and pocketing their keys. The final exhortation might do a play on the words "lock-it" and "pocket."[13]

Bizarre thinking allows both the writer and the audience to explore an innovation rather than merely contemplate a command. Church festivals, for instance, are often promoted by PSAs that make frequenting these events seem like just another dull duty on behalf of a boringly 'good cause.' Consequently, non-church members see no reason for attending, and even those in the flock look for ways to avoid showing up. But through application of bizarre thinking and a simple special effect, the Basilica Block Party in Figure 13.4 is positioned as a lighthearted affair at which everyone can enjoy responsible partying "of a higher order."

2. One Concept to a Cause, Please

Presenting a PSA in a clear and compelling manner also means sticking to one main image/idea. Given the usually intangible or remote nature of the PSA's audience benefit, every sound and picture must help flesh out the single key conclusion that our message was commissioned to communicate. Even in the case of television's audio and video capabilities, multiple copy points only guarantee that, no matter how much information is originally taken in, little, if any, will be retained. When it comes to radio, of course, very little will even *be* taken in if there is no single concept on which the listener can focus. The radio message that follows is also built around a "block party." But here, that party is not the PSA's subject, but a cohesive analogy through which the real subject can gradually register in listeners' minds.

WOMAN #1:   A block party?

WOMAN #2:   All the neighbors can bring potluck and their favorite beverage.

WOMAN #1:   Oh, what a marvelous idea!

WOMAN #2:   Do you want to help me put together an invitation list?

WOMAN #1:   Of course! But should we invite the new family at Twenty-oh-three?

WOMAN #2:	I haven't met them yet, but I hear they're very friendly.
WOMAN #1:	But aren't they Black?
WOMAN #2:	Oh, are they? They probably wouldn't feel comfortable.
WOMAN #1:	No, of course not. Well, what about the folks next door to them.
WOMAN #2:	The Goldbergs?
WOMAN #1:	Oh, aren't they Jewish?
WOMAN #2:	With a name like that?
WOMAN #1:	Oh, they seem so nice.
WOMAN #2:	Well, you just never know.
WOMAN #1:	Well, what about the people at the end of the block?
WOMAN #2:	They don't speak English!
WOMAN #1:	Well, then they wouldn't want to come to our party.
WOMAN #2:	Oh, of course not. Well, who's left? The Howards?
WOMAN #1:	His wife is in a wheelchair, she'd probably feel self-conscious.
WOMAN #2:	Hmmm, the Wilsons?
WOMAN #1:	They're in their seventies --- they wouldn't want to come.
WOMAN #2:	No. The Morgans? Their son is coming back from college.
WOMAN #1:	Oh, I understand he's a homosexual.
WOMAN #2:	No!
WOMAN #1:	Yes! Well, how many people do we have on the list so far?
WOMAN #2:	Well, there's me and you---
WOMAN #1:	---and that makes two. Well, what about your husband?
WOMAN #2:	Well, I'd invite him, but he's --- bald!
WOMAN #1:	Oh, my goodness!
WOMAN #2:	Yeah, he'd just be embarrassed.
WOMAN #1:	Oh, maybe you'd better not come either.
WOMAN #2:	No.
WOMAN #1:	Well, how many does that make?
WOMAN #2:	One.
WOMAN #1:	Doesn't sound like much of a party!
ANNCR:	The Leadership Conference Education Fund and the Advertising Council remind you that our strength depends on our diversity. Stop the hate.

(Courtesy of Dick Orkin, Dick Orkin's Radio Ranch)

OPEN ON FATHER
O'CONNELL AT THE
BASILICA.

HE'S CARRYING A
CLIPBOARD.

FATHER O'CONNELL: For
our upcoming block
party, July 7th and 8th,
we've got...

WE SEE THE CHECKLIST.

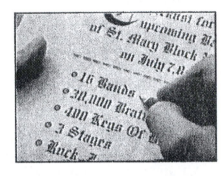

FATHER O'CONNELL:
...16 bands, 30,000
bratwurst...

CUT BACK TO MEDIUM
SHOT OF FATHER
O'CONNELL.

FATHER O'CONNELL:
...at least <u>400</u> kegs
of beer.

CONTINUE ACTION

FATHER O'CONNELL:
But I caution you, don't
over-do it.

FIGURE 13.4 (Agency: Odney Advertising; Art Directors: Chris Lincoln, Greg Dutton; Writer:
John Arms; Creative Director: Chris Lincoln; Production Company: Dublin Productions; Producer:
Greg Pope; Director: Rich Dublin)

A SMALL STATUE IN THE
BACKGROUND
EXPLODES AS IT'S HIT
BY LIGHTNING.

SFX: KABLAM!!!!!

SMOKE DRIFTS UP
FROM THE BLACKENED
SPOT THAT USED
TO BE A STATUE.

FATHER O'CONNELL
HAS A "GET WHAT I'M
SAYING?" LOOK ON
HIS FACE.

FATHER O'CONNELL:
Because we also have
one <u>serious</u> bouncer.

CUT TO BLOCK PARTY
LOGO.

(SUPER: For Tickets Call
333-4433)

ANNCR (VO): The
Basilica Block Party.

A party of a higher
order.

3. Bolster Believability

The single-concept PSA also makes it easier for the audience to grasp how the issue impinges on their own lives. Like an involving short story or an engaging commercial, the believable PSA is one whose simplicity enables people to put themselves in the picture --- to participate mentally and emotionally in the little vignette being spun out before their eyes and/or ears.

PSA believability is enhanced by the presence of three key factors: (1) sincere-sounding copy; (2) trustworthy testimonials; and (3) for television, comfortable yet contemporary photographic values.

Sincere-sounding copy is the element over which the copywriter obviously wields the greatest control. Sincere copy can make unknown talent seem just as familiar as (and perhaps more believable than) the famous folks who are usually beyond a public service's budget. The sincere message *makes honest sense,* and makes it in a way that strikes the audience as neither pompous nor patronizing:

WOMAN: I'll never forget my best friend Lanie's wedding. It was right before the ceremony and I walked into her bathroom without knocking because like I said, she was my best friend. And there she was in her gorgeous white lace dress, leaning over the sink with a straw up her nose. I says, 'Hey, what are you doing?' She jumps up and says, 'Shut the door, shut the door.' Then I see the white powder and I froze. She says, 'Hey, it's cool.' Then she leans over the sink and I say, 'Move it off or I'll blow it off.' She says, 'You do and I'll kill you.' Then she started to cry. And I started to cry. And we held each other real tight. Then I blew the coke off the sink and bolted outta there. I sent her a silver flower bowl, but she never wrote to thank me. I felt bad; so after three months, I broke down and called her. I thought maybe we could bury the hatchet because like I said, she was my best friend. But it was too late. They already buried Lanie.

ANNCR: If you think you can't live without drugs, don't worry. Pretty soon you may not have to. Partnership for a Drug-Free America.

(Courtesy of Joy Golden, Joy Radio)

As the above message also demonstrates, *trustworthy testimonials* add credibility to your PSA when the individuals who deliver them speak from experience. Particularly in the life-enveloping subjects with which many PSAs deal, average people rather than celebrities beget much more realism --- unless the celebrity has demonstrated personal involvement in the problem or cause you're discussing. Even then, some audience members may still doubt the veracity of the spot and perceive the star merely to be playing some phony, self-serving role.

Our final believability element, *comfortable yet contemporary photographic values,* positions the video PSA in a productional middle ground. The effective nonprofit pitch does not exude an institutional coldness in direction and pacing of its shots. Nor, on the other hand, are its cinematic techniques so hotly experimental that only spaced-out digital freaks understand them.

Unfortunately, some PSA writers tend to swing from one extreme to the other in their visual stylings. They try either to respect some assumed propriety mandate from the sponsoring organization or, on discovering that to be an imaginary constraint, go wild in a self-indulgent attempt to out-hip the most outlandish commercial treatment around. It is as though a public service announcement must be either more straitlaced or more radical than anything else on the screen in order to command viewer attention. This, of course, is anything but the case. Provided the central concept has been well-honed, a PSA can compete with any other commercial or continuity fare on the air or the Web --- and compete in the productional mainstream rather than on the uptight or far-out fringes. In the Figure 13.5 photoboard, the central concept is given full rein through an imaginatively angled, but by no means disorienting, pictorial progression.

MUSIC: SPOOFY, 1960's SITCOM STYLE

DAD: Son, did you clean that asbestos out of the attic like I asked you?

SON: Sure, dad. But isn't that dangerous?

DAD: Ooooh, poor little baby. Like I never exposed you to a group A carcinogen before!

SFX: FAMILY LAUGHING

ANNCR: Secondhand cigarette smoke is now a group A carcinogen — the same as cancer causing materials like asbestos and radon. Don't take chances with your family's health . . .

MOM: More lemonade dear? It's got radon in it.

ANNCR: Eliminate secondhand smoke today.

DAD: Make mine a double!

FIGURE 13.5 *(Courtesy of Marcie Brogan, Brogan & Partners)*

4. Liberate the Visual

However they are shot and amalgamated, PSA pictures must not be smothered by excessive soundtrack verbiage. Unfortunately, some television copywriters are like circuit-riding preachers trying to jam four weeks' worth of sermons into a single appearance.

Granted, the subject of your piece is laudable, humane, and vital. And it may be aired quite infrequently. But packing it with so much copy that the viewer must become primarily a *listener* throws away video's unique advantage. The perceptive PSA writer knows that the silent speech of gestures, facial expressions, and other camera revelations can have much more impact when not weighted down with wall-to-wall dialogue or voice-over copy. Certainly, the PSA's "product" is more difficult to delineate than a soft drink, cereal, or tennis shoe. But talking your script to death is no way to exploit video's potential. In all your video writing, and particularly in PSAs, where the tendency to pontificate is so strong, write copy as sparingly as a compelling picture will allow. In this way, the words you *do* use will possess special force and significance. For the thirty-second treatment below, any more words would detract from its stark visual analogy for a 'criminally' debilitating disease.

Video	Audio
ESTAB. HOUSE EXTERIOR. INTRUDER BREAKS INTO BASEMENT AND CREEPS AROUND. HE SHINES HIS FLASHLIGHT ON BREAKER BOX	FEMALE (VO): I was 28 when it happened.
CU OF CENTRAL NERVOUS SYSTEM DIAGRAM	It struck my central nervous system.
CU INTRUDER'S EYES AS HE SHINES FLASHLIGHT OVER LIST INSIDE BREAKER BOX	Now everything in my body is all mixed up.
INTRUDER SETS TO WORK MIXING UP THE BREAKERS	Some days I can barely see.
HE GIVES A HANDFUL OF WIRES A TUG FOR A FLASH OF SPARKS.	Other days I can't walk.
CUT TO BLACK. WOMAN'S HAND LIGHTS A CANDLE	
DIZ TO SUPER: Multiple Sclerosis Society of Canada	Multiple Sclerosis. Please help us connect with a cure.
DIZ TO SUPER: We <u>can</u> connect with a cure.	

(Courtesy of Terrence O'Malley, Vickers & Benson Advertising Ltd.)

5. Tag with Discretion

As with commercials, the most resounding element of an audio or video PSA is often the tag line. Further, in order to be accepted for airing, public service tags must usually identify their sponsoring institution. This tag ID needs to be neither extensive nor detailed, but it should include the name and (in video media) the logo of the originating institution.

If your intention is to have audience members email or call, then ample time must be allowed to permit registering and repetition of the phone number, email address, or Website URL. On radio, if the number or address is not mentioned at least twice, there is little or no chance of listener recall. On television, this "supered" information should be held for at least five seconds. In the PSA that follows, the writer has given the contact means ample time to register on the video side and follows this with a supered tag that exposes the serious purpose behind the previous anal puns.

Video	Audio
OPEN ON MAN AND DOCTOR TALKING IN EXAMINATION ROOM	MAN: So what you're saying, Doc, is a colonoscopy could really save my butt?
	DOC: You bet your booty!
	MAN: Well, let me probe further. Will it hurt?
	DOC: It doesn't. And I'm behind you all the way.
	MAN: So, I guess we should take a crack at this thing?
	DOC: Yeah, you're over 50 now.
	MAN: Up yours, Doc.
	DOC: No, actually it's up yours!
	VO: If joking helps you talk about it, that's okay.
	DOC: When it comes to your health, you should shoot for the moon.
CUT TO NURSE IN DOORWAY	NUR: Try Uranus.
BACK TO MAN/DOC	VO: Talk to your doctor. Get tested. Caught early, colorectal cancer is 90 percent curable.
SUPER: 1-800-872-3000 www.nccra.org	
ADD SUPER: Don't die of embarrassment.	
ADD NCCRA LOGO	

(Courtesy of Rich Tlapek, GSD&M Advertising)

Conversely, if you don't expect people to write or call, don't bother with an address or phone number. Fundraising appeals, for instance, are normally successful only when conducted via direct mail or telemarketing (phone calls to prospects). In such cases, your PSA's goals should be to pave the way for recognition and favorable response when the actual mail or phone solicitation later is received.

Whether a short or long tag is used, there is no need in a video environment to waste valuable time and audience attention with the words "This message is brought to you by . . . ." Simple verbalization or graphic conveyance of the organization's name will cue in viewers to the source of the piece.

6. Localize to Your Advantage

As we previously discussed, provided the spot is well-produced, stations and cable systems are more likely to select PSAs that address local needs, because airing such messages shows these outlets to be more community responsive. Therefore, anything the copywriter can do to bring a local slant to the subject increases the message's chances of outlet as well as audience attention. Even if the campaign is national in scope, it can be customized on radio by leaving "holes" for local copy insertions.

Video messages can likewise accomplish the same localization by leaving such holes for voice-over adaptation and/or providing screen-space for basic end-frame supers, as in this donor registry approach:

Video	Audio
OPEN ON GRAVESTONE ENGRAVER IN HIS SHOP.	ENGR: Business has slowed down some. There seems to be less funerals lately.
CUT TO ROOM FULL OF BLANK GRAVESTONES	ENGR (VO): So I've begun to adjust my craft accordingly.
CUT TO SMALL GRAVESTONE IN SUBURBAN BACKYARD READING Pee Wee Peppler	Gerbil gravestones have been a real test of my skills. Getting the gerbil's first and last name on such a small stone is no easy feat.
	LOCAL VO: Last year there were (approximate number) fewer funerals in (city or state) thanks to organ donors.
CUT TO ENGRAVER WITH TINY TOOLS AND MAGNIFYING GLASS WORKING ON SMALL STONE	But there are still hundreds of our neighbors waiting for transplants.
SUPER: Say Yes (state or city name)	Be an organ and tissue donor.
CUT TO END TITLE:	Join the Donor Registry. (City/state phone number and Website URL)

(Courtesy of Jonathan Schoenberg, TDA Advertising & Design)

7. Instruct—Don't Order

Whether PSAs are local or national, research has shown that they face an uphill battle in trying to convince people to alter certain counterproductive behaviors. However, evidence from the Stanford Heart Disease Prevention Program found that behavior change *can* be attained "if public service messages instruct audiences how to cease their negative practices."[14] A Washington State University study suggests further that "a skills-training PSA can help people learn how to dissuade their friends from driving drunk --- especially when the skills are demonstrated by a person typical of the target audience."[15]

In other words, spots that provide simple, direct instruction on how to modify harmful or self-defeating conduct are much more effective than are scare-tactic mandates. This holds true for both older and younger people --- as long as they can identify with the PSA character doing the demonstrating:

<u>Production Note</u>: Man and Woman are both elderly but NOT feeble-voiced.

(SFX: ESTABLISH SHOPPING MALL SOUNDS AND UNDER)

MAN: Didn't I see you get out of the bus in front of the mall?

WOMAN: That was me.

MAN: Where's your car?

WOMAN: I haven't been driving lately, I'm getting too old.

MAN: C'mon Jennie. I'm older than you and I'm still driving. I took a refresher course and just changed my driving habits a bit.

WOMAN: What do you mean?

MAN: Well, our eyes and hearing and reflexes change as the years go by. It's natural. So it's best to drive during daylight and avoid heavy traffic and bad weather. Just a few adjustments and we can stay on the road. Give it a try.

ANNCR: A lifestyle suggestion from (station ID) and the Motor Vehicle Manufacturers Association.

(Courtesy of James O'Donnell, NTN Film & Video Productions)

8. Don't Re-wage the Crusades

Few PSA wordsmiths set out to intimidate their audiences. But because they believe so strongly in their client's cause, copywriters often become much more strident in their public service scripts than they would ever think of being when selling a tube of toothpaste or a liquid breath freshener. As a London *Times* reviewer once observed about media content in general, "Good causes do not automatically beget good programs." Assaulting the consumer with shrill self-righteousness only invites that consumer to retaliate by tuning out.

Imagine the understandably defensive reactions of San Diego residents if a water conservation message snarled like this:

ANNCR: Unless you want sand coming out of your faucets, you had better stop wasting water. Selfish people are indulging themselves and their manicured lawns at the expense of the welfare of everyone else in the county. In just the last couple of hours, you probably squandered gallons of water --- water that could have been conserved for more vital purposes. It's time you economized to preserve our fragile environment. Call 297-3218 to learn how you can stop being a water waster. That's 297-3218 to find out 24 simple ways to reform your water use practices. Only hoodlums squander H-2-O.

Such a pronouncement virtually begs the listener to counter with clever rejoinders like "Who says?" "How do you know?" "Go douse yourself!" or several more colorful and unprintable responses. Certainly, the listener would be energized by such a message --- but toward all the wrong actions. In the actual PSA below, on the other hand, the copywriter covered much the same ground on behalf of the San Diego County Water Authority, but in a much less combative, more positive manner:

ANNCR: This (SFX: THREE FIRM TAPS ON METAL BUCKET) is a bucket. And this (SFX: ONE DROP HITTING BUCKET BOTTOM) is a drop in the bucket. And if I asked you to promise me to cut back the water you use each day by 10 percent, well, you'd probably think that all you'd be doing is (SFX: ONE MORE DROPLET). But now that San Diego County is in another year of drought, if you (ANOTHER DROPLET) and I (ONE MORE HIGHER-PITCHED DROPLET) and everyone else (MULTIPLE ACCELERATING DROPLETS) in San Diego County---. Hey, eight years ago we faced a similar water shortage, and during that summer we all pitched in and voluntarily cut water usage by 15 percent, (ONE DROPLET) one drop at a time. So find out 24 simple ways to save water by calling 297-3218. That's 297-3218. And don't worry. We didn't waste any water making this commercial. It was all done with sound effects. (ONE VERY TINNY DROPLET). Your San Diego County Water Authority.

(Courtesy of James R. Melton, San Diego County Water Authority)

Arriving through the extremely personal electronic media, the PSA is a guest in people's homes, or a rider in their cars. It must behave as a guest is expected to behave or the consumer has every right to kick it into the street. Don't push your cause with waving banners and blazing eyeballs. Don't try to re-wage the Crusades in your copy or you'll just be as futile as they were.

9. Remember That Stodginess Stinks

Conducting a Crusade is not the only way to defeat your public service purpose. Another surefire method for producing PSAs that fail is to use tedious word arrangements. Copy traits that are merely moldy in commercials can reek in PSAs, where we generally start out with a subject that is harder to freshly package than a commercial product pitch. Thus the following three stale writing tendencies are especially to be avoided: *'five-dollar' words*, *redundancy*, and *periodic sentences*.

As a class, PSAs have acquired a reputation for a certain, ponderous, bureaucratic copy style. Using *'five-dollar words'* --- bigger words than we require --- will reinforce rather than counter this stereotype:

ANNCR: The voluntary expropriation of your hemoglobin is a matter of unquestioned importunateness as Municipal Hospital endeavors to replenish its sorely depleted inventory.

Besides the use of some inaccurate terminology, why couldn't the copywriter just say the community was badly in need of blood? Overblown prose doesn't make the appeal seem more urgent --- only more unapproachable.

Redundancy, our second stodgy stink, differs from aromatic *emphasis* chiefly because of word placement. Both devices use the same word or phrase several times. But redundancy also puts it at the same place in a number of recurring sentences and thereby saps listener interest. Emphasis, conversely, varies the placement so the word or phrase is exposed at novel and unanticipated junctures. In its deft juxtaposition of "wait" and "waiting," the following PSA illustrates beneficial emphasis:

ANNCR: Waiting for some things is a part of life. We wait in line at stores, gas stations, movies; waiting is simply a fact of life. Except when you're hungry. Except when you're poor, jobless, under-employed. Then waiting destroys. The Campaign for Human Development believes in people working together to solve their common problems so that no person in America must wait to live a decent life. The Campaign for Human Development, United States Catholic Conference.

(Courtesy of Francis P. Frost, United States Catholic Conference)

Redundancy, on the other hand, would negate this cumulative sense of suspense by giving the repeated phrase an all-too-predictable and monotonous position:

ANNCR: Waiting for some things is a part of life. Waiting in line at stores. Waiting at gas stations and movies. Waiting is simply a fact of life. Waiting is endurable except when---

Another mechanism for repeating a point with emphasis rather than redundancy is to split it among several speakers, as in the following multivoice spot titled "Schoolyard Wisdom." Each character's mirroring of juvenile misconception mutually reinforces the spot's central premise without becoming monotonous.

Production Note: All 'kid' voices are different. Quick, hard edits.

(MUSIC: HAUNTING BACKGROUND LULLABY)

KID 1:   If you put your books under your pillow at night, you won't have to study.

KID 2:   If you work in a video arcade you don't have to pay taxes.

KID 3:   My cousin says when you run out of gas you can use ginger ale.

KID 4:   If you're not 18, they can't arrest you.

KID 5:   I know a guy who can drink a whole milkshake through his nose.

KID 6:   A good college can run your parents about 400 bucks a year.

KID 7:   Driving is easy, it's just like on video games.

KID 8:   Ask anybody, a dog won't bite if you smile at it.

ANNCR: Your kids hear everything from their friends. And sooner or later, they're going to hear about marijuana. Which is exactly why your kids should learn about marijuana --- from you.

KID 9:   You can jump off a five-story building and only twist your ankle. Look at Jackie Chan.

KID 10:   People who can do stuff with their left and right hands are amphibious.

ANNCR: Tell them what marijuana is, what it does and what you think about it. Talk to your kids, They need the truth. Call 1-800-788-2800 for help.

KID 11:   Try this stuff. It's not gonna hurt you.

ANNCR: To find out more, call 1-800-788-2800. The Partnership for a Drug-Free America.

(Courtesy of Jim Price, Oink Ink Radio)

Beyond varying word placement and speaker variety, redundancy also can be avoided by checking your writing for such 'double statements' as:

negative problem	bad stench
most favorite	accidental disasters
informative news	excess waste
giving charity	sad tragedy
the thrill of excitement	unwanted embarrassment
very unique	confused disorder

Periodic sentences, the final contributor to overripe discourse, are constructions that force the audience to hold several phrases in mind while waiting for the main verb to give it all meaning. Pretentious even for print, the following periodic sentence is pure torture on radio or as a video voice-over. The receiver must juggle long clauses with one ear and strain for the verb with the other:

ANNCR: The need for help, for donations of time and money, for the tools of farming and hygiene education, for a care that negates the neglect of the past and the abject futility of the future, all of these needs <u>can be met</u> with a Community Chest contribution.

In contrast, observe the craftsmanship in this Michigan Department of Health PSA. Here, the copywriter has placed the verbs near the front of compact idea units rather than burying them at the rear of overextended ones. This technique gives the message more impact --- and more clarity.

VICTIM: I didn't know I had AIDS until I saw it on my baby's death certificate. I did drugs for 20 years and I never thought I'd hurt anyone but myself. But I gave it to my wife, and she gave it to our daughter. I got AIDS by sharing my friend's works. He had it in his blood. Sure I'm scared of dying, but what's worse is that I destroyed my baby and my wife.

ANNCR: Don't share a bed with someone who shares a needle. Michigan Department of Public Health AIDS Prevention Program.

(Courtesy of Marcie Brogan, Brogan & Partners)

Five-dollar words, redundancy, and periodic sentences release obscuring fumes that do not rise from copy that is fresh. They simply confirm people's worst suspicions about PSAs' mustiness. In short, such stodginess stinks.

10. Banish Commercialism

The final Public Service Postulate reminds us that true PSAs serve nonprofit causes exclusively. Never use a public service announcement as a Trojan horse for some commercial pitch. At the very least, that practice incurs the understandable animosity of the outlet, which you have duped into airing an *advertisement* for free. At worst, it flagrantly deceives the listening/viewing public. Avoid copy like the following, and you'll similarly avoid such dangers and damage:

ANNCR: The Greencrest Brownie Troop is hosting its semi-annual bake sale at the Selkirk Hardware store, Cherry Street and Main. That's Selkirk's Hardware --- where you can also obtain the finest selection of tools, lumber, and all-round building supplies available anywhere in the area.

Everything occurring after the street address constitutes commercial copy. If Selkirk wanted a pitch, he should have sold a few more nails and *purchased* the airtime himself.

A SAMPLE CAMPAIGN

Despite their nonprofit motive, PSA campaigns should be developed via the same market and client analysis conducted in planning a commercial campaign. (We examine campaign planning procedures in detail in the following chapter.) Below is the objective for the United States Catholic Conference's Campaign for Human Development, together with a spot to illustrate how each of the objective's *subgoals* is to be reached. By defining the parts, the subgoals thereby help collectively to characterize the campaign as a whole.

Objective: To heighten adult awareness of the problems of poverty as well as to illuminate some of the solutions such as [subgoals] community organizing, caring, and working together.

Subgoal #1 --- Community Organization

Video	Audio
CONVENTION SCENE AS CAMERA MOVES DOWN CENTER AISLE	MEETING CHAIR (VO): The Third Annual Convention of the Northeast Community Organization is hereby called to order.
CU PLACARDS: Trinity United Methodist, NE Mothers for Peace, Our Lady of Lourdes	ANNCR (VO): A convention --- but a different kind.
WOMEN WORKING AT SIGN-UP TABLE	The elderly, the poor, the little people getting together
MAN STANDING AT MICROPHONE. SIGN BEHIND HIM READING: Strength in Action	to stand up against big wrongs in their neighborhood. Wrongs like industrial pollution,
CU INDIVIDUALS SPEAKING INTO MIC	landlord abuse --- wrongs they didn't think they could change until they got together.
CU PEOPLE APPLAUDING	SFX: APPLAUSE
CUT TO FULL SCREEN GRAPHIC Campaign for Human Development U.S. Catholic Conference Washington, D.C. 20005	Campaign for Human Development

Subgoal #2 --- Caring

Video	Audio
TWO INDIAN WOMEN WITH INFANT WALKING IN BARREN FIELD	MUSIC: MALE VOCALIST WITH GUITAR(VO) It's the same old earth It'll always be
QUICK CUTS OF PEOPLE INCLUDING: TRUCK DRIVER TRAINING MEN STUDYING ENGINE	Livin' with the joy of bein' free---
HISPANIC RADIO ANNOUNCER PARKING LOT ATTENDANT	CHORUS: bein' free---
TWO WOMEN OUTSIDE STORE, FAMILY EATING HOTDOGS, GIRL SELLING FLOWERS ON STREET	SOLOIST: you and me.
CAB DRIVER, OFFICE WORKERS (MALE & FEMALE), TRAFFIC COP, STONE MASON, GIRL ON BIKE, CHILD IN DENTIST CHAIR	CHORUS JOINS SOLOIST: The joy of people workin' together. People determined to win. Building for tomorrow. Startin' to dream again.
HARDHAT WOMAN AT WORKSITE, UTILITY WORKER ON POLE	ANNCR(VO): The Campaign for Human Development is all of us --- together with hope --- learning to care.

Video	Audio
FREEZE FRAME: ELDERLY MAN WAVING	<u>CHORUS</u>: Learnin' how to care. Learnin' how to live and hope. And learnin' how to share.
LOWER THIRD SUPER: Campaign for Human Development U.S. Catholic Conference Washington, D.C. 20005	ANNCR (VO): Campaign for Human Development. United States Catholic Conference.

Subgoal #3 --- Working Together

HARRY: All right, (SFX: RATTLING OF DICE) let's see if you can get past me on this turn, Joe.

JOE: All right, let's see Harr, let's see. (SFX: DICE ROLL AND STOP) OH, no, no, look at that!

HARRY: Looks like you didn't make it, Joe, and is it going to cost you!

JOE: Oh, I guess, but Harry, that's it. I'm wiped out.

HARRY: Too bad, old buddy, but that's life.

ANNCR: For too many people, that <u>is</u> life. But we believe it shouldn't be. The Campaign for Human Development. People together --- with hope. The United States Catholic Conference.

(All of the above courtesy of Francis P. Frost, Creative Services, U.S. Catholic Conference)

WHAT'S IN IT FOR THE COPYWRITER

With the substantial billings, media/production budgets, and on-air exposure that major commercial assignments offer, why do copywriters and their agencies (and outlets) voluntarily work on PSAs? Because, as group creative director Robert Osborn explains,

> Creatives choosing PSAs as a way to showcase their talents come as close to agency heaven as possible: They choose whom they work for. Creative is in control of the end product. Clients are appreciative of the concern taken in their cause. Meanwhile, the agency is viewed as a socially active, moral member of the community. It all adds up to a situation ripe for good advertising.[16]

Industry reporter Cathy Madison observes further that "while providing legitimate contributions to worthy causes, high-quality, high-profile work also advertises the agency, helps recruit talented employees and boosts morale among staff plagued by down time or the creative shackles of regular clients."[17]

The most visible of this *pro bono* (donated) PSA work is coordinated by the Advertising Council. The organization was founded as the *War Advertising Council* in

1942 by the American Association of Advertising Agencies and the Association of National Advertisers. Its original efforts promoted war-related cost-saving and resulted in citizen planting of countless victory gardens and the purchase of $35 billion in war bonds.[18] The very first Ad Council campaign was produced by the McCann Erickson agency to promote a scrap metal and fat drive.[19] At the end of World War II, the Council dropped *War* from its name and began to direct its services toward national civilian charities.

The Advertising Council pairs member volunteer advertising agencies with government organizations or nonprofit groups. As its past president, Ruth Wooden, explains, "A sponsoring organization must also be willing to fund a national campaign [meaning pay production costs] for a minimum of two years. The campaign must address a problem faced by every part of the country and must not promote a controversial point of view --- such as gun control --- that forces the Ad Council to take a political position. . . . The campaign must do more than publicize a social problem: it should suggest things individuals can do."[20] Ad Council campaigns are given significant electronic exposure. In recent years, they have expanded from radio and television placement to Web and personal communication devices. Whatever the medium, the volunteer advertising agencies prepare the actual messages, which the Council subsequently reviews and distributes to cooperating media.

Organizations whose needs cannot be serviced by the Ad Council are free to seek out *pro bono* help on their own, of course. And because the Council's roster of agencies is limited to the largest shops in the country, there is a great deal of *pro bono* work contributed outside its auspices by both station and smaller agency copywriters.

Whether accomplished inside or outside the Ad Council, these voluntary creative efforts are examples of copywriter *enlightened self-interest* at its finest. As writer Daniel Clay Russ observes,

> *Pro bono* gets into award shows and helps recruiters and creative directors see who is out there who might want a higher paying job in a better city on great accounts. This is important if you remember that the creative portfolio isn't some self-congratulatory exercise. It is the writer's or art director's meal ticket. It is how they feed their families.[21]

"For most employees," adds advertising journalist Stephen Battaglio, "*pro bono* assignments give them a chance to exercise a level of creative freedom not often permitted on an average packaged-goods account, as well as a personal satisfaction that comes from handling work for a good cause."[22] Taking on these 'freebie' jobs may be even more advantageous for *the junior* copywriter. As veteran creative Dave Halloway points out, "if you're a young creative, you'll get the chance to do things years before you would at your day job. It'll help build your confidence too. Clients will trust you. In turn, you'll gain your own voice. And perhaps even speak up more in meetings. You can make mistakes with less pressure. And lower stakes. You can take more chances. And even try a new discipline. Plus you'll have something to look forward to outside of work."[23] "Doing *pro bono* is every kid's dream," Bozell Worldwide's chief creative officer Jay Schulberg concludes. "The chance to hit the home run. To be creatively brilliant. To show the world you exist."[24]

PSA spots and campaigns, therefore, possess the potential to play a vital role in your professional career --- from both selfish and selfless standpoints.

PITCHING FOR 'THE PUBLICS'

Before concluding this chapter, there is one specialized aspect of 'public service' copywriting that needs exploration --- the fashioning of pledge drive and underwriting spots for noncommercial stations.

Most stations conduct periodic on-air campaigns to encourage audience donations that help keep the outlet running and attractively programmed. At their worst, these 'beg-fests' can become far more intrusive than the advertising breaks on commercial broadcasting. But when well-scripted and well cast, they can actually enhance the entertainment or informational value of the programming around which they appear. One proven technique is to take advantage of talent visiting your area by bringing them into the studio to record a short pledge pitch. If talent are associated with a program to be aired during the pledge period, so much the better. But even if they are not, their message can still be tailored to match the generic type of shows that will be broadcast. Thus a classical performer can record a spot to bumper an orchestral or opera presentation or a stage actor can cut an announcement to appear near a featured drama offering.

Below are two examples of pledge pitches that "make the ask" but in a way that integrates the talent and the programming with the potential donor's *enlightened self interest*. The first utilizes a single talent pitching directly to the audience. The second precedes such a pitch with a conversation among multiple talent, a conversation that could easily be converted into an audio spot for airing on a sister radio station. If your outlet is also producing the program, the availability of such quickly customizable spots (by matting the appropriate phone number at the end) is an added incentive for other stations to carry your show.

Video	Audio
MLS COOK ON STOOL IN FRONT OF PROJECTED *SMOKEY JOE'S* LOGO	COOK: <u>Smokey Joe's Café</u> is a mix of street-corner quartets, stunning solos, and a bunch of cooool cats singing together to create some of the greatest songs ever written.
LOWER THIRD SUPER: Victor Trent Cook	'On Broadway,' 'Yakety Yak,' 'Hound Dog,' 'Stand By Me,'—these are the great creations of Jerry Leiber and Mike Stoller. I'm so thrilled to have been a part of the cast.
LOSE SUPER; DIZ TO FOOTAGE OF AUDIENCE GIVING STANDING 'O'	While on tour, we received (ADD AUDIENCE APPLAUSE UNDER) heartfelt standing ovations from the audience. As a performer, that's when I know I've done my job. (SNEAK APPLAUSE OUT)
DIZ MS OF COOK	Now, we're bringing the show to Public TV and hoping you'll also
SUPER: Pledge phone number	give us a standing O with your call of support. That's how Public TV knows that they're doing their job. Have we heard from you yet?

Video	Audio
OPEN ON M2S OF BACHMAN AND CUMMINGS ON PLEDGE SET	BACHMAN: I'm Randy Bachman.
	CUMMINGS: And I'm Burton Cummings.
	BACHMAN: Burton and I have been partners in the music business for 40 years and it's been a lot of fun.
MATTE THEIR CONCERT FOOTAGE BEHIND THEM	<u>MUSIC: SOT FROM FOOTAGE, FEATURE AND UNDER</u>
	CUMMINGS: Yeah, it's been a blast and I'm looking forward to the next 40 years, Randy.
	BACHMAN: (Turns to camera) Well, you might wonder what it takes for a great partnership like ours to last? For one thing, it takes commitment,
	CUMMINGS: And hard work.
FADE OUT FOOTAGE	BACHMAN: Just like us, (<u>FADE OUT MUSIC GRADUALLY</u>) you have a partnership with public television.
CUT TO NEW, SLIGHTLY TIGHTER ANGLE ON CUMMINGS	CUMMINGS: Your local public station relies on you to keep it going, to support it. In return you receive great television programs 365 days a year.
WIDEN TO 2-SHOT	BACHMAN: Let's keep this partnership alive.
SUPER: Pledge phone number	CUMMINGS: Call now with your pledge.

(Both the above courtesy of Jamie Jendrzejewski, Detroit Public Television)

Underwriting announcements are another way in which noncommercial broadcasters raise money. Also referred to as "donor spots," these messages may seem much like commercials but cannot *be* commercials in order to preserve a station's non-commercial status. Even while promoting the entity that donated the cash, current FCC regulations require that the copy NOT contain four types of statements:

1. *Price information*. Your script could say:

Great Northern Fruit Company; purveyors of a wide variety of jams and jellies.

but not:

---a wide variety of low-cost jams and jellies---

2. *Comparative or qualitative descriptions*. Avoid writing:

---the widest variety (or) the best jams and jellies in Minnesota.

3. *Inducements to purchase*. You could not add:

Visit a Great Northern store before the end of October and receive a free jar of our gooseberry jam.

4. *A call to action*. It would be acceptable to state:

With stores in Brainerd, St. Cloud, Hibbing and Duluth.

but not:

Visit us soon at one of our stores located in Brainerd, St. Cloud, Hibbing and Duluth.

Brand and trade names can be used as long as they are not presented in a comparative or qualitative way. And stating the number of years a company has been in business is also not considered qualitative description. Thus an attractive and acceptable underwriting announcement for this client might be scripted like this:

ANNCR: This program brought to you in part through a grant from Great Northern Fruit Company, making the pickings of a Minnesota summer available all year long. Great Northern Fruit Company; purveyors of a wide variety of jams and jellies for 64 years. And also offering a full line of Keebler brand crackers. With stores in Brainerd, St. Cloud, Hibbing and Duluth. All open seven days a week. Great Northern Fruit Company. Fruit from Minnesota fields.

If this were a donor spot for television, the visual could include such things as the Great Northern name, logo and "value-neutral" slogan (such as "Fruit from Minnesota fields"). However, stay away from pictures (such as a smiling child holding up a handful of big, juicy strawberries) that might be ruled to constitute qualitative statements. Graphics giving store locations and non-comparative/qualitative slogans such as "a wide variety of jams and jellies for 64 years" would also be permissible.

Conversely, here is an alleged donor spot that the FCC found unacceptable:

ANNCR: Planning a special occasion? Tasty Freeze, at the airport exit off of I-70, has ice cream cakes for that office celebration, birthdays, anniversaries, or for that special event you've planned. These cakes, tastefully decorated by Bobby Tim, are available in 8 or 10 inch. Tasty Freeze, at the airport exit off of I-70 is open 7 days a week from noon until 10 p.m. Also available at Tasty Freeze: Hearth and Home Ohio Bicentennial candles by lum-lite, ice cream treats or ice cream cakes, its Tasty Freeze, 588-9314.

In ruling on this announcement, the FCC Enforcement Bureau wrote that, "The announcement made on behalf of Tastee [sic] Freeze characterizes the underwriter's ice cream products in prohibited qualitative terms, by noting that they are 'tastefully decorated,' and by attempting to induce patronage by asking listeners whether they are 'planning a special occasion' which might require use of the underwriter's products."[25] FCC rulings have not always been consistent in evaluating what is and is not acceptable in donor spots, so you are well advised to interpret these guidelines conservatively—or risk your station incurring significant fines. Like public service announcement writing in general, underwriting spots offer even greater challenges to the copywriter than do commercial assignments. That is why writers often choose to include effective responses to such assignments in their portfolios.

14 Electronic Media Campaign Construction

U p to this point, our concern has focused on the prewriting analysis, script creation, and post-draft evaluation of individual pieces of copy. Now it is time to view the process in compound form; to examine how an entire campaign is constructed and the individual messages within it coordinated into a mutually reinforcing whole. Even though the discussion in this chapter centers primarily on *commercial* strategies, keep in mind that the same basic steps and procedures can, and usually should, be followed in forging well-aimed outlet promotion, program promotion, and PSA packages as well. It should be noted, too, that cross-media campaigns in which both print and electronic media are employed would also conform to the same basic mode of creation.

ISOLATING BRAND CHARACTER

Any product, service, media outlet, or community institution has a name. And, as marketing professor Terance Shimp points out, a good brand name can evoke feelings of trust, confidence, security, strength, and many other desirable associations.[1] What the copywriter must do is to tap into the essence of this brand identity to discover *brand character*—the unique property that this name now reflects—or could reflect given proper campaign exposure.

Alex Kroll, former chairman of Young & Rubicam, further defined brand character as the sum of what he calls the "four FRED indexes": familiarity, relevance, esteem, and differentiation.[2] In the script below, for instance, *familiarity* is epitomized by the man's preemptive turning to Hallmark for help in a conflict situation with which almost everyone can identify. *Relevance* is demonstrated by the verse's prepackaged applicability to his particular problem and the slogan: "If you could say it like Hallmark, you wouldn't need Hallmark." *Brand esteem* (a separate quality from the emotional appeal of consumer esteem) accrues from this same line and also from the compliment that the effect of the company's verse draws from the eavesdropper.

Finally, *differentiation* is established by the end super ("No one says it like Hallmark") and the distinctive card-back logo that reinforces this super.

Video	Audio
30-ISH COUPLE RUN THROUGH RAIN. THEY'RE HAVING A FIGHT. THEY FIND SHELTER UNDER GAS STATION CANOPY	SFX: RAIN GUY: Debbie --- would you just stop?
HE IS VISIBLY STRUGGLING TO FIND RIGHT WORDS WHILE ANOTHER MAN WORKING ON HIS CAR EAVESDROPS	All I want to say is--- all I want to say is--- Come with me to a quiet place where the sun and breeze and grass erase trouble, conflicts, senseless chatter.
HE FINISHES, WAITS SHEEPISHLY FOR HER REACTION	Come with me and find what matters most. Holding you, I find my heaven close.
SHE PAUSES, THEN LOOKS LOVINGLY AT HIM	GAL: (Captivated) Ohhh---
CUT TO CARD MAN RECITED	SFX: BIRDS TWITTERING VO: If you could say it like Hallmark, you wouldn't need Hallmark.
CUT TO BACK OF CARD WHERE WE SEE HALLMARK LOGO SUPER: No one says it like Hallmark	
WS COUPLE WALKING AWAY WITH OTHER GUY IN FRAME	OTHER GUY: Nice save. GUY: Thanks.

(Courtesy of Mandy Way, Leo Burnett/Toronto)

How do you come up with a strategy that achieves brand character and passes four-FRED muster? And how do you ascertain whether that brand character needs reinforcement, amplification, or transformation? The best way is to construct a paper-and-pencil inventory of the existing marketing situation. Not only will this inventory process acclimate you to the client's world, but it will also make you feel more a part of it because you have injected some of your own words into this world, if only in list form. Making lists starts you grappling with campaign strategy and the brand character that this strategy is calculated to sculpt and promote.

Of course, before you can construct any list, you have to find out as much as possible about your subject. There are many ways to do this. After his agency acquired the Texaco account in 1934, Jack Cunningham, one of the founders of Cunningham & Walsh, "spent two weeks wearing the Texaco star, pumping gas, greasing axles and changing oil. From his time at the point of sale, Cunningham learned that customers cared more about the cleanliness of a service station's restrooms than they cared about the gasoline sold there. For several years to follow, it was clean restrooms that sold Texaco's petrol."[3]

Seventy years later, JWT/NY Chief Creative Officer Ty Montague spent a week at client Domino's Pizza Prep School, learning about store operations in the mornings and spending afternoons in a Domino's store where he took, prepared, and delivered orders. "I did it because I honestly believe in order to do great work, it is essential to understand how your client's business really operates," Montague reflects. Meanwhile, agency veteran Steve Bowen recalls riding through the Alps and Death Valley, California, with executives from client BMW motorcycles. "Until you've ridden on a rainy day on a freeway going 80 miles an hour, passing a truck and spray comes up . . . you're not going to have the authenticity in your language that will resonate with people who do that," Bowen recounts.[4] In search of such resonance, Proctor & Gamble CEO A. G. Lafley goes so far as to require all fifty of his senior managers to spend time every three months with target consumers in their homes or on their shopping trips, immersing themselves in customer lifestyles and buying behaviors.[5]

We must do whatever it takes to acquire an in-depth knowledge of our client's enterprise. Creative director Steven Penchina encourages copywriters to

> go to focus groups, client orientations, store checks, plant tours and client meetings so you can learn first-hand about the client's products and customers. You'll gain a better understanding of the client's problems and how you can solve them. Nothing beats a client's "gut feel." One time, when I was striking out on a campaign for Burroughs computers, I spent three days at the company's Detroit headquarters. I'll admit I caught up on some much needed sleep during the operating software presentations, but I did come back with the creative hook I needed.[6]

On projects to which you are assigned, you may not always have the time to go to such lengths. But all of these examples illustrate just how central first-hand product/market knowledge is to brand character isolation.

"In today's tough competitive world," counsels Bozell Advertising's Chief Creative Officer Jay Schulberg, "successful campaigns usually result from identifying a pinpoint, an insight, a nuance, a nugget of information gleaned from reams of research or sometimes from an intuitive understanding of a quirk of human nature. Successful campaigns are based on such gems."[7] An intrinsic part of this process is isolating the precise culture of the client because "a client's culture has a lot to do with its success and its brand story," creative director Bart Cleveland points out. "If we do not immerse ourselves in clients' cultures, we are missing a huge opportunity to discover truths that will help them successfully market their brands."[8] Once you have gained this first-hand understanding of client, brand, and market specifics, by whatever means, the list-making process can proceed in the assurance that it is based on fact.

1. List the Positive Attributes

The first and most obvious portion of your inventory should encompass all the reasons that someone (or different groups of someones) would want to utilize/patronize the product or service. Set down each of these in a consumer-benefit form and include at least one for each of the SIMPLE rational motivations discussed in Chapter 4. Keep an entirely open mind at this point, for you can never predict which benefit may, once the total analysis is completed, exhibit the greatest success potential. Write down every conceivable product merit, no matter how bizarre, and allow the process to isolate the *most* meritorious later.

Marketing professors Rita McGrath and Ian MacMillan divide positive attributes into three categories: (1) non-negotiables; (2) differentiators; and (3) exciters.[9] *Non-negotiables* are things people take for granted in the product. We expect any laundry detergent to get our laundry clean, so if that is all your copy talks about, it will do nothing to improve your brand's standing against the competition. *Differentiators* move beyond this expected attribute to favorably distinguish your product. For example, our detergent not only cleans clothes, but is concentrated to do more loads than competitors' same-size bottles. Finally, an *exciter* (if you can find it) not only distinguishes you from the competition but provides an additional benefit that delights the consumer and may even constitute the trigger for their decision to buy: our detergent's natural base of citrus and sodas rinses completely from the fabric, leaving no residue to damage its fibers and their elasticity. In other words, your favorite clothes, when washed in our product, look and feel good much longer.

2. List the Weaknesses

The perfect product or service never existed in this imperfect world, and don't assume yours will break the pattern. The honest and ultimately triumphant campaign always takes its client's drawbacks into consideration and proceeds accordingly. McGrath and MacMillan likewise divide weaknesses into three types: (1) tolerables; (2) dissatisfiers; and (3) enragers.[10] *Tolerables* are drawbacks common to every product in our category so are unavoidable no matter what brand a consumer buys. All potato chips lose their crispiness if stored for too long in an opened bag. *Dissatisfiers* do differentiate you from the competition --- but in a negative way. For instance, we do not package our chips in bags as small as our competitors --- so there is a greater chance our chips will remain in opened packages longer before they are fully consumed, thus increasing the chance for limp chips. *Enragers* are disadvantages so acute that they motivate consumers to actively boycott our product and perhaps even warn others away --- such as our chips having a higher per-serving sodium content than almost any other brand. If the client can't or won't correct such an enrager element, we must, at the very least, steer clear of any approach that seems to trigger it. Thus for our high-sodium chips, avoid anything that even obliquely suggests the subject of nutrition or healthy snacks.

As you may recall from Chapter 1, the in-house agency sometimes lacks the capability or willingness to acknowledge and inventory weaknesses in its company's products or services. Such self-imposed blinders too often ignore marketplace realities and consumer concerns. A negative attribute skimmed over in campaign planning is almost certain to surface like a dead, bloated whale once that campaign has been launched. Get all the product or service drawbacks out on paper, where you can see and deal with them *in advance.*

3. Retrieve the Exploitable Weaknesses

Once you've made a candid appraisal of product limitations, see if you can't transform them into positive attributes by casting them in a new light. This process can harvest the most persuasive brand character because it shows consumers that what they thought was a negative factor is really, on closer examination, a laudable characteristic. Thus for a certain candy mint, "you pay a few cents more, but for a breath deodorant it's worth it." Similarly, an insurance company's inability to contact personally every household is explained away by the popularity of the policies that are keeping its agents so busy. And, as revealed in the classic ten-second spot below, our hostelry's lack of a lounge may save both your ears and your wallet some pain:

Video	Audio
OPEN MS MARTIN MULL SEATED IN OVER-DECORATED COCKTAIL LOUNGE, LEANING ON BAR NEXT TO SEQUIN-DRESSED, PORTLY WOMAN WHOSE BACK IS TURNED. BEHIND MULL IS MALE SINGER WITH GREASED HAIR AND TASTELESS BLUE-PLAID DINNER JACKET	MULL: You know, you'll always pay less at Red Roof Inns because you don't have to pay for extras like a lounge.
	SINGER: (Off-key) Uh, uh, goo goo face---
	MULL: Aren't you glad?
LS STANDARD RED ROOF INN EXTERIOR AT DUSK WITH CAR PULLING IN	VO: Next time, hit the roof. Red Roof Inns.

(Courtesy of Ed Klein, Doner Advertising)

In fact, retrieving an exploitable weakness might even save the business itself. The story is told of the small salmon packing plant that was gradually losing more and more market share because its steam-based canning processes turned the naturally pink salmon meat to *white.* Though the process was just as hygienic as the methods employed at bigger plants, and though the steaming did not adversely affect taste, potential new customers were suspicious of white salmon. The plant did not have the money to install another process, and all seemed lost until an astute copywriter unearthed the perfect exploitable weakness theme:

(Company name) Salmon --- the only salmon guaranteed not to turn pink in the can.

In one stroke, the conventional became the unacceptable and the regional market for *white* salmon jumped to an all-time sales high.

4. Amalgamate the Benefits and Excuses

Next, take all the positive attributes from list #1 and all the feasible excuses from list #3. Merge them into one composite slate and condense this to the fewest possible essentials. You want to have a comprehensive catalog of benefits related to your product or service without a confusing and potentially replicative overlap. At this juncture, you should now have before you the total range of differentiated options, each of which may conceivably be selected as a main campaign theme, depending on the demographic/psychographic profile of your client's target audience. This comprehensively sets the stage for the winnowing process that follows.

5. List the Client's Past Approaches

Since we began with the assumption that you are planning a new campaign, it must also be assumed that the current approach is not working or has run its course, as did the other approaches that might have preceded it. Generally, it is deemed undesirable to revisit a previously abandoned theme from which all the usable fruit has already been picked and consumed. Thus list #5 serves to eliminate items from #4 that have been stressed in the past. Should you *want* to resurrect an earlier theme, however, crosschecking it with list #4 should ascertain whether there is a solid and readily identifiable current benefit from which that theme can issue. It may be discovered that the particular approach failed to work before because it really didn't relate to true brand character or mismatched an advantage with an inappropriate target audience, such as pitching a tire's durability to high-income types who only buy tires with a new car attached.

6. List What the Competition Is Stressing

This particular catalog may be long or short depending on how many major competitors there are and how many different campaigns each may be running. In our own campaign, we usually attempt to emphasize some aspect that the "other guys" are not reflecting in order to differentiate more effectively our character from theirs. Nevertheless, if your product is unequivocally and demonstrably superior to a competitor in terms of the element that competitor is currently stressing, you may want to take them on at their own game. In either event, list #6 gives you a playlist of what tunes the others are singing. It can therefore serve to eliminate their approaches from your composite list of options --- or it can alert you to the fact that encroaching on any of these "occupied" themes may set up doubtful brand recall and/or perilous comparative advertising considerations.

7. Weigh the Options That Remain

After crossing off those benefit approaches from list #4 that are (1) undesirably replicative of past campaigns or (2) dominated by the competition, you are left with a final and residual slate of possibilities. From this slate, and in conjunction with client representatives and their target audience specifications, select the benefit-expressing campaign theme. For maximum effectiveness, all subsequent advertising for the product, service, program, or outlet should be expressed in terms of this theme. Otherwise, you run the risk of advertising against yourself --- of seeming to promote two separate and competing brand characters.

8. Pick a Product Personality

Based on your theme and the benefit it conveys, a *product personality*, expressed in a consistent and meticulously tailored writing style, should be allowed to emerge. "Products are made in the factory," says veteran advertising executive Ed Vick, "brands in the mind."[11] This manufacturing job inside the consumer's head is what building brand character is all about. And product personality is brand character's hallmark. "Branding means nothing more (and nothing less!) than creating a distinct personality," business guru Tom Peters asserts, "and telling the world about it --- by hook or crook."[12] "A brand is a living thing," adds entertainment marketer Alan Rose, "and its personality is what defines it for consumers and separates it from the competition."[13]

A product personality will come through in your copy whether you want it to or not, so take the initiative to fashion one that is most appropriate to the campaign, the client, and the target audience that client is attempting to reach. Too many campaigns are afflicted with vapid or even schizoid image traits because, though the benefit theme has been carefully determined, the verve and style of the words conveying that theme have not been scrupulously monitored from assignment to assignment. In such cases, the product or client may, for instance, sometimes come across as somber, at other times appear simply businesslike, and on still other occasions appear downright dictatorial.

Product personality is the single most perplexing concept for a novice writer to grasp because, though certain personalities seem generally associated with particular benefit themes or product categories, there are now lighthearted insurance companies as well as deadly serious breakfast cereals. Like an old friend whose actions have a comfortable and reassuring predictability, a product personality's familiarity flows from a distinctive yet elusive way of saying and doing things.

Copywriters need to "dimensionalize brands like people," argues marketing executive Fred Posner. "If you're describing a friend, you don't say she has a head, two arms, and two legs. You say, she's reliable, sincere, trustworthy, warm. The brands that will have staying power . . . are the ones with similarly identifiable and affective personality traits."[14] "Each of your friends has something you like about them: a good sense of humor, a way of making you feel good about yourself," point out agency executives Bill Heater and Jeff Lawson . . . Loyal brands are steadfast. They earn trust by being there when you need them. A brand-friend can change itself on the outside—just like a friend can get a new haircut—but *inside* the values are rock solid."[15] Consistent projection of these 'rock-solid values' usually becomes so ingrained in a copy group, in fact, that major personality modification can in most cases be accomplished only when the account changes agencies.

If you still don't understand the dynamics of product personality, compare the Figure 14.1 commercial for the Guardian Plan with the following script for Australian-based No Frills Funerals & Cremations.[16] Imagine if the personalities were reversed. Could a senior citizen–aimed product that stresses "caring" for others do so with an edgy economy appeal? Would a company called "No Frills" want to project a warm glow of sentimental people interest to people who'd rather spend money on living? Probably not. Instead, the tightly shot and lovingly intimate feelings expressed by the Guardian Plan convey a personality of respectful concern for others, while the unvarnished No Frills approach is the curmudgeonly pal you can always expect to be brutally honest.

(SFX: MUSIC. CROWD SOUNDS.)

HARRIET (VO): Oh Mary, I'm so sorry. John was so loved.

JOE (VO): John took care of everything. He did it with The GUARDIAN PLAN program.

LEWIS (VO): Makes you think. Advance funeral planning makes a lot of sense.

PETER (VO): Yes...I remember John saying something about it.

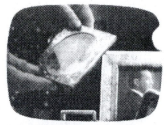

JOE (VO): He took care of all the details so Mary wouldn't be burdened.

HARRIET (VO): Ummh-huh. The GUARDIAN PLAN program.

LUKE (VO): I have one. Decided on everything in advance...even price.

ANN (VO): My Walter talked about getting one...but he never did.

KAY (VO): Well I'm certainly going to do something about it. I'm alone now too.

SON (VO): Mom.
MOTHER (VO): Your father was a wonderful, loving man.
SON (VO): I know.

ANNCR (VO): Call 1-800-9-CARING for your copy of our booklet. It's yours free from The GUARDIAN PLAN insurance funded prearranged funeral program.

FIGURE 14.1   *(Courtesy of Steven Hunter, Moss and Company Inc.)*

Video	Audio
BLACK SCREEN	
ADD SUPER: This is what it looks like when you're buried in a $25,000 funeral.	
LOSE SUPER/BACK TO BLACK	
ADD SUPER: This is what it looks like when You're buried in a $2,000 funeral.	
LOSE SUPER/BACK TO BLACK	VO: When you're gone, you're gone.
ADD 'NO FRILLS' LOGO	

(Created by Saatchi & Saatchi/Sydney)

If you think all the list making required to uncover brand character is a lot of work --- you are right. And if you think this results in overthinking a project --- you are probably right again. But as creative director Mac McLaurin points out:

> Great ideas come from great insight and great insight comes from information. Information that's been personally collected, stored and ruminated on by you. There are no shortcuts. Information is gathered from researching, thinking and rethinking about your client's business. Sometimes this information helps you to reject ideas. And sometimes this information helps you to revise and revise and revise the ideas. Regardless, the process of overthinking is essentially always good.[17]

As former Ogilvy & Mather president Rick Boyko adds, all of this labor is "about finding what's true and powerful about a brand and what's the best way to express that idea through all its different touch points first rather than coming up with a good TV idea, or an ad, and then figuring out how to spread that over everything else."[18]

CONCEPT ENGINEERING—FASHIONING THE CAMPAIGN PROPOSAL

This panoramic idea that is propelled by the power of the brand is captured in the formal *campaign proposal*. Frequently, a senior copywriter is called on not only to compose creative treatments but also to take a hand in the vital preliminary preparation that leads to this proposal's development. Unlike Brand Character Isolation's previously discussed lists, which remain the copywriter's private working sketches, campaign proposals are submitted to a variety of other people within both the agency and client organizations. The quality of a formal proposal must be high because scripts may never be produced, the business never won, if this document lacks clarity, precision, and persuasiveness. Writing solid proposals is the prerequisite to attracting entire accounts --- entire accounts that may bring in the means to pay your entire salary. Campaign proposal realization is normally the sum of five component steps:

1. Client analysis
2. Competition analysis

3. Advertising Objective (AO) development
4. Creative Selling Idea (CSI) construction
5. Sample message creation

Let's take a careful look at each phase of the process.

1. Client (Internal) Analysis

The more you know about the firm whose products you're seeking the opportunity to sell, and the more you know about each of those products, the larger will be the range of options that open themselves to you. (That is why our previously discussed list-making and the information-gathering it requires are so important.) The comprehensive client analysis shows the firm you are courting that you have taken the trouble to learn a lot about its operation and have compiled all the relevant facts needed to marshal a proper campaign response. Thus the client analysis stage comprises the gathering of the raw data out of which those brand character-isolating lists of positive attributes and weaknesses can easily and accurately be assembled.

Even though clients can usually be counted on to supply a great deal of information about themselves, smart campaign creators have learned not to rely exclusively on such materials. This is because client-originated dossiers may be flawed or incomplete for either of two reasons:

1. Clients are so close to their business, they fail to take note of elements that, though mundane to them, may be of unusual appeal to lay consumers. One brewer, around his firm's copper tanks all his life, was surprised that a touring creative team took such interest in them. When exploited in a "gleaming copper kettles" approach, however, this client-dismissed aspect became a successful and tangible referent for the beer's fire-brewing benefit. As writers, we are (fortunately) as initially ignorant of the operations of most of the businesses for which we write as are the consumers at whom we aim our messages. We, sometimes better than the client, can therefore isolate those methods and modes of operation that are of greatest potential interest to current or prospective customers. We can spotlight an implement or process that, while unremarkable to the client, can be of great benefit-illustrating significance to us and the lay audiences to whom we are writing.
2. Client-originated information may also be deficient because top management is afraid to lay bare product/corporate weaknesses. Managers (or their nervous underlings) try to "gild the lily" and treat the copywriter or agency as just one more consumer of their company's public relations plaudits. Then they wonder why the subsequent advertising blows up in their faces because the public wasn't told about the mandatory eight-week delivery delay or that the kitchen cleanser couldn't be used on marble surfaces. Experienced copywriters and market-wise clients have discovered that the firm's public relations department is usually *not* the best liaison with its advertising agency. To do its job, the agency needs the ugly truth rather than the rosy glow that emanates from the PR office.

Take the data that the client or prospective client provides and thoroughly evaluate them as filtered through your own appraisal of client/product strengths and weaknesses. As we advocate earlier, visit the firm's office, store, or plant. Take note of everything, for you can never tell when a seemingly insignificant on-site discovery can later be the key to a blockbuster campaign. Above all, cautions marketing consultant William Bartolini, be certain you have honed in on your client's "real business as determined by the consumer who uses your product. For instance, Black and Decker is not in the business of selling drills, they sell 'easy holes.' Similarly, you may work for a station but the station's real 'business' is probably entertainment."[19] And the GSD&M agency helped low-cost carrier Southwest achieve great success by taking it out of the drab airline business and into the democratizing "freedom business" with its brilliant "You are now free to move about the country" campaign.

2. Competition (External) Analysis

Once you have briefed yourself and *been* briefed on all available account data, you are in a position to define and scrutinize the competition's scope and character. Putting it another way, you are ready to complete a broadened framework for Brand Character Isolation's list #6.

The first requisite of a functional competition analysis is the *competition yardstick,* a definitional framework that separates the real from the imagined rivals. Because the client analysis has already provided you with a clear portrait of your own account, it is relatively easy to isolate its main wares and use these as discriminatory criteria. If your client's restaurant caters to the cocktail crowd, you probably should not worry too much about threats posed by family eateries and pizza places. In short, your client's key activities become the central qualities that any other firm must possess in order to constitute real competition. Here are some sample yardsticks, each of which would usually be preceded by the phrase "Competition for (client/ product name) would include. . . ."

> any gas station within eight miles that also features complete engine repair service;
>
> any store that sells shoes for the whole family;
>
> every all-seasons sporting goods establishment whether self-contained or part of a 'big box' store;
>
> every presweetened cereal intended primarily for consumption by children;
>
> any residential plumbing and heating contractor that handles both installation and maintenance;
>
> every metro-area full-service financial institution with its own trust department.

Once yardsticks such as these ferret out the *primary* rivals, a work-up statement on each of these rivals can be prepared. Such statements are not required to possess the depth of the original client analysis, but instead need concentrate only on describing each competitor's condition *relative to the strengths and weaknesses of your own account.* Hopefully, a pattern will at this point begin to emerge, and you will discover that your client or product is consistently superior (or, at least, *different from*) all competitors in regard to certain specific qualities or ways of doing business.

It might be that your firm has longer hours, a more convenient location, or a wider selection than any of its rivals. Or, your product may be less expensive, faster to use, or easier to store than those manufactured by other companies. Whatever the case, such distinctive advantages have now been identified as potential prime agents for the total campaign strategy.

As the last part of our competition analysis, it is necessary to uncover which advertising vehicles the competition is using and what approaches they are taking via these vehicles. You want your message to be clearly distinguishable from your opponents, and you also must consider their level of electronic media spending. You can't, for instance, outspend a much larger rival, so you may want to consider capitalizing on that very size discrepancy through copy that orchestrates your benefit to the tune of an underdog motif (we're the little company that does more for you because we need your business more).

3. Advertising Objective (AO) Development

With the completion of steps 1 and 2, all the results are in; it is now time to make the unequivocal choice of the central theme that all advertising for this particular product will be designed to promote. Bolstered by an incisive and hopefully unblushing appraisal of marketplace realities, we are now in a position to adopt an approach calculated to achieve the most positive recognition possible for the client whose aims we are serving.

From a workability standpoint, the AO must be narrow enough to delineate your client clearly from the competition, yet broad enough to encompass several related subthemes (or *subgoals* for PSA clients) that may later evolve in campaign fine-tuning. We want to provide growing room for our overall approach without making the AO so vague that we lose the sense of client uniqueness. If, for example, that same Advertising Objective could be put to use by a rival, it should never have been selected. As in the following classic examples, the AO usually includes a specification of target audience (universe) and a delineation of our key client benefit or benefit complex:

> Assure women forty-five and over that Second Debut moisturizing lotion is an effective cosmetic ally for the good and productive years that lie ahead.[20]

> Persuade the under-45 soft-drink user that Dr Pepper is neither a root beer nor a cola but a popular beverage for every occasion.[21]

> Convince blue-collar males that Miller High Life Beer possesses the traditional American attributes of "value, worth and quality."[22]

> Convince middle-aged and older blue-collar workers in the tri-state market that Buick is an affordable as well as a desirable car.[23]

> Tell physically active women that Pretty Feet & Hands is indispensable as an all-around skin care/repair application.[24]

> Demonstrate to men and women ages eighteen to forty-five that, unlike other haircut chains, Supercuts will give you the great looking haircut you want, with no surprises.[25]

> Help consumers age fifty and up understand that the Guardian Plan (revisit Figure 14.1) is the sensible way to complete funeral arrangements so that loved ones won't be burdened.[26]

Communicate to above-average-income families with children that Pizza Hut restaurants employ dedicated people whose primary responsibility is to serve customers.[27]

Show kids that Milk Duds is America's longer-lasting alternative to the candy bar.[28]

Introduce women ages twenty-five to fifty-four to Snuggle's *low-priced* fabric softening and static-cling-reducing capabilities.[29]

The selected advertising objective is then recast into a *positioning statement* that allows the essence of the AO to be articulated in the spot. You would never want to use the above Pizza Hut objective as copy, for example, but the positioning statement "our people make our pizza better" expresses its central tenet in a more abbreviated and conversational form that easily lends itself to script inclusion. Likewise, "when a candy bar is only a memory, you'll still be eating your Milk Duds" is a swingy, copy-ripe translation of the necessarily clinical AO whose cause it promotes. And "snuggly softness that's really less expensive" deftly works in the Snuggle product name as a benefit adjective while still mirroring its AO motivator. Keep in mind that advertising objectives are MARKETER TALK, whereas the positioning statements that flow from them are PEOPLE TALK.

As the Radio ad-Lab summarizes in its copywriter training materials, the positioning statement is "a handle on the business consumers can grab hold of that is "easy to remember, really stands for something and is based on your #1 appeal."[30]

Carelessly selected or crafted positioning statements may still have an impact --- but in a client-maiming way. Imagine the consumer reaction to this copywriter-created line on behalf of a bank whose embezzling vice-president had skipped the country only months before:

Your money goes farther at Assurity National Bank.

Or think about the derision that greeted this TV news positioning statement:

If it happens in Metroville, it's news to TV-6.

Here are some other positioning lines that are calculated only to drive the writers who created them to the unemployment lines:

Beneville Auto Repair. Try us once, you'll never go anywhere again.

No matter what your raincoat is made of, Mira-Spray will make it really repellent.

When you're tired of cleaning yourself, let Jiffy Maid do it.

Woodcrest four-poster beds --- perfect for antique lovers.

The positioning statement is the short encapsulation of the marketing strategy known simply as "positioning." As defined by its cofounder Al Ries, "The goal of an ad program should not be to communicate, but to occupy a 'position' in the prospect's mind."[31] Positioning is the discipline of "looking for a hole that doesn't belong to someone else."[32] Once this hole is located via the analytical procedures we've been discussing, the copywriter chisels a perceptual brand shape to fill it. To DDB's former CEO Keith Reinhard, "the essence of positioning is sacrifice --- deciding what's unimportant, what can be cut away and left behind, reducing your perspective to a very sharp point of view. Once that's done, you have to apply all of your energy, talent, heart and resources toward making your point of view a guiding star for your people."[33] "Positioning," concludes advertising legend Phil Dusenberry, "is really staking a claim to whatever part of consumers' lives you want your brand to dominate: what unique role it can play, what problems it can solve, what special needs it can fulfill."[34]

Positioning, ultimately, is what all of our earlier-mentioned lists and proposal steps have been geared to facilitate. We are trying to find what might be called the high ground of advantage --- the consumer-benefit orientation toward our product or service that clearly and auspiciously sets it apart from the competition and, says marketing professor Conrad Nankin "continually resonates within the minds of a public that is inundated with between 3,000 and 5,000 commercial messages a day."[35] According to Mr. Ries's long-accepted tenets:

> The first rule of positioning is this: You can't compete head-on against a company that has a strong, established position. You can go around, under or over, but never head-to-head. The leader owns the high ground . . . Too many companies embark on marketing and advertising programs as if the competitor's position did not exist. They advertise their products in a vacuum and are disappointed when their messages fail to get through.[36]

The associated technique of *re*positioning entails the application of a prime product characteristic to a new consumer-use benefit. Not long after its founding way back in 1846, the makers of Arm & Hammer baking soda came to realize people were using this product for much more than a leavening agent. Ultimately, the brand was repositioned as a trusted cleansing agent. The baking soda also came to be marketed as an odor-fighting "nice little secret for your refrigerator." Meanwhile, brand extension products made possible by this evolved positioning resulted in the launch of Arm & Hammer brand laundry detergent (1970), toothpaste (1988), deodorant (1994), and cat litter (1998).[37]

Similarly, Sara Lee offset a big decline in frozen dessert sales by moving from an image of plebeian pound cake convenience to that of purveyor of "Elegant Evenings" cheesecakes and croissants, hawked by a Parisian-sounding actress who queried, "Zis Sarah Lee, she is French, no?" Decades earlier, Miss Clairol hair color was saved by the studied repositioning repetition of the "Does She or Doesn't She?" question. "Previously," recalls marketing consultant Faith Popcorn, "the only women who dyed their hair had been blue-haired or of questionable reputation. Clairol's repositioning of hair coloring made it a legitimate option for self-respecting proper American women of any age."[38]

More recently, Prudential Insurance Company's century-old 'Rock of Gibraltar' symbol needed to be recast. "A rock is inflexible, and impersonal," perceived Fallon Advertising's chairman Pat Fallon. So his agency suggested changing Prudential's longstanding "Own (later, 'grab') a piece of the rock" slogan to "Be your own rock"—and won the $60 million account.[39] Even more succinctly, the California Prune Board and its associated growers won Food and Drug Administration approval to change the name *prunes* to *dried plums*. "Prunes [are seen] as an old person's fruit, and as a laxative," says Sunsweet's marketing vice-president Howard Nager, who feels the change makes the fruit more appealing to younger consumers. "There's nothing wrong with the name to those of us who know prunes and love them," asserts Richard Peterson of the California Prune Board. "But to some, it conjures up other images. 'Dried plums' sounds more appealing and contemporary."[40]

Positioning/repositioning statements, and the advertising objectives that motivate them, are clearly of extreme importance for both old and new products. They are also a prime indication that today's copywriter must be part creator and part market strategist --- a professional at home in both worlds. In fact, advertising pioneer David Ogilvy observed that campaign mastery depends less on "how we write your advertising than on how your product is positioned."[41]

In the twenty-first century, heritage brand Campbell Soup found its traditional image as 'the nutritious comfort liquid Mom served' was no longer resonating with the lifestyle needs of younger audiences. Sales were steadily falling. So it perceptually got out of the soup business and started marketing its product not as a line of 'soup,' but as 'easy to carry and easy to prepare hot meals.' This, accordingly to Campbell chief strategy officer Carl Johnson, enabled the company to "take what had been a narrow soup-against-soup positioning and broaden the competitive frame" by playing on the idea of a convenient soup that eats like a meal.[42] On the other side of the Atlantic, Heinz Microwave Soup was similarly establishing itself among younger British consumers as the easy meal in just two minutes. In the following award-winning commercial, there is no focus on the product's nutrition, cost or "just like Grandmother's" taste. (In fact, grandmothers are deliberately the last thing this scenario brings to mind.) Instead, the soup is potently positioned as the sensory satisfaction young consumers can achieve --- even in the most abbreviated of situations.

Video	Audio
OPEN ON YOUNG MAN AND WOMAN LYING IN BED. MAN ROLLS OVER ONTO HIS BACK WITH A SIGH. WOMAN STARES UP AT CEILING. THEY'RE BOTH RED-FACED, WITH RUFFLED HAIR.	SFX: ENVIRONMENT SOUNDS
MAN HAPPILY BLOWS THROUGH PUFFED CHEEKS, LOOKS PLEASED WITH SELF. WOMAN LOOKS NOT TOO PLEASED.	
WOMAN GETS UP AND LEAVES ROOM.	
CUT TO KITCHEN AS WOMAN ENTERS. SHE WALKS STRAIGHT OVER TO MICROWAVE. AS SHE REACHES IT, DIGITAL DISPLAY READS:	
1:58, 1:59, AND 2:00.	SFX: MICROWAVE 'ping'

Video	Audio
WITH A SIGH, SHE OPENS MICROWAVE AND TAKES OUT POT OF CREAM OF TOMATO. WISPS OF STEAM RISE FROM RICH BUBBLING SOUP. SUPER: Heinz Microwaveable Soups. Ready in two minutes.	

(Courtesy of Erika Moore, Leo Burnett Ltd./London)

4. Creative Selling Idea (CSI) Construction

From the AO, and the positioning statement that mirrors it, are spun a number of related, more detailed, and more focused applications. Each of these *Creative Selling Ideas* can, in turn, form the skeletal frame for a spot or flight of spots. Definitionally, a CSI is:

> **1.** a consumer-related *benefit*
>
> (+)
>
> **2.** a *technique* for presenting it
>
> (as applied to)
>
> **3.** this specific product or service.

CSIs (often referred to in PSA campaigns as *subgoals*) must be very carefully constructed if they are to contain all the above ingredients as well as relate unmistakably to their umbrella Advertising Objective.

Frequently, a novice writer will construct CSIs that are long on technique but in which the benefit is buried if not missing altogether:

Zoo spots in which trainer walks into various big cats' cages while eating from a bag of Acme Potato Chips.
(Product benefit?)

Or, the benefit may be there, but its execution is vague or unworkable within the creative and budgetary confines of the campaign:

Demonstrate distinct crunch of Acme Potato Chips by featuring it in a variety of international settings.
(What kind of settings? Why international? How does the setting document 'crunch'?)

Worst of all, the benefit and technique may show real thought and promise but fail to showcase the product properly or are totally outside the parameters set by the coordinating AO. This last defect, of course, would result in the sort of campaign fragmentation that all the previous stages of proposal development have worked so diligently to preclude. It would create multiple positions for the brand that, states positioning theory's co-founder Jack Trout, "are like multiple personalities or schizophrenia. Whether it is products or people, all it does is generate confusion. You have to stand for something in the mind or you become nothing."[43]

Advertising executive Paul Goldsmith describes what can happen when the coordinative AO is disregarded:

> When a creative person sits down to conceive an advertisement, he will often find it tempting to wander away from the agreed-upon strategy. Clearly, a desired quality is the discipline to keep the work within the confines of the product positioning. A scintillating piece of copy for a new car that highlights the fact that you need never carry a spare tire, when the strategy talks about better mileage, is a flop no matter how clever or brilliantly executed. "That's brilliant!" "That's funny!" "Beautifully done!" All are wasted words when the client says, "This is not the strategy we agreed upon."[44]

As Professor Brett Robbs discovered in a survey of advertising executives, "There is one creative skill that respondents seem to value over all the others. That's conceptual strength. It's the ability to transform the strategy statement [the AO] into an idea [a CSI] so astonishing that it makes the familiar seem new and enables the target to see both the product and its benefit as if for the first time. . . . In fact, conceptual strength is so important that survey respondents suggested that it can cause prospective employers to overlook other weaknesses."[45]

Below is an Advertising Objective for Marlene's Apparel Emporium and three *disciplined* CSIs that flow from it. Notice how each includes all three components of a good Creative Selling Idea and how each relates back to the umbrella AO. Note too that each CSI could constitute the basis for a single spot as well as for a whole series of closely related spots that would thereby comprise an *integrated flight:*

Advertising Objective:
Attract over-40 women to Marlene's by stressing the shop's concern for sensible fashions.

Creative Selling Ideas:

1. Multivoice spots featuring female school teacher(s) who find(s) Marlene's blouses are comfortable to teach in and still look smart.
2. Gift-giving husband testimonials to the economical altering service Marlene's provides to "tailor-make" their clothes --- even after the sale.
3. Marlene talks to women about her fashionable yet adaptable scarves.

As another example, here is how an eatery might be positioned through AO/CSI framing:

Advertising Objective:
Establish for area lower-income families and singles that Taco Heaven is the place to go for inexpensive and appealing Mexican food.

Creative Selling Ideas:

1. Multivoiced spots of teens enjoying an after-school snack at Taco Heaven --- affordable munchies even on an allowance budget.
2. Testimonials by blue-collar and clerical workers that eating at Taco Heaven converts lunchtime into a mini Mexican vacation.
3. Dialogue spots in which one homemaker tells another how Taco Heaven's menu entices her children to eat fresh vegetables, and for a lower-than-grocery-store cost.

5. Sample Message Creation

As the final step in your proposal development, you are ready to engage in what most copywriters (vocationally, at least) like to do best. You can now create a sample series of announcements that reflect all the market data and decision making with which the first four stages of the proposal are preoccupied. The messages constructed and presented at this, the final stage of the proposal, may either all relate to a single CSI—and thereby constitute an integrated flight—or they may derive from several different CSIs in order to demonstrate the range of campaign possibilities that exist within the framework of the advocated AO.

The two television spots below, for instance, are part of a single-CSI integrated flight that shows McDonald's as an ideal place for parent/child bonding. The "overarching" AO was *to demonstrate to middle-class parents that McDonald's is more than fast food --- it's an opportunity for gladdening family experiences.*

Video	Audio
SUPER: 'First Order" LOGO: McDonald's OPEN ON MOM AND LITTLE DAUGHTER INSIDE MCDONALD'S RESTAURANT SITTING ACROSS FROM EACH OTHER AT TABLE.	MOM: It's your first time. So remember what to say.
CU OF MOM	O.K?
CU OF DAUGHTER	DAUGHTER: O.K.
MOM HANDS HER MONEY	MOM: All right. And you pay with this. O.K.?
DAUGHTER WALKS TOWARD COUNTER	SINGER: She's growing up so quickly. I wish she didn't have to do.
DAUGHTER AT COUNTER	DAUGHTER: Um . . . cheeseburger, milk
DAUGHTER TURNS AROUND AND LOOKS AT MOM WHO MOUTHS THE WORD 'FRIES'.	SINGER: But go ahead and grow my little one.
DAUGHTER TURNS BACK TO COUNTER	DAUGHTER: ---and fries.
CU TO MOM SMILING	SINGER: It's so beautiful to see.
	DAUGHTER (VO): Thank you
DAUGHTER TAKES TRAY OF FOOD BACK TO MOM	SINGER: It's a good time
	DAUGHTER: (WHISPERS) Mommy. I got it!
SUPER: It's a good time for the great taste	MOM: (Laughs)
LOGO: McDonald's	SINGER: McDonald's.

Video	Audio
OPEN IN CLASSROOM. BOY IN SEAT POKES HIS HEAD OUT FROM DESK AND LOOKS BEHIND HIM AT GALLAGHER	MUSIC: THEME UP AND UNDER BOY: Hey, Gallagher, coming to lunch?
GALLAGHER THROWS CRUMPLED PAPER INTO WASTE BASKET	GAL: Nope --- going to see someone.
CUT TO GALLAGHER WALKING ALONG STREET	SINGER: Someone's thinking of you. Of that moment together---
CUT TO GALLAGHER'S HAND RECEIVING CHANGE AFTER BUYING FOOD AT MCDONALD'S. HE GRABS FOOD IN MCDONALD'S BAG	GAL: Thank you
CUT TO GALLAGHER ON STREET, CARRYING BAG. CUT TO HIM ARRIVING AT OFFICE. HE SITS ON RECEPTION COUCH. RECEPTIONIST IN BG	SINGER: ---that's just between you two. RECEP: Paging Mr. Gallagher.
CUT TO SIDE PROFILE GALLAGHER AS MEN WALK THROUGH FRONT DOORS IN BG. CUT TO GALLAGHER SMILING, CUT TO DAD NOTICING HIM AND SMILING BACK.	SINGER: There's a boy that makes you happy 'cause he's always there for you.
CUT TO SON AND DAD WALKING DOWN HALL TOGETHER	GAL: Hi dad. I hope you aren't too busy. SINGER: Together---
RECEPTIONIST LEANS OVER DESK AND SHOUTS DOWN HALL AFTER THEM	RECEP: Mr. Gallagher, you're needed in production.
CUT TO DAD. HE POINTS FINGER AT SON	DAD: Mr. Gallagher's needed right here.
CUT TO DAD AND GALLAGHER EATING IN OFFICE SUPER: McDonald's and You LOGO: McDonald's	SINGER: McDonald's and you.

(Courtesy of Terrence J. O'Malley, Vickers & Benson Advertising Ltd.)

In contrast, the following two TV commercials relate to two *different* CSIs within the same campaign. Here, the coordinating Advertising Objective is *to demonstrate to parents that Staples is the one-stop resolution to their back-to-school needs as well as those of their children.* CSI #1 unveils Staples' range of school supplies for younger students, and CSI #2 showcases the store's computer equipment for launching college-bound offspring.

Video	Audio
OPEN ON EMPTY AISLE AT STAPLES	MUSIC: "THE MOST WONDERFUL TIME OF THE YEAR" (MALE VOCAL) FEATURE AND UNDER
GROWN MAN ENTERS FRAME DANCING DOWN AISLE WHILE PUSHING CART	VO: It's that time of year again.
HIS KIDS ENTER FRAME BEHIND HIM, DEPRESSED AND HANGING THEIR HEADS	They're going back!
FATHER STOPS CART, AND BEGINS TAUNTING KIDS WITH SCHOOL SUPPLIES, DANGLING HIGHLIGHTERS IN THEIR FACES, FANNING OUT NOTEBOOKS, ETC.	It's back to school time at Staples.
FATHER SKIPS DOWN AISLE, LEAVING TWO KIDS ALONE, STARING UP AT HUGE WALL OF SUPPLIES. PRICE BUBBLES APPEAR ON VARIOUS PRODUCTS	Over 5,000 school supplies at the guaranteed low price.
FATHER ENTERS/EXITS FRAME RIDING ON TOP OF SHOPPING CART	
CUT TO STAPLES ANIMATED STAPLER LOGO SPELLING WORD 'Staples"	Staples. Yeah, we've got that.

Video	Audio
OPEN ON DAD AND COLLEGE-AGE SON IN DRIVEWAY IN FRONT OF FULLY-LOADED CAR. DAD HELPING LOAD COMPUTER INTO CAR ON TOP OF EVERYTHING ELSE	MUSIC: SOFT EMOTIONAL INSTRUMENTAL THROUGHOUT
	DAD: So this is it huh --- you're off to college.
	SON: Yeah---
DAD MOTIONS TO COMPUTER BOXES, TRYING TO PROLONG CONVERSATION	DAD: Pretty high-tech stuff you got here.
	SON: Yeah, but the guy at Staples explained everything when I bought it.
	DAD: Good --- well, good luck.
UNCOMFORTABLE PAUSE AS SON LOOKS BACK TOWARD HOUSE	SON: Isn't Mom gonna say good-bye?
DAD SHAKES HEAD 'NO'	DAD: She's still up in your room, getting used to the idea.
SON GRABS DAD, HUGS HIM	SON: Well, I love you, Dad

Continued

Video	Audio
CUT TO DAD IN DRIVEWAY AS SON'S CAR PULLS OUT	
CUT TO DAD UPSTAIRS IN DOORWAY OF SON'S ROOM, TALKING TO MOM	DAD: He's gone. What do you think?
CUT TO MOM IN SON'S ROOM EXCITEDLY MEASURING WALLS WITH TAPE MEASURE	MOM: Only 9-and-a-half feet. We're gonna need 10 for the hot tub!
	DAD: Well, this wall's gonna have to come down---
CUT TO IN-STORE DISPLAY OF STACKED COMPUTERS	VO: Staples has computers and 7,000 supplies at the guaranteed low price. Staples. Yeah, we've got that.

(Courtesy of Arthur Bijur and Catherine Abate, Cliff Freeman and Partners)

Well-designed outlet promotional campaigns likewise are built via Concept Engineering principles. In the following television spots for Detroit's CW-50, the objective was *to convince blue-collar males that the station's evening syndicated sitcoms are habit-forming guy fun.* Or, as the positioning statement put it, "Contagious Watching with CW-50." Each CSI pertained to a different show in the outlet's pre- or post-network time blocs, with all the promos tied together by a consistently male-oriented irreverence. The first spot below focuses on an 'access period' (pre-prime time) program and the second on a show that followed the evening's CW network-originated offerings.

Video	Audio
GRAPHIC: Tales in Contagious Watching	VO: And now, Tales in Contagious Watching --- on CW-50
BLUE-COLLAR GUY SEATED IN BLACK VOID, SPEAKING TO OFF-CAMERA INTERVIEWER	GUY: I work the swing shift at the plant. And before I leave for work at 7, I always watch *King of Queens* at 6:30 on CW-50. I appreciate the hilarity of Doug's comedic manifesto for the American working class. Plus his wife on the show is way hot. Last week, the show was so good, I decided to stay for the second episode at 7. I didn't even care if I was late for work. Well, I found out later that there was a tanker truck explosion on I-75 right <u>where I would've been</u> if I'd left on time! If not for my love of *King of Queens* and CW-50 --- well, I don't even wanna think about that.
BACK TO TITLE GRAPHIC	VO: Contagious watching with CW-50.

Video	Audio
GRAPHIC: Tales in Contagious Watching	VO: And now, Tales in Contagious Watching --- on CW-50.
BLUE-COLLAR DAD SEATED WITH TEENAGE SON, IN BLACK VOID, SPEAKING TO OFF-CAMERA INTERVIEWER	DAD: I wasn't a very good father while my son was growing up. But after years of watching *That '70s Show* --- weeknights at 10:30 on CW-50 --- I saw how Red imparted his wisdom to Eric and his friends. And I learned what it takes to be a good father. SON: I love you, Dad. DAD: Shut up, dumb-ass.
BACK TO TITLE GRAPHIC	VO: Contagious watching with CW-50.

(Courtesy of Tadd Van Cleve, CW-50)

Looking at our total five-stage proposal process in retrospect, it schematically suggests an hourglass, such as that diagramed in Figure 14.2. We start off as broadly as possible, gathering and analyzing client data from every conceivable source and perspective. This leads to developing a discriminatory competition yardstick and a consequent narrowing of focus to encompass only those other firms and products that meet the yardstick's specified criteria. From this we taper the process even more in the construction of an Advertising Objective and associated positioning statement. Together, these set the boundaries within which our product can be discussed and revealed to its greatest advantage. Several applied Creative Selling Ideas or subgoals branch out from this coordinating AO. These CSIs and subgoals, in turn, can each give birth to several closely associated spots and even flights of spots.

Through it all, the AO functions as central coordinating device. The first two stages of proposal development are devoted to a diligent narrowing of focus and the last two stages to that focuses' amplification and attainment. The Advertising Objective, in short, constitutes the *synergism* [look that up in your Noah Webster] between broad-based market research and multifaceted creativity.

Whatever you do, don't assume your spots will automatically conform to your AO specification. "The search for great ads is like jumping up and down in a box without a roof," says Swedish agency president Bo Ronnberg. "Creatives can, and should, jump as high as they can. But they have to keep within the four walls. Remember: Advertising is in the field of business, not entertainment. Part of the exhilaration and challenge of advertising is to be both brilliant and on strategy."[46] To meet this challenge, make sure the conceptual sand flows undiverted from the top to the bottom of your own proposal hourglass --- in other words, down to the spots themselves. "Strategy is only as good as the creative it produces," declares McCann-Erickson vice-chairman Peter Kim. "Strategy is discipline in pursuit of passion, while creative is passion in pursuit of discipline. By limiting strategic options, we'll open up creative options. Your strategy should be able to dance on the head of a pin. When you narrow it that much, it opens up incredible creative depths."[47]

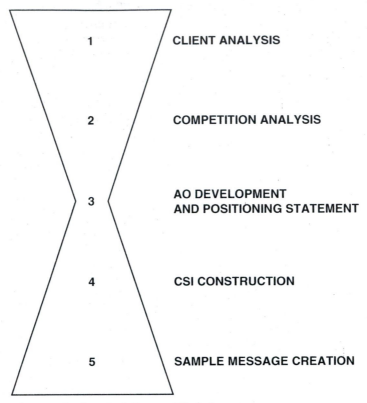

FIGURE 14.2   Concept Engineering's Proposal Hourglass.

PROPOSAL-RELATED ACTIVITIES AND IMPLEMENTS

Particularly as an in-station, cable, or Website copywriter, you may never be called on to construct a full-scale proposal of the type just described. Your local accounts especially may have long since been presold or attracted by an advantageous price structure or positive ratings reports that your outlet's salespeople are pushing. Under such circumstances, your main responsibilities will be to write the copy for these established customers in the manner to which they and/or your sales staff are accustomed. If, for instance, client merchants insist on being personally featured in the message, you accept the fact that they are spending money primarily to sell themselves rather than their businesses, so you showcase these people as best you can.

Prospects File

There comes a time, however, when even the most prosperous station/system/site needs to solicit some new accounts or, due to changing marketing or client management conditions, to revamp existing copy strategies. Perhaps a new competitor has emerged for your client or that client has moved into a new line or area of endeavor that presents a whole new slate of competitors. Under such conditions, the *prospects file* becomes a crucial resource --- and one for which you, the copywriter, may be responsible.

Simply put, the prospects file is made up of profiles of businesses that are either potential clients or potential or actual competitors of current clients. Each profile usually consists of a somewhat abbreviated version of proposal stage #1 (client analysis) plus a semi-standardized stage #2 (competition analysis).

Because you don't have the time, or the immediate need, for truly comprehensive client analyses in this prospects file resource bank, each sketch will normally just set down the main characteristics of each business and any advantages or weaknesses for which it is particularly noted. The limited depth of these profiles, in turn, makes it impossible to draw up *detailed* and customized competition analyses from them. As the prospects file is an initial familiarizer rather than a finalized product, extended and separate competition analyses for a bunch of businesses that may never become your clients would be wasted effort.

Instead, categorized competition surveys can be written in such subject areas as restaurants, financial institutions, auto repair shops, and so on. Copies of these surveys can be placed with each prospective client profile belonging to that category. If the classification is an especially large one given the market situation, you can also break down these categories into subunits. Restaurants, for example, can be divided into fast-food places, pizza parlors, and family and formal dining establishments, with separate competitive summaries written for each segment.

For purposes of illustration, let's say that one of your station's sales personnel is trying to woo business from a furniture emporium that has not previously advertised on your outlet. This salesperson should be able to obtain from the prospects file a prewritten, generic competition analysis covering local furniture stores as a whole. This can be supplemented with the individual sketches on each of the stores, including, of course, the profile on the store being courted. As that store becomes more interested and requests more detailed advertising suggestions, its abbreviated profile can be expanded and updated on the basis of the information to which it now gives you or your sales staff access. The generic competition analysis can also be customized to take into account the particular strengths and activities of this store and, if necessary, the other three stages of a full-dress proposal can now be prepared.

If the furniture store joins your list of clients, the pre-research will have immediately paid off. But even if the store decides to forgo business with your outlet or through your agency at this time, all the effort has not been wasted. For, in the courting process, you have acquired a great deal more information about that store and, therefore, about the furniture business in the market. This information can help you serve that firm more quickly in the future. And even if the store *never* signs a contract with you, your prospects file has still been enriched by much more specific and comprehensive material about it --- material that can be very useful in constructing pitches or formal proposals for that store's competition.

Spec(ulative) Writing

A closely allied procedure in which the copywriter may be involved is called *spec writing*. In spec writing, you prepare sample spots for businesses that are not yet your clients. There are two types of spec work: *specific* and *generic*. In *specific* projects, you are making a new business pitch to a particular company in the hope that it will assign you its advertising work. When done for a prospective rather than an existing client, the last stage of our just-discussed Concept Engineering process can constitute a *specific* spec writing situation.

Unfortunately, specific-project spec spots usually are not capable of getting any actual airplay. Indeed, one of the most irritating aspects of this kind of writing is that even account-winning creative seldom sees the light of day. This is because clients never *fully* brief the prospective media agency (and its copywriter) on business details until after they hire them. Such a guarded situation can lead to poor choices by clients who forget this spec work is not fully grounded in the core realities of their business. So the spec work lacks staying power. "I've gone through enough reviews to know that asking an agency to do spec work is ridiculous," asserts Heineken's marketing head Steve Davis. "I've been in situations where an agency was able to strike lightning with the creative spec project. Then you find out six months down the road they were a one-hit wonder."[48]

In addition, because it is part of a new business pitch, clients are likely to "get really comfortable, safe work. The spec creative process creates an incentive to please you [the client] first and consumers second," says Young & Laramore's president Tom Denari. "Unfortunately for pitch-dependent advertisers, the campaigns that usually engage consumers and drive sales are the ones that are surprising and unexpected. They start with what's important to the consumer, not the advertiser."[49] Even if it is aired, such spec work is therefore unlikely to achieve subsequent marketplace success.

Nevertheless, spec spots have become an ever more important element in the winning of new business, so be prepared to create them --- hopefully in a way that lays the groundwork for a successful rather than dead-on-arrival campaign. The following 'specific' spec spot is designed to show a fitness club how radio can be used to dramatize its seasonal specials in ways that resonate with customer lifestyles.

(MUSIC: HALLOWEEN SPOOKY – ESTABLISH AND UNDER)

ANNCR: It's the week after Halloween, and you're *still* eating all your kids' candy. 'But they're just tiny little treats,' you say. True, but a couple handfuls of 'fun-size' candy bars can lead to a 'super-size' butt. You see, Halloween is the start of the over-eating season.

(MUSIC: CROSSFADE SPOOKY MUSIC TO 'OVER THE RIVER AND THROUGH THE WOODS' INSTRUMENTAL)

ANNCR: In just a couple weeks, you can add turkey, mashed potatoes, and pumpkin pie girth to those candy calories.

(MUSIC: CROSSFADE TO CHRISTMAS EFFECT)

ANNCR: Then it's a month of Christmas cookies and eggnog. If you're waiting until January first (MUSIC: QUICK CROSSFADE TO 'AULD LANG SYNE') to start exercising, you're already ten pounds behind.

(MUSIC: 'SYNE' GRINDS TO A HALT, TRANSITIONS TO CONTEMPORARY UPBEAT)

ANNCR: Lakeside Fitness on Humphrey Street is giving you a chance to stay in shape for the holidays. Come in now for the 'November New Year's Resolution' special. Sign up for a one-year membership, and Lakeside Fitness will give you a 20% discount. Power off those pounds just as soon as you put them on with Lakeside's personal trainers, aerobics classes, and free weights. But don't sit on this offer. If you do, your spare tire will still be there --- but this chance for savings won't. Come into Lakeside Fitness before Thanksgiving to receive your 20% discount on a one-year membership. Let Lakeside Fitness help you power your way through the holidays.

(Courtesy of Craig Allen, Citadel Communications)

In the other category of spec work, *generic,* you are not pitching a particular client. Rather, you are writing broad categorical advertising into which a specific company can be dropped. Thus the same treatment may be usable for different clients in different markets. Obviously, such spots can never be as tailor-made for a company as will commercials built from the ground up through application of Concept Engineering discipline. Nevertheless, for businesses unable to afford campaigns designed exclusively for them, a well-chosen "off-the-rack" generic approach can at least increase their brand awareness --- unless this approach is too close to that of an established competitor.

The following generic spec spot by master copywriter Dick Orkin can be used to promote the core attribute of virtually any economy furniture store. Underlined sections can be removed and replaced with another emporium's name without compromising the integrity of the concept. While such spots will never reflect a particular store's unique character, they can at least project a clear consumer benefit in a high-profile way.

WIFE: Charles, it's not necessary for you to build all our furniture yourself!

MAN: But where could you find a couch like this?

WIFE: This is not a couch!

MAN: What is it then?

WIFE: This is a lot of bleach bottles stapled together and covered with an old shower curtain.

MAN: But think of all the money we're saving!

WIFE: There's a better way to furnish our home! Brandon Furniture! They're inexpensive, but they offer a wide selection of stylish furniture.

MAN: Like our coffee table.

WIFE: This is just an old tire.

MAN: So?

WIFE: So where do you put stuff on it?

MAN: I didn't say it was perfect.

WIFE: Take me to Brandon Furniture so we can get rid of this junk!

MAN: This dining room table you call junk?

WIFE: Because it's our old worn out screen door balancing on two garbage cans---

MAN:	But think of the money we're saving!
WIFE:	<u>It's nothing compared to what we'd save at Brandon Furniture.</u>
	For example, this lamp you're making out of tuna fish cans. What's it costing you?
MAN:	Um --- well, let's see. 500 cans of tuna fish, at $800, plus two kitty cats to eat the tuna---
WIFE:	Charles---
ANNCR:	<u>Think how much farther your money will go during Brandon Brothers Fall Clearance. Everything on the floor is up to one-half off now through the end of the month. Save now during Fall Clearance prices at Brandon Brothers Furniture. Jupiter Road at Kingsley.</u>

(Courtesy of Fran Sax, FirstCom)

Generic spec spots can be fashioned for television as well. The Figure 14.3 storyboard, created by a firm that specializes in generics, positions a catering service as the trouble-free, economical way to throw a successful party. Many small businesses cannot afford to produce treatments such as this from scratch, but they can benefit from generics written in such a way that the customization process is both easy and seamless.

In crafting specific and generic spec spots, use whatever product classification parameters and data are available to you in orienting your hypothetical approach to the very real marketplace consumers at whom this approach is supposedly aimed. Even if you have been given only the broadest description of the types of business or services to which your spec spots are expected to appeal, you can, at the minimum, make sure each announcement you write includes a rational appeal, at least one emotional appeal, a consumer-involving benefit, and the other main qualities we discuss in the previous thirteen chapters. Spec spots take a lot of work, so don't waste them by forgetting their ultimate purpose. "Spec spots are only for prospects on the fence," cautions radio creative services director Steven Steinberg. "They are not a prospecting tool. A spec spot isn't something you bring to a first meeting with a client. It is designed to close a deal, not open discussions."[50]

FOUR CASE STUDIES

A discussion of electronic media campaign construction and its motivating creative strategies would not be complete without the presentation of some classic illustrative examples of campaign development in action. The cases that follow do not articulate every step in proposal evolution. That would require an entire book in and of itself. Instead, they collectively serve to exemplify the interaction of market factors and analyses with creative design and development.

Case #1: Calavo Avocado Guacamole[51]

A carefully directed radio campaign can have just as much impact as can a television plan --- even in cases where the product category itself is in basic need of defining. Such a definitional problem was met head-on and solved by the old Anderson-McConnell agency in an historic campaign on behalf of its client, the Calavo Growers of California.

AUDIO VOICE OVER:

Planning a wedding reception or party

at "YOUR NAME CATERERS"

We'll organize the party of your life

We'll supply the furniture and decorations

fine food and our bar services

together with a tailor made menu of gastronomical delights

Elegantly served by our experienced staff

and remember when we set it up, we clean it up!

Whatever your taste in budget

we do it all for one low price.

Call

"YOUR NAME CATERERS

555-FOOD

FIGURE 14.3   *(Courtesy of Michael Mills, Thumbnail Spots Ltd.)*

The product to be marketed was Calavo's guacamole --- a frozen avocado dip that, though one-of-a-kind as to its ingredients, had to compete with the much better-known dip flavors manufactured and promoted by much larger corporations.

With a small budget that made radio the only feasible broadcast delivery system, the Anderson-McConnell creative group went about their analytical work. Given the uniqueness of the product and its name, an extensive client and competition analysis was unnecessary. The Advertising Objective, after all, was virtually automatic:

To identify and introduce to party-givers what guacamole is and who makes it.

Because avocados were still a fairly exotic item in many parts of the country, it was doubtful that consumers would make that key original purchase simply for their own snacking as they would, say, a new brand of potato chips. Rather, special foods are purchased for special occasions --- for parties, in other words. So people whose social and economic status enabled them to give parties became the campaign's target audience. And since parties are supposed to be fun, a light, humorous approach seemed not only natural, but almost mandatory --- as long as the humor did not decrease the attention given to product definition. Here are two of the spots that executed this concept.

Spot #1 (30 secs.)

(MUSIC: COCKTAIL DANCE-BEAT BEGINS)

(SFX: INTERMINGLE PARTY SOUNDS)

WOMAN: Would you like to try the avocado dip?

MAN: Sure, is it anything like the tango?

(MUSIC: UP AND STOPS FOR:)

MAN: Do you realize that Calavo is the only one in history to successfully freeze a ready-to-serve avocado dip?

MAN 2:   Holy guacamole!

(MUSIC: STARTS AND STOPS FOR:)

WOMAN: Listen --- if <u>she's</u> serving this jazzy avocado dip, it must be easy to serve. Why, it takes her two hours to make instant coffee.

(MUSIC STARTS WITH FOLLOWING VOICES OVER IT)

MAN: GWA-ka-mole, eh?

WOMAN: <u>WA</u>-ke-mole. Calavo Avocado Guacamole.

MAN: (In rhythm) Calavo Avocado Guacamole (BEAT) Dip.

ALL: (In rhythm) Calavo Avocado Guacamole (BEAT) Dip.

          (Fading off) Calavo Avocado Guacamole (BEAT) Dip.

          (Repeat to fade out at time.)

<u>Spot #2 (60 secs.)</u>

<u>(MUSIC: COCKTAIL DANCE-BEAT BEGINS)</u>

<u>(SFX: INTERMINGLE PARTY SOUNDS)</u>

<u>(MUSIC: STOPS FOR:)</u>

MAN:	(Pompous) It's a scientific breakthrough, do you hear? Frozen avocado dip, fully prepared and ready to release its provocative flavor at the touch of a can opener. What do you say to that, eh?
MAN 2:	What <u>can</u> I say? Holy guacamole!

<u>(MUSIC: STARTS AND STOPS FOR:)</u>

WOMAN:	Calavo Avocado Guacamole, Roger?
MAN 3:	You're talking my language, Elaine.

<u>(MUSIC: STARTS AND STOPS FOR:)</u>

MAN:	Honey, did you know that this avocado dip is frozen at 300 degrees below zero?
WOMAN 2:	Speaking of that, dear, did you notice I'm the only woman at this party without a fur coat?

<u>(MUSIC: STARTS:)</u>

MAN 2:	GWA-ka-mole, eh?
WOMAN 3:	<u>WA</u>-ka-mole. Calavo Avocado Guacamole.
MAN 3:	(In rhythm) Calavo Avocado Guacamole (BEAT) Dip.
ALL:	(In rhythm) Calavo Avocado Guacamole (BEAT) Dip. (Repeat to fade out at time.)

Definition, boisterous brand memorability, and continuing universe-oriented interest made this historic Calavo campaign a legendary low-budget success story. As it unmistakably proved, careful campaign planning can bring significant dividends to small as well as large accounts.

Case #2: Nationwide Buying Group[52]

Registering a single brand is one thing. But it is quite another task to promote a client whose outlets are known by different names and sell multiple products.

That was the situation Lawler Ballard Advertising faced in creating a campaign for the Nationwide Buying Group. Nationwide is a purchasing consortium comprised of six different chains. Thus the task became one of deriving a single, generic approach that each entity could use in its own marketing area as a distinctive and cohesive campaign.

Lawler Ballard knew that clients of this type require a number of low-cost commercials rather than one or two blockbusters. Further, flight cohesion would have to be maintained over a long string of season-oriented ads while still keeping production costs down. Video (rather than the more expensive film) seemed the obvious budgetary choice and, when thinking about genres usually shot on tape, soap operas came to the creatives' minds. Out of this brainstorming gradually emerged "Monica," a continuing soap opera that propelled the title-role heroine through a number of pun-raising spots in which the advertised sale was the payoff to each dramatic episode. Monica's exploits were so campy, and the puns they motivated so shameless, that the campaign "serial" soon acquired a loyal following among audiences in Norfolk, Virginia, where the Nationwide stores bore the name Northeast.

Each succeeding "Monica" installment was tied to seasonal event with the concluding tag frame easily customizable via a single graphic and voiceover line to identify the particular chain found in each respective market. Because so much retail advertising looks like it was created on a photocopy machine, "Monica" truly stood out as a high-profile and easily extendable concept that raised viewer attentiveness and sale awareness levels. Three of "Monica's" sequenced episodes appear below.

Video	Audio
FALL CLEARANCE SALE	
MONICA ENTERS LIVING ROOM, SETS DOWN BAG, TURNS ON ANSWERING MACHINE	SFX: BEEP
	GRANT (VO): Hey, Monica. This is Grant. Can't wait till tonight.
SHE TAKES OFF HER COAT AS SHE LISTENS	SFX: BEEP
	RODNEY (VO): Hey, baby, it's Rodney. I had a cancellation tonight. You're on.
MONICA MOVES CLOSE TO MACHINE	SFX: BEEP
	DADDY (VO): Hey you little filly. Sugar Daddy here. I'm at the airport and on my way.
MONICA TURNS OFF MACHINE. WE SEE GUY IN BATHROBE COMING OUT OF KITCHEN WITH WINE AND GLASSES	GUY: Surprise, Monica!
GRAPHIC: Fall Over-Stocked Sale	VO: Too bountiful a fall --- selected appliances, TVs, home entertainment systems and more. 10 to 50 percent off.
ADD CUSTOM GRAPHIC: Northeast	The Fall Overstocked Sale, at Northeast.
THANKSGIVING SALE	
MONICA AND JASON AT FRONT DOOR; HE TURNS AS SHE HELPS HIM ON WITH HIS COAT	JASON: That was some Thanksgiving dinner, Monica.

Video	Audio
HE ADMIRES HIMSELF IN MIRROR	But you know what really made the meal? The wine I brought.
	SFX: CAB HONKS OUTSIDE
	MONICA: There's your cab.
JASON OPENS DOOR	JASON: Oh, if my Christmas plans fall through, maybe I'll give you a call.
GIVES HER PECK ON CHEEK; SHE CLOSES DOOR WITH SHOCKED DISGUST	SFX: DOOR SLAM
GRAPHIC: After the Turkey's Gone Sale	VO: Now that the turkey's gone, we've trimmed our prices to the bone.
ADD CUSTOM GRAPHIC: Northeast	The After the Turkey's Gone Sale at Northeast.

CHRISTMAS SALE

Video	Audio
MONICA AND NOEL ON COUCH, TOASTING WITH WINE GLASSES. CHRISTMAS TREE IN BG	NOEL: Forever, Monica.
	SFX: PHONE RINGS
MONICA LEAVES ROOM AFTER BLOWING HIM KISS; NOEL PICKS UP PHONE	Hello? Oh, hello! (Nervous whisper) Tiffany, I can't talk to you right now --- Monica's here. What??? You left them here???
NOEL LOOKS UP TO SEE SCOWLING MONICA IN DOORWAY HOLDING UP A BLACK LACY NYLON STOCKING	
GRAPHIC: Stocking Stuffer Sale	VO: Anything you can stuff in a sock --- from cell phones to iPods. Now 30% off.
ADD CUSTOM GRAPHIC: Northeast	The Stocking Stuffer Sale, at Northeast.

Case #3: SelectCare[53]

Nationwide Buying Group had to establish multiple identities. SelectCare, a new Detroit-area health care insurance plan, needed to register just one name --- but it had to achieve this recognition in a market that had long been dominated by advertising for competitor Blue Cross/Blue Shield.

   To promote its client, Whitmore Communications realized that targeting *employees* would be at least as important as reaching employers. If workers wouldn't sign up for SelectCare, employers wouldn't offer it as a health-plan option. In the resulting campaign, radio and television were chosen as the best media to reach a broad cross-section of wage-earners.

Whitmore's market research discovered that Blue Cross/Blue Shield enjoyed a 70 percent penetration of the Detroit market. Yet as a group, the 'Blues' cardholders were very antagonistic toward it, with many complaints about claims servicing. These people felt, however, that there was no financially stable alternative so, for security's sake, stuck with this long-established monolith. The consumer interviews also showed Whitmore that financial stability concerns about SelectCare were allayed when prospects were told the names of the owner hospitals that formed SelectCare. The agency further discovered that copy points about "new ideas," "worldwide coverage for emergencies," and "more coverage than traditional insurance" strongly appealed to younger participants in the interview groups.

These findings became the basis for the resulting radio and television advertising. The campaign began with a full-sing radio spot that introduced SelectCare to the airwaves in a soft-sell, identity-raising manner:

SOLO SINGER:	When you get the best out of life And make the most of your health Then you know you're living well And that's an art all by itself. You want to go the distance Getting better every day And the people at SelectCare Are with you all the way.
SOLOIST/CHORUS:	SelectCare for the way you live SelectCare anywhere Worldwide SelectCare The New Standard in Health Care.
SOLOIST BRIDGE:	You like to live the way you choose Select a plan that you can use.
SOLOIST/CHORUS:	SelectCare for the way you live SelectCare anywhere Worldwide SelectCare The New Standard in Health Care.

Three weeks later, the first television spot debuted—a spot so successful that one of the named member hospitals was deluged with phone calls that very first day. This happened despite the fact that no phone number appeared in the commercial! The next day, the agency added a super of SelectCare's master 800 number to divert calls to the proper office.

Video	Audio
SHOT OF BLUE CROSS/BLUE SHIELD BUILDING (EXACTLY AS SEEN DOWNTOWN). INTERESTING SKY IN BG; ROCKY CLIFFS BEHIND	VO: Health care coverage used to be so simple.

Video	Audio
PULL BACK FROM BUILDING TO REVEAL WAVES LAPPING AT ITS BASE	Some people think it still is.
WAVES WIPE OUT A LUMP OF THE BUILDING, REVEALING THAT IT'S MADE OF SAND	But health care coverage has changed. Some forms of insurance may not measure up.
CU OF MORE AND MORE OF BUILDING DISSOLVING, EVEN BLUE CROSS/BLUE SHIELD EMBLEM WHICH SPILLS BLUE INK DOWN ITS SIDE AS WAVE HITS IT	
LUMP OF SAND ON THE BEACH IS ALL THAT'S LEFT; A MIX OF BLUE INK SPILLING INTO THE MEDITERRANEAN BLUE WATERS	One company has new ideas you should know about. The company was founded by Beaumont, Oakwood, Providence and Saint John Hospitals.
PAN UP TO ROCKY CLIFFS, WHERE SUN HITS THE ROCKS IN SUCH AS WAY AS TO SPOTLIGHT/ANOINT WORD CARVED MONUMENTAL STYLE ON FACE OF THE CLIFFS	It'll cover you in an emergency, anywhere. Worldwide.
CENTER ON WORD: SelectCare	This company is called SelectCare.
SUPER LOWER THIRD: The new standard in health care.	It's the new standard in health care.
ADD SUPER: 1-800-334-3122	

Blue Cross/Blue Shield felt so threatened by the announcement's impact that the company's executives began phoning complaints about it to the board members of SelectCare's owner hospitals. Having established SelectCare's visibility so powerfully, the company and the agency therefore replaced the contentious commercial with one called "Silence." In this spot, nothing was said about the 'Blues.' In fact, nothing was said on the audio track at all! Instead, the visual carried a starkly written "believe what you read" crawl that now presented SelectCare as though there were no real competition worth mentioning:

Video	Audio
WORDS APPEAR OVER BLACK, REVERSED OUT IN WHITE, UNDERNEATH STONE LOGO OF SELECTCARE WHICH REMAINS ON SCREEN FOR ENTIRE SPOT	MUSIC: CONFIDENT STATEMENT OF ORCHESTRA AFFIRMATION, FIRST 5 SECONDS
CRAWL: We're sponsoring a few seconds of silence so you can consider something new in health care.	

Continued

Video	Audio
WORDS CONTINUE TO APPEAR, SLIDE UP UNDERNEATH LOGO AT WHAT WOULD BE NORMAL SPEAKING RATE IF VOICED.	MUSIC OUT

CRAWL: SelectCare, founded by Beaumont, Oakwood, Providence and Saint John Hospitals offers a family of health plans. By design, our plans provide more coverage than traditional health insurance. We cover 100 percent of outpatient services such as X-rays and lab work. In many cases, physicians' office visits are fully covered. With one of our plans, you can keep your present doctor. SelectCare also covers you world-wide in emergencies. We think this is something to think about

SelectCare.

AS FOLLOWING WORDS APPEAR, THEY HOLD ON FRAME UNDERNEATH THE STONE LOGO AND THE 800 NUMBER DISSOLVES IN:

CRAWL: The New Standard in Health Care.
1-800-334-3122

(Courtesy of Ruth Whitmore, Whitmore Communications)

About one month after the campaign's run, an independent research firm hired by SelectCare found that an unusually high 47 percent of the people surveyed still recalled the campaign, with 77 percent of those expressing that they either "liked it" or "liked it very much." Even more dramatically, name awareness of SelectCare, which had been 6 percent in the target group before the broadcast campaign, now registered a whopping 66 percent. There is no better testament to the power of strong copy backed by pertinent objective-honing research.

Case #4: Chicago Wolves[54]

Advertising agency Cramer-Krasselt was hired to help launch a new International (now American) Hockey League team, the Chicago Wolves. The huge challenge was that even though the IHL was one step below the major-league National Hockey League (NHL), the Wolves would be playing in a city that already took pride in the Chicago Black Hawks, an NHL "original six" franchise with a sixty-eight-year history.

Wolves ownership felt they had two key advantages. First, with much lower player salaries, IHL ticket prices were a fraction of what an NHL team like the Black Hawks had to charge. Second, the Wolves' home arena (The Horizon) was in the suburbs in much less challenging surroundings than the Black Hawks' downtown venue. So the client felt that a good positioning statement would be: "Value-priced family hockey in a safe suburban environment."

But on taking over the account, Cramer-Krasselt detected major weaknesses with this positioning. Chicago, in the words of agency senior vice-president Don Brashears, "is a rough and tumble town. And the positioning statement we inherited suggested 'sissy hockey' --- the last thing in the world that would appeal to our target market." Besides, location and price structure were readily apparent. The target audience knew where The Horizon was situated and was fully aware that IHL-level tickets would be comparatively low-priced. So a much different strategy was mandated.

Brashears and his account team first defined a three-tier target market: (1) hockey fans --- people who had either gone to a hockey game in the last twelve months or had watched at least three televised games during that period; (2) suburban teens who were interested in or actually played hockey; and (3) sportswriters --- the people who could generate the greatest word-of-mouth about the Wolves. To reach these people, and to capitalize on the team's name, the agency developed a very different positioning: *"These guys are animals."*

A print and television campaign promoting this image and season-ticket sales was launched fifteen weeks before the Wolves' inaugural game. As the following thirty-second script demonstrates, the 'animal' quality of the team is unmistakably projected. There is no trace of a second-class or 'sissy hockey' attitude:

Video	Audio
OPEN ON SHOTS OF RINK SURFACE	MUSIC: HOCKEY ORGAN CHANT UP AND UNDER
HATS BEGIN TO LAND ON ICE IN SLOW MOTION	VO: When a hockey player scores three goals in a game, it's customary for the fans to throw hats on the rink.
CUT TO SHOT OF CLEAR ICE	When a player for the new Chicago Wolves scores three
HUNKS OF RAW MEAT BEGIN TO LAND ON THE ICE	goals in a game, somehow hats just don't cut it.
CUT TO LOGO; The Chicago Wolves at The Horizon	The Chicago Wolves. These guys are animals.
CUT TO GRAPHIC: 1-800-The Wolves	

After only six weeks of advertising (still nine weeks before the season opener), target audience awareness of the new franchise had jumped to 65 percent and 3,000 season tickets had been sold --- exceeding client expectations fourfold. Then, just before the season began, the Wolves got an unexpected boost when the National Hockey League locked out its players in a labor dispute. This put the Chicago Black Hawks temporarily out of the picture. Cramer-Krasselt quickly developed creative like the Figure 14.4 print ad that capitalized on the situation while still maintaining campaign consistency. This same approach was carried over into television treatments. Such flexibility is the mark of a well-wrought strategy. The strategy is not only clear and focused but also has the resilience to stretch in order to cover unforeseen circumstances.

WE COULD NEVER LOCK OUT OUR PLAYERS. THEY'D BEAT US UP.

HISTORIC OPENING WEEKEND

FRIDAY, OCTOBER 14, 7:30 DETROIT VIPERS   SUNDAY, OCTOBER 16, 7:00 MINNESOTA MOOSE

FOR INDIVIDUAL GAME TICKETS CALL TICKETMASTER 312-559-1212. FOR SEASON TICKETS CALL 1-800-THE-WOLVES

THE CHICAGO WOLVES AT THE HORIZON

THE CAMPAIGN DYNAMIC

Having studied Brand Character and Concept Engineering, and after your exposure to four separate case studies, you should have developed a working sensitivity to the components of electronic media campaign construction. It should be clear by now that successful campaigns are neither generated by, nor aired in, a vacuum. Rather, they are the outgrowth of a great deal of laborious research and step-by-step intellectual analysis. As advertising agency chairman Paul Harper once remarked at a seminar for his staffers:

> It is the right combination of shoe leather and scholarship that eventually leads you to a key fact about the market that everyone else has overlooked. It is only by separating truths from half-truths, straw from chaff, that you eventually find the shining needle—a competitive weakness, a proprietary strength—that nobody perceived before in quite the same way.
>
> That is the beginning of advertising victory.[55]

Much of this "shoe leather and scholarship" moves beyond the specifics of any single marketing problem and embraces your total awareness of the environment in which you, your clients, and your target consumers reside. So to become a truly great campaign copywriter, advises creative director Helayne Spivak, you must

> keep reading . . . keep aware of the world around you. Stay in touch with popular culture; know what people are reading, seeing, thinking. You can't isolate yourself . . . You need to be immersed in the culture of our times. It's not enough to be obsessed with advertising. You need to be obsessed with *life*.[56]

CHAPTER

15   Outro

By this juncture, you've been acclimated to the overall dimensions of electronic media copywriting, have suffered the rigors of scribbling for radio, and been exposed to the discipline of creating for video: television, placed-based, broadband and mobile. Finally, you have endured at least a small measure of the struggle that occurs between market conditions and creative inclinations, grappling that is the necessary prologue to a well-fashioned electronic campaign—whether in the service of commercial or public cause.

Nevertheless, despite diligent effort and cooperative attitude, "Many times, the end product might not be all you hoped for," counsels creative director Thomas Hayo, "leaving you to wonder where along the journey you might have made one too many compromises. Even if everything worked out exactly as one hoped, sometimes for unknown reasons the magic just doesn't happen. And that's what is really frustrating—yet also extremely exciting—about making commercials: no matter how much certain people want it to be a science, it's not."[1]

Instead, whether we are writing commercials or handling the many other types of assignments discussed in this book, electronic media wordsmithing is most often an art. And because all art is ultimately a delicate balance between the discipline of form and the discipline of content, promising copywriters remain stimulated by the whole pitfall-riddled mess. Much of this stimulation comes from realizing, as does industry icon George Lois, that "advertising, when pursued with love and talent, especially talent, can become a mass language that explains and illuminates the meaning of daily life through powerful and succinct images and ideas."[2]

These ideas usually have to be filtered through a client, of course, which adds additional challenges --- even if, as in the case of in-house accounts, that client is an executive within your own organization. Clients are intent on *ROI* --- return on investment. Concepts that don't appear to contribute to this objective are frowned upon or dismissed out of hand, no matter how brilliant you may believe that concept to be or how hard you have worked to sculpt it. Coming up with the idea and the script that expresses it is a dead-end exercise unless you can demonstrate its relevance and effectiveness to the people on the other side of the table.

This can be a bruising process in which some of what you believe are your best submissions have to be discarded when the client simply won't buy them. This happens with even the best of clients who politely reject what you have offered up and give an incisive reason why. Unfortunately, it happens much more infuriatingly with the worst of clients who are anything but polite in bludgeoning your idea and irrationally lambaste you for your 'stupidity' in even presenting it. You will discover, as has Richard Kirshenbaum, co-founder of Kirshenbaum + Partners, that: "There is a quadrant of clients [see Figure 15.1]: smart and nice, dumb and nice, smart and mean and dumb and mean. The only clients we're not interested in are the dumb and mean ones. There are some clients I haven't respected intellectually, and t hat's OK, but when they're mean to the agency, that's unacceptable."[3] As you grow as a copywriter, you will learn how to approach clients in the other three quadrants --- and strategies for defending yourself against the fourth until you can be reassigned to another account or your agency and the dumb/mean client finally part company.

It should be of some comfort to know that, once beyond that entry level job, you will be paid increasingly well for your efforts --- provided you take those efforts seriously. In fact, observes longtime New York agency executive Malcolm MacDougall: "The words that appear in advertising today are the most expensive words ever written [with the possible exception, as Phil Dusenberry once quipped, for the words in ransom notes.] Each and every one should be agonized over, crunched into a ball and tossed into the wastebasket, until just the right word is found --- the word that perfectly fits the selling message, the word that has that special power to arrest, to penetrate, to persuade, to create customers."[4]

While engaged in the agonizing and the crunching, you may occasionally hit the wall and develop the malady long known as writer's block. You will lessen the number of times this occurs if you do not pre-censor yourself by trying to be both

FIGURE 15.1 The client quadrant.

KIRSHENBAUM'S CLIENT QUADRANT

Smart and Nice	Smart and Mean
Dumb and Nice	Dumb and Mean

writer and editor. "You have to be able to separate the editing part of your brain from the making-up-stuff part of your brain," advises Carmichael Lynch's executive creator Jim Nelson. "Instead of coming up with an idea and deciding whether it's good, I turn it over and try to come up with another one. And I just keep doing that. The next day, some of that stuff will have changed in your head, and it will suddenly start to become good."[5] You can then take one or two of those product stories that are 'starting to become good' and proceed to make them truly so.

Good stories are what copywriting is all about. So good copywriters are numbered among the ranks of good storytellers. Through their narrative skills, effective storytellers "move us, inspire us, change us, drive social change and sometimes --- yes, sometimes --- sell us something," marvels Wieden + Kennedy's director of digital strategies Renny Gleeson. "In advertising, when we are at our best, we build a message around a fundamental human truth, we engage the heart, and we tell compelling stories that create meaning for brands awash in a rising quagmire of white noise. And yes, we sell stuff."[6]

There is nothing wrong with 'selling stuff' as long as we do it with integrity by being accurate in what we say and appropriate in who we say it to. Sometimes this means walking away from a client or a requested approach --- even if there are big bucks involved. "Money has a voice," admits British agency head John Hegarty, "[but] it doesn't have a soul. Too many creative people get tempted by the money, and eventually it destroys them."[7]

On the other hand, making a career of selling stuff *with integrity* serves an important social function. No less a luminary than President Franklin Delano Roosevelt once professed:

> If I were starting life over again, I am inclined to think that I would go into the advertising business in preference to almost any other. This is because advertising has come to cover the whole range of human needs and also because it combines real imagination with a deep study of human psychology. Because it brings to the greatest number of people actual knowledge concerning useful things, it is essentially a form of education . . . It has risen with ever-growing rapidity to the dignity of an art. It is constantly paving new paths . . . The general raising of the standards of modern civilization among all groups of people during the past half-century would have been impossible without the spreading of the knowledge of higher standards by means of advertising.[8]

As Roosevelt recognized, what we write can enlighten and refine society. However, despite this high-minded purpose, don't take yourself and your task *too* seriously. Don't become so intense in your illumination efforts that you experience personal and premature burnout, like the kid who expends all his July 4th sparklers before it gets dark enough to see them shine.

Instead, try to follow the long-trusted advice of veteran copywriter and creative director Don Cowlbeck and---

> Listen very carefully for the sound of your *own* soda-straw starting to suck bottom. When you hear it, go fishing. We are in a pressurized profession. "I need that next Tuesday." "We have to do something about our marketing situation in

Phoenix." "I don't know what --- that's what I pay you people for." "It's no big problem; how's about we discuss it tomorrow at a breakfast meeting. Say, 4 AM?"

What fun! What a challenge! How much better than the hum-drum, ho-hum, another-day-another-dollar existence of others less fortunate than we.

But there comes a time when each of us, under pressure, becomes cranky, finds his energies dissipated, himself unproductive and unhappy. My final secret—and perhaps most valuable one—is when your personal straw starts to suck bottom --- go fishing.[9]

As your author and guide through the world of broadcast/broadband copywriting, let me wish you every success as a wordsmith and leave you with one final and (after fifteen arduous chapters) heartfelt word:

S-S-S-SSLURP! (I hope the bluegills are biting.)

ENDNOTES

Intro and Acknowledgments

1. Ann Cooper, "The Way They Work," *Adweek* (December 4, 1995), 27.
2. Keith Reinhard, "What I Learned," *Advertising Age* (March 28, 2005), 30.
3. "What You Think of the Ad Business," *Adweek* (April 12, 2004), 18.
4. Dennis Brown, "Students Need More Writing Instruction, Not Less," *Chronicle of Higher Education* (October 19, 1988), B3.
5. Sally Hogshead, "Work Ethic, Ugh," *Adweek* (September 16, 2002), 10.
6. Curvin O'Reilly, "Why Some People Have More Ideas," *Adweek* (February 15, 1988), 57.
7. Mitch Albom, "These Days with Morrie," *TV Guide* (December 4, 1999), 42.
8. Mark Fenske, "How to Know When You've Done a Good Ad," *Creativity* (June 2002), 91.

Chapter One

1. Alice Flaherty, "Writing Like Crazy: a Word on the Brain," *Chronicle of Higher Education* (November 21, 2003), B6.
2. Ibid.
3. Guy McCann, "The Relationship between Psychological Type and Performance in a Copywriting Course." Paper presented to the Association for Education in Journalism and Mass Communication 1989 Convention (Washington, DC), 1.
4. Paris Barclay, remarks to the Broadcast Education Association Convention, April 29, 2006 (Las Vegas).
5. James Baker, "Creative Moonlighting," *Adweek* (June 2, 1986), S.S. 12.
6. Howard Good, "Teaching Writing as a Beautiful and Bleak Passion," *Chronicle of Higher Education* (July 17, 1991), B3.
7. Bob Cox, "Virtual Talent," *Adweek* (June 13, 1994), 22.
8. Charlotte Beers, "Where Great Minds Become Good Friends," *Advertising Age* (August 4, 1997), 20.
9. Alison Rogers, "Lancers for Hire," *Winners* (August 1989), 4.
10. Kandy Kramer, "The Freelance Life: Nice Work and Susie Burtch Has It," *Adweek* (October 28, 1985), 38.
11. Marcio Moreria, "The Idea Debate," *Adweek* (February 19, 2001), 10.
12. Ann Cooper, "Have Book, Will Travel," *Adweek* (January 9, 1995), 22.
13. "Agency Freelancers Thrive in San Francisco Scene," *Advertising Age* (December 11, 1995), 30.
14. Cooper, 24.
15. Alison Rogers, "The Freelance Life," *Winners* (August 1989), 54.
16. Mindy Charski, "Me, Myself and I," *Adweek* (November 22, 2004), 32.
17. Steve Smith, letter to the editor, *Adweek* (March 27, 1995), 18.
18. Eleftheria Parpis, "Top Guns," *Adweek* (October 25, 1999), 24.
19. Eleftheria Parpis, "Ideas for the Making," *Adweek* (April 7, 2008), 31.
20. Jim Colasurdo, "Life as a Copywriter: It Ain't Easy," *Adweek* (March 24, 1986), 22.
21. Gregory Solman, "Designers on Demand at All Types of Agencies," *Adweek* (March 10, 2008), 6.
22. Tony Benjamin, "10 Reasons to Think Small," *Adweek* (July 31, 1989), 24.
23. John Leonardi, "Greener Pastures," *Adweek* (May 1, 2006), 24.
24. Luke Sullivan, "The Small Agency as Challenger Brand," *one. a magazine* (Fall 2002), 7.
25. Jerry Fields, letter to the editor, *Adweek* (February 24, 1992), 30.
26. Barry Rosenthal, "What Drives the Creative," *BPME Image* (December 1990), 12.
27. Linda Kaplan Thaler, "Bringing Up Baby," *Adweek* (April 17, 2000), 20.
28. Steven Penchina, "Gone Are the Glory Days," *Adweek* (March 4, 1991), 32.
29. Joan Voight, "Hidden Talent," *Adweek* (May 29, 2006), 18.
30. Andrew Cracknell, "New Shapes, New Problems," *Adweek* (February 20, 1995), 29.
31. Richard Morgan, "Separation of Church and State: Can Tarlow Be Both Agency and Client?" *Adweek* (August 14, 1989), 2.
32. Gary Cozen, "The Real Deal: Improve Local Ad Campaigns," *Broadcasting & Cable* (November 11, 2004), 31.
33. Eleftheria Parpis, "You Say You Want a Revolution," *Adweek* (December 13, 1999), 32.
34. "Perusing the Portfolios," *ASAP* (May/June 1989), 27.
35. "Ad School Review," *Creativity* (September 2004), 58.
36. Mark Gale, "Creatives Fail Key Test," *Advertising Age* (August 5, 2002), 21.
37. Mae Anderson, "Lay Off the Astroturf," *Adweek* (March 11, 2004), 30.
38. Brett Robbs, "The Advertising Curriculum and the Needs of Creative Students," *Journalism Educator* (Winter 1996), 31.
39. "Perusing," *ASAP*, 28.
40. Ibid.
41. Robbs, 29.
42. Dave Willmer, "Portfolio Do's and Don'ts," *Adweek* (October 9, 2006), 14.
43. Mindy Charski, "Judging by the Cover," *Adweek* (February 27, 2006), 41.

44. Willmer, 14.
45. Ty Lifeset, "More on the Mini Book," *Adweek* (December 17, 2001), 11.
46. "Perusing," *ASAP* , 27.
47. Charski, 41.
48. Willmer, 14.
49. Aaron Copland, *Music and Imagination* (Cambridge, MA: Harvard University Press, 1952), 2.
50. Michael Kaplan, "The Last Temptation of Phil Dusenberry, *Winners*" (October 1988), 11.

Chapter Two

1. Jennifer Owens, "What Shines Online?" *Adweek* (May 8, 2000), 76.
2. George Lois, *What's the Big Idea?* (New York: Penguin, 1991), 79.
3. Paul Goldsmith, writing in "Monday Memo," *Broadcasting* (September 22, 1980), 12.
4. Ann Cooper, "The Way They Work," *Adweek* (December 4, 1995), 27.
5. "The Creativity 50," *Creativity* (March 2006), 39.
6. Marilyn Moore, "What Women Want," *Adweek* (May 5, 2008), S-2.
7. Ibid.
8. Mark Dolliver, "Do You Feel Commercials Talk Down to You?" *Adweek* (March 25, 1996), 26.
9. John Fiske, "British Cultural Studies and Television," in Robert Allen (ed.), *Channels of Discourse* (Chapel Hill: University of North Carolina Press, 1987), 269.
10. "Quips, Quotes, Gripes, Swipes," *Winners* (November 1988), 88.
11. Joyce King Thomas, "Priority One," *Adweek* (October 16, 2000), 18.

Chapter Three

1. "Quips, Quotes, Gripes, Swipes," *Winners* (December 1987), 48.
2. James Kilpatrick, "Good Writing Depends on 'Comma Sense,'" (Mt. Pleasant, MI) *Morning Sun* (February 12, 1993), 4.
3. Pico Iyer, "In Praise of the Humble Comma," *Time* (June 13, 1988), 80.
4. Lynne Truss, *Eats, Shoots & Leaves* (New York: Gotham Books, 2003), dust jacket.
5. Iyer, 80.
6. Mark Harmon, "Crossing a Question Mark with an Exclamation Point," *Chronicle of Higher Education* (July 28, 2000), B7.
7. George Will, "Best Seller Puts Focus on Commas, Dashes, and More," (Mt. Pleasant) *Morning Sun* (May 20, 2004), 4A.
8. Truss, 171.
9. Ibid., 165.
10. "Immigrants/Emigrants," *Canada Today*, (1&2, 1985), 6.
11. Thomas Sheridan, *A Course of Lectures on Elocution* (London: J. Dodsley, 1787).
12. *Daily Report from The Chronicle of Higher Education* (February 13, 2001), 3.

13. Whit Hobbs, "Same Old John," *Adweek* (April 6, 1987), 36.
14. Bruce McCall, "Taking the Cure," *Adweek* (September 14, 1992), 32.
15. Gabriele Zinke. Presentation to the Broadcast Education Association Convention, April 18, 1993 (Las Vegas).
16. Wendy Leibowitz, "Technology Transforms Writing and the Teaching of Writing," *Chronicle of Higher Education* (November 26, 1999), A67.
17. Dylan Landis, "Creatives and Computers: An Uneasy Alliance," *Adweek* (April 22, 1985), 22.
18. Bonnie Morris, "When the Pen Met the Blank Page: A Writer's Farewell to the 20th Century," *The Chronicle of Higher Education* (December 10, 1999), A72.
19. Leibowitz, A67.
20. Bob Killian, "In Defense of a Low-Tech Secret Weapon," *Adweek* (August 30, 1993), 38.
21. Abbey Klaasen, "Clear Channel Cuts: Jury Still Out on :30s," *Advertising Age* (February 7, 2005), 31.
22. Kevin Neathery, *Copy Writing and Campaign Development* (Jonesboro, AR: Triple FM, 2008), 10.
23. Klaasen, 31.
24. Steve McClellan, "Radio Takes the Lead in Cleaning Up the Clutter," *Adweek* (February 7, 2005), 9.
25. "For Some Hollywood Fare, Radio Mini-Ads Are a Perfect Fit," *latimes.com* (August 21, 2007), http://latimes.com/business/la-fi-clear21aug21, 1, 35798.
26. Noreen O'Leary, "Is Longer Better?" *Adweek* (February 13, 1995), 32.
27. Ira Teinowitz, "First Smoke, Then Fire," *Advertising Age 50 Years of TV Advertising* (Spring 1995), 30.
28. "Alberto-Culver Wins Split-30 Battle," *Broadcasting* (March 19, 1984), 42.
29. George Fabian, "15-Second Commercials: The Inevitable Evolution," *Journal of Advertising Research* (August/September 1986), RC 3-4.
30. Roberta Asahina, "The Creative Evolution of the 15-Second Television Commercial: Creative Structure and Impact upon the Shorter Message Format." Paper presented to the Association for Education in Journalism and Mass Communication 1989 Convention (Washington, DC), 3.
31. Jack Feuer, "Tools of the Trade," *Adweek* (April 10, 2000), 32.
32. Asahina, 6-7.
33. Ibid., 7.
34. Ibid., 6.
35. M. H. Moore, "'Wired': A New Accessory for Brits," *Adweek* (April 10, 1995), 14.
36. Tim Nudd, "Now You See It," *Adweek* (September 23, 2002), 38.
37. Laura Petrecca, "Five Second Ads Try to Counter TiVo," *USA Today* (July 5, 2006), http://www.usatoday.com/money/advertising/2006-07-05-5-second-ads-usat_x.htm.
38. Kamau High, "Pete Favat on the Spot," *Adweek* (January 15, 2007), 32.
39. Michael Applebaum, "In Mid-Stream," *Adweek* (October 15, 2007), 25.

40. Kris Oser, "Blink and You Might Miss Caddy's Latest on Net," *Advertising Age* (July 11, 2005), 29.
41. Brian Morrisey, "Will the 30-Second Spot Get a Second Life Online?" *Adweek* (June 11, 2007), 13.
42. Fabio Fernandes, "Heating Things Up in Brazil," *one. a magazine* (Summer 2001), 6.
43. Bernard Owett, writing in "Monday Memo," *Broadcasting* (October 13, 1975), 11.

Chapter Four

1. Barbara Lippert, "The Right Brain Gains Share of Mind at Agencies," *Adweek* (June 10, 1985), 29.
2. Don Stacks and William Melson, "Toward a Hierarchical Processing Model of Audio Advertising Messages." Paper presented at the Association for Education in Journalism and Mass Communication 1987 Convention (San Antonio), 8.
3. Sharon Livingston, "Emotional Intelligence," *Adweek* (November 26, 2007), 16.
4. *DMAD* (Direct Marketing Association of Detroit) *Response* (February 1999), 3.
5. Kim Foltz, "Psychological Appeal in TV Ads Found Effective," *Adweek* (August 31, 1987), 38.
6. Noreen O'Leary, "A Blueprint for Campaigns That Travel around the World," *Adweek* (October 31, 1994), 43.
7. Drusilla Menaker, "O & M Rightford Established a New Harmony," *Advertising Age* (April 15, 1996), S 5.
8. Jeff Graham, "A Difference of Opinion," *Adweek* (February 22, 1999), 12.
9. Dick Orkin, *Radio: Adcrafting with Soul* (Los Angeles: The Radio Ranch, 1995), 3.
10. Faith Popcorn, "All Wrapped Up in a Cocoon Boom," *Adweek* (August 26, 1991), 24.
11. Michael Wilke, "Kiwi Gives Safety Theme a Lift in Ads," *Advertising Age* (July 15, 1996), 4.
12. Orkin, 5–6.
13. Jon Berry, "Agencies Respond to Uncertain U.S. Economy," *Adweek* (July 30, 1990), 23.
14. Debra Goldman, "Marketing's Biggest Myths," *Adweek* (January 27, 1992), 29.
15. Paul Price, "Unleash Emotions for Business Growth," *Advertising Age* (March 12, 2007), 20.
16. Kathleen Sampey, "Box Office Smash," *Adweek* (January 29, 2001), 47.
17. Barbara Lippert, "Attitude Unbecoming," *Adweek SuperBrands '97* (October 7, 1996), 38.
18. Esther Thorson and Jacqueline Hitchon, "Effects of Emotion and Product Involvement on Responses to Repeated Commercials." Paper presented at the Association for Education in Journalism and Mass Communication 1990 Convention (Minneapolis), 14.
19. Jacqueline Hitchon and Esther Thorson, "Effects of Emotion and Product Involvement on the Experience of Repeated Commercial Viewing," *Journal of Broadcasting and Electronic Media* (Summer 1995), 386.
20. Single exposure studies cited by Thorson and Hitchon that demonstrate "consistent superiority in performance of emotional over non-emotional commercials" include the following: David Aaker, Douglas Stayman, and Michael Hagerty, "Warmth in Advertising: Measurement, Impact and Sequence Effects," *Journal of Consumer Research* 12(4), (1986), 365–381; Young Choi and Esther Thorson, "Memory for Factual, Emotional and Balanced Ads under Two Instructional Sets." In A. D. Fletcher (ed.), *Proceedings of the American Academy of Advertising* (Knoxville: University of Tennessee, 1983); Esther Thorson and Thomas Page, "Effects of Product Involvement and Emotional Commercials on Consumer's Recall Attitudes." In David Stewart and Sid Hecker (eds.), *Nonverbal Communication in Advertising* (New York: Academic Press, 1989); Esther Thorson, and Marian Friestad, "The Effects of Emotion on Episodic Memory for TV Commercials." In Pat Cafferata and Alice Tybout (eds.), *Advertising and Consumer Psychology* (Lexington, MA: Lexington Press, 1989).
21. Jon Berry, "Bonneville Puts Emotion on the Screen," *Adweek* (February 6, 1989), 34.
22. Celeste Ward, "Jeff Odiorne On the Spot," *Adweek* (May 9, 2005), 30.
23. "Pre-Fab Nostalgia," *Adweek* (December 13, 1993), 19.
24. Christine Coyle in Peter Orlik, *The Electronic Media: An Introduction to the Profession*, 2nd ed. (Ames: Iowa State University Press, 1997), 416.
25. Richard Rudisell, *Mirror Image: The Influence of the Daguerreotype on American Culture* (Albuquerque: University of New Mexico Press, 1971), 215.
26. Jonathan Bond and Richard Kirshenbaum, "Excerpts from 'Under the Radar: Talking to Today's Cynical Consumers,'" *Adweek* (November 8, 1999), 54.
27. Marc Weinberger and Charles Gulas, "The Impact of Humor in Advertising: A Review," *Journal of Advertising* (December 1992), 35.
28. "A Laugh Riot," *Adweek* (February 7, 1997), 17.
29. "What's So Funny," *Creativity* (September 2001), 41.
30. Paul La Monica, "The Problem with TV Ads," *CNN Money.com* (March 21, 2007), http://money.cnn.com/2007/03/21/commentary/mediabiz/index.html.
31. Bob Garfield, "Kia SW's Tale Is Tall, but Humor Is Small," *Advertising Age* (August 3, 1998), 43.
32. "Romantics," *Adweek* (November 3, 1989), H. M. 18.
33. Jon Berry, "Spotlight: Kids," *Adweek* (April 15, 1991), 32, 34.
34. Tom McElligott, "Great Advertising Breaks the Rules," *Adweek* (May 6, 1985), 46.
35. Tiffany Meyers, "Marketers Learn Luxury Isn't Simply for the Very Wealthy, *Advertising Age* (September 13, 2004), S-2.
36. Michael Kaplan, "The Last Temptation of Phil Dusenberry," *Winners* (October 1988), 8.
37. Steve McClellan, "Mind Over Matter," *Adweek* (February 18, 2008), 17.
38. "Wit and Wisdom from 'Chairman Leo,'" *Advertising Age* (July 31, 1995), LB 14.
39. Richard Vaughn, How *Advertising Works: An FCB Strategy Planning Model* (Los Angeles: Foote, Cone & Belding Communications unpublished monograph, 1979).

40. Dolf Zillman. Remarks to the Broadcast Education Association Convention, April 28, 1989 (Las Vegas).

41. Betsy Sharkey, "The Scribble That Won an $80-Million Account," *Adweek* (November 25, 1991), 31.

42. Gary Goldsmith, "Mr. Goldsmith Goes to Manhattan," *Adweek* (May 6, 2002), 2-3.

Chapter Five

1. "Little Caesars, Ortho Tie," *Advertising Age* (May 26, 1997), S 8.

2. Alan Monroe, *Principles and Types of Speech*, 3rd ed. (Chicago: Scott, Foresman and Company, 1949), 310.

3. Ken Sacharin, "Grand Entrance," *Adweek* (November 27, 2000), 40.

4. Paul Bolls, "Producing Effective Radio Ads: The New Bag of Tricks." Presentation to the National Association of Broadcasters Convention, April 23, 2001 (Las Vegas).

5. Bob Garfield, "When Wrong Brand Can Stick You," *Advertising Age International* (September 1996), I 12.

6. Jeffrey Hedquist, "How to Get 'Em to Take Action," *Radio Hed Lines* (September 1, 2007), 2.

7. "Event Marketing Adds to Radio's Coffers," *Broadcasting* (June 17, 1991), 35.

8. Ron Gales, "Mind Games," *Adweek* (October 30, 1989), M.O. 62.

9. "At Large: Henry Julian Kaufman," *Broadcasting* (June 25, 1979), 72.

10. James Ogilvy, "From Universal Needs to Particular Wants: A Vertigo of Possibilities," *Marketing Communications* (November 1986), 15-16.

11. "Death Knell for Demos?" *Advertising Age* (July 25, 1974), S 2.

12. Joan Voight and Wendy Melillo, "Study: Clients Want Multiple Partners," *Adweek* (May 14, 2007), 20.

13. "One More Thing Marketers Ought to Heed in Targeting Older Consumers," *Adweek* (May 24, 1993), 17.

14. "Oh Give Them a Ranch-Style Home," *Adweek* (April 5, 1993), 18.

15. Stephanie Thompson, "Spin City," *Adweek* (May 10, 1999), 18.

16. Betsy Sharkey, "The Father of VALS Looks Ahead," *Adweek* (December 1984), F 6.

17. See SRI Consulting Business Intelligence website: www.sric-bi.com

18. Carolyn Wall, remarks to the International Radio & Television Society Faculty/Industry Seminar, February 7, 1991 (New York).

19. Mike Drexler, "Media's Midlife Crisis," *Adweek* (February 9, 2004), 20.

20. Debra Goldman, "The Latest Census Figures Redefine Politics Not Marketing," *Adweek* (January 8, 2001), 13.

21. Michael Conrad, "Sharing the Spotlight," *Adweek* (October 18, 1999), 18.

22. Noreen O'Leary, "Best Laid Plans," *Adweek* (March 1, 1993), 25.

23. David Baldwin, "Planning Works. Got It?," *one. a magazine* (Spring 2002), 4.

24. Steve McClellan, "P&G Still TV's Best Friend?" *Broadcasting & Cable* (April 24, 2000), 28.

25. Jane Newman, "New York to Nairobi," *Adweek* (July 26, 2004), 22.

26. "The Mind of the Hot Creative," *Creativity* (March 2003), 41.

27. Lisa Sanders, "Fight for the Streets," *Advertising Age* (May 31, 2004), 58.

28. Kevin Roberts, "Living in the Age of Attraction," *Advertising Age* (January 29, 2007), 12.

29. Amy Rosenthal, "No Really, I Love It. I've Always Wanted a Jumbo Pencil with a Troll on the End," *Adweek* (November 29, 1993), 46.

30. Al Ries, "Auto Industry May Be Hampered by Overabundance of Creativity," *Advertising Age* (May 29, 2006), 15.

31. Greg Farrell, "Marketing Is a New Game in the Old East Germany," *Adweek* (October 29, 1990), 24.

Chapter Six

1. Richard Morgan, "A How-To on Managing Creatives Has More Clues Than Answers," *Adweek* (May 18, 1990), 2.

2. Leo Burnett, *Confessions of an Advertising Man* (Chicago: private printing, 1961), 20-21.

3. Amy Mangel, "Creativity According to Ogilvy, Bernbach," *Adweek* (October 5, 1992), 16.

4. Eleftheria Parpis, "Creative Cannes," *Adweek* (June 21, 1999), 26.

5. Alice Flaherty, "Writing Like Crazy: a Word on the Brain," *Chronicle of Higher Education* (November 21, 2003), B6.

6. Mallorre Dill, "Successful Ads 101," *Adweek* (November 1, 1999), 32.

7. "David Harner and David Johnson," *Adweek* (March 30, 1992), 24.

8. Bob Garfield, "'Creative' Pringles Spot Says It All Without Saying a Word," *Advertising Age* (February 23, 2004), 45.

9. Mike Turner, "Inside the Box," *Adweek* (November 19, 2001), 10.

10. Dave Dufour in *From the Radio Ranch Bunk House*, flyer published by Dick Orkin's Radio Ranch (Los Angeles), 1994.

11. Dick Orkin. Presentation to Central Michigan University students, September 17, 1994 (Mt. Pleasant, MI).

12. Bob Kodzis, "Natural Born Creativity Killers," *create magazine* (Fall 2006), N20.

13. Cliff Bleszinski, "Chasing Childhood," *Creativity* (March 2007), 10.

14. Allen Rosenshine, "Advertising's Demise Greatly Exaggerated," *Advertising Age* (March 20, 1995), 15.

15. Bob Kuperman, "Risky Business," *Adweek* (December 11, 2000), 50.

16. "Life with Lubars," *Advertising Age* (July 30, 2007), 5.

17. "Quips, Quotes, Gripes, Swipes," *Winners* (December 1987), 48.

18. Jeff Hedquist, "Radio Commercial Specifics," *Radio Hed Lines* (June 1, 2008), 3.

19. "Format Gold Rush: Staking a Claim in Oldies," *Broadcasting* (June 17, 1991), 36.

20. Barbara Lippert, "Woman of the Years," *Adweek* (November 21, 1994), 38.

21. Paul Connors, "Copywriting and the Importance of the Offer." Presentation to the Direct Marketing Educational Foundation Faculty Institute, June 4, 1986 (Chicago).

22. Jay Woffington, "Rx Ads Mired in '50s Tactics," *Advertising Age* (May 5, 2003), 20.

23. Brian Dillon, "Met Any People Lately?" *Adweek* (May 30, 1994), 20.

24. "Quips, Quotes, Gripes, Swipes," *Winners* (January 1988), 48.

25. Eleftheria Parpis, "Dan Wieden On the Spot," *Adweek* (June 16, 2003), 30.

26. Ellen Rooney Martin, "Agency Staffers' Youth Causes 'Ageism' in Ads," *Adweek* (May 8, 1995), 4.

27. Ann Cooper, "Creatives Forum," *Adweek* (July 5, 1993), 36.

28. Noreen O'Leary, "The Boom Tube," *Adweek Upfront* (May 18, 1998), 52.

29. Nora FitzGerald, "Selling Stories," *Adweek* (September 15, 1997), 36.

30. Deborah Potter, remarks to the Great Lakes Broadcasting Conference, March 8, 2005 (Lansing, MI).

31. "Creative Theft: A Primer in Advertising's Grand Tradition," *Adweek* (May 2, 1988), 30.

32. Robert Noel, "Of Elves and Gnomes," *Advertising Age 50 Years of TV Advertising* (Spring 1995), 35.

33. Cathy Taylor, "Wieden & Kennedy," *Adweek* (March 23, 1992), R. C. 9.

34. Valerie Graves, letter to the editor, *Adweek* (February 27, 1995), 17.

35. Kenneth Jacobsen, "David Ogilvy," *Adweek* (January 28, 1991), 16.

36. Shelly Lanman, "A Creative Philosophy or Two (or Three)," *Advertising Age* (April 28, 2003), C-12.

37. Craig Stoltz, "Weighing In," *Adweek* (June 1, 1992), 22.

38. "FTC Power on Corrective Ads Left Untouched by Supreme Court," *Broadcasting* (April 10, 1978), 80.

39. Stoltz, "Weighing In," 22.

40. Alicia Mundy, "Balancing Act," *Adweek* (June 13, 1994), 21.

41. Craig Stoltz, "The Enemies List," *Adweek* (October 28, 1991), 28.

42. Eleftheria Parpis, "A Dose of Creativity," *Adweek* (August 4, 2003), 19.

43. Fred Steingold, "Dealing with Customers," *Sound & Video Contractor* (May 20, 1993), 10.

44. Christy Fisher, "How Congress Broke Unfair Ad Impasse," *Advertising Age* (August 22, 1994), 34.

45. David Kelly, "Rainbow of Ideas to Trademark Color," *Advertising Age* (April 24, 1995), 20.

46. Martha Jacobs, "Flush with Anger, Tootsie Roll Sues," *Adweek* (September 4, 1989), 6.

47. Rebecca Flass, "Done That," *Adweek* (April 22, 2002), 21.

48. "High Court's Hard Line on Ad Bans," *Advertising Age* (May 20, 1996), 57.

49. Ira Teinowitz, "Court Further Bolsters Commercial Speech," *Advertising Age* (May 27, 1996), 47.

50. "Bag the Gag," *Broadcasting & Cable* (June 21, 1999), 82.

51. Bob Garfield, "Monster Scores By Eschewing Sports Glory in Olympics Spot," *Advertising Age* (August 9, 2004), 25.

52. Barbara Holsombach, "Ad Agencies Feel Piercing Glare of Watchdogs," *Adweek* (December 3, 1990), 18.

53. Joan Voight and Wendy Melillo, "Rough Cut," *Adweek* (March 11, 2002), 28-29.

54. Ira Teinowitz and Stephanie Thompson, "CARU's Medicine Hard to Swallow," *Advertising Age* (November 28, 2005), 3.

55. Howard Bell, "Independence Preserved," *Advertising Age* (December 2, 1996), c6.

56. Ira Teinowitz, "New NAD Director Brings Experience as Regulator," *Advertising Age* (April 28, 1997), 36.

57. Holsombach, 18.

58. Tanya Gazdik, "Truckers Have Feelings Too," *Adweek* (September 29, 1997), 51.

59. "Why Comparisons Work," *Adweek* (February 14, 1994), 18.

60. Rich Thomaselli, "Industry Wrestles with Comparative Ads," *Advertising Age* (October 27, 2003), 10.

61. Leah Rickard, "New Ammo for Comparative Ads," *Advertising Age* (February 14, 1994), 26.

62. Joe Marconi, "Total Recall," *Adweek* (March 27, 2000), 52.

63. Dottie Enrico, "On the Spot," *TV Guide* (November 28, 1998), 6.

64. James Astrachan, "When to Name a Competitor," *Adweek* (May 23, 1988), 24.

65. Robert Wood, "Attacking Ageism," *Media & Values* (Winter 1989), 8.

66. Noreen O'Leary, "What If 10 Out of 10 Doctors Agree?" *Adweek* (February 1, 1988), 4.

67. George Stevens, "Contractual Offers in Advertising," *Journalism Quarterly* (Spring 1990), 34.

68. Tom Darbyshire, "Sensibility Guides for Ads in PC-Land," *Advertising Age* (May 8, 1995), 24.

69. Eleftheria Parpis, "Going Over a Ledge in the Quest to Be Edgy," *Adweek* (February 19, 2007), 6.

70. Ibid.

71. Sarah Stiansen, "Subtitle This Book 'The Joy of Advertising,'" *Adweek* (October 12, 1987), 46.

72. Reprinted with permission of Nightingale-Conant Corporation, Chicago, 1979 copyright, producers of the Earl Nightingale radio program "Our Changing World."

73. Whit Hobbs, "Biting the Brands That Feed You," *Adweek* (October 4, 1982), 20.

Chapter Seven

1. "The Marriage of Radio Advertising and New Product Lines," *Broadcasting* (June 22, 1987), 43.

2. "Stakelin Accentuates the Positive of Radio," *Broadcasting* (May 20, 1985), 85.

3. Bert Berdis, "Radio: The Writer's Award," *Advertising Age* (October 17, 1994), R-10.

4. Tom Monahan, "The Radio Wasteland," *Communication Arts Illustration Annual 1994*, 198.

5. Mallorre Dill, "Radio Days," *Adweek* (June 14, 1999), 23.

6. Claudia Puig, "A Special Holiday Roast with Satirist Stan Freberg," *Los Angeles Times* (November 28, 1991), F13.

7. Greg Farrell, "Jay Williams," *Adweek* (June 14, 1993), 38.

8. Beth Heitzman, "Tom O'Keefe," *Adweek* (June 14, 1993), 44.

9. Donna Petrozzello, "The Art of Making Radio Spots Sing," *Broadcasting & Cable* (February 12, 1996), 43.

10. Reed Bunzel, "Garrison Keillor: An American Radio Romance," *Broadcasting* (January 6, 1992), 86.

11. Himan Brown, "They Say Your Name," *On the Air* (Summer 1999), 17.

12. Jeffrey Hedquist, "Radio Scripts—Case, Typeface and White Space," *Radio Hed Lines* (June 1, 2006), 2.

13. Dick Orkin, *Radio: Adcrafting with Soul* (Los Angeles: The Radio Ranch, 1995), 35.

14. "The Best Ads," *Adweek* (September 7, 1992), 32.

15. Emery Dobbins, writing in "Monday Memo," *Broadcasting* (May 18, 1970), 14.

16. Robert Potter, Annie Lang, Paul Bolls, "Identifying Structural Features of Radio: Orienting and Memory for Radio Messages." Paper presented at the Association for Education in Journalism & Mass Communication 1998 Convention (Baltimore), 14.

17. Martin Lindstrom, "Follow Your Nose to Marketing Evolution," *Advertising Age* (May 23, 2005), 136.

18. William Stakelin, writing in "Monday Memo," *Broadcasting* (December 10, 1984), 26.

19. G. J. Gorn, "The Effect of Music in Advertising on Choice Behavior: A Classical Conditioning Approach," *Journal of Marketing*, vol. 46 (1982), 94-101.

20. Alan Salomon, "Copland Tunes Rev Up TV Spots for Olds, Beef," *Advertising Age* (March 13, 1995), 12.

21. Martin Pazzani, "Making the Most of Music," *Advertising Age* (June 11, 2007), 21.

22. Elizabeth Myers, "Music to Your Ears," *Adweek* (September 1, 2003), 15.

23. Aaron Baar, "Ira Antelis On the Spot," *Adweek* (July 7, 2003), 24.

24. Monahan, 198.

25. Paul Bolls, "Producing Effective Radio Ads: The New Bag of Tricks." Presentation to the National Association of Broadcasters Convention, April 23, 2001 (Las Vegas).

26. Deborah Potter, "Storytelling Strategies." Presentation to the Radio Television News Directors Association Convention, April 8, 2002 (Las Vegas).

27. "Financial Communications Society Portfolio Award," *Advertising Age* (March 27, 1995), P-8.

28. "Orchestrating the Commercial," *ASAP* (January/February 1988), 17.

29. Curtis Feldman, "Bill Heater's Reality," *Winners* (July 1988), 6.

30. Matt Roush, "The Best Show You're Not Watching," *TV Guide* (March 11, 2000), 16.

31. S. I. Hayakawa, *Language in Thought and Action* (New York: Harcourt Brace and World, 1964), 262.

32. Petrozzello, 43.

33. Tim Nudd, "The Bard of Campbell-Ewald," *Adweek* (February 3, 2003), 62.

34. Robert Pritikin, writing in "Monday Memo," *Broadcasting* (March 18, 1974), 22.

35. Ibid.

36. George Lois, *What's the Big Idea?* (New York: Penguin, 1991), 53-54.

37. Mark Paul, "Joy Radio Casting," *Creativity* (June 2003), 63.

38. Bolls, "Bag of Tricks."

39. James Kilpatrick, "A Writer Tries His Hand at Teaching," (Mt. Pleasant, MI) *Morning Sun* (May 24, 1993), 4.

40. Ira Schloss, "Chicken and Pickles," *Journal of Advertising Research* (December 1981), 47-49.

41. William Lozito, "A Name's Sake," *Adweek* (April 24, 2006), 12.

42. Gary Provost, "Sound Advice," *Writer's Digest* (June 1986), 34.

43. Judson Jerome, "How Words Work," *Writer's Digest* (June 1986), 34.

44. Susan Korones, "Something's Burning," *Winners* (October 1987), 17.

45. "Ad Agency Creativity: Radio's Needed Dimension," *Broadcasting* (June 25, 1990), 46.

46. Ed Butler, "Why Creatives Avoid Radio," *Adweek Radio Issue* (October 1983), R.R. 38.

Chapter Eight

1. F. Joan Roger, "The Ecology of Radio," *NAB RadioWeek* (October 3, 1988), 8.

2. Michelle Nelson and Jacqueline Hitchon, "Loud Tastes, Colored Fragrances and Scented Sounds: How and When to Mix the Senses in Persuasive Communications," *Journalism & Mass Communication Quarterly* (Summer 1999), 366.

3. Ibid., 359.

4. "Adweek Midwest Creative All-Star Team," *Adweek* (June 5, 1992), 54.

5. "Eureka!" *Radio Ranch Wrangler* (Fall 1991).

6. Jeffrey Schoot, "Virgil Shutze and His American Dream Machine," *Winners* (July 1988), 39.

7. Dick Orkin, *Radio: Adcrafting with Soul* (Los Angeles: The Radio Ranch, 1995), 36.

8. Jeffrey Hedquist, "The Ultimate Radio Production Tool." Presentation to the National Association of Broadcasters Convention, April 10, 1995, (Las Vegas).

9. Gary Provost, "The Secrets of Writing Powerful Dialogue," *Writer's Digest* (August 1987), 30.

10. "Ad Agency Creativity: Radio's Needed Dimension," *Broadcasting* (June 25, 1990), 46.

11. Jim Crimmins, "Cut It Out," *Adweek* (August 13, 2001), 14.

12. Brooke Capps, "More Than Just Jingles: One Shop Uses Sound to Give Brands Voices," *Advertising Age* (April 16, 2007), 9.

13. Stephen Arnold, "That Jingle is Part of Your Brand," *Broadcasting & Cable* (January 24, 2005), 78.

14. "The Funniest Spots," *Adweek* (June 22, 1987), 42.

15. Tim Nudd, "Give Me a Jingle," *Adweek* (December 4, 2000), 18.

16. Robert Snodell, "Why TV Spots Fail," *Advertising Age* (July 2, 1984), 18.

17. Eleftheria Parpis, "Turn Up the Noise," *Adweek* (July 14, 2008), 23.

18. Marvin Waldman, "Stop the Music," *Adweek* (December 4, 2000), 18.
19. Mae Anderson, "The Beat Goes On," *Adweek* (March 10, 2003), 29.
20. Ibid., 28-29.
21. Peter Viles, "$10 Million Pepsi Buy," *Broadcasting & Cable* (July 26, 1993), 83.
22. Stephen Ford, "You, Too, Can Be a 'Music Man,'" *Adweek* (April 16, 1984), 18.
23. Mark Dolliver, "Takes," *Adweek* (July 2, 2001), 21.
24. David Fowler, "A Monster Is Born," *Beyond the Ratings: Radio* (Summer 1993), 12.
25. Richard Mercer, writing in "Monday Memo," *Broadcasting* (May 23, 1966), 24.
26. From *Light in August* by William Faulkner. Copyright 1932 and renewed 1960 by William Faulkner. Reprinted by permission of Random House, Inc., and Curtis Brown, Ltd., London.
27. Gary Provost, "Sound Advice," *Writer's Digest* (December 1985), 34.
28. Michael Spear, ". . . Such Bitter Business—This 'Rule' on Prepositions," *Journalism & Mass Communication Educator* (Winter 1999), 77–78.
29. Jeffrey Hedquist, "Magic Pronouns," *Radio Hed Lines* (January 1, 2008), 2.
30. Calvin Duncan and James Nelson, "Effects of Humor in a Radio Advertising Experiment," *Journal of Advertising*, XIV/2 (1985), 38.
31. Claudia Puig, "A Special Holiday Roast with Satirist Stan Freberg," *Los Angeles Times* (November 28, 1991), F13.
32. Duncan and Nelson, 38-39.
33. Anthony Chevins, writing in "Monday Memo," *Broadcasting* (May 18, 1981), 22.
34. "Some Serious Talk about Laughs and Learning," *ASAP* (November/December 1989), 31.
35. Barrie Gillies, "Funny Business," *Winners* (October 1987), 22.
36. Robert Sawyer, "Ries Forgot Important Test for Slogans," *Advertising Age* (June 9, 2008), 22.
37. Steve Cone, "Help Taglines Regain Lost Glory," *Advertising Age* (April 14, 2008), 42.
38. Martin Bihl, "Out of Time," *Adweek* (January 6, 2003), 12.
39. Julie Schwartzman, "The Touchy Task of Talking to Teens," *Adweek* (April 6, 1987), H.M. 13.
40. Caroline Jones, letter to the editor, *Adweek* (January 31, 1983), 22.
41. Emily DeNitto and Riccardo Davis, "Ethnic Efforts Take on Year-Round Scope," *Advertising Age* (February 7, 1994), 36.
42. Ron Bliwas, "You've Lost that Selling Spirit," *Adweek* (July 14, 2008), 12.
43. Kenneth Chaffin, "Voices from the Broadcast Tower," *ASAP* (January/February 1988), 25.
44. Gerry Hartshorn, "Marketing without Formal Research," *NAB RadioWeek* (March 4, 1991), 5.

Chapter Nine

1. Dennis Soapes, "Making Your Automation Sizzle," *Broadcast Programming Newsletter* (April 1990), 8.
2. Donna Petrozzello, "Jingles Are Music to Stations' Ears," *Broadcasting & Cable* (August 29, 1994), 42.

3. Jim Cooper, "How to Position Radio Stations," *Broadcasting & Cable* (March 28, 1994), 46.
4. Rob Balon, "How to Talk to Listeners," *Broadcast Programming Newsletter* (April 1990), 10–11.
5. Jim Teeson, "What's Your Programming Position?" *NAB RadioWeek* (March 13, 1989), 6.
6. Jon Follmer, "The Concept-Driven Image," *BPME Image* (August/September 1990), 13.
7. "Event Marketing Adds to Radio's Coffers," *Broadcasting* (January 17, 1991), 36.
8. Maureen Bulley, "Ten Great Radio Promotions," presentation to the National Association of Broadcasters Convention, April 6, 1998 (Las Vegas).
9. Kevin Neathery, *Copywriting and Campaign Development* (Jonesboro, AK: Triple FM, 2008), 30-31.
10. Andrew Giangola, "Station Production: A Valuable Tool," *NAB RadioWeek* (November 7, 1988), 6.
11. Richard Szathmary, "Direct Response Creativity at Its Most Accessible," *ADS Magazine* (November 1984), 27.
12. Thomas McAlevey, letter to the editor, *Adweek* (August 12, 1991), 26.
13. Mark Dimassimo, "Brand Direct," *Adweek* (August 21, 2000), 18.
14. Joe Mandese, "Getting a Direct Unit Going," *Adweek* (October 20, 1986), D.M. 16.
15. Jennifer Owens, "Eyada.com Rolls Out Audio-Enabled Banners," *Adweek* (April 17, 2000), 51.
16. Ron Bliwas, "A Direct Response Shop's Challenge: Can Your Agency Do This?" *Adweek* (November 8, 1993), 66.

Chapter Ten

1. Jim Hanas, "All in the Wrist," *Creativity* (June 2001), 72.
2. Peter Putman, "I Can See It Now—the Fine Art of Storyboarding," *Video Systems* (April 1996), 52.
3. Brett Shevack, "Open Up to a New Way to Develop Better Ideas," *Point* (June 2006), 8.
4. "Storyboards That Really Control Production and Save Money Too," *ASAP* (May/June 1988), 12.
5. Peter Kellogg, "Artful Deception Fills a Copywriter's Day," *Adweek* (April 16, 1984), 38.
6. Hanas, 72.
7. Cathy Madison, "Desktop Video Editing Has Ad Makers Clicking," *Adweek* (March 11, 1991), 47.
8. Rick Boyko, "The Artful Dodgers," *Adweek* (December 13, 1999), 60, 62.
9. Joan Voight, "Mascot Makeover," *Adweek* (July 7, 2003), 21.
10. David Altschul, "The Balancing Act of Building Character," *Advertising Age* (July 4, 2005), 14.
11. Dominick Morra, "The Marrying of Mind and State of the Art," *BPME Image* (October 1992), 19.
12. Tom Stefani, "Cartoon to Boardroom: Animation for All Audiences," *Video Systems* (February 1992), 36.
13. Steve Mayer, "Effects Solutions," *Video Systems* (July 1992), Sup. 16.
14. Jim Hanas, "Rotoscope Redux," *Creativity* (February 2002), 40.
15. Michael Schrage, "Mediamorphosis," *Adweek* (January 31, 1994), 24.

16. Barbara Lippert, "Pump 'n' Grind," *Adweek* (January 30, 1995), 23.
17. Ron Gales, "Fateful Attractions: Rollicking Raisins and a Manic Noid," *Adweek* (October 12, 1987), 54.
18. Moyra Rodger, "Clay Animation: A Life of Its Own," *BPME Image* (October 1992), 25.
19. Stephen Wershing and Tanya Weinberger, "Corporate Communications Come to Life with Animation," *Educational and Industrial Television* (March 1986), 42-43.
20. "Getting Animated," *one. a magazine* (Summer 2001), 38.
21. Ibid., 39.
22. Bob Bennett and John Javetski, "Automated Animation," *Video Systems* (January 1991), Sup. 14.
23. Jeffrey Cohen, "Are Corporate Graphics Losing Their Punch?" *Corporate Video Decisions* (November 1988), 32.
24. Stuart Elliott, "To Thwart TiVo, a Nod to Television's Golden Age," *New York Times* (May 21, 2008), http://nytimes.com/2008/05/21/business/media/21adco.html.
25. Steve McClellan, "'Kimmel' Revives Live Spots," *Hollywood Reporter* (April 15, 2008), 25.
26. Kevin Ransom, "Brent Bouchez On the Spot," *Adweek* (October 4, 2004), 36.
27. Bob Fisher, "A Man of All Seasons," *International Cinematographers Guild Magazine* (January 2000), 51.
28. Maria Grabe, Shuhua Zhou, and Brooke Barnett, "Explicating Sensationalism in Television News: Content and the Whistles and Bells of Form." Paper presented at the 1998 Association for Education in Journalism and Mass Communication Convention (Baltimore), 16.
29. Ibid., 24.
30. Richard Kiernan, writing in "Monday Memo," *Broadcasting* (August 15, 1983), 24.
31. Tim O'Leary, "Dot.comedy of Errors," *Adweek* (February 21, 2000), 14.
32. Cathy Madison, "Midwest MVP: Pat Burnham," *Adweek* (February 20, 1989), 19.
33. "The Whys and Hows of AP Video," *Broadcasting & Cable* (September 27, 1993), 45.
34. Barbara Lippert, "The New Terseness," *Adweek* (February 1985), C.R. 1.
35. Ken Kerschbaumer, "Sound Is More Important Than Ever," *Broadcasting & Cable* (July 26, 2004), 36.
36. Barbara Lippert, "Playing It Straight," *Adweek* (March 29, 1993), 36.
37. M. H. Moore, "On the Scene and on the Rise," *Adweek* (October 31, 1994), 33.
38. Charles Kuralt, speaking at the Writing for Television Seminar, Center for Communications, Inc. (New York), November 12, 1985.
39. Jim Dale, "Budget TV," *ADS Magazine* (June 1985), 96.
40. Roy Williams, "When to Use the Client's Voice," *Radio Ink* (January 7, 2008), 15.
41. Julia Miller, "Star Struck," *Advertising Age: 50 Years of TV Advertising* (Spring 1995), 31.
42. Cathy Yingling, "Beware the Lure of Celebrity Endorsers," *Advertising Age* (September 24, 2007), 19.
43. Abhilasha Mehta and Clive Davis, "Celebrity Advertising: Perception, Persuasion and Processing," Paper presented to the 1990 Association for Education in Journalism and Mass Communication Convention, 14-15 (Minneapolis)
44. Jim Hanas, "Lois Misses the Outrageous Ads Surrounding Stars," *Advertising Age* (February 20, 2006), S-2.
45. Kemba Johnson, "Generation X Finds a Voice for Ads," *Advertising Age* (September 18, 1995), 12.
46. Stephen Barr, "Voiceover Talent Turns Warm and Fuzzy," *Corporate Video Decisions* (August 1990), 18.
47. Ken French, "Producing an Effective Voiceover," *AVC Music Mart* (April 1990), 47.
48. Debbie Seaman, "Voiceover Study Shouts Down Male Superiority Notions," *Adweek* (September 22, 1986), 58.

Chapter Eleven

1. Thomas Cooper, "Communication as Corporate Callosum: A Reorganization of Knowledge," *Journalism Educator* (Spring 1993), 86.
2. Jacqueline Hitchon, Peter Duckler, and Esther Thorson, "Effects of Ambiguity and Complexity on Consumer Response to Music Video Commercials," *Journal of Broadcasting & Electronic Media* (Summer 1994), 292-293.
3. David Dole, writing in "Monday Memo," *Broadcasting* (February 12, 1990), 17.
4. Richard Morgan, "The Decline of Me-Too Advertising," *Adweek* (February 1984), C.R. 8
5. Kevin Roberts, "10 Principles of the Attraction Economy," *Advertising Age* (January 29, 2007), 14.
6. John O'Toole, writing in "Monday Memo," *Broadcasting* (April 17, 1978), 14.
7. Cleveland Horton, "Spots: Cheaper Is More Effective," *Advertising Age* (July 4, 1994), 6.
8. Alison Fahey, "The Big Picture," *Adweek* (March 29, 1999), 26.
9. "Adweek's Creative All-Star Team," *Adweek* (February 4, 1991), C.R. 14.
10. Mallorre Dill, "Cheryl Berman," *Adweek* (June 19, 2000), 36.
11. Eleftheria Parpis, "On the Spot: Phil Dusenberry," *Adweek* (March 10, 2003), 32.
12. Theodore Roth, "Buick Says Its Ads Outsmart Zappers," *Adweek* (July 16, 1990), 1, 4.
13. Stephanie Kang, "Why DVR Viewers Recall Some TV Spots," *Wall Street Journal* (February 26, 2008), http://online.wsj.com/article/SB120398730105292237.html.
14. Anne Marie Fink, "Press Fast-Forward for TV Salvation," *Advertising Age* (June 20, 2005), 18.
15. Kang, "Why DVR Viewers Recall Some TV Spots".
16. Lee Garfinkel, "Watch What You Say," *Adweek* (August 9, 2004), 17.
17. Freeman Gosden, "Marketing and Making an Offer," *Adweek* (April 30, 1984), 68.
18. Steve McClellan, "For a Whole New DRTV Experience, Call Now," *Adweek* (September 5, 2005), 10.

19. "Teleshopping Nothing New Under Broadcasters' Sun," *Broadcasting* (September 1, 1986), 90.
20. Tim O'Leary, "Old Hand at Infomercials Offers Tips to Newcomers," *Advertising Age* (January 17, 1994), 24.
21. Richard Zoglin, "It's Amazing! Call Now!" *Time* (June 17, 1991), 71.
22. Steve Dworman, "Important Notes from the Editor," *Adweek's 1994 Infomercial Sourcebook Issue*, 5.
23. Don Easdon, "Long Form," *Adweek* (December 7, 1992), 24.
24. "From Down Louisville Way: Some Shrewd Advice on Selling While Keeping Local Image," *Broadcasting* (January 16, 1978), 55.
25. Rich Zahradnik, "Turning to the Tube," *Adweek* (May 23, 1988), B.M. 20.
26. Andrew Jaffe, "The Big Guys Get Serious," *Adweek* (May 23, 1988), B.M. 6.
27. Ibid., B.M. 4.
28. Mark Dolliver, "Takes," *Adweek* (June 21, 2004), 29.
29. George Lois, *What's the Big Idea?* (New York: Penguin, 1991), 79-80.
30. Mark Dominiak, "Opportunity: It's All in the Presentation," *TelevisionWeek* (April 16, 2007), 14.
31. Cele Otnes, Arlo Oviatt, and Deborah Treise, "Views on Advertising Curricula from Experienced Creatives," *Journalism Educator* (Winter 1995), 24.
32. Helene Kalmanson, "Call to Attention," *Adweek* (August 10, 1992), 23.
33. Phillip Stella, "Communicating to Your Audience," *Audio Visual Communications* (December 1990), 33.
34. George Rike, "What's So Funny About That? One Man's Primer," *Advertising Age* (May 16, 1994), 32.
35. Cleve Langton, "What Breaks—or Makes—a Presentation," *Advertising Age* (June 9, 2008), 18.
36. Debbie Seaman, "Creatives Take Their Problems to Creative Therapy," *Adweek* (September 24, 1984), 50.
37. April Winchell, "The Good News: Your Idea Is Accepted. The Bad News: The Ad Gets Done," *Adweek* (July 31, 1995), 22.
38. Alfred Goldman, writing in "Monday Memo," *Broadcasting* (May 1, 1967), 20.
39. Debra Goldman, "Why Is This the Most Wanted Man in Advertising?" *Adweek* (March 28, 1994), 35.
40. Tarquin Cardona, "Are Directors Overshadowing Agency Art Directors?" *Adweek* (October 19, 1987), C.P. 8.
41. Chuck Phillips, "Pennant-Winning Pitching," *Adweek* (June 22, 1987), 55.
42. Barry Day, "'84's 10 Best," *ADS Magazine* (December 1984), 32.

Chapter Twelve

1. Tony Quin, "The Perils of Fragmentation," *BPME Image* (September 1992), 18-19.
2. John Chavez, "Network/Affiliate Packages," *BPME Image* (January 1989), 13.
3. Elizabeth Rathbun, "Marketers Take Promax Spotlight," *Broadcasting & Cable* (June 12, 1995), 12.
4. Steve McClellan, "Cohen: One Channel, One Network," *Broadcasting & Cable* (June 10, 1996), 8.
5. Bob Klein, "Survival Guide to Station Image Development," *NATPE Programmer* (January 1986), 124.
6. Karl Sjodahl, "The Station's Image," *BPME Image* (March 1988), 17.
7. Bruce Bloom, writing in "Monday Memo," *Broadcasting* (October 6, 1986), 24.
8. Ken Kerschbaumer, "A Very Special Trend in Network Promos," *Broadcasting & Cable* (June 29, 2005), 24.
9. "The Inside Story: John Larkin," *BPME Image* (January 1991), 4.
10. Jim Moloshok, writing in "Monday Memo," *Broadcasting* (October 2, 1989), 30.
11. Frank Brooks, "Maintaining the Leading Edge in Syndication/Promotion," *BPME Image* (October 1991), 15.
12. Joe Mandese, "NBC Entertains New Viewer Hook," *Advertising Age* (September 5, 1994), 8.
13. "Snypes and Squeezes," *Broadcasting & Cable* (June 21, 2004), 22.
14. Mallorre Dill, "Coming Attractions," *Adweek* (August 23, 1999), 21.
15. Ibid., 20.
16. "Coming to a Movie Theatre Near You: On Screen Advertising," *Adweek* (June 21, 2004), 16.
17. Jack Feuer, "Consumers Give Movie Ads a Thumbs Up," *Adweek* (May 19, 2003), 10.
18. Mallorre Dill, "Sleeper Hit," *Adweek* (December 9, 2002), 17.
19. Christine Champagne, "True Confessions," *Adweek* (March 26, 2007), 16.
20. Fred Cohn, "Getting It Down on Paper," *Corporate Video Decisions* (June 1989), 25.
21. Chris Petersen and Guillermo Real, "Muster Your Clusters," *Audio-Visual Communications* (November 1987), 53.
22. Robert Lindstrom, "Presentations-wise, We've Lost Our Tails," *Adweek* (October 5, 1998), P14.
23. Larry Eder, "Is Your Video a Success?" *Video Systems* (July 1995), 47.
24. Ed Neal, "The Overnight Scriptwriter," *Video Systems* (February 1995), 26.
25. Ibid., 27.
26. Eric Paulsen, "Lessons From a Life in Scriptwriting," *Video Systems* (August 1995), 20.
27. Ibid.
28. Sam White, "The Power of Music," *Video Systems* (August 1988), 48.
29. Ibid., 46.
30. "Orchestrating the Commercial," *ASAP* (January/February 1988), 17.
31. Paulsen, 21.
32. Fred Cohn, "PR Enters the Video Age," *Corporate Video Decisions* (March 1989), 34.
33. Ibid., 36.

34. Ibid.
35. Hugh Aoki, "Generating One Success Story after Another," *Marketing with Video, DVD and CD Rom* (*Adweek Supplement*, July 12, 1999), 10.
36. Junu Kim, "Marketing with Video," *Advertising Age* (May 22, 1995), S-4.
37. Barry Hampe, "Lessons from Losers," *Video Systems* (May 1999), 70.
38. Geoffrey Foisie, "CAB Promotes Non-Regulated Revenue Source," *Broadcasting & Cable* (April 12, 1993), 71.
39. Amanda Plotkin, "Digital Insertion Products Open Local Ad Gateways," *Advertising Age* (March 25, 1996), 32.
40. J. P. Cortez, "Media Pioneers Try to Corral On-the-Go Consumers," *Advertising Age* (August 17, 1992), 25.
41. "Ghost Stories," *Adweek* (March 27, 2000), IQ 8.
42. Pat Hinsberg, "In-Flight Advertising Hits New High," *Adweek* (July 17, 1989), 48.
43. Laura Blum and Steve McClellan, "Selling Where People Buy: The Rise of In-Store TV," *Adweek* (July 17, 2006), 11.
44. Claudia Kienzle, "Caveat Emptor," *Video Systems* (June 2000), 32.
45. Blum and McClellan, 11.
46. Steve McClellan, "Pump TV: Selling to a Briefly Captive Crowd," *Adweek* (May 21, 2007), 10.
47. Jean Halliday, "Captivate to Expand Network," *Advertising Age* (May 17, 2004), 152.
48. Richard Tedesco, "Web Ads Get Glitzy, Savvy," *Broadcasting & Cable* (November 8, 1999), 48.
49. Jeff Goodby, "Promised Land.com," *Adweek* (August 23, 1999), 14.
50. "The Changing Game," *Creativity* (August 2008), 30.
51. Jack Neff, "How You Can Get the Most from Digital Ads," *Advertising Age* (March 17, 2008), 13.
52. Carl Lindemann, "Eight Tips for Web Producers," *Broadcasting & Cable* (March 19, 2001), 46.
53. Abbey Klaassen, "When Web Branding Works," *Advertising Age* (July 16, 2007), 33.
54. Stan Ferguson. Remarks to the Broadcast Education Association Convention, April 6, 2000, (Las Vegas).
55. Richard Ting, "Taking Creativity to the Streets," *Adweek* (February 25, 2008), 13.
56. Allen Adamson, "Does Your Brand Have Portability Potential?" *Advertising Age* (July 23, 2007), 17.
57. Andrew Jaffe, "Burnett's Donald Gunn on What Wins at Cannes," *Adweek* (June 6, 1994), 46.
58. Jamie Barrett, "Truth in Advertising," *Adweek* (March 20, 2006), 12.

Chapter Thirteen

1. Ann Cooper, "Spreading the News," *Adweek* (December 20, 1993), 18.
2. "A Matter of Judgment Strategy," *Ad Council Special Advertising Section* (Spring 2002), 15.
3. Joe Mandese, "PSAs: Too Many Issues, Not Enough Time," *Adweek* (May 18, 1987), 52.
4. Ruth Wooden, "Education Should Be Sole Purpose of PSAs," *Advertising Age* (May 19, 1997), 40.
5. Paul Bloom, "Everyone's Waxing Philanthropic These Days, But It Pays Off—If You Do It Right," *Advertising Age* (May 26, 2008), 18.
6. Ronald Bishop, "Brought to You as a Public Service: How Public Service Announcements Are Placed On the Air at Commercial Radio and Television Stations," *Journal of Radio Studies* (December 2002), 233.
7. David Barash, "The Conflicting Pressures of Selfishness and Altruism," *Chronicle Review* (July 18, 2003), http://chronicle.com/weekly/v49/i45/45b00701.htm., 2.
8. Virginia Roark, "Take a Bite Out of Problems: PSA Research Reviewed and Extended." Paper presented to the 1993 Association for Education in Journalism and Mass Communication Convention (Kansas City), 21-22.
9. J. A. Edell and M. C. Burke, "The Power of Feelings in Understanding Advertising Effects," *Journal of Consumer Research*, V.14 (1987), 423.
10. Ruth Wooden, "PSAs Can Make a Difference, But It Takes Time," *Advertising Age* (March 14, 1994), 23.
11. Debra Goldman, "Behavior Modification," *Adweek* (June 22, 1998), 70.
12. Bishop, 234.
13. Jim O'Donnell. Letter to Peter Orlik. June 12, 1992.
14. "PSAs Should Demonstrate and Teach," *NAB RadioWeek* (October 31, 1988), 10.
15. Ibid.
16. Robert Osborn, "Viewpoint," *Winners* (May 1988), 3.
17. Cathy Madison, "The City That Put 'Pro' in Pro Bono," *Adweek* (January 1, 1991), 17.
18. Jane Hodges and Susan Taras, "Born in War, Ad Council Still Thrives," *Advertising Age* (July 31, 1995), 30.
19. "Advertising Council Formed," *Advertising Age* (January 24, 2005), 16.
20. "Ruth Ann Wooden," *Broadcasting* (November 2, 1992), 79.
21. Daniel Clay Russ, "Oh, No, Pro Bono," *Adweek* (September 2, 1991), 17.
22. Stephen Battaglio, "Giving at the Office," *Adweek* (January 1, 1991), 15.
23. Dave Halloway, "Pro Pro-Bono," *one. a magazine* (Winter 2005), 31.
24. Jay Schulberg, "Reality Bites," *Adweek* (December 10, 1994), 30.
25. Harry Cole, "FCC Rejects Love, Family and Tastefulness in NCE FM Underwriting Announcements," *Fletcher, Heald & Hildreth Memorandum to Clients* (May 2008), 11, 15. See http://www.fhhlaw.com/memo_clients/2008/0508.pdf

Chapter Fourteen

1. Terance Shimp, *Promotion Management and Marketing Communications*, 2nd. ed. (Hinsdale, IL: Dryden Press, 1990), 67.
2. Scott Hume, "A Few Good Seats Are Left on the Brand Bandwagon," *Adweek* (June 20, 1994), 38.
3. Chuck Reece, "Admen Remember Jack Cunningham," *Adweek* (March 4, 1985), 2.
4. Mindy Charski, "Hands-On Training," *Adweek* (September 5, 2005), 32.
5. Jack Neff, "P & G Kisses Up to the Boss: Consumers," *Advertising Age* (May 2, 2005), 20.
6. Steven Penchina, "Peace Offering," *Adweek* (November 29, 1993), 20.
7. Jay Schulberg, "Sell the Client's Product, Not Just Creativity," *Advertising Age* (April 8, 1996), C-20.
8. Bart Cleveland, "Here Are Four Ways to Build the Trust It Takes to Keep Your Clients Around," *Advertising Age* (March 3, 2008), 16.
9. Rita McGrath and Ian MacMillan, "When in Doubt, Simplify," *Point* (April 2005), 8.
10. Ibid.
11. Richard Morgan, "It's Veni, Vidi, Vick in San Francisco," *Adweek* (January 11, 1993), 38.
12. Tom Peters, "Brands Still Rule Supreme," *Advertising Age* (January 26, 1998), 26.
13. Alan Rose, letter to the editor. *Adweek* (May 27, 2002), 11.
14. Debra Goldman, "Study: Advertisers Aren't Talking to Consumers," *Adweek* (August 27, 1990), 25.
15. Bill Heater and Jeff Larson, "Life Lesson," *Adweek* (September 20, 1999), 14.
16. Mark Dolliver, "Mixed Blessings," *Adweek* (August 31, 1998), 17.
17. Mac McLaurin, "Give It Some Thought," *Adweek* (January 7, 2008), 17.
18. Teressa Iezzi, "O & M Thinks Big," *Creativity* (November 2002), 31.
19. William Bartolini, "Marketing Planning as a Team Effort," *BPME Image* (April/May 1989), 8.
20. Mel Rubin, writing in "Monday Memo," *Broadcasting* (July 9, 1979), 10.
21. Frank DeVito, writing in "Monday Memo," *Broadcasting* (February 16, 1981), 24.
22. William Meyers, "The Campaign to Save a Flagging Brand," *Adweek* (April 1985), F.C. 22.
23. Don Ferguson, writing in "Monday Memo," *Broadcasting* (May 28, 1973), 14.
24. John Muhlfeld, writing in "Monday Memo," *Broadcasting* (August 21, 1978), 16.
25. Extracted from materials courtesy of Kathy Kane, Foote, Cone & Belding/San Francisco.
26. Lisa Paikowski, "Funeral Marketer Breaks New Ground in Traditional Trade," *Adweek* (August 3, 1987), 17.
27. Sam Moyers, writing in "Monday Memo," *Broadcasting* (July 21, 1975), 10.
28. Al Ries, writing in "Monday Memo," *Broadcasting* (August 26, 1974), 11.
29. Merri Rosenberg, "Snuggle: A Hard Sell in a Cuddly Package," *Adweek* (April 1985), F.C. 36.
30. Kevin Neathery, *Copy Writing and Campaign Development* (Jonesboro, AK: Triple FM, 2008), 11.
31. Al Ries, "What I Learned," *Advertising Age* (March 28, 2005), 32.32. Ries, "Monday Memo," 11.
33. "Keith's Beliefs," *Adweek* (May 29, 1989), 14.
34. Philip Dusenberry, "What's Your Position?" *Adweek* (November 4, 1996), 68.
35. Conrad Nankin, "Positioning Still Relevant and Practical Technique," *Advertising Age* (July 19, 2004), 16.
36. "Do's and Don'ts of Broadcast Promotion Star at BPA Seminar," *Broadcasting* (November 26, 1973), 30.
37. Andrew Newman, "Apply Liberally," *Adweek* (July 14, 2008), 20.
38. Faith Popcorn, "Repositioning with Real Sell," *Adweek* (December 12, 1983), 42.
39. Mark Gleason, "Solid Creative Strengths Put Fallon in the Driver's Seat," *Advertising Age* (April 15, 1996), S-4.
40. T. W. Siebert, "A Prune by Any Other Name," *Adweek* (July 10, 2000), 54.
41. Craig Tanner, "Taking a Leaf from Ogilvy's Book," *Adweek* (March 7, 1983), 32.
42. Stephanie Thompson, "Souping Up a Classic," *Advertising Age* (May 2, 2005), 1.
43. Jack Trout, "Branding Can't Exist Without Positioning," *Advertising Age* (March 14, 2005), 28.
44. Paul Goldsmith, writing in "Monday Memo," *Broadcasting* (September 22, 1980), 12.
45. Brett Robbs, "The Advertising Curriculum and the Needs of Creative Students," *Journalism Educator* (Winter 1996), 28.
46. Bo Ronnberg, "Speaker's Corner," *Adweek* (May 19, 1997), 26.
47. Greg Farrell, "The New Man at McCann," *Adweek* (October 17, 1994), 40.
48. Eleftheria Parpis, "Debating Spec Work," *Adweek* (November 23, 1998), 19.
49. Tom Denari, "Why Spec Creative Doesn't Pay," *Advertising Age* (February 12, 2007), 15.
50. Steven Steinberg, "Spectacular Results From Spec Spots," *Radio Ink* (January 8, 2007), 42.
51. Extracted from Clinton Rogers, writing in "Monday Memo," *Broadcasting* (June 10, 1968), 18.
52. Extracted from materials courtesy of Marlene Passarelli, Lawler Ballard Advertising.
53. Extracted from materials courtesy of Ruth Whitmore, Whitmore Communications.
54. Extracted from materials courtesy of Don Brashears, Cramer-Krasselt.
55. Paul Harper, *Victory in Advertising* (New York: Needham, Harper & Steers, 1980), 4.
56. "Helayne Reigns," *Adweek* (March 23, 1992), R.C. 11.

Chapter Fifteen

1. Thomas Hayo, "Guest Critic," *Adweek* (December 12, 2005), 21.
2. George Lois, *What's the Big Idea?* (New York: Penguin, 1991), 5.
3. Kamau High, "Richard Kirshenbaum On the Spot," *Adweek* (November 12, 2007), 24.
4. Malcolm MacDougall, "The Advertising Cliché' Code," *Adweek* (April 22, 1985), 52.
5. Aaron Barr, "Jim Nelson On the Spot," *Adweek* (January 12, 2004), 32.
6. Renny Gleeson, "Last Word," *Creativity* (March 2008), 48.
7. Mae Anderson, "John Hegarty On the Spot," *Adweek* (April 12, 2004), 60.
8. Bradley Johnson, "A Man Who Ran Great Campaigns," *Advertising Age* (January 20, 1997), 8.
9. Don Cowlbeck, writing in "Monday Memo," *Broadcasting* (March 20, 1972), 19.

INDEX